David Mamet

D0075231

David Mamet

A Research and Production Sourcebook

David K. Sauer and Janice A. Sauer

Modern Dramatists Research and Production Sourcebooks, Number 18
William W. Demastes, Series Adviser

Belmont University Library

Westport, Connecticut
London

Library of Congress Cataloging-in-Publication Data

Sauer, David K., 1944–
      David Mamet : a research and production sourcebook / David K. Sauer and Janice A. Sauer.
         p. cm.—(Modern dramatists research and production sourcebooks, ISSN 1055–999X ;
      no. 18)
      Includes bibliographical references and index.
      ISBN 0–313–31836–0 (alk. paper)
         1. Mamet, David—Criticism and interpretation.   2. Mamet, David—Dramatic production.
      3. Mamet, David—Stage history.   I. Sauer, Janice A., 1944–   II. Title.   III.   Series.
      PS3563.A4345Z877   2003
      812'.54—dc21   2003053635

British Library Cataloguing in Publication Data is available.

Copyright © 2003 by David K. Sauer and Janice A. Sauer

All rights reserved. No portion of this book may be
reproduced, by any process or technique, without the
express written consent of the publisher.

Library of Congress Catalog Card Number: 2003053635
ISBN: 0–313–31836–0
ISSN: 1055–999X

First published in 2003

Praeger Publishers, 88 Post Road West, Westport, CT 06881
An imprint of Greenwood Publishing Group, Inc.
www.praeger.com

Printed in the United States of America

The paper used in this book complies with the
Permanent Paper Standard issued by the National
Information Standards Organization (Z39.48–1984).

10 9 8 7 6 5 4 3 2

PS
3563
. A4345
Z877
2003

CONTENTS

PREFACE

We believe that reference books such as this one are valuable tools for students, scholars and practitioners engaging in analysis of performance. From the time we began this endeavor in 1992 with the first issue of *The David Mamet Review*, we have watched the field of drama criticism change as scholars began citing performance reviews of the plays they examined. The performance dimension became standard in the discussion—though it was built into the first books on Mamet by C. W. E. Bigsby and Dennis Carroll. Individual sensitivity to performance can be expanded by reading the full panoply of reviews for a given play and especially in discovering how a play itself changes from cast to cast, as well as from decade to decade. Using this approach, a play is closer to a Rorschach test than a work of fixed meaning. Examining the reviews of *American Buffalo* we discover the range to which the text can be stretched in actual performance. Nussbaum's paranoia, Kellin's seedy pretending, Duvall's insane rage, Pacino's frustration, and Macy's comic self-delusion together create an understanding of the complexity of the character of Teach. Similarly, Madonna, whose ability as an actor was initially pilloried by many critics, gained their respect when they came to appreciate the ambiguities of the role as played by Felicity Huffman in New York, Rebecca Pidgeon and much later by Kimberly Williams in London. Scholars are now coming to the same appreciation of the possible interpretations of any role. We hope this work will facilitate criticism by students, scholars and practitioners who love the living theatre as well as the text.

A Note on Use

The librarian-half of this team is particularly concerned about the ease with which a researcher can use this book. It is organized by major play rather than by year because we think this is how students and scholars most often approach this material. Each play title is assigned a short code, as are Mamet's essay collections (M), the dissertations (D), film scholarship (F), and the bibliographies and reference books (BR) in order to facilitate cross references. Within each chapter the productions, designated by a lowercase *p,* are chronological. Reviews, beginning with a lowercase *r,* are alphabetical by author. Scholarly articles are marked with a lowercase *s.* We consider the production reviews as historical artifacts; thus we use past tense. The scholarly articles are part of an ongoing conversation and therefore are in the present tense.

Because of page limits we were not able to include every production and review that we considered valuable. For the same reason, we could not cover reviews of films, adaptations, books, poems and the myriad ways that critics both praise and skewer David Mamet's forms of artistic expression. We also are aware that we may have missed obscure, and maybe not so obscure, primary items and can only say—there wasn't room for everything anyhow.

A major concern we have is that many of the scholarly articles do not deal with a single play, but address an issue across two or more plays. We have placed the scholarly annotations for these with the most extensively covered play whenever we could make that determination. For those articles in which one play does not dominate the discussion, we have created a separate chapter called "Multiple Plays" and have attached *see also* references to them at the end of the relevant chapters. The criticisms covered under "Multiple Plays" may be as valuable as those annotated within the play chapter itself and should not be regarded as less important.

Acknowledgments

This book was prefigured by our annual bibliographies for the *David Mamet Review*. We are grateful to Leslie Kane and Chris Hudgins for their dedication to the David Mamet Society and its *Review* which gave us the inspiration and rationale for this book. Many people facilitated this work. We thank our deans, Dr. Noreen Carrocci at Spring Hill College and Dr. Richard Wood at University of South Alabama, for giving us sabbatical time to get the work well underway. We thank our colleagues who covered for us, helped with translations, and listened to us for the past two years—especially Michael Kaffer and Colette Windush. Our research wouldn't have been possible without our Interlibrary Loan librarians, Brett Heim, Debbie Cobb, Cubie Joor, and Tamilla Peyton. The Special Collection department of the Harold Washington Chicago Public Library, Teresa Yoder, Archival Specialist, above all, as well as the wonderful clippings files and the TOFT collection of the New York Public Library Performing Arts Library at Lincoln Center and its reference librarians (who unfortunately prefer anonymity) were indispensible. In addition, we are grateful for the Westminster Reference Library and the excellent theatre and microform collection of the Tulane University Library. Series editor, William Demastes, was most encouraging and helpful to us, and our Greenwood editors gave us clear direction for the book's construction. Scholars came to our aid by supplying us with information and articles—most notably Johan Callens, Harry Elam, Steven Price and Gerald Weales. Our personal thanks to Calvin Jones, our translator, friend and neighbor, and to Jeremy Sauer, proofreader extraordinaire. Geoff Sauer's knowledge of computers and print production and Ellen Sauer's experience in academic publishing got us started and kept us going. We are forever indebted to the friends and family who put up with our absences and our excuses and got us through this project with our partnership intact.

Most especially, we remember Rhoda Hafner, our dear friend, with whom we wish we had had more time. She is with us in our minds and hearts, and to her memory we dedicate this book.

LIFE AND CAREER

References to Mamet's autobiographical essays are listed in Selected Short
Writings, page 21, and coded as M1, M2, M3, M4, M5, M6, M7.

David Mamet was born November 30, 1947, in Chicago, the son of attorney Bernard Morris and teacher Lenore June, nee Silver. He remembered growing up in a
South Shore neighborhood of Chicago where his grandmother "spoke in what could
have been Yiddish, Polish, or Russian" to the shopkeepers; they lived on Euclid
Avenue, and his grandparents were Ashkenazi Jews from Poland ("Seventy-first
and Jeffrey" M1 125-28). He went to Parkside School. He recalled those days in
"When I was Young—A Note to Zosia and Willa" (M4 154-57). There he remembered the stickball played in the street and in drama recollects old times in Chicago
with a childhood friend in *The Disappearance of the Jews,* the first act of *The Old
Neighborhood.* He discovered acting when his Uncle Henry "was a producer of
radio and television for the Chicago Board of Rabbis. And he gave me jobs as a kid
and my sister jobs as a kid, portraying Jewish children on television and radio. And
through him I got into community theater in Chicago" (M7 196).

His mother and father divorced in 1958, and when his mother remarried, they
moved to a suburb amidst the cornfields where he described the psychological
and physical abuse of his sister and, as he later discovered of his mother when she
was a girl ("The Rake" M1 3-11). The play "Jolly," the second act of *The Old
Neighborhood* depicts a similar story, recollecting childhood abuse and resentments particularly after a divorce and the introduction of stepfather, stepbrother
and sister. *The Cryptogram* tells the story of a broken marriage, with a focus on
the boy whose mother and father have separated.

In high school he "hung around Second City [Chicago's renowned improvisation troupe] quite a bit," later working there as a busboy, and later, in tribute to its

stars, lived as they had at "The Hotel Lincoln" (M1 95-99). In the mid 1960s, after graduation from high school, he worked in a factory, living on the North side near Addison Avenue, and commuting to work near Cicero (western border of Chicago) where he worked welding, and spraying weeds around the building and in maintenance, tearing out asbestos ceilings to which he attributed years of weak lungs, "which seems to me a more dramatic story than twenty-five years of tobacco" ("The Truck Factory" M1 77-81). He also drove a cab in Chicago ("Cops and Cars" M2 17-19).

In 1965 Mamet worked at a roadside diner in Trois-Rivières, Provence de Quebec. In an essay he also described working in 1967 at Montreal's Expo '67 as an "acro dancer" in a Maurice Chevalier show, *Toutes voiles dehors!!!* (*"P.Q."* M1 25-30). In his twentieth year Mamet studied at the Neighborhood Playhouse School of Theater of Sanford Meisner ("A Tradition of Theatre as Art" M5 19-23) where he learned two first principles to which he devoted himself as he recalls in the preface to *Writing in Restaurants*: "(1) every aspect of the production should reflect the idea of the play; (2) the purpose of the play is to bring to the stage the life of the soul" (viii). In 1969 he graduated from Goddard College with a B.A. degree.

About that time he lived at 71st and Columbus Circle in New York City and worked "as an usher, then house manager, then assistant stage manager for *The Fantasticks*." In the summer he got a job in "summer stock out on the tip of Long Island, and it may have been the only time, or at least one of the few times, I was ever hired as an actor" ("Salad Days" M2 8-11). In 1970 he became a special lecturer in drama at Marlboro College, replacing a former acting teacher who was on sabbatical and where *Lakeboat* was first produced (M7 17).

Afterward, Mamet returned to Chicago where he sold real estate "to unsuspecting elderly people" (M7 17). In 1971-72 he was artist-in-residence in drama at Goddard College. Mamet had a 1969 Karmann Ghia bought in 1972 to drive in Vermont ("Karmann Ghia" M2 81-85). While at Goddard he formed the St. Nicholas Theatre Company with students William H. Macy and Steven Schachter who performed the first versions of *Duck Variations* and *Sexual Perversity in Chicago*.

In 1972 he returned to Chicago. *Duck Variations* and *Litko* were performed at the Body Politic Theatre. By 1974 *Sexual Perversity in Chicago* was also done by the Organic Theatre Company, and won a Chicago's Joe Jefferson Award. Mamet revived the St. Nicholas Theatre Company there and October 10 premiered *Squirrels*. "The Company is named for Nicholas of Maya, Patron of mountebanks, prostitutes, and the demi-monde." These notes, from the program, also included the Company's purpose: "Using Stanislavsky's definition that 'Acting is living truthfully under imaginary circumstances,' we have worked to establish a common vocabulary, and a common method which will permit us to bring to the stage (not through our insights, but through our craft) this truth in the form of action." In "Stanislavsky and Squirrels" in the *Sun-Times* on October 6, 1974, Mamet amplified, "the philosophy that life on the stage is not an imitation of anything, but is real life on the stage."

In 1975 Gregory Mosher directed *American Buffalo* at the Goodman Theatre's Stage 2. The production moved to St. Nicholas's theatre on Halsted Street. *Sexual Perversity* and *Duck Variations* opened off-off Broadway at the St. Clement's Theatre in New York, and won an Obie for best new play. Mamet then wrote *Revenge of the Space Pandas* for that company. He also wrote *Marranos* and *Mackinac* for Youth Theater of the Bernard Horwich Jewish Community Center.

In 1976 he lived in New York which he describes in "Memories of Chelsea" (M1 13-23). Mamet's big impact occurred 1976-1977 when productions hit New York in quick succession. Mosher's production of *American Buffalo* came to St. Clement's in New York in January, 1976, and won an Obie and Jefferson. *Sexual Perversity* and *Duck Variations* moved to the Cherry Lane in June, 1976. In an interview with Gerald Fraser (rSPC 3.6) Mamet explained: "Voltaire said words were invented to hide feelings. That's what the play is about, how what we say influences what we think. The words that the old [character] Bernie Litko says to Danny influences his behavior, you know, that women are broads, that they're there to exploit." Critic Gerald Weales used these lines as keystones of Mamet's world, because instead of characters having thoughts which require words, the order is reversed into postmodernism: words define the kinds of thoughts that are possible (sMP 52).

Ulu Grosbard directed *American Buffalo* with Robert Duvall on Broadway in February 1977, winning a New York Drama Critics' Circle Award. Meantime, *Life in the Theatre* opened in Chicago at the Goodman Stage 2, and moved to the Théâtre de Lys in New York. In May, *Water Engine* was staged by the St. Nicholas Company in Chicago while *Reunion* and *Dark Pony* premiered at the Yale Repertory Theatre. *Space Pandas* was staged at the St. Nicholas and Flushing Town Hall, Queens. *Sexual Perversity* and *Duck Variations* were performed in London at the Regent's Theatre. In November, Mamet directed Peter Weller and Patti LuPone at the St. Nicholas in *The Woods*. In December of 1977, Mamet married actress Lindsay Crouse.

Water Engine began as a short story, then a film script, and was always rejected—until Howard Gelman of Earplay commissioned a radio drama from Mamet, and it found its first medium. In 1978 *Water Engine* aired on Earplay, National Public Radio as did *Prairie du Chien* (M5 13). From the experience Mamet writes he became a better playwright: "More than any other medium it teaches the writer to concentrate on the essentials, because it throws into immediate relief that to *characterize* the people or scene is to take time from the story—to weaken the story" (M5 14).

In January of 1978 the Public Theatre in New York staged *The Water Engine*; it then moved to Broadway's Plymouth Theatre. In 1979, the Public Theatre also staged *The Blue Hour: City Sketches* and *The Woods* in 1978. A musical, *Lone Canoe, or the Explorer* was unsuccessful at the Goodman. PBS aired *A Life in the Theatre*. Mamet directed *Reunion, Dark Pony* and *Sanctity of Marriage* at the Circle in the Square in 1979.

In 1980 Mamet reworked *Lakeboat* for the Milwaukee Repertory Theatre. The Long Wharf Theatre redid *American Buffalo* with Al Pacino as Teach. This production transferred to Off Broadway, Circle in the Square, and opened on June 3rd, 1981. With cast changes, but still Pacino, the production was revived on Broadway at the Booth Theatre, October until December 17, 1983. The same production also showed at London's Duke of York's Theatre in August of 1984 with one cast change.

Mamet turned to film in 1981, writing his first screenplay for a remake of Cain's *The Postman Always Rings Twice*. He also worked on a script for *The Verdict* for which he received an Academy Award nomination in 1982. In that year as well, Mamet's *Lakeboat* was produced at both Long Wharf and the Goodman, and *Edmond* premiered at the Goodman, then went to New York where it received an Obie: "There are moments of real beauty in the play, and I think that rather than being about violence, it's a play about someone searching for the truth, for God, for release. [. . .] 'Edmond' presents the tragic view of a man who doesn't think faith exists. He is committing the modern New York heresy of denying the life of the soul'" (rE 2.14).

The Goodman Theatre was the site of his adaptation *Red River* and "The Disappearance of the Jews" a one act done with plays by Elaine May and Shel Silverstein. He sent the script of *Glengarry Glen Ross* to Harold Pinter asking for advice, and Pinter said simply, "the only thing it needed was to be produced" (rGGR 3.2). So Pinter sent it to the National Theatre which mounted a production that won both an Olivier and Society of West End Theatres' Award. In 1984 Mosher directed a production with an American cast at the Goodman, and then moved it to Broadway where it won the Pulitzer Prize, Drama Critics' Award for Best Play, and four Tony Nominations. Mamet described his job to Mel Gussow in this play "to create a closed moral universe, and to leave evaluation to the audience'" (rGGR 3.17).

When Henry Schvey asked him about sympathy for Roma in that play, however, Mamet replied, "I always want everyone to be sympathetic to all the characters. Because when you aren't, what you are doing is writing a melodrama with good guys and bad guys. Drama is really about the conflicting impulses in the individual. That is what *all* drama is about" (M7 65). Reviewers and scholars have not accepted this point of view; most pick sides and denounce one character or another. Christopher Hudgins is one scholar who used Mamet's idea of sympathy for all characters to construct his interpretation (sMP 23).

In 1985-86 Mamet's one acts were staged in various venues—Mosher used *The Shawl* and *Prairie du Chien* to reopen the Lincoln Center Theatre for which he became artistic director in 1985. That year Mamet's adaptation of Chekhov's *The Cherry Orchard* appeared at the New Theatre Company, which he founded in New York with Mosher. Mamet first collection of essays also appeared in 1986, *Writing in Restaurants*. And the following year, Mamet moved toward film, doing the screenplay for *The Untouchables* and writing and directing his first film, *House of Games* starring his wife Lindsay Crouse and Joe Mantegna. In *On*

Directing Film, lectures he gave at Columbia in 1987, he proposes that "the *only* thing I know about film directing" is Eisenstein's theory of montage. Rather than following a character around with a camera, Mamet's method is "*a succession of images juxtaposed so that the contrast between these images moves the story forward in the mind of the audience*" (2). Like the blackout method of his first plays, *Lakeboat, Sexual Perversity in Chicago,* and *Duck Variations,* this approach asked the audience to make the connections, rather than making them for the audience. In 1988 the second film he wrote (with Shel Silverstein) and directed, *Things Change,* was released, and the American Repertory Theatre debuted his adaptation of *Uncle Vanya.*

In 1988 *Speed-the-Plow* premiered on Broadway to great acclaim and controversy. Mantegna and Ron Silver were nominated for Tonys for their performances, but Madonna's role was so underplayed that Richard Hornby (rSTP 1.11) actually concluded that she was "not nearly sexy enough for the role." When queried by Billington about biting the hand that feeds him in the play, however, Mamet replied: "The people I'm attacking in *Speed-the-Plow* [. . .] are not the movie makers but the hucksters who manipulate them. Hollywood itself has been princely to me. People there won't take revenge on you unless you cost them money" (M7 105).

In 1989 the play moved to the National Theatre with similar acclaim and more positive reviews of Rebecca Pidgeon as Karen. The saga continued in a short play "Bobby Gould in Hell" which Mamet told John Lahr was one of the works "that surprised him in performance" (M7 117). Macy and Mamet had founded The Atlantic Theatre Company in 1985 and did Mamet's adaptation of *Three Sisters* in 1990. Mamet divorced Crouse in 1990—they had two children, Willa and Zosia.

In 1991 Mamet also wrote and directed *Homicide.* Bill Macy at the "Mamet at 50" conference told the story of acting in *Homicide* under Mamet's direction. In this instance, Macy said he played Mantegna's sidekick in the story of discovery of lost Jewish identity. In the scene, Macy was filling out a passport form when Mantegna came in and said, "You're like my family, Tim." Macy's line was "Bob . . . I *am* your family . . ." so he looked up and said it meaningfully, thinking this a key line to the Mantegna's sense of identity. But Mamet stopped him after the take, and said "Just fill out the paperwork." On the second take, Macy didn't look up, but said the line as meaningfully as he could—and Mamet stopped him again and said, "Just fill out the paperwork." So on the third take, he said the line tonelessly, not looking up from the paper—and thought this the perfect way to do the line and scene. This theory of underplay was most evident in Madonna's performance in *Speed-the-Plow*, and was the basis of Mamet's subsequent book, *True and False: Heresy and Common Sense for the Actor.*

He married Rebecca Pidgeon in 1991 and she starred with William Macy in Mamet's most controversial play, *Oleanna,* which he directed in 1992 at the ART, and then moved to the Orpheum Theatre in New York. In 1993 Pinter directed an earlier draft of the play in London. Markland Taylor interviewed Mamet (rO 1.7) in which he said, "The point of the play is, at the end, to ask, 'How did we get here?' The professor adores his students and prides himself on being a good teacher. How did he wind up thrashing a student?" His answer was that language "ceases to be a transparent medium of communication, translating thoughts and feelings clearly and unequivocally from one mind to another. Instead, language spins its wheels and gets nowhere. If you break the rhythm, you break the meaning" On the characters, he told Benedict Nightingale he still sympathizes with both: "I agree with what she says as much as with what he says. She may do some things that are dishonourable, but then so does he. For me, it's a play about the uses and abuses of power, and the corruption on both sides" (rO 4.28). In 1994 he wrote and directed a film version of the play with Macy and Deborah Eisenstadt who replaced Pidgeon, pregnant with their first child, Clara. His screenplay of *Hoffa* was also made into a film in 1992.

In that year Mamet's screenplay for *Glengarry Glen Ross* was filmed with an all-star cast. In 1994 André Gregory's film *Vanya on 42nd Street* was made using Mamet's adaptation. In London, Sam Mendes directed a revival of *Glengarry* at the Donmar Playhouse to great reviews. Greg Mosher directed *Cryptogram* at Ambassadors Theatre and this play extended Mamet's work into a family setting and into the world of mystery. In 1995 Mamet directed the play in Boston and later Westside Theatre in New York. John Lahr said the play "dramatizes a child's emotional abuse in a way that no other American play has ever attempted: from the child's point of view. [. . .] the new play bypasses reason and prompts deep, visceral feelings about the past which have a way of making the memory of the play implode in the imagination. 'People may or may not say what they mean,' Mamet says. 'But they always say something designed to get what they want'" (rC 2.16).

In the same year, his one-act "An Interview" appeared in *Death Defying Acts* with plays by Woody Allen and Elaine May. Mamet directed J. B. Priestley's *Dangerous Corner* for the Atlantic Theatre Company. The same company revived *Edmond* in 1996. Ensemble Theatre did two one-acts of Mamet's, and the film of *American Buffalo* was released. Mamet put together three of his one-acts into the single work, *The Old Neighborhood* in 1997 at ART with Tony Shalhoub and Brooke Adams directed by Scott Zigler. The production then moved to Booth Theatre, New York City with Patti LuPone and Peter Riegert; both featured Pidgeon as Deeny. The same year Mamet's screenplays for *The Edge* and final revision for *Wag the Dog* were released as was *The Spanish Prisoner* which he also directed.

In 1998, *The Old Neighborhood* debuted at the Royal Court with Colin Stinton and Zoë Wanamaker. The film of Mamet's screenplay *Ronin* was released and so was his adaptation of *The Winslow Boy*, also directed by Mamet. He also co-produced the HBO production of his screenplay *Lansky*.

In 1999 Mamet directed *Boston Marriage* at ART and also directed and wrote the film *State and Main*. *Lakeboat*, directed by Joe Mantegna, was released in 2000. Mamet wrote and directed the popular film *The Heist* in 2001. *Boston Marriage* was done at the Donmar in London in 2001. It came to New York to the Public Theatre in 2002, when the Mamets moved to Los Angeles from New England. He was inducted into the Theatre Hall of Fame on January 27, 2003.

CHRONOLOGY

For additional information on any titles listed here see the Primary Bibliography.

1947 Born, Chicago on November 30
1967-8 Studies under Sanford Meisner, N.Y.
1968 *Camel* (Goddard College) BA Thesis in English Literature
1970 *Lakeboat* Marlboro, VT, Marlboro Theatre Workshop
1971 Founds St. Nicholas Theatre Company at Goddard College, VT
1972 *Duck Variations* and *Sexual Perversity* Boston
 Litko and *Duck Variations*. St Nicholas at the Body Politic, Chicago.

1974 *Sexual Perversity in Chicago* premieres, Organic Theater, Chicago,
  June.
 Receives Joseph Jefferson Award for Best New Chicago Play
 Works with Illinois Arts Council
 Squirrels premieres, St. Nicholas Theatre Company, Chicago, October
 Mackinac. Bernard Horwich Jewish Community Center, Chicago,
  November

1975 Directs O'Neill's *Beyond the Horizon*, St. Nicholas Theatre Company,
  February
 Sexual Perversity and *Duck Variations*. St. Clements and Cherry Lane
  Theaters, N.Y., November and June. Obie for Best Play
 The Poet and the Rent St. Nicholas Theatre Company, June
 Plays Theseus/Oberon in Oak Park Festival Theatre's *A Midsummer
  Night's Dream*

Marranos. Bernard Horwich Jewish Community Center, Chicago,
    November
American Buffalo premieres, Goodman, October then to St. Nicholas
Visiting lecturer on drama at University of Chicago
St. Nicholas starts a school of acting
Contributing Editor of *OUI* magazine

1976   *Reunion* premieres St. Nicholas Theatre, Chicago, January
        Squirrels benefit performances at St. Nicholas, January
        American Buffalo St. Clements's, N.Y. January
        Leaves as Artistic Director of St. Nicholas Company; moves to N.Y.
        American Buffalo wins Chicago's Joseph Jefferson Award for Out-
            standing Production
        CBS fellowship in Creative Writing at Yale University
        Rockefeller award
        Sexual Perversity and Duck Variations Cherry Lane, N.Y., June
        Children's Theater grant from NY State Council on the Arts
        Obie special award [Best New Play] for *Sexual Perversity in Chicago*
            and *American Buffalo.*

1977   *A Life in the Theatre* premieres, Goodman, Chicago, February
        American Buffalo Broadway's Barrymore Theatre, N.Y., February
        American Buffalo gets the New York Drama Critics' Circle Award for
            Best American play
        All Men Are Whores: An Inquiry Yale Cabaret Theatre, February
        The Water Engine premieres, St. Nicholas, Chicago, May
        Reunion and *Dark Pony* Yale Repertory, October
        Creative Writing Fellowship New Haven, October
        A Life in the Theatre Theatre de Lys, N.Y., October
        The Water Engine airs on Earplay, National Public Radio, September
        The Woods premieres St. Nicholas Theatre, November
        *The Revenge of the Space Pandas; or, Binky Rudich and the Two
            Speed-Clock* St. Clements Co., Queens, June; St. Nicholas
            Theatre, Chicago, November
        Sexual Perversity and *Duck Variations* Regent Theatre, London,
            December
        Marries Lindsay Crouse, December

1978   *The Water Engine and Mr. Happiness* N.Y. Shakespeare Festival, January
        The Water Engine and *Mr. Happiness* Plymouth Theatre, N.Y., March
        Artistic director and playwright-in-residence at Goodman, March
        Prairie du Chien airs on BBC and NPR
        American Buffalo National Theatre, London, June
        Outer Critics Circle Award for contributions to American Theater

1979   *A Sermon* and *Sexual Perversity* Apollo Theatre, Chicago, January
        The Blue Hour: City Sketches N.Y. Public Theater, February
        The Woods N.Y. Public Theater, April
        Prairie du Chien premieres, National Public Radio "Earplay," April
        Lone Canoe or The Explorer Goodman, May
        The Poet and the Rent Circle in the Square, N.Y., May
        A Life in the Theatre Open Space Theatre, London, July
        A Life in the Theatre (filmed telecast of Theatre de Lys performance)
            PBS airs, October
        Reunion, Dark Pony and *The Sanctity of Marriage* Circle Repertory,
            N.Y., October
        Shoeshine. Studio Theatre, NY, December

1980   *Lakeboat* Milwaukee Repertory Theatre, April
        American Buffalo Long Wharf Theatre, New Haven, October
        Directs *Twelfth Night* Circle Repertory, N.Y., December

1981   *A Sermon* Circle in the Square, N.Y.
        Dark Pony and Reunion King's Head, London, February
        The Postman Always Rings Twice is released, March
        American Buffalo Circle in the Square, N.Y,, June

1982   *Lakeboat* Long Wharf Theatre, New Haven, February
        Frog Prince Goodman, Chicago, May
        The Woods Second Stage in N.Y., May
        Edmond premieres Goodman Theatre Studio, June
        Edmond Provincetown Playhouse, N.Y., October
        The Verdict is released, December
        Willa Mamet is born

1983   *The Red River* adaptation Goodman Theatre, Chicago, May
        Five Unrelated Pieces [Two Conversations, Two Scenes, and Yes, But
            So What] Ensemble Studio Theatre, N.Y., May
        Academy Award nomination for Best Adaptation for *The Verdict*
        The Disappearance of the Jews Goodman Theatre, Chicago, June
        The Dog, Film Crew, 4 A.M. Jason's Park Royal Hotel, New York, July
        Glengarry Glen Ross premieres National Theatre, London, September
        Society of West End Theatres' Award in London for Best Play
        American Buffalo Broadway's Booth Theatre, October
        Playwriting Obie Award for *Edmond.* Shared with Caryl Churchill,
            Tina Howe and Harry Kondoleon

1984   *Glengarry Glen Ross* Goodman Theatre, Chicago, February
        Glengarry Glen Ross John Golden Theatre, Broadway, March
        Litko and *Shoehorn* Hartley House Theatre, N.Y.
        Participates in Sanford Meisner documentary
        Glengarry Glen Ross awards:
                Pulitzer Prize for Drama, April
                New York Drama Critics' Circle Award for Best American
                    Play
                Antoinette Perry (Tony) nomination for best play
                American Theater Wing award for best play
                Dramatists' Guild Hall-Warriner Award, 1984.
                Tony nomination for Best Reproduction for *American Buffalo*
        The Frog Prince Milwaukee Repertory Theatre, April
        Vermont Sketches [Pint's a Pound the World Around, Deer Dogs,
            Conversations with the SpiritWorld and Dowsing] Ensemble
            Studio, N.Y., May
        American Buffalo Duke of York's, London, August

1985   *The Cherry Orchard* Goodman, March
        The Shawl premieres and *The Spanish Prisoner* Briar Street, Chicago,
            April
        The Water Engine Goodman Theatre, May
        Goldberg Street and *Cross Patch* WNUR Radio, Northwestern U.,
            March
        Founds Atlantic Theater Company, N.Y.
        Summer workshop in Vermont (with Macy and Mosher)
        "Vint" plays American Rep's tour of *Orchards*, September
        About Last Night is released
        The Shawl and *Prairie du Chien* Mitzi Newhouse Theatre, N.Y.,
            December
        Edmond Royal Court, London, December

1986   *Glengarry Glen Ross* Mermaid Theatre, London, February
        The Shawl and *Prairie du Chien* Royal Court, June
        The Untouchables is released, June
        Writing in Restaurants is published
        American Academy and Institute of Arts and Letters Award for
            Literature.

1987   "Wasted Weekend" is aired, January
        Cameo acting role in *Black Widow*
        Series of lectures at Columbia Film School, fall
        House of Games is released, October

1988   *Uncle Vanya* American Repertory Theatre, Cambridge, MA., April
        Speed-the-Plow premieres Royal Theater, N.Y., May
        "Where Were You When It Went Down?" in *Urban Blight* at the
            Manhattan Theatre Club, N.Y., May
        "Cross Patch" in *Sketches of War*, Boston, October
        House of Games is nominated for a Golden Globe for best screenplay
        The Untouchables is nominated for a Writers Guild for best screenplay
            based on material from another medium
        Lip Service is aired October
        Things Change is released, October
        Warm and Cold is published
        The Owl is published
        Zosia Mamet is born

1989   *Speed-the-Plow* National Theatre, London, January
        Tony nomination for best play for *Speed-the-Plow*
        We're No Angels is released
        The Water Engine Hampstead Theatre, London, August
        Life in the Theatre Theatre Royal, London, October
        Some Freaks is published
        Bobby Gould in Hell Mitzi E. Newhouse, N.Y., November

1990   *Squirrels* Annenberg Center, Philadelphia, January
        Uncle Vanya Goodman Theatre, Chicago, May
        Three Sisters Atlantic Theater Company at Festival Theatre in
            Philadelphia, Summer
        Hero Pony is published
        Completes screenplays for *The Deer Slayer, High and Low* and *Ace in
            the Hole* (never produced)
        Divorces Lindsay Crouse

1991   *Uncle Vanya* BBC/PBS broadcast, February
        Bobby Gould in Hell Lyric Studio, London
        Homicide [film] is released
        Yiddish Cinema (documentary) actor
        Father dies
        Marries Rebecca Pidgeon

1992   *Oleanna* premieres American Repertory Theater, Boston in May then
            Orpheum Theater, N.Y., October
        Glengarry Glen Ross [film] is released
        Adapts *The Water Engine* for TNT television; also appears in bit part
        Hoffa release

1993   *Squirrels* King's Head Theatre, London, March
        Oleanna John F. Kennedy Center, Washington D.C. May
        Oleanna Royal Court, June; then Duke of York's, London, September
        A Life in the Theater TNT is aired, October
        Rising Sun [film] is released

1994   *Ricky Jay & His 52 Assistants* directs at Second Stage, N.Y., February
        Oleanna Tiffany Theater, Los Angeles, February
            Tiffany Theater, Los Angeles, February
        The Cryptogram premiere, Ambassadors Theatre, London, June
        Glengarry Glen Ross Donmar Warehouse, London, June
        A Whore's Profession; Notes and Essays is published London, June.
        The Village is published, October
        Vanya on 42nd Street [film] is released, October
        Oleanna [film] is released, November
        Texan is written for Showtime Television
        Collaborates with wife, R. Pidgeon, on lyrics for her album *The Raven*
        Clara Mamet is born

1995   *The Cryptogram* directs, Walsh Theater, Boston, February, then
            Westside Theatre, N.Y., March
        No One Will Be Immune Ensemble Studio, N.Y., May
        Dangerous Corner directs J. B. Priestley's play, Atlantic Theater
            Company, N.Y., October
        Obie Award for Best Play for *The Cryptogram*
        An Interview [Death Defying Acts] Variety Arts Theater, N.Y., March
        Passover is published, April

1996   *The Cryptogram* Steppenwolf, Chicago June.
        The Cryptogram Studio Theatre Washington D.C. 1996-97 season
        Edmond. Atlantic Theater, N.Y., October
        Ricky Jay & His 52 Assistants [TV] directed HBO special
        American Buffalo [film] is released
        Make-Believe Town is published
        The Duck and the Goat is published

1997   *The Woods* Producer's Club, N.Y., January
        Old Neighborhood premiere at Hasty Pudding April in Boston then
            moves to Booth Theatre, N.Y., November
        The Edge is released
        Wag the Dog is released
        The Spanish Prisoner is released
        The Old Religion is published
        True and False: Heresy and Common Sense for the Actor is published

1998   *Lakeboat* Lyric Studio, London, February
        Jade Mountain, Ensemble Studio, N.Y., June
        The Old Neighborhood Royal Court Downstairs, London, June
        Ronin released, October
        Columbia Lectures on American Culture
        Three Uses of the Knife is published

1999   *Lansky* is aired on HBO television
        The Winslow Boy is released
        Boston Marriage premieres, ART in Cambridge, MA, June
        The Water Engine and *Mr. Happiness* Atlantic Theater, N.Y., October
        Agrees to serve for one-year as a contributor to *Premiere* magazine
        Noah Mamet is born
        Henrietta is published
        Bar Mitzvah is published
        Chinaman is published

2000   *Sexual Perversity* and *Duck Variations* Atlantic Theater, January
        Glengarry Glen Ross McCarter Theater, Princeton, NJ, February
        American Buffalo Donmar Warehouse, London, February
        American Buffalo Atlantic Theater, N.Y., March
        Speed-the-Plow New Ambassadors, London, March
        Space Pandas Atlantic Theater, N.Y., March
        State and Main [film] is released
        Contributes cartoons to *Boston* magazine
        Lakeboat [film] is released
        Catastrophe by Beckett is directed and aired
        The Audition Monologue: A Practical Guide for Actors published

2001   *Boston Marriage* Donmar Warehouse, London, March
        Boston Marriage New Ambassadors, London, December
        Heist is released
        Hannibal is released

2002   *Boston Marriage* N.Y. Public Theater, November

2003   *Whistle* (forthcoming)
        The Shadowbox (forthcoming)
        Diary of a Young London Physician (forthcoming)

PRIMARY BIBLIOGRAPHY

Plays

[The date given is for the first production. See individual plays for publishing information]

American Buffalo (1975)
Bobby Gould in Hell (1989)
Boston Marriage (1999)
The Cryptogram (1994)
Dark Pony (1977)
The Duck Variations (1972)
Edmond (1982)
The Frog Prince (1982)
Glengarry Glen Ross (1983)
An Interview (part of *Death Defying Acts*) (1995)
The Jade Mountain (1998)
Lakeboat (1980)
A Life in the Theatre (1977)
Mackinac (1974)
Mr. Happiness (1978)
The Old Neighborhood (1997 includes three previously solo plays: *The Disappearance of the Jews, Jolly,* and *Deeny.*)
Oleanna (1992)
The Poet and the Rent (1975)
Prairie du Chien (1979)
Reunion (1976)
Revenge of the Space Pandas or *Binky Rudich and the Two-Speed Clock* (1978)

The Sanctity of Marriage (1979)
Sexual Perversity in Chicago (1974)
The Shawl (1985)
The Spanish Prisoner (1973)
Speed-the-Plow (1988)
Squirrels (1974)
The Water Engine, An American Fable (1977)
The Woods (1977)

Play Collections

Five Television Plays. New York: Grove Weidenfeld, 1990. (includes *A Waitress in Yellowstone or Always Tell the Truth, Bradford, The Museum of Science and Industry Story, A Wasted Weekend, We Will Take You There*.)

Goldberg Street: Short Plays and Monologues. New York: Grove, 1985 (includes *Goldberg Street* (1985), *Cross Patch* (1985), *The Spanish Prisoner* (1985), *Two Conversations, Two Scenes, Yes But So What, Vermont Sketches* (1984); *The Dog, Film Crew, Four A.M.*(1983); *The Power Outage* (1977), *Food, Columbus Avenue, Steve McQueen, Yes, The Blue Hour: City Sketches* (1979), *A Sermon* (1979), *Shoeshine, Litko: A Dramatic Monologue* (1972), *In Old Vermont, All Men Are Whores: An Inquiry* (1977)

No One Will Be Immune. New York: Dramatists Play Service, 1994. (includes *Almost Done, Two Enthusiasts, Sunday Afternoon, The Joke Code, A Scene-Australia, Fish, A Perfect Mermaid, Dodge, L. A. Sketches, A Life with No Joy in It, Joseph Dintenfass, No One Will Be Immune* (1995)

Short Plays and Monologues. New York: Dramatists Play Service, 1981. (includes *The Blue Hour: City Sketches, Prairie du Chien*, A Sermon, *Shoeshine (1979), Litko* (1981), *In Old Vermont, All Men are Whores: An Inquiry*)

The Spanish Prisoner and The Winslow Boy: Two Screenplays by David Mamet. New York: Vintage, 1998.

Three Children's Plays. New York: Grove, 1986. (includes *The Poet and the Rent* (1974), *The Frog Prince*, and *The Revenge of the Space Pandas or Binky Rudich and the Two-Speed Clock*)

Three Jewish Plays. New York: S, French, 1987. (includes *Disappearance of the Jews, Goldberg Street, The Luftmensch*)

Unpublished

Addiction (1985)
Lone Canoe or The Explorer (1979),
Makinac (1974)
Marranos (1975)
Where Were You When It Went Down (1988)

Adaptations

The Red River adapted from Pierre Laville's *Le Fleuve Rouge* (1983)
The Cherry Orchard by Anton Chekhov, Trans. Peter Nelles (1985). New York: Grove, 1987.
The Three Sisters: A Play by Anton Chekhov. Trans. Vlada Chernomordik. New York: Grove, 1991.
Uncle Vanya by Anton Chekhov. Trans. Vlada Chernomordik (1988). New York: Grove, 1989. (1994)
"Vint." *Orchards: Seven Stories by Anton Chekhov and Seven Plays They Have Inspired.*(1985) New York: Knopf, 1986. 39-48.

Poetry

Warm and Cold. Illus. Donald Sultan. New York: Grove Press, 1988.
The Hero Pony. New York: Grove Weidenfeld, 1990.
The Chinaman. New York: Overlook, 1999.

Children's Books

Bar Mitzvah. Illus. Donald Sultan. New York: Little, Brown, 1999.
The Duck and the Goat. Illus. Maya Kennedy. New York: St. Martin's, 1996.
Henrietta. Illus. Elizabeth Dahlie. Boston: Houghton Mifflin, 1999.
The Owl, with Lindsay Crouse. Illus. Stephen Alcorn. New York: Kipling, 1987.
Passover. Illus. Michael McCurdy. New York: St. Martin's, 1995.

Nonfiction: Essays, Speeches, Lectures and Collections

3 Uses of the Knife: On the Nature and Purpose of Drama. New York: Columbia UP, 1998.
The Audition Monologue: A Practical Guide for Actors, with Karen Kohlhaas. New York: Atlantic Theatre Company, 2000.
The Cabin: Reminiscence and Diversions. New York: Turtle Bay, 1992.
Jafsie and John Henry. New York: Free Press, 1999.
Make-Believe Town: Essays and Remembrances. Boston: Little, Brown, 1996.

Notes for a Catalogue for Raymond Saunders, with Raymond Saunders. San Francisco: Stephen Wirtz Gallery, 1985.

On Directing Film. New York: Viking-Penguin, 1991.

Some Freaks. New York: Viking, 1989.

South of the Northeast Kingdom. Washington, D.C. : National Geographic Society, 2002.

True and False: Heresy and Common Sense for the Actor. New York: Pantheon, 1997.

A Whore's Profession: Notes and Essays. London: Faber, 1994.

Writing in Restaurants. New York: Viking-Penguin, 1986.

Fiction

The Old Religion. New York: Free Press, 1997.

The Village. Boston: Little, Brown 1994.

Wilson: A Consideration of the Sources. London: Faber, 2000.

Others' Plays—Directed

Beyond the Horizon by Eugene O'Neill, at Grace Lutheran Church, Chicago (1975).

Catastrophe by Samuel Beckett, television, London (2000).

Dangerous Corner by J. B. Priestley, Atlantic Theatre Company, New York (1995).

Ricky Jay and his 52 Assistants. (1994; HBO, 1998).

Ricky Jay on the Stem. Second Stage Theatre, New York (2002)

Twelfth Night. Circle Repertory (1980)

Films and Television

1979   *Life in the Theatre* (filmed telecast of theatrical performance) —writer

1981   *The Postman Always Rings Twice*—screenplay based on James M. Cain novel, Paramount

1982   *The Verdict*—screenplay based on Barry Reed novel (Academy Award Nomination for Screenplay Based on Material from another Medium), Columbia.
            Malcolm X—screenplay never produced

1984   *Sanford Meisner* (documentary)—himself, Films for the Humanities

1986   *About Last Night* (adapted from Mamet's *Sexual Perversity in Chicago)*, RCA/Columbia

1987   *Black Widow*—actor (Herb), 20th Century Fox
           The Untouchables—screenplay based on a novel *Untouchables,* Paramount
           "Wasted Weekend" episode of *Hill Street Blues* (television)—writer,
                typescript at NYPL
           House of Games—co-writer and director, British Film Critics Circle Award
                for Best Film in 1988, Orion Pictures (New York: Grove, 1987; London:
                Methuen, 1987)

1988   *Things Change*—co-writer with Shel Silverstein and director, Columbia
                (New York: Grove, 1988; London: Methuen, 1989)
           Lip Service (television)—executive producer, Prism, HBO, Filmhaus

1989   *We're No Angels*—writer (as suggested by play and movie of *My Three
                Angels*), Paramount (New York: Grove, 1990)

1990   *The Deer Slayer, High and Low,* and *Ace in the Hole*—screenplays never
                produced

1991   *Homicide*—writer and director, Columbia (New York: Grove, 1992)
           Yiddish Cinema (documentary)—himself, National Center for Jewish Film
           Uncle Vanya (television)— teleplay from a literal translation of Chekhov's
                play

1992   *Hoffa*—writer and associate producer, 20th Century Fox
           Glengarry Glen Ross—writer and screenwriter, New Line Cinema
           The Water Engine (television)—writer and actor (brown-haired man),
                Amblin Television

1993   *A Life in the Theatre* (television)—writer, teleplay and executive
                producer, Turner Entertainment
           Rising Sun—screenwriter (uncredited) 20th Century Fox

1994   *Oleanna*—writer, screenwriter and director, Samuel Goldwyn
           Vanya on 42nd Street (film)—adaptation of Chekov's play, Film Four
                International
           Texan (television)—writer, Chanticleer Films

1996   *American Buffalo* (film)—writer and screenwriter, Samuel Goldwyn

1997   *Wag the Dog* (film)—co-screenwriter of Larry Beinhart book (Academy
                Award nomination for Best Adapted Screenplay and Golden Globe
                nomination for Best Screenwriter), New Line Cinema
           The Spanish Prisoner—writer and director, Sweetland Films
           The Edge—(working title *Bookworm*) writer, 20th Century Fox

Ronin—co-screenwriter (as Richard Weisz), MGM
Ricky Jay and His 52 Assistants (television-HBO)—director

1999   *The Winslow Boy*—screenwriter and director of Terence Rattigan play
        Lansky—(television) screenwriter based in part on book, *Meyer Lansky:
        Mogul of the Mob*, and executive producer, HBO

2000   *State and Main*—writer and director, Fine Line Pictures. (London: Methuen,
        2001)
        Lakeboat—writer, Oregon Trail Films
        Catastrophe—(television) screenwriter and director of Samuel Beckett play,
        London: Clarence Pictures

2001   *Heist*—writer and director, Morgan Creek Productions
        Hannibal—screenwriter of Thomas Harris novel, MGM

2003   *Whistle*—screenwriter of James Jones novel (forthcoming)
        The Shadowbox—screenwriter of Michael Cristofer play (forthcoming)
        Diary of a Young London Physician—screenwriter and director
        (forthcoming)

Selected Short Writings

Many of Mamet's articles have been gathered into these collections:

M 1 *The Cabin*. New York: Turtle Bay, 1992.

M 2 *Jafsie and John Henry: Essays*. New York: Free Press, 1999.

M 3 *Make-Believe Town*. New York: Little, Brown, 1996.

M 4 *Some Freaks*. New York: Viking, 1989.

M 5 *Writing in Restaurants*. New York: Viking, 1986.

M 6 *A Whore's Profession*. London: Faber and Faber, 1994. (Contains *The Cabin, Writing in Restaurants, Some Freaks* and *On Directing Film*)

M 7 *David Mamet in Conversation*. Ed. Leslie Kane. Ann Arbor: University of Michigan Press, 2001.

1974   "Stanislavsky and Squirrels." *Chicago Sun-Times* 6 Oct. 1974, sec. 3.

1977   "The Power Outage (Short Story)." *New York Times* 6 Aug. 1977: 17.

1978   "Learn to Love the Theater." *Horizon* Oct. 1978: 96.
        "A National Dream-Life." *Dramatists Guild Quarterly* 15 (1978): 30-32. Rpt. in *Writing in Restaurants*.

"Realism." *New York Arts Journal* Nov.-Dec. 1978: 21. Rpt. in *Writing in Restaurants.*

1979   "A Tradition of the Theatre as Art." *New York Theatre Review* Feb. 1979: 24. Rpt. in *Writing in Restaurants.*
"Playwrights on Resident Theaters: What Is to Be Done?" *Theater* 10.3 (1979): 82.

1980   "A Playwright Learns from Film." *New York Times* 20 July 1980, sec. B: 6.

1981   "Final Cut: Special Delivery: David Mamet." *Cinema* 6 Mar. 1981.
"First Principles." *Theater* 12.3 (1981): 50-52. Rpt. in *Writing in Restaurants.*
"Living Playwrights in the Living Theatre: Lanford Wilson." *Dramatics* May 1981: 31.
"Mamet in Hollywood." *Horizon* Feb. 1981: 56-57.
"My Kind of Town." *Horizon* Nov. 1981: 56-57.

1982   "Air Plays." *Horizon* May-June 1982: 20-23.

1983   "Tennessee Williams: March 26th, 1911-February 25th, 1983." *Rolling Stone* 14 Apr. 1983: 124. Rpt. in *Writing in Restaurants.*

1984   "Why I Write for Chicago Theatre." *Vanity Fair* Nov. 1984.

1985   "Conventional Warfare." *Esquire* March 1985: 110-14. Rpt. in *Some Freaks.*
"Don't Tense Me In." *Mademoiselle* Nov. 1985: 136.
"Heat." (book review) *New York Times Book Review* May 1985.
"Las Vegas, Love it or Leave it." (book review) *New York Times Book Review* 19 May 1985: 15.
"A Playwright 'Plinker' Finds Joy in the Practice of Shooting Pistols." *Sports Illustrated* 4 Nov. 1985: 96+. Rpt. in *Some Freaks.*
"Too Much Sex, Too Little Love: What Ails the U.S. Male." With C.D.B. Bryan, Roy Blount, Stephen King, Robert Coles, Tom Biracree. *Mademoiselle* Nov. 1985: 134+.

1986   "Address to the American Theater Critics Convention." *Horizon*. Rpt. in *Writing in Restaurants.*
"Against Amplification." *Dramatists Guild Quarterly*. Rpt. in *Writing in Restaurants.*
"Chicago." *Horizon*. Rpt. in *Writing in Restaurants.*
"Concerning the *Water Engine.*" *Daily News* [New York]. Rpt. in *Writing in Restaurants.*

"An Embarrassment of Liberty When a Young Nation Grows Old, It Turns Its Back on the Huddled Masses." *Chicago Tribune* 29 June 1986: 6.

"Epitaph for Tennessee Williams." *Rolling Stone*. Rpt. in *Writing in Restaurants*.

"Family Vacation." *Vogue*. Rpt. in *Writing in Restaurants*.

"Introduction." *A Practical Handbook for the Actor.* Ed. Melissa Bruder, Vintage, 1986.

"National Dream-Life." *Dramatists Guild Quarterly*. Rpt. in *Writing in Restaurants*.

"Oscars." *Gentleman's Quarterly*. Rpt. in *Writing in Restaurants*.

"Playwright in Hollywood." *Horizon*. Longer version rpt. in *Writing in Restaurants*.

"The Pool Hall." *Rolling Stone* 17 July 1986: 52+. Rpt. in *Writing in Restaurants*.

"Radio Drama." *Horizon*. Rpt. in *Writing in Restaurants*.

"Schoolyard Law." *Harper's* Oct. 1986: 273+. Excerpt from *Writing in Restaurants*.

"The Things Poker Teaches." *New York Times Magazine* 20 Apr. 1986: 52. Longer version rpt. in *Writing in Restaurants*.

"True Stories of Bitches." *Vanity Fair*. Rpt. in *Writing in Restaurants*.

1987   "Caribbean Therapy." *Vogue* Feb. 1987: 298+.

"I Lost It at the Movies." *American Film* 12.8 (1987): 19-23.

1988   "In Losing, a Boxer Won." *New York Times* 7 Oct. 1988: A35. Rpt. as "The Laurel Crown" in *Some Freaks*.

"One April, 1988." *Paris Review* 107 (1988): 197. Rpt. in *The Hero Pony*. Poem.

"Speed-the-Plow." *(*excerpt) *Interview* Apr. 1988: 99+.

1989   "Chicago's Unique Cultured Voice of Home: WFMT" *Chicago Tribune* 1 Aug. 1989: 113. Rpt. in *The Cabin*.

"Dodge." *(*play) *Harper's* Feb. 1989: 43-44.

"Fighting Words." *Playboy* Dec. 1989: 118.

"Raymond Saunders: Notes for a Catalogue Essay." *Artspace* 13.2 (1989): 40. Rpt. in *Writing in Restaurants*.

"Sexual Perversity in Chicago." *Playboy* Jan. 1989: 200.

"A Time for Mickey Mouse." *Playboy* Aug. 1989 Rpt. as " A Party for Mickey Mouse" in *Some Freaks*.

"Talk of the Times: New Works in the Playwright's Art." *Harper's* Feb. 1989: 37+. With David Hare and Harold Pinter.

"The Truck Factory." *Chicago Tribune* 10 Dec. 1989: 11. Rpt. in *The Cabin*.

1990   "Back Street of Dreams; Coming of Age on Wabash Avenue, a World of
        Wonder Under the 'L'." *Chicago Tribune* 7 Oct. 1990: 34. Rpt. in
        The Cabin.

"Chelsea Days." *Conde Nast's Traveler* Apr. 1990: 168. Rpt. in *The Cabin.*

"Cold Toast." *Conde Nast's Traveler* Nov. 1990. Rpt. in *The Cabin.*

"Fine, I Gave Up Cigars. Now Cut the Music." *Chicago Tribune* 11 May
        1990: 23. Rpt. in *The Cabin.*

"He's the Kind of Guy Who . . ." *Theater Week* 22 Jan. 1990.

"Hot Tea and Cold Toast." *Conde Nast's Traveler* Apr. 1990: 150.

"In the Company of Men." *Playboy* Apr. 1990: 102. Rpt. in *Some Freaks.*
        New York: Viking, 1989. 85-91.

"Some Lessons from Television." *Dramatics* 61.9 (1990): 12.

"Two Men." (poem) *Paris Review* Spring 1990: 43. Rpt. in *The Hero
        Pony.*

1991   "Canned Applause." *Conde Nast Traveler* Oct. 1991: 146+.

"A Joe from Chicago." *Vogue* Apr. 1991: 308-11.

"A Life with No Joy in It." (play) *Antaeus* 66 (1991): 291+.

"Reminiscing without Reservations: Salad Days at the Hotel Lincoln."
        Chicago Tribune 8 Dec. 1991. Rpt. in *The Cabin.*

1992   "71st and Jeffery." *Chicago Tribune* 26 Apr. 1992, sec. 10: 23. Rpt. in
        The Cabin.

"The Cabin; On Failures of the Imagination and Lonely Days in the
        Woods." (excerpted from *The Cabin*) *Los Angeles Times* 6 Dec. 1992:
        42.

"First Person; the Buttons on the Board: A Playwright's Modest Collec-
        tion Transports Him to Places Unknown and Unknowable." *Art &
        Antiques* Nov. 1992: 35-37. Rpt. in *The Cabin.*

"Home Guide." Rev. of *Dodsworth. Premiere* Sept. 1992: 139.

"Homespun Fop." *New York Times Magazine* 21 June 1992: 14+. Rpt. in
        Make-Believe Town.

"Hotel Atlantic." (poem) *Grand Street* 41 (1992): 145-47. Rpt. in *The
        Chinaman.*

"I Was a Teenage Off-Broadway Gofer." *Observer* [New York] 2 Nov.
        1992: 22.

"In Vermont." *M* Oct. 1992: 77+. Rpt. in *The Cabin.*

"Memories of Off Broadway." *New York Observer* 2 Nov. 1992. Rpt. in
        Make-Believe Town.

"*Oleanna*: Creative in Our Rage." *American Repertory News* 12.3 (1992): 18.

"The Rake: A Few Scenes from My Childhood." *Harper's* June 1992:
        69-72. Rpt. in *The Cabin.*

"Screen: Cut to the Bone." *Guardian* 13 Feb. 1992: 27.

1993   "Girl Copy." *Allure* Oct. 1993. Rpt. in *Make-Believe Town.*
       "In the Mamet Manner." *Elle Decor* Apr. 1993: 70-75.
       "Mamet on Playwriting." *Dramatists Guild Quarterly* Spring (1993): 8-14.
       "*Oleanna.*" (playscript) *Theater Heute* 10 (1993): 35-43.
       "Two Colors." (poem) *New Yorker* 15 Nov. 1993: 80. Rpt. in *The Chinaman*
       "The Watch-Memoir." *Playboy* 1 Jan. 1993: 142.
       "The Waterworld." (poem) *Ploughshares* Spring 1993: 187. Rpt. in *The Chinaman.*

1994   "Anguished Games of Psychic I-Spy." *Observer* 3 July 1994, sec. Review: 22.
       "Deer Hunting." *Men's Journal* Fall 1994. Rpt. in *Make-Believe Town.*
       "Delsomma's." German *Vogue* Feb. 1994. Rpt. in *Make-Believe Town.*
       "The Diner" *Land's End Catalog* Feb. 1994: 14-15. Rpt. in *Make-Believe Town.*
       "A Gambler For Life." *Playboy.* Jan.1994. Rpt. in *Make-Believe Town* as "Gems from a Gambler's Bookshelf."
       "Manhattan Memories and Chelsea Mornings." *Observer* 21 May 1994, sec. Review: 2.
       "Movie Master Class." *Guardian* 16 June 1994: T10.
       "The Northern Novel." *Los Angeles Times Book Review* 9 Oct. 1994. Rpt. in *Make-Believe Town.*
       "The Village." (excerpt) *Playboy.* Sept. 1994: 78.
       "Why Schindler Is Emotional Pornography [How Jews Are Portrayed in Hollywood]." *Guardian* 30 Apr. 1994: 30. Rpt. in *Make-Believe Town* as "The Jews for Export."

1995   "Editing Among Friends." (obituary for Michael VerMeulen) *Guardian* 30 Aug. 1995: T15. With Christopher Silvester.
       "The Last Hand." *Men's Journal* 1995. Rpt. as "Six Hours of Perfect Poker" in *Jafsie and John Henry: Essays.*
       "Passover." (short story) *Los Angeles Magazine* Apr. 1995: 84-89.
       "The Room." (short story) *Grand Street* Spring 1995: 163-66.
       "Smash Cut." *Scenario* 1995. Rpt. in *Jafsie and John Henry: Essays.*
       "Tough Talk on Entertainment (forum on violence)." *Time* 12 June 1995: 32+.
       "Uncle Vanya." *Literary Cavalcade* (March 1995): 11.

1996   "Between Men and Women." *Nation* 1 Jan. 1996: 34-35. Rpt. in *Here Lies My Heart: Essays on Why We Marry, Why We Don't, and What We Find There.* Eds. Deborah Chasman and Catherine Jhee. Boston: Beacon Press, 1999.

"Blue Valentines." (a short story, published with stories by Kathryn Harrison and Pearson Marx) *Vogue* Feb.1996: 240+.

"Diary of a Sweater." *Esquire* March 1996: 42-43. Rpt. as "Black Cashmere Sweater" in *Jafsie and John Henry: Essays.*

"Domicile." *Architectural Digest* 1996. Rpt. in *Jafsie and John Henry: Essays.*

"Driver's Ed Series: The Chicago Rules." *Chicago Tribune* 28 Aug. 1996: 3.

"Hollywood Not Confidential; David Mamet Would Like to Share Some Choice Tidbits; Art as Prop and Other Tales of 'Those' People." *Los Angeles Times* 5 May 1996: 22.

"L.A. Homes." *Los Angeles Times* 1996. Rpt.in *Jafsie and John Henry: Essays.*

"Mad Hatters." *Esquire* Jan. 1996: 22. Rpt. as "Caps" in *Jafsie and John Henry: Essays.*

"Mamet on Playwriting." (an edited transcript of his answers at a Q & A session) *Dramatist's Guild Quarterly* 1996: 8-14.

"Nice Butt, Shame About the Script." *Guardian* 22 Nov. 1996: T6.

"Noach" *Genesis As It Is Written*. Ed. David Rosenberg. Harper: San Francisco, 1996. 59-62.

"Off with the Old Love." (short story) *Vogue* Feb. 1996: 240-42.

"Resorts." *Esquire* 1996. Rpt. in *Jafsie and John Henry: Essays.*

"Scotch." *Playboy* Feb. 1996: 106+. Rpt. as "Scotch Malt Whisky Society" in *Jafsie and John Henry: Essays.*

"Soul Murder." *Granta* Aug. 1996: 73.

"We Take the Brash View." *Time* 2 Sept. 1996: 42.

1997   "Business Is Business." *American Theatre* Nov. 1997: 16-17. (excerpted from *True and False*. New York: Pantheon, 1997)

"A Charade." (poem) *Ploughshares* Winter 1997: 93. Rpt. in *The Chinaman.*

"It's Genius! Artists Cheer the Best of the Year." *Village Voice* 7 Jan. 1997: 24+.

"Karmann Ghia." *Black Book* Fall 1997: 12. Rpt. in *Jafsie and John Henry: Essays.*

"Men without Women" *Mirabella* Nov./Dec. 1997: 168+.

"Restoration Drama." *Architectural Digest* Feb. 1997: 116+.

"Soul Murder: a Family Matter." *Utne Reader* Jan./Feb. 1997: 37. (excerpted from the Autumn 1996 issue of *Granta*)

1998   "Bad Boys." *Black Book* Fall 1998: 162-63. Rpt. in *Jafsie and John Henry: Essays.*

"K-22." *Black Book* Winter 1997/98: 146-50.

"The Deer Hunter." *Sports Afield* Winter 1998/99: 86+. Rpt. in *The Best American Sports Writing* 1999. Ed. Richard Ford. Boston: Houghton Mifflin, 1999. Rpt. as "Late Season Hunt" in *Jafsie and John Henry: Essays.*

"I'm on the Corner: A Distinguished Playwright's Advice to Actors." *Dramatics* 69.5 (1998): 18.

"Knives." *Men's Journal.* 1998-99. Rpt. in *Jafsie and John Henry: Essays.*

"Producers." *Black Book* Summer 1998: 142-43. Rpt. in *Jafsie and John Henry: Essays.*

"Prosody." *Black Book* Winter 1997/98: 149-50.

"Public as Sacrifice." *Black Book* Spring 1998: 32-33.

"Racing Demon." *Travel & Leisure* Oct. 1998: 126+. Rpt. as "Race Driving School" in *Jafsie and John Henry: Essays.*

"Salad Days." *Grand Street* Spring 1998: 144+. Rpt. in *Jafsie and John Henry: Essays.*

"The Screenplay and the State Fair." *Zoetrope* 1998. Rpt. in *Jafsie and John Henry: Essays. Zoetrope: All Story* 5 Jan. 2003 <http://www.all-story.com/issues.cgi?action=show_story&story_id=36>.

"Spanish Prisoner." (screenplay) *Scenario* Spring 1998: 102-49.

1999   "The Fireman's Child." *Tikkun* Mar./Apr. 1999: 32.

"Fix." *Tikkun* July/Aug. 1999: 32+.

"In Memoriam, David Mamet Eulogizes an Old Pal. [Kenny Lilliebridge]" *Chicago Tribune* 16 Feb. 1999, C1.

"Passions: Vermont's River Run." *Food & Wine* June 1999: 78+.

"The Question." *Tikkun,* Nov./Dec. 1999: 31.

"Samson, or Homage to Shel." *Tikkun* Sept. 1999: 32.

2000   "Burning House, and Other Tales from the Van." *New York Times* 10 Sept. 2000, sec 2: 53.

"The Humble Genre Novel, Sometimes Full of Genius." *New York Times* 17 Jan. 2000: E1.

"Love in a Warm Sweater." *Daily Telegraph* [London] 22 Feb. 2000. Rpt. from *Jafsie and John Henry* which was rpt. from "Diary of a Sweater." *Esquire* March 1996: 42.

"One or Two Steps Behind." (short story) *Playboy* Jan. 2000: 186.

"Whisky Galore." *Independent* 12 Feb. 2000: 33+. Rpt. from "Scotch." *Playboy* 1 Feb. 1996: 106+. Rpt. in *Jafsie and John Henry.*

2001   "A Beloved Friend Who Lived Life the Chicago Way." [Shel Silverstein] *New York Times* 14 Oct. 2001: AR7.

"The Cheap Hello." (short play) *Harvard Review* Fall 2001.

"A Day at the Beach." *Conde Nast Traveler* Nov. 2001: 162+.
"The Goon Squad (tales of movie location crews)." *Guardian* 2 Feb.
2001: S5.
"Ira Glass: He Has Retuned Radio with Old-Fashioned Storytelling."
Time 9 July 2001: 84.
"Jean and Eddie." (short play) *Harvard Review* Fall 2001.
"Moving Pictures." *Premiere* Sept. 2001: 73. With Brigitte Lacombe.

2002   "Be Happy You're In a Real Business." *Across the Board* Mar./Apr. 2002: 11-12.
"Crisis in Happyland." *Sight & Sound* Jan. 2002: 22+.
"Hearing the Notes That Aren't Played." *New York Times* 15 July 2002: E1.

SELECTED INTERVIEWS AND PROFILES

Leslie Kane collected twenty-six interviews, *David Mamet in Conversation,* published by the University of Michigan Press in 2001. Those reprinted in *Conversation* are so indicated below.

1974 Christiansen, Richard. "The Man Who Writes About the Squirrels." *Chicago Daily News* 7 Nov. 1974.

1975 Oliver, Edith. "David Mamet of Illinois." *New Yorker* 10 Nov. 1975: 135-36.

1976 Fraser, C. Gerald. "Mamet Plays Shed Masculinity Myth." *New York Times* 5 July 1976, sec. A: 7.
Wetzsteon, Ross. "David Mamet: Remember That Name." *Village Voice* 5 July 1976: 101+. [*Conversation* 9-15]
Winer, Linda. "David Stages a Victory over a Village Goliath." *Chicago Tribune* 12 Aug. 1976, sec. F: 2.
Zweigler, Mark. "Solace of a Playwright's Ideals." *Dance* [After Dark] Aug. 1976: 42-44. [*Conversation* 16-21]

1977 Barr, Richard. *David Mamet* (Interview). Emerging Playwrights series. New York State Education Dept. Albany, N.Y.: Center for Learning Technologies, 1977. (30 minute videocassette with excerpt of *Duck Variations* at TOFT.)
Bilowit, Ira and Henry Hewes. "Round Table Discussion: Henry Hewes, David Mamet, John Simon and Joe Beruh." *New York Theatre Review* (1977): 29-33. [*Conversation* 22-26]

Kaplan, Sherman. WBBM Radio/78 18 Nov. 1977.

Kroll, Jack. "The Muzak Man." *Newsweek* 28 Feb. 1977: 79.

Leogrande, Ernest. "A Man of Few Words Moves on to Sentences." [Sunday] *Daily News* [New York] 13 Feb. 1977, sec. C: 3. [*Conversation* 27-30]

Preston, Marilynn. "The Dream Rises to Top in Mamet Theory." *Chicago Tribune* 16 Nov. 1977, sec. 2: n.pag.

Raidy, William A. "Playwright with Paid-up Dues." *Los Angeles Times* 27 Nov. 1977: 72.

Saunders, Dick. "Rising Stars: Mamet Play Keeps Bravos Coming." *Chicago Sun-Times* 8 May 1977.

Swope, Martha. "A Sad Comedy About Actors." *New York Times* 16 Oct. 1977, sec. B: 7.

Terry, Clifford. *Chicago Tribune Magazine* 8 May 1977.

Wahls, Robert. "Jogging with Mamet." *Daily News* [New York] 23 Oct. 1977, sec. Leisure: 4.

Winer, Linda. "A Mamet Stage Marathon Races toward a Dead End." *Chicago Tribune* 27 Nov. 1977.

Witz, David. *Chicago Theater* Feb. 1977.

1978   Eder, Richard. "David Mamet's New Realism (Profile)." *New York Times* 12 March 1978, sec. 6: 40+.

Gottlieb, Richard. "The Engine That Drives Playwright David Mamet." *New York Times* 15 Jan. 1978: B1+.

"David [Alan] Mamet." *Current Biography Yearbook*. Ed. Charles Moritz. New York: H. W. Wilson Co., 1978. 274-77.

Drake, Sylie. "The Lunching of a Playwright." *Los Angeles Times* 5 Feb. 1978, sec. Calendar: 1+.

Dzielak, Steven. "David Mamet: An Interview." *New York Arts Journal* (1978): 13-14. [*Conversation* 31-38]

1979   Witt, Linda. "David Mamet." *People* 12 Nov. 1979: 58-63.

1980   Cherubin, Jan. "Two on an Island." *Daily News* [New York] 15 Dec. 1980: M8.

Vallely, Jean. "David Mamet Makes a Play for Hollywood." *Rolling Stone* 3 Apr. 1980: 44-45.

1981   Chase, Chris. "At the Movies." *New York Times* 20 Mar. 1981, sec. C: 6.

Christiansen, Richard. "Postman' Script: David Mamet's Special Delivery." *Chicago Tribune* 15 Mar. 1981, sec. F: 5+.

Duka, John. "Hollywood's Long-Running Romance with James M. Cain." *New York Times* 5 April 1981, sec. B: 15.

Earley, Michael. "An Interview on Scripting the 'Postman Always Rings Twice and the Playwright as Screenwriter." *Performing Arts Journal* 5.3 (1981): 36-40. Rpt. in *Conversations on Art and Performance*, Eds. Bonnie Marranca and Gautam Dasgupta. Baltimore, Johns Hopkins UP, 1999: 259-62.

Leahey, Mimi. "The American Dream Gone Bad." *Other Stages* 4 Nov. 1982: 3.

Lefko, Elliott. "Playwright's Talent Tapped." *Toronto Star* 14 April 1981, sec. D: 1.

Lewis, Patricia and Terry Browne. "David Mamet." *Twentieth-Century American Dramatists*, Part 2. Ed. John MacNicholas. Vol. 7. Detroit: Gale Research Co., 1981. 62-70.

O'Toole, Lawrence. "Broadway to Hollywood." *Film Comment* Nov.-Dec. 1981: 22-25.

Shewey, Don. "David Mamet Puts a Dark Urban Drama on Stage." *New York Times* 24 Oct. 1982, sec. B: 1+.

Taylor, Clarke. "Mamet and the Hollywood Wringer." *Los Angeles Times* 28 March 1981, sec. B: 10.

Yakir, C. "Postman's Words." *Film Comment* Mar./Apr. 1981: 21-24. [*Conversation* 39-45]

1982 Blum, David J. "David Mamet's Wealth of Words." *Wall Street Journal* [May or June] 1982.

Leahey, Mimi. "The American Dream Gone Bad." *Other Stages* 4 Nov. 1982: 3.

1983 Becker, Robert and Scott Heiser. "Donald Sultan with David Mamet." *Interview*, March 1983: 56+.

1984 Cantwell, M. "Bulldog of the Middle Class." *Vogue* July 1984: 279-81.

DeVries, Hilary. "In David Mamet's Hands a Pen Becomes a Whip." *Christian Science Monitor* 21 Mar. 1984: 21.

Taylor, Clarke. "Mamet Is 'Thrilled' by His Pulitzer." *Los Angeles Times* 19 April 1984, sec. F: 7.

1985 Baughn, Ted. "David Mamet (interview)." Videocassette. *Emerging Playwrights* 5 Albany, NY: Center for Learning Technologies, 1985.

Benson, Alan. prod. dir. "Profile of a Writer: David Mamet." London Weekend Television Co., March 24, 1985. 55 min.

Freedman, S. G. "The Gritty Eloquence of David Mamet." *New York Times Magazine* 21 Apr. 1985: 32+.

Nuwer, Hank. "A Life in the Theatre: David Mamet." *Rendezvous: Journal of Arts and Letters* 21.1 (1985): 1-7.

Nuwer, Hank. "Two Gentlement of Chicago: David Mamet and Stuart Gordon." *South Carolina Review* 17 (Spring 1985): 9-20. [*Conversation* 54-59].

1986   Roudané, Matthew C. "An Interview with David Mamet." *Studies in American Drama, 1945-Present* 1 (1986): 73-81. [*Conversation* 46-53] Also rpt. in *Speaking on Stage*. Ed. Philip Kolin. Tuscaloosa: U Alabama P, 1996.
        Guernsey, Otis, Jr. ed. *Broadway Song and Story*. New York: Dodd, Mead, 1986. 405-413.

1987   Brantley, Ben. "Pulitzer-Power Playwright Takes on Screen Challenge." *San Francisco Chronicle* 30 Aug. 1987. [*Conversation* 82-85]
        Freedman, Samuel G. "Games Men Play—on Film and Stage." *New York Times* 15 Mar. 1987, sec. 2: 1+.
        Haupt, D. E. "*Life* Visits David Mamet & Lindsay Crouse." *Life* Oct. 1987: 64+.
        Lehrer, Jim. "MacNeil/Lehrer Newshour." PBS, GWETA-TV 12 Oct. 1987. [*Conversation* 86-90]
        Oken, Stacey. "Postgraduate Pioneers of the 'Mamet Method'." *New York Times* 2 Aug. 1987: B5+.
        Savran, David. "Trading in the American Dream." *American Theatre* Sept. 1987: 12-18. Rpt. in *In Their Own Words: Contemporary American Playwrights*. New York: Theatre Communications Group, 1988. 132-44. [*Conversation* 27-30]
        Sessums, Kevin. "Dammit Mamet!" *Interview* Oct. 1987: 140+.

1988   Carr, Jay. "Things Change for Mamet." *Boston Globe* 9 Oct. 1988: B7. [*Conversation* 91-95]
        Harriott, Esther. "David Mamet." *American Voices: Five Contemporary Playwrights in Essays and Interviews*. Jefferson, NC: McFarland, 1988. 77-97.
        Lacombe, Brigitte. "Fast Forward." *Interview* Nov 1988: 104+.
        Ranvaud, Don. "Things Change." *Sight and Sound* Autumn 1988: 231-2.
        Schvey, Henry. "Celebrating the Capacity for Self-Knowledge." *New Theatre Quarterly* 4.13 (1988): 89-96. [*Conversation* 60-71]
        Stayton, Richard. "A Mamet Metamorphosis." *Los Angeles Herald Examiner* 21 Oct. 1988, sec. Weekend: 6-7. [*Conversation* 96-99]

1989   Billington, Michael. "Dream Sequence." *Guardian* 16 Feb. 1989: 21. [*Conversation* 105-108]
        Blowen, Michael. "David Mamet Pulls No Punches." *Boston Globe* 13 Dec. 1989: 61.
        Case, Brian. "Hard and Fast." *Time Out* 4-11 Jan. 1989: 29-30. [*Conversation* 100-104]
        Christiansen, Richard. "The 'Plow' Boy." *Chicago Tribune* 19 Feb. 1989: Arts 18.
        —. "Sexual Perversity in Chicago." *Playboy* Jan. 1989: 200.
        Clinch, Minty. "Mamet Plots His Revenge" *Observer Magazine* 22 Jan. 1989: 47-50.

1990   London, Todd. "Chicago Impromptu." *American Theatre* July/Aug. 1990:
        14+.

1991   Brunette, Peter. "Mamet Views Cops through a New Lens." *New York
        Times* 10 Feb. 1991.
        Trussler, Simon. "Introduction." *File on Mamet.* Ed. Nesta Jones and
        Steven Dylces. London: Methuen, 1991.
        Kane, Leslie. "Mantegna Acting Mamet." *American Theatre* Sept. 1991:
        18+.

1992   Stayton, Richard. "Enter Scowling." *Los Angeles Times* 23 Aug. 1992,
        sec. Magazine: 20+.
        Story, Richard David. "David Mamet Raises Outrage to an Artform in
        'Oleanna.'" *New York* 14 Sept. 1992: 58.

1993   Billington, Michael. "Man Trouble." *Guardian* 12 June 1993. sec.
        Weekend: 6-9.
        Nightingale, Benedict. "More Aristotle Than Hemingway." *Times* [Lon-
        don] 15 Sept. 1993: 37.
        "Playwright of Oaths and Testosterone: David Mamet, on Trial at the
        Court of Feminism." *Independent* 3 July 1993: 16.

1994   Bragg, Melvyn. "South Bank Show." London Weekend Television, 1994.
        [*Conversation* 143-56]
        Cammuso, F. and H. Seely "Glengarry Glen Plaid." [fashion catalog
        comic] *New Yorker* 9 May 1994: 108.
        Gross, Terry. "Fresh Air with Terry Gross." WHYY [Philadelphia] 17
        Oct. 1994. [*Conversation* 157-62]
        Nightingale, Benedict. "A Portrait of David Mamet, Foreign Playwright
        of the Year." *Theater Heute* Special Issue 1994: 44-45.
        Rose, Charlie. "Charlie Rose Show." WNET-TV (Channel 13, New York)
        11 Nov. 1994. [*Conversation* 163-81]
        Weber, Bruce. "Thoughts from a Man's Man." *New York Times* 17 Nov.
        1994: C1.

1995   Gerard, Jeremy. "Atlantic: Theater Is Rising." *Variety* 18 Sept. 1995: 39+.
        Haugen, Peter. "A Rare Glimpse inside the Mind of David Mamet." *Sac-
        ramento Bee* 14 May 1995: EN7.
        Hurwitt, Robert. "Mamet Has All the Answers for His Critics." *San Fran-
        cisco Examiner* 19 May 1995: C15.
        Norman, Geoffrey and John Rezek. "Playboy Interview: David Mamet."
        Playboy Apr. 1995: 51+. [*Conversation* 123-42]
        Stamberg, Susan. "Interview with David Mamet, Felicity Huffman, Ed
        Begley, Jr. And Shelton Dane." *All Things Considered.* (Natl. Public
        Radio.) 6 Feb.1995.

1996   Mosher, Gregory. "How to Talk Buffalo." *American Theatre* Sept. 1996.

1997   "Charlie Rose Show." WNET-TV Channel 13 [New York] 11 Nov.1997.
        [*Conversation* 182-91]
        Covington, Richard. "David Mamet." *Salon* Oct 1997. 2 Dec. 2002
        <www.salon.com/feature/1997/10/cov_si_24mamet.html>.
        "David Mamet on the Old Religion." *Tikkun* 12.6 (1997): 10.
        Lahr, John. "The Art of Theater." XI *Paris Review* 39.142 (1997): 51+.
        [*Conversation* 109-22]
        Holmberg, Arthur. "It's Never Easy to Go Back." American Repertory
        Theatre 1997. webpage. <http://www.amrep.org/past/neighborhood/
        neigh2.html>. accessed 10 Jan. 2003.
        James, N. "Suspicion-Why is David Mamet Dabbling in Edwardiana?"
        Sight and Sound, 1998.
        Koch, John. "David Mamet: The Interview." *Boston Globe* 9 Nov. 1997: 16.
        Lahr, John. "Fortress Mamet." *New Yorker* 17 Nov. 1997: 70-82. Rpt in
        Times [London] 25 Jan. 1998. sec. Magazine: 14+. Also rpt. in *Show
        and Tell: New Yorker Profiles.* Woodstock, N.Y: Overlook, 2000. 27-51
        Shulgasser, Barbara. *City Arts & Lectures* 20 Nov. 1997: Herbst The-
        atre, San Francisco. [*Conversation* 192-210]

1998   Boerner, Margaret. "From Aristotle to David Mamet: The Half-Moral
        World of America's Most Successful Dramatist." *Weekly Standard* 5
        Oct. 1998: 31.
        Denerstein, Robert. "Mamet on the Games Mamet Plays." *Rocky Moun-
        tain News* [Denver] 1998, sec. D: 6. [*Conversation* 226-229]
        Edwards-Jones, Imogen. "Man of Few Words." *Times* [London] 16 May
        1998.
        Fuller, Graham. "April's Favorite Fooler." *Interview* Apr. 1998: 66.
        Gross, Terry. "Fresh Air with Terry Gross." WHYY [Philadelphia] 26
        June 1998.
        Isaacs, Jeremy. "Face to Face." BBC2 23 Feb. 1998. [*Conversation* 211-
        25]
        Howell, Peter. "Mamet: Man of Many Words is a Good Listener." *Toronto
        Star* 24 Apr. 1998: C1.
        MacDonald, Marianne. "God or Mamet?" *Observer* 26 Apr. 1998: 4+.
        Whitty, Stephen. "Mamet Speaks." *Star-Ledger* [Newark, NJ] 19 Apr.
        1998, sec. 4: 1+.
        "Writing and Directing *The Spanish Prisoner*: A Q &A with David Ma-
        met." *Scenario* Spr. 1998: 99-101.

1999   Archer, John. "Practical Theories." *Herald* [Glasgow] 2 Sept. 1999: 4.
        Graham, Renée. "Mamet with Manners." *Boston Globe* 2 May 1999:
        N1+. [*Conversation* 230-34]
        Jenkins, David. "England of His Dreams." *Daily Telegraph* [London] 28
        Aug. 1999. <http://www.telegraph.co.uk>.

Johnston, Sheila. "Writer in a Class of His Own." *Times* [London] 12 Aug. 1999.

Kalb, Jonathan. "Casting New Light on the Most Visible of Playwrights." *New York Times* 7 Nov. 1999, sec. 2: 8..

2000   Dretzka, Gary. "David Mamet and Hollywood: A Rocky, Fruitful Relationship." *Los Angeles Times* 30 Dec. 2000.

Moss, S. "Home is the Hunter." *Guardian* 19 Feb. 2000: 6-7.

Rigney, Melanie. "Literary Trails: David Mamet's Chicago." *Writer's Digest* June 2000: 43.

Stein, Joel. "David Mamet [Arts/Q & A]." *Time* 25 Dec. 2000: 164.

Wallace, J. "Academia, Go F**k Yourself." *Times Higher Education Supplement* 1425 (2000): 19.

2001   Beith, Malcolm. "Movie Time." *Newsweek* 3 Dec. 2001: 6.

2002   Brown, Hannah. "Schmoozing with David Mamet." *Jerusalem Post* 26 July 2002: ART 16.

McKinley, Jesse. "A Memory of Houdini and, No Escaping It, It's a Gabfest." *New York Times* 16 June 2002: AR 5.

PLAYS: SUMMARIES, PRODUCTIONS, OVERVIEWS, REVIEWS AND SCHOLARLY CRITICISM

AMERICAN BUFFALO

Dedicated to: J. J. Johnston
Scene: Don's Resale Shop. A junkshop.
Time: One Friday. Act One takes place in the morning. Act Two starts around 11:00 that night.
Characters:
Don Dubrow, a man in his late forties and the owner of the shop.
Walter Cole, called Teacher, a friend and associate of Don.
Bob, Don's gopher.

Editions:
American Buffalo. New York: Grove Press, 1976.
American Buffalo. London: Methuen, 1977.
American Buffalo: A Drama in Two Acts. New York: S. French, 1977.
Nine Plays of the Modern Theater. New York: Grove, 1981.
The Obie Winners. Ed. R. Wetzsteon. New York: Doubleday, 1981.
Best American Plays. 8ᵗʰ Series, 1974-1982. New York: Crown 1983. 439-72.
American Buffalo: A Play. David Mamet and Michael McCurdy. San Francisco: Arion Press, 1992. Wood Engravings by Michael McCurdy.
American Buffalo. Dir. Michael Corrente. Samuel Goldwyn Co., 1996. (film)
David Mamet Plays: 1. London: Methuen, 1996. 147-257.

Awards:
Obie Award, Best New American Play for both *American Buffalo* and *Sexual Perversity in Chicago* in 1976.
Citation for Best American Play of 1976-77 from the New York Drama Critics' Circle.

Plot Outline:

As the play opens, Bobby apologizes for losing someone he was supposed to keep track of. Don gives sententious advice and recounts last night's poker game held in the shop. Teach enters complaining of Ruthie and Grace—Ruthie was the big winner at poker; he and Don both were losers. Teach is told about a man who came in the shop and bought a nickel for $90—Don asked the man what he'd offer and took that offer, but Don is sure that it must have been worth more. He's posted Bobby to keep a watch on the buyer, so that Bobby can break in and steal back that coin and others in the man's collection. During the act, Teach suggests he'd be a better break-in man than former drug-addict Bobby, and pushes Don into separating friendship and business. Don tells Teach they need more help—Fletch, whom Don admires as a real man. Teach is upset with the idea, but goes off to get some rest before the job.

In Act Two, Bobby arrives at the shop to get money from Don to buy a coin—ultimately he returns and gives Don a nickel for which, as it turns out, he paid $50. He is told by Don that they won't be doing the job now, but he gives Bob some money for keeping watch. Dismissing Bobby, they wait for Fletch and call "the guy" to see if he's really gone for the weekend as Bobby reported. Bobby arrives with news that Fletch was beaten up and is hospitalized. Teach assumes that Bobby is lying, and they call the hospital; no Fletch. Teach hits Bobby with a pig iron, making his ear bleed, and then Ruthie calls reporting that Fletch is indeed hospitalized at a different hospital. Teach trashes the store, then leaves to get a car to drive Bobby to the hospital. Don apologizes to Bobby for betraying him; Bobby apologizes for lying about the nickel, and about the object of the robbery, whom he'd lost much earlier. Don forgives him.

Production:

pAB 1 American Buffalo premiered at the Ruth Page Auditorium in the Stage 2 series of the Goodman Theatre in Chicago on October 23, 1975, then on weekends through November 9, 1975.

Director:	Gregory Mosher
Set Design:	Michael Merritt
Lighting:	Robert Christen
Graphics:	Francois Robert
Cast:	
Donny:	J. J. Johnston
Teach:	Bernard Erhard
Bobby:	William H. Macy

Overview:

Only Christiansen was positive about the play for its "humor, suspense, and a keen insight into the human spirit." Cassidy, the old doyen of Chicago critics, denounced it for "filthy language;" Syse thought the characters were too much a "dreary slice of life." Dettmer and St. Edmund both thought the play too long and shapeless—even Christiansen thought it could be trimmed. Macy was widely admired for his performance; Erhard was usually criticized as too mechanical.

Reviews:

rAB 1.1 Cassidy, Claudia. Rev. of *American Buffalo*. *WFMT Radio* [Chicago] 26 Oct.
1975. [typescript].

Negative review for "a foul mouthed episode that might be subtitled 'Waiting for Fletch.' [. . .] David Mamet has an interesting talent for characterization,
a strong sense of the suddenly shifting moods, the hazardous imbalance, the
vicious undercurrents of the rootless, shiftless and unstable momentarily lured
by the gleam of something for nothing. [. . .] Does the Goodman's Stage Two
really believe that filthy language is a substitute for drama?"

rAB 1.2 Christiansen, Richard. "*American Buffalo* a Theater Triumph." *Chicago Daily
News* 24 Oct. 1975: 5.

Very positive review of "poetically heightened reality": "Merritt's setting,
a Sargasso Sea of trash, and Robert Christen's shadowy lighting make visible
the cluttered backwater of these lives. And the acting [. . .] is so close to flawless that it becomes poetically heightened reality. Mamet's mesmeric dialog,
which turns gutter language into vibrant music, is perfectly paced and unerr-
ingly delivered."

rAB 1.3 Dettmer, Roger. "*American Buffalo* a Roamer." *Chicago Tribune* 24 Oct.
1975: sec. 3.

Negative review which liked only Macy, but found Erhard's Teach a
role "which holds too many contradictions for any consistency of characterization." The play itself was the problem: "Whether the author, young David Mamet, can organize almost two hours of bleep-rated dialog into a
beginning, a middle, and an end is altogether more problematical. [. . .] And
we come away with the feeling that Mamet writes dialog first, then characters to fit it, and lastly tries to relate them coherently and meaningfully."

rAB 1.4 St. Edmund, Bury. "Like a Play, Only Longer." *Reader* [Chicago]. No other
information available.

Mixed review which saw the script as too long. St. Edmund liked Johnston
and Macy, but not Erhard who was too mechanical: "The script's foremost
achievement is the comically bitter (bitterly comic?) emotional core of these
characters and their chemistry together. While there is little in the way of physical action—in the Mametian universe no one knows what the hell they're doing, and very rarely attempts to do it anyway—'American Buffalo' has a great
deal of plot. [. . .] The ending of the play dissolves rather than resolves."

rAB 1.5 Syse, Glenna. "*American Buffalo* Needs More Work." *Chicago Sun-Times*
24 Oct. 1975.

Negative review of the play and the social caste of characters: "At this point
it is just a dreary slice of life that needs tightening, focusing and clarifying.
Shortening? Yes, but if they took out all the four-letter words, it would last ten
minutes and somewhere along the line it needs an ending."

Production:

pAB 2 This Goodman Theatre production moved to the St. Nicholas Theatre, Chicago, previewed on the 19th and 20th, opened December 21, 1975, then it ran on weekends. The run was extended until February 15 with one cast change: Mike Nussbaum as Teach. The play was nominated for three of Chicago's Joseph Jefferson Awards and won this award for Outstanding Production of 1975.

Overview:

Reviewers were most enthusiastic and perceptive about the play in ways that the later New York critics were not always able to be. Offen saw the "round robin intrigue and manipulation" with Donny as father figure, and Teach as his mentor. The violence also was clearly germa.ne in this interpretation. Powers went where many scholars and critics later arrived: "the type of language determines the type of action." Winer saw Nussbaum as an improvement because he didn't do the "deadpan delivery" of the other two actors, a style Mamet actors have become (in)famous for using. Christiansen, Mamet's biggest supporter, noted the changes in text already—the strengthening of plot line, the tragic recognitions at the end, and Macy bringing tears to the audience in the final pathos.

Reviews:

rAB 2.1 Christiansen, Richard. "Bravos for a Play and a Theater." *Chicago Daily News* 22 Dec. 1975.

Rave review from a critic who noted changes: "Mamet has reworked the play's ending, so that a kind of horrible awareness dawns in the brain of the poor, tortured Bobby, thus hammering a final nail of irony in the coffin of these wasted lives. The author also has embellished some speeches in order to make the 'plot' development stronger. [. . .] J. J. Johnston, now strong and secure as Donny, and the wonderful William H. Macy, so sad in his final pathetic moments as Bobby that he makes one weep, are back from the original cast, joined now by Mike Nussbaum as Teach, giving the play new intensity with his bottled-up fury and vengeful paranoia."

rAB 2.2 Offen, Ron. "*American Buffalo* Coined to Valuable Theater." *Lerner Skyline Newspapers* 7 Jan. 1976.

Very positive review of the play's "deeper, subtextual relationship that exists between the three which is the more significant and which provides the flesh and bones of the play. Here we see that Donny is a father figure to Bobby, while Teach is a kind of mentor to Donny. Each plays off of the other's vanities, weaknesses and self-images in a round robin of intrigue and manipulation."

rAB 2.3 Powers, Ron. "A Playwright with the Chicago Sound." *Chicago Sun-Times* 7 Jan. 1976.

Very positive view which perceived that language determines actions: "'I've always been fascinated by the art of semantics,' Mamet said. 'Words cause specific behavior. The same phrase in Chicago will not produce the same behavior

as it will in New York. Words involve a dynamic interchange; a moral interchange. It is impossible to perform a nonmoral action. And the type of language determines the type of action.'"

rAB 2.4 Winer, Linda. "A Timely Move by St. Nicholas." *Chicago Tribune* 26 Dec.
1975, sec. C: 3.
    Very positive review with an interesting note on Nussbaum's Teach: "Ma-
met's gift is character, language, here almost poetic in its patter profanity, the
dry stylized rhythms and rich reality of the sounds. Gregory Mosher has directed the trio for character depth and comedy pace, though Mike Nussbaum—the
one new cast member—smartly avoids the Sgt. Friday kind of deadpan delivery I think intentionally stamps W. H. Macy's sweet junky kid and J. J. Johnston's
sympathetic hulk of a storekeeper-thief stealing American buffalo nickels. Sty-
listically Mamet or not, Nussbaum's overbearing but endearing lesson-monger
Teach is classic Nussbaum."

Production:
pAB 3 Theater at St. Clement's, New York. January 23 through February 7, 1976.

Director:	Gregory Mosher
Set:	Akira Leo Yoshimura
Lighting:	Gary Porto
Costumes:	Danny Mizell
Stage Manager:	Lynn Gutter
Cast:	
Donny:	Michael Egan
Teach:	Mike Kellin (won Obie Award for Performance)
Bobby:	J. T. Walsh

Overview:
Reviewers were very positive about this New York debut and Obie winning production. Gussow saw the play illustrating the gap between words and emotion, but thought
the "final outburst of violence seems to have strayed from a different work." Feingold
thought the language as the most remarkable feature: "Mamet's writing catches the
magical in the everyday." Oliver noted the three plays that came to New York as impressive for humor and the contrasting styles. But she thought the violence at the end of the
play a shock—"inconceivable" that such "clucks could turn so ruthless and cruel."

Reviews:
rAB 3.3 Feingold, Michael. Rev. of *American Buffalo. The Village Voice* 16 Feb. 1976: 135.
    Spectacular review and appreciation: "Mamet's criminals—a portly fence,
a bumbling professional thief, and a young drifter who hangs around with them—
are like other people, except for the fact of their being criminals, and their supreme unconsciousness (used for great comic effect) of how different that fact
makes them. Without being romantically drab, Mamet's writing catches the
magical in the everyday: in the complex overlapping of simple lines of thought,
the complex defensiveness and caution of simple people, the way the reasoning
of the inarticulate—all of us at certain times—twists back into irrationality."

rAB 3.2 Gussow, Mel. "St. Clement's Presents 3-Character Play." *New York Times*
28 Jan. 1976: 28.

Positive review: "The author also knows the disparity between words and
emotions, how tempers flare and words fail. The comedy comes not just from
the accuracy of the dialogue but from the delivery. [. . . Kellin and Egan] have
an air of undeniable authenticity as a seedy pair of friends and pretenders, the
first edgy and excitable, the second more amiable (but explosive when talking
to an unresponsive telephone). [. . .] The second act is sharper than the first,
until the two men harass nice young Bobby, played by J. T. Walsh. The final
outburst of violence seems to have strayed from a different work."

rAB 3.3 Oliver, Edith. "Off Broadway: Journey into Brooklyn." *New Yorker* 9 Feb.
1976: 78-81.

This first New York production ran only briefly, but got a rave review from
Oliver, noting: "Mamet has now shown an aptitude for vernacular and character in three contrasting milieus, and [. . .] 'American Buffalo' is just as funny,
and this time the undercurrent of greed and treachery is so far under (or else we
are so diverted from it by laughter at the conversation—the marvelous idiom—
of Dubrow and Teach) that the play's violent ending comes as a shock."

Production:
pAB 4 Previewed at the Ethel Barrymore Theatre, Broadway, February 8, opened
February 16, transferred to the Belasco on April 12, and closed on July 11,
1977 for 135 performances.

Director:		Ulu Grosbard
Set:		Santo Loquasto
Lighting:		Jules Fisher
Cast:		
	Donny:	Kenneth McMillan
	Teach:	Robert Duvall
	Bobby:	John Savage

Overview:
Surprisingly, the reviews were mixed. Some reviewers didn't get it at all and thought
the plot fizzled out. Watt was the most extreme in this vein: "the three dimwits become increasingly boring and their stupidity and fumbling efforts, however realistic,
simply add to the confusion of a play that promises much more than it delivers." Beaufort thought Mamet reached for too much and missed. Barnes was appreciative, seeing both Duvall's "psychotic nature" as well as "the touching belief they have in their
own cleverness." Porterfield and Kissel saw it as an opportunity for three major acting performances. But Gottfried went furthest in seeing both the attack on capitalism
as well as how this plays into Duvall's acting of the piece: "His ignorant and incompetent leadership of the shopkeeper, his frustration by the junkie, his fright and anger
and capacity for violence make him the mesmerizing center of a mesmerizing situation. Along with the other two, he presents a working class America whose basic,
informal self has been reduced to animal impulses."

Reviews:

rAB 4.1 Barnes, Clive. "Stage: Skilled *American Buffalo.*" *New York Times* 17 Feb.
1977: 50. Rpt. in *New York Theatre Critics' Review* 38.3 (1977): 364.

A very positive review which focused on relationships: "Mamet most clearly shows his skills and quality [. . .] in his depiction of the three men, particularly the relationship between the oldest and the youngest, and the psychotic nature of the middle man who takes violent eccentricity beyond the point of madness. [. . .] Both actors are clever at suggesting a relationship that may be homosexual and certainly has a great deal of affection in it. [. . .] Duvall's role is complex and nervy. He alternates between self-pity and wild gusts of paranoid fury. His body is like a clenched fist, his manner has the danger of a rattlesnake, and he talks with a childlike tone of pure, sweet unreason."

rAB 4.2 Beaufort, John. Rev. of *American Buffalo. Christian Science Monitor* 23
Feb. 1977. Rpt. in *New York Theatre Critics' Review* 38.3 (1977): 368.

Negative review: "Mr. Mamet appears to be grouping [sic] for an extended metaphor. He possesses the knack for accurately recording the scabrous vocabulary, jerky rhythms, half-formulated thoughts, and nonsequiturs of his ludicrously inept hoodlums. But the knack becomes a trick and the trick grows monotonous. Furthermore, the playwright's observations (psychological, sociological, etc.) are too superficial to waste time upon."

rAB 4.3 Christiansen, Richard. "Mamet Scores a Hit with Broadway Critics." *Chicago Daily News* (about 18 Feb.) 1977.

First surveying the positive reviews of New York critics, Christiansen noted that "Duvall pays off brilliantly in his relentless portrayal of the petty hood who spits out Mamet's beautifully structured speeches of gutter language with the intensity of a raging poet. Kenneth McMillan is right up there with Duvall as Donny, the decent, stupid slob shopowner, dominating the stage like a grizzled, foul-mouthed Buddha. Only John Savage's twitchy performance as Bobby, the dope addict kid, left me unsatisfied, for, to tell the truth, that role will forever be engraved in my mind through the luminous, touching portrayal by William H. Macy in Chicago."

rAB 4.4 Clurman, Harold. Rev. of *American Buffalo. Nation* 12 Mar. 1977: 313.

This is a positive review which recognized the technique: "He employs the language of people who have not yet arrived at the stage of integrated personality; they are void of coherent inner experience. Words, barely assimilated, casually picked up from the public media, rattle around in their consciousness only to come out in half-finished, involuted and convoluted spurts of verbiage, more gibberish than meaning. The effect is sometimes very funny and strangely disheartening. Millions speak so. [. . .] The fragmentation and vagueness of the play's plot and dialogue constitute its meaning."

rAB 4.5 Coe, Richard L. "*Buffalo*: Is This Drama?" *Washington Post* 30 Mar. 1977: B9.

Negative review of Mamet's treatment of character: "No characters have altered one whit, nothing has happened. [. . .] Is this drama? The play has been praised as expressing the loneliness of the three men and for the 'beautiful language' of Mamet as illustrative of 'pure street talk.' I didn't believe most of the dialogue, accurate as snatches of it may be. In fact, I found Mamet rather patronizing of his characters, mocking their ignorant pretensions from a perch of superiority. [. . .] One may summon compassion for such unfortunates, but to label, as some have, this leaden excursion into meanderings of inarticulate, failed criminals as 'the best American play of the year' is merely to reflect what a trashy theater season New York has had."

rAB 4.6 Duberman, Martin. "The Great Gray Way." *Harper's* May 1978: 79-87.

This overview of American drama found Thomas Babe superior to Mamet and Innaurato—on Mamet he was totally negative: "They are preparing, you see, to steal a reputedly valuable coin collection. They never do. Why? Apparently—as the dialogue attests—because no one can get up the energy. They prefer to sit around and repeat each other's opaque non-statements, for diversion, occasionally converting declaration ('No') into query ('No?'). They also, now and then, languorously collide. We're never sure about what. And we soon cease to care."

rAB 4.7 Gill, Brendan. "No News from Lake Michigan." *New Yorker* 28 Feb. 1977: 54-55.

Negative review of an "offensive" work, "less because of the language of which it is composed—every third word is either scatological or obscene; street language attempting in vain to perform the office of eloquence, as it does in so many black plays—than because it is presumptuous. The playwright, having dared to ask for our attention, provides only the most meagre crumbs of nourishment for our minds."

rAB 4.8 Gottfried, Martin. "*Buffalo* Is a Rare Broadway Coin." *New York Post* 17 Feb. 1977. Rpt. in *New York Theatre Critics' Review* 38.3 (1977): 365.

Positive review of the play as a comment on America: "Mamet means for the situation to represent America and its capitalistic system—the go-getters, the seekers after quick profits, and the legacy of it all as represented by the love-starved junkie. It is a point that he never gets around to resolving but the characters, the dynamic of the situation and the eerie suspension of this world are the play's fascination. The character of Teacher energizes the work. A disorganized organizer, an illogical logician, stupidly crafty and feverishly open [. . .] he makes one of the funniest and most striking characters ever to walk on an American stage."

rAB 4.9 Hughes, Catharine. "New American Playwrights." *America* 16 Apr. 1977: 363-64.

Neutral review: "But these three small-time crooks can really do nothing beyond talk, frequently, indeed almost obsessively, in obscenities and other undeleted expletives, celebrating their own imagined (or fantasized) cleverness. That they will not succeed in their robbery is foreordained."

rAB 4.10 Kerr, Walter. "Language Alone Isn't Drama." *New York Times* 6 Mar. 1977, sec. 2: 6+.

Negative review of language: "Something of what he hears is funny, something of it is wickedly human. [. . .] Okay. We're left with the things the three say to one another as they fatuously, foolishly, furiously speculate and quarrel over the proper way to proceed, decorating their outbursts liberally with obscenities that no longer shock or even interest us, staking everything on the verbiage that is the only thing left to them or to us."

rAB 4.11 Kissel, Howard. Rev. of *American Buffalo. Women's Wear Daily* 17 Feb. 1977. Rpt. in *New York Theatre Critics' Review* 38.3 (1977): 364-65.

Positive review focusing on the performances: "Mamet's play is to actors what a jam session is to jazz musicians—it invites the most experienced kind of playfulness and risktaking. [. . . Duvall] fills the stage with a wacky, manic energy. Kenneth McMillan, as the crusty shopowner, is masterful at suggesting authority in spite of apparent wheeziness. He has the best of Mamet's dialog and brings it off beautifully. In some ways the most impressive performance is John Savage's as the apprentice burglar—his is the most cryptic role and Savage's choices are marvelous: he has one of the most expressive, nuanced deadpans in the business."

rAB 4.12 Kroll, Jack. "The Muzak Man." *Newsweek* 28 Feb. 1977. Rpt. in *New York Theatre Critics' Review* 38.3 (1977): 364.

Kroll does three plays in one review: *American Buffalo, Sexual Perversity* (Off Broadway), and *A Life in the Theater* (Chicago's Goodman Theater). Mamet "is a cosmic eavesdropper who's caught the American aphasia. Not that he's the proverbial tape recorder, picking up speech like lint. Mamet is an abstract artist; his characters speak in a kind of verbal cubism, they address one another with the forked tongues of paranoia, insecurity, hostility, desperation. [. . . The characters] are brutes who need each other, but their words are like punches that almost casually build to real violence."

rAB 4.13 Lape, Bob. Rev. of *American Buffalo. WABC-TV* 7 16 Feb. 1977. Rpt. in *New York Theatre Critics' Review* 38.3 (1977): 368.

Very negative review that found nothing happened: "Well, playwright David Mamet took his shot and missed. The planned burglary aborts when an unseen fourth character [. . .] gets mugged first. Some perfectly reasonable actors got mugged in *American Buffalo*, and the whole play aborts. Duvall, who has shown a fine range of acting skills [. . .] is wonderfully profane, dense, and determined here. But there is so little light shed by the play that all he winds up with is a buffalo chip."

rAB 4.14 Porterfield, Christopher. "David Mamet's Bond of Futility." *Time* 28 Feb. 1977: 54+. Rpt. in *New York Theatre Critics' Review* 38.3 (1977): 367.

Positive review of the depths of the play: "Mamet has an infallible ear for the cadences of loneliness and fear behind the bluntness, and he also knows how to make the bluntness very funny. [. . .] Jittering between [Bobby and Don] like an arc of electricity between positive and negative poles is Robert Duvall as the older predator. Lashing out with desperate nihilism, Duvall crackles with the quality that Ingmar Bergman once said he looked for above all others in an actor: danger. [. . .] At the end they draw together in a fragile bond of shared futility, human castoffs alongside the inanimate ones."

rAB 4.15 Rich, Alan. "Living by Words Alone" *New York* 7 Mar. 1977: 71.

Extremely positive review of both staging and play: "Behind this smoke screen *American Buffalo* is a dark comedy that oozes into tragedy imperceptibly, frighteningly, dazzlingly." It offered "an interweaving of glorious performances by Robert Duvall, Ken McMillan, and John Savage. Santo Loquasto's set, an assemblage of tons of trash, artfully splayed on hooks and racks to mirror lights and shadows, is a wonder."

rAB 4.16 Rogoff, Gordon. "Albee and Mamet: The War of the Words." *Saturday Review* 2 Apr. 1977: 36-37. Rpt. in *Theatre is Not Safe*. Evanston: Northwestern, 1987. 141.

A mixed review of a low-class, no-plot play: "Mamet is imitating a hundred Bogart, Cagney, Robinson, and Brando movies, and he's not bad at the job. His dialogue has some of the vivacity missing from those movies. They were better at plot, however; and they didn't always treat Bogart and company like dummies. In *The Maltese Falcon*, Wilmer wasn't bright, but he had dignity. Mamet patronizes his trio: he is out to kill and get laughs. Modest ambitions, modestly achieved."

rAB 4.17 Stasio, Marilyn. "Hunting the Buffalo." *Cue* 19 Mar.-1 Apr. 1977.

Profile and interview: "Not that there's any significant difference between the 'stealing' that goes on in a Madison Avenue advertising agency and in an Eighth Avenue stickup," Mamet contends. "The corporate classes perform busywork, make-believe work; but they still call it work. But what's the difference between a man who works as a censor for CBS and makes $250,000 and a man who works as a guard in a record shop for $2.50 an hour? Both are performing imaginary jobs. Neither man's work has any value. The economic realities of our lives are based on the flimsy and transparent lie that anyone can get ahead by fealty to a nation or a corporation."

rAB 4.18 Watt, Douglas. "Stuck in a Junk Shop." *Daily News* 17 Feb. 1977. Rpt. in *New York Theatre Critics' Review* 38.3 (1977): 366.

This is a negative review about "dimwits." "Cunningly performed by a male cast of three and staged with artful simplicity, last night's 'American Buffalo' at the Barrymore is nevertheless a poor excuse for a play." It's " little more than character sketches of three oafish men in a junk shop."

rAB 4.19 Wilson, Edwin. "A Phlegmatic *American Buffalo.*" *Wall Street Journal* 23
Feb. 1977. Rpt. in *New York Theatre Critics' Review* 38.3 (1977): 367-68.
Mixed review which intuited poetry and critique of capitalism: "Mr. Mamet in a strange way is able to make these inarticulate men speak, to find in
their profanities a crude kind of poetry, and in their groping, half gestures to
convey communication between them. [. . .] Perhaps Mr. Mamet is trying to
make some statement about capitalism and the decline of morals in America. If
so, his symbols are interesting but they won't stick, and the play is not heavy
enough to support the weight of such ideas."

Production:
pAB 5 Opened at London's National Theatre, The Cottesloe, on June 28, 1978.

Director:		Bill Bryden
Set:		Grant Hicks
Lighting:		Andy Phillips
Cast:		
	Donny:	Dave King
	Teach:	Jack Shepherd
	Bobby:	Michael Feast

Overview:
Reviewers were mostly positive for many different reasons—Lewis saw it as a "comic piece," Barber as a depiction of "longing," Chaillet about the suspension of the
ethical sense, and Billington, "the lunacy of acquisitiveness." In his view the play was
notable for its quick reversals. For Barber, the play was complex on multiple levels,
and for Coveney the language was most astonishing. Gussow, however, found the
production "shortchanges the author's intent" by making it purely comic in contrast
to the Duvall version.

Reviews:
rAB 5.1 Barber, John. "Interest Caught By Vigorous New Play." *Daily Telegraph* 2
Dec. 1978: 15.
Positive review of "a complex American play which seems to me of interest on about 17 different levels. [. . .] You hear too their yearning for loyalty,
their efforts to contain the violence by which they live, and their longing to find
some bedrock of trust beneath the shifty evasions that have rotted their minds.
This, further, is a play about a real crisis—Don's discovery of whom he cannot
accept and whom he must love."

rAB 5.2 Billington, Michael. "Wiles in the Windy City." *Guardian* 29 June 1978: 12.
Positive review which noted the set as key, as well as the reversals of tone:
"And even more shocking than the violence is the way after it people revert to
the easy rhythm of friendship, as if smashing a man's face in were simply a
rougher version of tennis, but Mamet also understands that the theatre can make
its points through a central visual symbol: in this case a junk-shop which [. . .]
represents the ultimate lunacy of acquisitiveness."

rAB 5.3 Chaillet, Ned. "*Buffalo* Mamet at the National." *Times* [London] 19 June
1978: 6.
This is a promotional article which quoted Mamet who said the play "is
about an essential part of American consciousness, which is the ability to suspend an ethical sense and adopt in its stead a popular accepted mythology and
use that to assuage your conscience like everyone else is doing."

rAB 5.4 Coveney, Michael. Rev. of *American Buffalo*. *Financial Times* 29 June 1978: 12.
Positive review which focuses on the language: "David Mamet brings you
to the edge of your seat with language. Not just the force of it, but the cunning
deployment of everyday American speech patterns that cut corners and pure
grammar to distill hard meaning and veiled threats from the frenzied banter of
a trio of articulate burglars in a downtown junk shop. Hearing Pinter for the
first time must have been something like this."

rAB 5.5 Gussow, Mel. "David Mamet Breaks the Oceanic Barrier." *San Francisco
Chronicle* [*New York Times* on strike] 16 Sept. 1978.
Gussow compared productions. The difference was too great—King, a comedian, playing Donny, "is the bulwark of the national production." Shepherd,
as Teach, was at best "quirkily amusing." But Gussow most disliked Michael
Feast playing Bobby as "a fey urchin, turning the hint of latent homosexuality
into something almost explicit." The resulting production "becomes much more
of a comedy—clever, funny, and so fast-moving that at the performance that I attended, it sped by in two hours [. . .] much quicker than it was ever played in New
York. This is a palatable, brisk 'Buffalo', and one that shortchanges the author's
intent."

rAB 5.6 Lewis, Peter. "Perhaps Dave Was Wise Not to Read This!" *Daily Mail* 29
June 1978.
Mildly negative review which found it "hard to discover why" the play
was named best of 1977. "It is a comic piece—Mamet has been compared to
Pinter—in which the trio wrestle to express themselves in fractured Chicagoese, laden with expletives. Communication takes place without mentioning anything by name. Crime is 'business.' The robbery is 'the thing.' "

Production:
pAB 6 Long Wharf Theatre, New Haven, opened October, ran until November 9, 1980.

Director:	Arvin Brown
Set:	Marjorie Bradley Kellogg
Costumes:	Bill Walker
Lighting:	Ronald Wallace
Cast:	
Donny:	Clifton James
Teach:	Al Pacino
Bobby:	Thomas Waites

Overview:
Rich claimed that the play had "a falling off in Mr. Brown's pacing in the evening's early stages; the pauses in the rapid-fire dialogue occasionally widen into gaps." There was some sense among the critics that this was an ensemble performance as Kissel noted. Critics sympathized with the characters and concluded that the play "remains an involving, unsettling, blackly comic vision that finds redeeming human qualities" (Sterritt) in the lowest characters. Those who made comparison with Duvall's production, however, noted how much more humor Brown/Pacino had found in the role and the play, and most thought this less frightening version more in tune with the play. Sterritt alone preferred Duvall's "electricity, bite, the raw nerve." While Sterritt also says this is the "twitchiest" performance, all critics thought Pacino's actions were used to punctuate the words. The finale of Duvall's performance was seen as an explosion of anger/insanity, as opposed to a frustrated self in Pacino's version.

Reviews:
rAB 6.1 Gussow, Mel. "Al Pacino Put His Stamp on *American Buffalo*." *New York Times* 26 Oct. 1980: B3. Rpt. in *Theatre on the Edge*. New York: Applause, 1998. 205-06.
Positive review which compared it to the other versions. In Mosher's production: "Even at his angriest, Mr. Kellin's Teach seemed hapless, a habitual offender magnetically drawn into petty crime." The emphasis was on "the seedy authenticity of the locale." In Duvall's "the play became larger and more dramatic. It was charged with intensity. [. . .] He exuded menace; he was tough and mean. The director stressed the tautness of the situation." The British "was the broadest of the four productions," Bobby as punk rocker; Shepherd's Teach as "flashy East End hoodlum." The change here was that "The Long Wharf production restores the humor, but unlike the London version it is genuinely funny. [. . .] In Mr. Pacino's hands, the character becomes street-smart, cocksure and self-mocking. [. . .] He chooses to look for the comic insecurity. He is always on the move, restlessly skittering through the junk shop as if it were a cage. [. . .] Without losing the character's willfulness, Mr. Pacino makes him seem perplexed; his reactions are intuitive rather than conceptualized."

rAB 6.2 Novick, Julius. Rev. of *American Buffalo*. *Nation* 15 Nov. 1980: 521-22.
While finding this production inferior to the original, Novick noted that this was: "the best American play of several seasons; nothing written since, by Mamet or anyone else, tells so much American truth so powerfully, so keenly." Don and Teach "are failures by conventional American standards; to realize themselves in their own and other people's estimation, they are constantly dispensing American wisdom in wonderfully unconvincing terms, constantly trying to raise themselves by the frayed bootstraps of their language. [. . .] The play shows how the rhetoric of business provides a license, exerts a pressure, for personal betrayal."

rAB 6.3 Rich, Frank. "*American Buffalo* is Revived with Pacino." *New York Times* 21 Oct. 1980: C8.

Mainly positive review of Pacino, but hesitant about the rest of the production: "By constantly changing the inflections, contexts, and pauses of repeated phrases, Mr. Mamet steadily fills the evening with hidden betrayals and complex relationships—including some involving offstage characters. After a while, simple expressions like 'that is swell' or 'I understand' come to mean the exact reverse. When a character says nothing—or, for that matter, mutters 'nothing'—it can mean everything."

Production:

pAB 7 The Long Wharf production was transferred to Off Broadway, Circle in the Square with no changes, previewed on May 22, opened on June 3rd, 1981 and closed July 11, 1982 for 276 performances and 13 previews.

Reviews:

rAB 7.1 Barnes, Clive. "*Buffalo* Returns with Al Pacino Riding Herd." *New York Post* 5 June 1981. Rpt. in *New York Theatre Critics' Review* 32.14 (1981): 187.

Positive review which preferred Pacino to Duvall: "Pacino is funnier, full of cocky street-smarts, ironic. Duvall was colder, meaner, more menacing. In a scene of violence at the end Duvall almost literally went mad in a thunderclap of a moment. Pacino, and Brown, play this down, so it does not dominate the play as it did, perhaps wrongfully, on Broadway. Also Pacino is the more convincing punk failure."

rAB 7.2 Kerr, Walter. "Al Pacino's Supercharged *Buffalo*." *New York Times* 14 June 1981: D3.

Kerr faulted the plot, but appreciated the tension between language and lack of action: "the actor seems to make himself representative of a sizable species, victims of a vast evolutionary error. It is as though, somewhere along the long, long way, the evolutionary process itself had made a thumping mistake and had allowed one unlucky branch of the human family to learn to talk before it had learned to think. In this parrot-like process thinking had been skipped and left behind, never to be recovered. The species survives; but its members have minds whose contents are as unclassified as the stuff in junk-shops, though words tumble ready-made and meaningless from their lips."

rAB 7.3 Kissel, Howard. Rev. of *American Buffalo. Women's Wear Daily* 5 June 1981. Rpt. in *New York Theatre Critics' Review* 32.14 (1981): 189.

Positive review of Pacino who "has always made use of a certain nervousness in his personality, not always as carefully as he does here. During the whole first act he gives the impression of a wary sparring partner, a skittish alley cat—there is a menace lurking just beneath the surface, but it is overshadowed and heightened by an uneasiness, a vulnerability that make him both comic and even innocent. [. . .] [W]hatever he does grows out of the other actors' work."

rAB 7.4 Rich, Frank. "Al Pacino in *American Buffalo*." *New York Times* 5 June 1981. Rpt. in *New York Theatre Critics' Review* 32.14 (1981): 188. Rpt. in *Hot Seat*. New York: Random House 1998. 85-87.

Very positive review of Pacino's humorous additions: "Duvall was taut and mean in the part: after fumbling away his burglary, his self-hatred drove him to lash out like a killer. Mr. Pacino, by contrast, is slovenly and abstracted. With his baggy clothes and pasty, ill-shaven face, he's a tabby rather than an alley cat. And he's very, very funny. [. . .] Yet by the time 'American Buffalo' is over, it, too, has pounded away at the American dream of success until it is left in soiled, hideous tatters."

rAB 7.5 Sterritt, David. Rev. of *American Buffalo*. *Christian Science Monitor* 16 June 1981. Rpt. in *New York Theatre Critics' Review* 32.14 (1981): 190.

Sterritt preferred Duvall's interpretation and saw Pacino's as too mannered: "He makes the role of a loquacious hood entirely his own, however, by unleashing a score of body mannerisms that parallel and accent the vociferous speeches of his character. He lacks the electricity, the bite, the raw nerve that Robert Duvall had. [. . .] Still, there is an amazingly eccentric vitality to his performance, which must be the twitchiest of his career. [. . .] 'American Buffalo' remains an involving, unsettling, blackly comic vision that finds redeeming human qualities in the most squalid of circumstances."

rAB 7.6 Watt, Douglas. "*Buffalo* in Mint Condition." *Daily News* [New York] 5 June 1981. Rpt. in *New York Theatre Critics' Review* 32.14 (1981): 188-89.

Positive review of Pacino's both funny and scary Teach: "The obscenities as well as the more homely exchanges compose a litany of the underworld, and Mamet has caught the tone precisely, knowing full well that the trio's words and actions are a form of prayer of the dispossessed. Pacino makes it all fall into place with his richly expressive, funny, only slightly scary picture of Teach, slouching about the shop in deep thought and with a mind as cunning as, but no more so, than a wharf rat's. He is simply marvelous, at times hilarious, in a perfectly coordinated performance."

rAB 7.7 Wilson, Edwin. "Pacino on Stage." *Wall Street Journal* 26 June 1981. Rpt. in *New York Theatre Critics' Review* 32.14 (1981): 186-87.

Mixed review of a "petty" play, but admired Pacino's performance: "The men planning the robbery are emblems of scheming businessmen. The play, however, never supported such themes: The criminals come off as too petty and Mr. Mamet fails to provide insight into his subject. [. . . Pacino] has developed more twitches than a horse swatting flies in the summertime—an aggressive shrug of the shoulder, the chin jutting out, hands thrust in front of him, a grab at his crotch—and each move is a convincing gesture of futility, an attempt to locate an identity, or break through to a world that does not hear him."

Production:

pAB 8 This is another revival of the Long Wharf Production at Broadway's Booth
    Theatre. Previews began October 20, 1983; officially opening October 27;
    closing February 4, 1984 for 102 performances with only the following
    changes to the 1980 production [see pAB 6]. [11 minute ABC-TV Joel Siegel
    excerpt and review at TOFT].

> Cast:
>
> | Donny: | J. J. Johnston |
> | Teach: | Al Pacino |
> | Bobby: | James Hayden |

Overview:

Rich and Barnes both lamented Pacino as becoming too mannered, too much a star
turn. Kissel, however, thought this the "most balanced" performance he'd seen. Watt
was most enthusiastic about this production, "an uproariously funny evening" both
because Pacino had refined his humor, and Brown had directed for even more humor.

Reviews:

rAB 8.1 Barnes, Clive. "Pacino Is Back for a Knockout in *Buffalo*." *New York Post* 27
    Oct. 1983. Rpt. in *New York Theatre Critics' Review* 34.14 (1983): 143-44.

> Still positive about the play and production, but Pacino should move on:
> "Duvall as Teach gave a performance that should have turned your insides out.
> Indeed it did. Duvall's final madness had a quality of abject desperation that
> Pacino doesn't try for. Pacino's triumph—and he has narrowed down his per-
> formance approaching the pinpoint of his concept—is something that needles
> savage ordinariness. Pacino runs through the play like an electric wire. And
> eventually that wire faults. He knows why. He shows us why."

rAB 8.2 Beaufort, John. "*Buffalo* Is Back — Tragicomedy Starring Al Pacino." *Chris-
    tian Science Monitor* 8 Nov. 1983. Rpt. in *New York Theatre Critics' Review*
    34.14 (1983): 144.

> Positive review: "In a recent *Daily News* interview, Mr. Mamet said he
> wanted it to be about 'three guys trying to be excellent.' To which Mr. Brown
> added: 'That's what we've sort of done. For them, life is infinitely possible. That's
> where both the humor and the sadness of the piece comes from, their perennial opti-
> mism and belief that you can bull your way through anything.' The problem with
> 'American Buffalo' for this reviewer is that the pathos never really catches up with
> the ludicrousness of the basic situation—funny as that can sometimes be. [. . .] Mr.
> Pacino plays him like a man on a string—taut, voluble, and potentially violent."

rAB 8.3 Cunningham, Dennis. Rev. of *American Buffalo*. WCBS TV2 27 Oct. 1983.
    Rpt. in *New York Theatre Critics' Review* 34.14 (1983): 145.

> Very positive review of play and production. Pacino "is phenomenal as he
> shakes and slams the current timid Broadway season into full and vivid life.
> [. . . Johnston and Hayden] the two other denizens of a junk shop where three

people playing up to, off and against each other are, in fact, just hanging out...
and just hanging on. [. . .] But playwright David Mamet has arranged it all so
brilliantly, it is very like intricate music, a wonderfully profane fugue."

rAB 8.4 Gill, Brendan. "Interlude 1983: *American Buffalo.*" *New Yorker* 31 May 1993:
91. Reprint of 1983 review.

Positive review of a "classic American comedy" for which, Gill admitted,
"I was plainly unready," partly due to "Grosbard's direction." However, in
Brown's production, the "tiresomely monosyllabic drumbeat of obscenities"
heard in the first production became "lyric" in Pacino's. Now, too, the characters are classic con-men of American literature, like those of "Melville, Twain,
and Frost," as well as "Malamud, Bellow and Roth." "They are every hypocrit-
ical Wall Street rags-to-riches story turned inside out and upside down; not for
the world would we be one of them, but not for the world dare we exclude them
from the gross national product of American energy, optimism, and cunning."

rAB 8.5 Kissel, Howard. Rev. of *American Buffalo. Women's Wear Daily* 28 Oct.
1983. Rpt. in *New York Theatre Critics' Review* 34.14 (1983): 142-43.

Positive review of this revival: "Each production I have seen of 'American
Buffalo' has had its own virtues, but here the performances seem most in balance. Al Pacino, as the roughest of the trio, seems more controlled than he did
two summers ago. He still gives the impression of being highly combustible,
but there are fewer tics, implying greater strength and perhaps greater frustration."

rAB 8.6 Rich, Frank. "Al Pacino, *American Buffalo.*" *New York Times* 28 Oct. 1983.
Rpt. in *New York Theatre Critics' Review* 34.14 (1983): 142.

A rather negative review of this production: "Still, the heat and blood are
gone. As Mr. Brown demonstrated before, 'American Buffalo' is as much about
friendship as about business. Teach, the volatile con artist played by Mr. Pacino, is desperate to win his cronies' approval. He'll do anything to prove himself
the smartest, most manly guy on the block. It's typical of the decline in Mr.
Pacino's once-vital performance that he now usually faces the auditorium rather than the other actors on stage."

rAB 8.7 Watt, Douglas. "Pacino's *Buffalo* in Mint Condition." *Daily News* 28 Oct.
1983. Rpt. in *New York Theatre Critics' Review* 34.14 (1983): 145.

Positive review of this revival: "Surely what started out in the 1977 Broadway production as an unsettling and somewhat skimpy comedy of menace has
now developed into an uproariously funny evening about the three Chicago
grifters who gather in Donny Dubrow's junk shop to plan a theft that is never
consummated. And that is largely because Pacino, having taken the measure of
his loony role, plays it to the hilt and has great fun with it in the process."

Production:

pAB 9 The Long Wharf production next moved from Broadway to London's Duke of York's Theatre with previews opening July 24th and officially on August 2nd, 1984 with one change in cast: Bruce MacVittie took over as Bobby.

Overview:

Critics found Pacino too "mannered," too Method. Radin was most sympathetic in noting that he "provides the fire—surprisingly modestly" because of his build, "short, stocky" and "rather plump." She went to some length to discuss meanings—particularly in Mamet's view of these characters as victims, at the same time letting the audience identify "the little person in all of us," an American view she found alien to British playwrights. Others, like de Jongh, found the play empty of meaning, merely gestures by Pacino and Mamet. Finally, there was a third contingent that found Pacino an impediment to recognition of the play's deeper sense of characters' "often touching dependence on and loyalty to each other" (Hirschhorn). Most thought the intention was to make the characters sympathetic in some way.

Reviews:

rAB 9.1 Coveney, Michael. Rev. of *American Buffalo. Financial Times* 3 Aug. 1984. Rpt. in *London Theatre Record* 30 July-12 Aug. 1984: 654.

Rather negative view of Pacino's mannerisms: "Pacino flicks a left-eye every so often at the audience and dispels a round of welcoming applause with a broadside of vitriol. Grace and Ruthie, the last night's card game, the rain: all that is giving him a bad time, which he channels through a cold house store of Method tics and cliches. He keeps touching his hair, checking the parting, tucking his shirt in the top of his pants, splaying his legs, preening and primping generally like a man either afflicted with fleas or stricken with the St. Vitus Dance according to Lee Strasberg. The rhythm and pace of the play has to hang around while all this is going on, unrelieved by the dour monotony of J. J. Johnston's shop keeper."

rAB 9.2 de Jongh, Nicholas. Rev. of *American Buffalo. Guardian* 4 Aug. 1984. Rpt. in *London Theatre Record* 30 July-12 Aug. 1984: 655.

Negative review of Pacino being more than the play: "Earlier as he prowls, grim-faced and didactic, the perfect know-all with a captive audience, he is sometimes in danger of becoming all manner and no matter."

rAB 9.3 Gordon, Giles. Rev. of *American Buffalo. Spectator* 11 Aug. 1984. Rpt. in *London Theatre Record* 30 July-12 Aug. 1984: 656.

Positive view of "funny and compassionate play." Pacino's "performance of a neurotic, small-time crook has all the nervy detail and lack of stage projection which 'film stars' are heir to when they return to the boards. He keeps running his fingers through his hair as if afraid he'll go bald, hitches his trousers in fear of revealing all, and mumbles the Chicago demotic."

rAB 9.4 Grant, Steve. Rev. of *American Buffalo. Time Out* 9 Aug. 1984. Rpt. in *London Theatre Record* 30 July-12 Aug. 1984: 653.

Somewhat negative review of Pacino as trying too hard: "It's busy, fussy even, a technical tour de force but ultimately little more. [. . .] Maybe he was trying too hard on the first night: certainly the extrovert style, the continual movements and facial gestures are related to the character—but sometimes it's hard to escape from the feeling that the 'performance' is winning out."

rAB 9.5 Hirschhorn, Clive. Rev. of *American Buffalo. Sunday Express* 5 Aug. 1984. Rpt. in *London Theatre Record* 30 July-12 Aug. 1984: 656.

Positive review of the whole ensemble: "Forget the tenuous plot (Mamet almost does) and, if you're able to detach yourself from Pacino's mesmeric tour de force, concentrate instead on the characters, their often touching dependence on and loyalty to each other, the subtle performances of Johnson and MacVittie and on the writer's raw highly individual use of language."

rAB 9.6 Hurren, Kenneth. Rev. of *American Buffalo. Mail on Sunday* 5 Aug. 1984. Rpt. in *London Theatre Record* 30 July-12 Aug. 1984: 656.

Mixed review: "Pacino, four-letter perfect, gives a restless, edgy display, all busy hands, hunching shoulders and thrusting pelvis."

rAB 9.7 King, Francis. Rev. of *American Buffalo. Sunday Telegraph* 5 Aug. 1984. Rpt. in *London Theatre Record* 30 July-12 Aug. 1984: 655-56.

Rather negative review: "Though the story has irony and pathos, it is far too slim to provide a whole evening in the theatre."

rAB 9.8 Radin, Victoria. Rev. of *American Buffalo. Observer* 5 Aug. 1984. Rpt. in *London Theatre Record* 30 July-12 Aug. 1984: 654-55.

Very positive view of Pacino's rage and vulnerability: "These three failed crooks are the waste products of the American belief in free enterprise. But while Mamet shows them as victims, it is without patronage and with respect and even love for these little people who, as he somehow makes one feel, resemble the little person in all of us. [. . .] Although his rage is frightening (and Pacino is very good at rage), you never forget his vulnerability. It's there in his face, as in Mamet's text, without mawkishness: the whole raw bleeding horror of what led up to putting Reagan in the White House."

rAB 9.9 Shorter, Eric. Rev. of *American Buffalo. Daily Telegraph* 3 Aug. 1984. Rpt. in *London Theatre Record* 30 July-12 Aug. 1984: 653.

Positive review of Pacino as both "limited" yet "riveting": "His arms are semaphores; his hands are so restless that sometimes he has to clap them. Indeed, he becomes so jumpy as the outsider with ideas for a robbery which never comes off that we wonder if his nervousness hasn't something to do with his first London stage appearance as well as with the character whose big talk (and small vocabulary) disconcerts the owner of the shop and his young assistant."

rAB 9.10 Shulman, Milton. Rev. of *American Buffalo. Standard* 3 Aug. 1984. Rpt. in *London Theatre Record* 30 July-12 Aug. 1984: 655.

Mixed review of Pacino: "Although there have been attempts to give it some more philosophical dimension [. . .] Mamet's comedy is actually about little, inarticulate people trying to make a dishonest dollar. [. . .] Al Pacino's facial muscles and windmill arms give the impression they have been galvanised by electric shocks. It is a performance both hypnotic and tiring to watch."

rAB 9.11 Tinker, Jack. Rev. of *American Buffalo. Daily Mail* 3 Aug. 1984. Rpt. in *London Theatre Record* 30 July-12 Aug. 1984: 656.

Rather negative review of American acting: "There is no respite from the posturing that passes for energy, no shelter from the array of cynical quirks with which he guards the real nature of his character, Teach—a bantam cock loser with whom we are supposed to sympathise. Thumbs pick at teeth, hands sweep the hair, fingers tug and readjust the waistband of his baggy trousers."

rAB 9.12 Woddis, Carole. Rev. of *American Buffalo. City Limits* 10 Aug. 1984. Rpt. in *London Theatre Record* 30 July-12 Aug. 1984: 656.

Rather negative view of Pacino: His "extraordinary performance as Teach, the petty crook with desperation writ large in his every action, is the most monumental piece of egotistical acting I've seen since Olivier's 'Othello.' [. . .] But from a text meant for quickfire exchanges, Pacino wrings pauses reaching back to yesterday, dowsing the lines in a Wagnerian ponderousness, as though responding to some intense, inner script."

Production:

pAB 10 Co-production with the Atlantic Theatre Company at the Donmar Warehouse in London, previewed January 28, opened on February 3, and closed February 26, 2000.

Director:	Neil Pepe
Set:	Kevin Rigdon
Costumes:	Laura Bauer
Lighting:	Howard Werner
Cast:	
Donny:	Philip Baker Hall
Teach:	William H. Macy
Bobby:	Mark Webber

Overview:

Critics were divided over Macy's performance. Some took it as a "wonderfully funny performance" (Taylor). Others wanted the old interpretation: "Macy quite misses the sense of desperation and fury that ought to fire role and production alike" (de Jongh). The best point on the set was Taylor's recognition of a grandfather clock with no hands—with a dummy human fist lying at the bottom: "This useless timepiece sums up the trio's talents for the synchronised heist." Billington noted Kennedy and Lincoln portraits, as well as the smashing of Buddha as a direct allusion to Pinter's *The Caretaker.*

Reviews:

rAB 10.1 Billington, Michael. Rev. of *American Buffalo. Guardian* 4 Feb. 2000. Rpt. in *Theatre Record* 29 Jan.-11 Feb. 2000: 126.

Positive review of this production for not making Teach a "star-turn": "Macy brilliantly shows Teach to be a nervy outsider who desperately wants to be part of the game. But he also brings out Teach's bullying vanity: almost his first action is to stare at himself in a compact and virtually his last is to shelter behind Donny when he interrogates the injured Bobby. Philip Baker Hall's grizzled Donny is good without quite conveying his final moral awakening but Mark Webber's Bobby has the right tremulous desire to please [. . .]."

rAB 10.2 Brown, Georgina. Rev. of *American Buffalo. Mail on Sunday* 6 Feb. 2000. Rpt. in *Theatre Record* 29 Jan.-11 Feb. 2000: 127.

Positive review of the play as a critique of business: "And it is utterly compelling. I guess Mamet is presenting a metaphor for the way business—a word that frequently pops up—is done in America. For this play is also about the way men talk to one another, about the lies and strategies of language, about friendship and treachery, the power struggles, the using and abusing, the games, verbal games and more devious psychological stuff—that men play."

rAB 10.3 Butler, Robert. "Malcontents with a Mission." *Independent on Sunday* 6 Feb. 2000. Rpt. in *Theatre Record* 29 Jan.-11 Feb. 2000: 127.

Positive review of Macy's balance: "There's a touch of the jerk in Macy's persona. He treads the line between the comic and serious through sheer earnestness. [. . .] Macy can scrunch his nose, crinkle his forehead, and clamp on an expression of fixed intent that carries a hint of panic."

rAB 10.4 Coveney, Michael. Rev. of *American Buffalo. Daily Mail* 4 Feb. 2000. Rpt. in *Theatre Record* 29 Jan.-11 Feb. 2000: 127.

Positive view of Macy's Teach: "Whereas Pacino was self-obsessed and angrily wound-up, Macy is a faster, funnier buffoon, out of his depth in the shallowest water. He resembles a worried spaniel, clean-shaven and neat but desperate to succeed, which he never will."

rAB 10.5 de Jongh, Nicholas. Rev. of *American Buffalo. Evening Standard* 4 Feb. 2000. Rpt. in *Theatre Record* 29 Jan.-11 Feb. 2000: 122.

Negative review of the production which denigrated the play as bearing "the softness and flabby sprawl of middle age" as compared to young American Neil LaBute's *Bash*. "Macy's aggrieved, self-important Teach is angry and his speedy manners energise Neil Pepe's far too placid production. He is pleasingly ridiculous too as he hustles, snarls, and flatters his way into the shop-owner's confidence. It's a limited performance, though. Macy quite misses the sense of desperation and fury that ought to fire role and production alike."

rAB 10.6 Foss, Roger. Rev. of *American Buffalo. What's On* 9 Feb. 2000. Rpt. in *Theatre Record* 29 Jan.-11 Feb. 2000: 125.

Positive review of the actors, but not of the director: "Hall is the affable but bent shop-keeper; Mark Webber, making his stage debut, is stunningly inarticulate as his teenage gopher, while Macy gets the laughs as the treacherous Teach who mangles his words and spits them out like chewed-up bubble gum. But in Neil Pepe's production, tension seems to be missing and the play's articulation of cheap culture always on the make is rarely penetrated deeply enough to reveal the sudden bursts of anger and the creeping paranoia."

rAB 10.7 Gore-Langton, Robert. Rev. of *American Buffalo. Express* 4 Feb. 2000: 47. Rpt. in *Theatre Record* 29 Jan.-11 Feb. 2000: 122.

Very positive review: "We are deep in Mamet country here—and Macy is wonderfully at home. The sharp hair, the suit, the cussing—everything about him is loaded with reptilian charm and ferocity. [. . .] But it's the edge, the paranoia, the human betrayals which bring this to a dramatic boil."

rAB 10.8 Gross, John. Rev. of *American Buffalo. Sunday Telegraph* 6 Feb. 2000. Rpt. in *Theatre Record* 29 Jan.-11 Feb. 2000: 125.

Mixed review: " it is an image of America itself. Personally, I don't find it much more than an anecdote. But I'd concede that it illuminates some aspects of America as it goes along; and within its anecdotal limits it is undeniably trenchant and shrewd."

rAB 10.9 Hagerty, Bill. Rev. of *American Buffalo. News of the World* 13 Feb. 2000. Rpt. in *Theatre Record* 29 Jan.-11 Feb. 2000: 125.

Mixed review which liked Macy, but not Hall: "With pencil moustache and a personality no more than an explosion of anger away from psychotic, Macy's Teach dominates the action like a fox in a chicken coop. He's deadly convincing. Philip Baker Hall isn't, for me, tough or rough enough as Don."

rAB 10.10 Kellaway, Kate. Rev. of *American Buffalo. Observer* 6 Feb. 2000. Rpt. in *Theatre Record* 29 Jan.-11 Feb. 2000: 121.

Positive review of Macy's energy: "The language is crazy junkshop too. It's the sheer energy of the writing that is so staggering, and there is an enjoyable challenge in reading between the lines to guess what these crooks actually feel or think. Teach is superbly played by [Macy. . .]. He charges about like a buffalo, his anger indiscriminate."

rAB 10.11 Macaulay, Alastair. "Mamet's Gem Set in a Junk Shop." *Financial Times* 7 Feb. 2000. Rpt. in *Theatre Record* 29 Jan.-11 Feb. 2000: 127-28.

Positive review: "You start to laugh at the absurdity of his choice of words—earlier on he has said 'the only way to teach people is to kill them'—but his despair wipes any hope of laughter off your face. What point does any of these three lives have? The ending, in which Don at least looks after the wounded Bobby, offers some glimmer of minor hope amid the major hopelessness."

rAB 10.12 Morley, Sheridan. "Power Play." *Spectator* 12 Feb. 2000: 47. Rpt. in *The-atre Record* 29 Jan.-11 Feb. 2000: 122.

Very positive review of the edginess of the play: "What makes Mamet dis-tinct [from Miller's *The Price*] in this three-card trick is the way he deals in danger, with the suggestion that mayhem and murder are never more than min-utes away; the play rattles like a snake, but there's a street poetry here, as well as an awareness that all three of these men are playing an unending game of power poker in which relationships can turn quite literally on a dime."

rAB 10.13 Nathan, David. Rev. of *American Buffalo. Jewish Chronicle* 11 Feb. 2000. Rpt. in *Theatre Record* 29 Jan.-11 Feb. 2000: 125.

Very positive review of Mamet's going beyond sympathy for characters: "David Mamet's crooks talk big-time, but small-time runs through them like the writing in a stick of Blackpool rock. Arthur Miller would have found com-passion for them, but in 'American Buffalo,' which gets a powerful all-Amer-ican production at the Donmar, Mamet mercilessly cuts into their dumbness, using their own words as a scalpel to pare away their pretensions."

rAB 10.14 Nightingale, Benedict. "Brilliant, Plain and Simple." *The Times* [London] 5 Feb. 2000. Rpt. in *Theatre Record* 29 Jan.-11 Feb. 2000: 125-26.

Positive review of Macy's interpretation: "behind the frustration, anger, bravado, sententious rhetoric and comically self-serving contradictions, he's an over-age infant dimly aware that he'll never claw his way out of the urban ashcan. Macy misses some of that insecurity and secret desperation: but he catches the character's fierce paranoia. [. . .] We, too, have been half-convinced that ultimately there is no honour, loyalty or friendship when self-interest strikes. But the final evidence is that, yes, there are values even down there, in the grottier reaches of the lower depths."

rAB 10.15 Price, Steven. Rev. of *American Buffalo. David Mamet Review* 7 (2000): 4.

Positive review: "Macy's performance captures what is at stake when ac-tions no longer seem grounded in meaning. In the other productions I have seen, Teach has been a ranter, unaware that his verbal self-contradictions will precipitate a catastrophe. A feature of Macy's acting, however, has always been the ability of that cherubic face to fall in an instant, and the effect of this in the tiny space at the Donmar is electrifying. As words come out of his mouth this Teach will pause, the facial expression indicating full awareness of the absurdi-ty of what he is saying. And yet he continues compelled, it seems, more by syntax than by logic to complete the sentence."

rAB 10.16 Spencer, Charles. "Genius with Greed." *Daily Telegraph* 7 Feb. 2000: 19. Rpt. in *Theatre Record* 29 Jan.-11 Feb. 2000: 127.

Positive review of this production's compassion: "The eyes are those of a man who knows deep down that he is second-rate. It's a persuasive reading, which explains not only the terrible frustration underlying Teach's hilarious profanity, [. . .] but also his brutality to Bobby. Teach, you suddenly realise, regards even this broken down boy as a threat, and his climactic violence is a mark of the fear that corrodes him from within. [. . .] Both these characters, and even Teach, thanks to Macy's penetrating performance, reveal Mamet as a far more compassionate dramatist than he is usually given credit for. Testosterone may be in short supply [as Germaine Greer remarked to the reviewer of this production]; the pity that underlies all great dramatic tragedies certainly is not."

rAB 10.17 Taylor, Paul. Rev. of *American Buffalo*. *Independent* 7 Feb. 2000. Rpt. in *Theatre Record* 29 Jan.-11 Feb. 2000: 122.

Very positive view of Macy: "Macy's wonderfully funny performance as Teach drives that point home in style. He sounds like a sonorous, spuriously sincere voice-over on an ad for the Republican Party and the good old American way; he looks, with his slick-backed, cut-price dapperness and ridiculously natty moustache, like a failed used car salesman. And underneath his humorless know-all swagger; there is an ignorant, raging insecurity which erupts in furious tirades which, brilliantly timed by Macy, have an elaborate illogicity that is almost baroque."

rAB 10.18 Woddis, Carole. Rev. of *American Buffalo*. *Herald* 9 Feb. 2000. Rpt. in *Theatre Record* 29 Jan.-11 Feb. 2000: 128.

Mixed review: "Macy's Teach has the mock respectability of an insurance salesman amid a puffed up, expletive-filled language that goes nowhere and betrays a world of frustration, misogyny and hate. For the original 'muscular' macho play, Neil Pepe's production is surprisingly underwhelming, only fitfully hitting its comic targets, though, perhaps for that very reason, capturing something touchingly, at once pathetic and universal."

rAB 10.19 Wolf, Matt. "Abusive American Tales Storm Stages in London." *Variety* 14 Feb. 2000: 49-50.

Noting the parallel with Neil LaBute's *Bash*, Wolf was negative about this production, which missed Mamet's "bitter" thesis while "the production settles for belly laughs. [. . .] Where is an awareness of the stakes for which Mamet's three hapless anti-heroes are playing, as they bungle a coin heist that threatens to make brutes of them all?" He finds Macy's Teach too "small-time" and the production "a comedy of bungled manners that has yet to cast a chill."

Production:
pAB 11 The co-production with Donmar Warehouse moved intact to the Atlantic Theatre Company, New York and played from March 12 to May 21, 2000.

Overview:
Brustein began by contrasting Duvall who was "more menacing and explosive" than Macy, "who underlines the character's nervous tension, edginess, and weak nature. Both interpretations are correct." Feingold too came to Macy's defense: "but who ever said Teach was a heavy character or the play a ponderous piece of work?" Isherwood, Lahr, Rivera, and Zinman, however, thought the production disappointing

because of Macy's unconventional Teach. Brantley was the most balanced, finding Macy's "brittle anxiety" a "fresh angle" and legitimate interpretation. But he felt the production more distanced than any other, and so less effective.

Reviews:

rAB 11.1 Brantley, Ben. "The Blue Language Pales but Not the Mamet Music." *New York Times* 17 Mar. 2000, sec. B: 4.

Positive review of "a brisk, oddly breezy revival." Most surprising was that four-letter words no longer shocked: "With the novelty of the play's brusque, blue dialogue long worn off, it's the careful, bravura manipulation of language to thematic ends that seems most apparent now." Macy's performance was the main interest. He specialized in "brittle anxiety. [. . .] Applying this self-consciousness to Teach isn't inappropriate. It certainly makes you see the character from a fresh angle, and it's fun watching the variations on the dance of aggression and retreat that provides the central rhythm of Mr. Macy's performance."

rAB 11.2 Brustein, Robert. "Plays Fat and Thin." *New Republic* 17 Apr. 2000: 64.

Positive review of "ensemble balance": "Duvall was far more menacing and explosive in the part than Macy, who underlines the character's nervous tension, edginess, and weak nature. Both interpretations are correct. And playing opposite Philip Baker Hall's avuncular Don and Mark Webber's goofy Bobby, Macy achieves an unerring ensemble balance, proving that, in the hands of good actors, there is no such thing as a definitive performance."

rAB 11.3 Feingold, Michael. "Stepping Lightly." *Village Voice* 28 Mar. 2000: 69.

Positive review of Macy's new interpretation: "Robert Duvall [. . . was a] borderline psycho who, from his very first entrance, seemed more than likely to kill someone by the final curtain. Al Pacino's Teach [. . . was a] heavy stylized portrait of underworld disappointment, with a windup—toy walk, a glassy-eyed stare, and hands held, finlike, at shoulder height. [. . . Kellin] poured a streak of Duvall's savagery into a sardonic sense of failure far realer than Pacino's. [. . . A] little classier and younger than his predecessors, [Macy] links the character's out-for-blood drive to his sense of inadequacy. The jittery body and the final smashup suggest a jailbird on a rampage; the hapless, perplexed line readings evoke Bob Hope. [. . .] This lightened version ends up showing you more rather than less of its complex material."

rAB 11.4 Isherwood, Charles. "Bland *Buffalo* Roams Stage of the Atlantic." *Variety* 20 Mar. 2000: 36.

Negative review of the production and of Macy: "With a valiant but sorely miscast William H. Macy playing the jittery, volatile grifter Teach, and Philip Baker Hall offering a gruff but bland Donny, the play runs on empty for the entire first act, and only fitfully sputters to life in the final, wrenching minutes. [. . .] But beneath the tinfoil bluster of their words are black reservoirs of insecurity and bitterness and alienation that are only hinted at obliquely in Mamet's scabrous, profane dialogue."

rAB 11.5 Lahr, John. "The Theatre: The Vicious Campfire." *New Yorker* 27 Mar. 2000:
     121-22.
          Mixed review of the production: "If there is a better comedy about Ameri-
     can business and the nation's lost soul, I don't know it. [. . .] The characters in
     'American Buffalo' can't define their feelings because they don't have the words.
     It's Mamet's awesome achievement to at once show and comment on these
     despoiled minds. [. . .] Macy's performance as Teach has grown in ferocity as
     the production has journeyed from a sold-out London run to New York. [. . .]
     Teach's desperate vacancy is never quite clear or clinched. Both he and Kevin
     Rigdon's set are too tidy and too contained, and this mutes the play's sense of
     impoverishment."

rAB 11.6 Rivera, Elaine. "Retreading the Boards." *Economist* 20 May 2000: 101+.
          Mixed review: "With 'American Buffalo,' Mr. Mamet created both the
     straight talking, anti-corporate themes and the tough, defiant characters that
     resurface in many of his later works—and in many tired imitations. Yet the
     current production by his Atlantic Theatre Company, with its quiet, deliberate
     direction and understated performances, only heightens the bitter themes for
     which Mr. Mamet's distinctive, biting dialogue was meant."

rAB 11.7 Simon, John. "Switch-Hitters." *New York* 27 Mar. 2000: 103.
          Mixed review: "The play is to be perceived as a satire on big business,
     which these piddling rogues try to emulate and, in their puny way, supposedly
     mirror. The suggested equation is questionable, and there is nothing likable about
     any character; yet as an actors' exercise the play succeeds."

rAB 11.8 Zinman, Toby. Rev. of *American Buffalo. David Mamet Review* 7 (2000): 3.
          Negative review of the production because the three characters "should be,
     as I understand the play, repulsive and dangerous as well as pathetic, but here
     they seem merely inept jerks. This shifts the emotional burden of the drama: it
     becomes painful without being frightening. [. . . Macy's] Teach is merely a
     blowhard, a cheezy braggart, and not a cruel creep, despite his bashing of Bob-
     by and his trashing of the store, Macy's exit into the rain at the play's conclu-
     sion, wearing a hat he made out of newspaper, checking himself in a
     old-fashioned handmirror which is lying around, is a golden moment—the kind
     of inspired gesture that speaks both the actor and the character."

Scholarly Overview:
Required reading is Andrew Harris for the history of the play's development in early
productions. The chapter raises an issue key to response over whose play this is—
Teach's or Donny's. Language is the favored approach—some see the debased language, mainly of Teach, creating debased thoughts and actions (Dean, Garner, King,
Williams); others see Teach as more manipulative and in control of words (Schleuter,
Vorlicky). Similarly, critics split over the view of business. If it is Teach's play, then it
is a satire of American business (Barbera, Moran, Zeifman). But if it is Donny's, the
play is a tragedy of betrayal (Kane, Malkin). The ending of the play is accordingly a

matter of debate—some find it comforting and healing (Kane, Vorlicky), others find it despairing (Bigsby, Dean, Malkin, McGowan). Thematically, critics as usual divide over Mamet as a misogynist (McDonough) or not (Haedicke, Kane).

Scholarly Articles:

sAB 1 Barbera, Jack V. "Ethical Perversity in America: Some Observations on David Mamet's *American Buffalo*." *Modern Drama* 24.3 (1981): 270-75.

An early scholarly defense of "a play of intellectual content" (275) based on two criteria, language and themes: "friendship, looking out for oneself, business, and being knowledgeable" (272). The first three themes are interwoven and mutually contradictory; the fourth comes from Clurman who noted that while "being knowledgeable" is prized, none of the characters has any real knowledge. In conclusion, Barbera notes: "For 'buffalo' read the slang verb 'to intimidate.' It is because he does not know anything that Teach must try to buffalo Don. [. . .] Knowledge creates divisions among people, divisions of power and wealth, but such divisions can seem undemocratic, un-American. So robbing and cheating are attempts to restore justice" (274-75). Mamet is "satirizing such corrupt notions" (275).

sAB 2 Bigelow, Gary E. "Marginacion y Amistad en Mamet y Sastre: El Caso de *American Buffalo* y *La taberna fantastica*." *De lo particular a lo universal: El teatro espanol del Siglo XX y su contexto*. Ed. John P. Gabriele. Frankfurt: Vervuert Verlag, 1994. 112-18.

A comparison of the two plays as critiques from the marginalized: "The more obvious similarities between *American Buffalo* and *La taberna fantistica* are: first, both narratives are strongly critical of their own countries; second, all the actions happened in one day, in one place (the store 'El Gato Negro'); third, all the characters of Mamet and almost all of Sastre are marginal people, among whom there is fighting over who is to be a friend and who an enemy; fourth, those men are associated by the same occupation or by alcohol; fifth, the person who does any destructive action is a colleague, pal, or familiar of the victim; sixth, the marginal people speak in a colloquial language, from the abbreviated Chicago accent of Mamet to the Spanish slang from the inner neighborhoods of Madrid" (114).

sAB 3 Bigsby, C. W. E. "*American Buffalo*." *David Mamet*. Contemporary Writers. London: Methuen, 1985. 63-85.

This chapter covers the themes and culture of the time, but also does an extended analysis of Thorstein Veblen's influence on Mamet: "The language of classic liberalism survives. The idea of a social contract to which individuals subscribe in order to preserve individual freedom still registers. [. . .] But such phrases have lost all meaning. There is no longer a community to which they may relate. The final irony is that they have been uttered by those who have been instrumental in eroding their meaning" (77). This construction allows for no meaning. "And although the play appears to end with a gesture of reconciliation—the simplified dialogue suggesting that deceit and treachery may have been temporarily laid aside—it is difficult to credit this with much substance, given the moral inversion of the world they inhabit" (84).

sAB 4 Callens, Johan. "Mr. Smith Goes to Chicago: Playing out Mamet's Critique of Capitalism in *American Buffalo.*" *European Journal of American Culture* 19.1 (1999): 17-29.

Callens roots the split in Adam Smith's origins of capitalism between the need for "sympathy" in *The Theory of Moral Sentiments* and "self-interest" in *The Wealth of Nations.* The article interestingly notes how the card game conflates the two realms which are polarized in Don's "compassion and forgiveness" (20) as opposed to Teach, a "gamester, trickster, gambler, or conman" (24) for whom "business is paradoxically figured as a dutiful game with stringent rules" (24).

sAB 5 Carroll, Dennis. "Business." *David Mamet.* Modern Dramatists series. New York: St. Martin's, 1987. 31-50.

Carroll's interpretation draws attention to how the play was initially misinterpreted as purely realistic, and where that fails, and why the metaphoric interpretation makes more sense as an analysis of America itself: "The play, a little inconsequential at face value, leaves a provocative residue in the mind. A dialectical principle is again in operation. If the play is interpreted as 'realism' only, the action is practically non-existent, the characters small-time, the scope limited, underlined by the final scenic image of a stage full of trash doubly 'trashed'. But metaphorically the implications are considerable. It is partly *because* the action in the microcosm is so trivial that the validity of the macrocosm is so effectively questioned. *American Buffalo* confronts the validity of an entire national mystique, and the premises on which many enterprises and dreams of great moment are founded" (40).

sAB 6 Dean, Anne. "*American Buffalo.*" *David Mamet: Language as Dramatic Action.* Rutherford, New Jersey: Fairleigh Dickinson UP, 1990. 85-118.

Dean constructs a sympathetic reading of Teach by looking beneath the surface to find unstated motives and desires which humanize him: "The world Mamet creates is charged with terror; the characters can barely articulate their rage or sense of impotence and so they often react in the only way known to them—by indulging in deception, betrayal, and violence. Even a man like Teach, though seriously disturbed and profoundly affected by lack of stability in his society, remains at base a sad and desperate character; he is not a psychopath or fundamentally evil man, but one who uses his manipulative powers to buy affection and respect" (95). Teach "gathers up what he sees as the essence of disparate incidents and binds them together into a workable narrative" (100).

sAB 7 Garner, Stanton B., Jr. "Deixis and the Site of Utterance: Breaking the Silence, *American Buffalo*, Not I." *Bodied Spaces: Phenomenology and Performance in Contemporary Drama.* Ithaca, NY: Cornell UP, 1994. 124-36.

Garner uses Teach's speech about losing at cards to illustrate the idea of "deictic speech" which points towards specifics: "The words *I, you, it, this, that, those, here, there, now* refer directly to the situation of utterance and its participants" (126). He notes that the unified subject, "I," has been under "a counter-pressure to complicate the discursive 'I' and displace it from its expressive origins in the speaking subject [. . .] from the start of modern drama" (127). Then he examines how "all of Mamet's characters [. . .] tend to talk at each other, and this is reflected in their dominating use of speech regularly oriented in terms of the speaking I" (129). Garner observes how often Teach uses the words "say" and "talk" and so the speech takes on a "metadiscursive quality" (129).

sAB 8 Haedicke, Janet V. "Plowing the Buffalo, Fucking the Fruits: (M)Others in *American Buffalo* and *Speed-the-Plow*." *Gender and Genre: Essays on David Mamet*. Eds. Christopher C. Hudgins and Leslie Kane. New York: Palgrave, 2001. 27-41.

The bold purpose here is to challenge "the claim of most feminists that Mamet and misogyny ring simultaneous" (27). Noting that Mamet's early plays were episodic, and that later, more linear narratives imply a realistic inscribing of women, Haedicke counters that view: "As the language cracks under its excess, so, too, does the realism as Mamet's characters frantically strive to perform into existence a stable, objective reality in which identity is fixated or gendered and such binaries as male/female, professional/personal, and rich/poor remain reassuringly hierarchical. These performances emerg[e] as parodies of the Oedipal quest" (29). So, for example, "Mamet's repetition of the word 'thing' over sixty times in the play as well as the junk 'things' in Don's shop not only render ironic the clawing search for an objective reality and fixed identity but also indict the inevitable violence in this 'thing' of Oedipal Individualism, where it is 'either him or us'" (32).

sAB 9 Harris, Andrew B. "*American Buffalo*." *Broadway Theatre*. London: Routledge, 1994. 97-112.

Harris's work is unique in that it traces the evolution of the play from its earliest Chicago productions through to Broadway. Harris claims that Ulu Grosbard, the Broadway director, was influential in getting Mamet to revise the script through six drafts in the four months before opening. The changes he wanted were "more consistent characterization. This meant eliminating ambiguities and anchoring every significant detail of the action in psychological motivation" (105). A consequence was "to refocus the play on Teach" for whom Grosbard would only accept Robert Duvall with whom he had worked in past productions. The result was a diminishing of Donny's role. "In the rewritten script, Teach was unpredictable, uncontrollable, and psychotic" (106). Finally, he notes that Mamet saw the play with Donny as tragic hero; a few Chicago critics saw this, none did in New York. Instead, Harris traces a conflict between Kerr and Barnes in the *New York Times* who denounced the play, and Feingold in the *Village Voice* who praised it as a "post-Watergate" work of incompetent third-rate burglars.

AB 10 Kane, Leslie. "The Comfort of Strangers." *Weasels and Wisemen: Ethics and Ethnicity in the Work of David Mamet*. New York: St. Martin's, 1999. 23-56.

The morality theme is evinced clearly and directly: "the key to understanding *American Buffalo* [. . .] is that our moral responsibility to others testifies to our humanity, a lesson evident in the play's concluding image implicitly affirming the value of father-and-son unity and of male bonding" (56). She sees this theme in the opening: "I believe that from the first, Don's lecture on the business of life—eat well, watch your back, do a job right—sets high standards of obligation and conduct and is far more revealing, ironic, and indeed prophetic than is his discussion on life in business" (31). Don's recognition comes from Bob: "Don learns to be an 'excellent man' from Bob, whose *menschlekeit,* practical knowledge born of genuine caring and will to virtue, embodies above all the Jewish injunction to remember" (55). Surprisingly, though, Teach is not demonized as an evil tempter, but rather, contra Dean and Zinman, as Jewish. Teach "is an extraordinarily complex character whose attitudes, philosophy, entrepreneurial instincts, and ethnicity are revealed in his discourse. At once a parody of the loud-mouthed, pushy Jew obsessed with money [. . .]" (51).

sAB 11 King, Thomas L. "Talk and Dramatic Action in *American Buffalo*." *Modern Drama* 34 (1991): 538-48.

Using Saussure, King argues that Teach's approach to language is fundamentalist, based on assumed connection of words and things into "facts." Donny, by contrast, is more of a semiotic relativist: "Teach in his interest in 'facts' seems to desire talk as an accurate representation, whereas Don is satisfied with what is better for him to believe" (541). Thus, Teach becomes frustrated when facts do not correspond, so he attacks Bobby, and later the shop itself. "In a sense, *American Buffalo* teaches its audience that language is action in that its practical effect is more important than its referent and that 'truth is what it is better for us to believe.' At the end of the play, Don transforms the beating that Teach has given Bobby into an accident. This is what it is better for them and for the hospital to believe. This is the practical side of the matter which Don actively creates with his words" (545).

sAB 12 Malkin, Jeanette R. "Language as a Prison: Verbal Debris and Deprivation: David Mamet: *American Buffalo* and *Glengarry Glen Ross*." *Verbal Violence in Contemporary Drama*. Cambridge: Cambridge UP, 1992. 145-61.

Malkin makes the play a tragedy of betrayal of Bobby by Don, using a Mamet quote to justify the interpretation: "Mamet writes about the impossibility of human contact or compassion among the verbally and morally debased" (147). As a consequence, lines which are open to interpretation become closed. Language is divided: "Mamet creates two types of language which correspond to this opposition of personal relations and business relations, and like the opposition itself, the two interpenetrate and undermine each other. [. . .] As Teach says, 'I am a businessman, I am here to do business. I am here to face facts' (p. 83). Such self-confident platitudes are more than slightly ludicrous since the 'facts' change at whim, and neither he nor Don is capable of the logical analysis which such statements imply" (150).

sAB 13 McGowan, Todd. "From Enjoyment to Aggressivity: The Emergence of the New Father in Contemporary Society." *Journal for the Psychoanalysis of Culture & Society* [Kent, Ohio] 3.1 (1998): 53-60.

Using a Freudian/Lacanian framework, McGowan argues that the Primal Father of Freud whose enjoyment of women was total, gives way to the new anal father of late capitalism who submits "all cultural life to the process of commodification" (54). As a result, this new father "presides over a society crawling with" enjoyment— "All his enjoyment doesn't bar us from enjoying" (54). In *American Buffalo* McGowan contends that Fletcher is "the anal father of enjoyment" (54). This anal father of enjoyment is all action, not talk. But, in a perfect reversal mirroring the play, this anal father is declared to be one who cheats, who works in the underworld, and who is "threatening yet ridiculously impotent" (55) as is Fletcher revealed to be at the end when he is beaten and hospitalized. The consequence of the father's impotence is reminder of the subjects' "constant sense that they are not enjoying enough, that they unknowingly sacrificed the thing that they see the father enjoying" (56). He concludes that the play "reveals to us that the aggressivity associated with the idea of stolen enjoyment is the result of a mistake, a mistake rooted in paranoia" (58).

sAB 14 Moran, Daniel. "An Overview of *American Buffalo*". Gale, Literature Resource Center 1998. <http://www.galenet.com/servlet/Lit>. 1 Aug. 1998.

An overview of the play for undergraduates, the focus is on a straightforward betrayal. Teach talks Don into dropping Bobby so he can take his place in the theft. Theme: "members of the proletariat (lower class) have fully ingested and accepted the myths of American Capitalism; as the play progresses, the characters are seen (in various ways) bowing down to the 'God of Business.' This God, which dictates the way these petty thieves behave, allows them to excuse any betrayals or underhandedness in His name." (par. 2).

sAB 15 Rabillard, Sheila. "The Seductions of Theatricality: Mamet, Tremblay and Political Drama." *Autralasian Drama Studies* 29 (1996): 33-42.

Rabillard examines what she terms Brecht's "culinary theatre" which includes both "a refusal to perpetuate the current social system" as well as "a deep unease with illusion" (34). "Brecht showed us that 'culinary' theatre lulled the audience into a satiated tolerance of the status quo; Mamet and Tremblay reveal that we are quite capable of thus entertaining ourselves" (35). She sees this in Mamet, whose "dialogue reveals itself gradually as an established script, daily rehearsed" (35). She then argues that "In each play we are shown the destructive effect of the ludic impulse turning action into game: into a drama" (36). Thus Teach's "criminal fantasy of the Big Score" indulges in "socially-dictated scripts, the fantasies of capitalist fulfillment" (36).

sAB 16 Schlueter, June and Elizabeth Forsyth. "America as Junkshop: The Business Ethic in David Mamet's *American Buffalo*." *Modern Drama* 26.4 (1983): 492-500.

    Teach is the center of the play and betrayal is an outgrowth of his business ethic. "The junkshop, with its piles of once treasured, now rejected cultural artifacts, proves to be a powerful image for an America in which the business ethic has so infiltrated the national consciousness and language that traditional human values have become buried under current values of power and greed" (499). Teach's "notions of right and wrong, fair and unfair, are tangled up in his vision of the American myth of opportunity: [. . .] for this reason, he translates the robbery into a business deal and begins negotiations by persuading Don that there would be little wisdom in including Bob" (494). The failure of the enterprise is because "Teach is plagued by the constant threat of failure. Neither true friend nor true businessman, he experiences abrupt mood swings from that of the authoritarian leader to that of the child wounded by imagined offenses" (498).

sAB 17 Vorlicky, Robert. "Realizing Freedom: Risk, Responsibility, and Individualization." *Act Like a Man*. Ann Arbor: U. Michigan P., 1995. 213-29.

    Using his optic of sociopersonal dialogue, Vorlicky shows how Teach drives a wedge between Don and Bobby: "Teach never forgets that he is talking business, or social dialogue, with Don. However, he skillfully and selectively draws from the codings in personal dialogue to capitalize on the sentiments (and power) of friendship that he knows underlie Don's (his listener's) fundamental communicative dynamic. Using features of the two dialogues, with emphasis on the *socio*personal, Teach appeals to the Don who is gendered, culturally coded male—one who prefers material success over the male bonding of friendship" (219). His analysis of the conclusion of the play is in contrast to most other critics: "The world of *American Buffalo* is not, finally, as Hersh Zeifman suggests, 'literally ruthless and graceless' (129); it is a world in which charity and responsibility can be, and are, present" (227). Vorlicky's reads the final exchange of Bob and Don as "open and sincere, and not 'pointless words of apology and forgiveness' as Malkin argues" (154). Their attempt through language to fill a "missing intimacy" (Bigsby 1985, 22) is an uncommon feature in male-cast drama. It is a particularly unique communicative interaction for (white) heterosexual male characters, made all the more paradoxical in its inarticulate, fragmented presentation" (227).

sAB 18 Williams, Daniel. "Harry Secombe in the Junkshop: Nation, Myth and Invention in Edward Thomas's *House of America* and David Mamet's *American Buffalo*." *Welsh Writing in English: A Yearbook of Critical Essays* 4 (1998): 133-58.

    Using the approach of myths of nationalism (Barthes, Anderson), Williams examines how Mamet uses invented myths about America: "Much of the play's humour lies in this use of pious maxims, derived from national history and frontier mythology, to justify morally questionable ends" (137). Quickly, however, he moves beyond these myths to analyze how the language itself creates its own myths finally exceeding those limits totally: "The moment Teach blames Don for making assertions that have no basis in reality marks a point where their discussion becomes wholly self-referential; words cease to have a referent in an external social reality. An idealism, based on national myth of prosperity and self-reliance, is unceremoniously dismissed in the dramatic action, only to re-enter as verbal exuberance" (144). By the conclusion of the play, there is no connection between what is said and the real, so that Williams argues reconciliation is indicated by the words, but not by the actions or delivery.

sAB 19 Zeifman, Hersh. "Phallus in Wonderland: Machismo and Business in David Mamet's *American Buffalo* and *Glengarry Glen Ross.*" *David Mamet: A Casebook*. Ed. Leslie Kane. New York: Garland, 1992. 123-36. Rpt. in *Modern Dramatists: A Casebook of Major British, Irish, and American Playwrights*. Ed. Kimball King. New York: Routledge, 2001. 167-76.

Zeifman analyzes the exclusion of women from the play, and the sense of "homosocial order" requiring that as well as otherizing of homosexuals—both combined in Teach's epithet for Ruthie: "The patently illogical has been transformed into the patently tautological: in Teach's pantheon of abuse, 'dyke' and 'cocksucker' are simple equivalencies" (127). At the end of the essay, Zeifman observes that this otherizing of women, even if relegating them to positive realms of "compassion, tenderness, empathy, spirituality [which] are seen as threatening to their business ethos" (124-25), still risks the charge of stereotyping and therefore antifeminist (132-33). The article also analyzes satire in *Glengarry:* "The homosocial world of American business so wickedly critiqued [. . .] becomes [. . .] a topsy-turvy world in which all values are inverted by characters who think with their crotch" (125-26).

See also the annotations for the following articles covering multiple plays:

sMP 7 Blumberg, Marcia. "Eloquent Stammering in the Fog: O'Neill's Heritage in Mamet."

sW 2 Brown, John Russell. "The Woods, the West, and Icarus's Mother: Myth in the Contemporary American Theatre."

sMP 10 Chakravartee, Moutishi. "Open Theatre and 'Closed Society': Jean Claude Van Itallie and Mamet Reconsidered."

sMP 17 Esche, Edward. "David Mamet."

sMP 18 Gale, Steven H. "David Mamet: The Plays, 1972-1980."

sMP19 Geis, Deborah R. "David Mamet and the Metadramatic Tradition: Seeing 'the Trick from the Back.' "

sMP 21 Herman, William. "Theatrical Diversity from Chicago: David Mamet."

sMP 23 Hudgins, Christopher C. "Comedy and Humor in the Plays of David Mamet."

sWE 3 James, Justin. "Individual Responsibility and the Disintegration of Social Values in David Mamet."

sMP 32 Lundin, Edward. "Mamet and Mystery."

sMP 35 McCarthy, Gerry. "New Mythologies: Mamet, Shepard and the American Stage."

sMP 36 McDonough, Carla J. "David Mamet: The Search for Masculine Space." .

sMP 37 McDonough, Carla J. "Every Fear Hides a Wish: Unstable Masculinity in Mamet's Drama."

sMP 40 Price, Steven. "'Accursed Progenitor': Samuel Beckett, David Mamet, and the Problem of Influence."

sMP 45 Roudané, Matthew C. "Mamet's Mimetics."

sMP 50 Smith, Susan Harris. "En-Gendering Violence: Twisting 'Privates' in the Public Eye."

sMP 52 Weales, Gerald. "The Mamet Variations."

sMP 54 Zinman, Toby Silverman. "Jewish Aporia: The Rhythm of Talking in Mamet."

Bobby Gould in Hell

Scene: Anteroom to Hell
Editions:
    Oh, Hell!: Two One-Act Plays. New York: S. French, 1991.

Plot Outline:
Bobby Gould is in Hell where an Interrogator and Assistant demand that he confess to being bad. He refuses, claiming he was B minus throughout his life. They cite things he said to a young woman, but he insists on his innocence. She is brought to Hell, irritates everyone by her attitude, and is sent back. Bobby contends her attitude justifies his treatment of her, and the Interrogator finally agrees he can go back and restart his life without guilt. Bobby refuses to go demanding to know what the catch is. As he makes this demand, he realizes, in his refusal, he lost his soul. He finally admits, "I am a Bad Man." The Interrogator agrees, "You were cruel, without being interesting." With his recognition Bobby is told to go home.

Production:
pBGH 1 Double-billed with Shel Silverstein's *The Devil and Billy Markham* under the title *Oh, Hell* at the Mitzi E. Newhouse Theater, Lincoln Center, New York City from November 7 to December 31, 1989 with 32 previews and 32 performances.

Director:	Gregory Mosher
Sets:	John Lee Beatty
Costumes:	Jane Greenwood
Lighting:	Kevin Rigdon
Sound:	Bill Dreisbach
Effects:	George Schindler

Cast:

Bobby Gould:	Treat Williams
Interrogator:	William H. Macy
Interrogator's Asst.:	Steven Goldstein
Glenna:	Felicity Huffman

Overview:

All the critics found the play funny, but beyond that there were significant divisions. Some thought it was only funny (Barnes, Christiansen, Kirkpatrick, Nelson, Simon, Stearns, Watt). Others took the play more seriously, especially in its view of women (Disch, Henry, Kramer, Rich). Indicative of the division, Brustein dismissed the play because he liked Mamet's "scalpel" not his "whimsy." However, Winer noted that Mamet is "always a moralist," yet when he becomes ardent, as in *Edmond*, he is too harsh; his satire is better when mixed with humor. The "funny" critics thought Treat Williams merely sleepwalking in his pjs (Kirkpatrick) and incapable of having enough "pizzazz in him to pursue the earthly vices attributed to him." Kramer alone argued the brilliance of the casting by having: "Gould played here not by the wicked, swift, subtle Joe Mantegna (who created the character in 'Speed-the-Plow') but by Treat Williams, with a look of dumb suffering and the demeanor of a dog who can't understand why he's been put out for the night." She had similarly insightful things to say about Huffman's performance (in contrast to the "flat, dead toneless deliveries he elicited from Lindsay Crouse"). Her final recognition and what separated these interpretations is the satirical Mamet whose purpose was the final "tour-de-force" in which "he makes us echo the play's single blasphemy."

Reviews:

rBGH 1.1 Barnes, Clive. "Double Dose of Fiendish Fun." *New York Post* 4 Dec. 1989.
Rpt. in *New York Theatre Critics' Reviews* 50.17 (1989): 95.
    Positive view but seen as a minor piece: "Mamet is here at his most relaxed and playful—the ideas are paper-thin but fun, the situation amusing and until the punchline is unaccountably pulled, this innocent piece of diablerie provides its director and players ample chance to work the room."

rBGH 1.2 Brustein, Robert. Rev. of *Bobby Gould in Hell. New Republic* 29 Jan. 1990: 28.
    Brustein saw no connection between *Speed-the-Plow* and this play: "Mantegna's Bobby Gould was ruthless, fast-talking manipulator prepared to sacrifice friendship to expediency, and vulnerable only to sexual confidence games. Treat Williams's version of the character is oddly diffident and defensive, shy and puzzled in his bathrobe and pajamas, hardly a candidate for such remorseless diabolical attention."

rBGH 1.3 Christiansen, Richard. "1-Liners Propel Mamet's Latest to Hell and Back." *Chicago Tribune* 15 Dec. 1989: A26.
    Christiansen likened the play to "an exuberant college sketch" lasting an hour—in contrast to Mamet's "determinedly moral work, in which the author is trying to come to grips with the transitory, imperfect nature of life that he sees in himself and all other men."

rBGH 1.4 Disch, Thomas M. Rev. of Oh, Hell. *Nation* 29 Jan. 1990: 143.

Disch noted that critics worried about "what they think Mamet may be saying. Often enough [. . .] he's not saying anything—his art is all in how he says it. No one can crack wise like David Mamet, and there is music like Mozart's in hearing W. H. Macy. [. . .] Mamet's critics are wont to scold him for misogyny, but how else should a satirist depict that half of humanity who are women, if not satirically?"

rBGH 1.5 Henry III, William A. "Having a Hell of a Time." *Time* 18 Dec. 1989. Rpt. in *New York Theatre Critics' Reviews* 50.17 (1989): 97.

Positive review which viewed the play as moral: "The stage is ablaze with hellfire and brimstone, aroar with howls and explosions. [. . .] His subject is how to live morally in this world rather than penitently in the next, and the dynamic that fascinates him is why people make excuses, time and again, rather than attempt to be better."

rBGH 1.6 Kelly, Kevin. "Mamet Devilish, Silverstein Bad in Twin Bill." *Boston Globe* 13 Dec. 1989: 63.

Glowing review: "Mamet's piece is one of his best." The reason for it was "a blistering, quick-run exchange [. . .] behind which is a steady argument about the necessity of taking responsibility for all our actions. [. . .] Mamet keeps this going with absolute dramatic assurance. The immediate inside argument spins dizzily to an outside acceleration about Jewish guilt, as well as Christian worry."

rBGH 1.7 Kirkpatrick, Melanie. "Hellish Evening at Lincoln Center." *Wall Street Journal* 12 Dec. 1989. Rpt. in *New York Theatre Critics' Reviews* 50.17 (1989): 97-98.

Mildly positive review of all the actors but Williams who "perhaps inspired by the PJ's he's wearing, sleepwalks through the role of Bobby. It's hard to believe he had enough pizzazz in him to pursue the earthly vices attributed to him. At least the others in the cast often make the babbling bearable. Mr. Macy is a suitably oily, smooth-talking Satan, and Ms. Huffman is amusingly maddening as the woman scorned. But it's Steven Goldstein, as the Interrogator's Assistant, who is the most fun to watch. He's fussy, exacting, and fawning when the Interrogator is around and officious and accusatory to Bobby."

rBGH 1.8 Kramer, Mimi. "Double or Nothing" *New Yorker* 25 Dec. 1989: 77-79.

In this positive extended examination of the connection to Mamet's other works, especially *Speed-the-Plow,* Kramer noted that Mamet's archetypal hero is "the man who is eminently criticizable by the lights of conventional morality (because he lies, cheats, steals, and blasphemes as a way of life) but whom we come to view as a sort of hero, either because his language charms us (the blasphemy-as-poetry syndrome) or because he does what he does so exceedingly well. The Mamet hero is a self-avowed crook, but he's honest about what he is; that's the one thing he's straight about—not being a good man." Kramer noted the link with Shaw's Don Juan—"He's Everycad." Of the performances, she noted that Williams has none of Mantegna's swift edge as Bob—only "a look of dumb suffering." With Huffman, however, she thought that Mosher/Mamet had gone beyond the flat, toneless delivery of Lindsey Crouse and Madonna— "It didn't matter that the woman never got her say: we didn't know who she was." But in this play the view of woman was much more complicated, and Huffman fit that as the actor who took over the role of Karen, creating "an ambiguity rather than a nonentity." In this play, however, "he does give Miss Huffman a chance to tell Bobby Gould off, and after turning the ultimate female revenge fantasy into a misogynist's nightmare he brings Gould round to the point where, I think, most women would want to see the men about whom they have this particular dream. The tour de force is that he makes us echo the play's single blasphemy. [. . .] by the time he does we're guilty of the very thing that Bobby Gould has been put on trial in Hell for."

rBGH 1.9 Nelson, Don. "'Hell': Hot and Cold Deviled Ham." *New York Daily News* 5 Dec. 1989. Rpt. in *New York Theatre Critics' Reviews* 50.17 (1989): 96.

Positive review of a hilarious play for all actors but Williams: "The interaction of these three—and an assistant devil—supplies the evening's hilarity. There is fine work from Felicity Huffman as the woman and Steven Goldstein as the assistant devil. Treat Williams' talent as Gould, however, seems minimal when placed alongside the others."

rBGH 1.10 Rich, Frank. "Mamet's Tasteful Hell for a Movie Mogul." *New York Times* 4 Dec. 1989. Rpt. in *New York Theatre Critics' Reviews* 50.17 (1989): 94.

Rich focused on the role of women: "It takes only a few minutes of psycho-babble-flecked hectoring for Glenna to bring the previously antagonistic Gould and Interrogator together in a male bond. [. . . Huffman] is most amusing here as she stubbornly and humorlessly stands her ground. When Mr. Williams responds with the exasperating cry, 'There was no pleasing her!' he seems to express a masculine bafflement as timeless as the Old Testament imperatives underlying the play's tongue-in-cheek view of heaven and hell."

rBGH 1.11 Simon, John. "Beelzebubee." *New York* 18 Dec. 1989: 105.

Breezy review: "Mamet is smart, smart-aleck, smart-ass, the whole gamut. But mostly smart in the senses of 'brisk' and 'impudent.'"

rBGH 1.12 Stearns, David Patrick. "Burning Questions Light up *Oh, Hell.*" *USA Today* 13 Dec. 1989. Rpt. in *New York Theatre Critics' Reviews* 50.17 (1989): 95-96.

Positive review of a humorous play: "Mamet's devil is obviously a product of the guilt-free generation. This ineffectual Satan launches into helplessly jumbled theological tirades—appropriate for someone who's heard it all for thousands of years, but definitely lacking menace. Amid Mamet's hilarious non sequiturs—made more dazzling by Gregory Mosher's buoyant direction—his accusations against Bobby Gould (mildly played by Treat Williams) are a verbal house of cards, so insignificant that when Gould reminds him 'I'm a good man,' he can't even argue. The play has all the fantasy that Mamet's relentlessly naturalistic works have often lacked—and it's wickedly funny."

rBGH 1.13 Watt, Douglas. "When 'Hell' Is Cool." *Daily News* [New York] 15 Dec. 1989. Rpt. in *New York Theatre Critics' Reviews* 50.17(1989): 96.

Positive view: "The performances are right on the mark under Gregory Mosher's direction. [. . .] Macy, who ends the short work with a terrific punchline, is as reasonable and companionable a Devil as you're likely to wind up with."

rBGH 1.14 Winer, Linda. "Mamet's Devil and the Double Bill." *Newsday* 4 Dec. 1989: B7.

Winer wondered if this is the same Bobby Gould as in *Speed-the-Plow* because that Bobby: "took glee in knowing he was a 'secure whore' while this one claims he's a 'good man.'" Winer thought it "is not as tightly written as Mamet's major work, but it is a lovely, silly, smart little piece—filled with typical Mamet double-speak poetic patter [. . .]." She noted, however, that "it has Mamet's first complex powerful woman character in a long time."

Production:

pBGH 2 As in the earlier production it was double-billed with Shel Silverstein's *The Devil and Billy Markham* as *Oh, Hell.* It was presented by the Mandrake Theatre Company at the Lyric Studio, London from September 12 to October 5, 1991.

Director:	Aaron Mullen
Sets:	Michael Vale
Lighting:	Gavin McGrath
Cast:	
Bobby Gould:	Nic D'Avirro
Interrogator:	Steven O'Shea
Interrogator's Asst.:	Martin Sadofski
Glenna:	Nancy Crane

Overview:

Like the New York critics, there was a division between those who thought the play merely funny (Eryes, Jones, Peter, Rutherford) and those who saw serious issues beneath the humor (Billington, Neslen). Billington was particularly interesting in his construction of Mamet as a moral absolutist.

Reviews:

rBGH 2.1 Billington, Michael. Rev. of *Bobby Gould in Hell. Guardian* 14 Sept. 1991. Rpt in *Theatre Record* 10-23 Sept. 1991: 1129.

Positive review which recognized the deeper questions the play raises: "What is revealing about the play is Mamet's belief in moral absolutes. [. . .] Under the Shavian whimsy and lurking chauvinism (the garrulous Glenna, having got to Hell, obstinately refuses to quit), Mamet also makes some troubling points: the quarrelling ex-lovers would rather risk damnation than pardon each other's faults as if all life and death were a process of prolonged self-vindication. Bobby's suggestion that sin stems from loneliness and the fact that 'we want God to notice us' sets up all kinds of reverberations."

rBGH 2.2 Donald, Caroline. Rev. of *Bobby Gould in Hell*. *Independent* 20 Sept. 1991:
Arts 17. Rpt in *Theatre Record* 10-23 Sept. 1991: 1129.

Positive review which recognized the play's humor: "Nancy Crane plays a
girlfriend with whom life would indeed be hell on earth. After an encounter
with her, hell itself doesn't seem so bad at all."

rBGH 2.3 Eyres, Harry. Rev. of *Bobby Gould in Hell*. *Times* [London] 16 Sept. 1991.
Rpt. in *Theatre Record* 10-23 Sept. 1991: 1129.

Dismissive review: "The play is, I suppose, quite clever: but my impression
grows that Mamet's inability to write character—the fleshless, bloodless quality
of his drama—is a weakness increasingly shown up by the waning of his manic
humour."

rBGH 2.4 Jones, Rick. Rev. of *Bobby Gould in Hell*. *Time Out* 18 Sept. 1991. Rpt in
Theatre Record 10-23 Sept. 1991: 1130.

The reviewer appreciated the humor, but little else: "Mamet gets stuck with
the end and the final joke feels like a cop-out, but Aaron Mullen's neat direction
makes a divine comedy of the whole evening."

rBGH 2.5 Neslen, Arthur. Rev. of *Bobby Gould in Hell*. *City Limits* 19 Sept. 1991.
Rpt. in *Theatre Record* 10-23 Sept.1991: 1129.

Twisty and positive review with an interesting slant on the Interrogator:
"Bobby arrives at the gates of Hell and attempts to persuade his redneck
fisherman interrogator that there really has been a terrible mistake. Hindered
by his dotty ex-lover and a Cecil B. DeMillean clerk, he achieves salvation
only through accepting damnation."

rBGH 2.6 Peter, John. Rev. of *Bobby Gould in Hell*. *Sunday Times* 29 Sept. 1991. Rpt
in *Theatre Record* 10-23 Sept. 1991: 1129.

Mildly positive review: "The piece is written for five voices rather than
characters, which is probably why, even though Mamet is constitutionally
incapable of writing a dull line, the thing comes over in the end as a distinctly
minor piece of fireworks."

rBGH 2.7 Rutherford, Malcolm. Rev. of *Bobby Gould in Hell*. *Financial Times* 19
Sept. 1991: Arts 17. Rpt in *Theatre Record* 10-23 Sept. 1991: 1129.

Positive review of the play for both humor and ideas: "This is a witty, zany
play, full of theatrical tricks down to the use of fireworks and corny jokes. It
falls into no obvious pattern, but provides a great deal of fun and some thought.
Is Bob Gould a good man or not? Steven O'Shea in waders and fishing gear is
a splendid interrogator [. . .]."

See also the following scholarly article that covers the Bobby Gould plays:

sSTP 16 Zinman, Toby Silverman. "So Dis Is Hollywood: Mamet in Hell."

BOSTON MARRIAGE

Scene: A drawing room.
Characters: Anna and Claire, two women of fashion. The Maid, Catherine.
Editions:
  Boston Marriage. New York: Vintage, 2000.
  Boston Marriage. London: Methuen, 2001.

Plot Outline:
In Act One, both Anna and Claire reveal new relationships, Anna's with a male
benefactor and Claire's a planned liaison with a young woman. While Anna sees
her protector to be the financial savior of the women's independent lifestyle, she
sees Claire's infatuation as betrayal. Claire tries to recruit Anna to help with the
seduction, but it is abandoned when Claire's young woman turns out to be the
daughter of Anna's lover.

Act Two, Scene One explores the history and intricacies of the women's relationship. They plan to regain their credibility by arranging a séance and pretending to be mediums. In Scene Two the seance falls through and Claire decides to
leave. She reconsiders their friendship when Anna proclaims that she will be jailed
for the loss of some jewelry. Claire exits; Anna returns the recently proclaimed
lost jewels and the play ends. Throughout the play with its high-flown, outrageous (sometimes contemporary) wordplay, Anna and Claire deride their Scottish maid, Catherine, whose peasantry and language counterpoint the drawing
room setting.

Production:
pBM 1 American Repertory Theater at the Hasty Pudding Theatre, Cambridge,
  Massachusetts. June 4 to June 27, 1999.
     Director: David Mamet

Set Designer:		Sharon Kaitz and J. Michael Griggs
Lighting:		John Ambrosone
Costumes:		Harriet Voyt
Asst. Dir.:		Robert Milazzo
Prod. Asst.:		Mitchell Sellers
Cast:		
	Anna:	Felicity Huffman
	Claire:	Rebecca Pidgeon
	Catherine:	Mary McCann

Overview:

This play took a new direction for Mamet, and many of the critics were disconcerted by the change. The first shock was the set. Instead of his usual minimalism, his designers took the opposite extreme creating a "Dufy with squiggles and splashes of bold color" (Lyons), a "cartoon" (Byrne), in which "The walls are done in stripes of red, orange, pink, and black, a kind of post-modern mockery of the late Victorian period. A goofy lavender settee with zebra stripes dominates the stage. All the furniture is mismatched, ugly, and absurd" (Mason). Not only was this Mamet's only play set in a historical period, the cast was all-female. The critics tended to reduce it to Mamet in drag. For Karam, "Like Mamet's men, the women use language to conceal and deceive; it is an essential tool in life's battles." For Mason the play "does for hard-edged female characters what many of his others have done for hard-edged males—expose the cruelty, venality, and predatory impulses in them." Byrne was more reductive: "these gals exhibit as much testosterone as any Mamet male." And Brantley concluded, Mamet "is flamboyantly exhibiting his command of Wildean artifice, which he sends up even as he precisely follows its rules. It is as though a football player had decided to dance in the ballet, pointing out as he soars through grands jetés that the skills of the two disciplines are not all that dissimilar." Yet those who saw past the differences from earlier plays (Mamet's or Wilde's) found this one rewarding. For Gale, "the playwright has a premise here concerning the circumscription of women's lives by male dominance. It's one that his critics may be surprised by, if they have the wit and objectivity to see it." Clay saw the play more "about the shifts and sacrifices, jockeying and jealousies, even the duplicity, endemic to any long-surviving 'unity of two.' What makes the play, which does not run deep nor mean to, such brilliant fun was its marriage of glinting period artifice and contemporary frankness."

Great fun was found in the juxtaposition of the two languages. Not to be distracted by verbal slights of hand, Lyons concluded that Mamet "has a sweet ace up his sleeve. Two aces, actually, for both Anna and Claire have been after something we didn't quite see the whole time. The final joke in this delicious play is that all language—from elegant Henry James to streety David Mamet—is a blind, a distraction, a ruse."

Reviews:

rBM 1.1 Brantley, Ben. "Victorian Women? From Mamet? Well, #@%*!" *New York Times* 16 June 1999: E1.

Mixed review. This play "presents a world hermetically sealed by its dense language. But the ripe street vernacular of early Mamet has been replaced by perfumed locutions of improbable archness. Well, mostly anyway. Obscenities explode every so often, rather like stink bombs at a garden party. [. . .] It is an exceptionally clever exercise, a pastiche carried out with knowing and subversive detail. But there is a distancing air of contempt to the proceedings, a faint disdain for the emptiness of posturing estheticism."

rBM 1.2 Brucher, Richard. Rev. of *Boston Marriage. David Mamet Review* 6(1999): 1-2.

Positive review which saw the play as "a witty, incisive satire of decorous vulgarity, barely repressed desire, and class hostility." But in detail there was more than satire. "Anna and Claire have passions that, however self-indulgent, rebel against gender restrictions, class roles and proprieties, even clothes and furnishings. The wit and thrill of the play issue from these tensions." Most notable about the production was the set in which the walls "resemble a modernist painting, say a rough Mondrian, with blocks of color. A character seated against the back wall (I recall a forlorn Anna in act two) creates an arresting visual composition, one that contrasts eras, attitudes, and styles."

rBM 1.3 Byrne, Terry. "'Marriage' Works with Mamet's Cast." *Boston Herald* 11 June 1999: S08.

Positive review of a play that: "often feels more like a linguistic exercise than an exploration of a couple of characters. But Mamet does manage to create some wonderfully funny contrasts between the artifice of that era and the bluntness of today. [. . .] As director, Mamet smartly backed away from his usual control over every beat and let his actresses create their own rhythm. [. . .] The result is some delicious parrying between Anna and Claire, who, despite their extensive vocabulary, remain remarkably featherbrained."

rBM 1.4 Clay, Carolyn. "Altared State: Mamet Goes Wilde in 'Boston Marriage.'" *Boston Phoenix* 10-17 June 1999.

Positive review: "Within that framework, [. . .] the three actresses lounge and sweep and bustle with panache, impeccably putting forward Mamet's fast, furious mix of period formality and bitchy sniping, arcane construction and cheeky contemporaneity. [. . .] McCann, in her more demure and servile way, gives as good as she gets. So, though his epigrams aren't on a par with Wilde's, does Mamet."

rBM 1.5 Donahue, Anne Marie. "Dear David? Felicity Huffman on the Mirthful Mamet." *Boston Phoenix* 3-10 June 1999.

In a promotional piece Huffman explains: "Yes, they're lesbians, and their relationship is sexual in nature. But the play is more about the marriage, about the negotiations that go on, about what each person needs and what they're willing to give up. What makes it deep and interesting is that they're outside of society, on the fringe. They have to figure out how they're going to keep themselves in the manner to which they are accustomed, how they're going to survive, not just in society but within their marriage, within their love."

rBM 1.6 Gale, William K. "'Boston Marriage' Is First-Rate Mamet." *Providence Journal-Bulletin* 15 June 1999: 4F.

Positive review: "Rail-thin, with a high, imperious demeanor, Huffman manages to catch the underlying desperation of Anna's life, one that seems almost totally dependent on a man. Pidgeon nicely counters with the brightly expectant eyes of someone beginning an affair, and later shows us that she can be as devious as, well, as any man."

rBM 1.7 Karam, Edward. "Mamet's Feminine Side." *The Times* [London] 22 June 1999.

Mixed review: "They hone their skills in arias and duets that often have the air of the dramatist showing off his prodigious vocabulary ('But could such a Byzantine rodomontade restore the girl to me?'). Still, to hear Huffman rhapsodise on the importance of a pie in seduction is sublimely absurd. [. . .] However, for all its verbal pyrotechnics and Mamet's own well-paced direction, 'Boston Marriage' often feels like an intellectual exercise. Anna and Claire are grand caricatures of upper-class snobbery, but neither Huffman nor Pidgeon can make one believe they were capable of ever loving each other. Their most passionate moments are spent tormenting Catherine."

rBM 1.8 Lehman, Jon L. "Too-Cute Dialogue Stifles 'Boston Marriage.'" *Patriot Ledger* [Boston] 12 June 1999: 35.

Somewhat negative review: "Mamet has undertaken a period comedy of manners—although what period it's set in is not completely clear—and his verbiage sounds as if he's been caught in a crossfire between Henry James and Noel Coward. But what Mamet is doing behind the tedious, too-cute wordplay is trying to show us women's lives from the inside out."

rBM 1.9 Lyons, Donald. "A Play on Language." *New York Post* 14 June 1999: 42.

Positive review: "Mamet amuses himself by structuring 'Boston Marriage' as a three-act farcical melodrama. [. . .] But as they decamp, it emerges that our playwright, the inventive trickster who devised 'The Spanish Prisoner', has a sweet ace up his sleeve. Two aces, actually, for both Anna and Claire have been after something we didn't quite see the whole time. The final joke in this delicious play is that all language—from Elegant Henry James to streety David Mamet—is a blind, a distraction, a ruse."

rBM 1.10 Mason, M. S. "*Boston Marriage*: Barbs beneath Victorian Propriety."
    Christian Science Monitor 18 June 1999, sec. Arts & Leisure: 20.
        Very positive review: "Claire's and Anna's barbarity to the maid and
    to each other, their greedy appetites, and their shallow self-concern would
    be as alarming as Mamet's macho madmen's were it not for the gleam-
    ing surface of upper-class propriety, the elegant language (and even more
    elegant carriage) of the actors, the humor, and the fact that no one seems
    to feel the barbs too keenly. [. . .] Absurd, too, are the crude, contempo-
    rary idiomatic expressions that break out every once in a while, disturb-
    ing the graceful surface of Mamet's language— albeit, always to reveal
    something about the mental state of one of the women: the vulgarity of
    the maid, the predatory selfishness of the lovers."

rBM 1.11 Siegel, Ed. "At Art, a *Marriage* Made by Mamet." *Boston Globe* 11
    June 1999: D1.
        Mildly positive review: "There is a nice balance that Mamet strikes
    between the women's prim and proper reserve and the anger and sexual-
    ity simmering beneath it. [. . .] Pidgeon and Huffman engage in a bizarre
    form of Mamet-speak, one that allows for almost no facial expression.
    That's obviously what he wanted, given that he's also the director. They're
    quite good at the Thelma-and-Louise-with-parasols poses, and the earthi-
    ness and emotionality of McCann's maid is a welcome counterpoint. I
    wonder, though, if 'Boston Marriage' wouldn't play better with a Wilde-
    er, Maggie Smith-like approach to the parts."

rBM 1.12 Taylor, Markland. Rev. of *Boston Marriage. Variety* 21 June 1999: 88.
        Negative review: "The central characters could just as well be a man
    and a woman or two men—Mamet's point, presumably, is that relation-
    ships are much the same, whatever the sex of the partners. The trouble is
    that his two central characters are essentially just mouthpieces for end-
    lessly wordy banter and bitchiness. This lack of characterization is fur-
    thered by Mamet's highly stylized direction, which requires actresses [. . .]
    to declaim their dialogue rather than act it. They almost never interact,
    and mostly come across as two shrill and straining Maggie Smith
    wannabes."

Production:
pBM 2 Donmar Warehouse, London. Previewed March 8, opened March 16 and
    ran to April 14, 2001. It then transferred to the New Ambassadors Theatre.
    (See next production.)

Director:	Phyllida Lloyd
Set Designer:	Peter McKintosh
Lighting:	Rick Fisher
Music:	Gary Yershon

Cast:

Anna:	Zoë Wanamaker
Claire:	Anna Chancellor
Catherine:	Lyndsey Marshal

Overview:

Surprisingly, British critics were divided—when in the past they had usually been more positive about Mamet than those in New York. Benedict Nightingale opined that "Every major dramatist should be allowed the odd ghastly error." Others were more direct: "art it ain't' (Foss); "tiresome lark" (Gore-Langton); "a little bit like Henry James [. . .] a little bit like Restoration comedy (but not nearly as witty), mostly like nothing at all" (Gross); "unattractive nonsense" (Koenig); "like a male camp comedy obligingly performed by actresses" (Basset); "its misogynistic jokiness left me feeling I rather wish he hadn't" (Woodis).

Yet a number of them were quite positive, usually citing the precedent of Joe Orton and Ronald Firbank—as John Lahr did: "Farcical detachment is a great comic game; and, on this score, it seems, Mamet can hold his own with past masters." Morley went further, arguing that great dramatists break their own mold, revealing "the quality of surprise." Others justified it with a theme most perceived: "exposing the raw, demotic urges that underlay the polite circumlocutions of cultivated New England drawing-rooms" (Billington); "the crude passions that lurked beneath 19th century decorum" (Spencer, Gross); "affected language and Victorian pretension can conceal anger, jealousy, and manipulation" (Nightingale). De Jongh however, perceived more than the language: "In Mamet, what people say often conceals more than it reveals. So too here. Are the women seriously jealous of each other? Is their relationship under threat or are they playing a fantasy game, a ritual of power and abasement as in Genet's 'The Maids'?"

Reviews:

rBM 2.1 Bassett, Kate. Rev. of *Boston Marriage. Independent on Sunday* 25 Mar. 2001. Rpt. in *Theatre Record* 17 Apr. 2001): 339-40.

Mildly positive review: "It's high on style but low on meaning. Though our protagonists question love and howl about fate, it's all a big joke. Maybe Mamet's unflattering picture of lesbians is meant to be as polemical as his antifeminist 'Oleanna', only these women barely seem connected to real life. Actually, the piece feels like a male camp comedy obligingly performed by actresses."

rBM 2.2 Billington, Michael. "Linguistic Fun and Games at the Donmar." *Guardian* 17 Mar. 2001: 27. Rpt. in *Theatre Record* 17 Apr. 2001: 340.

Positive review: "Even if the dialogue is better than the plot, Phyllida Lloyd's well-paced production, set in a chintz-covered drawing-room, boasts three excellent performances. Zoe Wanamaker is brilliant as Anna precisely because she belongs convincingly to a world of whaleboned snobbery and crooked little fingers yet also one of emotional desperation: she handles the language with kid gloves while coming out with phrases like, 'Tell it to the

marines.' Anna Chancellor's Claire is also a hilarious mix of social refine-
ment and predatory lust and Lyndsey Marshal as the maid neatly blends
naivete with a shrewd grasp of sexual powerplay. All language, Mamet
suggests, is a facade: his skill lies in exposing the painful reality under the
fancy filigree phrases."

rBM 2.3 Brown, Georgina. Rev. of *Boston Marriage. Mail on Sunday* 25 Mar.
2001. Rpt. in *Theatre Record* 17 Apr. 2001: 338.
Mildly negative review: "Imagine David Mamet's fast and filthy dialogue and macho posturing translated into more refined, restrained 19th century drawing-room conversation between two erstwhile female lovers. What
you get is this: 'One must keep a civil tongue in one's mouth. It need not be
one's own.' Or 'I've lost my most precious possession.' 'Your rapier wit?'
The sniping, scabrous and scatological urges that boil beneath the veneer
of civility and propriety erupt like blisters." The play is "no more than an
exercise in pastiche."

rBM 2.4 Clapp, Susannah. Rev. of *Boston Marriage. Observer* 25 Mar. 2001.
Rpt. in *Theatre Record* 17 Apr. 2001: 342.
Negative review: "Trying to resolve the tensions that have arisen between them, the characters slide between violently contrasting styles of
dialogue. Most of their talk is made up of contorted sentences batted speed-
ily at each other, as if Henry James were playing ping-pong with himself:
they 'garner', they 'opine', and they drawl: 'Did I say abjure hypocrisy?'
But then suddenly they lurch from the la-di-da to the direct and demotic,
bursting out with: 'get off my tits', 'tell that to the marines'. The effect is
quite often funny, quite often dirty. [. . .] But to what purpose?"

rBM 2.5 Coveney, Michael. Rev. of *Boston Marriage. Daily Mail* 17 Mar. 2001.
Rpt. in *Theatre Record* 17 Apr. 2001: 339.
Positive review: "The subsequent banter, flecked with interruptions by
a docile maid, is like a Henry James story revved up by Joe Orton and spun
into decadent confusion by Jean Genet. We are talking style here, not great
drama. [. . .] The froth of wordplay is invaded by surprise slang and in-
sults—'While I was admiring your muff, your parts came' and 'Bite through
your wrists and die' are two of my favourites—until the stage reels with a
heady concoction no less wrong-footing than what actually happens."

rBM 2.6 de Jongh, Nicholas. "Boston Tee-Hee Party." *Evening Standard* 19 Mar.
2001: 57. Rpt. in *Theatre Record* 17 Apr. 2001: 338-39.
Positive review: "In Mamet, what people say often conceals more than
it reveals. So too here. Are the women seriously jealous of each other? [. . .]
Since the women speak rather as Henry James wrote, in a style of abstruse,
stately circumlocution, you're uncertain until a final revelation. But since
talk is peppered with modern vulgarities their inflated language probably
screens elemental emotion."

rBM 2.7 Edwardes, Jane. Rev. of *Boston Marriage. Time Out* 21 Mar. 2001. Rpt.
in *Theatre Record* 17 Apr. 2001: 340.
    Neutral review: "The three women are fanciful creations and director
Phyllida Lloyd takes the production at breakneck speed, as if afraid that
any pause for breath would reveal how little lies beneath the froth of their
witty one-liners, tears, and tantrums. As Anna, Zoe Wanamaker superbly
exposes her jealousy, snobbery, and fear of aging."

rBM 2.8 Foss, Roger. Rev. of *Boston Marriage. What's On* 21 Mar. 2001. Rpt. in
Theatre Record 17 Apr. 2001: 338.
    Negative review: "This vicious mix of contemporary street language,
chintzy drawing room politeness, seething jealousy and dykey histrionics."

rBM 2.9 Gore-Langton, Robert. Rev. of *Boston Marriage. Express* 23 Mar. 2001.
Rpt. in *Theatre Record* 17 Apr. 2001: 339.
    Negative review: "Behind the polite, witty, Wildean linguistic curli-
cues, these ladies are bitching and jockeying for sexual advantage just as
viciously as any of the Mamet's male reptiles. Words like 'reticule' and
'rodomontade' are bandied about, although the characters often slip into
'kiss my ass' vernacular to keep the laugh quota up. I didn't buy it."

rBM 2.10 Gross, John. Rev. of *Boston Marriage. Sunday Telegraph* 25 Mar. 2001.
Rpt. in *Theatre Record* 17 Apr. 2001: 339.
    Negative review of a work whose purpose was "to lay bare the crude
passions concealed behind the façade of New England decorum, but the
main impression you carry away is of the horrible congealed lingo which
Mamet has devised for his characters—a little bit like Henry James (but not
remotely as subtle), a little bit like Restoration comedy (but not nearly as
witty), mostly like nothing at all. The sooner Mamet gets back to tough
guys the better."

rBM 2.11 Koenig, Rhoda. "Carry on Camping." *Independent* 20 Mar. 2001: 11.
Rpt. in *Theatre Record* 17 Apr. 2001: 341.
    Negative review: "'Boston Marriage,' with its hoity-toity dialogue, is
not just effete, it's phony. Anna, a grande dame of 100 years ago, has not
only conquered her hatred of chintz to please her paramour Claire, covering every domestic surface in cabbage roses; she has set aside her distaste
for heterosexuality, submitting to a wealthy lover in order to keep the two
of them in style."

rBM 2.12 Lahr, John. "Lust Be a Lady; David Mamet Makes Merry." *New Yorker*
2 Apr. 2001: 94.
    Positive review of the play; negative of the production: "In this folde-
rol, there is no psychological subtext for the actors to impart; the nature of
the characters—that sense of willful self-inflation that makes the women
sidesplitting foils for each other—is inherent in the breathing it takes to

make Mamet's lines play. If the actors get the rhythms right (and, in this production, they sort of do), the very intakes of air necessary to speak the words at speed force them into the vain, strutting posture that is their characters' hilarious essence. In Mamet's serious work, language is opaque, probing, and ambiguous. Here it is all on the surface. His usual theatrical impulses have been turned upside down. [. . .] Despite her prowess, Wanamaker has neither the natural swank nor the lightness of touch to properly punch it up. And, for her part, Chancellor never quite hits the pure note of comic outrageousness."

rBM 2.13 Macauley, Alastair. "Master of Modern Life Turns to Period Camp." *Financial Times* 20 Mar. 2001, sec. Arts: 20. Rpt. in *Theatre Record* 17 Apr. 2001: 341.

Positive review: "'Boston Marriage' is wonderfully funny. The audience hangs open-mouthed on its bizarre inventiveness and on the twists of a plot that in many another playwright's hands would be cheerless farce—but what makes it disarming is that all three of its bisexual characters are manoeuvering each other in a power-play that calls to mind the more sinister pages of Laclos or Balzac. [. . .] The play—exquisitely wrought—is as light, deadly, and unique as a cyanide sorbet confected by Escoffier. Mamet camp! I can't get over it."

rBM 2.14 Morley, Sheridan. Rev. of *Boston Marriage*. *Spectator* 31 Mar. 2001. Rpt. in *Theatre Record* 17 Apr. 2001: 342.

Positive review: "Lloyd directs three strong performances from Zoe Wanamaker and Anna Chancellor as the two high-society dames, and especially Lyndsey Marshal as their put-upon, warm-hearted, constantly misunderstood and undervalued housemaid; there may not, deep down, be much of a play here but there is an intermittently hilarious comedy of appalling manners."

rBM 2.15 Nathan, John. Rev. of *Boston Marriage*. *Jewish Chronicle* 23 Mar. 2001. Rpt. in *Theatre Record* 17 Apr. 2001: 339.

Mildly positive review: "The verbal sparring in David Mamet's latest work, 'Boston Marriage', is less a battle for supremacy than a courtship ritual between lovers. [. . .] The performances are impeccable, but while director Phyllida Lloyd is right to avoid histrionics, the central relationship is perhaps too often based on an irony instead of emotion."

rBM 2.16 Nightingale, Benedict. "Sapphic Odour." *Times* [London] 19 Mar. 2001. Rpt. in *Theatre Record* 17 Apr. 2001: 338.

Negative review: "Every major dramatist should be allowed the odd ghastly error. [. . .Mamet] should be forgiven for perpetrating what the characters in his latest play (who wear Victorian dresses and talk in capital letters) would call a Ghastly Error or even a Heinous Piece of Veritable Pseudepigrapha."

rBM 2.17 Peter, John. Rev. of *Boston Marriage. Sunday Times* 25 Mar. 2001.
Rpt. in *Theatre Record* 17 Apr. 2001: 340-41.

Mildly positive review: "The writing is all tongue-in-cheek ornate respectability: it could be Joe Orton parodying Edith Wharton, punctuating
the formal exchanges with louché wisecracks and the odd completely incongruous obscenity, as if to reassure you that every silver cloud has a dirty
lining."

rBM 2.18 Rosenthal, Daniel. "The Winner Takes It All." *Times* [London] 5 Mar.
2001.

This promotional article noted that Howard Davies was to direct but
withdrew. Phyllida Lloyd was delighted to take over: "It's just such a spec-
tacular text, [. . .] Mamet writes with almost musical notation. It needs
fantastic virtuosity from the actors. It's actually scarcely relevant that the
characters are female, because he's really writing about what happens in a
marriage or a partnership when one person wants to have an affair. He's
celebrating a couple whose sexual life, one feels, is very much based on
fantasy and talk. There are hints of Beckett and Genet; the women's civilised
language is what prevents them from killing each other."

rBM 2.19 Spencer, Charles. "An Affair to Remember." *Daily Telegraph* 19 Mar.
2001: 19. Rpt. in *Theatre Record* 17 Apr. 2001: 340.

Positive review: "Nevertheless, Phyllida Lloyd's production has exactly the right ironic, poised assurance, and the performances are terrific.
Wanamaker, with her jolie laide face and beady currant eyes, poignantly
captures the desperation of an ageing woman who will stop at almost nothing to hang on to her lover. As Claire, the statuesque Anna Chancellor
powerfully signals a seething sexual desire beneath her prim skirts, while
Lyndsey Marshal is a comic delight as the much-abused maid who is nothing like as innocent as she appears."

rBM 2.20 Woddis, Carole. Rev. of *Boston Marriage. Herald* 20 Mar. 2001. Rpt.
in *Theatre Record* 21.6 (17 Apr. 2001): 341-42.

Negative review: "This is a queer fish. [. . .] Mamet delights in atmo-
spheres of antagonism, mystery, and super-charged demotic language. But
in 'Boston Marriage' he has adopted the self-conscious, arch style of a Henry
James in a three-hander of perplexing rhythms and intentions, sardonic
possessiveness, and financial intrigue."

rBM 2.21 Wolf, Matt. Rev. of *Boston Marriage. Variety* 16 Apr. 2001: 39.

Negative review of a "peculiarly fruity prose that suggests Oscar Wilde
crossed with Genet. [. . .] But once it becomes clear that this play is for real,
its overriding archness takes root. It's been some time since high-style language has been less pleasing on the ear. [. . .] As usual, Mamet is writing
about coercion and money and sex, this time with his preferred social

echelons and genders changed. It's the suffocating nature of the talk that seems new, with even as seasoned a pro as Wanamaker stymied in trying to make it sing."

Production:

pBM 3 The Donmar Warehouse production was transferred intact to the New Ambassadors Theatre, West End, London, previewing on November 28, opening December 3, 2001, and closing 16 February 2002. (Lyndsey Marshal was nominated for the *Evening Standard* Theatre Award as Outstanding Newcomer for *Boston Marriage* and *Redundant* in 2001.)

Overview:

Nearly all the reviews were negative about the play. Largely they thought it an exercise rather than a serious work. Expectations about language were a focus. They found the surprising interjection of only three four-letter words (the first at 45 minutes Young observed) the main source of humor and yet didn't fit with the Henry James diction most noted: "precious rhetoric" (Nightingale), "stylish if misogynistic mockery" (Woddis), "double entendres and muff jokes" (Taylor). All but one thought the production well-directed and acted. There were only two positive reviews. John Thaxter noted and loved the sets and costumes as well as the production. Alastair Macaulay, the most positive, saw the point of the whole play and production as "style," in which "Anna is a subtly scheming, heartlessly artificial, pretentiously witty, elaborately rhetorical, dazzlingly camp, lesbian voyeuse and minx." Most other reviewers, however, saw no irony and simply found the play excruciating: "snail's pace" (Young).

Reviews:

rBM 3.1 Gardner, Lyn. "Mamet's Camp Night Out." *Guardian* 5 Dec. 2001: 16.
    Negative review: "And why write about a relationship in which you clearly have no real interest, except as a theatrical parlour game that allows you to show off your verbal dexterity?"

rBM 3.2 Gore-Langton, Robert. Rev. of *Boston Marriage. Express* 7 Dec. 2001: 50.
    Negative review: "All this is an exercise in drawing-room banter (set in what looks like a brothel from the set of a Western) in which both women sound as if they've swallowed several dictionaries plus the entire works of Henry James to boot—sexual passions bubbling away beneath their bodices and sentences that seem to go on forever."

rBM 3.3 Logan, Brian. Rev. of *Boston Marriage. Time Out* 12 Dec. 2001: 149.
    Negative review: "Mamet's comic technique here involves splicing the refined language of the New England drawing room with four-letter vulgarities—the better to denote the lusts for sex and power bubbling beneath all that corseted gentility. The occasional hilarity that ensues owes little to character or situation and everything to writerly pyrotechnics."

rBM 3.4 Macauley, Alastair. "Mamet's Marriage Is Made in Heaven." *Financial Times* 5 Dec. 2001: Arts 18.

Very positive review: "Seen a second time, however, it starts to resemble all-male Mamet classics like *American Buffalo*: talk, talk, talk, and gathering agitation about a project that goes awry. And the talk is all-important. *Boston Marriage* is the wittiest new play I have seen in years, and the wittiest work of Mamet's that I have yet encountered. Plays like this do not change the world—that is not what works of art do—but they change your ear, your appetite, your responsiveness. Mamet understands that the true subject matter of art is style itself. Rhythm, phrasing, structure, texture, instrumentation: a play happens to an audience like a sonata, as expressive as a piece by Hayden or Shubert."

rBM 3.5 Nightingale, Benedict. "A Bit of Camp Squib." *Times* [London] 5 Dec. 2001: Features.

Negative review, after not liking it at Donmar, though still liking the actors: "Ninety minutes being sprayed with lines such as 'Adversary Implacable, what does one not sacrifice upon the altar of your merciless caprice?'—is at least 60 too many, even if they're intermittently interrupted by 'kiss my ass' and other modernisms."

rBM 3.6 Spencer, Charles. "Uneasy Marriage of Old and New." *Daily Telegraph* 5 Dec. 2001: 23.

Negative review: "The second time around, however, the joke seems thin and grotesquely overextended. This is a 20-minute revue sketch stretched out over 90 minutes, and, though the acting is outstanding and Phyllida Lloyd's direction deft, I was almost screaming with boredom long before the end."

rBM 3.7 Taylor, Paul. Rev. of *Boston Marriage. Independent* 8 Dec. 2001: 8.

Negative notice: "The posters quote from a review of the original outing: 'As light and deadly as a cyanide sorbet.' It's a great selling line, but wrong. 'Boston Marriage' is as cold and pointless as one."

rBM 3.8 Thaxter, John. Rev. of *Boston Marriage. Stage* 6 Dec. 2001: 12.

Positive review: "But the transfer to a proscenium arch has transformed Peter McKintosh's design into an overwhelming setting of flowery chintz—winning an enthusiastic round when the curtain first rose. [. . .] The plot may be gossamer thin, the comedy springing from the sly disjunctions. But this is a brilliantly acted, deliciously entertaining diversion, never more so than in Marshal's droll bollywood medley, delivered downstage, for reasons too complicated to explain."

rBM 3.9 Woddis, Carole. Rev. of *Boston Marriage. Herald* [Glasgow] 15 Dec. 2001: 17.

Mildly negative review: "I have to admit to the undoubted tour de force

it is—a glittering literary and verbal bon bouffe with Zoe Wanamaker's
fluting but viperish Anna just about winning out on points over her 'partner'
Anna Chancellor's statuesque Claire. [. . .] Somewhere in there, you get the
feeling of a subconscious jibe at female hunger. "

rBM 3.10 Young, Toby. "Strange Union." *Spectator* 8 Dec. 2001: 66.
Negative review, which contends: "The plot of *Boston Marriage* is
exactly the same as that of *House of Games, The Spanish Prisoner* and *The
Heist.* [. . .] The experience wasn't made any easier by the wildly uneven
performances of Zoe Wanamaker and Anna Chancellor as the two leads.
Neither was capable of sustaining an American accent for more than a few
seconds and Chancellor, in particular, gave some very eccentric line
readings."

Production:
pBM 4 Martinson Hall in the Public Theater, New York. Previewed November 5,
opened November 20 and ran to December 22, 2002.

Director:	Karen Kohlhaas
Set Designer:	Walt Spangler
Lighting:	Robert Perry
Cast:	

	Anna:	Kate Burton
	Claire:	Martha Plimpton
	Catherine:	Arden Myrin

Overview:
The reviews were mixed. Winer and Gardner both liked Mamet's move into a
new approach, but Brantley thought it a mere exercise, and Feingold faulted it as
a mixture of "tolerable foolery; some is interestingly resonant seriousness. Most
of it, though, is archness posturing in a void, as if the 1890s were not a different
time but a different planet, and women not an alternative gender to men but a
different species altogether." Lyons faulted Kolhaas's direction.

Reviews:
rBM 4.1 Brantley, Ben. "A Boy's Idea of Girl Talk, from Mamet." *New York
Times* 21 November 2002: B1, 5.
Negative review of "principally a gymnastic exercise of language" in
which: "The tedium quotient is more pronounced in this staging than it was
in Cambridge, where Mr. Mamet directed [. . .]" because the cast was not
balanced as Mamet's was. Plimpton "here goes for an exaggerated Wildean
absurdity" while Burton "though every bit as arch as her role requires, comes
close to creating a real person."

rBM 4.2 Feingold, Michael. "Vagina Dialogues, &c." *Village Voice* 3 Dec. 2002: 66.
Feingold's response was negative on direction: "'Boston Marriage' takes
place in a room where the color of the walls changes dramatically, from a lush
red-orange down to a pale cherry-blossom pink. (Reviewers who ascribe the

change to set designer Walt Spangler are being unfair to lighting designer Robert Perry.) The heavily noticeable color alterations match the shifts in emotional temperature, as if the action were happening in a room-size thermometer or polygraph. This exteriorizing is superfluous, since Karen Kohlhaas's staging is all heavily gesticulated emotive signals. It's the late 19th century in Mametworld, and no sentence may be spoken without semaphoring." Curiously, however, he also faults the play for failure to be realistic: "Characters in Mamet plays tend to be isolated from the larger reality around them—his lack of interest in social history as a source of dramatic material is near total—but they usually drop a clue or two that help you place them. Few have seemed as insular as Claire and Anna. Where they come from, what they do all day, how they lived before Anna went admirer-hunting, are all completely blank."

rBM 4.3 Gardner, Elysa. "Mamet's Women Have Edge in 'Marriage.'" *USA Today* 21 November 2002.

Positive review of the new direction because "the duo is up to the challenge—and so is their creator. For all their vain, catty and deceitful tendencies, these women are no less complex and no more ruthless than Mamet's male characters have been. And in the end, Anna and Claire emerge as more resourceful and sympathetic than many of the guys who have slithered through the playwright's oeuvre. Briskly directed by Karen Kohlhaas, the production emphasizes these strengths and contradictions while making it plain that Mamet is on new ground."

rBM 4.4 Lyons, Donald. "Mamet's 'Marriage' Fails." *New York Post* 22 Nov. 2002: 39.

Although "one of the funniest comedies in years" this production doesn't match Mamet's "precise and hilarious" direction. Kolhaas "manifests no grace or pace or rhythm. As Anna, Kate Burton comes on like Hedda Gabler (whom she played last year) on speed. Martha Plimpton's Claire is somewhat better. She at least has an inkling of the purpose of the wacky wordplay. But neither woman seems really comfortable in Mamet's tricky, deceptive world."

rBM 4.5 Winer, Linda. "Couple Has Words, Courtesy of Mamet." *Newsday* 21 Nov. 2002.

Mixed review that Mamet has returned to "verbal playfulness is certainly back [. . . in this] elegant production. Instead of giving us the Mamet he knows his audience wants and expects, however, he is somewhere else again—challenging himself, or teasing us, or paying off a bet, or, most likely, filling the space in another new way until he figures out where his prodigious abilities will take him next. [. . .] Burton has a creamy viciousness as the manipulative Anna, and Plimpton—no longer the nubile starlet—is a revelation of sardonic poise as the hungry Claire. Both deftly juggle Mamet's outlandish verbiage—wise epigrams plus convoluted showing-off, winking anachronisms and both archaic and contemporary raunch. Walt Spangler's drawing room set is aptly, erotically garish [. . .]."

THREE CHILDREN'S PLAYS

The Revenge of the Space Pandas or
Binky Rudich and the Two-Speed Clock

Time: The Present
Scene 1: The Rudich House, Waukegan, Earth
Scene 2: Various Spots around Crestview, Fourth World in the Goolagong System
Scene 3: Back at the Rudich House
Characters: Leonard (Binky) Rudich, a scientist; Vivian Mooster, an associate; Bob, a sheep; Mrs. Rudich, Leonard's mother; George Topax, a supreme ruler; Edward Farpis, an ex-matinee idol; Various Space Pandas, Retainers, Jesters, Announcers, Residents of Crestview
Editions:
Mamet, David.
  *The Revenge of the Space Pandas: or, Binky Rudich and the Two-Speed Clock:
  A Comedy*. Chicago: Dramatic Pub. Co., 1978.
  Three Children's Plays. New York: Grove, 1986.

Plot Outline:
Three friends from Waukegan leave the earth by means of a two-speed clock escaping a mother's insistent calls to come to a casserole lunch. The two space pandas, whom they encounter on the planet Crestview, take them to a lunafish casserole lunch where they meet George Topax, who almost whacks them all out with a giant pumpkin until he realizes Bob is a sheep. George, the chief, says he will shoot them back to earth via a spatial relocator after a tour of the planet, but tries to seize Bob, the sheep, because he needs wool, as he is allergic to synthetics. The three travelers escape and the planet's residents are mobilized to hunt for

them with the threat of missing a viewing of the original film version of *Penguins on Parade* starring Edward Farpis. The real Edward Farpis shows up as a derelict, turns them in, then rescues them from the great pumpkin execution, revealing his true identity to his Crestview fans. The heroes reclaim the two-speed clock and return home in time for a casserole lunch.

Production:

pRSP 1 Opened June 11, 1977 at Theater of St. Clement's, Stage Company, Flushing, N.Y. on June weekends, then moved to St. Clement's for July weekends.

Director:	Matthew Elkan
Set Design:	Joe Kallopos
Costumes:	Margot La Zaro
Lighting:	Bob Barnes
Cast:	
Leonard (Binky) Rudich:	Michael Gennaro
Bob the Sheep:	Michael Shapiro
Bill The Retainer:	Earl Michael Reid
Vivian Mooster:	Patti Walker
Edward Farpis:	Peter Van Norden
Donald, Buffy (a Space Panda):	Jamie Farbman
Boots, Jester:	Katherine Farrell
Newscaster, Executioner, Mrs. Rudich:	Margo Martindale
George Topax:	Joseph Bergmann

Overview:

All the reviews were positive and focused on the gap between child and adult responses.

Reviews:

rRSP 1.1 Dace, Harold. "Binky, Mooster, Topax and Farpis." *The Soho Weekly* 14 July, 1977: 40.

Positive review by seventh grader who recommends "a very interesting science fiction children's play that kids between the ages of about five and twelve will love, though when strange jokes were told between scenes I heard many men and women laughing hysterically."

rRSP 1.2 Enright, Joe. Rev. of *The Revenge of the Space Pandas. Show Business* 16 June 1977: 19.

Positive review of the response of kids, but notes: "Changes were being introduced as late as show time and some of the best script was written the previous night." Moreover, "even Mamet admits some rewriting could be done. Areas for rewrite, he notes, are easily identifiable since the children's attention wanders at these points."

rRSP 1.3 Field, Bruce. "Mamet's Gamut: 'Buffalo' to Bears." *Daily News* 14 June 1977: 49.

Positive review of "charming new children's play" which concluded with a question and answer session: "Mamet admitted the inspiration for his play originated in his hatred of Waukegan, Ill., and other suburban towns he refers to as 'a poor man's hell.'"

rRSP 1.4 Shepard, Richard F. "Mamet's *Space Pandas*." *New York Times* 24 June 1977: C3.

Positive review: "There is a good deal of nonsense in the lines, and it all belongs. Some of it may be above the heads of young children but the audience at hand last Saturday seemed to giggle all the way through, except for the few who worried about the fate of the three kids."

Production:

pRSP 2 St. Nicholas Theater Company, Chicago, from November 19, 1977 to January 1, 1978.

Director:	Steven Schachter
Set Design:	David Emmons
Costumes:	Julie A. Nagel
Lighting:	Tom Herman
Music:	Alaric Jans
Cast:	
Leonard (Binky) Rudich:	Mark K. Nutter
Bob the Sheep:	Kathleen Gavin
Vivian Mooster:	Barbara E. Robertson
Mrs. Rudich, Retainer, Newsperson:	Donna Porter
Buffy (a Space Panda):	Jim Scholle
Buffy (Space Panda)/ Edward Farpis:	Robert Falls
George Topax:	Jay Jans
Executioner, Court Jester:	Jeremy Pollack

Overview:

All the reviews were positive and all reviewers thought the play worthwhile for both adults and children. Saunders noted how much fun the cast had performing it. St. Edmund and Winer liked the wisecracks and Winer thought it a relief to have "none of the traditional Mamet wordplay."

Reviews:

rRSP 2.1 Andrew, Edward. "*Panda* Is a Bear of a Play." *Gay Leisure* [Chicago] week of 24 Nov. 1977.

Positive review because Mamet "has written *Binky Rudich* with a sharp eye focused upon the impressions of how children perceive the adult world. There is a good deal of satire, irony and parody involved in this play which children won't perceive, but then that's what makes this hour long play worth the viewing time for both adults on the intellectual and children on the literal levels."

rRSP 2.2 Christiansen, Richard. "Whacko *Space Pandas* in a Socko Kiddy Show."
Chicago Daily News 21 Nov. 1977: 43.

Very positive review: "If nothing else, the show proves forever that
Mamet can indeed devise complicated plots. [. . .] Filled with running gags
and outrageous wordplay (in which the Space Pandas dine on 'lunafish'
casserole), the play has inventive humor for both kids and oldsters. Crestview
(so named because its founders thought it would attract investors) is where
the worst punishment imaginable is that nobody gets to go to the movies
and where the latest scenic attraction is the new car wash."

rRSP 2.3 Nelson, Jeff. Rev. of *Revenge of the Space Pandas. News Gazette*
[Urbana-Champagne, IL] 24 Nov. 1977.

Positive review. "Mamet's glib, fast-paced dialogue is full of droll one-
liners that move the story well, and provide some laughs for the older patrons.
The adults almost have more fun that the children watching Jay Jans play
the 'cruel' ruler of the planet Crestview. [. . .] His show-stealing performance
has grown-ups laughing and children answering his lines."

rRSP 2.4 St. Edmund, Bury. Rev. of *Revenge of the Space Pandas. Reader* 2 Dec.
1977.

Positive review: "Haven't heard so many Waukegan jokes since Jack
Benny went off the air. But they're not cheap shots, folks, they all have
legitimate artistic links to the situational and motivational needs of Binky
Rudich. [. . .] Director Steven Schachter climbs to new depths with this
production, whipping his cast through Mamet's wise-guy dialogue at
breakneck speed, playing with props and lights as if they were dimestore
magic tricks, riffling through one inventive piece of schtik after another."

rRSP 2.5 Saunders, Dick. "A Luna-Fish Casserole for the Kids." *Chicago Sun-
Times* 23 Nov. 1977.

Positive review: "The production is a bit ramshackle, but that makes it
all the more endearing—at least to us kids who are sick of being told that
neatness counts. The actors bring a special kind of joy to their work—as
only people worth taking seriously can when they kick up their heels. The
same goes for David Mamet. And if there's a better way to introduce
youngsters to the theater than through the special imagination of America's
hottest young playwright, I don't know what it is."

rRSP 2.6 Winer, Linda. "*Pandas* Is Lively, Inventive." *Chicago Tribune* 25 Nov. 1977.

Positive review that reminds us "that good children's theater is childlike
without being childish. [. . .] The script has none of the traditional Mamet
wordplay which, at this point in his stylistic evolution, is something of a
relief. The show [. . .] includes digs at TV news, cross-cultural language
lessons, and enough adult wisecracks to make parents glad they tagged
along."

Production:
pRSP 3 Atlantic Theater Company, N.Y., from March 2, 2000.
       Director: Robert Bella
          Cast:
              Leonard (Binky) Rudich: Joshua Dickens
                    Bob the Sheep: Chris Papagapitos
                    Vivian Mooster: Diana Ascher

Review:
rRSP 3.1 Graeber, Laurel. "A Tale Wild and Woolly.' *New York Times* 2 March
      2000: part 2: 45.
          Positive review of a production which "might be described as 'Back to
the Future' on hallucinogens" in which "young theatregoers are urged to
yell out, 'Waukegan!' instead of something like 'Abacadabra!' or 'That
way!'" and "includes lots of silliness and racing through the aisles."

The Poet and the Rent:
A Play for Kids from Seven to 8:15

Dedication: ". . . dedicated to W. H. Macy in the hopes that he and I may continue
to be aware of what the other is thinking; and, Ladies and Gentlemen, to Patricia
Cox."
Setting: "This play takes place in a theater. All of the characters, at various times,
address the audience directly, and most men and women in their time play many
parts."
Characters: Aunt Georgie, a camp counselor; Sergeant Albert Pressman, a
mountie; Kodiac Prince, a wonderdog; The Poet, a poet; The Landlord, a
landlord; The Girlfriend, a young woman; Spuds O'Malley, a cop who keeps
his eyes peeled; The Factory Owner, a capitalist; The Wacko Woman, an
advertising copywriter; Gene, a thief; Boots, a thief; Various other people

Plot Outline:
This camp one-act, presented as a staged fairytale, revolves around the adven-
tures of the poet trying to acquire $60 dollars to pay his overdue rent. He first tries
to sell his poems in a park, then becomes a nightwatchman in a factory, then a
thief, a jailbird and finally returns to his poetry. Throughout the story a variety of
eccentric characters become involved including: a cop obsessed with potatoes, a
woman who writes ads for Wacko, a product of undetermined use, a girl who
turns out to be wealthy and generous, an intelligent dog, Aunt Georgie who continually gets whacked in the face with pies and several others.

Production:
pPR 1 St. Nicholas Theater Company at Jane Addams Theatre of Hull House. June
      19, 1975 then Saturdays and Sundays through July in different venues, at
      midnight.

Director:	William H. Macy
Set:	David Stettler
Costumes:	Tim Rose
Music:	Alaric Rokko Jans & Annie Hat
Cast:	

Uncle Georgie:	Penelope Court
Sergeant Preston:	David Stettler
Yukon King, The Wonder Dog:	Claudia Bohard
Poet:	David Novak
Girl Friend:	Patricia Anderson
Landlord/Factory owner/Ad exec.:	Terri Silverstone
Spuds, the Cop:	Russell Fear
Thief 1 (Tony):	Linda Clink-Scale
Thief 2(Maurice):	Larry Weiss
Girl:	Fran Roth

Overview:

Only Dettmer panned the play. McShane replied that Dettmer didn't understand children's theatre. Christiansen liked it for not being typical of children's fare. VerMeulin and Finn noted the rough spots in the production, but liked it nonetheless.

Reviews:

rPR 1.1 Christiansen, Richard. "A New Play to Cheer; Happy Days Are Here." *Chicago Daily News* 20 June 1975: 20.

Very positive review of the play as atypical for children: "The play, thank heavens, is not 'for children.' It's free of all the usual fairy tale fustian that adults seem to believe youngsters like. Instead, Mamet has just let his own abundant, antic imagination loose on a sweet, silly fable. [. . .] There are custard pies, pratfalls, intellectual puns, Jewish gags, theatrical satire, an Irish policeman who's just crazy about potatoes and a wonderful song about bananas."

rPR 1.2 Dettmer, Roger. "Mamet's *"Lesson"* Just One Big Drag." *Chicago Tribune* 20 June 1975.

Negative review of the play, not the production: "Tots in the audience were bored with the gag by the second time [but not the last] that someone pasted Uncle Georgie with a pie. Mamet's multilingual puns—visual as well as verbal—went over their heads, mercifully. The direct address of homilies condescended, and those kids knew it."

rPR 1.3 Finn, Jane. ". . . Worth Learning for Kids 7 To 100." *The World* 29 June 1975, sec. B: 2.

Positive review by a high school student: "On the whole, the show is very amusing with only a few rough spots that time will mend. [. . .]The story is narrated by a character looking a great deal more like a track coach than a storyteller named Uncle Georgie (Penelope Court). Poor Georgie receives many pies in the face along with plenty of laughs."

rPR 1.4 McShane, Timothy. "*Poet*: A Lesson in Comic Form." *The World* 29 June 1975, sec. II: 2.

Positive review: "It is the comedy of incongruity, of absurd juxtapositions, where it is possible for an actor to be called offstage to answer a phone call from his mother. It is also, as Roger Dettmer's damning review in the *Chicago Tribune* pointed out, a lesson. And although Dettmer is right on that score, his preconceived notions of children's theatre, and Mamet's in particular, ought to keep him away from this genre which values naivete so highly."

rPR 1.5 VerMeulen, Michael. Rev. of *The Poet and the Rent. Reader* 27 June 1975.

Very positive review of the play: "Very simply, *The Poet and the Rent* is an unusually strong and appealing script. It's the kind of play innocuous words like 'delightful' were coined to describe. And even though the St. Nicholas Theater Company's production contains some prominent flaws, Mamet's work alone makes the show a success."

Production:
pPR 2 Circle in the Square Repertory Theater, New York, May 9, 1979.

Director:	R. Stuart White
Music/additional Lyrics:	Andrew Mishkind
Cast:	
Aunt Georgie:	Joyce Reehling
The Poet:	Burke Pearson
The Girlfriend:	Maura Swanson
Sgt. Preston:	Jeff Daniels

Review:
rPR 2.1 Gussow, Mel. Rev. of *The Poet and the Rent. New York Times* 10 May 1979: C22.

Rather negative review: It "is billed as an entertainment for children and adults, and may appeal to the very youngest in both categories."

Frog Prince

Production:
pFP 1 Goodman Theater, Chicago, 17 May, 1982 (reading)

Scholarly
s 1 Adler, Thomas P. "Mamet's Three Children's Plays: Where the Wilder Things Are." *Gender and Genre: Essays on David Mamet*. Ed. Hudgins and Leslie Kane Eds. Christopher C. New York: Palgrave, 2001. 15-27.

Thomas Adler opens the anthology with an insightful essay which argues that Mamet's theatricalism in the children's plays reflects the work and vision of Thornton Wilder—especially that of *Our Town*. Adler makes a good case by citing addresses in *The Revenge of the Space Pandas* which mirror Emily's as well as the sense of never knowing good things until they have passed in *The Frog Prince*. Along the way, however, he also discovers more bald statements and visions of Mamet's rejection of business and capitalism: "In Mamet's retelling, the clear implication is that all property is suspect, because it entails an usurpation of what perhaps should be shared, if not communally, at least with those who have less" (18). And in *The Poet and the Rent* Adler notes, "The anti-business bias of the play, with its criticism of a society that deems the artist superfluous and expendable because he 'ain't got no marketable skills' and therefore is of 'no use'" (24). Most intriguing, however, is the implied but never fully developed sense of Mamet's vision of the metatheatrical in this last play.

THE CRYPTOGRAM

Dedicated to: Gregory Mosher
Scene: A living room.
Characters: Donny, a wife and mother; John, her son; Del, a family friend
Editions:
  The Cryptogram. New York: Vintage Books, 1995.
  The Cryptogram. New York: Dramatists Play Service, 1995.
  The Cryptogram. London: Methuen Drama, 1995.
  David Mamet Plays: 4. London: Methuen, 2002.
Award: Obie for Best Play of 1995.

Plot Outline:
It is the night before John is to go on a camping trip with his father, and he can't sleep. As Donny, his mother, and Del, a family friend, try to calm John down and get him to sleep, Donny tries to figure out why Robert has not yet come home from work. She and Del share memories of the past, and John comes down to ask questions. When John goes back upstairs, he sees a note on the mantlepiece—it is a note from Robert to Donny saying he is leaving her.

The next night, Del returns having been out looking for Robert and buying medicine for John. John asks question after question about what things mean, and why Robert hasn't come for him, but the adults put him off, and send him up to sleep. Donny then probes Del about discrepancies in his story of going camping with Robert and about a knife. Del finally admits he wasn't camping—but let Robert use his hotel room. Donny, outraged both at her husband's cheating and Del's betrayal of her— demands that he leave as she cries "Bobby, Bobby, Bobby." John then comes down the stairs to tell of his dream vision of voices, someone walking and a candle outside.

A month later the third act opens with the room "denuded. Various packing boxes are seen." John enters and asks if Donny has ever wished that she could die. She avoids answering him: "Things occur. In our lives. And the meaning of them … the *meaning* of them … is not clear." When Del enters she continues, telling John that each person is alone, each person has a story. She sends John up to sleep. Del apologizes, but she refuses to accept his gift offering—the knife and a book he borrowed. John returns, begs for a blanket which is packed in the attic—she sends him to get it. The fight continues as Donny says all men betray her, and John returns. She is irate, having told him to go to bed—but he can't cut the twine around the box. Del gives him the book to read and knife to cut the twine. As John ascends the stairs holding the knife; he returns to talking about the voices which are calling to him.

Production:

pC 1 *The Cryptogram* premiered at the Ambassadors Theatre, West End, London on June 29, 1994.

Director:	Gregory Mosher
Set Designer:	Bob Crowley
Lighting:	Rick Fisher
Cast:	
Donny:	Lindsay Duncan
Del:	Eddie Izzard
John:	Danny Worters, Richard Claxton

Overview:

British reviewers divided over the play depending on whether they recognized that it was told from a child's perspective. The *Express* critics were most negative. Hirschhorn denounced the play as "the tic-infested doodling of a formidable dramatist temporarily (one hopes) adrift in the doldrums. What he has written boils down to a 20-minute sketch about the corrosive effects of betrayal and deception have on a marriage." This view was similarly articulated by Paton, that the play is "underwritten and no more than a scene setter that never develops." She also focused on "Endless repetition, logic-chopping and fragments of conversation" of "the Chicago housewife agonising over every clue, however trivial, to her husband's disappearance." For most critics however, "we are seeing the action through his [John's] sleepy, non-comprehending eyes" (Smith; see also Gross) and so "He is the vulnerable central character caught up in a swirl of adult emotions" (Edwardes). These critics were less frustrated by the lack of full revelation of fact as in a modernist realist play, but they tended to account for the murkiness by contending that Mamet was confronting painful memories that were too personal to reveal fully. Wardle: "Was Mamet also in the dark when he wrote this play; or is he deliberately withholding material that is too painful to disclose?" Spenser: "you get the impression of a writer confronting submerged traumas, and attempting to keep pain at a distance by the discipline of controlled, enigmatic dialogue." Nightingale came close to this too: "Am I wrong to sense private griefs in his portrait of John, with his insomniac terrors, his interest in suicide, and the ominous voices he hears 'calling my name'?" Billington soared over all the others in his reading: "Mamet's point is that we are held spiritually captive by our bluster and evasions." Kane found a more positive meaning in the ending which "signals an intimate night journey inherently dangerous, painful and ultimately enlightening."

The actors were unanimously praised in Mosher's production. Izzard was a big surprise to all who had known him as a stand-up comedian who performs in drag. de Jongh described his "shambling, dejected Del lifts the character from the depths of gay cliché." Crowley's set was also widely praised. He "has designed a high room which is stark at the same time as being cluttered" (Peter). Billington noted how it aided interpretation: "marvelously conveys the sense of a world askew." Taylor noted as well how the set "shows you the house from the boy's overwrought, incipiently pubertal perspective." Though its most notable feature, the scrim walls, didn't work for Hoyle: "suddenly transparent walls that give glimpses, big deal, of a kitchen or child's bedroom though no sign of the emperor's clothes."

Reviews:
rC 1.1 Barnes, Clive. "Mamet's Cry from the Heart." *New York Post* 29 Aug. 1994: 30.
    Positive review: "'The Cryptogram' seems like Albee without Albee. But once Mamet shows his hand and gets the play's themes of betrayal and childhood loss of innocence under way, his work grows incandescent with feeling. [. . .] The mother is seen to be a self absorbed shrew, the family friend a shiftless Judas, and the son—caught on the cusp of the age that first questions the unanswerables—finally arms himself for life."

rC 1.2 Billington, Michael. "World Premiere: A Cracking Code." 24 June 1994, sec. 2: 13. Rpt. in *Theatre Record* 18 June-1 July 1994: 799.
    Most perceptively Billington observed: "Like Pinter's 'Betrayal' Mamet's play suggests that deception is an endless spiraling process that eventually corrodes the soul." The explanation of corrosion is in words: "we use words as a destructive social camouflage to lie to others and ourselves. [. . .] And here through all the repetitions, half sentences and echoing encounter of one question with another, you feel the characters devalue experience through their use of language. As Del cries in desperation at the end, 'If we could speak the truth for one instant, then we would be free.' Mamet's point is that we are held spiritually captive by our bluster and evasions."

rC 1.3 Core, Susan and George. "Americans in London." *Sewanee Review* 102.4 (1994): 694-99.
    Negative review which saw only insanity: "The psychology of the action, including the mysterious geometry of relations among the three characters, turns upon the madness of a ten-year old boy. Nothing is done to explain his sickness. [. . .] The fragmentation is complete as the betrayed and raving mother watches her suicidal child choosing his obvious last resort—a knife."

rC 1.4 Coveney, Michael. Rev. of *Cryptogram*. *Observer* 3 July 1994. Rpt. in *Theatre Record* 18 June-1 July 1994: 797-98.
    Rather negative about the play, ("both dense and infuriatingly slight") but positive about the production which "brilliantly evokes a fear of the dark and of terror at the top of the stairs." In general, however, "All three characters, and

the audience, are engaged in a game of psychic I-Spy that turns on the emergent truth of Del's relationship with the unseen father and husband. They have been camping together in more ways than one."

rC 1.5 de Jongh, Nicholas. Rev. of *Cryptogram. Evening Standard* 30 June 1994. Rpt. in *Theatre Record* 18 June-1 July 1994: 799.

Negative review of a play that was: "puzzling and not that alluring. [. . .] Donny tells her son: 'Things occur in our lives and the meaning is not clear at the time.' And her words speak for the world of the play. Mamet's elliptic, evasive dialogue, his manipulation of symbols and signs, his thinly rendered characters in their dissociated speaking serve to make 'The Cryptogram' seem a desultory charade, which never rises to full dramatic potential."

rC 1.6 Doughty, Louise. Rev. of *Cryptogram. Mail on Sunday* 10 July 1994. Rpt. in *Theatre Record* 18 June-1 July 1994: 801.

Negative review of Donny: "Her character is a black hole in the place where an emotional centre should be. Like Izzard, Duncan struggles to make sense of her part, her frustration with its limitations as real and as physical as the sofa in her living room. Somewhere inside 'The Cryptogram' there is a play struggling to get out, but what we have here is a snapshot, an anecdote about absent husbands and screwy wives who bequeath their resentment to their children."

rC 1.7 Edwardes, Jane. Rev. of *Cryptogram. Time Out* 6 July 1994. Rpt. in *Theatre Record* 18 June-1 July 1994: 800-01.

Mixed review. John is "the vulnerable central character caught up in a swirl of adult emotions." Donny is "a rare example of a female Mamet character of some substance." She was slightly critical of Izzard who "looks neatly accurate as a '50s queen and although I can think of other, less famous actors who would dig deeper, the nervous distance that he creates between him and his role is oddly affecting. Danny Worters is so good as John that one fears for his welfare."

rC 1.8 Gross, John. Rev. of *The Cryptogram. Sunday Telegraph* 3 July 1994. Rpt. in *Theatre Record* 18 June-1 July 1994 798.

The play was too cryptic. He viewed the play through John: "He can't sleep; he hears voices calling him; he teases away at the meaning of things like a precocious philosopher. It is as though he already sensed that his world was about to break up. [. . .] The cryptogram in this sense is adult behaviour seen through a child's eyes—so confusing, so unfair, so unreliable. And while John's story doesn't particularly take us anywhere, the details accumulate with a dark force."

rC 1.9 Hagerty, Bill. Rev. of *Cryptogram. Today* 30 July 1994. Rpt. in *Theatre Record* 18 June-1 July 1994: 799-800.

Positive review: "David Mamet's slip of a new play—an hour and a half that appears to speed by in half the time—is set in the Chicago of 1959." But the play would do better without an interval for drinks.

rC 1.10 Hirschhorn, Clive. Rev. of *Cryptogram. Sunday Express* 3 July 1994. Rpt. in *Theatre Record* 18 June-1 July 1994: 800.

Negative review which denounced the play: "the tic-infested doodling of a formidable dramatist temporarily (one hopes) adrift in the doldrums. [. . .] This slender thread of narrative unravels at a funereal pace and is spun out to an indefensible 90 minutes."

rC 1.11 Hoyle, Martin. "Mamet Goes Minimalist." *Financial Times* 1 July 1994: 17. Rpt. in *Theatre Record* 18 June-1 July 1994: 796-97.

Negative review of a play that is: "an insubstantial wisp of memory. [. . .] Bob Crowley's sets desperately attempt to add something to this flimsy meandering: a dark room, a staircase, suddenly transparent walls that give glimpses, big deal, of a kitchen or child's bedroom though no sign of the emperor's clothes."

rC 1.12 King, Robert L. "Versions." *North American Review* 279.6 (1994): 51.

This negative review assumed the play must be autobiographical: "His [John's] last words reveal some dark anxiety about the voices he hears as he would sleep: 'They're calling my name.' Some darkly creative power must be waiting to shape his future; armed with a parachutist's escape knife, he will presumably confront his destiny."

rC 1.13 Kane, Leslie. "*The Cryptogram* 23 July 1994." *The David Mamet Review* 2 (1995): 1+.

Kane saw the play through Donny's explanation to John: "Things occur. In our lives. . . . the meaning of them . . . is not clear." But the reason for this was found in the set whose stairs suggested "the fluidity between states of consciousness and unconsciousness." Rather than moving in a psychological direction, however, Kane then moved toward the religious: "As setting, the home is a rarity in Mamet's canon, and coupled with the night-time scene and the evocative power of three—the heavenly number of the soul, the human family, the triads of truth, courage, and compassion, and past, present, and future—it signals an intimate night journey inherently dangerous, painful and ultimately enlightening." The set is seen to figure into this at the end of the play: "Beautifully complementing the complexity and mysticism of *The Cryptogram*, Bob Crowley's set, resembling a Rothko painting, and expertly lit by Rick Fisher, is dominated by a huge staircase that seems to disappear into the shadows, and is especially effective in the final disturbing moments."

rC 1.14 Lahr, John. "Betrayals." *The New Yorker* 1 Aug. 1994: 70-73.

In a positive review published a month after the opening, Lahr refuted the British critics who criticized the play: "Mamet chose to attack the world, and 'The Cryptogram' goes some way toward illuminating the source of the cruelty and faithlessness that his characters generally find in it. The shifting ground of the play makes it hard to engage with, but its aftershock is enormous. 'The Cryptogram' may be short, but it is not miniature. The oblique, brilliant dialogue is not underwritten, nor are the characters unexplored. With remarkable concision and insight, Mamet has mapped out the dynamics of a soul murder. This daring, dark complex play got respectful though mixed notices in London, but I suspect that in time it will take its place among Mamet's major works" (73).

rC 1.15 McCue, Jim. "Will Somebody Please Tell Him?" *Times Literary Supplement* 15 July 1994: 21.

Negative review: "The problem with *The Cryptogram* is that the adults don't know what they want and the boy always looks destined to be thwarted. [. . .] In so little as it's about anything specific, this is a play about betrayal of a child by insecure adults. It is unfair, and increasingly common, to treat a child as a grown-up or to confront him prematurely with the sad truth that a parent is not God. But childish needs, met or unmet, lack the tension of contradictory adult wishes. And because John has no power, he cannot unleash any drama. [. . .] Well, it's not a disgrace. Good dramatists sometimes write bad plays. But who will be unmannerly enough to tell him it needs fixing."

rC 1.16 Morley, Sheridan. "A House of Horrors." *Spectator* 9 July 1994. Rpt. in *Theatre Record* 18 June-1 July 1994: 801.

Negative review. Morley placed it in the genre of "a memory play" and concluded: "there's a fatal lack of dramatic energy, what holds the attention here is the way that everything is seen and heard through the eyes of the boy. [. . .] He alone still has a handle on the truth, still knows that things not clear now will become clear later if only his hold on the truth an be maintained. The two adults have lost that, and are left with the consequences of the lies they have told to keep themselves going."

rC 1.17 Nathan, David. Rev. of *Cryptogram*. *Jewish Chronicle* 8 July 1994. Rpt. in *Theatre Record* 18 June-1 July 1994: 801.

Perceived two levels to the play: "the first seems to be about betrayal." This was the adult plot. But the second level dealt with John: "Coded messages often deal with facts too brutal for plain language. What are we to make of a couple who, filled with anger at their own lives, give a knife to a small, sleepless boy who hears voices and is unafraid of death? At this point a great sense of evil wells up from Bob Crowley's dark, shabby and red-stained set, and betrayal seems a weak incongruous metaphor for the act we have just witnessed."

rC 1.18 Nightingale, Benedict. "Coded Display of Private Suffering." *Times* [London] 1 July 1994. Rpt. in *Theatre Record* 18 June-1 July 1994: 797.

Mixed review of a not too successful play: "Am I wrong to sense private griefs in his portrait of John, with his insomniac terrors, his interest in suicide, and the ominous voices he hears 'calling my name'? [. . .] Somewhere here is the true key to 'The Cryptogram' and it eludes dramatic definition."

rC 1.19 Paton, Maureen. Rev. of *Cryptogram*. *Daily Express* 30 July 1994. Rpt. in *Theatre Record* 18 June-1 July 1994: 800.

Negative review: The play was "underwritten and no more than a scene setter that never develops. [. . .] Endless repetition, logic-chopping and fragments of conversation" of "the Chicago housewife agonising over every clue, however trivial, to her husband's disappearance."

rC 1.20 Peter, John. "Mamet's House of Secrets." *Sunday Times* [London] 3 July 1994. Rpt. in *Theatre Record* 18 June-1 July 1994: 795.

Positive review: "Mamet has often been compared to Pinter, but the differences are as important as the similarities. Both understand the great secret dramas of insecurity; but Pinter's characters are refugees seeking asylum, while Mamet's are prisoners, chained or cheated or both, struggling for freedom. Put more simply: Pinter's characters are trying to get in, Mamet's are fighting to get out."

rC 1.21 Smith, Neil. Rev. of *Cryptogram*. 7 July 1994. Rpt. in *Theatre Record* 18 June-1 July 1994: 800.

Very positive review: "We realise that we are seeing the action through his sleepy, non-comprehending eyes. [. . .] But if you can surrender yourself to the play's hypnotic speech rhythms and haunting insight into family trauma it's a play that will stay with you for a very long time."

rC 1.22 Spencer, Charles. "Mamet Devastates with a Tale of Growing Pains." *Daily Telegraph* 30 June 1994: 9. Rpt. in *Theatre Record* 18 June-1 July 1994: 798-99.

Spenser praised: "Mamet's elusive, harrowing new play [. . .] the writing is at first cool and minimal. [. . .] You get the impression of a writer confronting submerged traumas, and attempting to keep pain at a distance by the discipline of controlled, enigmatic dialogue."

rC 1.23 Stuart, Jan. "A Puzzle of Portent from Mamet." *Newsday* 1 July 1994: B2.

Praise for direction: "Mosher musters considerable tension with the minimalist material, achieving a fluidity of performance that eludes the author in his self-directed efforts ('Oleanna' and the film 'House of Games'). Mosher knows how to take the clunkiness out of Mamet's conversational mannerisms, but neither he nor the actors know how to de-clunk the odd clichés that often give 'The Cryptogram' the feel of a B-movie trailer."

rC 1.24 Taylor, Paul. "Brute Strength." *The Independent* 1 July 1994. Rpt. in *Theatre Record* 18 June-1 July 1994: 796.

The only critic who confronted the final moment: "And what about the husband's German combat knife, the (alleged) reward to Del for his complicity, which turns out to have been a purchase, not a real trophy of war, and is thus farcically devalued in sentimental terms. An ambiguous emblem of deception and of cutting yourself free, it winds up in the hands of the boy—resulting in a final picture which, like much of the proceeding play, remains potently cryptic."

rC 1.25 Tinker, Jack. Rev. of *Cryptogram*. *Daily Mail* 30 June 1994. Rpt. in *Theatre Record* 18 June-1 July 1994: 801-02.

> Disliked the play, but loved the production: While "I found the play itself hardly worth a quick re-reading, the production of it is quite extraordinary." His unique point of access was Del, whom he assumed at first was the father, "so comfortable is he in her home and with her son [. . .] not until much later that he reveals his true needs to be admitted as a member of their family."

rC 1.26 Waites, Aline. Rev. of *The Cryptogram*. *Plays and Players* July/Aug. 1994: 9.

> Positive review: "Donny is obsessed with betrayal. She feels she has been betrayed by her husband, her friend Del and also by her son. She, in turn, betrays him, betrays John without realising it. The play is directed by Gregory Mosher with an awesome realism which is in stark contrast to the darkness at the top of the stairs created by designer Bob Crowley and lighting designer Rick Fisher."

rC 1.27 Wardle, Irving. Rev. of *Cryptogram*. *Independent on Sunday* 7 July 1994: 14. Rpt. in *Theatre Record* 18 June-1 July 1994: 798.

> Positive on Worters: "the stunning performance of Danny Worters, who decisively initiates every turning point in the action, and radiates authority from his opening show of defiance (while swinging on the bannisters) to his unsmiling curtain call."

rC 1.28 Wolf, Matt. "Mamet's Bleak New *Cryptogram* a Mystery Waiting to Be Decoded." *Chicago Tribune* 5 July 1994: 16.

> Positive review of the play, less so of the production: "As the title suggests, the play exists to be decoded, and those attuned to the writer's ever-darkening palette will find it a hypnotic task. Involving three characters over three short scenes, 'The Cryptogram' cloaks its painful story of abandonment and betrayal in language acknowledging its obliqueness; at times, the play seems to be deconstructing itself. [. . .] Mosher's direction of his British cast could be sharper: Too often, the actors falter with Mamet's unique rhythms, as if struggling with an alien dialect, and Duncan's typically cool presence keeps sympathy at bay. Izzard['s] likability heightens the frisson of the play's cruel twists."

Production:

pC 2 Walsh Theater, Boston on February 5, 1995. It moved intact to the Westside Theatre/Upstairs, New York and opened March 28 and played till 4 June, 1995 for 62 performances.

Director:	David Mamet
Designer:	John Lee Beatty
Lighting:	Dennis Parichy
Costumes:	Harriet Voyt
Cast:	
John:	Shelton Dane
Donny:	Felicity Huffman (Obie Award for Performance)
Del:	Ed Begley, Jr.

Overview of Boston and New York Critics:

The New York critics were more sharply divided over this play than previous critics had been. Nearly half seemed to see the production as no more than Mamet posing and Mamet-speak exercises. They found no meaning in the experience. For others, however, it was a harrowing experience of probing psychological depth. One critic remarked that we are used to stories of abuse which are physical; but not those that are psychological. Feingold went furthest in seeing the positive dimensions of this production—making the link to Mamet that no other reviewer was able to do. In Boston, Kalb was most enthusiastic in seeing the play as a revelation of Mamet's meaning behind the stylistic quirks—he saw it as one might see a stuttering child reveal the initial trauma that caused his inability to communicate. In New York, Feingold found the fulcrum of the play in Donny: "The play's emotional weight rests on Huffman, whose fierce, precise assurance on every elliptical line makes you marvel even while she's wrenching your heart out."

In marked contrast was the London production, which tended to dismiss Donny's character as central to the play—there the focus was on the child. The only critic to compare the productions, Clive Barnes, however, much preferred the London production for directing and for each character—"The big difference is in Felicity Huffman's stiffly unattractive and deliberately unappealing wife. This portrayal presumably represents the playwright's current intent, but is far less credible than the complex and richly textured portrait (of a woman who a man, particularly a son, could love) offered earlier by Lindsay Duncan." Linda Winer, however, seemed to see the tragedy as Donny's equally with John's: "Huffman, a Mamet specialist, exquisitely deteriorates from scene to scene as the worn-down woman is increasingly incapable of handling her son."

Those who were moved by the production saw this balance in tragedy between Donny and John—so it was not just the child's perspective that was given, but the perspective on the adult world. For such reviewers, the critical line was Donny's, "I don't like you but I still love you." Robert Vorlicky, however, was startled by Donny's lashing out at Del: "Yet, in a glaring choice of language, the playwright assigns to Donny, at the height of her emotional intensity, the words he usually reserves for the (now absent) straight white male. As Donny humiliates (the apparently spineless) Del by screaming at him and shaming him as a 'faggot,' a 'queer' and a 'fairy,' echoes of Richard Roma's voice fill the air, in the naming that is meant deliberately to diminish, to dominate and to marginalize the other." There was more sense in these reviewers of the strain which Donny experienced which explained her lashings out, seeing John's perpetual questions as an irritant to her, rather than his search for meaning as the main focus of the play.

Reviews:

rC 2.1 Austin, April. "Mamet Fires Off a Scorching Play." *Christian Science Monitor*
       24 Feb. 1995, sec. Arts: 13.
              Positive review: "It's easily Mamet's most haunting and emotionally
       wrenching play. [. . .] The eloquence comes not so much from the jumble of
       words or communication misfires, but in spite of them. It's truly a play in which
       subtext rules."

rC 2.2 Barnes, Clive. "A Tale of the Cryptic." *New York Post* 14 April 1995. Rpt. in
National Theatre Critics' Reviews 56.7 (1995): 212.

Negative in comparison with the London production: "This time round,
the play has been directed by Mamet himself—possibly a mistake, because the
play seemed somewhat stronger in London. The action moved at a less formal
gait, and the playing was altogether more naturalistic, which added to the story's
poignancy, and the sense of a child looking back mostly into his life and finding,
if only vaguely, that defining point of character."

rC 2.3 Canby, Vincent. "Mamet in a Bleak Living Room of Childhood." *New York
Times* 10 Feb. 1995, sec. C: 3. [Boston]

Extremely positive review: "Young John is the play's focal point. He's an
astonishing character. Not in any contemporary stage literature that I know has
childhood been as movingly invoked as it is in 'The Cryptogram.' John is
certainly not an average child, but he's not necessarily some budding genius of
a playwright. He's a particular child whose loneliness and prescience about
doom give his mind a special alertness." [. . .] 'The Cryptogram' is first rate."

rC 2.4 —."David Mamet's Attempt to Decode Family Life." *New York Times* 14 Apr.
1995: C3. Rpt. in *National Theatre Critics' Reviews* 56.7 (1995): 209-10.

Very positive review: "The play is thick with spare Mamet language, which
is delivered in such a relentless way that commonplace words take on an edge
and a ferocity that have little to do with the meanings and emotions they usually
evoke. [. . .] His direction is as cool and formal as his intricately designed
dialogue. This is spoken by [. . .] the members of his extraordinary ensemble
cast, with the sort of intense dispassion that allows us to understand the sense of
things while being aware of every syllable. It's as if Mr. Mamet were
deconstructing language to make us think more clearly."

rC 2.5 Christiansen, Richard. "No Words Wasted in Mamet's *Cryptogram*." *Chicago
Tribune* 21 Feb. 1995, sec. 1: 14.

The play was "one of Mamet's finest and most deeply moving works. [. . .]
For the first time in a very long while, a Mamet play cuts so deeply and sharply
with its emotional power. [. . .] Huffman's passionate limning of the tortured,
torturing wife and mother, Donny, emphatically demonstrates the macho Mamet
can indeed write sympathetic roles for women. Pathetically wailing in despair
and cruelly lashing out in rage, Huffman shows both the injustice and the just
cause of her plight. Ed Begley Jr.'s portrayal of the hapless family friend, Del,
a gay man caught in domestic turmoil, is a wonder of wit and compassion. He
makes each vocal and physical nuance count in creating the character of this
silly, funny, lonely man. When Donny scornfully calls him 'fairy' and 'faggot,'
the pain caused by that outburst of betrayal is almost palpable."

rC 2.6 Fanger, Iris. "Mamet's Latest Family Drama Rises to the Heights of Tragedy."
Boston Herald 9 Feb. 1995, sec. S: 46.

Positive review: "Mamet has directed the terrific ensemble [. . .] to speak the lines in a maddening cadence that comes close to operatic recitative. However, as the disclosures come—and they do, despite the many unanswered questions—the actors break down in heartstopping ways. You'd have to be a stone to remain unmoved by their individual and collective plights. [. . .] Where other dramatists are writing melodrama about the dysfunctional family, Mamet has written high tragedy."

rC 2.7 Feingold, Michael. "Codehearted." *The Village Voice* 25 Apr. 1995: 97. Rpt. in *National Theatre Critics' Reviews* 56.7 (1995): 208-09.

Positive review: "The central figure is a child, but the action is conducted in rigidly adult terms, a puzzle that a child can only decipher in retrospect. It feels like a deep-buried memory of the playwright's own, striking with a force at once more personal and more profound than his other works. Under the cold, terse phrases, the spare structure, the formalized tableaux, its vulnerability is tangible. [. . .] Beatty's Hopperish set seems to stretch up to a dark infinity: the son's last slow ascent of it [. . .] makes the audience gasp as intensely as Cherry Jones' final curtain climb in 'The Heiress.' Like other objects in the play, the knife too turns out to be a deceit, its obvious meaning false, the ones it will carry in retrospect more complex and numerous: a parting gift, a death wish, a symbol of the father's phallic betrayal, a memento that's also a manufactured lie. This is man's inheritance: Every memory is bittersweet, every object from the past as false as it is precious. [. . .] The play's emotional weight rests on Huffman, whose fierce, precise assurance on every elliptical line makes you marvel even while she's wrenching your heart out."

rC 2.8 Gerard, Jeremy. Rev. of *Cryptogram. Daily Variety* 17 Apr. 1995: 45. Rpt. in *National Theatre Critics' Reviews* 56.7 (1995): 211-12.

Positive review, particularly of the "quietly shattering finale that caps 80 of the most densely packed, emotionally searing minutes this season. [. . . John's] incantatory wail cannot penetrate Donny's own hurt. Her inability to hear, let alone comfort him, horrifies us; it makes us want to take to the stage and save both of them before they are lost to a despair beyond salvation. And when Donny allows Del to give John his father's knife—ostensibly to open the box holding his blanket—she seems to be giving him implicit permission to do something quite different. [. . .] Indeed what's overwhelming about that final scene is how Mamet's signature speech rhythms—the halting, staccato delivery the half-finished sentences, the constipated emotional outbursts—seem completely natural, pouring forth from a confused, hurt boy, the fitful patterns of a child who cannot—who will never be able to—comprehend why he has been treated so cruelly. It's as if the playwright were telling us: This is the way it has been, all along. Suddenly the obsessiveness of Mamet's style is revealed in the thwarted, truncated attempts at communication by a baffled child."

rC 2.9 Heilpern, John. "*The Cryptogram*: More Mametspeak, More Provocation." *Observer* 24 April 1995. Rpt. in *How Good Is David Mamet Anyway?* New York: Routledge, 2000. 220-224.

"*Irr. . .irr, irr, irr, irritating*" is Heilpern's description for this play. "The self-conscious surface style, the convolutions and cadences, are only a part of the problem." Heilpern, however, sees how it works: "We, in turn, are meant to project our fears for the child—and perhaps our own childhood problems—onto the play, as we might a fearful message onto a blank canvas."

rC 2.10 Kalb, Jonathan. "Crypto-Mamet." *The Village Voice* 28 Feb. 1995: 83.
Negative review: "In directing this desiccated production of 'The Cryptogram' he seems at loggerheads with actors who either cannot or have been told not to animate his mannered language, invest it with their own creativity. [. . .] One must look behind and between the sparse and fragmentary facts. The three characters talk over and through one another, for instance, continuing what they were saying two lines or two pages before, regardless of what the other person just said, so that even the basic plot is hard to follow in performance."

rC 2.11 Kissel, Howard. "Mamet's Murky *Cryptogram*: Is a Puzzlement." *New York Daily News* 14 April 1995. Rpt. in *National Theatre Critics' Reviews* 56.7 (1995): 212-13.
Negative review: "Perhaps the most charitable way of viewing David Mamet's new play 'The Cryptogram' is as a plea for help. 'Save me!' Mamet seems to be crying. 'I have become a prisoner of my own style!'"

rC 2.12 Kroll, Jack. "Phantoms in the Dark." *Newsweek* 20 Feb. 1995: 72.
Positive review: "To see little John uttering his perfectly timed Mametgrams is spooky and exciting. As the play moves towards its implicitly shocking climax, we're witnessing both a tragedy to the character and the genesis of a sensibility for the playwright. [. . .] The actors, especially young Dane, perfectly project Mamet's fiercely unsentimental triptych of a self-cannibalizing family. Staging his own play must have been both a victory and an exorcism."

rC 2.13 Lahr, John. "Talk of the Town: 'David Mamet's Child's Play." *The New Yorker* 10 Apr. 1995: 33-34.
The play "dramatizes a child's emotional abuse in a way that no other American play has ever attempted: from the child's point of view. [. . .] John's quest taps into the audience's own search. Unlike Mamet's polemical 'Oleanna,' which prompted argument, the new play bypasses reason and prompts deep, visceral feelings about the past which have a way of making the memory of the play implode in the imagination. 'People may or may not say what they mean,' Mamet says. 'But they always say something designed to get what they want.'"

rC 2.14 Lyons, Donald. "To Paris and Back in a '20s Dream." *Wall Street Journal* 14 Apr. 1995, sec. A: 7. Rpt. in *National Theatre Critics' Reviews* 56.7 (1995): 213.
Mixed review: "The master Mametian idea here is that the breakup of family can be expressed in a breakdown of language. Words here are as dysfunctional as people, with everybody repeating, interrogatively, what they've just heard. [. . .] Indeed, this stylistic tic is not only the form but the only content of his

plays. Here, it is slower than usual and is deployed in aid of exposing the hollowness of the '50s family—a project by now so overdone that true originality would lie only in celebrating the myths of the era."

rC 2.15 Minor, Kyle. "Breaking the Code of Mamet's *Cryptogram*." *Minuteman* 16 Feb. 1995, B21-22.
Positive review which notes that Boston papers have speculated about the autobiographical connections which Mamet has denied: "'The Cryptogram' is fascinating, frustrating, and enticing all at once. [...] Mamet is quite comfortable in this terrain. [...] Though not as topical or incendiary as 'Oleanna,' it raises just as many if not more questions. It will also leave you just as uneasy."

rC 2.16 Siegel, Ed. "Mamet's Puzzling, Poignant *Cryptogram*." *Boston Globe* 10 Feb. 1995: Living 47.
Rather positive review: "'The Cryptogram' often seems like a missile aimed at the new nostalgia for the fixed values of the 1950s. This is what people want to go back to? Women who pour their identity into that of wife and mother? The love that dare not speak its name? But everyone was closeted then; the moral certitude was not so certain. These lives, these times, were built on lies and no one paid for those lies more than the children. Even the heroism of World War II, Mamet seems to be saying at one point, was not what it was cracked up to be."

rC 2.17 Simon, John. "Verbal Mastication." *New York* 24 Apr. 1995: 76+. Rpt. in *National Theatre Critics' Reviews* 56.7 (1995): 209.
Negative review of the play, but not of the production: "The form is dramatic fetishism: object after object is verbally idolized. The slippers, the teapot, the blanket John wraps himself in against the cold. [...] About language, then? Yes, if you like rambling monologues that, merely because they occasionally connect, pretend to be dialogue—and don't even connect so much as encroach on one another. Mamet is the man who mistook the hat he was talking through for his muse. Felicity Huffman moved me: Here is a capable actress who clearly believes in what she is doing to the point of imagining a role where there is none."

rC 2.18 Stearns, David Patrick. "David Mamet's Family Values *Cryptogram* Analyzes Morality." *USA Today* 22 Feb. 1995: D5.
Positive review: "While the play could be seen as an indictment of the faithless male sex—or of the female sex that drives them to be so—it also questions what both sexes are passing on to children. The central image is a German paratrooper's knife that is passed between characters and symbolizes the emptiness and destructiveness of male bravado. Finally, it falls to the boy— with the ominous implications of a slasher movie."

rC 2.19 Taylor, Markland. Rev. of *The Cryptogram*. *Variety* 13 Feb. 1995: 59-60.
   A mildly positive review that questioned whether another cast could do it. Dane, as the boy, projects: "remarkable self-assurance and unfaltering ability to handle the difficult dialogue. [. . .] Huffman is an actress with the blessed ability to be perfectly still and silent while continuing to project a vivid characterization. And the way she seems to age and disintegrate from scene to scene is laudable. Begley subtly injects a prissy quality into his performance. [. . . But] He never goes too far and is not afraid to be the 'pathetic' bachelor he says he is while refusing to wallow in self-pity or be less than likable and believable."

rC 2.20 Vorlicky, Robert. "*The Cryptogram* 28 May 1995." *The David Mamet Review* 2 (1995): 3-4.
   Positive review of two realities: "In the New York production, John Lee Beatty's stark set design is as sparse as the play's elliptical, clipped language: a worn couch, a stuffed chair and ottoman, and an area rug, all positioned conspicuously beneath a looming, steep staircase that dominates the surroundings upstage center. The staircase links the two worlds of the play—the 'reality' bound living room space, and the elevated world of the unseen attic and bedrooms, upstairs spaces that, at least in this staging, are meant to exist beyond the house/theatre, beyond the sight of one's opened eyes." And Vorlicky implied a higher reality might emerge from absent Bobby's betrayals: "Each character, as time passes, must deal with the mysteries that either initiate or inform his or her sense of loss and betrayal—prompted by Bobby's offstage (in)actions—, mysteries that must be confronted if not penetrated in order for one to know how to go on [. . .] truthfully and lovingly." But Vorlicky's conclusion was instead a negative and earth-bound one: "As Donny humiliates (the apparently spineless) Del by screaming at him and shaming him as a 'faggot,' a 'queer,' and a 'fairy,' echoes of Richard Roma's voice fill the air, in the naming that is meant deliberately to diminish, to dominate and to marginalize the other. Curiously, Mamet's recognizable canonical code of maleness remains intact, here in the words of a female character. It is the one conspicuous feature— now, a type of Mametian dramaturgical 'certainty'—that somehow reduces a captivating, infinitely yielding new work that otherwise values the voices of others—their faults and all—without initially (although, sadly noted, finally) marking them as 'other.'"

rC 2.21 Weiss, Hedy. "*Cryptogram* Echoes Mamet's Childhood." *Chicago Sun Times* 13 Apr. 1995, sec. FTR: 36.
   Positive review, especially of Mamet's production which: "is maddeningly effective and impeccably performed, with not a single sign of affection— physical or emotional—demonstrated between mother and son. Huffman fiercely resists any attempt to sentimentalize her character and turns in a riveting portrayal. And Begley is extraordinary—bitter, cagily effeminate and weak. [. . .] And Mamet's

stylized language has never seemed more apt or more infused with pain than when it comes from Dane's mouth. Here is the damaged child with every nerve end exposed—an artist (or a damaged man) in the making."

rC 2.22 Winer, Linda. "An Emotional Puzzle from Mamet." *New York Newsday* 14. Apr. 1995. Rpt. in *National Theatre Critics' Reviews* 56.7 (1995): 210-11.

Positive review of a play of "pure agony": "The emotions may be as close-to-the-bone as Mamet has ever peeled in public. The voice is Mamet at his most extreme, lean and elegant, fingernails on the blackboard anxious and Chinese-water-torture mirthless. [. . .] Huffman, a Mamet specialist, exquisitely deteriorates from scene to scene as the worn-down woman is increasingly incapable of handling her son."

rC 2.23 Zoglin, Richard. "Cryptic Game." *Time* 20 Feb. 1995: 76.

Somewhat negative review: "His new work is an elliptical, fragmented 75-minute conversation among three characters who use words, words, words to disguise (and maybe salve) their spiritual isolation. [. . .] The play is an assured, carefully crafted work, but also something of a disappointment. The ricocheting dialogue verges on self-parody, and it doesn't have the realistic underpinnings (or the humor) of *American Buffalo* or *Glengarry Glen Ross*."

Scholarly Overview:
Unlike reviewers, scholars are more at ease with Mamet's departure into the underdetermined (in contrast to the overdetermined *Oleanna* which provoked so much controversy). Martin Schaub, however, rejects the reviewers' consensus that at the end of the play, John is off to commit suicide. That interpretation was more dominant in performance. Leslie Kane cites her interview with Gregory Mosher: "'dark pools of light' created by Dennis Parichy's lighting (of his production) created the Rothko-like impression that reinforced (or inspired) the response of critics and audiences alike that the hunting knife in John's hand was a tool of death." She extends his point: "an impression augmented by the dark set and frighteningly steep staircase that disap-peared into the flies in this production" (352). Kane observes that Haedicke constructs the knife as "the father's instrument of castration." Haedicke herself takes Lahr's two options for the ending: "John may use the knife on himself, finishing the job that his father has begun, or on the box in the attic, retrieving the torn blanket and redeeming the past" (16). And Kane has a "mystical, metaphysical interpretation" of John as Jacob ascending a ladder "starved for sleep, has a terrifying dream from which he awakens in a fright, fears being cast into hell, ascends a ladder connecting the secular and sacred worlds, hears a powerful insistent voice at night, is privy to revelation, and sees a fire in the form of an individuated light" (224). Schaub's view is also rather mystical: "As we watch the play through John's eyes, Mamet explains to us the words and symbols whose meaning John can only grasp intuitively. Like John, we come to understand that encrypted codes vouch for a 'truth.'"

Scholarly Articles:

sC 1 Dorff, Linda. "Reinscribing 'the Fairy': The Knife and the Mystification of Male
Mythology in *The Cryptogram.*" *Gender and Genre: Essays on David Mamet.*
Eds. Christopher C. Hudgins and Leslie Kane. New York: Palgrave, 2001. 175-91.

Using a Lacanian psychoanalytic approach, Dorff argues that Mamet's fears
of castration and loss of masculinity are dramatized in his works. In *The
Cryptogram* "by subtracting the (heterosexual) patriarch, it masquerades as a
drama of Others, focusing on a woman, a gay man, and a child. But rather than
exploring the marginalized identities as alternate subjects of drama, the characters
negotiate their relationships to each other through a system of mythical objects
that refer to the absent father, positioning him as the (present) subject of this
play" (176). However, she argues that "The emphasis upon failure and absence"
is what characterizes the father, yet they are "cloaked by Mamet in mysticism,
in order to maintain belief in the fictional equation between the penis [male]
and phallus [power]" (178). Her conclusion is that "The end of *The Cryptogram*
suggests that John's death occurs at a symbolic level, almost without his use of
the 'real' knife, but an imaginary one" (187).

sC 2 Gidmark, Jill B. "Violent Silences in Three Works of David Mamet." *Midamerica
XXV: The Yearbook of the Society for the Study of Midwestern Literature* [East
Lansing] (1998): 184-92.

"Speech is evasive or elided or aborted; no one knows how to interpret the
codes of another. [. . .] Donny and Del, who by all indications seem to be very
close friends, will never be lovers; they aren't even intimate to tell each other
the truth" (187). This is the level of discussion in this article that also deals with
Oleanna and *Passover.* She notes the costumes in the two plays, nicely decoding
the changes of Carol and Donny through the three acts. The conclusion notes
the similarity of silence and potential for death at the end of *Cryptogram* and
Passover. The article ends with Mamet's explanation of the *Three Uses of the
Knife,* for the knife is the concluding prop in each work.

sC 3 Haedicke, Janet V. "Decoding Cipher Space: David Mamet's *the Cryptogram*
and America's Dramatic Legacy." *American Drama* 9.1 (1999): 1-20.

Haedicke begins with a substantive theoretical reexamination which reverses
the usual feminist objections to realism ("foundationalist ideology of linearity,
transparency of language, and stability") finding Mamet instead "exposes the
mythologized, politically capitalized Family as a system providing a prototype
for the economic system" (2). In *The Cryptogram* the characters, "a parodic
Oedipal triangle," are 1959's Others: the housewife, the homosexual, the child.
All of them seek realism's "stability" in objects, in certainty, in a fixed past—
but none of them find it. As a result, Haedicke is able to attack the "reviewers'
consensus" and argue instead that Donny is not "stonewalling" John, but rather
"urging John to navigate the inevitability of chaos and to create his own narrative
as a decentered subject" (14). Similarly, she rejects the critics' consensus that
John is going to commit suicide at the end of the play. "If these outsiders can

break the chains of betrayal in ideology's perceptual prison and celebrate the performance of perception, they may perturb the order of masculinized hegemony with the chaos of feminized Otherness" (16).

sC 4 Kane, Leslie. "Coming Home." *Weasels and Wisemen: Ethics and Ethnicity in the Work of David Mamet.* New York: St. Martin's Press, 1999. 185-225.

Kane's interpretation of *The Cryptogram* is rather stretched to make Del a homosexual equivalent of a 1900 stereotype of male Jew as demasculinized (190), Donny as typical Jewish mother (198), and John as the resultant angst-ridden Jewish boy (193). Perhaps as a consequence, Kane takes a balanced and sympathetic view of all three characters: "Donny brings to her pursuit of the truth the same attention to detail, precision, intellect, concentration, and passion she previously brought to clarifying the photograph, locating its meaning in an amalgam of time, place, and persons, and anchoring it to memory" (209). Such an essentialist interpretation in which Donny "separates fact from fiction" (209) takes much of the cryptic out of the play. John is the final focus, in that his "confusion functions as a filter through which we perceive the madness that surrounds him," but also "led him to newly acquired wisdom" (213). "John has learned that not only does hell exist [. . .] it is the absence of truthful, caring, ethically responsible people" (213). Most fascinating are the footnotes with excerpts from interviews with Huffman, Dane, Mosher, and Mamet's notes to Begley.

sC 5 London, Todd. "Mamet vs. Mamet." *American Theatre* July/Aug. 1996: 18+.

The article contrasts Mamet's theories with his productions: "Mamet the playwright knows things that Mamet the director doesn't. [. . .] A guiding problem of his whole body of work may well be to say the *unsayable* in such a way that it gets heard" (18-19). In *The Cryptogram* "even the most quotidian objects—a photograph, a blanket, and a tea kettle—contain mysteries; severed from their significance and history, they become puzzles within puzzles of the title" (19). "The damage done to *The Cryptogram* seemed greater to me, because it's a finer, more elusive play. The confused, angry, intelligent, trapped woman of the script lost the stage to the cold, narcissistic mother and unfeeling friend" (20). London regrets Mamet's approach as a director because his minimalism implies a clarity that is counter to a play's mystery: "in his direction of *Oleanna* this rigid approach to production reinforced the play's reductivism. Other directors have worked to explore and heighten Carol's unspoken motives or even the dynamics of attraction and repulsion between teacher and student. Mamet ruthlessly refused to consider anything but words (as spoken) and verbs (as enacted)" (20).

sC 6 Pearce, Howard. "'Loving Wrong' in the Worlds of Harold Pinter's *Moonlight* and David Mamet's *Cryptogram*." *Journal of Dramatic Theory and Criticism* 15.1 (2000): 61-79.

Pearce examines a twilight state between dreaming and waking and places the experience of Bridget and John in the two plays into the center of meaning: "John is trying to make stories from the vantage point of an interim state, from the insights that arise from the play between worlds" (68). After centering the play around John, however, Pearce goes on to consider Donny and Del, and lapses back into the old thematicism—"a need for community" (74). "Expressions and acts of love, of the need for harmonious relations, are easily undermined, and good intentions often become deflected (74).

sC 7 Schaub, Martin. "Magic Meanings in Mamet's *Cryptogram.*" *Modern Drama* 42.3 (1999): 326-37.

    Schaub demonstrates a nice grasp of the postmodern predicament, as he playfully overstates the case: "Has postmodern theory not obliterated 'truth' as an intellectual curiosity long ago?" (326). He uses this to set up his argument that "In Mamet's dramatic universe 'things do mean things'—even though, and maybe also because, his characters are constantly denying it" (326). Having it both ways, Schaub notes that Mamet atypically uses the family setting, but it is a place of "almost total disassociation from home and family. He stages a harrowing theatrical celebration of the 'truth' that we postmoderns long for communion, confession, and forgiveness in an amoral and aleatoric universe, and that, not finding it, we become sad witnesses to the haunting 'reality' of these 'truths'—mostly against our will" (328). The article is notable for the negative view of Donny: "A mother unable to come to terms with her life refuses to love and be loved and passes on her pain to her child, offering innocent tears to propitiate ghosts from the past" (329). His sympathy is with John completely: "John begins to understand that in his world the meanings of things that are customarily held to carry meanings—books, buildings, the globe, history, thought—are collapsing. He faces the question of how he might live in a world (one that looks stunningly like our own!) where the meaning of things cannot be taken for granted any more" (331). "As we watch the play through John's eyes, Mamet explains to us the words and symbols whose meaning John can only grasp intuitively. Like John, we come to understand that encrypted codes vouch for a 'truth,' [. . .] recalling and remodelling memories of a childhood spent in an archetypal broken home, and reinventing the rhapsodic structure of a young mind's search for meaning" (334).

See also the following for the scholarly articles covering multiple plays:

sMP 4 Bigsby, C. W. E. "David Mamet: All True Stories."

sON 4 Kane, Leslie. "'It's the Way That You Are with Your Children': The Matriarchal Figure in Mamet's Late Work."

DUCK VARIATIONS

Scene: A park on the edge of a big city on a lake
Time: An afternoon around Easter
Characters: Emil Varec and George S. Aronovitz, two gentlemen in their sixties.
Editions:

  Sexual Perversity in Chicago, and, the Duck Variations: Two Comedies. New
  York: S. French, 1977.

  Richards, Stanley. *The Best Short Plays, 1977.* Radnor, Pa.: Chilton, 1977.

  American Buffalo; and, Sexual Perversity in Chicago; &, Duck Variations:
  Three Plays. Methuen's New Theatrescripts; No. 12, London: Eyre
  Methuen, 1978.

  Sexual Perversity in Chicago; and, the Duck Variations: Two Plays. 1st Evergreen ed. New York: Grove Weidenfeld, 1978.

  David Mamet Plays: 1. London: Methuen Drama, 1994. 1-43.

Plot Outline:
Fourteen short dialogues between two old men about the lives and habits of ducks,
about getting old, power, nature, competition, fate, and ultimately about loneliness,
friendship and the inevitability and acceptance of death.

Production:
pDV 1 *Duck Variations* was first produced at Goddard College in 1972. The Off-
  Off Broadway production was double-billed with *Sexual Perversity in*
  Chicago, and opened at St. Clement's Theatre, New York City during
  December 1975.

Director: Albert Takazauckas
    Cast:
        Emil: Paul Sparer
        George: Michael Egan

Overview:

The play was highly praised. Feingold was most enthusiastic, recognizing "the rhythms and repetitions of everyday speech." At the same time he thought that what they were talking about wasn't their real concern, which was rather "their own deaths." Gussow also liked the dry understatement and sense of humor, but thought it went on too long. Oliver saw both "a marvelous ring of truth" as well as the elaboration of "their preposterous notions."

Reviews:

rDV 1.1 Feingold, Michael. Rev. of *Duck Variations. Village Voice* 17 Nov. 1975: 122.

> Positive review: "In this early play, he weaves a chamber duet from the commonplaces of two old men sitting in a lakeside park. [. . .] Mr. Mamet's devotion to the actual rhythms and repetitions of everyday speech is sometimes as scary as the passionate internality of Gertrude Stein. [. . .] The old men find themselves facing their own distaste for the human world, their own lives, ultimately (though not visibly onstage) their own deaths."

rDV 1.2 Gussow, Mel. "Two Pungent Comedies by New Playwright." *New York Times* 1 Nov. 1975: 15.

> Rather positive review: "Even the wildest statements are dryly understated. The play goes on a bit too long—it is surprising how many things can be said about ducks—but the author never loses our attention or his sense of humor."

rDV 1.3 Oliver, Edith. "David Mamet of Illinois." *New Yorker* 10 Nov. 1975: 81.

> Positive review: "There is a marvelous ring of truth in the meandering, speculative talk of these old men—the comic, obsessive talk of men who spend most of their time alone, nurturing and indulging their preposterous notions."

Production:

pDV 2 This production transferred to Off Broadway, Cherry Lane Theatre, New York City. Double-billed with *Sexual Perversity in Chicago*, opened on June 16th, 1976, closed April 17, 1977 for 273 performances and 8 previews.

Overview:

This production's acting was well received, but not the production as a whole. The music was "jarring" consisting of quacks between scenes, breaking up the rhythm of the play. Several saw loneliness, others death; Hill, dignity and philosophical resignation; Kalem, friendship; Alan Rich, just killing time; Simon, the desire to outdo the other; but Douglas saw communication as ultimately connecting the two men.

Reviews:

rDV 2.1 Da Silva, Beatrice. "Prizewinning *Perversity*." *Villager* 24 June 1976.

Negative review of the play, not of the acting: "Mamet offers 14 'variations' to project his death image, Director Takazauckas has punctuated the 14 scenes with a moog synthesizer that wails 'quack' electronically. Only the actors [. . .] make the diseased script sufferable, and soar throughout on splendidly sensitive performances."

rDV 2.2 Eaker, Sherry. Rev. of *Sexual Perversity in Chicago and Duck Variations*. *Backstage* 10 Sept. 1976: 23.

Positive revelation that the men: "are actually reflecting upon their own lonely existences."

rDV 2.3 Frank, Leah. Rev. of *Sexual Perversity in Chicago and Duck Variations*. *WNYC Radio,* New York City. 17 June 1976.

Positive review: "The second play, *Duck Variations* is the more successful of the two because it makes an honest attempt to investigate the loneliness and fear of old age. It, too, is only a series of short scenes, but there's an underlying urgency that unifies this play."

rDV 2.4 Hill, Holly. "Play Captures Amoral Desperation of Singles." *Westchester Weekend* 9 July 1976.

Positive review: "The old men are no less lonely and displaced than the characters in *Sexual Perversity* but they have acquired dignity and a philosophical resignation to their disappointments."

rDV 2.5 Kalem, T. E. "Pinter Patter." *Time* 12 July 1976: 68.

Positive review of men who: "talk like lobotomized Talmudic scholars about the habits of ducks and other subjects of which they know virtually nothing yet speculate about with endless comic invention. What emerges is a vivid sense of their friendship, the fear of solitude, the inexorable toll of their expiring lives."

rDV 2.6 Oliver, Edith. Rev. of *Sexual Perversity in Chicago and Duck Variations*. *New Yorker* 9 Feb. 1976: 81.

While reviewing *American Buffalo*, Oliver provides a less negative view of *Duck Variations* than her November review of *Sexual Perversity*: "It's often charming and sometimes moving, and it features two fine actors. [. . .] Unfortunately, the scenes are separated by Quincy's jarring electronic music—here, also, the music stops the flow of the play without adding anything of substance."

rDV 2.7 Oppenheimer, George. Rev. of *Sexual Perversity in Chicago and Duck Variations*. *Newsday* 19 Sept. 1976.

Neutral review, but the plays: "go on too long. [. . .] with occasional non sequiturs and nonsensical comments that sound as if its author had wisely taken Ring Lardner's one-acters as his models."

rDV 2.8 Rich, Alan. Rev. of *Sexual Perversity in Chicago and Duck Variations.* *New York* 12 July 1976: 64.

Very positive review of: "a gorgeously written, wonderfully observant piece whose timing and atmosphere are close to flawless. Two Jewish bums sit on a park bench and make up things to talk about (mostly ducks), out of each one's inner desperation to hold someone's, anyone's, attention."

rDV 2.9 Simon, John. "Our Words as They Speak Us." *New Leader* 16 Aug. 1976: 21.

Positive review for a play that: "seems even less consequential on the surface, something larger looms beyond it façade of flimsiness. [. . .] Now, to acquire prestige, one must know more than the other fellow: disagree with him, correct him, outmaneuver him. Yet one also seeks approval by agreeing with, even praising the other chap's insights. The duologue becomes a curious mixture of argumentativeness and corroboration; often what is disputed is a fact plain enough to be a truism, whereas what is assented to is the most palpable fabrication."

rDV 2.10 Stasio, Marilyn. Rev. of *Sexual Perversity in Chicago and Duck Variations.* *Cue* 4 & 11 Sept. 1976: 9.

Negative view: "The same problem—slick without substance—plagues *Duck Variations*, a low-keyed sketch of two elderly gents philosophizing on a park bench. [. . .] the piece would be delightful at half the length."

rDV 2.11 Watt, Douglas. "A Serving of Sex and Ducks." *Daily News* [New York] 17 June 1976: 106.

Positive review: "Mamet's interest is the disconnected thoughts and pretended knowledge of people who manage, in spite of all odds, to communicate, with one another. Up to a point. But what's the point, as Aronowitz triumphantly inquires? Go see for yourself. You'll have a good time."

rDV 2.12 Wilson, Edwin. "A Broad Sampler from Area Stages." *Wall Street Journal* 20 July 1976.

Rather negative view because Mamet is trying: "to create a full impression from a series of fragments. [. . .] The play itself, though amusing in spots, is like any number of plays from the past in which septuagenarians on a park bench tell of their loneliness and the world's folly; breaking it up into fourteen parts has not made it more significant."

Production:
pDV 3 Regent Theatre, London, December 1977 with *Sexual Perversity in Chicago.*
>Director: Albert Takazauckas
>Cast:
>>Emil Varec: Bernard Spear
>>George S. Aronovitz: Gordon Sterne

Overview:
Chaillet liked Mamet's "fine ear;" Stothard, the "circling word formations;" Billington noted the humor of the language.

Reviews:
rDV 3.1 Billington, Michael. Rev. of *Duck Variations. Guardian* 2 Dec. 1977: 12.
>Positive review: "Gordon Stern (who looks oddly like Saul Bellow) and Bernard Spear play it sensitively, and if you find exchanges like 'No man is an island to himself—Or to anyone else,' as funny [. . .] you'll discover it's a springy, humourous appetiser for the main course."

rDV 3.2 Chaillet, Ned. Rev. of *Sexual Perversity in Chicago and Duck Variations. Times* [London] 2 Dec. 1977: 9.
>Negative reviews of both plays: "It demonstrates Mr. Mamet's fine ear for dialogue and the difficulty of saying serious things, but it demonstrates it very early on and goes no farther than that."

rDV 3.3 Stothard, Peter. Rev. of *Sexual Perversity and Duck Variations. Plays and Players* Feb. 1978: 30-31.
>Positive review which catches the verbal trick of the play: "After a time the circling word formations become uncannily catchy, uncomfortably so; you feel there ought to be something left behind that you can hum and yet all that remains is the miserable meaning of ordinary speech, the unremarkable exposure of two old men's humorously half-baked theories of natural science."

Production:
pDV 4 This Atlantic Theater Company, New York, production opened January 12th, 2000 to February 6 with *Sexual Perversity in Chicago.*
>Director: Hilary Hinckle
>Set: Alexander Dodge
>Costumes: Rick Gradone
>Lighting: Robert Perry
>Cast:
>>Emil Varec: John Tormey
>>George S. Aronovitz: Peter Maloney

Overview:
Feingold remains positive about the play as a depiction of "the looming presence
of death." For Simon, also positive, it is about broken communication since both
men are mostly wrong about life.

Reviews:
rDV 4.1 Feingold, Michael. "The History Channelers." *Village Voice* 1 Feb 2000: 65.
    Mildly positive review: "But under the seemingly nebulous, and
    sometimes outright goofy, chitchat is a sense of life coming to an end. Ducks
    die; ducks get shot; ducks get eaten (so one codger's theory runs) by blue
    herons. And people? Maybe it's better to talk about ducks."

rDV 4.2 Simon, John. "Two Early Plays Remind Us of a Time When David Mamet
    Still Mattered." *New York* 24 Jan. 2000.
    Positive review: "Most of it is about the ducks they are watching, much
    about life as they understand it, and about both they are mostly wrong. But
    it is also, in a sad way, funny. [. . .] Both plays are about the broken dialogue
    between people, the hollow inarticulateness that pseudo-savvy verbiage tries
    to plaster over. They are about us, idiot savants all, and the comic-pathetic
    ways in which we struggle to make do."

rDV 4.3 Zinman, Toby. Rev. of *Duck Variations. David Mamet Review* 7 (2000): 3.
    Positive review: "*Duck Variations* is, simply, wonderful: funny, warm,
    and philosophical. This tiny play honors the noble attempt to think—however
    confusedly—about the mysteries of the universe."

Scholarly Overview:
Bigsby sees the play as Theatre of the Absurd, but Miner sees it as a successor to
that movement. Goist sees the characters mouthing myths, but Carroll thinks they
use social roles to avoid "too much self-questioning." Kolin finds humor in a mock-
Socratic dialogue.

Scholarly Articles:
sDV 1 Bigsby, C. W. E. "*Duck Variations. The Woods.*" *David Mamet.*
    Contemporary Writers. London: Methuen, 1985. 46-62.
    Reading the play through Beckett Bigsby constructs the play as absurdist:
    "What is true of the fictions they invent is equally true of the characters. Their
    conversations amount to an elaborate series of attempts to make sense out
    of the apparent pointlessness of their lives—to place themselves inside a plot
    that guarantees them status, significance, and relief from their fear of death"
    (29).

sDV 2 Callens, Johan. "'Allemaal Mooie Woorden, de Eenden Leggen de Eieren'
    of David Mamets *Duck Variations.*" *Documenta* 5.4 (1987): 229-51.

sDV 3 Carroll. Dennis. "Learning." *David Mamet*. Modern Dramatists Series. New York: St. Martin's, 1987. 70-90.

"Each character, then, has a social role that shores him up against silence and too much self-questioning. While this restricts the depth of the friendship, it gives it a dynamic quality" (73).

sDV 4 Goist, Park Dixon. "Ducks and Sex in David Mamet's Chicago." *Midamerica: The Yearbook of the Society for the Study of Midwestern Literature* [East Lansing] 18 (1991): 143-52.

The first half of the essay recounts a number of points about Mamet's aesthetic and philosophy, then examines the two plays. "As the two old men in his previous play attempted, in their talk of ducks, to avoid the subject of death, so the young men and women in Chicago avoid dealing with human relationships by talking explicitly of sex" (149). "Mamet is dramatizing his experiences with the belief in the power of language; in this case, how a vocabulary borrowed from popular myths we share, helps shape the way we think and act. His characters reveal how 'The myths around us [are] destroying our lives'" (150).

sDV 5 Kolin, Philip C. "David Mamet's Duck Variations as a Parody of a Socratic Dialogue." *American Drama* 9.1 (1999): 21-32.

Kolin thinks: "Emil and George are profoundly funnier than critics may have thought." What makes it funny is when "[v]iewed from this historical perspective" it envisions the two old men's talk as a mock "Socratic dialogue [which] invariably concludes with a universal truth that unites past to present to future, applicable to all people in all times. But George and Emil end by comically severing their ties to history" (30). At the end of the essay he dismisses Gale's view of the play which focuses on the relationship between the characters. In contrast, Kolin ignores relationships totally in his analysis.

sDV 6 Miner, Michael D. "Grotesque Drama in the '70's." *Kansas Quarterly* 12.4 (1980): 99-109.

This article struggles to characterize the "Grotesque" as a new movement in drama, the successor to the Absurdists. "Mamet is transforming the shape of human perception to the shape of an immense intellectual duck, a grotesque enough vision feathered with humor, stoicism, pathos, and nostalgia. [. . .] Part of this grotesque effect stems from the clear association of the duck's problems and those of human beings." (104).

See also the following for the scholarly articles covering multiple plays:

sMP 9 Callens, Johan. "'You've Gotta Be Where You Are: David Mamet."

sMP 19 Geis, Deborah R. "David Mamet and the Metadramatic Tradition: Seeing 'the Trick from the Back."

sMP 21 Herman, William. "Theatrical Diversity from Chicago: David Mamet."

sMP 40 Price, Steven. "'Accursed Progenitor': Samuel Beckett, David Mamet, and the Problem of Influence."

sMP 49 Schvey, Henry I. "The Plays of David Mamet: Games of Manipulation and Power."

sMP 51 Storey, Robert. "The Making of David Mamet."

sMP 54 Zinman, Toby Silverman. "Jewish Aporia: The Rhythm of Talking in Mamet."

EDMOND

Dedication: Richard Nelson and Wally Shawn
Setting: New York City
Editions:

The Woods; Lakeboat; Edmond: Three Plays. New York: Grove Press, 1979.
Edmond: A Play. New York: Grove Press, 1983.
Edmond : A Drama. New York: S. French, 1983.
"Edmond." *The Best of Off-Broadway.* Ed. Ross Wetzsteon. New York: Mentor, 1984. 17-80.
Edmond. London: Methuen with Royal Court Writers Series, 1986.

Plot Outline:
In twenty-three short scenes set in New York City, Edmond Burke of West 79th Street goes to a Fortune Teller who tells him "You are not where you belong." He goes home to his wife, leaves her, and begins his descent into the city's underworld, going from bar to b-girl club, to peep show, to three-card monte to whorehouse. Beaten up and robbed, he goes to a hotel, a pawnshop, a subway, peep show, and coffeehouse. Here he meets Glenna who takes him back to her apartment where he kills her to get her to stop yelling for help. He goes to a mission where a woman he accosted in the subway calls a policeman. At the police station he is interrogated about the woman in subway, leaving his wife and the murder of Glenna. Visited by his wife, he has no explanation: "I think I'd just had too much coffee. (*Pause.*) I think there are just too many people in the world. I think that's why we kill each other." In his cell, Edmond reflects "I always knew that I would end up here. (*Pause*) (*To himself:*) Every fear hides a wish. I think I'm going to like it here." His large, black cellmate forces him into fellatio. When visited by the Chaplain he yells at the piety, but acknowledges "I'm sorry about everything." In the final scene he and his cellmate reflect on the meaning of life, Heaven and Hell. Then Edmond gets up, exchanges a goodnight kiss with him, and returns to his bed.

Awards:

Edmond won two *Village Voice* Off-Broadway awards [Obie Awards] in 1982-83. Howe, Kondoleon, and Mamet shared a $1000 prize for playwriting, and *Edmond* was named the best new American play. Mosher received an Obie for best direction.

Production:

pE 1 Premiered at the Goodman Theatre in Chicago on June 4, 1982.

Director:	Gregory Mosher
Setting:	Bill Bartelt
Lighting:	Kevin Rigdon
Costumes:	Marsha Kowal
Edmond:	Colin Stinton
Wife:	Linda Kimbrough
Man in a Bar, Hotel Clerk/	
Man in Back/Chaplain:	Bruce Jarchow
B-Girl/Whore:	Joyce Hazard
Fortune-Teller/a Manager/	
Woman in Subway:	Marge Kotlisky
Bartender/Bystander/Pawn	
Shop Owner/Interrogator:	Jack Wallace
Manager/Leafleteer/Customer/	
Policeman/Guard:	Rich Cluchey
Peep Show Girl/Glenna:	Laura Innes
Cardsharp/Guard:	José Santana
Shill/Pimp:	Ernest Perry, Jr.
Mission Preacher/Prisoner:	Paul Butler

Overview:

Most reviewers found the play to be a harrowing experience, "ruthless, remorseless, unremittingly ugly" (Brustein) but applauded it for that: "a play of shattering yet exhilarating ferocity" (Christiansen); "a brutish, unsparing, sleepless night of a play" (Gussow); "mesmerizing," (Morrison). Yet beneath the ugly surface, Christiansen found compassion and Syse a "sense of redemption, a curious serenity that promises catharsis." All praised Stinton's performance because of the many turns and inconsistencies he had, and all liked Mosher's stripped down staging simply rearranging tables, chairs, and bed for all the different scenes.

Reviews:

rE 1.1 Blum, David J. "David Mamet's Wealth of Words." *Wall Street Journal* 11 June 1982: 25.

A promo piece with an account of *Edmond*: "After the curtain, Mr. Mamet came onstage to answer questions from the audience of 100 or so. To each query that suggested a problem with the play, Mr. Mamet responded: How would you have done it? Could you have done it better? He left his audience silent and mystified—and perhaps angry. Few playwrights accept criticism well; David Mamet accepts it not at all. A few years ago, Mr. Mamet submitted the following to a New York magazine contest that sought 'The Best' of anything. He offered up 'The Best Review': 'I never understood the theater until this night. Please excuse everything I've ever written. When you read this I'll be dead. Signed. Clive Barnes.' "

rE 1.2 Brustein, Robert. "The Shape of the New." *New Republic* 12 July 1982: 23-24. Rpt. in *Reimagining American Theatre* New York: Hill and Wang, 1991. 49-52.

Positive review of the play despite its roughness: "As directed by Gregory Mosher, *Edmond* is a remarkably cruel play—ruthless, remorseless, unremittingly ugly. [. . . Mamet] has pushed in our faces into a world which most of us spend our waking hours trying to avoid, finding a kind of redemption in the bleakest, most severe alternatives. I don't think he will be thanked much for this, but I for one want to express gratitude—for the play, even in its current rough state, for the production, even though it lacks a scenic strategy, and for the brave performances of the entire company."

rE 1.3 Christiansen, Richard. "Mamet's *Edmond* Savage but Compassionate." Rev. of *Edmond*. *Chicago Tribune* 7 June 1982, sec. C: 14.

Positive review of the play for searching into the depths of experience: "When the drama stops briefly to allow Mamet, the philosopher, to contemplate man's destiny, it is in danger of becoming studied and pretentious in its dialogue. But when Mamet concentrates on the singular rage and futility of Edmond lashing out for some human feeling, the drama is a searing, stunning work of theatre. [. . .] 'Edmond' is a play of shattering yet exhilarating ferocity. Its savagery, which summons up the demons in all of us, is cleansing. And, for all its brutality, it is ultimately a most humane and compassionate work."

rE 1.4 Gussow, Mel. "Mamet Explores the Fall of *Edmond*." *New York Times* 17 June 1982: C17. Rpt. in *Theatre on the Edge*. New York: Applause, 1998. 207-08.

Positive view of the play's power: "It is not an easy play to like, but it will be a difficult one to forget." In Gussow's view, the parallel was with Buechner's *Woyzeck*. Edmond began with "a note of mysticism" but "Frustration turns him into a kind of urban vigilante. Before he realizes it, he is speaking and acting like a redneck racist and male chauvinist. He cannot prevent his descent into madness." In the end, "prison becomes a kind of final domicile for the annihilation of self. [. . .] A few tables, chairs and counters serve interchangeably although the locale shifts from bars to peep shows to prison. [. . .] But elaboration in writing and performance might act against the starkness of Mr. Mamet's vision."

rE 1.5 Morrison, Hobe. Rev. of *Edmond*. *Variety* 7 July 1982: 74.

This is a mixed review which objected to the different styles of the play as difficult: "The language in the play veers from realistic street talk to a very poetic or rhetorical style, sometimes in the same speech. The technique works well when the transitions are just right, but when they are not it's jarring and breaks the tight rhythm of the cascade of violent vignettes."

rE 1.6 St. Edmund, Bury. *Reader Chicago's Free Weekly* No Date: 46.

Rather negative review of an unerring production but which found the play unfocused: "less a play of ideas than a play of slogans, a plateful of bitter fortune cookies. [. . .] But too much of the presentation has an arbitrary, unfinished quality. Despite the wonderful image of Edmond being a sucker in every sense of the word from the first scene to last, he's too much of a walking mouthpiece without a character. His mistakes seem more tailored to plot demands than to a character with an IQ over 50."

rE 1.7 Syse, Glenna. "*Edmond* a Superb Odyssey of Raw Rage." *Chicago Sun-Times* 8 June 1982: Living 54.

Positive review with warning labels for kids and some adults: "It is strong stuff, black as midnight, mean as hell, raw as an open wound. But for all of its gutter talk, alley menace and unexpected sodomy, it concludes with an eery [sic] sense of redemption, a curious serenity that promises catharsis. I could be all wrong but I think that Mamet is telling us that we all have to chance the horrors of insanity to stay sane. We have to be found with our identification missing before we find out who we are."

rE 1.8 Valeo, Tom. "*Edmond*: Mamet Genius Shines Brilliantly." *The Daily Herald* 7 June 1982.

Positive review of a play: "which justifies calling David Mamet one of the most exciting playwrights alive. [. . .] Colin Stinton's performance brilliantly combines the apparent contradictions in Edmond's behavior—the emotional numbness and the frenzied energy, the smug righteousness and the profound uncertainty, the fear and the fury."

Production:

pE 2 The Goodman production moved to the Provincetown Playhouse, New York City with only one cast member change: Lionel Mark Smith took over as Shill/Pimp. It previewed October 20, opened on October 27, 1982, and closed January 2, 1983 for 77 performances. [A 71 minute videotape of this production is in the TOFT collection of the NYPL.]

Overview:

Reviewers were universal in praise of Mosher's direction of his fourth Mamet production. Particularly praised were the cinematic quick pace of the play and the use of all the actors as an ensemble (10 actors to play the 28 roles other than Edmond). Rich noted that the direction "adds another layer of artifice to the writing." Watt observed it was "without a wasted motion, and with some unforgettable pictures, scenes like bits of sculpture." Lighting and set were praised for their stark look. Barnes likened the production look to Bellows, while Kissel saw "the alienating, sometimes cryptic, haunting canvases of Balthus." Critics also were nearly unanimous in praising Colin Stinton as Edmond, Kalem noting that "Stinton is stubbornly and sensitively convincing in his search for the decontaminated self." Christiansen observed Stinton "is in amazing control of his furies. He is a shade too young for the part, but his passage from button-down businessman to wounded, raging animal is sustained without a flaw, and his final scenes, when he has come through the fire to an awesome serenity, are staggering in their hushed power." Reviewers were, however, divided over the play, depending on whether they took it literally or not. Rich denounced "authorial" clichés; Hummler noted "the hero's musings on human nature ('maybe we were the animals') were far from original." But Kissel recognized that the production undercut "moments of grandiloquence" with irony. The ending of the play was the subject of most clear critical disagreement, though the limits of reviewing preclude giving away the ending. Beaufort framed the issue "Edmond finds redemption and release in a homosexual relationship with his violator seems, at the least, simplistically contrived and incredible."

Reviews:

rE 2.1 Barnes, Clive. "New Mamet Play Is Simplicity Itself." Rev. of *Edmond. New York Post* 28 Oct. 1982: 45. Rpt. in *New York Theatre Critics' Reviews* 33.15 (1982): 162.

Positive review of a play which ends with transfiguration: "This parable about divisions and prejudice in today's society, as well as the predestination of hindsight provided by a chain of events, is told in terms as stark as a comic book." Trying to grasp the play's form, Barnes likened Edmond to "Dante without a Virgil to guide him" yet he is "not some downtrodden Everyman," and noted that Mamet cited Dreiser's *An American Tragedy* as an influence. In Barnes's view, Edmond "finally encounters death and transfiguration—and comes to terms with his fear-ridden hates." But he criticized the language: "Mamet always seems to be on the point of revealing something that eventually proves beyond him."

rE 2.2 Beaufort, John. "*Edmond* a New Play by David Mamet." *Christian Science Monitor* 8 Nov. 1982: 18. Rpt. in *New York Theatre Critics' Reviews* 33.15 (1982): 163.

Positive review which saw the ending unredemptive: "'Edmond' is a brutely surreal allegory about the hate, prejudice, violence and sexual aggression that imperils human relations and threatens the fabric of human society. [. . .] This pilgrim's progress through hell unfolds in Mr. Mamet's characteristic blend of rhythmic, often staccato exchanges and veristic colloquialism. [. . .] The writing is as controlled as the hero's behavior is wildly impulsive." But Beaufort rejected Barnes' ending: "the notion that Edmond finds redemption and release in a homosexual relationship with his violator seems, at the least, simplistically contrived and incredible."

rE 2.3 Feingold, Michael. "The Way We Are." *Village Voice* 9 Nov. 1982: 81.

Extremely positive review which saw the play in cinematic terms: "Against the bare brick walls of the theater, Mosher moves from scene to scene with a brusqueness that scorns anything so refined as a transition: one trick that suggests the French New Wave is to have the lights for each scene catch up with the dialogue a beat later, so that the audience is always being jerked forward into the new scene before they know where they are. Powerful as this tight-lipped approach is, it tends to dry out the juicy life in the script, leaving Edmond's spiritual odyssey strongly envisioned, but parchingly abstract—though this doesn't stop Colin Stinton's tough-jawed, deadpan performance from attaining considerable intensity. [. . .] What matters is that, for all its waywardness and eccentricity, its groveling in the flesh and its fumblings for the abstract, 'Edmond' states the problem of our lives and it does it with considerable power. It doesn't grasp everything it reaches for, but then, how could it, striving as it does to take on the whole world at once? [. . .] I rank it high, along with very few American works of recent years."

rE 2.4 Hummler, Richard. Rev. of *Edmond*. *Variety* 3 Nov. 1982: 80.

Negative review which saw the play as cliché: "Cleansing of the soul through degradation and depravity is a spiritual theme of ancient vintage. [. . .] The protagonist's need to pass through the crucible of self-destruction, to embrace what he fears the most, e.g. homosexuality and blacks, to achieve purification, is merely an authorial statement and not dramatized. [. . .] 'Edmond' is an ugly and unenlightening play that will not advance its author's reputation."

rE 2.5 Hurley, Joseph. "Mamet's Tour of Urban Depravity." *Other Stages* 4 Nov. 1982: 3-4.

Hurley's review was mixed, but praised the production: "Gregory Mosher's production is as chilly and as harshly effective as a meat locker; and Kevin Rigdon's lighting scheme that could be termed Balkan-police-interrogative is in perfect harmony. Mamet's scenes bleed into one another, and bleed is very much the applicable word, with one gritty tableau glued to the next in line by snatches of sound or speech from the forthcoming segment, with an ease which makes a cliché of the word 'cinematic.' Somewhere along the way, however, despite the brevity of the intermissionless evening and the staccato punchiness of most of the scenes, the beaten, groaning audience may be inclined to disconnect or switch off."

rE 2.6 Isaac, Dan. Rev. of *Edmond*. *Other Stages* 4 Nov. 1982: 2.

Isaac compared *Edmond* to David Hare's *Plenty*: "But both plays with their frigid inexplicable rage, alienate the audience in ways that somehow belong to the idiosyncracies of the playwright rather than anything Brechtian."

rE 2.7 Kalem, T. E. "I Hate New York." Rev. of *Edmond*. *Time* 8 Nov. 1982: 82. Rpt. in *New York Theatre Critics' Reviews* 33.15 (1982): 162.

"Mamet's problem in 'Edmond' is that his intuitional reach exceeds his dramatic grasp. He senses that the times are out of joint, that modern urban man is doing a slow dance on a killing ground, but he seems half in love with that gaudy, bawdy death." Like Barnes, however, Kalem saw hints of regeneration: "Edmond harbors horrified inner fears of blacks, homosexuals, and, possibly, women. Raised to consciousness, these fears are exorcised." He concluded that: "Stinton is stubbornly and sensitively convincing in his search for the decontaminated self-a journey to salvation through the precincts of Sodom and Gomorrah."

rE 2.8 Kaufman, David. Rev. of *Edmond. East Side Express* 25 Nov. 1982: 13.

Kaufman saw the production as an attempt to compensate for the play's flaws: "the production here seems to supercede the content. The pace and speed of the innumerable scenes, the simple production style with just two doors, and the use of 11 actors to play 29 roles all are evidence of the foregrounding of theatricality." The failure of the play is seen as indifference to Edmond: "While Edmond proceeds deeper into depravity, through pimps and whores and street gambling and subway encounters [. . .] Mamet refuses to take the stand. Finally, as drama, the idea is as disembodied as the main character whose soul we're to automatically perceive as dehumanized."

rE 2.9 Kerr, Walter. "Two New Plays That Focus on the Male Loner." Rev. of *Edmond. New York Times* 7 Nov. 1982, sec. Arts: 3.

Ultimately negative review of the play by Kerr which focused on the ending: "It would seem, Edmond now announces, that every fear we have hides a wish, and if we fear blacks and want to put them all in jail it is because we secretly want to be in jail with them. His cellmate, having had enough of that, promptly sodomizes him. This leads to a fadeout in which, come bedtime, the two hold hands for a bit before Edmond implants a kiss on his friend's cheek, having magically shed the racial hatreds that have cropped up so frequently but so erratically during the evening's journey. Judging by the radiance of his countenance, Edmond has also shed or satisfied whatever spur it was that first drove him onto the streets. But that's one of the things most wrong with the play. We can't define his itch to begin with. Though Colin Stinton does what is very likely a good job with the role, his curt, tight-lipped, monosyllabic thrusts-dictated by the script-refuse us intimacy, even information. 'Edmond' is an ambitious play, but an overly ambitious one."

rE 2.10 Kissel, Howard. Rev. of *Edmond. Women's Wear Daily* 28 Oct. 1982: 35. Rpt. in *New York Theatre Critics' Reviews* 33.15 (1982): 159.

Kissel recognized "Eddie Burke" as an allusion to Edmund Burke: "The extreme of liberty obtains nowhere; nor ought to obtain anywhere, because extremes, as we all know [. . .] are destructive." He saw the play as "anything but didactic. Though it often seems like a grotesque parody of a morality play." Noted "moments of humor" like "musical bit of dialog in a pawnshop" and the "arty conversation" with an actress before murder. He also observed the "lighting brilliantly accentuates the starkness and gives even moments of grandiloquence an ironic undertone" likening the images to "the alienating, sometimes cryptic, haunting canvases of Balthus."

rE 2.11 Kroll, Jack. "Hearts of Darkness." *Newsweek* 8 Nov. 1982: 82. Rpt. in *New York Theatre Critics' Reviews* 33.15 (1982): 161-62.

Mamet discovered the true story behind the news: "Edmond is the rock-bottom man, the man who's died inside, who can't be either happy or unhappy, only enraged at his own emptiness. So kill a president, kill a pop star, taint a Tylenol, saw the beaks off some pelicans. [. . .] Tell the cop you don't know why you did it, you don't know that you did it. It was a misunderstanding. It was the devil. It was the genes. It was the bad smell of your own life." [. . .] He concluded: "Edmond is neither good nor evil; he's modern man as a bundle of behavioral spasms that turn into a destructive epilepsy when the rotting social-psychological structure finally collapses."

rE 2.12 Oliver, Edith. Rev. of *Edmond. New Yorker* 8 Nov. 1982: 160.

Positive review of a "shocking and horrible" experience: "One aspect of David Mamet's talent, in play after play, has been his power to evoke a real time and place and to move convincingly from there (and then) into the private world of his imagination. 'Edmond' is as shocking and horrible as it is meant to be, and—to me at any rate—as mesmerizing. My reservations are afterthoughts: I don't understand the idea of destiny that opens and closes the evening as it applies to the circumstances of the play."

rE 2.13 Rich, Frank. "Mamet's "Edmond" at the Provincetown." *New York Times* 28 Oct. 1982: C20. Rpt. in *New York Theatre Critics' Reviews* 33.15 (1982): 161.

Reflecting on fate and the fortuneteller, Rich denounced the play for its language, which the critic took as Mamet's own sentiments: "Yet whenever Mr. Mamet wants to come to a point, he just announces it—in authorial lines like, 'The world seems to be crumbling around us' or 'You can't control what you make of your life.' [. . .] Mamet is spinning hooey and neglecting his valuable gifts. [. . .] The author's ear has gone tone-deaf, and his social observations have devolved into clichés." Rich rejected what he purported to be the play's main argument for causality: either that fate (embodied in the fortuneteller) or "the play's underlying knee-jerk sociological bromide that the dehumanized urban jungle reduces all that enter it into beasts."

rE 2.14 Shewey, Don. "David Mamet Puts a Dark Urban Drama on Stage." *New York Times* 24 Oct. 1982, sec. Arts: 2.

Interview with Mamet: "'Edmond' [is] a fairy tale, a myth about modern life. 'Because Edmond allows himself to express his hatred of blacks and homosexuals,' Mr. Mamet said, 'He thinks he's free, that he's faced the truth of himself. Only at the end of the play, after having completely destroyed his personality, does he realize how incredibly destructive and hateful an attitude that is. In fact, he winds up in a homosexual alliance with a black guy. Because of that alliance, because he resolves those basic dichotomies, I think it's a very, very hopeful play. [. . .] There are moments of real beauty in the play, and I think that rather than being about violence, it's a play about someone searching for the truth, for God, for release. [. . .] 'Edmond' presents the tragic view of a man who doesn't think faith exists. He is committing the modern New York heresy of denying the life of the soul.'"

rE 2.15 Simon, John. Rev. of *Edmond*. *New York* 8 Nov. 1982: 60.

> Not quite Simon's usual negative review: "*Edmond* is probably David Mamet's best play in quite a long time, which may not be saying all that much. [. . .] *Edmond* fails as a play because it cannot make us experience and share its thesis. But, except when its dialogue Pinterizes blatantly, it works scene by scene, thanks to harrowing spareness, eerie exoticism, and the odd patch of racily dim-witted dialogue."

rE 2.16 "Taut Drama Suffers from Murky Motives." *New World* 28 Oct. 1982: 3B.

> Positive view of the production, but the play had no depth: "But aside from pop philosophizing, there is no depth to 'Edmond'. Much of his motivation remains unrevealed. We see 'Edmond' acting and acted upon, but too much about him remains unexplored. The scenes are taut though, and the tension they generate grips your guts."

rE 2.17 Watt, Douglas. "'Edmond' Goes Round the Bend." *New York Daily News* 28 Oct. 1982: 85. Rpt. in *New York Theatre Critics' Reviews* 33.15 (1982): 160.

> Mixed review: "It has its unintentionally funny moments, and it ends, after a surprisingly static letter-writing scene, with a far-fetched apotheosis, but it is a play that blisters, disquiets, shatters, hurts." Watt concluded the play exhibited: "masterly control over a dizzying experience and it will knock you for a loop."

rE 2.18 Weales, Gerald. "American Theater Watch, 1982-1983." *Georgia Review* 37.3 (1983): 604-05.

> Positive review which focused on the ironic ending: "It is true that Edmond seems to have found a shelter, a home of sorts, in his prison cell and that his relationship with his fellow prisoner is apparently closer than that with his wife. This is not the crucifixion with which *From Morn to Midnight* ends, but I can find nothing but irony in the final scene, both in its coziness and its anchorless philosophical discussion of Hell and Heaven. Besides, the final image (in the New York production, which differs slightly from the printed version) is one of isolation. Edmond steps up on his bunk and kisses his cellmate in the bed above; he then gets down and, as he settles in his own bed, their hands, which have been touching, slowly separate. Only disconnect."

Production:

pE 3 Put on by the English Stage Company jointly with the Tyne-Wear Company, Newcastle-upon-Tyne at the Newcastle Playhouse on November 7, 1985. It was transferred to Royal Court Theatre, London on December 3, 1985.

Director:	Richard Eyre
Designer:	William Dudley
Lighting:	Mark Henderson
Sound Designer:	Dave Cross
Assistant Director:	Hettie Macdonald
Casting Director:	Serena Hill

Cast:

Edmond:	Colin Stinton
Fortune-Teller/ Peep Show Girl/ Glenna:	Miranda Richardson
Edmond's Wife:	Connie Booth
Man in Bar/Hotel Clerk/ Man in Back/Guard:	Linal Haft
B-Girl/Whore/ Woman in Subway:	Marion McLoughlin
Bartender/Shill/Pimp:	Cyril Nri
Manager/Cardsharp/Leafleteer/ Customer/Interrogator:	William Armstrong
Bystander/Pawnshop Owner/Policeman/Chaplain:	Sam Douglas
Preacher/Prisoner:	George Harris

Overview:

All reviewers of the play were positive except for Hirson who thought Eyre failed to make the play naturalistic. Recognizing the play as "filmic" (Grant), "picaresque fable" (Coveney), or "allegory" (Nathan) in 23 scenes, all reviewers praised Richard Eyre's production style, both for its speed of delivery, as well as for its performances and setting. Colin Stinton was universally praised for his "Everyman" quality—"chunky ordinariness" as Billington termed him. Miranda Richardson was also unanimously acclaimed as a "scatty" victim. Dudley's sets of iron stairways were seen as minimalism matching the language of the play. Reviewers seemed comfortable with the unusual form of the play, likening it to *Woyzek*, Wallace Shawn (Billington, Ratcliffe, Grant), Wertenberger and *Candide* (Shulman, Grant). Most saw it as a descent into hell.

Reviews:

rE 3.1 Barber, John. Rev. of *Edmond. Daily Telegraph* 5 Dec. 1985. Rpt. in *London Theatre Record* 20 Nov.-3 Dec. 1985: 1196.

    Positive review despite the philosophizing: "As usual, he is at his best as a reporter, and veers towards the maudlin when he philosophizes. [. . . But] the early glimpses of New York's lower depths [are] the most vivid and gripping part of the play—scenes which drive the hero to cry out, understandably, 'Is everyone in this town insane?' "

rE 3.2 Billington, Michael. Rev. of 'Edmond.' *Guardian* 4 Dec. 1985. Rpt. in *London Theatre Record* 20 Nov.-3 Dec. 1985: 1196.

    Extremely positive review of "chillingly good" play and production: "Richard Eyre's fleet production, played against a fine economical set by William Dudley full of iron stairways and black corrugated walls, boasts a splendid performance by Colin Stinton (who created the role at Chicago's Goodman Theatre in 1982) as Edmond: he has both the chunky ordinariness and subterranean panic of this modern Everyman eagerly embracing the selfish society."

rE 3.3 Coveney, Michael. Rev. of *Edmond. Financial Times* 4 Dec. 1985, sec. I: 13. Rpt. in *London Theatre Record* 20 Nov.-3 Dec. 1985: 1196.

Extremely positive review of production's style fitting the play: "Dudley's emblematic settings—a bar, a massage parlour, a pawnshop, a church exterior—materialising within a black box topped off with minimal steel girders and catwalks. [Stinton . . .] combines a curious emotional blankness with a persnickety sense of decency in every flagrantly indecent situation. There is here a remarkable sense of a character wanting to break free and going about doing so with rare indelicacy and inefficiency."

rE 3.4 Gardner, Lyn. Rev. of *Edmond. City Limits* 6 Dec. 1985. Rpt. in *London Theatre Record* 20 Nov.-3 Dec. 1985: 1195.

"Stunning" but mixed review: "Richard Eyre's production is a stunning theatrical experience but not a dramatic one, and this modern day pilgrim's progress set in a blasted New York landscape complete with eerie subways, brash bars and derelict wastelands is all style and no soul."

rE 3.5 Grant, Steve. Rev. of *Edmond. Time Out* 12 Dec. 1985. Rpt. in *London Theatre Record* 20 Nov.-3 Dec. 1985: 1195.

Very positive review of both play and players: "Except Edmond is a man—he must think out his actions even as they confound his thought processes. Richard Eyre's production has an acutely observed, filmic intensity which serves the economic turn of Mamet's writing well, while as Edmond Colin Stinton excellently conveys a mind on the edge of darkness."

rE 3.6 Hiley, Jim. Rev. of *Edmond. Listener* 12 Dec 1985. Rpt. in *London Theatre Record* 20 Nov.-3 Dec. 1985: 1197.

Positive review of acting and minimalism of the production: "Stinton makes Edmond's squat ordinariness compulsive. I liked, too, Miranda Richardson as Edmond's scatty victim, and—especially—George Harris as his prison companion. Richard Eyre's direction, William Dudley's sets and Mark Henderson's lighting are richly evocative without ever betraying this short, dark play's essential minimalism."

rE 3.7 Hirson, David. "Scare Tactics." *Times Literary Supplement* 13 Dec. 1985: 1428.

Hirson saw both play and production as misconceived: "So authentic-sounding is Mamet's fractured argot that it is frequently held to be documentary. Yet his brand of naturalism often warps his characters, through sheer aggression, into chilling Grotesques. *Edmond,* currently having its British premiere at the Royal Court, presents a world of grotesques form the start, and the result is confusing. [. . .] Richard Eyre's attention to the Dantesque aspects of Mamet's vision only undermines the play further. Potentially evocative scenes (such as Edmond's verbal assault on a woman on a subway platform) are robbed of any naturalistic force when entrances are staged as descents into hell."

rE 3.8 King, Francis. Rev. of *Edmond. Sunday Telegraph* 8 Dec. 1985. Rpt. in *London Theatre Record* 20 Nov.-3 Dec. 1985: 1197.

"Superb" production: "Despite the humour that intermittently flashes through it, like lightning through sulphurous darkness, it is a terrible story of self-degradation that David Mamet tells in 'Edmond'. [. . .] Colin Stinton, an actor whom I do not remember ever having seen before, makes one feel, unnervingly that one is watching Edmond ceaselessly falling, in slow motion, from the top of a skyscraper into a crowded street."

rE 3.9 Nathan, David. Rev. of *Edmond. Jewish Chronicle* 6 Dec. 1985. Rpt. in *London Theatre Record* 20 Nov.-3 Dec. 1985: 1198.

Positive review of hellish vision: "In 'Edmond' at the Royal Court the individual disappears and what emerges is an allegory on the banks of the Hudson; New York as an ante-room to hell where people scream at each other from fear and kill each other in order to fulfill expectations of murder."

rE 3.10 Ratcliffe, Michael. Rev. of *Edmond. Observer* 8 Dec. 1985: 25. Rpt. in *London Theatre Record* 20 Nov.-3 Dec. 1985: 1197-98.

Positive review of a "minor" work: "The prison ending is sentimental and abrupt, but the piece, though minor, is most sympathetically directed by Richard Eyre. [. . .] Stinton gives a performance of total truthfulness as a stocky, boxy, sensible, not overbright, violent sort of man."

rE 3.11 —. "London: Cherry on Top." *Drama* 160 (1986): 33+.

Mildly positive view: "Colin Stinton was faultless as the dull, stocky hero, but only one scene went on long enough to stretch into life of its own: Edmond's encounter with the silly, tender waitress Glenna (the marvelous Miranda Richardson). *Edmond* remains a minor exercise, a 75-minute miniature from a master hand."

rE 3.12 Shulman, Milton. Rev. of *Edmond. London Standard* 4 Dec. 1985. Rpt. in *London Theatre Record* 20 Nov.-3 Dec. 1985: 1198.

Very positive review: "Mamet reduces both speech and action to an almost Neanderthal level. It is a disturbing picture of ferocity and disintegration which leaves us uncertain about whether we have been witnessing a blunt morality play or an escapist dream. Colin Stinton, as Edmond, faces almost every horror and indignity with the bland resignation of an American Everyman. Even his occasional outbursts of passion and hate indicate an inner desire to be violated and rejected."

Production:
pE 4 Atlantic Theater Company, New York City previewed on September 17, opened October 1 and ran till October 27, 1996.

Director:	Clark Gregg
Set:	Kevin Rigdon
Lighting:	Howard Werner
Costumes:	Kaye Voyce

Cast:

B-Girl/Glenna:	Mary McCann
Edmond:	David Rasche
Wife/Peepshow girl/	
Whorehouse manager/	
Subway woman:	Maryann Urbano
Fortune teller/Whore/Shill:	Leslie Silva
Card Sharp/Pimp/	
Pawnshop Customer:	Kevin Thigpen
Shill/Policeman/Chaplain/	
Man in pawnshop:	Neil Pepe
Man in bar/Bystander/	
Prison guard/pawnshop owner :	Rod McLachlan
Manager/Interrogator/	
Hotel clerk:	Jordan Lage
Bartender/Leafleteer/	
Prisoner/Mission preacher:	Isiah Whitlock, Jr.

Overview:

Most reviews thought this production excellent—though they disagreed about the play itself. Waxman was very favorable about Rasche's performance "lending more weight to the play than the script justifies." Woodruff thought the performance excellent too, and the play of equal merit. Brantley thought this production redeemed the play from its original presentation revealing its true nature as a fable about the city itself. Mandell, however, thought the play dated; Lyons viewed it negatively as well.

Reviews:

rE 4.1 Brantley, Ben. "In Mamet's 'Edmond,' A Man on Empty." *New York Times* 2 Oct. 1996: C13.

Extremely positive review of the play as much better than in 1982. It took Mamet's view of the play as: "a fable, and hence beyond the standards of psychological realism. Mr. Gregg's production, anchored by Mr. Rasche, doesn't disguise a certain sanctimoniousness in 'Edmond.' But here the actors and the director, trusting in the dislocating rhythms of Mr. Mamet's dialogue, do indeed make a sinister, Grimm-like forest out of a New York that the playwright described as having 'lost its flywheel,' adding, 'It's spinning itself apart.'"

rE 4.2 Lyons, Donald. Rev. of 'Edmond'. *Wall Street Journal* 3 Oct. 1996: A12.

Brief notice which saw the play: "reveals only the writer's signature tics and his easy contempt for his cardboard targets."

rE 4.3 Mandell, Jonathan. "A Creep Creates His Own Hell." *Newsday* 2 Oct. 1996: B7.

Negative review of the play as dated: "'Edmond' can most charitably be thought of as a period piece, written in an era marked by both high and low, an era marked by both cocaine and crack, junk bonds and junkies. But even in this period, Mamet was capable of better."

rE 4.4 Waxman, Howard. Rev. of *Edmond*. *Variety* 7 Oct. 1996: 98.

> Very positive view of Rasche, less so of the play: "[But] there is little to indicate that this dolt's search for meaning would be of much interest to anyone were it not so fascinating to Rasche. He reacts to every bit of revelation as if he were Saul on the road to Damascus. And when Edmond finds a moment of repose, Rasche radiates his happiness like a Buddha with a winning lottery ticket. [. . .] Kevin Rigdon's big, brooding set is on par with Rasche's performance, lending more weight to the play than the script justifies."

rE 4.5 Woodruff, Greg. Rev. of *Edmond*. *David Mamet Review* 4 (1997): 1-3.

> Positive review of Mamet's company's revival based on a recurring motif: "What makes this image of Edmond looking out the window so enduring and meaningful is the result of brilliant theater. Director Clark Gregg handles Mamet's good script wonderfully. He has David Rasche look out for a considerable time at the audience out of the imagined window, skillfully 'created' by lighting designer Howard Werner. As if in a two-way mirror, Edmond considers himself while the audience looks to see what they can see of him in themselves. [. . .] Mamet's refusal to flinch at exposing our own relationship to such 'doomed' characters is what makes his writing so good and Rasche's acting so resonant."

Scholarly Overview:

Scholars have mirrored the reviewers in concerns about the ending and the initial motivation for Edmond's descent. Dean gives Edmond a pre-history: "He is too much a product of his upbringing, taking with him an excess of the constraints of a bourgeois life." McDonough views the play as an attempt by Edmond to gain power over women, only to reach the opposite fate: "In the penal institution, totally run and inhabited by men, where the male is supposedly the absolute master, femininity must be constructed out of masculinity—which is exactly what Edmond's cell mate does with Edmond" (79). Bigsby, however, takes the ending as irony: "*Edmond* is an ironic *Bildungsroman* in that its protagonist sets out on a quest for self-knowledge and experience which leaves him baffled and imprisoned" (105). Carroll, arguing that Mamet follows Joseph Campbell, sees clear stages, marked by Edmond's use of language. In the first he "constricts and distorts his talk" (101) as he represses his desires. In the second phase, "after his violence against the pimp, his words are freed, his sentences become staccato bursts of certitude" (102). "In the third phase, Edmond's inarticulacy reaches its nadir" (102). Carroll sees the final phase, not ironically, but reflecting a relationship which "is now clearly an authentic one marked by genuine rapport—and this latter condition is clearly indicated by the language" (103). None of the critics took note of the moving final scene as staged in the New York production noted by Weales and on videotape at TOFT.

Scholarly Articles:

sE 1 Bigsby, C. W. E. "The Culture of Narcissism: *Edmond*." *David Mamet*. Contemporary Writers. London: Methuen, 1985. 101-110.

> Using Lasch as a guide to the culture of the 1980s, Bigsby contextualizes *Edmond*, but he then uses the theatrical structure to support the theme: "His

failure to relate his fragmented experiences to some central meaning is equally the failure of his culture. [. . .] Mamet writes of a world in which alienation is a fundamental experience; he creates plays in which that fact is reflected in the linguistic and theatrical structure. They are, indeed, episodic for more than structural reasons. Discontinuity, disjunction, a disruption of coherence at almost all levels is fundamental" (109).

sE 2 Brucher, Richard. "Prophecy and Parody in *Edmond.*" *Gender and Genre: Essays on David Mamet.* Eds. Christopher C. Hudgins and Leslie Kane. New York: Palgrave, 2001. 61-77.

This article argues the influence of Veblen and O'Neill's *The Hairy Ape* as keys to *Edmond*—that the play is a satire, and not to be taken as psychological realism: "That is, Mamet offers a scathing indictment of late-twentieth-century American society, and perhaps even the possibility of middle-class tragedy, except that he keeps turning the play back in on itself, distancing us from Edmond as self-conscious victim, and so deflecting the tragic gesture with ironic comedy" (64). Brucher notes that Dean cites Mamet challenging a hostile female critic: "Didn't you feel any compassion for [Edmond]?" (62). But the parodic thesis doesn't really allow much room for complicated engagement/detachment from Edmond: "The philosophizing between Edmond and his cellmate, leading up to their goodnight kiss that ends the play, fails to resolve matters because Mamet intends the talk to be superficial and disconcerting" (64).

sE 3 Callens, Johan. "*Edmond* by David Mamet, Théâtre Varia, Brussels. 16 January 1995." *Journal of Dramatic Theory and Criticism* Fall 1996: 127-31.

This account is of an environmental production: "the opening two and the last four scenes, played in a transformed costume shop, an intimate room with risers facing each other across the floor, the rest of the play took place in the gutted house" (127) so that audience and players mingled in space. Other play references were changed to make them more Belgian (Edmond Burke became Eddie Dubruque). It also mixed film and live performance, "thereby answering its own questions, serving as a subtitle to *Edmond*: 'Du théâtre comme au cinéma: mission impossible?' "(129). The production was even followed by a twenty minute documentary of the making of the play, as actors explored and interviewed denizens of Brussels' red light district. Most interesting is the recognition that: "Ultimately, it was humor's subversive bent that helped to release the evening's participants, press-ganged into this 'American Rake's Progress,' this grueling ambivalent picaresque quest for freedom, sexual satisfaction, self-realization, human feeling and truth" (130).

sE 4 Carroll. Dennis. "Communion." *David Mamet.* Modern Dramatists Series. New York: St. Martin's, 1987. 91-117.

Carroll, arguing that Mamet follows Joseph Campbell, sees clear stages, marked by Edmond's use of language. In the first he "constricts and distorts his talk" (101) as he represses his desires. In the second phase, "after his violence against the pimp, his words are freed, his sentences become staccato bursts of certitude" (102). In the third phase, "Edmond's inarticulacy reaches its nadir, as he is asked why he killed Glenna and cannot complete a sentence" (102). Carroll sees the final phase, not ironically, but reflecting a relationship which "is now clearly an authentic one marked by genuine rapport—and this latter condition is clearly indicated by the language" (103).

sE 5 Combs, Robert. "Slaughtering Lambs: The Moral Universe of David Mamet and Wallace Shawn." *Journal of American Drama and Theatre* 13.1 (2001): 73-81.

Combs argues that both dramatists confuse the audience: "The result is tragicomedy the audience must sort out, which they cannot do, however, without admitting to themselves their own complicity with evil. This is a theatre of Swiftian satire with Orwellian message" (73). Foregrounding economics reconfigures the encounters with women: "Central to Edmond's psychology all along is a passive innocence of attitude he unconsciously maintains notably with women" (75). The result is class malaise: "Mamet has captured in this play not only the middle-class fear of losing its perhaps illusory privileges, but also a far greater fear, that of recognizing oneself as empty, irrelevant, eager for abnegation" (75).

sE 6 Dean, Anne. *"Edmond." David Mamet: Language as Dramatic Action*. Rutherford, New Jersey: Fairleigh Dickinson UP, 1990. 148-88.

In her analysis Dean makes Edmond a character with a pre-history: "Edmond leaves behind a loveless and joyless marriage, rejecting former friends and job ties to plunge headlong into a search for sensation and satisfaction. It is his tragedy that he can no more be a part of the chaotic and somewhat anarchic subculture toward which he flees than the mundane and routine domestic situation he leaves behind. He is too much a product of his upbringing, taking with him an excess of the constraints of a bourgeois life. Temperamentally unsuited to disorder and unscrupulousness, he cannot deal with the opportunism he finds to be rampant" (149).

sE 7 Dervin, Daniel. *"Edmond*: Is There Such a Thing as a Sick Play?" *Psychoanalytic Review* 73.1 (1986): 111-19.

For Derwin *Edmond* is a sick play ("unresolved, unhopeful and plain wrong") because it makes Everyman homosexual: "But the hero's journal from latent to overt is hardly Everyman's, though it may be a valid transition for Edmond; but nowhere is there any transition from the black's ruthless exploitation of his white prey to their mutual affection and respect at the end. The black's unmitigated contempt [. . .] is glossed over—denied, never allowed its intensity, complexity, depersonalizing effects, or necessary catharsis" (118). Mamet's blackout technique leads to "a sick play."

sE 8 Habib, Imtiaz. "Demotic Male Desire and Female Subjectivity in David Mamet: The Split Space of the Women in *Edmond*." *Gender and Genre: Essays on David Mamet*. Eds. Christopher C. Hudgins and Leslie Kane. New York: Palgrave, 2001. 77-95.

This is a difficult article because of its use of idiosyncratic reflexives: "She [Glenna] plays back to Edmond his transgressive shift from the assurance of the rightness of one's self-authoring to the oppressive projection of that self-authoring onto others, that is, the slide from male self-agency to self-aggrandizement, in three progressive critical movements, the last of which costs her her life" (85). The point of the essay isn't so complex that it requires such self-intensifiers: "Yet it is paradoxically the women who suffer most and are the most oppressed who are the most effective vehicles of Mamet's brilliant inquisition of male self-aggrandizement and of his agenda of contemporary spiritual reparation" (80). The point is that the women, most obviously the women in bar, peepshow, and the prostitute "each enact a systemic disruption that denies the play's male purveyor his enjoyment of the system" (81).

sE 9 Piette, Alain. "In the Loneliness of Cities: The Hopperian Accents of David Mamet's *Edmond*." *Studies in the Humanities* 24.1-2 (1997): 43-51.

Piette argues against the view that Mamet and Hopper are realists. Using no theory of realism, Piette's idea is that both writer and painter give the viewer: "portions of reality as if seen through a window whose frame allows us to see only a fragment of the total picture, forcing us to imagine the rest" (44). There are parallels to scenes in *Edmond*: "the peep show scene echoes a painting entitled *Girlie Show* (1941), the scene at the Allegro—a pick-up joint— has reminders of *Soir bleu* (1914), and the bar scene unmistakably suggests [. . .] *Nighthawks* (1942)" (44). Edmond and the audience search for meaning: "the rhythm of performance [. . .] prevents us from any empathy or identification with the character. This in turn produces a feeling of frustration in the spectator whose attention is constantly redirected to another vignette in the chain" (47). [. . .] "These composite fragments are not meant to be realistic: they are reconstructions of a reality that goes far beyond any immediate human experience, an experience that eludes both the character in the fragment and the viewer" (49).

sE 10 Savran, David. "New Realism: Mamet, Mann and Nelson." *Contemporary American Theatre*. Ed. Bruce King: St. Martin's P, 1991.

Savran is a gifted cultural critic, who here takes on the philosophical underpinnings of realism, then argues that the three playwrights: "renovated the very principles that Ibsen used to deconstruct the realism of his day" (67). The techniques include "populating their plays with figures unable to express their emotional turmoil or to understand how they are being manipulated, characters robbed of the ability to speak. [. . .] The subject is articulated by a discourse over which he or she has little control [. . .] either stammers out a broken and wounded speech or talks incessantly" (65). The final stage direction of *Edmond* is cited: "How has Edmond moved toward this act, both real reconciliation and its demonic parody? While carefully delineating the results of Edmond's homicide, Mamet just as studiously omits the steps to this erotic and spiritual apotheosis" (76). As a result, there is no disappearance of the author, but rather a reappearance, "now heard as a distant oracle, speaking a strange, lost tongue" (76).

sE 11 Solomon, Alisa. "Weeping for Racists, Rapists, and Nazis." *Performing Arts Journal* 7.1 (1983): 78-83.

Negative review of the play because Edmond is presented with some sympathy: "Like *Good*, *Black Angel* and *Edmond* shirk their issue through a new dramaturgical and intellectual glibness. They mold their intellectual simplicity to a dramatic form that might be called 'schmaltzified Brecht'—a form dependent on identification, despite its superficial nods to innovations of twentieth century dramaturgy. It is a style that makes nothing strange, but makes everything that ought to be regarded complexly—being a nice Nazi, becoming a murderer—familiar and complacent. [...] Indeed, *Edmond* bears out Lukacs' prediction that 'the more lonely men in drama become, the more the dialogue will become fragmented, allusive, impressionistic in form'. [...] The mechanism of empathy in 'schmaltzified Brecht' relies on the spectator's complicity in the dramatic illusion, as in naturalism, and on new dimension provided by narration, direct address, monologue within an illusionistic structure—the invitation into the protagonist's mind" (83).

See also the following scholarly articles covering multiple plays:

sMP 5 Blansfield, Karen. "Women on the Verge, Unite!"

sMP 7 Blumberg, Marcia. "Eloquent Stammering in the Fog: O'Neill's Heritage in Mamet."

sMP 8 Callens, Johan. "David Mamet."

sMP 15 Demastes, William W. "David Mamet's Dis-Integrating Drama."

sMP 30 Kim, So-im. "Sexual Myths in David Mamet."

sMP 32 Lundin, Edward. "Mamet and Mystery."

sMP 36 McDonough, Carla J. "David Mamet: The Search for Masculine Space."

sMP 47 Rouyer, Philippé. "David Mamet: Une Nouvelle Écriture Américaine."

sGGR 38 Tuttle, Jon. "'Be What You Are': Identity and Morality in *Edmond* and *Glengarry Glen Ross*."

sMP 53 Weber, Myles. "David Mamet in Theory and Practice."

GLENGARRY GLEN ROSS

Dedication: Harold Pinter

Scenes: Chinese restaurant and a real estate office

Characters: Shelly Levene, fifties; John Williamson, forties; Dave Moss, fifties; George Aaronow, fifties; Richard Roma, forties; James Lingk, forties; Baylen, forties

Editions:

Glengarry Glen Ross: A Play. New York: S. French, 1983.

Glengarry Glen Ross. New York: Grove 1984.

Glengarry Glen Ross. London: Methuen, 1984.

Best Plays of 1983-1984. Guernsey, Otis. L., Jr., Ed. New York: Dodd, Mead, 1984, 201-16

Best American Plays: 1983-1992. Barnes, Clive, Ed. Ninth Series. John Gassner Best Play Series. New York: Crown, 1993.

Glengarry Glen Ross. Dir. James Foley. New Line Cinema, 1992. [film]

David Mamet Plays: 3. London: Methuen Drama, 1996. 1-66.

Awards:

New York Drama Critics Circle Award for Best American Play, 1983

Society of West End Theatre Award for Best New Play, 1983.

Dramatists Guild Hall-Warriner Award, 1984

Pulitzer Prize for Drama, 1984

Dramatists Guild, Antoinette Perry ("Tony") Award nomination, 1984

American Theater Wing for Best Play, 1984.

Plot Outline:

The first act consists of three separate two-person scenes, all of which take place in the Chinese restaurant in Chicago across the street from the Real Estate office setting of the second act. All three scenes involve one speaking person, the other nearly silent. In the first, Shelly Levene, down on his luck salesman, tries to convince office manager John Williamson to give him some of the premium leads so that he can get back on "the board" of top salesmen. When all appeals fail, he offers a bribe, which Williamson will accept, but Levene hasn't the cash to deliver—and Williamson won't give them on credit. In the second, Dave Moss talks with George Aaronow about how the bosses exploit the workers today, everything is for a quick buck, no consideration for the customer—and then at the end comes the reversal. He wants Aaronow to break into the office that night and steal the premium leads, which they would then sell to a real estate competitor. When Aaronow declines, Moss threatens him with being an accessory before the fact because he listened. In the third two-hander, Ricky Roma seems merely to be delivering a monologue on the existential meaninglessness of life to another drinker—James Lingk. At the end, reflecting on how one must seize the moment to give meaning to life, Roma produces a brochure for Glengarry Highlands.

The second act takes place in the ransacked office in which the police are interviewing the salesmen. Levene enters on a high because he has sold eight units to a couple from the useless leads. Roma is also successful in having sold Lingk the last piece he needed to win a Cadillac. Moss and Aaronow exit sequentially from the inner office, outraged about their treatment by police. Lingk arrives to renege on his contract, and Levene quickly improvises the role of a satisfied big customer, helping Roma to keep the sale. But when Williamson emerges and tries to help, he tells Lingk the contract was sent to the bank, exposing Roma's bluff that it hadn't, and breaking off the sale. When Lingk leaves, Roma and Levene savagely rebuke Williamson, and Levene continues as Roma is called in for questioning. Williamson deflects criticism by noting that Levene's sale was bogus: those customers have no money, and just play with salesmen. When Levene rebukes Williamson for lying without knowing the game Roma was playing, the Office Manager suddenly recognizes that only the person who broke in could know that the contract wasn't sent to the bank. As Levene begs for mercy, offers bribes, etc., Williamson coldly declares he's turning Levene in to the police. Roma emerges to tell Levene they should be partners. When Levene is called in, Roma tells Williamson that the partnership is a sham, Roma should get all the profit, and reconfirms their deal to continue giving bribes for the premium leads. The play concludes with Aaronow entering to complain, "I hate this job."

Production:
pGGR 1 Cottesloe in the National Theatre, London, September 21, 1983.

Director:	Bill Bryden
Designer:	Hayden Griffin
Lighting:	Andy Phillips
Sound:	Caz Appleton
Cast:	
Levene:	Derek Newark
Williamson:	Karl Johnson
Moss:	Trevor Ray
Aaronow:	James Grant
Roma:	Jack Shepherd
Lingk:	Tony Haygarth
Baylen:	John Tams

Overview:
The immediate recognition of a hit was evident in the breathless excitement of the reviewers as they discussed the play. For example, Cushman in the *Observer* asserted this was "Only the best play in London" and lamented praising other plays in the past because of issues they raised, rather than a play which "mentions nothing" but "implies a great deal." Critics were nearly universal in praise of Jack Shepherd as Roma, in a white suit as "the most neurotic of the salesmen" (Barber); Derek Newark as Levene was praised as "a flannel-suited blusterer" (Billington). Mackenzie summed it up, "Bill Bryden's cast is the best in London." There was also praise for the realism of Hayden Griffin's set, especially the Chinese restaurant. Asquith noted that the two sets were flip sides of a coin of the world of the salesmen. Several critics saw a discrepancy between the fragmented scenes of the first act and unified plot of the second act. Coveney thought the "farcical" second act redeemed the first, and most regarded it as a "funny" play (Fenton)—though with deeper resonance—"a chillingly funny indictment of the world in which you are what you sell" (Billington).

Reviews:
rGGR 1.1 Asquith, Ros. Rev. of *Glengarry Glen Ross. City Limits* 30 Sept.-6 Oct.
   1983: 54. Rpt. in *London Theatre Record* 10-23 Sept. 1983: 822.
   Very positive on the play's depiction of the dehumanizing system: "These men are heading full tilt for coronaries. They're also microcosms of a system so distorted that it martials considerable human resources and intelligence in pursuit of the grand con. So this is a morality play. Bill Bryden's production occasionally flags, while his superb cast just now and then fail to milk the nuances of Mamet's brutish subtlety."

rGGR 1.2 Barber, John. Rev. of *Glengarry Glen Ross. Daily Telegraph* 23 Sept. 1983:
   15. Rpt. in *London Theatre Record* 10-23 Sept. 1983: 822.
   Positive review noting how language carries one to brutality: "But they are so in love with their verbal diarrhoea and the clackety-clack of their yakkety-yak, that you are carried along helpless, as on a roller-coaster—until eventually you are revolted by the brutality and ferocity beneath all the gobbledygook."

rGGR 1.3 Billington, Michael. Rev. of *Glengarry Glen Ross. Guardian* 22 Sept. 1983:
   15. Rpt. in *London Theatre Record* 10-23 Sept. 1983: 822.
   Very positive review of the play as an indictment of a world "filled with the spiralling obscenity and comic bluster of real-estate salesmen caught off-guard; yet underneath that there is fear and desperation. Mamet says that he admires his characters' pragmatic individualism, but to me the piece comes across as a chillingly funny indictment of a world in which you are what you sell."

rGGR 1.4 —. "Mamet Turns to the World of Salesmen." *New York Times* 9 Oct. 1983,
   sec. B: 6+.
   Positive review of the play's objectivity: "Mamet demonstrates rather than judges, observes rather than harangues: these salesmen are desperate, muddled human beings rather than counters in an attack on the capitalist ethic. And this

tone of moral neutrality is scrupulously preserved in the production at the National. The designer, Hayden Griffin, subtly contrasts the borrowed comfort of the Chinese restaurant, where most of the real work is done, with the tackiness of the sales office which stares out onto a white brick wall."

rGGR 1.5 Brook, Stephen. "On the Line." *New Statesman* 30 Sep. 1983: 34+. Rpt. in *London Theatre Record* 10-23 Sept. 1983: 824.

Very positive review of the play's construction and characters: "The play gives an unpleasing picture of entrepreneurial capitalism, in which the scavengers themselves are picked clean by their superiors' rapacity. Everybody's job is constantly 'on the line.'"

rGGR 1.6 Coveney, Michael. Rev. of *Glengarry Glen Ross*. *Financial Times* 22 Sept. 1983: 15. Rpt. in *London Theatre Record* 10-23 Sept. 1983: 824-25.

Positive review, especially of the second act: "Although the production sags a little in the first half, the farcical second act takes off like a rocket. The tricks of 'cold calling,' office politics (Karl Johnson is the blank and sallow bureaucrat) and competitive bidding are all demonstrated with relish."

rGGR 1.7 Cushman, Robert. "All American Boys." *Observer* 25 Sept. 1983: 33. Rpt. in *London Theatre Record* 10-23 Sept. 1983: 823.

Extremely positive review of a play "carving characters and conflicts out of language, is a play with real muscle: here, after all the pieces we have half-heartedly approved because they mentioned 'important' issues as if mentioning were the same as dealing with. 'Glengarry Glen Ross' mentions nothing, but in its depiction of a driven, conscienceless world it implies a great deal."

rGGR 1.8 Edwards, Christopher. Rev. of *Glengarry Glen Ross*. *Drama* 151 (1984): 23-24.

Positive review especially of language: "Mamet's real estate salesmen speak a language which, like army speech, is obscene by rote; it is spoken in Bryden's production exactly as it comes off the page; with the desperate velocity of sales patter where a pause would be an admission of doubt in the product. Mamet's main rhetorical device is the question—aggressive, sentimental, or dismissive—to which the character then provides his own answer, hardly ever brooking an actual response from the other person. The direct effect is comical; the cumulative effect turns the individual speaker's performance into a form of acute pleading for the staple comforts of trust and security."

rGGR 1.9 Fenton, James. "Okay, as a Favour, I'll Tell You What I'll Do." *Sunday Times* [London] 25 Sept. 1983: 39.

Very positive review of the play: "It is a very funny play. [. . .] Once you are convinced of that [authenticity], convinced that you have been offered a real insight into an absorbingly awful world, it is your curiosity that will carry you through the evening. You don't need metaphors. You don't want messages. What you want is to see this world as it works, its logic, its psychology, the sophisticated immorality it calls a philosophy of life."

rGGR 1.10 Gordon, Giles. "Transatlantic." *Spectator* 1 Oct. 1983: 27. Rpt. in *London Theatre Record* 10-23 Sept. 1983: 823.

Mildly negative review which saw realistic dialect as excessive: "Mr. Mamet, as in previous plays, reveals an exact ear for the rhythms and speech patterns of lower-middle-class America, even if he's borrowed Studs Terkel's Chicago tape-recorder for too long for his own good as an imaginative artist."

rGGR 1.11 Hayman, Ronald. "Following the Lead." *Times Literary Supplement* 30 Sept. 1983: 1042.

Very positive review of the play in performance: "In the duologues the interruptions, the cagey pauses, the exasperated expostulations could not have been played so well if each actor had not been familiar with the tricks and timing of his partner. [. . .] At the same time they manage to give convincingly American performances, which is less a matter of accent than of rhythm, delivery and modulation. They are helped by the precision and incisiveness of Mamet's writing, but in this grueling play even the more taciturn characters live on the verge of hysteria, and the most impassioned never seem uncontrolled."

rGGR 1.12 Hirschorn, Clive. Rev. of *Glengarry Glen Ross*. *Sunday Express* 1983. Rpt. in *London Theatre Record* 10-23 Sept. 1983: 824.

Positive view that the second act redeemed the first: "Happily, in Act Two (set in the office itself), Mamet's tensile, idiosyncratic and hard-hitting dialogue is harnessed to some action, and both plot and play move excitingly into top gear. Indeed, the second half of the evening is a dazzler, and under Bill Bryden's vigorous direction, the all-male cast [. . .] puts paid to the shibboleth that British actors are never convincing playing Americans."

rGGR 1.13 Lahr, John. "Winners and Losers." *New Society* 29 Sept. 1983: 476-77.

Very positive review of men deceived by the system: "In their blindness as to how the system works, the salesmen despise themselves for failing. [. . .] And they hate the guys who close big, having bought the capitalist propaganda that winners are somehow better than losers. They don't understand that capitalism insists on 'losers' for there to be 'winners.' They see prowess in this hunt for profit and hate anyone who gets in the way. [. . .] Betrayal and manipulation are the only ways to get by. The future that both the winners and losers worry about can only be one of loss."

rGGR 1.14 Mackenzie, Suzie. Rev. of *Glengarry Glen Ross*. *Time Out* 1983. Rpt. in *London Theatre Record* 10-23 Sept. 1983: 823-24.

Positive view, especially of second act: "In a series of three duologues we meet the morally grey men, operators trying to wheel or deal their way into the driving seat of a Cadillac, steering with one hand, fighting off the rest of the world with the other. But in the second half comes the sting, audience, stooge, con men are duped in turn and Mamet's hypnotic, mellifluous sale-speak turns out to be the biggest con of all: the real manipulators don't talk, they set their faces in impassive sincerity and wait to strike."

rGGR 1.15 Say, Rosemary. Rev. of *Glengarry Glen Ross. Sunday Telegraph* 25 Sept. 1983: 16. Rpt. in *London Theatre Record* 10-23 Sept. 1983: 825.

Very positive review of the production: "Bill Bryden, the director, knows his well-tried cast, his author and what he is doing in this enclosed neurotic world with its tense momentum, its staccato speech rhythms and explosive reactions."

rGGR 1.16 Shulman, Milton. Rev. of *Glengarry Glen Ross. Standard* 22 Sept. 1983: 26. Rpt. in *London Theatre Record* 10-23 Sept.1983: 824.

Positive review of the power of the language: "There is a glib, breathtaking momentum in the speech rhythms that Mamet has devised for this pathetic flotsam of the capitalist system. As they talk of the deals and leads and contracts, their conversation is charged with the resentment, anger and frustration of failures."

rGGR 1.17 Taylor, John Russell. Rev. of *Glengarry Glen Ross. Plays & Players* Dec. 1983: 27-29.

Mildly negative review of the play as mannered: "The manner of the dialogue is a sort of Pinter naturalism: that is, the minute notations of how those evading communication really speak are completely convincing, yet the overall effect is one of extreme mannerism and meticulous, almost abstract patterning."

rGGR 1.18 Wardle, Irving. "Con-Men Sold on American Dream." *Times* [London] 22 Sept. 1983: 14.

Very positive review of how the play bought sympathy to its characters: "Hitherto when stories come up of trusting American citizens buying worthless strips of desert advertised as idyllic rural sites, my sympathies have been on their side; but the effect of David Mamet's fine new piece is to reveal the con-men as well as the clients as unhappy dupes. [. . .] His play does not include or invite moralizing, but is wholly concerned with the process of the game."

Production:
pGGR 2 Opened at the Goodman Theatre Studio, Chicago on February 6 and played through March 4, 1984.

Director:	Gregory Mosher
Set:	Michael Merritt
Lighting:	Kevin Rigdon
Costumes:	Nan Cibula
Cast:	
Levene:	Robert Prosky
Williamson:	J. T. Walsh
Moss:	James Tolkan
Aaronow	Mike Nussbaum
Roma:	Joe Mantegna
Lingk:	William L. Peterson
Baylen:	Jack Wallace

Reviews:

rGGR 2.1 Christiansen, Richard. "*Glengarry* Refines Map of Explored Terrain."
Chicago Tribune 7 Feb. 1984, sec. 5:2.
　　　Very positive review of the play which was so finely honed in Chicago:
"Shelly 'The Machine' Levene is a warped, 1980s version of Willy Loman [as
in 'Death of a Salesman'], a once-hot huckster who has hit what he calls 'a bad
streak' and is trying to hang on to his job by making a deal with the cold-fish
office manager. [. . .] Throughout the play, Mamet's poetic gutter language is
brilliantly displayed, as he reveals the nature of his characters through their
convoluted repetitions, aborted sentences, and rushed phrasing. [. . .] The
brilliance of the acting often is expressed in nonverbal ways: in the hang-dog
look plastered on Mike Nussbaum's hapless Aaronow, in the sweaty nervousness
of James Tolkan's infuriated Moss, and in the sick dread that crosses the face of
William L. Petersen's bamboozled customer."

rGGR 2.2 Syse, Glenna. "'*Glengarry Glen Ross*' Rings up Another for Mamet."
Chicago Sun Times 7 Feb. 1984: 44.
　　　Positive review, especially of language. "I don't mean that Mamet merely
records. Far from it. He takes this talk and he does dramatic surgery on it, ripping
it open to express the cavity of man's soul and carefully stitching it up so that
we can look at the character and know more about him than his own mother—
and all within a matter of minutes. He can even do it with silences—which is
no mean trick. [. . .] The ending is not yet working. It needs a moment for us to
look at the bottom line."

Production:

pGGR 3 The Goodman Theater production moved to the John Golden Theatre, New
York City, previewing on March 16, opening on March 25, 1984 and closing
February 24, 1985 for 378 performances and 11 previews. Lane Smith took the
role of Lingk in this NYC production. Vincent Gardenia and later Howard Witt
took over for Robert Prosky and J. J. Johnston replaced James Tolkan as Moss
during the run. [TOFT videotape, 86 minutes, taped on November 7, 1984.]

Overview:

There was a sense among the British reviewers of the premiere that this negative view
of the salesman was perfectly right in its depiction of the American Dream. In New
York, by contrast, there were some clearly offended critics. Such critics took it as "a
slice of life" (Hughes, Siegel, Watt) and as anti-business (Wilson); Cook, however, in
Forbes, thought it an accurate view of the problems faced in sales (Jenner). Others, of
course, thought this an "objective" depiction of "beasts of prey" (Brustein) exposing
the evils of their world (Barnes, Beaufort, Gill, Helbing, Kroll, Novick). These critics
often extolled the play for its refusal to sympathize with any of the characters (Simon,
however, thought Mamet "enjoys his characters too much"). Those who most appreciated the play, however, saw the salesmen as living in a corrupt system against which
they struggle (Holmberg, Hummler, Nelson): "an ugly symbol of all that is hollow
and vicious in the way of life his characters gallantly endure" (Rich); "Their struggle

for something like existence, for triumph, within that language is the real dynamics" (Kauffmann); "Mamet sees both the desperation of wasted lives and gallant energy with which these salesmen pursue their dreams" (Christiansen); "in Shelly's tale there is a glimpse of the possibility of achievement, of professional pride" (Weales). Munk alone argued that this desire to sentimentalize, to see them as "compelled to behave the way they do" was to cover up the real emptiness of this system and its victims. Many cited *Death of a Salesman* because Dustin Hoffman's production also opened in March. Usually they contrasted the "unsentimental and sleazy" (Allen) view of Mamet versus Miller (see Kauffmann); a number also likened it to *Front Page* ("souped up Hecht and MacArthur"—Allen)

Reviews:

rGGR 3.1 Rev. of *Glengarry Glen Ross. Variety* 28 Mar. 1984: 106.
Report on critics: "Opened Sunday (25) to eighteen favorable notices ... one mixed ... one unfavorable."

rGGR 3.2 Allen, Jennifer. "David Mamet's Hard Sell." *New York* 9 Apr. 1984: 38-41.
Profile of Mamet during rehearsals: "The characters are now less dependent on that Pinterian wordplay that glitters with dazzling nastiness or glaring stupidity, but that is really just an authorial trick of verbal one-upsmanship or one-downsmanship. Consider the casuistic combat in this exchange: 'The thing we are talking about' 'We are speaking about it.' The substitution of a synonym is supposed to chop the other fellow down to kindling, yet fails by being too clever for the speaker (or talker) and too facile for the author."

rGGR 3.3 Baker, Russell. "Playing for Keeps." *New York Times* 26 May 1984, sec. 1: 23.
Baker noted the viciousness of the characters: "The competition seems to be a game, but the stakes encourage so much cheating that it turns into real life. If there is a message in Mamet's play it is: If you think life is a game, friend, this knife in your back won't hurt a bit."

rGGR 3.4 Barnes, Clive. "Mamet's *Glengarry*: A Play to See and Cherish." *New York Post* 26 Mar. 1984:, sec. 2: 15+. Rpt. in *New York Theatre Critics' Reviews* 45.4 (1984): 336-337.
Extremely positive review of play's objectivity: "The nastily amoral world of unreal real estate is described with passionless objectivity. The humor—and it is a cruelly, wonderfully funny play—is meant to be totally unconscious. These little operators, petty gangsters of the bank-balance, brochure bandits, peddlers of false dreams, are seen as paranormal American businessmen. [. . .] They are simply crooks who have forgotten that what they are doing is crooked because they are lost in the legitimate rituals of salesmanship, with all its scoops, bonuses, and disappointments."

rGGR 3.5 Beaufort, John. "A Searing Look at the Sordid World of Salesmen." *Christian Science Monitor* 10 Apr. 1984: 25. Rpt. in *New York Theatre Critics' Reviews* 45.4 (1984): 339.

Positive view of the play's lack of pity for its characters: "Certain other of Mr. Mamet's plays that I have seen have invested even their desperate characters with a touch of humanity. Not so in 'Glengarry Glen Ross.' Its protagonists are detestable and despicable. Its one victim is inarticulately pitiful."

rGGR 3.6 Bennetts, Leslie. "New Face: Joe Mantegna, the Hot Shot Salesman of Mamet's 'Glengarry.'" *New York Times* 18 May 1984: C4.

Profile of Tony winner Joe Mantegna as Roma: "My big dramatic breakthrough was understanding that from Ricky's point of view he's not doing anything wrong; he's just doing his job the best way he knows how. Now I love this guy. He's a winner. He's very sure of himself, he's glib, he's funny, he feels subservient to no one, and he's very much of an individual."

rGGR 3.7 Brustein, Robert. "Show and Tell." *New Republic* 7 May 1984: 27-29. Rpt. in *Who Needs Theatre*. New York: Atlantic Monthly P, 1987. 67-71.

Viewed the play as a masterpiece "so precise in its realism that it transcends itself and takes on reverberant ethical meanings. It is biting, pungent, harrowing, and funny, showing life stripped of all idealistic pretenses and liberal pieties— a jungle populated with beasts of prey who nevertheless possess the single redeeming quality of friendship. It is a play that returns tragic joy to the theater."

rGGR 3.8 Christiansen, Richard. "Chicago Playwright David Mamet Wins Pulitzer prize." *Chicago Tribune* 17 Apr. 1984: 1+.

Reported on the Pulitzer Prize winners and Mamet's response: "'I really feel very warm and gushy,' said the playwright who has a home in Vermont. 'It beats the hell out of ignominious failure.'"

rGGR 3.9 —. "'Glengarry' Gets Rave, Coolly Favorable N. Y. Reviews." *Chicago Tribune* 27 Mar. 1984, sec. 5: 1+.

Very positive review of the play: "The play, its ending slightly changed, its pace tightened and its actors in top form, is even better in its third presentation."

rGGR 3.10 Cook, James. "Life of a Salesman." *Forbes* 21 May 1984: 56.

Positive view of the play as an accurate depiction of sales: "It is about the collapse of a man's pride in himself, but Miller somehow puts the blame on the system. Mamet's play deals instead with the 'life of a salesman,' what we would see Willy doing if we caught him out on the road. It's concerned simply with men doing what their jobs demand of them. 'If you're going to be that salesman,' Mamet says, 'You've got to say, "Irrespective of whether I hate the job, I've got to make the close." Those are the rules of the game, and whether or not you like the job, you've got to do that.'"

rGGR 3.11 Corliss, Richard. "Pitchmen Caught in the Act." *Time* 9 Apr. 1984: 105. Rpt. in *New York Theatre Critics' Reviews* 45.4 (1984): 338.

Mixed review dazzled by language: "Out of the mouths of these middle-class lowlifes comes the odd flowery word used for screwball effect: 'inured,' 'imperceptibly,' 'supercilious.' The rest of the rhetoric is a litany of abuse, invective and those four-letter words that describe things people do every day in the privacy of their bedrooms and bathrooms. [. . .] This is street slang refined and extended into the surreal, the baroque, the abrasive and the lyrical. And as spoken in blazing ricochet rhythms by his energized septet of actors [. . .] Mamet's absurdist riffs almost make sense."

rGGR 3.12 Cunningham, Dennis. Rev. of *Glengarry Glen Ross*. WCBS-TV 2. 25 Mar. 1984. Rpt. in *New York Theatre Critics' Reviews* 45.4 (1984): 338.

Extremely positive review: "David Mamet's *Glengarry Glen Ross* is a theatrical event, altogether extraordinary, an astonishing, exhilarating experience . . . and that rarest of Broadway achievements, a major American play by a major American playwright."

rGGR 3.13 Denby, David. "Stranger in a Strange Land; a Moviegoer at the Theater." *Atlantic* Jan. 1985: 37+.

Overview of current plays versus movies: "The first act of David Mamet's new play is thrilling. I don't know when I've heard on stage words so eager to be spoken, so charged in rhythm, so juicy to play, so completely 'overheard' yet poetic. [. . .] As we listen, we realize that Mamet has discovered a new mode of American speech—a language of pure intention, which darts ahead, anticipating objections and refusals, and then collapses anyway at the first sign of resistance. [. . .] I would guess that he heard it not only in offices (for a while in his youth Mamet worked in Chicago real estate) but also in such prime records of American felony as the transcripts of Nixon's talks with Dean, Halderman and Ehrlichman. In those weird, disintegrating dialogues, a mass of crooked intentions, literally unspeakable, broke language into semi-coherent shards, with only a glint of fact shining through the vague surface of allusion and deception."

rGGR 3.14 Freedman, Samuel G. "The Cast That Put Mamet on the Board." *New York Times* 18 Apr. 1984: C21.

Postscript on the production: On the winning of the Pulitzer prize, how the cast was chosen and spontaneously bonded together. Discussed an improvisation in which J. T. Walsh made up the contest with the Cadillac, and the responses of the others in character.

rGGR 3.15 Gill, Brendan. "The Lower Depths." *New Yorker* 2 Apr. 1984: 114.

Rather positive review: "Mamet has something much more substantial on his mind; evidently he is indignant at the rat's maze through which his corrupt, anguished salesmen are forced daily to drive themselves in pursuit of rewards characteristic of our contemptible consumer society—flashy cars, Sun Belt condos, and the like. One can hardly pretend that the indictment is a novel one, but Mamet's howl of protest is both very funny and unexpectedly convincing, thanks in large part to the excellence of the cast."

rGGR 3.16 Gluck, Victor. "The Time of the Salesmen." *Wisdom's Child* 16 Apr. 1984: 7.

Positive view of the play's appeal to the society it critiqued: "I have been bemused by the fact that *Glengarry Glen Ross*, a portrait of American society at its most loathsome which is even more clearly metaphorical than its predecessor *American Buffalo*, in no way frightens or annoys the establishment. [. . .] though given the nature of the Reagan administration, it's one that rather hits you in the face."

rGGR 3.17 Gussow, Mel. "Real Estate World a Model for Mamet." *New York Times* 28 Mar. 1984: C19.

Preview of the play with profile of Mamet: "'My job,' he said, 'is to create a closed moral universe, and to leave evaluation to the audience.'"

rGGR 3.18 Harvey, Stephen. Rev. of *Glengarry Glen Ross*. *The Nation* 28 Apr. 1984: 522-23.

Positive view focusing on a key moment of silence: "Mamet's characters love to loathe, and all that bluster and bravado is their way of proving they exist. So it's pretty terrifying when, just before the end of the last act, a leaden silence clamps down on the stage. [. . .] We know that something dreadful is happening, unheard and unseen by us, within a locked private office in an upstage corner. Meanwhile the play's prime scam artist stands a center stage, oblivious but uneasy, acting out the longest preen in theatrical memory—a slow twist to the fat knot of his tie, a series of reflexive twitches at the shoulders. After the elaborate setup comes Mamet's unsettling payoff: a final burst of quiet that hurts more than catharsis and is considerably more truthful. We realize that somebody's future has been squished in that room, and that nothing fundamental has changed. Mamet has honored the audience by keeping the details discreetly out of sight and permitting it to grasp the essentials for itself."

rGGR 3.19 Helbing, Terry. "Desperate Salesmen." *New York Native* 23 Apr. 1984: 42.

Positive view of the depiction of "desperate" characters: "One powerful scene follows another as these angry violent desperate men attempt to save the fragile structure of their crumbling lives and careers. Lying, cheating, and stealing comes so naturally to them and is so much a part of their scam (and of all American business?) that when the office manager inadvertently lets the meek customer know his deal can be called off, Roma lets off a vituperative stream graphic enough to make your ears burn. (Naturally the worst name he can think to call Williamson is a fairy. When will homophobia like this stop?)"

rGGR 3.20 Holmberg, Arthur. "Playwrights Who Take a Dim View of Business." *New York Times* 2 Dec. 1984, sec. 2: 3.

Positive view of "blinded" characters in a piece on Weller, Rabe, Miller and Mamet: "What is particularly disturbing about Mr. Mamet's portrayal of business as usual is not that his characters are driven by the profit motive, but that they are blinded by it. They cannot see past today's bottom line. Their mindset is strictly short-term. Social responsibility, even as enlightened self-interest, doesn't exist for these men, who grab what they can and in the process destroy friendship and loyalty, solidarity and trust. Mr. Mamet's real concern is how the human personality adapts to cutthroat competition and how a decent man becomes a beast of prey in the Darwinian struggle for profits."

rGGR 3.21 Hughes, Catharine. "Salesmen." *America* 28 Apr. 1984: 320.
      Rather negative view of depicting the "substream": "Like Mamet's *American Buffalo*, it is a scathing and scatological portrait of a substream of American life. And, like it, it never quite manages to rise above its mundane and mendacious setting. Mamet captures its rhythms and vocabulary with striking fidelity and acuteness, but fails to endow them with more than transitory interest."

rGGR 3.22 Hummler, Richard. Rev. of *Glengarry Glen Ross*. *Variety* 28 Mar. 1984: 104.
      Positive review focusing on Roma: "Also of prize caliber is the work of Joe Mantegna as the cocksure blusterer who'll let nothing deter him from landing a sales fish. Mantegna's character best exemplifies Mamet's subtheme of language as power. In Mamet's world, those who are most adept at using language, either as a club or a shield, come out ahead of their less verbally deft opponents. [. . .] Mamet probably intends his predatory hustlers to be seen as victims of a money-and-status-mad society rather than perpetrators."

rGGR 3.23 Jenner, C. Lee. Rev. of *Glengarry Glen Ross*. *Stages* May 1984: 6-7.
      Positive review of the play's focus on sales: "Like the carnival barker and the medicine show doc before them, these fellows are not just merchants but actors in performance, improvising their spiels as they go. [. . .] The excitement of the matches, their crackling energy, the skills of the gamesters make you root for the salesman surviving by his wits. In the exhilaration of the battle you forget momentarily that the sales are as violent as rape."

rGGR 3.24 Kauffmann, Stanley. "American Past and Present." *Saturday Review* Nov./ Dec. 1984: 58-59.
      Very positive view which saw language issues beneath the critique of business: "But this is not just one more moan about the emptiness of business life, no Arthur Miller pseudo-tragedy about the pot of gilt and guilt at the end of the American rainbow. Mamet's eclectic work [. . .] deals with social and psychological transformation, with men to whom aggressive selling has become a means of defense and attack, of self-identification and of being. [. . .] Their struggle for something like existence, for triumph, within that language is the real dynamics of this pungent play."

rGGR 3.25 Kissel, Howard. Rev. of *Glengarry Glen Ross*. *Women's Wear Daily* 27 Mar. 1984: 20. Rpt. in *New York Theatre Critics' Reviews* 45.4 (1984): 335-336.
      Very positive review which focused on how the verbal contrasts with the visual: "The set, with its banal Oriental motif, creates a marvelous theatrical exercise, since no one stands and only once does someone actually slide any significant distance across the shiny red vinyl. The rest of the time the figures

remain stationary, as if in accord with some ancient esthetic. The lack of physical movement, however, does not mean that the mood is static. To begin with, intense animation comes from Mamet's brilliant dialog, the vulgar sounds one hears on any street corner shaped into a jarring, mesmerizing music. An equal amount of animation comes from the very look of the 'puppets' all of whom seem to have been painted by Jack Levine, a master of understanding the grotesque in everyday American life. [. . . Prosky] carries himself with considerable pride. The strain shows itself not in his carriage but in his face, creased from years of smiling confidently, years of presenting a mask of bluster to the world. The smile by this time is as poignant as it is comic."

rGGR 3.26 Kroll, Jack. "Mamet's Jackals in Jackets." *Newsweek* 9 Apr. 1984: 109. Rpt. in *New York Theatre Critics' Reviews* 45.4 (1984): 337-338.
    Very positive review of the "Aristophanes of the inarticulate": "Mamet's pitchmen sandbag their gullible customers and slash away in cutthroat competition with each other, trying to win the 'sales contests' their bosses use to drive them on. [. . .] Their code is pathetically macho; yet they have their own mystique, a perverse chivalry of chiselers. [. . .] His antiphonal exchanges, which dwindle to single words or even fragments of words and then explode into a crossfire of scatological buckshot, make him the Aristophanes of the inarticulate."

rGGR 3.27 Lawson, Carol. "Mamet's New Play About Real Estate to Open in March." *New York Times* 24 Feb. 1984, sec. C: 2.
    Preview and interview with Mamet: "The play was originally scheduled for the Goodman Theater, but I was having trouble with the script, so I sent it to Harold Pinter," Mr. Mamet says, "I was bollixed up. I said to him, 'What do you recommend?' He said: 'Just stage it. I've given it to Peter Hall at the National.' That was the first time I've ever asked another writer for advice."

rGGR 3.28 Levett, Karl. Rev. of *Glengarry Glen Ross*. *Drama* 153 (1984): 42-43.
    Extremely positive review centering on Levene: "Mr. Prosky is a salesman who appears to expand and deflate with the play's climatic changes. It is a performance devoid of sentimental appeal, yet it catches a touch of pathos before disappearing behind the glass door. [. . .] Here he has a fine time orchestrating his expletive arias with lyrical fervor. In these arias, Mamet, the artist, demonstrates his great affection for these salesmen; this affection would seem to conflict with his obvious indictment of such salesmen."

rGGR 3.29 Merschmeier, Michael. "Willy Loman Lebt Weiter: New York Szenen im Frühjahr." *Theater Heute* 6 (1984): 16-21.
    This is an overview of the Broadway season including photos of *Glengarry*.

rGGR 3.30 Munk, Erika. Rev. of *Glengarry Glen Ross*. *Village Voice* 17 Apr. 1984: 105.
    Negative view of the play as inadequate critique of power: "After all, the main question about such characters is: what would it be like to be in their

power? This is not a question that Mamet, his producers, or most critics ask, though given the nature of the Reagan administration it's one that rather hits you in the face. The virtue of the play is that you can draw your own conclusions. Its corollary vice is that those who should be most shaken by its portrayals conclude merely that the salesmen are, somehow, all right, and anyway are, somehow, compelled to behave the way they do."

rGGR 3.31 Nelson, Don. "Playwrights Mamet and Rabe: Abrasive Moralists." *New York Daily News* 8 July 1984: 5.

Positive view of characters trapped in a dehumanizing world: "From one point of view, they are great creative storytellers. From another, they are swindlers. But the point is they can do nothing about it. It's not only the wish to beat out the other guy on commissions; it's the knowledge that if they don't they won't survive."

rGGR 3.32 Nightingale, Benedict. "Is Mamet the Bard of Modern Immorality?" *New York Times* 1 Apr. 1984, sec. B: 1+.

View of the production as not quite up to the British premiere: "When these salesmen aren't manipulating and exploiting the customers, they're all too likely to be manipulating and exploiting each other. [. . .] It will still amuse you, alarm you, possibly touch you, and just occasionally make you feel that someone has stuck his teeth in the nape of your neck and given you a good shake. Broadway audiences don't seem to like being too drastically churned these days, and may of course find this a resistible recommendation."

rGGR 3.33 Novick, Julius. "Men's Business." *Village Voice* 3 Apr. 1984: 89.

Positive view of the play as a world in which no one was sympathetic: "But 'Glengarry Glen Ross' derives a special purity, a special power, from the fact that it is about nothing but the necessity to sell—which means, in this play, to bend other people to your will and take what you want, or need, from them. [. . .] Nobody is sympathetic in this world. [. . .] This is a deeply moral play that never moralizes."

rGGR 3.34 Rich, Frank. "A Mamet Play, *Glengarry Glen Ross*." *New York Times* 26 Mar. 1984: C17+. Rpt. in *New York Theatre Critics Reviews* 45.4 (1984): 334. Rpt. in *Hot Seat*. New York: Random House, 1998. 306-09.

Very positive view of the play and its performance: "There's particular heroism in Mike Nussbaum, whose frightened eyes convey a lifetime of blasted dreams, and in Joe Mantegna, as the company's youngest, most dapper go-getter. When Mr. Mantegna suffers a critical reversal, he bravely rises from defeat to retighten his tie, consult his appointments book and march back to the Chinese restaurant in search of new prey. Mr. Prosky, beefy and white-haired, is a discarded old-timer: in the opening scene he is reduced to begging for leads from his impassive boss. [. . .] But there's no color in the salesman's pasty, dumbstruck face—just the abject terror of a life in which all words are finally nothing because it's only money that really talks."

rGGR 3.35 —. "Theatre's Gender Gap Is a Chasm." *New York Times* 30 Apr. 1984, sec. 2: 1. Rpt. in *Hot Seat*. New York: Random House 1998. 328-32.

Gender issues in Rabe's *Hurlyburly*, Shepard's *Fool for Love*, and *Glengarry Glen Ross*.

rGGR 3.36 Richards, David. "The Lives of the Salesmen: From Miller and Mamet Lessons for the Stage." *Washington Post* 29 April 1984, sec. H: 1.

Comparison of Miller and Mamet: "The evening's duplicities are acted with stunning veracity by a superlative cast, which seems to thrive on vituperation and mistrust. Prosky, especially, goes through a remarkable transformation, his body alternately puffing up with ruddy self-congratulation and then collapsing wanly in on itself as his fortunes rise and fall. The pride is appalling, the emptiness frightening."

rGGR 3.37 Sauvage, Leo. "Corrupted Salesmen." *New Leader* 16 Apr. 1984: 20-21.

Negative view of the play as presenting stereotypical characters: *"Glengarry Glen Ross*, which was hailed at its premiere in London as the best play of the season before it was embraced by the Broadway critics, is neither a valid social drama nor an intelligent satirical comedy—if only because its characters are exaggerated stereotypes. Admittedly, such caricatures can be commercially rewarding."

rGGR 3.38 Siegel, Joel. Rev. of *Glengarry Glen Ross*. New York: WABC-TV7, 1984. Rpt. in *New York Theatre Critics' Reviews* 45.4 (1984): 339.

Positive view of the play as presenting the real world: "The language is raw; it will offend you, but so will the nerves Mamet exposes; they will offend you as well. The structure bothered me that two acts seemed too much like two separate plays. When the curtain comes down it stops rather than ends. But I did carry the conflicts out of the theatre."

rGGR 3.39 Simon, John. "Salesmen Go, Salesmen Come." *New York* 9 Apr. 1984: 72-74.

Negative view saw Mamet as sympathizing with immoral characters: "Yet here the trouble is that the author enjoys his characters too much, that he revels in their brazen, agile crookedness. This strikes me as reprehensible, immoral. It would be all right in a totally cynical work such as *Volpone*, where the victims are merely inept versions of the villains; but the dupe in *Glengarry* is a pathetic nonentity, which makes the others monsters."

rGGR 3.40 Syna, Sy. "Mamet's '*Glengarry Glen Ross*' Gripping Play of Hustlers, Suckers." *New York Tribune* 26 Mar. 1984: 5B.

Mixed review which found the plot unreal: "But Mamet pulls several switcheroos, at least one of them so unrealistic it destroys any further belief in the situation. These flaws damage his play severely, but his overall portrait of a business (which stands for a society) grown so grasping and materialistic that the only morality is scoring, is more than disturbing—it's terrifying."

rGGR 3.41 Templeton, Jane. "Broadway Revives the Myth of the Salesman." *Sales & Marketing Management* 13 Aug. 1984: 55.

Interviews with salespeople about Willy Loman and the salesmen of *Glengarry*: "Marjorie Perry, a sales representative for United Airlines, and a career salesperson says, 'I thought *Glengarry Glen Ross* was terribly powerful ... I was so depressed I just went to bed for a day. It's unfortunately the truth. We lose ourselves in the sale and we lose ourselves in the corporation. We look for approval, but the people you need to support you are never there, like Mitch and Murray. You work for them, but you don't get what you need from them.'"

rGGR 3.42 Watt, Douglas. "A 'Dearth' of Honest Salesmen." *New York Daily News* 26 Mar. 1984. Rpt. in *New York Theatre Critics' Reviews* 45.4 (1984): 337.

Negative review of the play as a "slice of life": "The play, which can't run to very much over an hour, not counting an intermission, has the effect of numbing our senses after a while because it gradually creates the impression of being an endless stream of vituperation. [. . .] To elevate it to the status of a bitter comment on the American dream would amount to cosmic foolishness. It is what it is, a slice of life that sends you out of the theater neither transported or even informed, just cheerless."

rGGR 3.43 Weales, Gerald. "Rewarding Salesmen: New from Mamet, Old from Miller." *Commonweal* 4 May 1984: 278-79.

Positive review which saw both condemnation and admiration for the characters: "Yet there is a revealing scene in Act II in which Shelly, at the insistence of the only other salesman who understands the art of the con, recounts his moves, his thoughts, his sense of triumph in closing a most unlikely sale. These men are jackals, for whom customers are fair game, but in Shelly's tale there is a glimpse of the possibility of achievement, of professional pride."

rGGR 3.44 Wilson, Edwin. "Lives of Salesmen." *Wall Street Journal* 4 Apr. 1984. Rpt. *New York Theatre Critics' Reviews* 45.4 (1984): 337.

Negative view of the play as anti-business: "For Mr. Mamet, American business is a jungle, a world of ruthless, corrupt, conniving petty thieves who will do anything to make a sale: lie, cheat, steal. In fact, this is about all they do. [. . .] At its best, 'Glengarry' is a corrosive, if extremely foul-mouthed, indictment of corruption. Despite its virtues, the play is severely limited."

Production:

pGGR 4 *Glengarry Glen Ross* opened at the Mermaid Theatre in London on February 24, 1986. This is a revival of the 1983 London production with the sound producer changed and one change of cast, Kevin McNally replacing Jack Shepherd as Roma. See pGGR 1 for complete cast.

Overview:

Interestingly several reviewers note the pace going so fast at the start that they couldn't keep up; the first reviewers seemed to recognize this as the playwright's technique.

Barber said, "The thing goes by at such a hurtling pace under Bill Bryden's direction, you can't tell at first what is going on." And de Jongh thought "the play's momentum is here lost in the sheer gabble of minor crooks" until the entrance of Roma. There was again universal praise for Newark as Levene and McNally "as the whizz-kid spieler with the almost manic drive. While his predecessor has faintly mad air at the best of times, Mr. McNally excels as the normal guy turned fanatic, obsessed with coming first" (Hoyle).

Reviews:

rGGR 4.1 Barber, John. Rev. of *Glengarry Glen Ross*. *Daily Telegraph* 26 Feb. 1986. Rpt. in *London Theatre Record* 12-25 Feb. 1986: 178-179.

> Very positive view despite the fast pace: "The thing goes by at such a hurtling pace under Bill Bryden's direction, you can't tell at first what is going on. [. . .] This is not a nice play, and the language is foul. A small masterpiece, all the same."

rGGR 4.2 de Jongh, Nicholas. Rev. of *Glengarry Glen Ross*. *Guardian* 22 Feb. 1986. Rpt. in *London Theatre Record* 12-25 Feb. 1986: 177.

> Positive review despite the speedy opening: "But the play's momentum is here lost in the sheer gabble of minor crooks until Kevin McNally, as the smoothest of these sharp-suited fellows, hooks his client—Tony Haygarth, bejeaned, mind-fuddled and giggling. And from then the play acquires a force and fury that hit has hitherto lacked."

rGGR 4.3 Gardner, Lyn. Rev. of *Glengarry Glen Ross*. *City Limits* 14 Mar. 1986. Rpt. in *London Theatre Record* 12-25 Feb. 1986: 177.

> Positive review of language: "Mamet goes straight for the jugular employing a litany of hustler's patois and obscenity to create a suffocating sense of desperate caged aggression. Very tense, very frightening and very butch. Bill Bryden and the boys do it proud."

rGGR 4.4 Hiley, Jim. Rev. of *Glengarry Glen Ross*. *Listener* 6 Mar. 1986. Rpt. in *London Theatre Record* 12-25 Feb. 1986: 178.

> Mildly positive review: "Mamet's people are small-minded and foul-mouthed, but their talk indicates an achingly vast sense of aspiration. In the tension between the two lies tragedy, and a startling critique of American life. [. . .] Much of the play is very funny."

rGGR 4.5 Hoyle, Martin. Rev. of *Glengarry Glen Ross*. *Financial Times* 25 Feb. 1986. Rpt. in *London Theatre Record* 12-25 Feb. 1986: 179.

> Positive review which focused on the changes in this production: "Kevin McNally replaces Jack Shepherd as the whizz-kid spieler with the almost manic drive. While his predecessor has faintly mad air at the best of times, Mr. McNally excels as the normal guy turned fanatic, obsessed with coming first. His outburst of fury when a profitable deal is sabotaged by the office manager raises the dramatic temperature appreciably, helped by powerful writing."

rGGR 4.6 Hurren, Kenneth. Rev. of *Glengarry Glen Ross. Mail on Sunday* 22 Feb.
1986. Rpt. in *London Theatre Record* 12-25 Feb. 1986: 178.
Negative review: "But the foul mouthed dialogue is about as authentic as a
three-dollar bill, and as an indictment of American capitalism it is superficial
tosh."

rGGR 4.7 Jacobs, Gerald. Rev. of *Glengarry Glen Ross. Jewish Chronicle* 28 Feb.
1986. Rpt. in *London Theatre Record* 12-25 Feb. 1986: 177.
Positive review of McNally: "Kevin McNally has replaced Jack Shepherd
in the role of super salesman Richard Roma bringing a sharp, acid focus to
compensate for the loss of rounded humanity that Shepherd always suggests."

rGGR 4.8 King, Francis. Rev. of *Glengarry Glen Ross. Sunday Telegraph* 3 Feb. 1986.
Rpt. in *London Theatre Record* 12-25 Feb. 1986: 177.
Very positive review: "Under Bill Bryden's relentless direction, there is a
whole Himalayan range of outstanding performance, with Derek Newark's
aging, embattled salesman as its Everest. If only there were some modern English
dramatist capable of writing with the same terseness, clarity, punch, and mastery
of the vernacular."

rGGR 4.9 Morley, Sheridan. Rev. of *Glengarry Glen Ross. Punch* 22 Feb. 1986. Rpt.
in *London Theatre Record* 12-25 Feb. 1986: 178.
Extremely positive review: "Mamet's is about what happens in that
[American] nightmare: men get bought and sold and divided as easily as the
worthless plots of Florida marsh they deal in, and even after three years there is
an energy and a manic fervour about this staging that you will find nowhere
else in London."

rGGR 4.10 Shulman, Milton. Rev. of *Glengarry Glen Ross. London Standard* 25 Feb
1986. Rpt. in *London Theatre Record* 12-25 Feb. 1986: 178.
Positive review: "[Mamet, Odets, Miller] reversed the gratitude of their
parents for being permitted to live in the land of opportunity and converted it
into resentment against a society in perpetual pursuit of the elusive buck. [. . .]
Derek Newark, as a salesman who realises he has lost his touch, is impressive
as a pathetic bag of bombast. Karl Johnson is frighteningly reptilian as the office
manager ready to exploit any of his colleagues for a crooked dollar."

rGGR 4.11 Tinker, Jack. Rev. of *Glengarry Glen Ross. Daily Mail* 25 Feb. 1986. Rpt. in
London Theatre Record 12-25 Feb. 1986: 179.
Positive review of the production: "Bill Bryden's piston-driven production, [. . .]
transfers with Kevin McNally now playing the role of the young over-achiever who
will turn a quiet drink in a bar into a high-pressure sales pitch—and very effective he
is, too. However, it is Derek Newmark's bull-necked loser who reveals the real price
of such unsavoury ethics. Behind his bucolic roaring is the panic of a truly
desperate man and when, finally, this over-inflated windbag is punctured the
play's secret heart is revealed. This is indeed the death of a salesman 1980s style."

Production:

pGGR 5 This production was staged at the Donmar Warehouse in London and
previewed from June 16 opening June 22 and running till August 27, 1994.

Director:	Sam Mendes
Decor:	Johan Engels
Lighting:	David Hersey
Sound:	Fergus O'Hare
Cast:	

Levene:	James Bolam
Williamson:	William Armstrong
Roma:	Ron Cook
Moss:	Anthony O'Donnell
Aaronow:	John Benfield
Lingk:	Keith Bartlett
Baylen:	Carl Proctor

Overview:

Critics were not unanimous about Mendes's revival. Billington thought the movie
better, because the British actors missed the "vibrant, expressive, body-language" of
American actors; they acted "from the neck up." Nightingale thought the original
production had an "odd and disturbing ambivalence" about the characters whereas
Mendes's "are plainly victims who can only survive by victimising others." Taylor,
however, took no note of the National production, instead comparing this to the movie
which he thought failed in every point. For example, "Presenting the man in all his
seedy, unlovable desperation, Bolam's Levene doesn't make false bids for sympathy.
Again unlike Lemmon, Bolam keeps you guessing about his responsibility for the
robbery until the last possible moment. Impressively uningratiating, like the production" (794). In fact, Bolam and Cook had primarily positive reviews.

The new approach to the set that aroused considerable comment. The set revolved
in the first act so that each pair of characters rotated into view. Taylor thought the
device "quasi-cinematic." Its effect "creepily reinforces the sense that they are being
observed like specimens." It reinforced the sense that Mendes had his own take on the
play, and didn't view the salesmen with the sympathy of the premiere production.

Reviews:

rGGR 5.1 Billington, Michael. Rev. of *Glengarry Glen Ross. Guardian* 24 June 1994,
sec. 2: 13. Rpt. in *Theatre Record* 18 June -1 July 1994: 792.

Positive vision of how the play had improved over time: "But, seeing the
play after a gap of 11 years, another point hits home: Mamet's insistence on the
decay of language. It's most obviously there in the way the competing salesmen
swap four-letter words and profanities to disguise their inner fear. But Mamet
implies that all American life is plagued by the gap between words and action.
One guy, being persuaded by a colleague to commit an office robbery, asks,
'Are you actually talking about this or are we just...' before his voice trails
expressively off. And after an apologetic client announces that his wife has
instructed him to cancel the deal, Roma replies 'That's just something she said.

We don't have to do that.' It is this devaluation of words to provisional bargaining chips that Mamet nails to perfection. But although this is also a play about the cruelty of capitalism, nothing seems urgently at stake in Mendes' revival."

rGGR 5.2 Coveney, Michael. Rev. of *Glengarry Glen Ross*. Observer 26 June 1994. Rpt. in *Theatre Record* 18 June -1 July 1994: 793.

Positive comparative review: "After the disappointing film version, Sam Mendes's cool revival is a real treat, setting the rhythmical, antiphonal dialogue in a sort of highlighting relief, for which relief much thanks. The restaurant, designed by Johan Engles, is a minimalised glass and brick façade. A single booth revolves, menacingly."

rGGR 5.3 de Jongh, Nicholas. "Powerful Tragedy in a Combat Zone Nightmare." *Evening Standard* 23 June 1994. Rpt. in *Theatre Record* 18 June -1 July 1994: 794.

Positive review of play and production: "Mamet's critique of this combat zone is so powerful because it avoids Arthur Miller's breast-beating melodramatics. And Mendes's hurtling production, with edgy impressions of threatening macho males in rivalry, is an authentic triumph. These men are as strutting, truculent and aggressive as the worst sort of Wimbledon finals."

rGGR 5.4 Doughty, Louise. Rev. of *Glengarry Glen Ross. Mail on Sunday* 26 June 1994. Rpt. in *Theatre Record* 18 June -1 July 1994: 792.

Positive review of a play without a moral center: "There is no moral centre to speak of in David Mamet's 'Glengarry Glen Ross' at the Donmar Warehouse in London. In his world of macho bonding, the greatest evil is to betray your buddy and the greatest good to screw the rest of the world on his behalf. It is an ethical vacuum which Mamet has filled with all the wretchedness of the competitive working atmosphere."

rGGR 5.5 Edwardes, Jane. Rev. of *Glengarry Glen Ross*. Time Out 29 June 1994. Rpt. in *Theatre Record* 18 June -1 July 1994: 791.

Positive view: "For his revival, director Sam Mendes has gone for psychological realism rather than explosive profanity. [. . .] Ron Cook as top dog Roma can spin a dream to make you sign your last buck away. [. . .] The disappointment is James Bolam; not only does his accent wander but he looks so seedy it's hard to believe that he was ever a success. Mendes captures the sweaty fear and despair but not the American energy of the bluster and expletives that make this a comedy."

rGGR 5.6 Gross, John. "Tragedies of Good and Bad Manners." *Sunday Telegraph* 26 June 1994. Rpt. in *Theatre Record* 18 June -1 July 1994: 788.

Positive view of plot and language: "Still, the plot is only a means to an end—the end being the depiction of life among a pack of manipulative, contending, interlocking personalities. And the play lives above all through its language; the brilliantly handled elisions, the perfectly timed verbal feints and body blows."

rGGR 5.7 Hagerty, Bill. "Slice of Life at a Bargain Price." *Today* 23 June 1994. Rpt. in *Theatre Record* 18 June -1 July 1994: 794.

Very positive view of the production: "[. . .] the stage revolves slowly, like a watchspring being coiled. You could cut the atmosphere with a knife if the blade wasn't busy plunging into someone else's back. A set change then presents the smoky, paper-strewn burgled office in which are played out the final desperate hours of Mr. Mamet's indictment of the twisted values we have been taught by tawdry example."

rGGR 5.8 Hirschhorn, Clive. Rev. of *Glengarry Glen Ross*. *Sunday Express* 26 June 1994. Rpt. in *Theatre Record* 18 June -1 July 1994: 791.

Extremely positive view: "Glengarry's opening three scenes, set in a Chinese restaurant, are particularly baffling—rather like looking at a vast painting with your eye only three inches away from the canvas. [. . .] its blazing theatricality and the force and originality of the dialogue are wonderfully explored by a fine cast. [. . .] Unmissable."

rGGR 5.9 Hoyle, Martin. "The American Dream Distorted." *Financial Times* 24 June 1994. Rpt. in *Theatre Record* 18 June -1 July 1994: 792.

Positive view of the critique of "a sad, half remembered distortion of a great American ideal: a dream, if not the dream, of independence and toughness, individual self-fulfillment in a territory bristling with dangers.[. . .] James Bolam, more Irish than American, as the salesman going over the hill to find a precipice on the other side, changes brilliantly from cock-a-hoop champ to aghast failure, his face sagging blankly in defeat. John Benfield's thicky is a little too dumb to have survived so long in this jungle; but Ron Cook's smooth-talking conner, spivvy and plausible, is a convincing golden boy of the soft sell. Only his lack of stature detracts from his fits of rage."

rGGR 5.10 Morley, Sheridan. "Theatre: Copacabana, Home, *Glengarry Glen Ross*." *Spectator* 2 July 1994: 42+. Rpt. in *Theatre Record* 18 June -1 July 1994: 792.

Positive review: "Mamet has seen a black farce about wheeler-dealers whose wheels have come off, and it has been given a suitably hothouse production by Sam Mendes."

rGGR 5.11 Nathan, David. Rev. of *Glengarry Glen Ross*. *Jewish Chronicle* 1 July 1994. Rpt. in *Theatre Record* 18 June -1 July 1994: 792-93.

Positive review focusing on Levene: "As a result, Levene escaped a society where he would have been persecuted, to inhabit one where he is both victim and oppressor. It is also another place where two languages are spoken, the glib sale-speak of instant friendship and the jagged unfinished sentences, obscenities spilling through the gaps, of men in fear of losing the one lousy job they can hold down. [. . . leaving] no doubt that Mamet is the most merciless chronicler of the greed-black values of commercial America."

rGGR 5.12 Nightingale, Benedict. "The Sharks Still Have Bite." *Times* [London] 24
June 1994. Rpt. in *Theatre Record* 18 June -1 July 1994: 793.
    Negative view of this production as meaner, nastier: "Sam Mendes's
direction has made the play's world uglier and less funny. Both Jack Shepherd
in London and Joe Mantegna on Broadway brought a sleek charm to the role of
Ricky Roma, [. . .] Ron Cook is just as verbally dizzying, but meaner, nastier.
This means that the play loses an odd and disturbing ambivalence. Back in
1983, I felt there was a side of Mamet that sneakingly admired these men. [. . .]
At the Donmar of 1994, they are plainly victims who can survive only by
victimising others. Their macho swagger is bluster concealing greed for money
and terror of failure, little else."

rGGR 5.13 Paton, Maureen. Rev. of *Glengarry Glen Ross*. *Daily Express* 2 July 1994.
Rpt. in *Theatre Record* 18 June -1 July 1994: 791.
    Positive view of a "cynical" play: "A first-rate cast is led by Joe Pesci
lookalike Ron Cook, a silver-tongued Prince of Darkness listing his amoral
articles of faith, and James Bolam, on shifty, bug-eyed form as a burnt-out case.
Intoxicating, supremely cynical stuff."

rGGR 5.14 Smith, Neil. Rev. of *Glengarry Glen Ross*. What's On 29 June 1994. Rpt.
in *Theatre Record* 18 June -1 July 1994: 793.
    Mildly negative view of this production: "Sam Mendes' revival at the
Donmar doesn't quite do it justice: his all-British cast can't grasp the howling
desperation that underpins the sly patter of the play's real estate salesmen (or
should that be conmen?), or keep us hooked as they fight to keep their jobs,
their sanity and their self-esteem."

rGGR 5.15 Spenser, Charles. Rev. of *Glengarry Glen Ross*. *Daily Telegraph* 24 June
1994. Rpt. in *Theatre Record* 18 June -1 July 1994: 794-95.
    Positive view of the play, and "almost heroic" characters: "A lesser
playwright would use all this as a cumbersome symbol for the failure of the
American Dream, a moralistic denunciation of the savagery of dog-eat-dog
capitalism. [. . .] Mamet simply seems to be presenting a documentary account of
these men in action, a fascinating study of duplicity and the dark arts of persuasion
and entrapment. [. . .] The playwright's attitude to his superbly drawn characters is
fascinatingly ambiguous: they are of course little better than crooks, preying on the
dreams of vulnerable people. But they are up against the wall, too, and there is
something almost heroic about their increasingly desperate strategies for survival."

rGGR 5.16 Taylor, Paul. "Brute Strength." *Independent* 24 June 1994. Rpt. *Theatre
Record* 18 June -1 July 1994: 793-94.
    Positive review of this production forcing the audience to do the work: "As
successive pairs of salesmen engage in intense conversation, they and their table
are rotated slowly on a central revolve. It creepily reinforces the sense that they
are being observed like specimens. One of the misjudgments of the film is to
add a laborious scene at the start explaining the terms of the new, inhuman

sales competition, whereas one of the glories of the play is that it pitches you right in with three fragmented scenes that assume a familiarity that you have, in fact, to acquire on the hop. Mendes paces the material with a sort of laconic violence, from the startling rise of the scrim at the start, to the sinister, finger-clicking percussion between scenes that is brilliantly in tune with the play's story-telling manner."

rGGR 5.17 Wardle, Irving. "A Crazy Way to Make a Living." *Independent on Sunday* 26 June 1994: 14. Rpt. in *Theatre Record* 18 June -1 July 1994 788-89.

More positive than of the original: "With its continual changes of perspective, this piece is ideally suited to the point-blank stage conditions of the Donmar. [. . .] But the whole show seems to be taking place on an imaginary revolve, successively bringing different aspects into view: from an exposure of the conspiratorial nature of professional life, to the cut-throat rivalry between the sales staff. They are allowed some dignity, as actors who must believe in their roles, and as foot soldiers who despise the top brass. Then the focus shifts again, and they shrivel into a malignant swarm in relation to the cheated client."

Production:
pGGR 6 McCarter Theater in Princeton, New Jersey on February 18, 2000.

Director:		Scott Zigler
Sets:		John Lee Beatty
Costumes:		Catherine Zuber
Lighting:		Howard Werner
Cast:		
	Levene:	Charles Durning
	Williamson:	Jordan Lage
	Moss:	Daniel Benzali
	Aaronow:	Sam Coppola
	Roma:	Ruben Santiago-Hudson
	Lingk:	Steven Soldstein
	Baylen:	Lionel Mark Smith

Overview:
All the reviewers were extremely positive about this production, and there was much talk, as Daniels suggested, of a Broadway run, but a theatre was not available at the right time. Critics focused on Durning who was "heartbreaking" in the role (Klein) playing Levene as alternately "pugnacious and pleading" (Hampton), and so infused both variety and power in building "a beautifully structured performance that grows in anguish and desperation" (Daniels).

Reviews:
rGGR 6.1 Daniels, Robert L. Rev. of *Glengarry Glen Ross. Variety* 6-12 Mar. 2000: 50.
Positive review which "can hardly imagine a better production than this staging" and notes that "the production [. . .] draws on both published working scripts, leaning toward the Grove Press edition." Durning "builds a beautifully structured performance that grows in anguish and desperation."

rGGR 6.2 Hampton, Wilborn. "Loman's Ghost Haunts Mamet's Turf." *New York Times*
23 Feb. 2000: E3.

Very positive review of the play which focused on Levene as "the stark,
dead-end reality of the American dream [. . . who] fights back with bluster and
bluff, with boasting and bravado. [. . .] Alternately pugnacious and pleading as
he [Levene] fights to keep his head above water, the actor uses subtle gestures
and tone—a hand to the forehead or the forced, hollow ring of a laugh—to
paint a gripping portrait of a man pushed to his limit. [. . .] Santiago-Hudson
breaks the stereotype, portraying him as a snake-oil hawker with the mellifluous
rhythms of a country Baptist preacher. [. . . Benzali and Copola] are hilarious in
the scene in which they plot a theft. Both are natural Mamet actors, turning
their fury and resignation into just another of life's little jokes. [. . .]"

rGGR 6.3 Klein, Alvin. "Some Creepy Predators from Mamet." *New York Times* 27
Feb. 2000, sec. 14NJ: 12.

Very positive review which focused again on emotions: "For those who
think Mr. Mamet's creepy predators cannot be unutterably moving, there is
Charles Durning's heartbreaking performance as Levene, declaring desperation
and totally inhabiting it."

Scholarly Overview:
Criticism on this play is particularly complex because the film and the stage versions
are not very clearly delineated, despite the best efforts of Hudgins and Lublin. One
division of scholars results from opposing responses to Levene; some sympathize
with him (Hudgins) while others quite despise him (Dean). The issue is further complicated in that Lemmon's self-pitying depiction was the opposite of the NY stage
version (Prosky/Gardenia) which depicted him as self-confident in the extreme, but
on a losing streak he expected to end any moment. Boon asks the key question—how
can a work which features so much immorality actually be extremely moral? Some
view the play with detachment and denounce its immorality (Berger, Brucher, Dorff,
Garaventa, Geis, Greenbaum, Jacobs, Klaver, Nelson, Price, Stafford, Vorlicky). Others sympathize with the characters and see deeper values implied (Hudgins, Kane,
Kolin, Rolf, Roudané, Worster). Boon, Cullick, Lublin, Price, Sauer and Tuttle walk
a middle ground seeing the immorality as a demand for the audience to supply the
morality lacking in the characters.

sGGR 1 Berger, Jason and Cornelius B. Pratt. "Teaching Business-Communication Ethics
with Controversial Films." *Journal of Business Ethics* 17.16 (1998): 1817-23.

Using the films of *Glengarry Glen Ross* and *House of Games* to teach
"interactive" business ethics for public relations courses, the authors view
salesmen as "professional con men who sell bogus land in Florida. They work
in shabby office where they reminisce about the 'go-go' days of the 1960s when
they earned huge sums of money by swindling 'easy marks' either on the
telephone or on a 'sit'" (1819). Students "indicate that public relations is indeed
in the sales business" (1821), the students enjoy Pacino's performance, and
males "said they wanted to be like Ricky" (1821). Students see ethics as lacking

in "business communications" and so misunderstand business communications using "stereotypes that equate business communications with propaganda" (1822).

sGGR 2 Bigsby, C. W. E. *"Glengarry Glen Ross." David Mamet.* Contemporary Writers. London: Methuen, 1985. 111-26.

This analysis examines the ideas of fiction and storytelling: "His salesmen are agents of the capitalist system which is destroying them; but they are also brilliant storytellers, improvising their lives, performing themselves and deploying language with a facility matched only by its misplaced function. The status of the salesmen is determined solely by their success, but it is in failure that anxieties are exposed, as the flow of language falters. They are not only selling property to other people but also struggling to maintain a sense of identity and meaning independent of that activity. The problem is that they have so thoroughly plundered the language of private need and self-fulfillment and deployed it for the purpose of deceit and betrayal that they no longer have access to words that will articulate their feelings" (123).

sGGR 3 Bishop, Ryan. "There's Nothing Natural About Natural Conversation: A Look at Dialogue in Fiction and Drama." *Cross-Cultural Studies: American, Canadian and European Literatures: 1945-1985.* Ed. Mirko Jurak. Ljubljana, Yugoslavia: English Dept, U. of Ljublijana, 1988. 257-66.

Arguing that "our judgments regarding 'natural' dialogue are determined by our literacy and literary tradition, not by reality" (257), Bishop sets out to demonstrate that dialogue, as in *Glengarry Glen Ross* is not "realistic" but literary. Using Ong, Bishop argues that written language is never the equivalent of spoken language. It is more formal, spoken without punctuation, so attempts to punctuate always impose form onto it. And overlapping is difficult to replicate but common in dialogue. In addition, "Everyday conversation is filled with backtracks and elliptical thoughts [as well as a] mixture of redundancies and references to shared knowledge, which often take the form of seemingly magnificent leaps in logic to an eavesdropper" (258). Furthermore, much of conversation is overlapping, which "gives a non-linear form to much conversation" (258). *Glengarry*'s dialogue "is full of interruptions, incomplete statements, backtracks, and referents unclear to the reader/audience" (264). But it also has the literary convention of "relevance" for though the characters' speeches are not really relevant to each other, we can see that each tries to manipulate the others, and so we recognize the "relevance."(265).

sGGR 4 Boon, Kevin Alexander. "Dialogue, Discourse & Dialectics: The Rhetoric of Capitalism in *Glengarry Glen Ross.*" *Creative Screenwriting* 5.3 (1998): 50-57.

After an examination of ideas of "discourse" and "ethics" drawn from Aristotle, Boon queries: "But what are we to make of Mamet's *Glengarry Glen Ross*, where much of the dialogue between and among the characters is clearly unethical. Yet the screenplay itself is not without ethics, inviting us to examine how a screenplay in which all characters are unethical manages to construct an

ethical point of view" (51). His answer is that "We provide the moral critique of
the discourse" (51). The article focuses first on Blake, then on the dialogue of
Moss and Aaronow: "As in Aristotle's paradigm, Aaronow is guilty because he
listened to unethical discourse without distinguishing it as untrue or unjust.
Listening without moral judgment is a crime just as much as robbery is a crime"
(57). In this way, "Mamet skillfully puts us in the position where we must judge
the rhetorical acts of these characters as unjust, or become accomplices in the
pervasive spread of blind avarice and the resulting decay of communal values" (57).

sGGR 5 Brawer, Robert A. *Fictions of Business*. New York: Wiley, 1998. 27-29.
      Roma is seen as defying Covey's rule "to listen first and talk afterward.
And yet, in his inimitable way Roma 'hears' his man perfectly. His gutter gossip,
his insistence on breaching life's constraints, and his apparent master of life's
contingencies add up to a big deposit on this's individual's Emotional Bank
Account. Roma has 'listened' empathetically" (27).

sGGR 6 Brucher, Richard. "Pernicious Nostalgia in *Glengarry Glen Ross*." *David
      Mamet's Glengarry Glen Ross: Text and Performance*. Ed. Leslie Kane. New
      York: Garland, 1996. 211-25.
      In this stimulating essay, Brucher examines the salesmen plays: *Death of a
Salesman, The Iceman Cometh*, and *Glengarry* through the optic of Emerson's
ideals of American self-reliance. All three are seen as ironic comments on these
ideals: "As a purveyor of possibility and unbridled individualism, Emerson is a
major creator of the cultural baggage that Theodore Hickey, Willy Loman, Shelly
Levene, and Richard Roma trade in. As a stoical antimaterialist and skeptic
about the ability of language to reveal reality, he is a progenitor of O'Neill,
Miller, and Mamet. I think that each of these writers deliberately travesties Emerson
and probably one another, to find an original and promising American thought" (223).

sGGR 7 Carroll, Dennis. "Business: *American Buffalo*; *Glengarry Glen Ross*."
      David Mamet. Modern Dramatists series. New York: St. Martin's, 1987. 31-50.
      Glengarry is seen as a parallel to *American Buffalo* with a number of
similarities. The differences are that the "plot of *Glengarry Glen Ross* again
centres upon a robbery, which this time does take place; and the chain of events
that ensues, linked by cause and effect, comprises elements of a conventional
'rising action'. But this plot is still not as important as the 'submerged' pattern
of interaction between the salesmen, the 'beats' limned by allegiances proposed
or aborted, competition smoothed over or stepped up. The plot and this other
pattern however, prove to be increasingly interrelated as the play goes on" (40).

sGGR 8 Cohn, Ruby. "'Oh, God I Hate This Job'." *Approaches to Teaching Miller's
      Death of a Salesman*. Ed. Matthew C. Roudané. New York: MLA, 1995. 155-62.
      Cohn examines briefly the sales trilogy: *The Iceman Cometh, Death of a
Salesman,* and *Glengarry Glen Ross*. "O'Neill and Miller are deliberately vague
about what their respective salesmen sell, but Mamet is ironic; what estate is
less 'real' than Florida swamplands with names resonant of romantic Scottish

highlands?" (159-60). And she concludes: "these theatre salesmen mark progressive disenchantment with the American dream of success. O'Neill's Hickey, proud of his sales prowess, imposes salvation on others so as to avoid his own atonement. Mamet's salesmen, wholly absorbed by their quasi-real estate, connive in the momentum of their own damnation" (161-62).

sGGR 9 Cullick, Jonathan S. "'Always Be Closing:' Competition and the Discourse of Closure in David Mamet's *Glengarry Glen Ross*." *Journal of Dramatic Theory and Criticism* 8.2 (1994): 23-36.

Cullick employs a binary system of oppositions in discourse: "The discourse of community is transactional, comprised of speech acts that communicate and invite responses. It is a language of mediation, negotiation, and cooperation—an open discourse. On the other hand, discourse of competition is adversarial, the language of manipulation, deception, self interest" (23). Thus Levene, lacking "status," must appeal to Williamson using the language of community. When that fails, he offers bribes, the language of mediation. Moss similarly first uses communal language of how it used to be, then shifts to language of mediation to get Aaronow to break into the office for him. Roma uses all communal language of men together in the third scene, but when Lingk returns in act 2, he first tries that language with Levene as satisfied customer, then resorts to negotiation of days with Lingk.

sGGR 10 Dean, Anne. "*Glengarry Glen Ross*." *David Mamet: Language as Dramatic Action*. Rutherford, New Jersey: Fairleigh Dickinson UP, 1990. 189-221.

Dean is sympathetic with all the salesmen: "but it is not merely their ability to construct stories that make Mamet's salesmen interesting; it is why they choose to do so. They sell not only real estate but also hope and consolation, as much to themselves as to their hapless clients. So alone in the world are they that they have subverted language to such a degree that they can barely articulate genuine needs and emotions. Selling is their whole lives, and they do not really exist outside of the workplace. Despite their corruption, they are worthy of our sympathy; a ruthless, capitalistic society has set them on the wheel, and for them there is no turning back" (220).

sGGR 11 —. "The Discourse of Anxiety." *David Mamet's Glengarry Glen Ross: Text and Performance*. Ed. Leslie Kane. New York: Garland, 1996. 47-61.

Dean interprets the fragmentary style. Levene "dares not finish his sentences lest Williamson should manage to speak" (51). Two kinds of fear are detected in the next scene, Aaronow's that he is "being irrevocably drawn into criminal conspiracy" (53), and Moss's ire about the injustice of the system. But when Moss goes on a rant, "He interjects new issues without concluding the previous sentence and his words race ahead, almost incoherently, toward a reminiscence of better times" (56). Roma's "arrogant frustration with the world in general" leads to his speaking style (56). When he is assured his sale went through, "His pent-up anxiety does not permit him to succumb to immediate relief on hearing the good news; his words rush ahead, punctuated only by commas, never pausing long enough to justify a full stop" (57). Lingk has all her sympathy for his "deep-seated fear of his wife" (59). "Roma utilizes his strategy of not allowing his pathetic victim to speak, his machine-gun sentences ricocheting off the walls" (59).

sGGR 12 Dorff, Linda. "Things (Ex)Change: The Value of Money in David Mamet's *Glengarry Glen Ross.*" *David Mamet's Glengarry Glen Ross: Text and Performance.* Ed. Leslie Kane. New York: Garland, 1996. 195-209.

In a clever variant on the Baudrillardian theme of the empty signifier which Klaver also explores in this book, Dorff follows the imagery of money and finds that there is no real cash in the play—Levene hasn't enough to bribe Williamson, the Nyborgs have none to pay Levene, the salesmen are detectives trying to find out who has money and where it is hidden (in socks and government bonds). And as Klaver and Stafford note, the "leads" become the currency of the play, though they have no real cash value.

sGGR 13 Garaventa, Eugene. "A Tool for Teaching Business Ethics." *Business Ethics Quarterly* 8.3 (1998): 535-45.

This article examines plays as a means to teach business ethics. Noting that there are two conflicting theories—one that business is amoral, the other that it should be based on personal morality, he questions how one should classify Roma's sales pitch and the procedure for allocating leads. He doesn't answer the question, but raises the ethical issues. Curiously, he doesn't deal with the crucial choices—the attempted deception of Lingk when he returns to void the contract—or Moss's argument that stealing the leads is not unethical in an amoral universe.

sGGR 14 Geis, Deborah R. "'You're Exploiting My Space': Ethnicity, Spectatorship and the (Post)Colonial Condition in Mukherjee's 'a Wife's Story' and Mamet's *Glengarry Glen Ross.*" *David Mamet's Glengarry Glen Ross: Text and Performance.* Ed. Leslie Kane. New York: Garland, 1996. 123-30.

Geis uses Muhkerjee's story to view Mamet's play through the eyes of an Indian woman who is affronted: "I don't hate Mamet. It's the tyranny of the American dream that scares me. First, you don't exist. Then you're invisible. Then you're funny. Then you're disgusting. [. . .] A play like this, back home, would cause riots. Communal, racist, and antisocial. This play, and all these awful feelings, would be locked up" (127). Very gently, Geis shows us this vision of the play from the outsider's point of view—whose space is taken by the white man laughing beside her: "the man's reaction points to the complicity of the spectators in accepting, appreciating, and appropriating the characters' sexism and racism (however ironic Mamet's intention in having his characters say these lines in the first place: the balance of judgment is a delicate one)" (127).

sGGR 15 Goldensohn, Barry. "David Mamet and Poetic Language in Drama." *Agni* [Boston] 49 (1999): 139-49.

Very stimulating thought piece by a poet who team-taught Shakespeare with Mamet. He asked Mamet about his influences—"Pinter, Beckett, and Kleist." Pinter and Beckett are seen as polar opposites, one writing dramatic, the other lyric poetry. Mamet is seen as poised between them. It concludes with an analysis of Roma's pitch to Lingk as dramatic poetry: "What makes this unlikely material poetic is the pointed brilliance of its satire, its Swiftian energy [. . .], the sense that not a word is out of place, nor a pause nor any aspect of rhythm, and its intense compression. [. . .] And it is entirely e mbedded in the action of the character and the play. It is realistic dialogue of stunning *dramatic* precision—as opposed to simple tape-recorder accuracy." (148). [It is worth adding that Richard Stayton's article "Enter Scowling," *Los Angeles Times* 23 Aug. 1992, Mag.: 20—observes: "Robert Prosky remembers seeing Mamet at the rear of the theater during rehearsals counting on his fingers the number of iambs in one speech".]

sGGR 16 Greenbaum, Andrea. "Brass Balls: Masculine Communication and the Discourse of Capitalism in David Mamet's *Glengarry Glen Ross*." *Journal of Men's Studies* 8.1 (1999): 33-43.

There isn't much original here—citations of Almansi, Cullick, Dean, McDonough, Radavich, Worster, Zeifman, and Zinman underly the rehashes of their points on masculinity, language, exile of the feminine, etc. Curiously, there is no Vorlicky, who is the expert on this topic. The one original bit is a set of references, a few stretched, which constitute "military imagery." The real originality is in the ascription of *Death of a Salesman* to "Henry Miller" and continual references to "Jerry Graft [sic]—Murray and Mitch's prime competitor."

sGGR 17 *Hartwick Classic Leadership Cases: Glengarry Glen Ross*. Oneata, NY: Hartwick Humanities in Management Institute, Hartwick College, 1994.

This business institute publishes case studies based on classic works of literature, philosophy, history, drama, and biography. The teaching module for *Glengarry Glen Ross* uses it to illustrate management styles and issues, such as Total Quality Management, path-goal theory of leadership, the basis of managerial power, boss-centered leadership, motivation and the ethics of business bluffing.

sGGR 18 Hasenberg, Peter. "'Always Be Closing': Struktur Und Thema Von David Mamets *Glengarry Glen Ross*." *Anglistik & Englischunterricht* [Heidelberg] 35 (1988): 177-91.

Hasenberg argues from the headnote: "The central aspect of Mamet's parable is the unattainability of striving for values, success, meaning and definitive certainty. 'Always be closing' says the salesman's maxim placed as a motto at the head of the play, a formula that describes the striving for closings (closure), for deals (actions) that have been consistently brought to an end."

sGGR 19 Hudgins, Christopher C. "'By Indirections Find Directions Out': Uninflected
      Cuts, Narrative Structure, and Thematic Statement in the Film Version of
      Glengarry Glen Ross." *David Mamet's Glengarry Glen Ross: Text and
      Performance*. Ed. Leslie Kane. New York: Garland, 1996. 19-45.

      With a thesis that Mamet's desire is an impossible quest ("I always want
      everyone to be sympathetic to all the characters."), Hudgins nevertheless tries
      to show how morality and a balanced view of characters emerges mainly from
      intercutting. He begins with the opening scene of Levene calling his daughter,
      intercut with Moss trying to connect by phone with a client: "Moss's disgust as
      he says with a similar desperation in his eyes, 'I'll call you back in ten minutes,'
      suggests that the two activities are very different, the one sincere, caring, centrally
      important in the most humane ways, and the other manipulative, hostile,
      inhumane and duplicitous" (24). Of course the neat separation implies discrete
      responses, but as Hudgins develops his argument, the desire to work for the
      daughter results in the desire to manipulate and deceive others. In the second
      scene, intercutting Moss and Aaronow getting into a car in the rain, bemoaning
      the job, and Levene leaving his car to make a call, allows the conclusion that
      "The second scene concretely illustrates the abstraction of the first" (25). In the
      play, of course, none of these connections are made for the audience; they must
      intuit connections as the three two-person scenes unfold in the first act. Hudgins,
      who is surely the most sympathetic reader of Mamet's characters, views Roma
      as "genuinely concerned for Lingk" (38) when he appears in the office to renege
      on their deal. He concludes that Roma is a real friend, and the film ends
      "emphasizing admiration for these men rather than criticism of the system" (41).

sGGR 20 Jacobs, Dorothy H. "Levene's Daughter: Positioning of the Female in
      Glengarry Glen Ross." *David Mamet's Glengarry Glen Ross: Text and
      Performance*. Ed. Leslie Kane. New York: Garland, 1996: 107-22.

      Jacobs argues that the "phallocentricity of this world is the language of
      contempt, hatred, and dehumanization that is insistently allied to matching
      attitudes towards women" (108) in an interesting companion piece to Vorlicky's.
      She concentrates on the absent women of the play, Harriet Nyborg, Jinny Lingk,
      and Levene's daughter. Her analysis of Harriet is not very convincing, because
      the same could be said of her husband, Bruce. But her interpretation of Jinny as
      the power character of the play is unique: "Jinny Lingk is male fear made audible,
      the domestic in combat-boots, the intruder into the male domain of business
      deals" (114). Jacobs concludes with an overview of Mamet's mistreatment of
      other women characters: "Mamet's on-stage women must be discarded" (118).

sGGR 21 Kane, Leslie. "Caught in the American Machine." *Weasels and Wisemen:
      Ethics and Ethnicity in the Work of David Mamet*. New York: St. Martin's Press,
      1999. 57-102.

      Isolating the Jewish Characters, Moses, Aaron, and the Levites (Moss,
      Aaronow, and Levene), Kane sees the play in terms of anti-Semitism embodied
      in Williamson who is insulted by Levene as "fucking white-bread" (97) and so
      takes his revenge: "the office manager prefers to rid himself and his office of

this pushy Jew" (100). Williamson reverses the work relationship, "makes it personal" (100) against the character the audience likes, Levene. "Mamet's take on this rhetoric is to uncover the mythical signifier for what it is: flagrant, abhorrent anti-Semitism" (100).

sGGR 22 Kane, Leslie. "A Conversation: Sam Mendes and Leslie Kane." *David Mamet's Glengarry Glen Ross: Text and Performance*. Ed. Leslie Kane. New York: Garland, 1996. 245-62.

Mendes, whose first film was *American Beauty*, became director of Donmar Warehouse in 1992, and there directed *Glengarry Glen Ross* in 1994.

sGGR 23 — *David Mamet's Glengarry Glen Ross: Text and Performance*. New York: Garland, 1996.

The articles in this book are individually annotated in this chapter, with the exception of those by Carroll and Gale which are listed in "Film Scholarship," and the bibliography done by Jan Sauer in "Bibliographies and Reference Books."

sGGR 24 Kim, Yun-cheol. "Degradation of the American Success Ethic: *Death of a Saleman, That Championship Season,* and *Glengarry Glen Ross*." *The Journal of English Language and Literature* [Seoul] 37.1 (1991): 233-48.

sGGR 25 Klaver, Elizabeth. "David Mamet, Jean Baudrillard and the Performance of America." *David Mamet's Glengarry Glen Ross: Text and Performance*. Ed. Leslie Kane. New York: Garland, 1996. 171-83.

This is an interesting thought piece more than an analysis. The real estate agents aren't selling reality, but only a simulacrum, at best, of real estate—a dream, an illusion of Glengarry Highlands: "are these parcels simply the signs of an American dreamscape completely divorced from any referential anchorage?" (177). Klaver goes further to argue that in both Mamet and Baudrillard is found "the capacity of signs to turn into each other and turning into each other at the same time" (179). Thus "Mamet lets the edge of criminality lurk behind every aspect of the real estate venture from the bribery of Williamson by Levene to the seductive lure of Roma's language to the final break-in and robbery" (178).

sGGR 26 Kolin, Philip C. "Mitch and Murray in David Mamet's *Glengarry Glen Ross*." *Notes on Contemporary Literature* 18.2 (1988): 3-5.

Taking the opposite approach to Hudgins, who sees Mitch and Murray as barely staying in business, Kolin sees them as invisible bosses who insulate themselves with middle management. Thus they are "the bosses in the consumer economy of the 1980s" (3). In Kolin's view, Mitch and Murray are "the new robber barons" who not only "epitomize the corrupt bosses of capitalism" but, worse, represent the pitfalls of "false friendship" (4). They show no loyalty to Levene who has slaved for them for so many years. And their salesmen mirror their values, as Roma does in bribing Williamson, or Williamson who "extorts a huge bribe" from Levene and then turns him into the police.

sGGR 27 Lublin, Robert I. "Differing Dramatic Dynamics in the Stage and Screen Versions of *Glengarry Glen Ross.*" *American Drama* 10.1 (2001): 38-55.

Lublin addresses the difference between the two versions. Though he does not attempt cinematic analysis *per se*, Lublin makes the argument that the addition of Blake to the film creates a simpler society in which the rich and powerful are in control, and the powerless are exploited. In the play, however, there is a much greater sense of poverty across the board, so that everyone is fighting the same desperation to survive, and cutting each other's throats to do so. Lublin shows how the salesmen are all living hand-to-mouth in the play. As a result, the play's salesmen are more sympathetic, but at the same time they are themselves responsible for the vicious world in which they live. Interestingly, Lublin does examine the references to Levene's daughter to show his sympathy, but doesn't go further to examine Lemmon's shift in portrayal of Levene as a loser who continually begs for sympathy, as opposed to the play's Prosky and Gardenia in the New York production whose Levene was a tough and confident salesman just on a losing streak.

sGGR 28 Malkin, Jeanette R. "Language as a Prison: Verbal Debris and Deprivation: David Mamet: *American Buffalo* and *Glengarry Glen Ross.*" *Verbal Violence in Contemporary Drama.* Cambridge: Cambridge University Press, 1992. 145-61.

Malkin analyzes the language games of *Glengarry Glen Ross*: "The act of talking, which already in *American Buffalo* is ambiguously treated by the characters themselves, is here developed into a schizophrenic term: to 'talk' is to act, talk is power, men know how to 'talk'" (156). "Levene opposes action (i.e. talk which sells) with the other meaning of 'talk' developed in the play: talk as 'the blah blah blah' (p.13), talk divorced from action, talk as theory, as idea" (157). "To talk is to become an accomplice; to listen is to be implicated ('Because you listened'). Words can only buy and sell, and they sell trust and friendship just as easily as land" (159). But for her the primacy of text over performance results in a static idea of a stable text with one possible interpretation: *"Glengarry Glen Ross*, in which ethical perversity and verbal restrictedness are totally interwoven and breed a bestiality which, Mamet seems to be saying, endangers an entire society" (161).

sGGR 29 Nasser, Maria Cristina A., Lilian Cristina Duarte. "The Myth of Success in David Mamet's *Glengarry Glen Ross.*" *Estudio Anglo Americanos* [Sao Paulo, Brazil] 17-18 (1993): 114-21.

sGGR 30 Nelson, Jeanne Andrée. "So Close to Closure: The Selling of Desire in *Glengarry Glen Ross.*" *Essays in Theatre/Etudes Theatrales* [Canada] 14.2 (1996): 107-16.

Rejecting the common view of capitalistic exploitation, Nelson sees instead that "inner conflicts" rather than outside pressures, are the cause of problems. Using Freud and Girard, Nelson examines "the patterns woven by imitation and envy in the play" (108). In scene one, Levene invites Williamson to imitate him, but when rejected, "he transfers his self-overevaluation to his boss" (111). Moss and Roma both use the same strategy: "The model here, seduces, cajoles, and finally points the way toward self-appropriation, and closure of identity" (112) but Aaronow rejects identification with Moss, while Lingk is seduced by Roma. "The market, modeled after human mimetic interactions, lures desire toward concrete possessions that will make others envious and will grant self-sufficiency to the subject who will settle in the promised land of eternal supremacy" (115). But for all this jargon of desire, there is no clear explanation of why all the sales fail.

sGGR 31 Price, Steven. "Negative Creation: The Detective Story in *Glengarry Glen Ross*." *David Mamet's Glengarry Glen Ross: Text and Performance*. Ed. Leslie Kane. New York: Garland, 1996. 3-17.

In an extremely smart examination of why Mamet would employ the retro "linear, realistic form" (13) of the detective story in his play, Price argues that Mamet invokes the myth only to debunk it. The myth involves a single guilty party who is exposed at the end, revealing the secret required by realistic form— but here instead there is also "the circular or fragmentary form of the absurd" (13). Along the way, Price offers an argument for a Freudian analysis of an oedipal plot "characterized by the metaphor of something or someone struggling to break free of the authority of the parent" (5). He also offers a fascinating explanation for the seeming irrelevancy of the theft of the telephones, and does nice work playing off the old saws opposing British and American detective stories, showing how both are invoked in this play. Through this approach, Price deepens the recognition of the play's view of "business as crime" (6), noting that Mamet's view of American myth (of the lone detective, of the frontier) "is decidedly lacking in nostalgic illusion" (8).

sGGR 32 Radavich, David. "Man among Men: David Mamet's Homosocial Order." *American Drama* 1.1 (1991): 46-60. Rpt. in *Fictions of Masculinity: Crossing Cultures, Crossing Sexualities*. Ed. Peter F. Murphy. New York: New York UP, 1994. 123-36.

Radavich surveys Mamet's plays looking for patterns that conform to Sedgwick's *Between Men*. He lists the homosexual, homophobic, anti-feminist allusions in each play to trace male bonding references. This results in some strange centering: "In yet another all-male play, the cast is now middle-aged, and the focus on male rape ('fucking up the ass') and enslavement (18). And the 'screwing' is not merely verbal" (53). This analysis of *Glengarry* leads to the conclusion: "In the ethos of Mamet's plays, a man symbolically deprived of his penis through personal insecurity or deprecation by other males is, by definition, a faggot or a cunt, debased both sexually and professionally" (54). This leads to a final view of Mamet as "essentially a comic satirist" (58) whose work gives "his dramatic view of a decadent, wounded patriarchy" (59).

sGGR 33 Rolf, Robert T. "A Japanese *Glengarry Glen Ross*." *David Mamet's Glengarry Glen Ross: Text and Performance*. Ed. Leslie Kane. New York: Garland, 1996. 227-43.

An interesting performance review of a Kabuki-influenced style of realism which allows much larger displays of emotion than Americans expect. Williamson was played as gay due to an overly literal interpretation of one of Roma's epithets, and "slumps in a chair and hangs his head," devastated from Roma's tongue lashing. (239) When his guilt is detected by Baylen, Levene gives a long, loud, anguished cry. Such raw expression of emotion is not called for in Mamet's stage directions" (239). Aaronow gave way to loud cries of anguish as did Lingk who even knocked Roma down as he exited in Act 2. "[...] the feeling was more of a group of lost, pathetic men in the same sad predicament, as if writhing in some Buddhist hell, than of a collection of 'sleazeballs,' as it were, forced by a system to do wrong" (240).

sGGR 34 Roudané, Matthew C. "Public Issues, Private Tensions: David Mamet's *Glengarry Glen Ross*." *South Carolina Review* 19.1 (1986): 35-47.

This is an analysis of "the puckish relationship between the individual's sense of public responsibility and his or her definition of private liberties" (35). This conflict is seen as a "Tocquevillian dialectic" and is traced through the early plays to *Glengarry*. Roudané concedes "Mamet's experiments with dramatic form at times place him within the post-modern movement" but Roudané sees his sympathies rather with "liberal humanism. Underneath his characters' hard boiled, enameled public bravado lies an ongoing inner drama, a subtext presenting the characters' quest for consciousness. The profound irony stems from the characters' inability to understand the regenerative powers of consciousness, or, worse, that such transcendent powers even exist" (36-37). In *Glengarry*, however, "Mamet deliberately dramatizes the Tocquevillian connection between the public self—the hurlyburly of those caught within a business-as-sacrament world—and the private self—the anguished characters' inner reality. For Mamet, public and private experiences become one" (39). Thus the private self is not presented in the play, but seemingly inferred by its absence. Roma is cited as the key example of someone with "no conscience" (43).

sGGR 35 Sauer, David Kennedy. "The Marxist Child's Play of Mamet's Tough Guys and Churchill's *Top Girls*." *David Mamet's Glengarry Glen Ross: Text and Performance*. Ed. Leslie Kane. New York: Garland, 1996. 131-56.

The basis of the parallel here is that both playwrights have given audiences superficial targets (men oppressing women, bosses oppressing salesmen) but in fact it is the system itself which corrupts all within it. As a result, the characters themselves destroy themselves. "The smaller corporate worlds of Mamet and Churchill are equally decentered—at least morally. Both begin with disorienting misdirection—making us think we are dealing with feminism, or real estate scams, and conjuring the illusion of a golden age when there was no exploitation. Then they change direction with internal contradiction or humor to give a different focus—on socialism and variant forms of dishonesty. In doing so, both present their characters as losing their way, behaving like children, and worse, hurting their own children by being unable to cope with the disorientation they feel" (152).

sGGR 36 Stafford, Tony J. "Visions of a Promised Land: David Mamet's *Glengarry Glen Ross*." *David Mamet's Glengarry Glen Ross: Text and Performance*. Ed. Leslie Kane. New York: Garland, 1996. 185-94.

This is more verbally playful, but not as philosophically challenging as Klaver's similar contemplation on empty signs. Clever wordplay teases out meaning from the title, the names of the characters, and other verbal signs, all under the rubric of "illusion," in the examination of which the names of the real estate properties are illusions of Highlands Scotland in flatland Florida swamp. The Chinese restaurant is a sign of China, not a reality. Illusions abound—though when analyzing the plot curiously Stafford ignores the one which makes the whole contest an illusion, Roma's bribery of Williamson to get the best leads.

sGGR 37 Temkine, R. "The Theatre of Dereliction." *Europe-Revue Litteraire Mensuelle* 79.861-62 (2001): 286-91.

This article recounts a Marseille production of *Glengarry* which was done realistically: "La piece n'a rein perdu de son actualité; au contraire peut-être en a-t-elle gagné" (289).

sGGR 38 Tuttle, Jon. "'Be What You Are': Identity and Morality in *Edmond* and *Glengarry Glen Ross*." *David Mamet's Glengarry Glen Ross: Text and Performance*. Ed. Leslie Kane. New York: Garland, 1996. 157-69.

Tuttle sees Edmond as someone who breaks out of the ideology everyone else accepts to a despairing view that: "there is NO LAW . . . there is no history . . . there is just now" (162). "For Teach, Edmond, and in fact all of Mamet's most negative characters, this *weltanshauung* becomes a rationale for breaking out of what Edmond calls the "fog" of imposed morality to indulge a self-interest untrammeled by conscience. As such it provides the strongest connective tissue between *Edmond* and *Glengarry Glen Ross*" (162). Using a thematic parallel, however, means that mainly Roma's speech to Lingk becomes the focus of analysis of man alone making his own rules. Levene's actions also work as a parallel. The purpose is that "Like Brecht, Mamet portrays extremes of behavior in order to encourage his audience to question his characters' choices" (167).

sGGR 39 Vorlicky, Robert. "The American Masculine Ethos, Male Mythologies, and Absent Women." *Act Like a Man: Challenging Masculinities in American Drama*. Ann Arbor: U of Michigan, 1995. 25-56.

This revolutionary approach to American drama studies all male-cast plays, examined in the light of feminist and queer studies. The result is a new understanding—"Mamet's dialogue resists any such private access to the individual. What results in *Glengarry* is a cryptic, inarticulate coding system that deliberately fluctuates between clarity of meaning and ambiguity while it propels the men's conversation forward. This social dialogue is narrowly confined to the topic of the men's employment" (27). He notes the two strategies that deflect language from the personal. The first act uses "metalinguistics" where the three conversations continually revolve around "talk about talk" which displays "their calculated skill in avoiding meaning—[and] propels their communicative interaction forward" (34). The second act uses "metatheatrics" in which, for example, Levene acts out his sale to the Nyborgs, or Roma and Levene act out a charade to deflect Lingk from breaking the deal. In both cases the implication is that one moves faster, the quicker to escape definition. Power, however, is analyzed at the end of the play as Roma, Williamson, and then Baylen successively invoke the authority of "the patriarchal system" (52).

sGGR 40 —. "Men among the Ruins." *David Mamet's Glengarry Glen Ross: Text and Performance*. Ed. Leslie Kane. New York: Garland, 1996. 81-105.

Vorlicky approaches language through the semiotic examination of codes of masculinity. He is particularly good in his analysis of Roma's sales pitch, and how it manipulates codes forcing Lingk to acquiesce in order to be a man. Vorlicky's construction of masculinity is derived entirely from plays as the social constructions of reality. For example, asserting that after men "discuss their perceived lack of power" their talk will next turn to "the power of violence to effect change." And to prove it: "From Martin Flavin's *Amaco* to Edward Albee's *The Zoo Story*, Charles Fuller's *A Soldier's Story*, and OyamO's *Let Me Live*, male characters repeatedly resort to violence as a final solution" to their conflicts (88).

sGGR 41 Worster, David. "How to Do Things with Salesmen: David Mamet's Speech-Act Play." *Modern Drama* 37 (1994): 375-90. Rpt. in *David Mamet's Glengarry Glen Ross: Text and Performance*. Ed Leslie Kane. New York: Garland, 1996. 63-79.

Using Stanley Fish as a model for applying "How to Do Things With Austin and Searle," Worster argues that the salesmen claim power and authority through their use of words: commanding, demanding that others listen, and using language as seduction. In every instance the use of language takes control of the other. Yet ironically, the salesmen all fail in their attempts. Worster develops the idea of silence through several variations, however, and even argues that Aaronow is ironically the strongest character because of his command of silence.

See also the following scholarly articles covering multiple plays:

sMP 2 Andreach, Robert J. "Exemplary Selves in Hell." *Creating the Self in Contemporary American Theatre*.

sMP 7 Blumberg, Marcia. "Eloquent Stammering in the Fog: O'Neill's Heritage in Mamet."

sSPC 3 Bruster, Douglas. "David Mamet and Ben Jonson: City Comedy Past and Present."

sMP 13 Cohn, Ruby. "Phrasal Energies: Harold Pinter and David Mamet."

sMP 15 Demastes, William W. "David Mamet's Dis-Integrating Drama."

sMP 19 Geis, Deborah R. "David Mamet and the Metadramatic Tradition: Seeing 'the Trick from the Back."

sMP 20 Geis, Deborah R. "Theatre as 'House of Games': David Mamet's (Con) Artistry and the Monologic Voice."

sMP 21 Herman, William. "Theatrical Diversity from Chicago: David Mamet."

sMP 23 Hudgins, Christopher C. "Comedy and Humor in the Plays of David Mamet."

sMP 28 Kane, Leslie. "Time Passages."

sMP 36 McDonough, Carla J. "David Mamet: The Search for Masculine Space."

sMP 37 —. "Every Fear Hides a Wish: Unstable Masculinity in Mamet's Drama."

sMP 40 Price, Steven. "'Accursed Progenitor': Samuel Beckett, David Mamet, and the Problem of Influence."

BR 23 Sauer, Janice A. "Bibliography of Glengarry Glen Ross, 1983-1995."

sMP 49 Schvey, Henry I. "The Plays of David Mamet: Games of Manipulation and Power."

sMP 50 Smith, Susan Harris. "En-Gendering Violence: Twisting 'Privates' in the Public Eye."

sAB 19 Zeifman, Hersh. "Phallus in Wonderland: Machismo and Business in David Mamet's *American Buffalo* and *Glengarry Glen R oss*."

sMP 54 Zinman, Toby Silverman. "Jewish Aporia: The Rhythm of Talking in Mamet."

LAKEBOAT

Dedication: John Dillon and Larry Shue

Scene: 28 scenes in the engine room, galley, fantail, boat deck and rail of the boat,
  T. Harrison.

Characters: Pierman, age 30s or 40s; Dale, Ordinary Seaman, 20; Fireman, Engine,
  60s; Stan, Able-Bodied Seaman, deck, 40s; Joe, Able-Bodied Seaman, deck, 40 or
  50; Collins, Second Mate, 30s or 40s; Skippy, First Mate, late fifties; Fred, Able-
  Bodied Seaman, deck, 30s or 40s.

Editions:

  The Woods; Lakeboat; Edmond: Three Plays. New York: Grove Press, 1979.

  Lakeboat: A Play. New York: Grove Press, 1981.

  Lakeboat: A Play. New York: S. French, 1983.

  David Mamet Plays: 2. London: Methuen Drama, 1996.

  Lakeboat. Dir. Joe Mantegna. Oregon Trail Films, Ltd, 2000.

Plot Outline:

Twenty-eight scenes aboard a ship carrying steel on the Great Lakes, depicting life
among the eight sailors, one of whom is a college student to whom the others confide
their hopes, fears, dreams and stories. The student was hired as a cook to replace
another who disappeared from the ship in Chicago, and there is much speculation
about why he disappeared.

Production:

First staged at a Theatre Workshop, Marlboro College, Marlboro, Vermont in 1970.

pLB 1 A revised version opened on April 24, 1980 at the Court Street Theater,
  Milwaukee Repertory Theater, Milwaukee, Wisconsin.

  Director: John Dillon

Settings:	Laura Maurer
Lighting:	Rachel Budin
Costumes:	Colleen Muscha
Cast:	
Pierman:	Gregory Leach
Dale:	Thomas Hewitt
Fireman:	Paul Meacham
Stan:	Eugene J. Anthony
Joe:	Larry Shue
Collins:	John P. Connolly
Skippy:	Robert Clites
Fred:	Victor Raider-Wexler

Review:

rLB 1.1 Jaques, Damien. Rev. of *Lakeboat*. *Milwaukee Journal* May 2, 1980.

"About halfway through the play, Mamet seems to shift gears. The humour is left behind, and we get a serious look at Joe, a weary veteran seaman who struggles with the difficulty of expressing his frustrations and broken dreams. Joe is haltingly eloquent about his youthful hope of becoming a dancer, the functional beauty of a bridge, his self destructive impulse."

Production:

pLB 2 Long Wharf Theater's Stage Two, February, 1982.

Director:	John Dillon
Settings:	Laura Maurer
Lighting:	Jamie Gallagher
Costumes:	Bill Walker
Stage Manager:	Robin Kevrick
Cast:	
Pierman:	Ed O'Neill
Dale:	David Marshall Grant
Fireman:	Walter Atamaniuk
Stan:	Clarence Felder
Joe:	Larry Shue
Collins:	Ralph Byers
Skippy:	Dominic Chianese
Fred:	John Spencer

Review:

rLB 2.1 Christiansen, Richard. Rev. of *Lakeboat*. *Chicago Tribune* 5 Mar. 1982.

Positive review: "Alone and fearful and bored, the men come together in search of warmth and comfort, absurd and silly creatures of sensitivity and dignity. Their talk is ridiculous, hyperbolic, touching, fantastic."

rLB 2.2 Gussow, Mel. "*Lakeboat*, Mamet's First at Long Wharf." *New York Times* 17 Feb. 1982: C23. Rpt. in *Theatre on the Edge*. New York: Applause, 1998. 205-06.

Positive review: "Sailing through the season's slough is David Mamet's

Lakeboat, a small gem of a play at Long Wharf Theater's Stage Two. *Lakeboat* is Mr. Mamet's *Life on the Mississippi*—the artist as young river pilot, or, in Mr. Mamet's case, lakeboat steward. Through his eyes, we see a cross-section of flavorful characters, imparting lore, both landlocked and seaworthy. [. . .] Time stands still on the boat—a suitably seedy design by Laura Maurer—a fact that often catches the characters off guard. [. . .] Watching the play, one is reminded not only of *Life on the Mississippi* but also of *Mister Roberts*, as the craft plies its path 'from Tedium to Apathy.' But there is no war to look forward to, and no tyrannical captain to rebel against. *Lakeboat* is like life, slightly askew."

Production:

pLB 3 Tiffany Theater, Los Angeles opened February 24 and closed March 13, 1994.

Director:	Joe Mantegna
Set/Costumes:	John Paoletti / Jeff Leahy
Lighting:	Geoffrey Bushor
Cast:	
Pierman:	Ian Patrick Williams
Dale:	Tony Mamet
Fireman:	Vincent Guastaferro
Stan:	J. J. Johnston
Joe:	Ed O'Neill / Dan Lauria
Collins:	George Wendt
Skippy:	Ron Dean
Fred:	Jack Wallace

Reviews:

rLB 3.1 Breslauer, Jan. "'Lakeboat's Actors Sail a Taut Ship." *Los Angeles Times* 26 Feb. 1994: F1.

Positive review of the production, less so of the play which "is more a chain of monologues and dialogues than a play. It's a high-order actors' vehicle with no real dramatic arc and an arbitrary ending. It wouldn't resonate on as many levels as it does here without first-rate performers adding dimension to the characters."

rLB 3.2 Scaffidi, Richard. Rev. of *Lakeboat*. *Drama-Logue* 3 Mar. 1994: 26.

Positive review of both cast and play of laughs which "is not so much a whole play with a central conflict or particular climax as it is a 90-minute series of scenes peering in on a group of 'manlymen' who work aboard a grubby ore freighter on the Great Lakes. But what scenes they are! Each of the eight colorful characters has his choice moments, propelled by vintage Mamet dialogue—all those staccato repetitions and bursts of rhythmic expletives—that seems particularly at home in the play's macho maritime milieu. Mantegna has mustered a terrific cast (heavy on the Chicago connection) and further attuned them to the precise Mamet style, being notably successful at naturalizing the dialogue and mining the quirky humor. This show finds more laughs than any Mamet play we've seen."

Production:
pLB 4 Lyric Studio, London from February 5 until February 28, 1998.

Director:	Aaron Mullen
Set:	Melanie Allen
Lighting:	Amanda Garrett
Costumes:	Victoria Lancaster
Cast:	

Pierman:	James Terry
Dale:	Joe May
Stan:	Simon Harris
Joe:	Jim Dunk
Collins:	Chris Porter
Skippy:	Brian Greene
Fred	Jon Welch
Fireman:	Peter K. Clark

Overview:
British reviewers were unanimously favorable—even to their own surprise since this is Mamet's first play (though the 1980 revision was used). Interestingly, several critics even thought this play much better than more mature efforts—Spencer preferred it to *Old Neighborhood*, and Taylor suggested he should return to it from recent plays "too cerebrally conceived." All critics noticed the dialogue—they were rather taken by the blackout intercutting of short scenes and longer ones as a different kind of dramatic structural technique. Likening him often to O'Neill (Billington, Taylor, Morley, but "less sentimentally"—Nightingale), most recognized that stories were the way the men filled empty lives, as if with meaning.

Reviews:
r LB 4.1 Billington, Michael. "The Insight: The Drunken Sailors; It's a Man's Life in the Navy—at Least When Mamet's at the Helm." *Guardian* 7 Feb. 1998: 7. Rpt. in *Theatre Record*, 29 Jan.-11 Feb. 1998: 128-29.

Very positive review of the play of fear and fantasy: "What is David Mamet's secret? The simple answer is that he writes great dialogue: that he captures, in a manner rivalled only by Pinter, the rhythms of colloquial speech. But, for me, Mamet's real genius is his understanding of the fear, isolation and fantasy that hermetic male groups camouflage through language of bullish bravado. The point is confirmed by *Lakeboat*, an early work getting its European premiere. [. . .] The whole work is built on the notion of subtext, through-line and the developing arc of the narrative. Mamet's characters curse, brag, bad-mouth women and exhibit all kinds of male crudity, yet underneath Mamet is saying that they are lost souls reduced by circumstance to a life of hopeless fantasy."

r LB 4.2 Butler, Robert. "Unperformed, Unknown and Unbelievably Good." *Independent on Sunday* 8 Feb. 1998: 8. Rpt. in *Theatre Record*, 29 Jan.-11 Feb. 1998: 129-30.

Very positive review of the play's depiction of a group: "Well, if *Lakeboat* was really Mamet's latest—which for us in one way it is—this debut by a massively talented young writer would be on the short-list for best new play. [. . .] They are talkative and inarticulate. The rebarbative mix of advice, abuse, and homespun philosophy takes on sex, drink, wives, racing, dreams and whatever happened to a guy called Guigliani. [. . .] Unhampered by any overt moral or political purpose, this energetic, candid, funny and observant piece smacks of life in the raw."

r LB 4.3 Cavendish, Dominic. Rev. of *Lakeboat*. *Time Out* 11 Feb. 1998. Rpt. in *Theatre Record*, 29 Jan.-11 Feb. 1998: 130.

Positive review which realized this could have been "never a dull moment, a catalogue of grit, sweat and tears." Instead, however, Mamet "opts for the kind of ambiguities and boredom-bred jagged exchanges that have been such a distinguishing feature of his later work. [. . .] Aaron Mullen's slick, well-cast European premiere passes as quickly as a dream, but in that time we catch poignant glimpses of life's drifters clinging to the flotsam of necessary fiction."

r LB 4.4 Clapp, Susannah. "Mamet Wrote This as a Student. He Could Still Learn from It." *Observer* 8 Feb. 1998: 11. Rpt. in *Theatre Record*, 29 Jan.-11 Feb. 199: 129.

Positive review of the play's language and the production: "Unlike many neglected early works, it is terrific. [. . .] This is a rich work, less needlingly argued and less stylised than some of Mamet's more recent plays, and more buoyant: even the older Mamet could learn something from his younger self. It dramatises an interesting world—one which is seldom seen on the stage and which is strongly realised in Melanie Allen's busy, compact design of pipes and planks and rails and ladders and ropes. It has a striking structure: a series of short scenes, some consisting only of a feed and a punchline, some wistfully and inconclusively reflective, others skillfully building up to an explosive moment, and then skillfully shrugging off the consequences."

r LB 4.5 Foss, Roger. Rev. of *Lakeboat*. *What's On* 11 Feb. 1998. Rpt. in *Theatre Record*, 29 Jan.-11 Feb. 1998: 129.

Extremely positive review of play and this production: "The production also marks director Aaron Mullen's third Mamet premier, and it is perhaps no wonder that the playwright has given him preference over the big boys at the National. In a series of brilliantly well-paced snapshot scenes, some clipped down to a single line, and one sexually charged below-decks scene consisting almost entirely of a breathtaking Pinteresque pause, Mullen is always true to the moody machismo of Mamet's writing as well as plumbing depths of meaning beneath these trapped characters' amazing swear word raps and cocky tale-telling. His whole cast gets right under the greasy skins of the crew. [. . .] Jim Dunk excels as the bear-like Joe confiding to Dale (Joe May) that he once dreamed of becoming a ballet dancer. Suddenly, there is a tenderness beneath the tough male exteriors that makes this play a real voyage of discovery."

r LB 4.6 Hewison, Robert. Rev. of *Lakeboat*. *Sunday Times* [London] 15 Feb. 1998. Rpt. in *Theatre Record*, 29 Jan.-11 Feb. 1998: 130.

Positive review of the play as poetic: "The piece is short, elliptical and closely observes the banalities of masculine conversation, giving them, like the voyage itself, their own kind of poetic significance."

r LB 4.7 Morley, Sheridan. Rev. of *Lakeboat. Spectator* 14 Feb. 1998. Rpt. in *Theatre Record*, 29 Jan.-11 Feb. 1998: 128.

Positive review of the depiction of lost lives: "Like another great American dramatist, Eugene O'Neill, who also set his early plays on the boats he then knew best, Mamet finds in his crew a whole series of richly detailed character portraits. [. . .] There's no real plot here, just eight men in conversations and monologues trying to make some kind of sense out of their lost opportunities, friendships, and in some cases lives. All of them [. . .] could have been contenders but by now they have forgotten quite what the contest was, or just how they were supposed to go about winning it. These men are every bit as wasted as the salesmen of *Glengarry Glen Ross*, only here there is no real competition, just a bleak sense of loss."

r LB 4.8 Nathan, David. Rev. of *Lakeboat. Jewish Chronicle* 13 Feb. 1998. Rpt. in *Theatre Record*, 29 Jan.-11 Feb. 1998: 130-31.

Very positive review of the play as touching and funny: "They talk to keep a corrosive sense of wasted lives at bay and to bolster their fragile egos and the biggest of them talks about his dream of being a ballet dancer so that he could catch graceful ballerinas in flight. And it is funny, but infinitely touching. [. . . It] shows a writer who infallibly catches not just the surface coarseness of men talking dirty but the underlying hunger for respect, even admiration."

r LB 4.9 Nightingale, Benedict. "Mamet's Voyage of Truth." *Times* [London] 9 Feb. 1998. Rpt. in *Theatre Record*, 29 Jan.-11 Feb. 1998: 130.

Positive view of an unsentimental depiction: "Like O'Neill, who spent much of his youth working on ships, Mamet uses these men's journey to suggest their rootlessness, aimlessness and vulnerability; but he does so less sentimentally, more harshly. Back home they are losers but cannot admit it; on the lake a day may consist of staring for eight hours at a pressure gauge. So they evade, fib, strike fake-powerful attitudes, incoherently philosophise, boast about drink and women, tell tall stories, create legends. [. . .] There and elsewhere, Mamet and a fine cast leave you feeling they have discovered dialogue, not invented it."

r LB 4.10 Spencer, Charles. "A Mean Mamet." *Daily Telegraph* 9 Feb. 1998: 19. Rpt. in *Theatre Record*, 29 Jan.-11 Feb. 1998: 130.

Positive review of the play as a "poetic" depiction with language "brutal, demotic, yet somehow transforming inarticulate speech into something rich, true, even poetic. The other major element is Mamet's familiar obsession—part attraction, part revulsion—with an unrepentantly masculine, macho world. [. . .] There's no real plot, just a series of often fragmentary dialogues and monologues which lay bare character with rare precision. [. . .] Mamet's point is that men need to make myths to ease hard and monotonous lives."

r LB 4.11 Taylor, Paul. "Black to the Future." *Independent* 9 Feb. 1998: 6. Rpt. in
Theatre Record, 29 Jan.-11 Feb. 1998: 129.

Positive review of the play as one of Mamet's best: "*Lakeboat* [. . .] is a
major event, period. It's one of the funniest, gutsiest, saddest, subtlest, and
most gratefully rhythmic works ever written by Chicago's number one
playwright. And Aaron Mullen's production gave it an expertly nuanced
knockout immediacy. [. . .] On Melanie Allen's strong two-tier set of girders,
scaffolding and a scrim-like bridge, the play proceeds as a series of snapshots
and blackguard sketches."

Scholarly:

sLB 1 Bigsby, C. W. E. "Story and Anti-Story" *David Mamet*. Contemporary Writers.
London: Methuen, 1985. 22-26.

Bigsby recognizes the excellence of the play as the repair of fragmented
lives with stories and theatricalizing: "Yet even in this early work his central
concerns are apparent: the sense of fiction as evasion and fiction as truth, a
social world deprived of transcendence, an absurdity to be held at bay by the
imagination or succumbed to in a collapse of will on the private and public
levels. The very structure of *Lakeboat* implies a discontinuity which becomes a
basic characteristic of the figures he creates, a fragmentation which is presented
as social fact (a sense of alienation bred out of American myths of competitive
capitalism), psychological reality (men and women divorced equally from one
another and their own sexuality) and historical truth (they are cut off from a
sense of the past). The gap between language and experience suggests a
discrepancy which is the source of their pain, and this they attempt to bridge by
theatricalizing their world, by redirecting their energy into pure invention."

sLB 2 Caltabiano, Frank P. Rev. of *Lakeboat. World Literature Today* 56.3 (1982): 518.

This is a review of the published text which dismisses Mamet as a favorite
of the "Eastern and Midwestern Cities" [the author is from Santa Clara].
Condescendingly, he sees potential for the play to be staged as "a mildly entertaining
evening by a group of interesting actors." He faults the work because Mamet "has no
real vision for raising the sights or bettering the plight of the ordinary guy caught in
the wake of the dissolving American dream." Instead, "Mamet chooses merely to
record their present state in much the same way that television sitcoms do."

sLB 3 Hinden, Michael. "'Intimate Voices': *Lakeboat* and Mamet's Quest for Community."
David Mamet: A Casebook. Ed. Leslie Kane. New York: Garland, 1992. 33-48.

Hinden uses Turner to define *communitas*, the desire for community. He
cites Mamet on Chekhov that "no one in that play, he insists, really cares about
the orchard" (34). In this play, what the characters talk about is not what they
desire: "Mamet's characters care less about sexual conquest and still less about
business (the topics that preoccupy them) than they do about loneliness and their

failure to construct a satisfying context for emotional security" (34). Hinden argues for community as what they desire: "I do not wish to attribute a Marxist message to the play [. . .]. But Mamet interprets the quarrel for them articulating a vision of communal identity that the characters of *Lakeboat* struggle to perceive" (45).

See also the following scholarly articles covering multiple plays:

sMP 20 Geis, Deborah R. "Theatre as 'House of Games': David Mamet's (Con) Artistry and the Monologic Voice."

sMP 25 Jacobs, Dorothy H. "Working Worlds in David Mamet's Dramas."

sMP 36 McDonough, Carla J. "David Mamet: The Search for Masculine Space."

sMP 54 Zinman, Toby Silverman. "Jewish Aporia: The Rhythm of Talking in Mamet."

A LIFE IN THE THEATRE

Dedication: Gregory Mosher
Scene: Various spots around a theater
Characters: Robert, an older actor and John, a younger actor
Editions:

A Life in the Theatre: A Play. New York: S. French, 1975.

A Life in the Theatre: A Play. New York: Grove Press, 1977.

A Life in the Theatre. Great Performances, PBS, June, 1979. [videotape]

A Life in the Theatre. London: Methuen Drama, 1989.

A Life in the Theatre. Dir. Gregory Mosher. TNT television. 9 Oct. 1993.
[videotape]

David Mamet Plays: 2. London: Methuen Drama, 1996.

Plot Outline:

Older, experienced actor Robert, and young rising actor, John are depicted in twenty-six scenes of repertory. The first takes place after a performance, with the text being an analysis of the audience and performance, and the subtext, Robert's angling for an invitation to dinner. References are to the theatre, but there is usually a second level of meaning—the relationship between the would-be mentor and tutor ("We are the explorers of the soul"). As John's star rises, however, he has less need for Robert. Six scenes are of old clichéd plays/films—hospital, war, lawyer's office, lifeboat, at tea, storming barricades. In the finale, John goes out with friends without inviting Robert who is left alone on stage, caught by John making up a thank-you speech to an imagined audience—and asked to leave so the theatre can be closed for the night.

Production
pLITT 1 Premiered at the Goodman Theater, Chicago, a Stage 2 series production,
   on February 3, 1977.

Director:	Gregory Mosher
Designer:	Michael Merritt
Costumes:	Marsha Kowal
Lighting:	Robert Christen
Music:	Stuart Klawans
Cast:	
John:	Joe Mantegna
Robert:	Mike Nussbaum

Overview:
In this original production, the onstage scenes were played to an invisible audience upstage—and there was an upstage curtain that would open when the actors
were playing to them. The remainder of the scenes, off-stage, were played facing
front.

Reviewers tended to polarize the play and the performances. Some liked the
view of actors seen backstage—egos and bitchiness (Gussow, O'Connor, and
Winer). Some found Mamet's script too harsh in its view of the actor/characters
(Soukup, Winer). Cassidy, Christiansen, Dreyer and Syse thought the play lacking because the on-stage scenes were disconnected from the off-stage ones. But
Christiansen saw two transcendent moments in which writing, performance, and
production fused together.

Reviews:
rLITT 1.1 Cassidy, Claudia. *WFMT Radio* 6 Feb. 1977. [Transcript]
   Positive review though the "play is a sketch full of holes." [. . .] The
   two performances are equal—Mike Nussbaum's self-contained despair as
   the actor soon to lose even his not very high shelf of security—not very
   high, but all he has; Joe Mantegna's quiet move from the amiable young
   disciple who might have stepped from a Renaissance canvas to one sensing
   his potential strength. They are amusing men full of backstage bitchery, but
   they are more."

rLITT 1.2 Christiansen, Richard. "Mamet's Touching Fable *A Life in the Theater*."
   Chicago Daily News 4 Feb. 1977.
   Christiansen noted this play is "a relatively early Mamet work, brought
   out of the trunk and polished up." As a result the writing "seems abrupt and
   mannered" and the on-stage scenes "reach too hard for laughs." However:
   "One scene brilliantly plays John's on-stage presence against Robert's off-
   stage voice, and the other focuses on Robert alone, standing in front of a
   work light and rehearsing a thank-you speech for an audience's tribute that
   we know will never come his way."

rLITT 1.3 Dreyer, Bruce. Rev. of *A Life in the Theatre*. *WNUR Radio* 8 Feb. 1977.
   Mixed review which saw "superlative staging" but "doesn't seem to

have very much to say here. [. . .] The play manages to be amusing, funny, occasionally (but not excessively) sentimental, but as far as I could see, aimless."

rLITT 1.4 Gussow, Mel. "Mamet Wins with 'Life in Theater.'" *New York Times* 5 Feb. 1977: 22.

Gussow thought both writing and performance "effortless": "Backstage, the actors are self-indulgent and super critical. Blame is always placed on other actors, except when it is leveled against the critics, the ones who praise bad performances, then turn around and pan 'a split-second of godliness.' Egos are transcendent—and so is the hilarity. [. . .] Pretending to be in performance, the actors turn their backs to us and face an imaginary audience upstage, behind footlights. For us, it is a little like being in the wings watching a magic show in which all the tricks fail."

rLITT 1.5 O'Connor, Sean. Rev. of *A Life in the Theatre. Gay Life* 18 Feb. 1977: 9.

Positive review of "a Pinteresque study of a prissy old actor and a brittle younger actor, their dependencies on and jealousies of one another. Mamet's strength is his ear for dialogue and he has listened to actors. The speech here is formal, pompous, considerably bitchy. [. . .] Mantegna and Nussbaum play the subtext for all its worth, giving the play a sense of continuity it might otherwise lack."

rLITT 1.6 Soukup, Alan. "No Second Banana at Stage 2." *DuPage Progress* 15 Feb. 1977: 15.

Very positive review of "a triumph of production and acting power over material." Soukup saw all the compassion coming from the actors, while the play is too much like *American Buffalo* in which "each is isolated by his inability to communicate except in clichés and obscenities (how sad)."

rLITT 1.7 Syse, Glenna. "Mamet Brings Backstage View Up Front, But ... Only for Theater." *Chicago Sun-Times* 4 Feb. 1977.

Unimpressed review which noted that: "It is simply a backstage view, sure to be amusing and perceptive to those who work in and around the theater. But for universal appeal it will be too much of a trade-script." But Syse had no trouble grasping the central premise: "At first the younger actor is puzzled by and deferential to his older colleague whose insecurity is masked by a condescending authority and a flowery pretentious phrase. By play's end, the tables are turned."

rLITT 1. 8 Winer, Linda. "Mamet Puts Life in Theater While He's Taking It Apart." *Chicago Tribune* 4 Feb. 1977.

Positive review—with reservations: "Mamet is ambiguous about his feelings toward the characters, a lack of commitment toward their growth and decay which leaves me wondering whether he cares about them at all. There is snideness in the sympathy that sometimes still chooses the clever words over clear intention." Yet Winer appreciated that "the men expose the paranoia of public exposure and the neurotic self-analysis that threaten people who put their egos on the public line."

Production:
pLITT 2 The first New York performance opened at the Theatre de Lys, Greenwich Village, New York on October 20, 1977 and closed July 9, 1978 for 288 performances.

Director:	Gerald Gutierrez
Set:	John Lee Beatty
Costumes:	John David Ridge
Lighting:	Pat Collins
Music:	Robert Waldman
Cast:	
Robert:	Ellis Rabb
John:	Peter Evans
Stage Manager:	Benjamin Hendrickson

Overview:
Gerald Rabkin noticed Mamet "is essentially unconcerned with their deeper motivations, their sexual preferences, their life outside the theater." This didn't stop most critics from looking for psychological depth. Simon lamented, "Neither actor is ever allowed to acquire a full personality" and wondered if Rabb is "meant to be a fruity old ham or a hammy old fruit." Most critics, however, were more concerned with whether this "love letter to the theatre" (Oliver; Beaufort, Gottfried, Lamb, Madd, Reed, Watt), was too "sentimental" (Kissel) or "too close to shoptalk" (Kalem; Jenner, Kerr, Novick). The division seemed to be between those who wanted psychology and sex lives as the focus, and those who accepted Mamet's innovative technique of blackouts, short scenes and long ones, which the audience itself must connect—all of the scenes in the workplace rather than the home, heralding a different approach to dramaturgy.

Reviews:
rLITT 2.1 Beaufort, John. Rev. of *A Life in the Theater. Christian Science Monitor* 28 Oct. 1977: 27.
> Positive review of the staging and play as: "theater to the life—a beguiling entertainment superbly acted and beautifully staged. The new comic slice of make-believe at the de Lys Theater begins and ends on a bare stage whose gloom is relieved only by the grudging beam of a work light."

rLITT 2.2 Clurman, Harold. Rev. of *A Life in the Theatre. Nation* 12 Nov. 1977: 504-06.
> Negative review of the play as inside joke: "I disliked *A Life*. [. . .] Very little of this has to do with the pain, the pleasure, the glamour, the fun, or follies of theatrical life. It is all an inside joke of which the real absurdity of the sophomoric response it has produced. But that is not Mamet's fault."

rLITT 2.3 Duberman, Martin. "The Great Gray Way." *Harper's* May 1978: 79+.
Mildly negative review of the play as a trifle: "At its best, *Life* is a mildly amusing diversion; at its more frequent worst, it is a tedious, offensively banal caricature of what daily life in the theatre is actually like."

rLITT 2.4 Gottfried, Martin. "Life in the Theater Surges with Love." *New York Post* 21 Oct. 1977: 42.
Positive review of the play as acted: "Evans sometimes seems uncertain about how to play the young man—as if the script says calculating but he reads it as human. He is generally excellent and achieves the fine edge of the hustler. His development of a staginess like Rabb's character is cannily graduated. The ambition behind his friendliness, his willingness to abandon the frail are the play's rough theme. [. . .] Despite Mamet's intentions, 'A Life in the Theater' overflows with good feeling and humanism. It confirms his profound abilities. It is surely the warmest (and often the funniest) play in town."

rLITT 2.5 Gussow, Mel. "Illusion within an Illusion." *New York Times* 21 Oct. 1977: C1. Rpt. in *Theatre on the Edge.* New York: Applause, 1998. 201-02.
Positive review of an improved production: "Since the Chicago premiere, Mr. Mamet has slightly expanded his play—as it now runs 90 minutes— and added a third, silent character, who changes the scenery. The original production had a free-flowing spontaneity and there was a balance between the performers, who performed as if it were Story Theater. Mr. Gutierrez's staging is more structured and the play is now more of a performance piece. Ellis Rabb wears his role as if it were a tailor-made theatrical cape of many colors. [. . .] Another change—and improvement—from Chicago to New York is John Lee Beatty's ingenious set. [. . .] The actors play to that imaginary audience, while we, behind the scenes, see and hear the artifice— the asides, whispers and blunders. In a poignant pair of scenes, each acts to an empty house and the other, not so silently, watches. We eavesdrop on the eavesdroppers—a triple Pirandello for this acrobatic playwright."

rLITT 2.6 Hughes, Catharine. "Great Expectations." *America* 10 Dec. 1977: 423.
Mildly positive review: "David Mamet's *A Life in the Theatre*, off-Broadway, isn't about to set the heart beating with hope for the American theatre, but it makes for a generally entertaining evening and confirms Mamet's reputation as a young writer of substantial promise."

rLITT 2.7 Kalem, T. E. "Curtain Call: *A Life in the Theatre.*" *Time* 31 Oct 1977: 94. Rpt. in *New York Theatre Critics' Review,* 144.
Praised the play because of its use of language: "The constant that knits them together is Mamet's ear, which is a precision instrument. He recognizes the shaping force of language—how it is used as a weapon or a shield depending on what a character wishes to convey or conceal. [. . .] Rabb can tango with words and he is a sly devil at milking an audience dry of laughter.

Peter Evans' John rolls his lines like dice in a crap game he dare not lose. For Mamet, this play is a five-finger exercise, but so nimble that he often seem to be using ten."

rLITT 2.8 Kerr, Walter. Rev. of *A Life in the Theater. New York Times* 30 Oct. 1977: D5.

Kerr viewed the play as only mildly amusing: "Rabb, his mouth as severely drawn as Cotton Mather's is amusing as he pursues neophyte Peter Evans's suggestion that he has let one of his scenes go brittle. 'Overly brittle?' Mr. Rabb wants to know. 'The whole scene?' But that's closer to target than the author generally gets during his basically sentimental, sometimes burlesque evening."

rLITT 2.9 Kissel, Howard. Rev. of *A Life in the Theatre. Women's Wear Daily* 24 Oct. 1977: 10. Rpt. in *New York Theater Critics' Review*: 336.

Positive view of the play for its humor and innovative staging: "These snippets of plays—like a hilariously wispy bit of pseudo-Chekhov—are performed with the actors' back to us. They play to an empty audience indicated by John Lee Beatty's witty set, which allows us to peer through the back of the scenery into the spotlights and red exit signs the actors face. The older actor is an amalgam of petty vanities and endearing affectations, the kind of part actors dream of playing but can easily overdo."

rLITT 2.10 Kroll, Jack. "The Muzak Man." *Newsweek* 28 Feb. 1977: 79.

Positive view of the play's balance: "This touching, pointedly ironic little play says a lot about the relationship between reality and theatre. [. . .] Mamet's ear is tuned to an American frequency, transmitting the calls for help, at once funny and frightening, which much of our speech barely disguises behind the bravado."

rLITT 2.11 Madd. Rev. of *A Life in the Theatre. Variety* 16 Nov. 1977: 92.

Positive view of the play as balancing humor and sentiment: *"A Life in the Theatre*, the brilliant David Mamet play which should enjoy a long life at the Theatre de Lys, does indeed provide devastating looks at backstage actor traumas. But it does so in such an engagingly funny and poignant way, that more universal human truths are strengthened rather than overshadowed in trivia."

rLITT 2.12 Novick, Julius. Rev. of *A Life in the Theatre. Village Voice* 31 Oct. 1977: 83.

Mildly negative view of the play as having scenes that are too short to develop: "Scenes keep ending before anything quite happens. Robert is clearly (sometimes repetitively) trying to get into John's life and affections, as a father figure and perhaps also as a homosexual lover. Robert is waspish, vain, touchy, insecure, sentimental, plangently sad about the passage of time [. . . and] he fits right into the old queen stereotype, though he never explicitly declares himself. But John is opaque. We don't see how he gets from expressions of boyish admiration to 'Will you please shut up.' The relationship doesn't develop; it just takes random jumps. And so the play doesn't seem to be going anywhere."

rLITT 2.13 Oliver, Edith. "Actor Variations." *New Yorker* 31 Oct. 1977: 115-16.
    Overall a positive review: "As Robert, Mr. Rabb is often funny, and he never misses a point, comic or pathetic, but his portrayal of this shrewdly observed hokey actor is too hokey and flamboyant. At any rate, I never entirely believed in him, being unable to lose him in the character or to separate his own stylistic flourishes from the dramatist's. As John, Mr. Evans does far more than just respond; bit by bit. He builds a credible and solid characterization of an interesting, confident young actor who is on his way. [. . .] Mr. Mamet has written—in gentle ridicule; in jokes, broad and tiny; and in comedy, high and low—a love letter to the theatre. It is quite a feat, and he has pulled it off."

rLITT 2.14 Rabkin, Gerald. "In Theater as in Life." *Soho Weekly News* 27 Oct. 1977: 53.
    Positive review of the play which noted little depth of character: "For this reason [a theme of evanescence in the theatre], his characters are shadowy psychologically; Mamet is concerned with the personal relationship of the actors John and Robert only insofar as it elucidates their professional relationship. He is essentially unconcerned with their deeper motivations, their sexual preferences, their life outside the theater. He focuses instead on the inevitable fact that one generation must transfer artistic authority to its successor."

rLITT 2.15 Reed, Rex. "Couple of Real Winners." *Daily News* [New York] 25 Oct. 1977: 72.
    Positive review of the play as revealing life itself: "Ellis Rabb is magnificent as the older actor, adding a soupçon of Barrymore and a pinch of Scaramouche to his grandiose movements. [. . .] What sad and wasted lives, we think, but 'A Life in the Theatre' shows with dignity, humor and passion why they can't do anything or be anything else. Actors are a breed apart and this play shows why they keep dancing on the lip of that volcano so recklessly, making life richer for the rest of us."

rLITT 2.16 Simon, John. Rev. of *A Life in the Theatre. New York* 7 Nov. 1977: 75-76.
    Negative review of the play as offering undeveloped characters: "Neither actor is ever allowed to acquire a full personality, a life beyond that of lines in a graph, or mannequins and mouthpieces for Mamet's jokey didacticism. [. . .] Ellis Rabb plays Robert well if he is meant to be a fruity old ham or a hammy old fruit, and Peter Evans is a good John if he is supposed to be amorphous under his ambitiousness—matters the author might have made clearer."

rLITT 2.17 —. Rev. of *Life in the Theatre. Hudson Review* 31.1 (1978): 154-55.
Mildly negative review of the play as caricature without definite target:
"But, ultimately, two problems weigh down *A Life in the Theater*. One is
that these are all anecdotes, quips, rivalries that can be hung on any theatrical
stick figures, which is, in fact, what John and Robert are. Under the all too
typical mockery, there are no human beings. True, this is intended as
caricature, but even caricatures are first of somebody specific. [. . .] Secondly,
I get tired of Mamet's eternal duologues. However many characters there
may be in a Mamet play (and there never seem to be more than four), just
about every scene is a twosome."

rLITT 2.18 Speck, Gregory. Rev. of *A Life in the Theatre. Show Business* 3 Nov.
1977: 22.
Negative review of the play because its scenes were drawn from movies:
"[. . .] with Mamet also, most of the visual and verbal punchlines are drawn
from old movies, or at least they give that impression. The moments he has
depicted are so stereotypical that they hardly seem authentic, and thus he
has defeated his own purpose, of allying himself still more closely with his
chosen art form."

rLITT 2.19 Stasio, Marilyn. Rev. of *A Life in the Theatre. Cue* 12-25 Nov. 1977:
22.
Extremely positive review of the play for humor: "In this treacherously
witty backstage comedy, the language is physical as well as verbal, as we
follow the careers of the two actors in what must be the doggiest repertory
company in the country. In a dream of a performance, Ellis Rabb glows in
the role of a veteran ham with impeccable diction and a monumental ego."

rLITT 2.20 Watt, Douglas. "A Comic Masterpiece by Mamet." *Daily News* [New
York] 21 Oct. 1977: 5.
Mildly positive review of the play as balanced: "The fact that all these
scenes are for two men only is a curiosity I don't feel is worth investigating.
The talk, by the way, is with the exception of a couple of usages, nothing
like the rough exchanges in the author's previous work. [. . .] The obviousness
of Mamet's theme, the concept of theater as life and life as theater, and the
danger of sentimentality are countered by the piece's humor."

Production:
pLITT 3 The Theatre de Lys stage production [pLITT 2] was videotaped for PBS
Great Performances, WNET 13 on October 3, 1979. [90 minute videotape
in the TOFT Collection of the New York Public Library]

Review:
rLITT 3.1 O'Connor, John J. "TV: Mamet's 'A Life in the Theater." *New York
Times* 3 Oct. 1979: C27.

Positive review which immediately recognized the reversal as Robert opens drinking champagne, and John "has to make do with a domestic jug wine in a paper cup." Slowly, "Robert begins to forget his lines, finds himself growing more dependent on John. The imposing facade begins to show unsettling cracks." Rabb's voice is likened to William F. Buckley, Jr. and "his gestures, his projection are marvelously ridiculous and irresistible." Locations for taping were in San Francisco.

rLITT 3.2 Rev. of *Life in the Theatre*. *Theatre News*, 11 (1979): 18-19.
Positive review: "As in the best of comedies, David Mamet has carefully, seemingly effortlessly drawn in poignancy as well. Slowly, the two men reverse their roles. Imperceptible at first, the 're-casting' grows clear; it is now Robert who needs John. Yet John has not taken life from Robert. He simply, as all good actors do, 'played with it, and made it his own.'"

Production:
pLITT 4 Open Space Theatre, London, July 18, 1979.

Director:	Alan Pearlman
Set:	Robert Dein
Lighting:	Francis Reid
Music:	Robert Waldman
Cast:	
Robert:	Freddie Jones
John:	Patrick Ryecart

Reviews:
rLITT 4.1 Coveney, Michael. Rev. of *A Life in the Theatre*. *Financial Times* 19 July 1979.
Positive review of the play, but, negative of the production: "I suspect that, played less portentously and a good deal faster, this could emerge as a very funny comedy." In the event, however, it wasn't. "The sketches themselves are hilarious. [. . .] Because Mr. Pearlman's production is so deliberate, you keep waiting for an ideological crutch that never comes. The backstage sketches are not capable of bearing the weight thrust upon them, and the play ends up punctuating blackouts and music rather than vice-versa."

rLITT 4.2 Ludlow, Colin. Rev. of *A Life in the Theatre*. *Plays and Players* Aug. 1979: 25+.
Rather positive review of Jones who captured: "the pathos of the older man with admirable control, never allowing his performance to verge into cheap sentimentality. There is great dignity not only in his portrayal of the character's pomposity and affectation, but also in the way he handles Robert's increasingly agonised awareness of his own failure and self-delusion. [. . .] The play is not an explosive piece of theatre, [. . .] its contained emotion and understated substance come as a welcome and refreshing change."

Production:
pLITT 5 Theatre Royal, Haymarket, London on October 31, 1989
   Director: Bill Bryden
     Set: Hayden Griffin
   Costumes: Adrian Gwillym
   Lighting: Rory Dempster
     Cast:
       John: Samuel West
      Robert: Denholm Elliot

Overview

Mamet revised the play slightly. Spencer noted that Mamet was "present at re-hearsals," and "extra scenes have been added, a few Americanisms that appear in the published text have been removed, and Mamet has now proved himself to be as effective a writer of English dialogue as he is of tough Chicagoese."

Critics were divided on the play, with negative reviews predominant, but all were positive about the production and Elliot's performance, especially when he satirized Gielgud and Coward. But the response reflected what Osborne thought was a division in the play between the satire of the old world of repertory, and the "tragic" drama that Spencer saw. Morley and Coveney loved the evocation of the old theatrical world; Billington alone thought the dramatic construction excellent. Most of the negative reviews thought it a plotless and pointless piece (especially Edwards and Nathan).

Reviews:

rLITT 5.1 Billington, Michael. Rev. of *A Life in the Theatre. Guardian* 2 Nov. 1989. Rpt. in *London Theatre Record*. 22 Oct.-4 Nov. 1989: 1491-92.
  A positive review: "a satiric valentine to a medium Mamet palpably loves." In the first scene: "On the surface, it is a nervous backstage encounter in which Robert is seeking reassurance that his performance went well: underneath it is about a lonely old actor's desire to be asked out to eat. Initially, John alone is 'famished'; at the end Robert echoes the word, signifying his grateful acceptance by the younger actor."

rLITT 5.2 Coveney, Michael. Rev. of *A Life in the Theatre. Financial Times* 1 Nov. 1989. Rpt. in *London Theatre Record*. 22 Oct.-4 Nov. 1989:1490.
  Positive review: "Elliott, who also has a field day as a Gielgud clone in a bath chair and funny hat, seething with wrinkle-nosed tetchiness. While avoiding over-the-top old-laddie-ness, this really wonderful actor, returning in triumph to the boards, conjures a vanished world of superstition, ephemeral reality, and regret."

rLITT 5.3 Edwards, Christopher. Rev. of *A Life in the Theatre. Spectator* 11 Nov. 1989. Rpt. in *London Theatre Record*. 22 Oct.-4 Nov. 1989:1491.
  Rather negative review by a critic who values Mamet: "'A Life in the Theatre' is essentially a series of sketches that become limper and limper as the evening wears on. Any two or three put together would make a nice

playlet. But strung together as they are here, you are struck more by their slightness than by any sense of dramatic shape. Only Denholm Elliot's performance keeps you from complete exasperation. Robert the actor is a wooden old ham, but Elliot manages to amuse us with this bad acting while, at the same time, giving a delicate study of disintegrating confidence. The desolation of the older man, his sense of the importance of his calling and his knowledge that he is being pushed to one side are memorably caught."

rLITT 5.4 Hassell, Graham. Rev. of *A Life in the Theatre*. *What's On* 8 Nov. 1989. Rpt. in *London Theatre Record*. 22 Oct.-4 Nov. 1989:1493.

A negative review: "For the most part a minimal script leaves the players to wrinkle out rounded personalities with nuance and gesture, which they do. Robert displays frustration-going-on-bitchiness hand waving agreement with John's assessment of an antagonistic actress colleague until hearing the contention that she trades on her beauty. He freezes, then explodes with rapturous aghast—'What beauty!'"

rLITT 5.5 Hiley, Jim. Rev. of *A Life in the Theatre*. *Listener* 16 Nov. 1989. Rpt. in *London Theatre Record*. 22 Oct.-4 Nov. 1989: 1488.

Positive view of the production, but not of the play: "Bill Bryden directs smoothly and designer Hayden Griffin conjures up some effective behind the scenes atmospherics. Elliot is in great form, waspish and wizened by turns, and Samuel West cleverly combines insouciance with gangling solemnity. But neither actor can conceal the dramatist's soft heart and unambitious ideas."

rLITT 5.6 Kennedy, Douglas. Rev. of *A Life in the Theatre*. *New Statesman & Society* 8 Dec. 1989. Rpt. in *London Theatre Record*. 19 Nov.-2 Dec. 1989:1657.

Mildly negative review: "It has its moments; especially in its spot-on observations of backstage paranoia—but it's ultimately too lightweight to be anything more than a series of interlinking sketches which don't amount to much."

rLITT 5.7 Morley, Sheridan. Rev. of *A Life in the Theatre*. *Herald Tribune* 8 Nov. 1989. Rpt. in *London Theatre Record*. 22 Oct.-4 Nov. 1989: 1492.

A positive review of: "the wonderful mix of sentimental love and cynical loathing that Mamet lavishes on his brief two-man play. [. . .] Denholm Elliot gives one of the finest performances of his career as the hammy old thespian facing competition from the young man (Samuel West, also in fine form) who has come to share his dressing-room and challenge his most basic assumptions about the greasepaint trade before effortlessly overtaking him on the road to Hollywood film fame."

rLITT 5.8 Nathan, David. Rev. of *A Life in the Theatre*. *Jewish Chronicle* 10 Nov.
1989. Rpt. in *London Theatre Record*. 22 Oct.-4 Nov. 1989: 1488.
    Negative review: "Of course it is funny, and the performances are fine
and Bill Bryden's direction is sharp, but, far from exploring all the paradoxes
of the theatre, where to act is to pretend to take action and where truth is
sometimes found by exploring fiction what we get are bad actors in snippets
from unlikely and awful plays to the cheers of an unseen and undiscerning
audience on the other side of the back curtain."

rLITT 5.9 Osborne, Charles. Rev. of *A Life in the Theatre*. *Daily Telegraph* 2
Nov. 1989. Rpt. in *London Theatre Record*. 22 Oct.-4 Nov. 1989: 1490-91.
    Positive review which noted it was not one play, but two—one is the
backstage satire, the other drama of character: "Frail egos hide behind
assertiveness, advice is sought only to be resented, and the relationship
between old Robert and young John moves from wariness to casual affection
to envy and occasional bursts of solidarity."

rLITT 5.10 Paton, Maureen. Rev. of *A Life in the Theatre*. *Daily Express* 1 Nov.
1989. Rpt. in *London Theatre Record*. 22 Oct.-4 Nov. 1989: 1490.
    Negative review: "Mamet's Pinteresque exercise lets the silences speak
louder than words to reveal the inadequacies underneath. The problem is
that you need a plot rich in incident to justify a play concerned with type
rather than character. Robert's failure to make contact in conversational
gambits that become soliloquies results in a series of anti-climaxes that are
death to any drama."

rLITT 5.11 Ratcliffe, Michael. Rev. of *A Life in the Theatre*. *Observer* 5 Nov.
1989. Rpt. in *London Theatre Record*. 22 Oct.-4 Nov. 1989: 1489.
    A somewhat negative review: "A slight, funny discursive but fragile
two-hander, its carefully fractured rhythms and bewilderingly
inconsequential narrative are spun even thinner by the decision to interrupt
them with a jolly old West End interval half-way through."

rLITT 5.12 Shulman, Milton. Rev. of *A Life in the Theatre*. *Evening Standard* 1
Nov. 1989. Rpt. in *London Theatre Record*. 22 Oct.-4 Nov. 1989: 1487.
    Rather negative review which found the play too much an in-joke: "You
have therefore been warned. In this affectionate tribute to the conversation
of theatrical digs you are unlikely to find anything new. [. . .] Elliott registers
a kaleidoscope of emotions as the florid heights of stage fantasy have to
give way to the mundane resentments of reality."

rLITT 5.13 Spencer, Charles. Rev. of *A Life in the Theatre*. *Sunday Telegraph* 5
Nov. 1989. Rpt. in *London Theatre Record*. 22 Oct.-4 Nov. 1989: 1487-88.
    Very positive review which saw the reversal as one in which: "a figure
of fun has become a character of tragic dimensions."

rLITT 5.14 Taylor, Paul. Rev. of *A Life in the Theatre*. *Independent* 2 Nov. 1989.
Rpt. in *London Theatre Record*. 22 Oct.-4 Nov. 1989: 1493.

Mixed review, shaded to the negative: "As John becomes more successful, Robert views his erstwhile protégé with a mixture of jealousy and pained possessiveness. Because theatre is an ephemeral, unreserved art form, Mamet implies, an actor's successors are his sole posterity and these, like children, move ungratefully on."

LITT 5.15 Tinker, Jack. Rev. of *A Life in the Theatre*. *Daily Mail* 1 Nov. 1989.
Rpt. in *London Theatre Record*. 22 Oct.-4 Nov. 1989: 1492.

Positive view of acting, but not of the play: "There are two performances at the Haymarket as sweet, as true, as funny and as touching as you are likely to see in a lifetime in any theatre. Unfortunately for both [Elliot and West] their brief evening of high artistry resembles nothing so much as two characters in search of a play."

rLITT 5.16 Wolf, Matt. Rev. of *A Life in the Theatre*. *City Limits* 9 Nov. 1989.
Rpt. in *London Theatre Record*. 22 Oct.-4 Nov. 1989: 1488-89.

Negative review: "Elsewhere, director Bill Bryden can do little to camouflage the ellipses in the script, and while one understands Mamet's desire not to bring the actors' offstage lives on-stage, surely he could have made John more than a quietly cunning figure of assent who says 'yes' enough times to fill a Pinter play."

Scholarly:
sLITT 1 Bigsby, C. W. E. "*Water Engine, Life in the Theatre*." *David Mamet*.
Contemporary Writers. London: Methuen, 1985. 86-100

Bigsby does some interesting questioning of Mamet's point about the relation between art and life: "As to the audience—ourselves—Mamet seems to imply that we too are manoeuvred into playing parts not of our own devising, speaking a language that is not our own, and enacting plots that are all too often distinguished neither by their metaphor—developed as it is by Robert out of his own insecurities—is perhaps suspect. The theatre is, as Robert remarks, 'part of life.' At times, indeed, it may seem all too accurate a reflection of it, as life turns itself into inferior art. The authority, however, is not yet complete. There are freedoms, privacies, and relationships not available to the actor. In this play the distinction is difficult to make, since theatrical and performed self coincide. But in eliminating the space between actor and self it seems to be make a plea for its restoration" (99-100).

sLITT 2 Carroll. Dennis. "Learning." *David Mamet*. Modern Dramatists Series.
New York: St. Martin's, 1987. 70-90.

Carroll takes his approach to performance through setting: "Though the theatrical environment is minimally shown, the result is not skimpy allegory but poetic suggestiveness, for appropriate costumes and props help create the theatrical ambiance" (78). The performance sense is most keen on it application to language: "As often in Mamet, the climactic lowering of social mask is signalled by changes in the dialogue. Earlier, Robert's speech is sprung with the certitude and confidence of an almost-iambic pattern, a spare and non-repetitive confidence of address. Clashes in different levels of language are smoothed over with assertive rhythms. But here Robert's rhetorical confidence drains away; he fumbles, pauses, repeats himself. The personal reaching-out, the confession of a personal need, involves not only the lowering of the mentor mask but, with it, the distance from which he maintains his authority" (81).

sLITT 3 Dean, Anne. *"Life in the Theatre." David Mamet: Language as Dramatic Action.* Rutherford, New Jersey: Fairleigh Dickinson UP, 1990. 119-45.

Dean reads beneath the words to find inner motives to the characters which make them sympathetic: "Mamet breaks up his sentences, making him begin again and again without finishing and inserting phrases such as 'of course,' 'of a sort, and 'I mean.' All this serves to undercut the portentousness—and pretentiousness—of the tone. Robert believes he has a truly important task to perform; however, he is constantly shown to be full of self-delusion and evasion and his hyperbolic remarks are therefore somewhat diminished in the light of our knowledge of his true state of mind. He struggles to find meaning in banality because to admit the frailty of his position as a third-rate actor struggling to make a living on the very fringe of the profession would be to invite terror and despair" (126).

See also the following scholarly articles covering multiple plays:

sMP 16 Ditsky, John. "'He Lets You See the Thought There': The Theater of David Mamet."

sMP 19 Geis, Deborah R. "David Mamet and the Metadramatic Tradition: Seeing 'the Trick from the Back.'"

sMP 21 Herman, William. "Theatrical Diversity from Chicago: David Mamet."

THE OLD NEIGHBORHOOD

Characters and Scenes:
"Disappearance of the Jews": Bobby, a man in his thirties or forties and Joey, his friend. The scene is in a hotel room. "Jolly": a woman in her thirties or forties; Bob, her brother; Carl, her husband. The scene is Jolly's house. "Deeny": a woman in her thirties and Bob [Bobby Gould]. The scene is set in a restaurant.

Editions:
The Old Neighborhood: A Play. New York: S. French, 1998.
The Old Neighborhood: Three Plays. New York: Vintage, 1998.
The Old Neighborhood. Royal Court Writers Series. London: Methuen, 1998.
David Mamet Plays, 4. London: Methuen, 2002.
"Jolly." *Best American Short Plays 1992-93.* Eds. Howard Stein and Glenn
    Young. New York: Applause, 1993. 93-119.

Plot Outline:
Bobby Gould returns to Chicago, his hometown, after many years and because his marriage is breaking up, seems to want to reconnect to his past. In "The Disappearance of the Jews" he and Joey reminisce in a hotel room about people they knew. They debate whether Bobby's son is a Jew, since his mother is not, and Bobby confesses that his wife once said "If you've been persecuted so long, eh, you must have brought this on yourself." In response, Joey confesses his fantasies—such as his wish they were back in the old world in a Jewish village. They conclude reminiscing as Bobby asks about Deeny who is divorced and works at Fields. In "Jolly" he and his sister talk in her home about their parents' divorce and the results on their lives and the anger it causes. There are old resentments over mother's remarriage, and Jolly is especially resentful of the stepfather's children, and their refusal to help her with money from a trust fund when she and her husband, Carl, needed help. Jolly confesses to be completely frustrated seeing herself as "some haggard, sexless, unattrac-

tive, *housewife*, with her kids in a station wagon." She assures Bobby that they love him and will support him through the divorce. In "Deeny" Bobby meets with an old love in a restaurant to find her also struggling to find meaning in her life. She has hopes of starting a garden, of being one with nature. They talk of passion and attraction, but she concludes, "I thought that I knew what you wanted" and they say goodbye.

Production:
pON 1 The first production of "The Disappearance of the Jews," was as a one-act with one acts by Elaine May ("Hot Line") and Shel Silverstein ("Gorilla") called *Mamet, May, Silverstein—3 New Plays*. It opened at the Goodman Theater Studio in Chicago on June 3 and ran till July 3, 1983.

Director:	Gregory Mosher
Set and Costumes:	Franne Lee
Lighting:	Rita Pietraszek
Sound:	Michael Schweppe
Cast:	
Joe:	Joe Mantegna
Bobby:	Norman Parker

Overview:
All the reviews were positive for the play and especially for the performances. Some saw the situation as universal—"memory of things lost"—and saw this as touching. Only two thought the issues as particularly Jewish (Kaplan and Valeo). Syse sensed that there was a good part of fantasy to the memories as did Christiansen who went further to examine "the secret truth" for which the friends quest. Christiansen and Valeo noted the characters' likeness to those in *Sexual Perversity in Chicago*.

rON 1.1 Cassidy, Claudia. "Open Sesame: The Search for Theatre Treasure." *Chicago* August 1983: 20+.
　　　　Positive review: "Here Joe Mantegna and Norman Parker share that vestigial memory of things lost, even if never known. [. . .] This is offhand, far from profound, yet a sense of loss clings like cobwebs."

rON 1.2 Christiansen, Richard. "One-act Goodman Plays Deliver a 1-2-3 Punch." *Chicago Tribune* 15 June 1983: Tempo.
　　　　Positive review: Joey is "tossing off his hopes, fears, and philosophies as if they were just popping into Bobby's ignorant, shallow but still deeply troubled mind." Likening the characters to Danny and Bernard of *Sexual Perversity*, now in their thirties, married, they were like *Edmond*: "worried about their future and yearning nostalgically for a bucolic past of simplicity and peace they never knew. Once again, they are searching for the secret of truth while they thrash about in a life that has become too restrictive and complex for them. Once again, there is the danger of violence and murder in their lives."

rON 1.3 Kaplan, Sherman. "Three New Plays: A *WBBM* Theatre Review." [Chicago] 15 June 1983.
　　　　Positive review focused on religious identity: "Above all, Mamet's play

is about a renewal of faith as a couple of thoroughly modern manlys [. . .] rekindle between them the communal bond they share not only as friends who have not seen each other for sometime, but as Jews struggling with their identities in a Gentile world."

rON 1.4 Morrison, Hobe. "Resident Legit Review: Three New Plays." *Variety* 22 June 1983: 96.

Enigmatically succinct recognition of the play's depths: "It is about language and the interstices where the concrete becomes symbolic and vice versa."

rON 1.5 Syse, Glenna. "These Serious Times Bring New Humor to the Theater." *Chicago Sun-Times* 15 June 1985.

Extremely positive review of dialogue and reminiscing which captured "the contradictions, the coverups, and the doubts." She also noted the fear of aging: "The wistful aroma of what might have been (or was it that way?) creeps in, as does the need for the comfort of family elders, the desire to embrace their roots and the disappointed confessions of how it is now, in fantasy and in reality."

rON 1.6 Valeo, Tom. "Silver Lining Makes 'Gorilla' Funniest of 3 Plays." *Daily Herald* [Hyde Park, Chicago]: 6+.

Positive review which saw "an uncanny resemblance" to *Sexual Perversity*— except that "the two men are no longer young, and they're both grappling with the disillusioning realities of adulthood. Bobby, played with world-weary lassitude by Norman Parker, believes he should have married a nice Jewish girl instead of a *shiksa*." He also quoted the line about how Jews brought the holocaust on themselves which no other reviewer noted.

Production:
pON 2 The three act play was first presented by the American Repertory Theater at the Hasty Pudding Theater, Cambridge, Massachusetts from April 11 to May 4, 1997.

Director:	Scott Zigler
Set:	Kevin Rigdon
Lighting:	John Ambrosone
Costumes:	Harriet Voyt
Cast:	
Bobby:	Tony Shalhoub
Jolly:	Brooke Adams
Joey:	Vincent Guastaferro
Deeny:	Rebecca Pidgeon
Carl:	Jack Willis

Overview:
Reviewers recognized immediately that the audience has to participate in assembling these fragments into a coherent narrative. Seigel, for instance, reminded the audience not to be impatient, "But the interplay is so rich [. . .] that we give Mamet the slack he deserves and the time he needs to get to wherever he's going. Most reviewers agreed

the second play was best, as Byrne did: "But tucked in between is a gem called 'Jolly.'"
For others, however, Mamet, as usual, remained enigmatic. Stearn's noted that it "leaves you annoyed at how coy and unfinished it seems—and how stubbornly Mamet refuses to reveal his underlying intentions. Then you remember: This is Mamet. Forget finished. Forget fun. Forget easy." For Karam, as for others who enter into Mamet's world, "this time pain is inescapable."

Karam, however, savaged the direction, and Pidgeon was controversial. He recognized that her "carefully modulated performance shows the discomfort underneath" and Lehman thought her "a little masterpiece of comic deadpan." *Backstage* and Cummings thought her "a cold fish."

Reviews:

rON 2.1 Rev. of *Old Neighborhood. Backstage* 16 May 1997: 13.

>   Positive review except of Pidgeon: "The only disappointment is Mamet's wife, Rebecca Pidgeon, who—as in *Oleanna*, when that play premiered here a few years ago—doesn't seem to get the rhythm of her husband's writing. She delivers her potentially funny and touching monologue in a monotone that makes her scene (the last of the three) a very long haul."

rON 2.2 Byrne, Terry. "Mamet's *Neighborhood* Is Blighted but for 'Jolly'." *The Boston Herald* 18 Apr. 1997, sec. S: 12.

>   Positive view of 'Jolly' alone: "'The Disappearance of the Jews' and 'D.' are two bland bookends that could have been lifted from earlier Mamet works. But tucked in between is a gem called 'Jolly.' It's a touching, powerful and quite affecting look at sibling ties. But it's almost as if Mamet fears 'Jolly' cuts too close to the bone. He surrounds it with scenes that keep his oft-used main character, Bobby Gould (Tony Shalhoub), at a distance. As long as people are talking at him, Bobby can blunt the impact of Mamet's language of attack. And as long as he can avoid becoming emotionally engaged, so can the audience."

rON 2.3 Cummings, Scott T. Rev. of *The Old Neighborhood. Village Voice* 6 May 1997: 103.

>   Positive review of the play and Shalhoub: "While his interlocutor rambles on about lifting a fallen tree out of the road or the ritual mutilations of distant tribes, Shalhoub manages to convey a strong impression of a man examining his past in an effort to get a bead on his future. Skillfully, Vincent Guastaferro takes Joey just to the edge of caricature and comes away with a genuine and robust Mamet 'guy.' Brooke Adams is likeable as the very unlikable and bilious Jolly, whose deep and unresolved fury with her mother (now dead) makes her a perpetual kvetch. Adams, Guastaferro, and Shalhoub all interact with an unforced comfort and honesty that evokes the warm, deep ties that bind. By comparison, Rebecca Pidgeon is a cold fish. [. . .] The character herself is something of a cipher, and Pidgeon compounds matters by making D. opaque and colorless."

rON 2.4 Fanger, Iris. "Mamet Goes Home Again in *Neighborhood*." *Boston Herald* 27 Apr. 1997: 50.

Positive view of the play's failures to communicate: "The unspoken words and interrupted sentences stand for the inarticulate manner in which Mamet's men communicate: afraid to say what they mean because they might utter thoughts too fearful to be examined in daylight.

rON 2.5 —. "Mamet's *Old Neighborhood* Rouses Yearnings of a Trip Home." *Christian Science Monitor* 28 Apr. 1997: 15.

Positive review of the play which forced the audience to fill in blanks: "Mamet's trademark paring down of language forces the audience to search for clues in the pauses and thoughts left unspoken as much as in the dialogue. He withholds information that other playwrights would let fall like so many breadcrumbs to mark a path through the forest. [. . .] To be sure, the image of 'The Old Neighborhood' is a metaphor for a past that seems to be the repository of dreams. But Mamet is too shrewd an observer and too suspicious of sentiment to suggest any comfort waits back home."

rON 2.6 Karam, Edward. "Bobby's Back, Disappointed." *Times* [London] 2 May 1997: 37.

Mixed review of a play in which "pain is inescapable" as well as "middle-aged melancholy and distress. The discussion of past relationships reveals disappointments that run deep among the characters. [. . .] Brooke Adams impressively shows Jolly's fragile self-esteem, veering between the self-assurance gained from the love of her husband Carl (Jack Willis) and the memory of her mother's cruelty. 'D' appears more self-possessed in a cafe with Bobby. In a virtual monologue, she rambles about gardens, the weather, and her dreams of primitive tribes that mutilate themselves. Although Pidgeon's carefully modulated performance shows the discomfort underneath, and the final goodbyes provide a bittersweet catharsis for the trilogy, the act drags. Better direction than that of Scott Zigler might have helped. Throughout the production, lines that are written to overlap or be interrupted are delivered in toto, followed by the next actor cleanly beginning the next line. The effect is a stiltedness that undermines Mamet's rhythms."

rON 2.7 King, Robert L. Rev. of *The Old Neighborhood. North American Review.* Sept.- Oct. (1997): 14.

Mixed review of the play which required audience involvement: "David Mamet's new play—unlike *Oleanna* and *Cryptogram*—uses evocative language that prompts active reflection from its audience. [. . .] Mamet, whose, tape-recorder ear and unmoored aphorisms have often wearied me, compresses a world of disturbed and disturbing values in the dialogue between Bobby and Joey. [. . .] Bobby spends most of Act III listening to his wife [sic] as she talks around the reasons for their separating. Again, merely talking about meaning substitutes for clarity of meaning, and this act like the three scenes of the previous one ends with one character quietly distinguishing what the other says."

rON 2.8 Lehman, Jon L. "New Mamet Play Looks at Midlife." *Patriot Ledger* 19
Apr. 1997: 35.

Positive review focused on the complexity of the work: "None of the
relationships here are explained, and some of them are complicated, so that the
viewer's mind is off-balance from the very beginning and always is racing to
put the pieces together. [. . .] This central playlet, with its oblique descent into
the hell of a disconnected family, of relationships based on greed, power and
hurt instead of on love, is powerful and unsettling, the more so because we only
gradually realize what it is we are hearing. [. . . Deeny], delivered in a tightrope-
walking performance of exquisite grace by Rebecca Pidgeon, is a little
masterpiece of comic deadpan. The memory of a youthful, physical relationship
hangs in the air, never mentioned by either, and we see the bright, almost
desperate energy that the woman is putting into creating a new image for herself."

rON 2.9 Siegel, Ed. "The Talk Is Rich in Mamet's *Old Neighborhood*." *Boston Globe*
18 Apr. 1997, sec. F: 1.

Positive review of the richly textured work that took "us along for the ride
back home, and it's hard not to admire the scenery as Gould looks back less in
anger than in sadness. His only source of real warmth is his sister.[. . .] Adams
gives her such radiance that our heart goes out to her in all her raggedness. [. . .]
Jolly, like Mamet's male characters, talks a good game about having all the
answers, but with a nod, a look away, or exhaling cigarette smoke, Adams lets
us know—without Mamet coming out and telling us—that perhaps she doesn't
really have it as together as she'd like us, and Bobby, to think. [. . .] The play
ends on a dreamlike note as creepy as anything in the playwright's larger works."

rON 2.10 Stearns, David Patrick. "A *Neighborhood* of Disconnected Lives." *USA
Today* 18 Apr. 1997, sec. D: 4.

Mildly negative review because the play "has Shalhoub unable to reconcile
with a former girlfriend (Rebecca Pidgeon) who was once considered intelligent
but now seems vapid. If the play is about anything, it's the end of love. [. . .
Shalhoub] is constantly seeing people he was once close to but hasn't seen in a
while. That underscores the sense that absence is a prevalent state here. The
one relationship that does have familiarity is that of Adams' character and her
husband, who for all their warmth don't have much to say to each other."

rON 2.11 Taylor, Markland. Rev. of *The Old Neighborhood*. *Variety* 23 June 1997:
105.

Mixed review: "The second and longest, 'Jolly,' probably contains Mamet's
best-written female character to date. And if 'D.,' the final play, is less satisfying
and more artificially stylized, it may well be because Mamet sees its pivotal
female character that way. 'The Old Neighborhood' isn't the full-scale
powerhouse play we've been awaiting from the Mamet of 'American Buffalo,'
but it'll do until the real thing comes along."

Production:

pON 3 Booth Theatre, New York City with previews from November 11, 1997, opening November 19. [A videotape of the January 16, 1998 performance of this play is held at TOFT.]. The cast and production staff were the same as above, except the replacement of Adams and Shaloub with:

Jolly:	Patti LuPone
Bobby Gould:	Peter Reigert

Overview:

Some New York critics began to appreciate Mamet's technique. Brantley explained that: "Mamet [is] a playwright whose baldness of dialogue is matched only by its indirection," and Canby described the effect: "Without warning, it draws you into depths where the terrors are less often physical than emotional, where cruelty is all the more damaging for being without point, as it can seem in childhood." The problem was that once the audience had filled in the blanks the story became theirs rather than Mamet's though they attribute the ensuing story to him. Thus, Stone constructed misogyny: "Bobby [. . .] isn't aware of this, isn't aware of how his willed dumbness is connected to the despair he feels about his choices and his confusion about being a man. Mamet resonates from blows to modern malehood."

Feingold, by contrast, used imagery from within the play to interpret not Mamet, but the absent center, Bobby Gould, who "is an enigma even to himself, a winner too self-effacing to crow, a driven man with nobody at the wheel. [. . .] He can't find his roots because, like most modern Americans, he's never really had any." For those unable to construct a center, disaster ensued, especially if they waited for the third play, "Deeny," to supply explanations. Its failure to do so was frustrating to Simon, Spencer, Stearns and Steyn; indeed, King, Deffaa and Scholer thought Deeny Bobby's wife. Such critics only saw a cipher at the center of the play. For Barnes, however, "This is a funny, moving evening in the theater—thoughtful, provocative and making demands of empathy and feeling as uncommon on Broadway as they are welcome."

Reviews:

rON 3.1 Rev. of *The Old Neighborhood. Variety* 24 Nov 1997: 72.

> Positive review: "Zigler isn't the only one who gets the rhythms and emotions just right—stars Peter Riegert and Patti LuPone are first-rate as a brother and sister coming to painful grips with their loveless upbringing. [. . .] Bobby would seem the most passive of protagonists, but Mamet is too sly for that. Like a cubist painting, Joey, Jolly and Deeny illustrate three angles of one man, three aspects of one life. Neither Bobby nor the audience knows where the character is headed at play's end, but both know where he's been."

rON 3.2 Barnes, Clive. "A Chip Off the Old Mamet Block." *New York Post* 20 Nov. 1997: 59.

> Rave review in that Mamet: "has found his unique voice. Moreover, his concept of a play as a journey—often with a hero wandering through like a careworn, careless Odysseus—is very much his own. [. . .] Yet it is a stylization that cleverly lulls you into hearing a subtext, sometimes of despair, sometimes

of evasion or deceit, sometimes simply of an unutterable vagueness suggestive of the long littleness of life. Bobby—so much in need of comfort—is cast in his inevitable role as a comfort giver. He listens with a frozen warmth, his smile painfully locked in sympathy with others as his needs churn."

rON 3.3 Brantley, Ben. "A Middle-Aged Man Goes Home, to Mametville." *New York Times* 20 Nov. 1997, sec. E: 1.

Positive view of a play of fantasies: "They speak in code, of course, the characters in 'The Old Neighborhood,' David Mamet's heart-piercing new play. Middle-aged people with shared pasts usually do: boyhood pals, former lovers, a brother and sister who recall the unhappy Christmases of their youth. [. . .] For the brother and sister in 'Jolly,' on the other hand, their past, a childhood warped by an emotionally abusive mother and stepfather, is and always will be the present. It is their central defining reality, and its particulars are recited and repeated like a litany. In 'Deeny,' what occurred between Deeny and Bobby remains unspoken, and the consequent vacuum resonates with an elegiac tone of loss. . . . But the most haunting and original element of 'Neighborhood' is its characters' fantasies of an alternative world, in which religion, family and erotic love have a formal, enduring substance."

rON 3.4 Canby, Vincent. "Mamet's Stunning Foray into the Past." *New York Times* 30 Nov. 1997, sec. 2: 4+.

Positive view of a play of terrors: "Though lean of line and calm of surface, 'The Old Neighborhood' is as dangerous as an uncharted vortex. Without warning, it draws you into depths where the terrors are less often physical than emotional, where cruelty is all the more damaging for being without point, as it can seem in childhood. [. . .] Mr. Riegert is fine as the troubled, sympathetic ear for the other characters. Mr. Willis, in a role that also requires that he spend most of the time reacting, is memorable. Mr. Mamet's women are not as vividly written, and that's a problem with this play. The thoroughly disciplined Ms. LuPone works hard and occasionally with good effect as the angry Jolly, but it's a big stretch. If Ms. Pidgeon (in private life the wife of the playwright) never quite finds the heart of Deeny, it may be because the character remains less dramatically ambiguous than simply unfinished."

rON 3.5 Deffaa, Chip. Rev. of *The Old Neighborhood*. *Backstage* 12 Dec. 1997: 1+.

Negative review, especially of "D" as "excruciatingly tiresome. It's far from top drawer Mamet, contains little tension, and few surprises. We know the characters' marriage is dead before they seem to. I don't see its purpose except perhaps to bring the overall length of the show up to 90 minutes and to provide an acting job for Rebecca Pidgeon [. . .], who is colorless in a colorless role."

rON 3.6 Evans, Greg. Rev. of *The Old Neighborhood*. *Daily Variety* 20 Nov. 1997: 72.

Extremely positive view of play and actors: "Jolly is a woman made both tough (she curses as much as any Mamet man) and heartbreakingly vulnerable by a loveless childhood. As loyal to her brother, husband and daughters as she is resentful toward her recently deceased mother, Jolly has scratched out a stable family life through sheer determination, but not without considerable psychic cost. [. . .] LuPone, a Mamet vet, is wonderful as the sister, her hard-boiled delivery barely concealing the catch of a sob. [. . .] So where is Bobby in all this? Playing sounding board to the dominant characters in each scene, Bobby would seem the most passive of protagonists, but Mamet is too sly for that. Like a Cubist painting, Joey, Jolly and Deeny illustrate three angles of one man, three aspects of one life. Neither Bobby nor the audience knows where the character is headed at play's end, but both know where he's been."

rON 3.7 Feingold, Michael. "Unsaying Substance." *Village Voice* 2 Dec. 1997: 97+.
      Positive view of the play as an overview of Bobby: "A reaction to the failed marriage, Bobby's trip to his old home base is an effort at reorientation, an inquiry into the roots of his instability. [. . .] Bobby learns, in effect, that his problems are rooted in rootlessness. He can't find his roots because, like most modern Americans, he's never really had any. The old European (or African, or Asian) folkways are engulfed in democracy's nondescript materialism; placelessness is the American version of urban anomie. Not irrelevantly, the conversation of Deeny, Bobby's ex, is all about gardening, transplanting, and greenhouses—'forcing houses,' as Deeny notes the British call them."

rON 3.8 Heilpern, John. *How Good Is David Mamet Anyway?* New York: Routledge, 2000. 225-28. Reprint of his review from the *New York Observer.*
      Heilpern saw Mamet as parallel to Warhol: "Everything's there, you just can't see it. It's all hidden in the coded subtext! You may wonder what's hidden there, exactly. And the answer is, a projection of yourself. Where, then, is the drama? It's up to you." The first act is "imagining a sentimentalized version of shtetl life" but "It's just small talk" and "is meant to convey the disappearance of the assimilated Jews and a desperate search for meaning and roots. Big and important issues—reduced to a shrug, a comedy turn, a vague slack nostalgia." He concluded: "*Jolly* is little more than a loud, prolonged whine from unforgiving, self-hating, foul mouthed sis."

rON 3.9 Kalb, Jonathan. Rev. of *Old Neighborhood. New York Press* 10 Dec. 1997: 58.
      Mixed review of a play with "the most astonishing range of production quality I've seen on a Broadway stage. It begins with acting as forcefully subtle and richly suggestive as the best of Mamet 'stars' such as Joe Mantegna and William H. Macy. Then, bizarrely, it ends with a performance by Rebecca Pidgeon that seems barely professional. Mamet didn't direct this show (Scott Zigler did), but since Pidgeon is Mamet's wife and a proven professional, it's safe to surmise that her affectless line readings are an attempt to serve his notoriously eccentric theories of acting."

rON 3.10 Kanfer, Stefan. "Diverting Sorrows." *New Leader* 29 Dec. 1997: 34+.
      Mixed review: "Scott Zigler has directed 'The Old Neighborhood' with panache. The quartet of actors have responded briskly. Riegert is especially

effective when he listens, and LuPone when she talks. Kevin Rigdon's sets and Harriet Voyt's costumes are suitably bleak. A pity these talents had to be squandered on an antique masking as postmodern art."

rON 3.11 Lyons, Donald. Rev. of *Old Neighborhood. Wall Street Journal* 21 Nov. 1997, sec. A: 20.

Negative review which saw the play as autobiography: "Directed by Scott Zigler in a way that heightens the text's torpor and stasis, these exercises reveal an emotionally blocked writer. Mr. Mamet is angry; Mr. Mamet is hurt; Mr. Mamet is unforgiving. He is not, though, willing to write a play that might offer, in terms of art, an objective equivalent for his feelings."

rON 3.12 O'Toole, Fintan. "Mamet Takes a Minor Detour." *Daily News* [New York] 20 Nov. 1997: 47.

Mixed review: "This is a triptych of small scenes from a midlife crisis, outlined in broad, bold strokes. The hand is that of a master, but the image is slight and unadorned. [. . .] The central problem is that Bobby, the character who links the scenes, is never more than a wry, melancholic presence. He acts mostly as a sounding board for the other characters' woes. Because he is never deeply engaged with them, his journey into the past feels more like emotional tourism than a voyage of discovery. The result is that the whole is never more than the sum of its small, beautifully crafted parts."

rON 3.13 Scholem, Richard. "Our Man on Broadway." *Long Island Business News* 15 Dec. 1997: 1+.

Review which confused life and art: "In ['Deeny'] Mamet and his wife (Rebecca Pidgeon) are breaking up. He is giving her the news. She is regretfully groping for reasons, for justification. She is sorry, but puzzled. Their parting is awkward, even embarrassing."

rON 3.14 Simon, John. "David as Goliath." *New York* 8 Dec. 1997: 69-70.

Extremely negative review: "It is hard to believe that David Mamet wrote some of *The Old Neighborhood* fifteen years ago. At that time, he still had some talent. Rather less than he had 25 years ago, but more than he has exhibited since, as witness the current piece, which is worse than bad, scandalous. [. . .] The piece drones along, resolving itself into a stream of complaints, their motto, 'Oh, Bobby, it's all gone. It's all gone.' [. . .] Mamet is the Quintillian of kvetch."

rON 3.15 Spencer, Charles. "Broadway Springs a Surprise." *Daily Telegraph* 28 Nov. 1997: 25.

Negative review: "In the third piece, the briefest and most infuriatingly elusive of them all, we watch Bobby and a girlfriend raking through the ashes at the end of an affair. Though well acted, these pieces have a fatal lack of dramatic energy and the maudlin gloom of the writing seems self-indulgent rather than affecting. At the end I felt like giving this usually electrifying writer a good shake and saying: 'Too bad, you big cry-baby.'"

rON 3.16 Stearns, David Patrick. "Mamet, in the *Neighborhood* of Babel." *USA Today* 21 Nov. 1997, sec. D: 20.

Negative review: "There's always a point in David Mamet's plays when you want at least one character to shut up. Mamet would take that as a compliment: It means he's confronting you with things you don't want to face. There are times, though, when his characters are just plain annoying. And in *The Old Neighborhood*, which opened Wednesday at Broadway's Booth Theater, the annoyance factor runs very high. [. . .] In Part 3, Riegert's character breaks up with a motor-mouthed Rebecca Pidgeon, whose far-flung speeches careen between definitions of good taste and musings on self-mutilation. [. . .] You know there's meaning, but you have to sift through so much mucky verbiage to find it."

rON 3.17 Steyn, Mark. "Peddling Air." *New Criterion* Feb. 1998: 40+.

Negative review which found nothing at the center: "Bobby is a cipher's cipher, a human being from whom all human impulses—emotion, reason, prejudice, attraction—have been squeezed dry. His three chums wear their lack of self-knowledge like medals. To be sure, all manner of great fictional characters have done that, but Mamet gives the impression that to force his dramatis personae to confront this lack would somehow be obvious or crass or conventional. [. . .] Engagement, shrugs Mamet, is squaresville; who needs it?"

rON 3.18 Stone, Laurie. "From Russia with Love." *Nation* 5 Jan. 1998: 33+.

Negative view of Mamet and his play: "In the first act we're presented with a sufferer who ricochets between nostalgia and rage but doesn't see this. Jolly is a broken record in love with disappointment and grievance, but she doesn't know why it's compelling to remain a victim. Deeny is a flake, presented presumably so we can observe that Bobby chooses women because of some attraction so detached from who they are that when they speak he is always surprised. He isn't aware of this, isn't aware of how his willed dumbness is connected to the despair he feels about his choices and his confusion about being a man. Mamet resonates from blows to modern malehood, living as he does in a world where male privilege is something you can be brought up on charges for collaborating with, a world that for men means sharing access and power in order not to be a pig. Does Mamet know what's on the menu (being a pig, or hating yourself for being a pig, or doing with less, which in time may be more and then again maybe it won't be in your lifetime)? Who the hell can tell from this play?"

rON 3.19 Winer, Linda. "A Harsh, Haunting Trip Home Again." *Newsday* 20 Nov. 1997: B11+.

Mixed review: "This is an archetypal carrot-on-the-stick work, which means it starts with a couple of hilarious Mamet guy's-guys reminiscing about broads and other tribal insecurities, then culminates in the bald, solemn, fingernails-on-the-blackboard style of his most elliptical, aggressively airless work. In 90 nonstop minutes, the evening becomes almost time-lapse photography of the evolution of this fascinating, always brilliant, often infuriating writer. The difference, this time, is that we also get a glimpse of the evolution of the man. [. . .] And—news flash—this time there is even a female character, played by Patti LuPone, who has the unpredictable flinty depth he has so consistently found in men."

rON 3.20 Winn, Steven. "Mamet Gets Personal. Shorenstein Hays Production Opens on Broadway — It's a Stretch for Playwright." *San Francisco Chronicle* 20 Nov. 1997, sec. D: 1.

    Mixed review: "Between the jokes and recollections and Pinteresque pauses come lines that verge on being simplistic captions for the play's explorations of mortality, loss, Jewish tradition and the fragility of connections." It then "concludes with a farewell-to-love line that even Riegert's quietly turbulent coda, suffused with longing, can't redeem from stating the obvious. While 'The Old Neighborhood' leaves plenty unsaid, its characters tend more toward transparency than the gnarly opaqueness often associated with Mamet."

rON 3.21 Zoglin, Richard. "Bad Memory." *Time* 8 Dec 1997: 85+.

    Mixed review: "Scott Zigler has directed with haunting spareness. And the acting is top-notch, particularly Patti LuPone, feisty and funny as Jolly. But raiding the memory bank has made Mamet lazy. His plays have never been much concerned with plot, but *The Old Neighborhood* has no forward propulsion at all. Bobby spends most of the time staring off into the distance, head cocked slightly, as if groping for memories, meaning, connection. So are we. Because the play, in its terse but meandering way, occasionally stumbles on a snatch of family observation to which we can all relate (Jolly complains that her parents never bought her skis), or wrestles with the intermittent big idea (Bobby's longing for his Jewish roots), some people may mistake this for profundity. But it's pretentious doodling."

Production:
pON 4   Royal Court Theatre Downstairs, London. Previewed June 17, 1998, opened June 23 and closed August 8.

Director:		Patrick Marber
Decor:		William Dudley
Lighting:		Rick Fisher
Sound:		Simon Baker
Cast:		
	Bobby:	Colin Stinton
	Joey:	Linal Haft
	Jolly:	Zoë Wanamaker
	Carl:	Vincent Marzello
	Deeny:	Diana Quick

Overview:
Critics were most pleased by Lionel Haft's Joey, and intrigued by the quick shifts of emotion of Zoë Wanamaker's Jolly, seen as "fiercely funny and moving" by Benedict, for instance, while Edwardes noted "Wanamaker, at her finest, plays Jolly with a mix

of exhausted bitterness, tender appreciation of the solid worth of her own husband, and concern for Bobby who had just left his wife." Stinton had little notice because of the passive role, though Butler observed that "Stinton catches a pained, slow-burning intelligence," and Kellaway, "It is impossible to believe that he is acting: he conveys with absolute naturalness—in the slumped way he sits, in his defeated way of listening—the weight of depression under which he lives." Critics did, however, see Bobby's experience as their own. Billington noted that he is the "epitome of anyone who returns to his past and is confronted by age, change, lost time and missed chances. This is Mamet at his most autobiographical and yet his most universal." And Brown saw the play similarly: "it's thematic concerns will strike painful chords in every one of us: that we are all products of our past, our blood and our roots."

Others, as usual, saw nothing at all in the plays (Gross, Gore-Langton, Morley, Smith). Usher, however, noted that audience might be confused, but offered guidance to get beyond it: "Playgoers accustomed to explication [...] will flounder. They haven't lost the plot, if that's any consolation, because there isn't one. Instead, in less than an hour-and-a-half, we get to know a man and his sister, their plight emerging gradually, like a photograph gaining definition in developer fluid. I found it engrossing, fitfully funny, frequently painful." Macaulay explained that Mamet's characters are not prejudged for us: "In Mamet, most of the characters always lay bare far more of themselves than they themselves see. That is not to say he tells you how to think about them." Playwright Patrick Marber was great praised as director of the production.

Reviews:

rON 4.1 Benedict, David. Rev. of *The Old Neighborhood*. *Independent* 24 June 1998. Rpt. in *Theatre Record* 4 June-1 July1998: 811.

Positive view of the understated play: "The most exciting thing about Mamet's writing for both actors and audiences lies in the pregnancy of what is left unsaid. Joey, (bluff, energetic Lionel Haft), is voluble and animated, but it is Bobby's reticence that quietly grips, and his clipped intimations of his unhappy marriage speak volumes."

rON 4.2 Billington, Michael. Rev. of *The Old Neighborhood*. *Guardian* 24 June 1998. Rpt. 23 June 1998 in *Theatre Record* 4 June-1 July1998: 808-09.

Positive review of Chekhovian play: "Filled with reminiscence and the corrosive sadness of missed chances, it is, if you can imagine such a thing, like a Jewish version of the Shallow-Silence scenes in Shakespeare's 'Henry IV Part Two.' [...] Although he is writing very specifically about the loss of Jewish identity and the perils of assimilation, he is also dealing with the great Chekhovian theme of what-might-have-been. Bobby becomes the moving epitome of anyone who returns to his past and is confronted by age, change, lost time and missed chances. This is Mamet at his most autobiographical and yet his most universal."

rON 4.3 Brown, Georgina. Rev. of *The Old Neighborhood*. *Mail on Sunday* 28 June 1998. Rpt. in *Theatre Record* 4 June-1 July1998: 807-08.

Positive review of a play which evoked memories which "will strike painful chords in every one of us: that we are all products of our past, our blood and our roots. [. . .] Again and again, Jolly scratches away at the old scabs, and the blood gushes as freely as when the wounds were originally inflicted. Mingling with fury, though, is her fierce determination to hold her family together and not let history repeat itself while Bobby who has left his wife and kids, knows his abandonment will ensure precisely that. [. . .] Marber speaks the same language as Mamet, and his fluent, eloquent production is marvelously alert to the changing tones and the trauma that lie just beyond the reach of words."

rON 4.4 Butler, Robert. Rev. of *The Old Neighborhood*. *Independent on Sunday* 28 June 1998. Rpt. in *Theatre Record* 4 June-1 July1998: 810.

Positive view of the charged language: "The dialogue in 'The Old Neighborhood' pulses with an electric charge. Characters keep rewriting what they say. Thoughts stack up. Replies are delayed. Mamet peppers his dialogue with 'heys,' 'huhs' and 'uh-huhs,' placed as precisely as musical notes. [. . .] But here it seems effortlessly natural. This London production drives the action forward, knocking 20 minutes off the New York one."

rON 4.5 Clapp, Susannah. "Wrong Kind of Loving." *Observer* 28 June 1998, sec. Review: 13. Rpt. in *Theatre Record* 4 June-1 July 1998: 808.

Positive view of the play as a mood piece: "Each play is an attenuated piece of mood music, a piece with a finely drawn but predictable arc which ends with too obviously clinching a conclusion. The final words [. . . are] an exchange which has the thumping sonority—is this goodbye to one lover or to all lovers, to romantic love or to all love?—of a Fifties pop song."

rON 4.6 de Jongh, Nicholas. Rev. of *The Old Neighborhood*. *Evening Standard* 24 June 1998. Rpt. in *Theatre Record* 4 June-1 July 1998: 807.

Positive view of the play's balance: "The play's appeal has to do with its bright nonchalance while masking desolate significance. There's a joshing lightness, an amused, amusing take upon the glee and rue of friends and family who treat Bobby's homecoming as a chance to raid the vaults of nostalgia and badmouth the past. Mamet's dark, ironic humor still holds."

rON 4.7 Edwardes, Jane. Rev. of *The Old Neighborhood*. *Time Out* 1 July 1998. Rpt. in *Theatre Record* 4 June-1 July 1998: 812.

Positive view of the play as Chekhovian: "Is Mamet getting soft? Poignancy is not a word one associates with [him] and yet there are moments in these three short plays that are tenderly despairing and full of a Chekhovian yearning for dreams that were never realised. [. . .] The pain of it lies in the way that old hurts still seem so raw; there is no compensation for those who have lacked maternal love. Zoë Wanamaker, at her finest, plays Jolly with a mix of exhausted bitterness, tender appreciation of the solid worth of her own husband, and concern for Bobby who has just left his wife."

rON 4.8 Fleming, Juliet. "Turning toward Death." *Times Literary Supplement* 3 July 1998: 17.

Very positive view of the play of recollection: "Mamet's formal rectitude operates as a principle of regulation within writing that otherwise pretends to be a realistic reflection of the indeterminacies and random compulsions of daily life. [. . .] In fact, both language and relationships have been invented and scripted by Mamet, whose spare texts wise actors follow word for word. [. . .] To Deeny falls the inchoate philosophizing that is the occasional task of Mamet's female characters. [. . .] Like any Mamet character, Deeny contradicts herself; if there is sense to her meditations it is not articulated at the conscious level. 'Deeny', which reads like the record of an analysis, begins with her 'vision' of a garden where she could shield and grow things. But Deeny knows to protect herself from the garden and its joys, and to follow the consolation that is 'turning... toward death.' This is the 'poignancy' that she shares with Bobby; he, poignantly enough, understands."

rON 4.9 Gross, John. "Too Many Tricks Spoil the Plot." *Sunday Telegraph* 28 June 1998, sec. Arts: 11. Rpt. in *Theatre Record* 4 June-1 July: 810.

Negative review of the play as thin because it "consists of three wafer-thin playlets by David Mamet. [. . .] But to what end? The characters, in so far as we get to know them, seem narrow and shallow—and, more to the point, a good deal narrower and shallower than we are asked to believe."

rON 4.10 Hepple, Peter. "Royal Court Downstairs: *The Old Neighborhood.*" *Stage & Television Today* 2 July 1998: 12.

Positive view of the play and production: "In 75 minutes, the time taken to perform the three short plays that make up David Mamet's latest work, the author manages to say a great deal about himself, the assimilation of the Jews in the United States, and the general self-obsession of its inhabitants. Yet this cultural deluge is accomplished in a pacy, rhythmic style which is the hallmark of one of America's most gifted and individual playwrights."

rON 4.11 Kellaway, Kate. Rev. of *The Old Neighborhood. New Statesman* 26 June 1998: 49.

Positive review of the play as "conducted like music. The dips and rises in register are always surprising, always right. And William Dudley's set ingeniously links the three different plays with an image of loss: a sepia montage of lost faces, like a suspended photograph album. [. . .] Tempting as it is to see Bob as someone who specialises in being a receptacle for the outpourings of women, there is a sense in which he always has the upper hand. When he finally tells Deeny he has come to say goodbye, the light fails altogether—like a heart missing a beat or the sudden onrush of night."

rON 4.12 Macaulay, Alastair. Rev. of *The Old Neighborhood. Financial Times* 24 June 1998. Rpt. in *Theatre Record* 4 June-1 July: 808.

Positive review of the play which revealed character: "In this quick-pouring series of brief phrases, there are more ironies, and absurdities, than Deeny is aware of. In Mamet, most of the characters always lay bare far more of themselves than they themselves see. That is not to say he tells you how to think about them. With one phrase, you burst out loud into laughter; with the next, the laughter is wiped off your face. And so his rhythm proceeds, constantly tragicomic."

rON 4.13 Morley, Sheridan. Rev. of *The Old Neighborhood. Spectator* 7 July 1998. Rpt. in *Theatre Record* 4 June-1 July: 812.

Negative review: "From that bleak and brilliant start we go rapidly downhill. [. . .] The trilogy lasts only 90 minutes in its entirety, but somewhere along the way we seem, on both sides of the footlights, to lose the plot."

rON 4.14 Nathan, David. Rev. of *The Old Neighborhood. Jewish Chronicle* 26 June 1998. Rpt. in *Theatre Record* 4 June-1 July: 811-12.

A positive view of the plays from which "the alienated Jew peers anxiously out, remembering how persecution and poverty were at least accompanied by certain certainties, such as a knowledge of who he was and where he came from. Before the play opens, a travel bag stands floodlit on one side of the stage and the lush sound of 'Dancing in the Dark' fills the theatre; director Patrick Marber clearly likes strong, unambiguous signposts. [. . .] Although these are essentially Jews and Mamet is clearly on a voyage of self-exploration, he writes so piercingly about lives from which meaning has drained away that in an evening that lasts no more than 80 minutes, he achieves an intensity and a universality that cut deep and are not confined to any particular experience."

rON 4.15 Nightingale, Benedict. "Hell Is Your Own People." *Times [London]* 25 June 1998: 40. Rpt. in *Theatre Record* 4 June-1 July: 810.

Positive review of play and production: "Everywhere Mamet's dialogue bustles and fizzes in its terse, staccato style; but when Zoë Wanamaker is playing Jolly, as Bob's sister is bizarrely misnamed, you get the feeling that words are about to fragment, like landmines."

rON 4.16 Peter, John. "A Matter of Good Faith." *Sunday Times [London]* 28 June 1998: 16-17. Rpt. in *Theatre Record* 4 June-1 July: 809.

Very positive review of the direction: "Patrick Marber directs with a breathtaking sense of psychological accuracy and lethal timing. The author of 'Dealer's Choice' and 'Closer' is a deeply English writer, but he is also the nearest thing to Mamet that we have: he can direct this quintessentially American text, full of naked self-exposure, vitriolic and defensive humour and painful riffs of anger and contrition, with such engrossing power partly, I think, because the same qualities, in their English guise, fuel his own writing."

rON 4.17 Spencer, Charles. "Dangerous Dave Meets Delicate David." *Daily Telegraph* 25 Jun 1998: 27. Rpt. in *Theatre Record* 4 June-1 July: 810-11.

Mixed review, positive on the production: "When I saw the plays on

Broadway last year they struck me as both self-indulgent and dramatically thin. In Patrick Marber's characteristically intense, exceptionally well-acted production, they seem more robust, though they strike me as interesting minor Mamet rather than great major Mamet."

rON 4.18 Tanitch, Robert. Rev. of *The Old Neighborhood*. *Plays and Players* August 1998: 13.

Positive review which compared the productions: "In New York I enjoyed the opening scene most, thanks largely to the actors' witty handling of the Mamet speech rhythms and to Vincent Guastaferro's performance as Joey. In London I enjoy the second scene most, thanks largely to Zoë Wanamaker's electric performance as Bobby's sister, Jolly, who remembers the ghastliness of a childhood in which she had been brought up by a mother and stepfather who did not love her."

rON 4.19 Usher, Shaun. Rev. of *The Old Neighborhood*. *Daily Mail* 26 June 1998. Rpt. in *Theatre Record* 4 June-1 July: 812-13.

Mixed review because the viewer must work at this: "Playgoers accustomed to explication [. . .] will flounder. They haven't lost the plot, if that's any consolation, because there isn't one. Instead, in less than an hour-and-a-half, we get to know a man and his sister, their plight emerging gradually, like a photograph gaining definition in developer fluid. I found it engrossing, fitfully funny, frequently painful. [. . .] Wanamaker [is] outstanding as a vulnerable woman whose rage and resentment over an unhappy childhood cannot hide sweetness, damaged yet persistent."

rON 4.20 Woddis, Carole. Rev. of *The Old Neighborhood*. *Herald* 26 June 1998. Rpt. in *Theatre Record* 4 June-1 July: 812.

Mixed review: "Running at under 90 minutes, that [three one acts have turned into a full evening] is perhaps debatable. All the same, Mamet being Mamet, it's still something of an event—if a slight one, the three plays adding up to an enigmatic portrait of roots and regret."

rON 4.21 Wolf, Matt. "Abroad: *The Old Neighborhood*." Rev. of *Old Neighborhood*. *Variety* 3 Aug. 1998: 45.

Wolf preferred Quirk's Deeny to Pidgeon's which "in New York seemed so encoded and abstract—and so robotically acted by its distaff player, Rebecca Pidgeon—that it vitiated the goodwill generated by its more accessible predecessors. In London, 'Deeny' (not to mention Deeny herself) still constitutes a cryptogram all its own; a tone poem that begins in medias res and ends with an ambiguously phrased (and, in the text, punctuated) farewell to passion. [. . .] Diana Quick is an immediately vital, sexual being—she's as stylishly dressed as Pidgeon was dowdily so. [. . .] The two preceding playlets repeat their New York zing."

Scholarly Overview:
The central issue is realism. In *TCI* Mamet's lighting designer observes that Mamet always backs away when things get too detailed or realistic. Bigsby similarly argues that the language conflicts with the set, undermining realistic interpretation. Nelson, too, treats only "The Disappearance of the Jews" and sees it as "a series of aborted beginnings." But Kane takes the three plays as very real depictions of issues of Jewish identity. Pearce takes "Deeny" as embodying the desire "to idealize."

Scholarly:
sON 1 Barbour, David. "You Can't Go Home Again." *Theatre Crafts International* 32.2 (1998): 10-11.

Interviewing lighting designer John Ambrosone reveals the minimalism of Mamet. "I think David would appreciate the fact that, if the play is successful, you don't really place it in a particular time frame or setting. For example, there was a discussion about the second play, which is set in the kitchen: Should there be a kitchen fixture over the table? But that was too specific."

sON 2 Bigsby, C. W. E. "Story and Anti-Story: *Lakeboat, Duck Variations, Dark Pony, Reunion, Disappearance of the Jews*." *David Mamet*. Contemporary Writers. London: Methuen, 1985. 22-45.

Bigsby notes that such "plays that might be thought to work with almost equal effect on the radio; what would be lost, however, is the contrast between an expansive and sometimes confident language and a manifestly reductive physical setting" (43). These disjunctions in the language reveal key moments for Bigsby: "Within the apparent harmonics of conversation are dissonances that suddenly expose the extent of alienation, the nature and profundity of personal and social anxieties. The plays exist for those moments. The reassuring worlds which his characters construct prove predictably fragile; the sound of their fracturing provides the background noise against which they enact their lives. Mamet has something of the artist's eye for creating painterly tableaux where realism is subtly deformed, as it is in art by the photorealists whose own portraits of urban vacuity combined realist aesthetics with self-conscious techniques that destabilize the reality they seemed to embrace" (44).

sON 3 Kane, Leslie. "Gathering Sparks." *Weasels and Wisemen: Ethics and Ethnicity in the Work of David Mamet*. New York: St. Martin's Press, 1999. 227-59.

Kane as usual gives an encyclopedic referencing to all the Jewish (and Chicago) allusions in the play. In these, she finds a thematic center to the three plays: "Principally concerned with the very uniqueness of American Jewish life—who or what defines a Jew, the responsibilities of Jewish men and women, the effects of deracination, the pitfalls of intermarriage, the illusion of assimilation, and the difficulty of maintaining ritual—*The Old Neighborhood* raises questions about the difficulty of being Jewish in America confronting both the issues of self-hatred and anti-Semitism in ways not previously addressed by Mamet" (231). The way of discovering identity Kane notes arises from "increasing interest in personal narratives that afford greater visibility to ethnicity" (231). Kane sees the most gripping moments in the play in "Jolly"—first when Bobby discovers that he's not returning to the marriage with Laurie; the second when Jolly, in the second scene, recounts the dream of her mother trying to get into her room to kill her (253). But the conclusion of the play she sees as open-ended because, despite Deeny's assertions of faith, it is unclear if Bobby will follow her path toward spiritual peace after his divorce (255).

sON 4 —. "'It's the Way That You Are with Your Children': The Matriarchal Figure in Mamet's Late Work." *Gender and Genre: Essays on David Mamet.* Eds. Christopher C. Hudgins and Leslie Kane. New York: Palgrave, 2001. 143-75.

In *The Cryptogram* Kane views Donny negatively as: "Turning her wrath on her vulnerable son, an 'equally marginalized figure' who hears voices and speaks of suicide" (156-57). Despite this, she sees John as "Virtually and metaphorically empowered to survive, he not only listens to himself, but to a Higher Voice that does not lure him to his death" (157). Her view of Jolly is sympathetic: "a loving mother and caregiver who has survived a destructive, abusive relationship with her own mother and stepfather, and finds herself paralyzed by ambivalent, conflicted emotions—mourning a woman she has long detested" (159). Kane sees no irony in this portrait, but takes it quite literally. Most perceptive is her recognition of a moment of Jolly breaking down, where the breaking off of dialogue implies overpowering emotion: "this nuanced, intimate moment in which the ambivalent nexus of loss, love, and rage is backlit" (166).

sON 5 Nelson, Jeanne Andrée. "A Machine out of Order: Indifferentiation in David Mamet's *The Disappearance of the Jews.*" *Journal of American Studies* 25.3 (1991): 461-67.

Nelson uses René Girard's theory of the use of scapegoats and violence to explain the final scenes of the play in which, in her view, characters have lost borders, lost Jewish identity, lost male identity, and seek a scapegoat to blame for their loss. "Joey's nostalgia is filled with religious, hierarchical, and patriarchal structures. He stands at the edge of the gap that separates him from these archaic systems, and by praising their virtues, he would like to erect a bridge that would allow him to cross over to his lost origin and to what he imagines to be its transcendence. But his fantasy does not insure his safe passage towards the idealized totality. The quest for a logocentric world fails repeatedly. The two friends draw no lesson from their succession of aborted narratives, and this is one of the reasons why the play does not progress, but rather remains a series of fragmented beginnings" (463).

sON 6 Pearce, Howard. "Illusion and Essence: Husserl's Epoché, Gadamer's 'Transformation into Structure,' and Mamet's *Theatrum Mundi.*" *Analecta Husserliana* 73 (2001): 111-28.

With a curious view of *theatrum mundi* Pearce examines the gap between the real and the ideal in Mamet's plays. "The plays *Cryptogram, The Water Engine, The Shawl,* and *The Old Neighborhood* might be suggested as instances that open up the fluctuating relationships between worlds and reveal the mystery and uncertainty of their making connections. The most startling reading is of "Deeny" as a world "of tranquillity and communion. The two characters are aware of their world's deficiencies and their own inadequacies, but they share a moment of harmony and love. The past evoked seems to nourish their spirits, as they explore their imaginations and memories for images of sustaining value. The idea of a garden becomes the paradigm of the happy place they have achieved, at least momentarily and metaphorically" (120).

sON 7 —. "Poiesis and the Withdrawal: The Garden-Motive in Henry James, Wallace Stevens, and David Mamet." *Analecta Husserliana* 75 (2002): 253-278.
    Starting with Heidegger's idea of "longing for idealized place" with that of pastoral, the article examines Henry James, Wallace Stevens, and Mamet. Instead of using *The Woods* which clearly fits the pastoral mode, Pearce uses "Deeny" the third play/act of *The Old Neighborhood*. He notes how Deeny "reverts to the past and its allowing of the dream, the impulse, to idealize" (261). At the end of the play Deeny and Bob confess "their defenselessness against time and change" (261-63).

See also the following article that covers "The Disappearance of the Jews."

sSTP 15 Zinman, Toby Silverman. "So Dis Is Hollywood: Mamet in Hell."

OLEANNA

Dedication: to the memory of Michael Merritt
Scene: John's Office
Characters: John, a professor in his 40s; Carol, a college student
Editions:
Oleanna. New York: Pantheon Books, 1992.
Oleanna. New York: Vintage Books, 1993.
Oleanna. New York: Dramatists Play Service, 1993.
Oleanna. London: Methuen Drama with the Royal Court Theatre, 1993.
Oleanna. Dir. David Mamet. Samuel Goldwyn Co., 1994. [film]
David Mamet Plays: 4. London: Methuen, 2002.

Plot Outline:
In the opening, John is on the telephone discussing the purchase of a house with his realtor. The telephone interrupts throughout the play. Carol slowly recognizes that he is buying a house, and is near to receiving tenure from the university. She is having trouble in his course. Despite reading his text, and writing down all he says in class, she cannot understand. John tries to explain his course, and when she complains that she must be just stupid, he says he too had trouble in school. He offers to teach her by private tutorials in his office, and to give her an A if she'll come to these meetings. When she becomes upset, he puts his arm around her to console her, and encourages her to tell him what she's never told anyone. As she's about to do so, the phone rings again. There is no problem with the house; his wife was trying to get him to come there for a surprise party. He explains he must go to the party, and leaves. In the second act, a little time has passed and Carol has brought charges against John for sexual harassment. She has come at his request to discuss her charges. She refuses to drop them and admit that she's been wrong. As she starts to leave, he tries to restrain her from leaving and she yells for help.

In the third act he has again requested a meeting. He's been at a hotel for two days; she reveals that she has brought charges against him for battery and attempted rape, and he is crushed realizing he has lost his house and position. Carol, firmly in control, says that she and her group of supporters might drop the charges if he agrees to their list of demands which, he discovers, involves dropping his book. He is outraged and tells her to leave and that he will fight these demands. When his wife calls, he reassures her. As he hangs up, leaving, Carol tells him not to call his wife, "Baby." At this he snaps, grabs her, hits her, knocks her to the floor, raises a chair to smash her, yelling "I wouldn't touch you with a ten foot pole. You little *cunt*." He then catches himself. Stops. ". . .yes. That's right," she says.

Production:
pO 1 Back Bay Theatre Company in association with American Repertory Theater at
     The Hasty Pudding, Cambridge, Massachusetts, May 1, 1992.

Director:		David Mamet
Set designer:		Michael Merritt
Costumes:		Harriet Voyt
Lighting:		Kevin Rigdon
Cast:		
	John:	William H. Macy
	Carol:	Rebecca Pidgeon

Overview:
The reviewers all noted the explosive nature of the play and its effect on the audience. Gale attributed it to Pidgeon who "is a coiled spring as Carol. Repressed and lashing out, her performance grows. She makes you feel the sting of her anger, of her displacement." Karam noted that the first act seemed to begin slowly, but "By the end of the play there was no such worry. [Mamet] had launched the dramatic equivalent of a Scud attack on political correctness." Kelly and Stayton both wrote about the angry and heated post play discussions.

Reviews:
rO 1.1 Austin, April. "Mamet Debuts New Play." *Christian Science Monitor* 21 May
      1992: 13.
         A brief notice contradicting itself almost instantly: "It's easy to sympathize
      with the student. She's paralyzed with doubt about her capacity to learn, but her
      search for knowledge quickly surges into anger [. . .]. The play, while ambiguous
      in many ways, shows Mamet to be firmly on the professor's side."

rO 1.2 Gale, William K. "New Mamet Play Typically Touches Nerves." *Chicago
      Tribune* 13 May 1992: C20.
         Positive review reported that most "applauded the work. [. . .] But those
      sharp boos, which seemed to come from men, were a signal that Mamet [. . .]
      has again struck a nerve, several in fact. [. . .] Repressed and lashing out,
      [Pidgeon's] performance grows. She makes you feel the sting of her anger, of
      her displacement. William H. Macy's John is an edgy portrait in covering up.
      This professor knows all the words, but not what to say. [. . .] The surface is
      ever shifting. We all, he seems to say, live on a fault line."

rO 1.3 Karam, Edward. "Pre-Emptive Strike on Feminism?" *Times* [London] 13 May
1992. LT: 3.

Positive review: "At the interval [. . .] an elderly gentleman asked an usher
hopefully, 'Is the play over?' He might have been forgiven, because the first act
of 'Oleanna' is uncharacteristically innocuous for Mamet. [. . .] By the end of
the play there was no such worry. [Mamet] had launched the dramatic equivalent
of a Scud attack on political correctness."

rO 1.4 Kelly, Kevin. "'Oleanna' Enrages— and Engages." *Boston Globe* 2 May1992: 34.

This review positively reported the effect on the audience. Mamet "sets up
a dramatic situation so innocent (and didactic) that the rampant danger, the
pervasive evil of its outcome leave you shaken. Like the play's protagonist [. . .]
you feel a need of action, desperate action, even violence. Syntax has lost
meaning. Interpretation is rabid, cause and effect scrabbled. You're drawn into
the second act of Mamet's 90-minute play—when the mouse turns on the cat—
to have reason and logic give way to a single thought of reprisal. Pushed to the
limit, the professor gives way to obscenity and force. You sit there powerless,
harboring rage."

rO 1.5 —. "Political Correctness Off Broadway with David Mamet." *Heterodoxy*
June 1992: 9.

Positive review of the play as theatre which "caused not only cool after-
the-fact discussion but heated arguments during performances. [. . .] If Mamet's
provocation resembles somewhat, say, the rabble rousing that spilled over from
an agitprop forerunner like Clifford Odets' famous *Waiting for Lefty*, it is activism
of the most intellectual kind. It asks penetrating questions, gives forceful and
then frightened answers, and compels a serious rebuttal of political correctness."

rO 1.6 Taylor, Markland. Rev. of *Oleanna*. *Variety* 11 May 1992: 127.

Mamet interview: "The point of the play is, at the end, to ask, 'How did we
get here?' The professor adores his students and prides himself on being a good
teacher. How did he wind up thrashing a student? [. . . Language] ceases to be
a transparent medium of communication, translating thoughts and feelings
clearly and unequivocally from one mind to another. Instead, language spins its
wheels and gets nowhere. If you break the rhythm, you break the meaning.
Rhythm conveys meaning. It's puzzling. I can't explain it. But my ear hears it."

Production:

pO 2 Back Bay Theatre Company's production moved to the Orpheum Theatre in
New York City for previews on October 13, 1992; opened officially on October
26; and ran until January 16, 1994, for 513 performances and 15 previews. [An
80 minute videotape of the January 20, 1993 resides in the TOFT collection of
the New York Public Library's Performing Arts Collection.] During the run
Macy and Pidgeon were succeeded by:

John:	Jim Frangione, then Treat Williams
Carol:	Mary McCann

Overview:
Generally, there were three responses to the play. One group thought John was mistreated, and saw the play as his tragedy (Henry, Kirkpatrick, Lahr, Barnes). Another, mainly feminist in origin, were outraged by Mamet's treatment of Carol and upset with the accusation of rape, seeing him as failing to be even-handed, and so mistreating women (Gerard, Resnikova, Rich, Russo, Solomon, Stuart). A third group found the handling to be balanced in its examination of the abuse of power, whoever is in charge (Feingold, Holmberg, Kaufman, Kroll, Silverthorne, Weales).

Most critics were outraged at John's mistreatment by Carol, likening her and her third act costume to the Chinese Red Guard (Kissel, Lahr, Rich, Solomon). But Kroll saw: "On the surface, her accusations seem frightening in their lethal absurdity. But inexorably we realize that she is telling the truth—*her* truth. His compliments ('Don't you look fetching') she sees as sexist put-downs coming from his position of power."

Nearly all faulted Mamet's direction of the play because they saw the actors as underplaying emotion. That is, the actors didn't display emotion when and where the reviewer expected it—to conform to his or her interpretation of the play. Barnes and Sterritt both saw "ritual" in Mamet's direction of the performances, and several saw a "debate." Simon, Barnes, and Watt noticed the "spare" staging, but none drew any significance from the lack of a realistic set.

Reviews:
rO 2.1 Barbour, David. "Academic Gowns [Costumes]." *TCI* 27.3 (1993): 8.
>Harriet Voyt, Mamet's assistant, also chose the costumes for *Oleanna*: "Written in the appropriately elusive Mametian style, the minimalist design [. . .] is nonetheless filled with telling details. 'I've worked for David for a few years now; we talked about how the characters should look.' Because of the overall minimal approach, she notes, every detail was given extra weight. 'We'd go through everything,' she says. 'We'd take a look at the socks and say, 'We have to change those.'"

rO 2.2 Barnes, Clive. "Mamet with a Thud." *New York Post* 26 Oct. 1992. Rpt. in *New York Theatre Critics' Reviews* 53.19 (1992): 359.
>Rather negative: "The professor has no contest in winning our sympathy at the hands of a deranged agent provocateur apparently acting on behalf of an extortionist multicultural group. [. . .] The physical production (it took 13 producers to raise the money for this!) looks so Spartanly bare (even chintzy—and not in the English sense) that it appears more suitable for a read-through than a staging. Adding to the anti-theatrical chill Mamet himself has directed his actors [. . .] into a stylized ritual, effetely artificial in phrase and pause, halfway between debate and conflict but irreversibly frozen."

rO 2.3 Feingold, Michael. "Prisoners of Unsex." *Village Voice* 3 Nov. 1992: 109. Rpt. in *New York Theatre Critics' Reviews* 53.19 (1992): 357.
>Positive review of "a tragedy built as a series of audience traps; the minute

you get suckered into thinking it says one thing, you're likely to find it saying the exact opposite. [. . .] [C]ertain lines at the performance I attended made audience members shout back, not a common event at a New York press opening. [. . .] The real horror of what happens is that it comes from a series of verbal misunderstandings, glaringly magnified by each and reflected back as a bigger misunderstanding onto the other. [. . .] And neither party, through the whole tortuous event, says a single word he or she does not sincerely believe is true."

rO 2.4 Frank, Glenda. "Past Politically Correct." *Chelsea Clinton News* 21 Jan. 1993: 10.
    Positive review: "Michael Merritt's emblematic set is as minimalistic as the dialogue and plot. Its teacher's desk is the academic power John abandons in order to reach out to Carol; the phone makes continuous economic and social demands on John's attention; the black backdrop is reminiscent of the omnipresent classroom blackboard and of a funeral. Harriet Voyt's green-toned costumes become graceful ensigns of victory and defeat."

rO 2.5 Gerard, Jeremy. Rev. of *Oleanna. Variety* 26 Oct. 1992: 76. Rpt. in *New York Theatre Critics' Reviews* 53.19 (1992): 353.
    Negative review: "Then again, it's also one of the nastiest contraptions to sputter down the pike in some time. [. . .] But by now, Carol has been transformed from self-doubting wallflower to a scourge of the Old Order. As tenure, home, even job slip away, John tries to reason with her, only to become more entangled in the sticky web she's spun. Carol's complaints aren't without merit, but they don't come close to representing the real sexism women confront on the campus, and that's where Mamet goes off the deep end. He stacks the deck against her with stunning ferocity. John may be a pompous, self-important bombast, but he's not evil and he's not a lech. [. . .] No one's going to believe that John's shortcomings merit the consequences he suffers."

rO 2.6 "He Said . . . She Said . . .Who Did What?" *New York Times* 15 Nov. 1992, B 6.
    Pundits commented on the play: Susan Brownmiller, Enrique Fernandez, Deborah Tannen, Mark Alan Stanley, Ellen Schwartzman and Lionel Tiger.

rO 2.7 Henry III, William A. "Reborn with Relevance." *Time* 2 Nov. 1992: 69. Rpt. in *New York Theatre Critics' Reviews* 53.19 (1992): 363.
    Positive review: "By the end the professor resembles the broken-spirited figures in anti-communist plays by Pinter or Havel, ready to comply with anything just to end the humiliation and pain. His ugly spiral downward is at once outlandish and entirely plausible, and it had this audience member virtually leaping out of his chair in fury at the injustice and unreason. Whatever the bumps—and there are a few in Mamet's staging of his text—the power to incense, like that to sadden or amuse, is reason enough to cheer for the future of the theater."

rO 2.8 Hornby, Richard. "Dramatizing Aids." Rev. of *Oleanna. Hudson Review* 46.1 (1993): 193-92.

Negative review: "Even if we accept that such an outrageous travesty of justice could actually occur (and I will grant that university campuses are weird places), Mamet's professor is so inept that we can hardly have any sympathy for him. [. . .] *Oleanna* backfires, shifting our sentiments to all the wrong places."

rO 2.9 Kane, Leslie. Rev. of *Oleanna*. *David Mamet Review* 1 (1994): 1-2.

Kane, who sat in on a rehearsal in Cambridge, viewed it positively as "an incendiary unnerving examination of the burning issues of sexual harassment and censorship." Her view was very anti-Carol: "If *Oleanna* enrages and engages—and it most certainly does (Pidgeon was hissed at several performances I attended)—it is largely because Mamet masterfully reveals the pernicious, pervasive evil of thought control, the McCarthyism of the 1990s. It is simply too easy to dismiss *Oleanna* as antifeminist, even misogynist. Male and female alike we understand that Carol's wilful misinterpretation of the truth—however much it costs her—has little to do with the abolition of elitism and sexism. What we are speaking about here is fascism masquerading as humanitarianism."

rO 2.10 Kanfer, Stefan. "Problems of Craft." *New Leader* 14 Dec. 1992: 26.

Negative review: "In this editorial cartoon both characters are wrong. Carol is more wrong than John, that's all. Incidentally, the title has nothing to do with the text or the personae."

rO 2.11 Kaufman, David. "The Hidden Agenda." *Downtown* 2 Dec 1992: 18.

Positive review: "Now it is John who says, 'I don't understand,' echoing Carol's lament from their first meeting with each other. Their roles have completely reversed, and we finally perceive that 'Oleanna' is, above all, a play about the transference of power. [. . .] As Carol continues to provoke him, John ends up beating her viciously, turning her accusations into a self-fulfilling prophecy."

rO 2.12 Kirkpatrick, Melanie. Rev. of *Oleanna*. *Wall Street Journal* 29 Oct. 1992. Rpt. in *New York Theatre Critics' Reviews* 53.19 (1992): 358-59.

Positive review: "The true victim might be the accused, not the accuser. This is the question Mr. Mamet poses, and it is also the question he is careful not to answer. The intellectual appeal of 'Oleanna' is that it is hard, if not impossible, to judge what happened between a young student (Rebecca Pidgeon) and her encouraging professor (William H. Macy)."

rO 2.13 Kissel, Howard. "Mamet's Campus Combat: It's PC or Perish for *Oleanna* Prof." *Daily News* [New York] 26 Oct. 1992. Rpt. in *New York Theatre Critics' Reviews* 53.19 (1992): 361.

Positive review: "Even when the lines are witty, W. H. Macy, presumably with Mamet's imprimatur, delivers them in a hard-edged manner. Perhaps this was to redress the balance between teacher and student. Mamet has written the role of the student unsympathetically, and Rebecca Pidgeon plays her with the deadly fanaticism of the Red Guard."

rO 2.14 Kroll, Jack. "A Tough Lesson in Sexual Harassment." *Newsweek* 9 Nov.
1992: 65. Rpt. in *New York Theatre Critics' Reviews* 53.19 (1992): 360.

Positive review which noted how perspective changed: "We don't know
what happened between Anita Hill and Clarence Thomas, but we see exactly
what happens with Carol and John. On the surface, her accusations seem
frightening in their lethal absurdity. But inexorably we realize that she is telling
the truth—her truth. His compliments ('Don't you look fetching') she sees as
sexist put-downs coming from his position of power."

rO 2.15 Lahr, John. "Dogma Days." *New Yorker* 16 Nov. 1992: 121+. Rpt. in *New
York Theatre Critics' Reviews* 53.19 (1992): 351-53.

Positive review of the play, less so of Mamet's direction: "The battle that
ensues brings the audience up against the awful spoiling power of envy disguised
as political ideology. Carol ends up trashing the professor's life. [. . .] Carol's
rigidity is a sign of her insecurity. Her ruthless orthodoxy is skillfully shown as
her means of controlling her enormous anxiety of ignorance. In this production,
the intelligence of Rebecca Pidgeon, who plays Carol, makes it hard to suspend
disbelief in her academic ineptness but also makes her puritan willfulness
powerfully credible. Dressed now, in the last of their three encounters, in a
loose-fitting black jacket, green chinos, and sensible black shoes, and peering
out from behind wire-rimmed glasses, Carol stands above John like some Maoist
enforcer. [. . .] Both Mr. Macy and Ms. Pidgeon are a bit under wraps here, at
once awed and cowed by Mamet's authority, which takes some of the acting
oxygen out of the air."

rO 2.16 Miracky, James. Rev. of *Oleanna*. *America* 15 May 1993: 16.

Positive review of the play with Jim Frangione: "On a deeper and more
successful level, the play is an often brilliant representation of the relationship
between language and power and a sobering exploration of the possibility of
human communication. [. . .] Does language reflect 'reality' or actually create
it? Is shared meaning possible, or does 'truth' boil down to individual
interpretations that are often in conflict? Is genuine human communication
ever possible? John moves from articulate professor to desperate man and Mary
[sic] transforms from awkward co-ed into confident opponent."

rO 2.17 Mufson, Daniel. "The Critical Eye: Sexual Perversity in Viragos." *Theater*
[New Haven] 24.1 (1993): 111-13.

Examined reviewers' conflicting views: "*Oleanna's* working title could have
been *The Bitch Set Him Up*." Mufson argued that the play is all one-sided: "one
of the two characters is a cardboard cut-out, a nightmarish phantom conjured
by the paranoid fantasies of a patriarchy peering over a cliff to see—gads!—
egalitarianism." Mufson asserted "The critics showed most integrity in their
views of *Oleanna* when they explicitly stated their political motivations for
liking the play." He made no such assertion about those who disliked it. In his
view they were just seeing reality, not their own ideology modeled before them.

rO 2.18 Nelsen, Don. "Macy Parades Talent." *Daily News* [New York] 8 Nov. 1992, sec. *City Lights*: 9.

Profile and promotional piece: "I thought [. . .] that women would be more upset with the play, and it's turned out to be the opposite. Men are more enraged, while women seem to be smarter about it. They see both sides. I'm sure it offends many women, and I don't get to talk to them because they don't want to talk to me, but the ones I do talk to who found it outrageous are at least intellectually titillated by it. It makes them think."

rO 2.19 Resnikova, Eva. "Fool's Paradox." *National Review* 18 Jan. 1993: 54-56.

Negative review of the play's imbalance: "because of the guile with which he sets up and manipulates the characters and the action. He purports to present an ambiguous situation in a balanced manner and then asks the audience to make up their own minds, based on the evidence. [. . .] At the end of the evening, when one tots up the character flaws, John emerges as a well-meaning fool, while Carol is an emotional terrorist who has no qualms about destroying not only John but his innocent wife and child as well."

rO 2.20 Rich, Frank. "Mamet's New Play Detonates the Fury of Sexual Harassment." *New York Times* 26 Oct. 1992: B1+. Rpt. in *New York Theatre Critics' Reviews* 53.19 (1992): 354. Rpt. in *Hot Seat*. New York: Random House 1998. 907-09.

Mixed review which saw the play as slanted toward John because: "Both Carol and John win scattered points as they argue, Rashomon-style, that a particular physical gesture or a few lines of suggestive conversation in their first office encounter may have been either menacing or innocuous. But once Carol inflates her accusations for rhetorical purposes before a faculty committee, Mr. Mamet's sympathies often seem to reside with the defendant. [. . .] Yet 'Oleanna' might be a meatier work if its female antagonist had more dimensions, even unpleasant ones, and if she were not so much of an interchangeable piece with the manipulative, monochromatic Mamet heroines of, say, 'House of Games' and 'Speed-the-Plow.' "

rO 2.21 Richards, David. "The Jackhammer Voice of Mamet's *Oleanna*." *New York Times* 8 Nov. 1992, sec. 2: 1.

Positive review of the visceral effect of the actors who "are in full possession of their roles—he, plunging from a smug complacency to the wild-eyed panic of one who feels the ground giving way beneath him and is helpless to do anything about it. Meanwhile, she's traveling in the other direction—from bewilderment to the kind of righteous self-assurance that can put the blaze of steel in a crusader's eyes. The anger and indignation of the two performers arouse in an audience transcend the confines of a mere play. In the head-to-head clashes, something elemental is being evoked—some poisonous sense of disparity that continues to divide the sexes.[. . .]"

rO 2.22 ——. "Mamet's Women: From Wimp to Warrior." *New York Times* 3 Jan. 1993, sec. B: 1+.

He noted Pidgeon's treatment as a villain: "Mr. Mamet purposely isn't saying whether he believes her to be truly aggrieved or just power mad. [. . .] Carol will stay on at the university. Rightly or wrongly, the professor is the one who is expelled. In many spectators' eyes, this makes her an outright villain. Ms. Pidgeon frequently gets hissed on stage."

rO 2.23 Russo, Francine. "Mamet's Traveling Cockfight." *Village Voice* 29 June 1993: 96.

Negative review of the woman-hating Mamet: "At *Oleanna*'s recent premiere in Stamford, 45 Coast Guard cadets packed the audience, smartly turned out in civvies. When the professor's fist smashed into the female student who'd accused him of sexual harassment, many of them whooped and cheered. 'Yeah!' they yelled. 'Yeah.' [. . .] There's been a lot of smart analysis of this play to prove it's weighted on both sides, but to experience *Oleanna*, you need to bring your nose as well as your intellect. The on-its-head world Mamet's written reeks of woman-hating, and his directorial choices spew a mean-spirited, unwholesome smog over the proceedings on and off-stage."

rO 2.24 Sheward, David. Rev. of *Oleanna*. *Backstage* 30 Oct. 1992: 48.

Positive review which noted Pidgeon "has a stiff British technique which contrasts starkly with Macy's more naturalistic approach. Her character emerges as a cipher. But that seems to be what Mamet intended. Carol is a blank page, easily written upon by her professor and then by an unseen 'group' which has pushed her to make charges. [. . . The play] does what theatre is supposed to do: it will make you angry, lead you to question your assumptions, and shake you until your teeth rattle."

rO 2.25 Showalter, Elaine. "Acts of Violence: David Mamet and the Language of Men." *Times Literary Supplement* 6 Nov, 1992: 16.

Reviewing the film of *Glengarry* and the staging of *Oleanna* Showalter presented the clearest argument that the play is unbalanced: "In making his female protagonist a dishonest, androgynous zealot, and his male protagonist a devoted husband and father who defends freedom of thought, Mamet does not exactly wrestle with the moral complexities of sexual harassment. What he has written is a polarizing play about a false accusation of sexual harassment; and that would be fair enough—false accusations of harassment, rape and child abuse indeed occur—if he were not claiming to present a balanced, Rashomon-like case. The disturbing questions about power, gender, and paranoia raised in *Oleanna* cannot be resolved with an irrational act of violence."

rO 2.26 Simon, John. "Thirteen Ways of Looking at a Turkey." *New York* 9 Nov. 1992: 72. Rpt. in *New York Theatre Critics' Reviews* 53.19 (1992): 361-62.

The usual negative review by Simon: "In truth, the language of the play is totally synthetic. John speaks mostly in pedantic convolutions, Carol in echoing vacuities. There is no drop of human reality anywhere. Deliberate? Maybe, but to what end? To generate sympathy? It doesn't."

rO 2.27 Solomon, Alisa. "Mametic Phallacy." *Village Voice* 24 Nov. 1992: 104. Rpt.
in *New York Theatre Critics' Reviews* 53.19 (1992): 355-56.

Negative review: "Her accusations are so obviously exaggerated [. . .] that
the audience audibly gasps with every new charge. I hoped that they were
gasping at Mamet's mounting mendacity, but by the end I had to accept that
they'd walked into his wicked trap: a few actually cheered at the end when the
professor beats the student up, convinced, no doubt, that she deserved it, she
provoked him, she brought it on herself. [. . .] What the play really dramatizes,
in other words, is how sexual harassment functions as a trumped-up weapon of
'political correctness.' Pointing out sexism, in Mamet's view, leads inevitably
to censorship and needless destruction."

rO 2.28 —. "He Said/He Said." *Village Voice* 2 Nov. 1993: 110+.

One year later, Solomon was upset by *Oleanna's* popularity: "But the
proliferation of *Oleannas* raises new questions, for it is not just another mildly
liberal 'issues play,' as works that mention AIDS or apartheid are called in
season-planning powwows. It's a twisted indictment of egalitarian impulses,
dramatizing how sexual harassment is used as a trumped up weapon of 'political
correctness.' In Mamet's view, pointing out sexism (or, by extension, racism,
homophobia, or anything else dismissed as so much p.c. harangue) leads
inevitably to censorship and the vindictive destruction of straight white men."

rO 2.29 Stayton, Richard. "Then He Created Woman." *Newsday* 25 Oct. 1992, sec.
Funfair: 7+.

Recounting that Brown students came to a preview and in the after play
discussion "admit they're confused by the play. [. . .] 'But this issue of date
rape,' interjects a woman in her early 20s, 'is this play politically irresponsible?
An audience, seeing her . . .' Mamet doesn't allow the student to make her
point: 'Politically irresponsible?! We call that art. Women by their sex are not
debarred from making a false accusation.' [. . . On the phone the next day with
Pinter] 'I almost lost it; I regressed,' Mamet confesses to Pinter. 'I felt like the
professor in my play. "Politically irresponsible." Can you believe it? I wouldn't
have felt more shocked if she'd said it was too Jewish.'"

rO 2.30 Stearns, David Patrick. "Mamet's Brutal Battle of the Sexes." *USA Today* 26
Oct. 1992. Rpt. in *New York Theatre Critics' Reviews* 53.19 (1992): 362.

Mixed review: "But this one gets under your skin and itches there for days.
It's impossible to tell if it's great or greatly manipulative."

rO 2.31 Sterritt, David. "Drama Touches on Political Power." *Christian Science
Monitor* 30 Oct. 1992: 12. Rpt. in *New York Theatre Critics' Reviews* 53.19
(1992): 358.

Positive review of Mamet's purpose: "a teacher's job is not to tell students
how to think, but to provoke them into drawing their own conclusions. Mamet
clearly sees his own job in similar terms—not to flatter his audience with voguish
formulations or time-tested truisms, but to explore the murkiest and most

turbulent depths of contemporary discourse, stirring up harsh passions the better to examine their contorted shapes and inescapable complexities [. . .]."

rO 2.32 Stuart, Jan. "Mamet's Reactionary Howl on Sexual Harassment." *Newsday* 26 Oct. 1992. Rpt. in *New York Theatre Critics' Reviews* 53.19 (1992): 356.

Negative review: "The message is as blunt as the seated figure with the bull's-eye chest on the 'Playbill' cover: [there were two covers, one with a male figure, the other with a female]: Self interest in feminist clothing has rendered our judiciary language so mushed-out and meaningless that every man in a position of authority is a sitting duck. Attaboy, Dave!"

rO 2.33 Watt, Douglas. Rev. of *Oleanna. Daily News* [New York] 30 Oct. 1992. Rpt. in *New York Theatre Critics' Reviews* 53.19 (1992): 360.

Negative review: "A tricky, ironic little work. Using an almost bare stage (desk, two chairs, bench), Mamet has staged 'Oleanna' as pointedly as possible. But it doesn't coalesce until the second half, and that's too late."

rO 2.34 Weales, Gerald. "Gender Wars." *Commonweal* 4 Dec. 1992: 15+.

Positive review of the characters' ambivalence: "John is either a well-meaning professor at first intent on helping a confused student or a sexist and elitist whose every casual word is an indication of his comfortable place in the power structure. Carol is either a victim of that structure or a radical feminist who wishes to replace the professor as power figure. Neither character, in so far as the two are characters rather than opposing points of view, is particularly attractive. Each in his/her way is a whiner and completely self-absorbed although both explain their words and actions in terms of some larger idea or entity."

rO 2.35 —. "American Theater Watch, 1992-1993." *Georgia Review* 47 (1993): 564-65.

Positive review which suggested that women saw John as "a perfect model of the condescending professor" and men saw Carol as "a paragon of political correctness." But "The two characters are so well drawn that both contain victim and victimizer. [. . . And] words dictate behavior and in which the speaker, particularly in the case of John, like the less-educated petty thieves in *American Buffalo*, cannot really hear what he is saying" (564).

rO 2.36 Weber, Bruce. "Sex Battles, No Codes." *New York Times* 30 Oct. 1992: C2.

At a recent performance when John lashed out at the end, "there was scattered applause in the audience, leading one woman, when the lights came up, to mutter angrily: "Let's find those guys who clapped." Also noted that in an interview that week Mamet explained that the first draft "was written some eight months before the Hill-Thomas hearings, but it was the hearings that led him to pull it out of a drawer and work on it again."

rO 2.37 Winer, Linda. "A Not-So-Shocking Secret in *Oleanna*." *Newsday* 30 Oct. 1992: 63.

Negative review of the play: "Because this is one of those rare times when, as far as I'm concerned, Mamet has failed to light the dynamite he obviously intended to bring to the theater. [. . .] What he has written is a didactic, one-sided argument that, if it weren't so deadly and unsubstantial, could have been a scary piece of work. [. . . Of John] nothing onstage makes us think, for a moment, that his transgressions—a vaguely off-color joke, a comforting arm around her shoulder—are grounds for destroying his life."

Production:
pO 3 The Back Bay Company's production playing at the Orpheum, also played at the Eisenhower Theatre of the John F. Kennedy Center for the Performing Arts. May 1 until May 23, 1993 with:

| John: | William H. Macy |
| Carol: | Debra Eisenstadt |

Overview:
The notable feature of this production, brought from New York by Mamet, was the blackboard in the lobby after the play which asked the audience to vote: Is he right? Was she wronged? Could it really happen? The idea was the Kennedy Center's, rather than Mamet's, Eisenstadt told us. Page and Rosenfeld comment on audience response. Rose liked Macy, not Eisenstadt—so he thought the production and play imbalanced.

Reviews:
rO 3.1 Macy, William, Deborah Eisenstadt and Liane Hansen. "David Mamet's Oleanna Raises Questions of Harassment." 2 May. NPR *Weekend Edition*, 1993.
Substantial reflections on acting in this play by both actors.

rO 3.2 Page, Clarence. "A Sexual Battle Onstage . . . And Off." *Chicago Tribune* 2 May 1993, sec. 4: 3.
A mixed review noted the blackboard "in the theater's lobby counted audience votes on two questions. Almost everyone thought the professor, not the student, was right (that was easy; Mamet stacks the deck) and that the staged situation could happen in real life. [. . .] Women want to be respected the same as men, yet 'hostile workplace' rulings ban much of the language and behavior men normally take for granted among other men."

rO 3.3 Rose, Lloyd. "Mamet's *Oleanna*: Too Long, Yet It Falls Short." *Washington Post* 26 Apr. 1993, sec. D: 1+.
Mixed review: "Macy has far and away the better of the two roles and he's a lot of fun to watch, skillful, exciting, often funny. You get the feeling, though, that the actress playing Carol could drop dead or miss an entrance and he'd give exactly the same performance; certainly he and Eisenstadt aren't connecting up there on the stage. A young, inexperienced actress in a difficult role, Eisenstadt can't keep up with Macy and this makes Carol and John's conflict even more one-sided than Mamet has written it. Mamet directed, and how much of this imbalance is deliberate on his part and how much simply inept is hard to figure

out. [. . .] Carol—who, it is implied, is a lesbian—destroys John for even daring
to be a sexual being, i.e. a man."

rO 3.4 Rosenfeld, Megan. "Exit Audience, Arguing: A Poll on Mamet's Uneven
Battle." *Washington Post* 30 Apr. 1993, sec. B: 1.
    Explained the votes: "The audience votes on blackboard. [. . .] 'Is he right?'
says one, 'Could it really happen?' the next, and 'Was she wronged?' the third.
[. . .] Tuesday, 61 percent of those who voted thought he was right, compared
with a week-long average of 79 percent. Thirty-nine percent thought she was
wronged, compared with the average 21 percent. And only 85 percent said
something like this could really happen, compared with the normal 96 percent."

Production:
pO 4 Opened at the Royal Court Theatre, London on June 24, 1993 then moved to the
Duke of York's Theatre, London on September 15, 1993.

Director:		Harold Pinter
Designer:		Eileen Diss
Lighting:		Gerry Jenkinson
Cast:		
	John:	David Suchet
	Carol:	Lia Williams

Overview:
Mamet's production lasted ninety minutes; the printed Royal Court script noted one
intermission and two hours and ten minutes duration to the production directed by
Pinter (though Marvin thought it 15 minutes shorter than New York). But reviewers
who had seen the New York production were nearly unanimous in praising this
one as superior because it had "more balance and ambiguity in the piece" (Taylor)
under Pinter's direction. Suchet was lauded for showing the "smugness" and self-
satisfied flawed side of John; Williams was praised for showing the shift from first
act to second between genuine bewilderment to become a "fury" (Rutherford).
Marvin, however, noted that she was too "gorgeous. The girl must be a sexless
spinster or the play is thrown off balance." But Wolf countered that with his view
that: "Whereas Mamet directed [. . .] Carol as a prim, sexless, schoolmarm, Pinter
understands that the play is much more disturbing if her gathering confidence allows Carol to develop a sexuality as well as a case." Pinter used a draft in which
Carol totally defeated John: "Here, shakily but with chilling single-mindedness,
Carol gets up from the vicious assault and finds the confession she wants him to
deliver before the whole school and list of books (including his own) the Group
wants banned. The broken man is reading this out to her as the play ends" (Taylor).

Reviews:
rO 4.1 Anthony, Andrew. Rev. of *Oleanna*. *Guardian* 7 July 1993. Rpt. in *Theatre
Record* 18 June -1 July 1993: 747.
    Positive review: "What was striking was the fact that they did not share the
same language. And, ultimately, it was Mamet's echo of Orwell's warning—

that the abuse of power lies in manipulating language—which proved more thought provoking to me than questions of gender and guilt."

rO 4.2 Back, Sophie. Rev. of *Oleanna*. *Plays and Players* Oct. 1993: 11.

Positive review: "This is Pinter's domain: ordinary situations where there is unexpressed violence between ordinary people. John is irritating and pompous, Carol is irritating and pathetic. However, Carol needs John's help. Their relationship which turns her into a jargon spouting non-entity, speaks reams about student-lecturer relationship as it should not be. [. . .] The tragedy of *Oleanna* is that her victory involves her own fall."

rO 4.3 Billington, Michael. Rev. of *Oleanna*. *Guardian* 1 July 1993. Rpt. in *Theatre Record* 18 June -1 July 1993: 740.

Very positive: "Pinter's production—far better than the one I saw in New York—which releases the mythic quality under the realistic surface." Mamet created "a superb mythic drama about the breaking of the social contract that makes all education possible: when John approaches Carol as a now-vulnerable human being, he is angrily rebuffed and told to 'stick to the process.' Mamet's point is that once people resort to ideological jargon or legalistic devices, then the whole idea of intellectual freedom breaks down. [. . .] Suchet in the first half is all intellectual condescension [. . .] by the second half he has become a stricken victim finally goaded to a fury he bitterly rejects. And Lia Williams makes Carol's transformation from a muddled despair to an iron certainty wholly convincing."

rO 4.4 Boycott, Rosie. Rev. of *Oleanna*. *Guardian* 7 July 1993. Rpt. in *Theatre Record* 18 June -1 July 1993: 747.

Negative review: "It is a riveting bit of theatre in terms of tension and it's extremely damaging to women because the complaints in the play that Carol makes to John are obviously untrue. [. . .] But although John is an unsympathetic shit who represents the unpleasantness of the educational elite, the final scene where he beats the hell out of her had me on his side."

rO 4.5 Caplan, Betty. "The Gender Benders." *New Statesman and Society* 2 July 1993: 34.

Negative review: "Mamet's best plays are those in which women don't even appear. [. . .] [N]o one seems to have noticed that Carol in *Oleanna* isn't actually a character at all. Even the feminist writer Elaine Showalter treats the play as if it had two equals. [. . . Instead,] a man with a life of his own and on the other hand, a nothing who destroys because, like the most desperate people in the world, she has nothing to lose. One character plus a heap of incongruent attitudes maketh not a play."

rO 4.6 Church, Michael. "To PC or Not to PC, That Is the Question." *Observer* 20 June 1993: 60.

Pre-opening interview with actors Lia Williams and David Suchet.

rO 4.7 Cook, William. Rev. of *Oleanna*. *Mail on Sunday* 1993. Rpt. in *Theatre Record*
18 June-1 July 1993: 740-41.

Rather negative review: "Suchet is perfect as the pompous professor put
upon by his blonde student (Lia Williams). But Harold Pinter's ponderous
direction hangs like a thick grey cloak around his shoulders. And this static,
stifling debate only bursts into life in the final few minutes."

rO 4.8 Coveney, Michael. Rev. of *Oleanna*. 4 July 1993: 56. Rpt. in *Theatre Record*
18 June-1 July 1993: 744.

Positive review contrasting the New York production in which Carol was
"a zombie" with Lia Williams who "does not wear spectacles and allows her
long hair to fall sensuously below her shoulders. David Suchet adds a leavening
of vanity to John, a thin smile, an ineradicable air of smugness about his book
and his son and his career. This restores equilibrium to the drama. [. . .] In
seeking to validate the piece as drama, Pinter exposes its weaknesses as a
polemic."

rO 4.9 de Jongh, Nicholas. "A Politically Correct Broadside for Men." *Evening
Standard* [No other information available], 1993.

Mixed review: "Last night there was a scattered applause for the Professor's
action. And you could say Mamet has designed this two-character play to elicit
such a response. For 'Oleanna' is a warning to the Politically Correct movement
in America, and the extreme feminists who blaze its trail. [. . .] Mamet tilts the
play too much against the female of the species. The unlikeable Carol becomes
a vehicle for lying fanaticism." He faults Pinter's direction of the two actors:
"Williams's Carol is humanised. She develops from disturbed waif into feminist
automaton but never fearsomely blazes." John is too moderate: "Mr. Suchet
misses panic and outrage, sinking into bland mildness. Even his violence is
restrained. Violence, Mamet suggests, is the Professor's only mode of retaliation."

rO 4.10 Edwardes, Jane. Rev. of *Oleanna*. *Time Out* 7 July 1993. Rpt. in *Theatre
Record* 18 June-1 July 1993: 745.

Negative review: Mamet's "rage burns so furiously that he is incapable of
making any kind of case for the other side and as hard as Lia Williams struggles
to give some substance to her character she still resembles a nostalgic throwback
to a WRP automaton. Rarely can there have been such a manipulative clarion
call to men's baser instincts. It's a very uncomfortable equation between the
rise of feminism and a decline in freedom of thought and more provocative
than any piece of theatre currently playing in London."

rO 4.11 Grant, Steve. "Pinter: My Plays, My Polemics, My Pad." *Independent* 20
Sept. 1993, sec. Living: 13.

Promotional piece and interview with Pinter: "The three of us, David Suchet,
Lia Williams and me, have tried so hard to avoid hysteria, and to find out where
they are both human. And that's why a lot of women do find the figure of this
girl is by no means a grotesque monster or a cripple, but a normal young woman

who is complicated and serious and vulnerable, and pretty ruthless when she gets going. [. . .] I find it striking how the male reaction at the climax has sometimes been total fury and delight, because they are actually cheering when a woman is almost being kicked to death. I want to get the arguments as clear as possible. What she's doing is a truly revolutionary thing, challenging a value-system that, no matter how liberal, is based on a male system."

rO 4.12 Gross, John. "The Mouse That Became a Monster." *Sunday Telegraph* 4 July 1993, sec. Arts: 7. Rpt. in *Theatre Record* 18 June-1 July 1993: 741.

Positive review: "Suchet suggests the professor's limitations—a certain glibness, a certain crudeness—without ever letting you doubt his fundamental decency. Lia Williams's Carol is a deadly study in dishonesty of the most dangerous kind, the kind that believes in what it is doing."

rO 4.13 Hassell, Graham. *What's On* 7 July 1993. Rpt. in *Theatre Record* 18 June-1 July 1993: 744.

Positive review: "Pinter's steadfast direction is equally scrupulous in balancing the contentious arguments. While what we witness pulls our emotions in one direction, Pinter continually engages our liberal consciences in the other: after all, hasn't Carol got a point?"

rO 4.14 Hirschhorn, Clive. *Sunday Express* 4 July 1993. Rpt. in *Theatre Record* 18 June-1 July 1993: 745.

Negative review: "Mamet's play is deeply misogynistic piece that is as manipulative as the actions of his vengeful heroine. [. . .] Yet, despite the dice-loading, 'Oleanna' is an enthralling, emotionally-charged battle of the sexes that reaches a heart-pounding climax and raises challenging questions about power, privilege, exploitation and the educational process."

rO 4.15 Karpf, Anne. Rev. of *Oleanna*. *Guardian* 7 July 1993. Rpt. in *Theatre Record* 18 June-1 July 1993: 745.

Negative review: "I went to see the play thinking Mamet had dramatised a debate between two viewpoints. What I found was the trouncing of one ideology by another. [. . .] He utterly discredits the student who accuses her professor of sexual harassment when we, the audience, saw that his behaviour was nothing more than an instinctive, if clumsy, attempt at kindness."

rO 4.16 Lawson, Mark. "Drama on the Stage, Outrage in the Stalls." *Independent* 29 July 1993: 18.

Negative review: "Twice in the past six months, I have seen Mamet's play in New York. On both occasions, the teacher's violent assault on his pupil provoked a round of applause from men in the audience. On my first visit, this was amplified by foot-stamping and the quite distinct comment—from a man sitting near me, who looked like a retired fund manager—of: 'Teach the cunt a lesson.' A relatively frequent theatre-goer for 15 years, I have never otherwise experienced such an ugly atmosphere at a play."

rO 4.17 Lewis, Peter M. Rev. of *Oleanna*. *Guardian* 7 July 1993. Rpt. in *Theatre Record* 18 June-1 July 1993: 746.

Positive review: "He says it was 'devoid of sexual content.' She says, 'It's not for you to say.' I agree; the meaning of a message isn't totally controlled by its sender—the receiver's interpretation is equally valid."

rO 4.18 —. "Provocative Drama Divides Sexes." *Independent* 1 July 1993, sec. Home: 6.

Report on audience response: "Couples emerged screaming at each other and cancelled post-theatre dinners. One group of women reportedly tried to 'get' the men who applauded when the exasperated lecturer does strike and kick the girl in the climax of this gripping play. Some men did indeed spontaneously applaud last night. [. . .] Luke Rittner, former secretary general of the Arts Council, said: 'It's a long time since I've seen people in an auditorium virtually fighting with one another at the end.'"

rO 4.19 Marvin, Blanche. Rev. of *Oleanna*. *London Theatre Reviews* June/July 1993: 17.

Preferred the New York production: "Lia Williams, who plays the bogus girl, has long blonde hair and is gorgeous. The girl must be a sexless spinster or the play is thrown off balance. [. . .] The first act clipped along, being 15 minutes shorter than in New York without changing a word. So much for the Pinter pauses Mamet directed in New York. The girl's frustration and her backwardness as a college student is much clearer here. Her support from the woman's group that leads her onto this aggressive behaviour is also much sharper. But one loses sympathy with the wimpy weak professor of David Suchet who tries ingratiating himself to the girl, not out of sympathy, but patronisingly. One believes her accusations of his need for power, called passive aggression these days."

rO 4.20 Morley, Sheridan. "Table for Two." Rev. of *Oleanna*. *Spectator* 10 July 1993: 38. Rpt. in *Theatre Record* 18 June-1 July 1993: 740.

This is a positive review on the issue of power. "By reverting to Mamet's original curtain, Pinter reminds us that this is in the end a play about who shall be given the power of deciding what things mean. [. . .] Like Lillian Hellman's *The Children's Hour*, which it much resembles in outline, this is also a play about pupil power and student revenge."

rO 4.21 Nathan, David. Rev. of *Oleanna*. *Jewish Chronicle* 2 July 1993. Rpt. in *Theatre Record* 18 June-1 July 1993: 745.

Positive review: "The real issue is whether the student Carol (Lia Williams), is a travesty or a representative figure in the feminist campaign to achieve equal rights and stop the sexual harassment of women students by male academics."

rO 4.22 Nightingale, Benedict. "Mamet Takes a Sharp Dig at McCarthyite Feminism." *Times* [London] 1 July 1993. Rpt. in *Theatre Record* 18 June-1 July 1993: 744.

Positive review, especially of this production: "Suchet gives a fine, true performance of a man clinging desperately to the values his foe rejects as patriarchal. Williams's task is harder, for she must change from an upset dimwit to an articulate feminist. [. . .] Her Carol uncynically believes that what John sees as a concern for his pupils is really a love of power, show and long words; and she is not utterly wrong. That makes for a more even-handed play, but, paradoxically, one with yet more force."

rO 4.23 —. "More Aristotle Than Hemingway." *Times* [London] 15 Sept. 1993: 37.
    Promotional interview with Mamet: "I agree with what she says as much as with what he says. She may do some things that are dishonourable, but then so does he. For me, it's a play about the uses and abuses of power, and the corruption on both sides."

rO 4.24 Peter, John. "That'll Teach Her." *Sunday Times* [London] 4 July 1993. Rpt. in *Theatre Record* 18 June-1 July 1993: 742.
    Positive review of "a play about power. For Mamet, political correctness is partly the product of a system which uses power with smugness and condescension. [. . .] Suchet catches, with a baleful brilliance, the ghastly egomaniacal sincerity of the teacher who does not really believe in teaching but relishes the opportunity to lay down the law. [. . .] The final confession, under a harsh bright light, has the atmosphere of the show trial about it. But no, thank you, I do not want the lesson read to me: the earlier ending, which left both characters humiliated, was much harder to take, like confronting your enemy in the dark. That was the proper finale to this brilliantly constructed and savagely even-handed play."

rO 4.25 Rutherford, Malcolm. Rev. of *Oleanna*. *Financial Times* 2 July 1993. Rpt. in *Theatre Record* 18 June-1 July 1993: 742.
    Positive review: "The real subject is witch-hunting or McCarthyism, whether from the left or the right. [. . .] The difference between the two of them is that the professor believes that words have a definable meaning while the student resorts to a group movement that prefers slogans. [. . .] Suchet catches to perfection that pedagogical sometimes patronising manner of a man trying to be rational against the odds struggling to find words for things that cannot be said because even language is imperfect as a means of communication. Ms. Williams is quiet and fumbling to start with, as the part demands. She becomes a fury, the essence of a semi-educated sub-culture taking over."

rO 4.26 Sierz, Aleks. Rev. of *Oleanna*. *Tribune* [UK] 9 July 1993. Rpt. in *Theatre Record* 18 June-1 July 1993: 740.
    Mixed review, but very positive of Pinter's direction: "By sympathising so overtly with John, Mamet turns this trial of strength into a kangaroo court. [. . .] Although the play's ideological deck is stacked, this version (brilliantly directed by Harold Pinter, who underlines the play's language games) restores Mamet's original ending with its deep sensation of failure."

rO 4.27 Spencer, Charles. "Bittersweet Battle of the Sexes." *Daily Telegraph* 15 Sept. 1993: 17.

Interview with David Suchet and Lia Williams.

rO 4.28 —. "Provocative View of an Epic Power Struggle." *Daily Telegraph* 2 July 1993: 19. Rpt. in *Theatre Record* 18 June-1 July 1993: 743.

Positive review of actors humanizing their roles: "There is a smugness and a coldness about Suchet's performance that repels sympathy, a hint that he might indeed be sexually interested in Carol. Meanwhile, Lia Williams suggests just how comforting it must be for a confused and lonely girl to seize on the glib certainties of the politically correct, and her body language visibly grows in confidence as the play progresses. The final explosion of violence has a terrifying, bruising intensity that instantly silenced the applause from some of the more blokeish chaps in the audience."

rO 4.29 Taylor, Paul. "Dramatically Incorrect." *Independent* 2 July 1993, sec. Arts: 15. Rpt. in *Theatre Record* 18 June-1 July 1993: 743.

Positive review: "At the start, the actress valuably pulls you into the character's confused feelings of being out of her depth. You then see how, instead of learning to swim, Carol latches on to PC as a way of shooting the swimming instructor. And, since this can only be achieved at the cost of intellectual suicide, the ending must be bleak for both of them."

rO 4.30 Tinker, Jack. "Battle of the Sexists, or How to Put the Boot into Nazi-Speak." *Daily Mail* 7 July 1993. Rpt. in *Theatre Record* 18 June-1 July 1993: 747.

Positive review of Pinter's direction to get "the enlightened, liberal audience of the Royal Court Theatre applauding the sight of a middle-aged man kicking the living daylights out of a gauche young woman. [. . .] Given two of the most powerful, combative performances in London today from David Suchet and Lia Williams, the play as directed by Harold Pinter has a far more even-handed feel to it than in New York—in spite of that chilling burst of approval when Mr. Suchet finally is sufficiently unhinged to put the boot in."

rO 4.31 —. Rev. of *Oleanna. Daily Mail* 3 July 1993. Rpt. in Theatre Record 18 June-1 July 1993: 747.

Mixed review: "She has cried 'sexual harassment' where only kindness was meant. She has screamed 'attempted rape' when only a restraining hand was laid upon her. When her professor addresses her as 'dear' she denounces him as a sexist. And in return for his bumbling attempts to make her feel at ease, she ruins his career and wrecks his life."

rO 4.32 Wardle, Irving. Rev. of *Oleanna. Independent on Sunday* 4 July 1993. Rpt. in *Theatre Record* 18 June-1 July 1993: 741.

Positive review of the direction because the "unspoken premise is that the characters are treading a sexual minefield. Anything may trigger it off; and the two performances wonderfully articulate Mamet's gift for converting tentative speech into dynamic rhythms, with words often bitten off in the middle, and John's apologies for interrupting Carol still preventing her from speaking. Even after war is declared, the voices remain quiet and reasonable."

rO 4.33 Weiss, Hedy. "Mamet's *Oleanna* Both Infuriating, Provocative." *Chicago Sun-Times* 14 Sept. 1993: 33.

This compared the productions. In New York 'Oleanna' "took the form of a vicious, unrepentant battle between the sexes, with the actors giving automaton-like performances. In London [. . .] it became more human. Though never less than a ferocious battle for power and control, the relationship between the two characters was enriched by layer upon layer of ambiguity. [. . .] The problem is that Carol seems to be Mamet's paradigm of the modern young woman, rather than the worst aberrational fringe element of the feminist movement. A serpent in sheep's clothing, she is the ultimate male nightmare of a castrating female in this age of 'sexual harassment' litigation."

rO 4.34 Wolf, Matt. "London *Oleanna* Deepens the Debate." *American Theatre* Nov. 1993: 77-78.

Wolf preferred Pinter's production to Mamet's, after noting the "geometric set" and lighting revealing the "study exists on the cusp of a black hole": "Indeed, Lia Williams's transformation from a cowed figure of a vengeful repression to a woman of almost shockingly sexy self-righteous is one of the triumphs of the evening. Whereas Mamet directed [. . .] Carol as a prim, sexless, schoolmarm, Pinter understands that the play is much more disturbing if her gathering confidence allows Carol to develop a sexuality as well as a case. Small wonder, too, that David Suchet's first-rate John responds with mixed signals of his own, freezing the audience on his admission that he will give Carol an A if she returns several more times. 'Why?' she asks. His response suggests the duplicitous Angelo in *Measure for Measure*—because 'I like you.'"

rO 4.35 Zeifman, Hersh. Rev. of *Oleanna*. *David Mamet Review* 1 (1994): 2-3.

Positive review of Pinter's improved version: "the power struggle between female student and male professor constantly seesawed throughout, as did the sympathies of the audience. Lia Williams's Carol was far more human, and therefore believable, than her New York counterpart—frightened and vulnerable in her initial helplessness, smug and arrogant as she slowly inched her way toward a painful, exultant, and decidedly Pyrrhic 'victory.' Similarly, David Suchet captured wonderfully the paradoxes and ambiguity of John; his surface generosity and concern could not entirely mask an underlying unctuousness and condescension that were deeply disturbing. Carol's battle for psychic 'territory' was reflected in Pinter's gradually allowing her to claim more and more physical space. [. . .]"

Production:
pO 5 Tiffany Theatre, Los Angeles, February 4,1994.

Director:	William H. Macy
Cast:	
John:	Lionel Mark Smith
Carol:	Kira Sedgwick

Overview:
Outside factors overshadowed the play itself. Macy was to direct and chose a cast, with Mamet, of their old colleague Lionel Mark Smith and Kyra Sedgwick. (Kendt, Shirley, Stayton). The Mark Taper Forum objected—they wanted to be in charge of casting. Macy moved the play from 750 seat Taper for the 99 seat Tiffany. Casting Smith foregrounded racial issues according to Lochte and Tucker—but as Tucker notes they cut both ways. Macy thought that they might be cancelled out. Tucker faced the issues head-on— "a black man stood over a white woman who had charged him with rape, a visual reminder of the horror inherent in racial stereotyping" and so the issue is a more complex than pure sympathy for the African-American.

Reviews:
rO 5.1 Byrne, Bridget. "Gifts of Gab." *Los Angeles Times* 7 Feb. 1994: E6.
> Gossip column chit-chat about the lobby of the opening night: "'I had trouble applauding that young lady because I wanted to give that little broad she played a punch in the stomach,' said Esther Williams."

rO 5.2 Foreman, T. E. "'Oleanna' is Theatrically Incorrect." *Press-Enterprise* [Riverside, CA] 15 Feb. 1994: A9.
> Negative review focusing on race: "Casting Smith as the professor simply exacerbates the flaws in what was already a flawed play. [. . .] A black teacher, however obtuse, with his own almost certain experience with prejudice and discrimination, simply would not react to the woman's charges of discrimination the way a white teacher might. Nor would he refer to 'the white man's burden' as John does. And he almost certainly would have been very cautious about putting his arms around a woman."

rO 5.3 Holt, Paula. "Counterpunch.' *Los Angeles Times* 21 Feb. 1994: F3.
> Producer Paula Holt complained of Shirley's review: "Shockingly, the only description the reader is given of Kyra Sedgwick's superb performance, which carries half the play, is that she is 'white,' and that she 'mastered most—although not all—of Mamet's rapid-fire dialogue.' Oh yes, and that she is too glamorous."

rO 5.4 Lochte, Dick. "The *Oleanna* Con." *Los Angeles Magazine* Mar. 1994: 120.
> Positive review: "Does either casting change the perception? Absolutely. A reference to 'the white man's burden,' for example, switches from sexist to racist without taking a breath. But, so what? [. . .] they are never quite what they seem. Is Sedgwick's character a perplexed, frustrated, inarticulate school-girl,

or a controlled, empowered and arrogant monster of feminism? Is Smith's a slightly pompous, ivory-towered intellectual or a beaten and very vulnerable man? And will they, as Mamet plays his final game with our heads, change one more time? This is a bristling, riveting play. Skin color is just one more element."

rO 5.5 Stayton, Richard. "The Storm over *Oleanna*." *Los Angeles Times* 30 Jan. 1994: 8.
Macy refused to give in; Smith said he was amazed that Bill and David ignored race in casting him for the role—never thought he'd be considered. Macy saw his own interpretation of the role as too race based—as a white professor, and wanted to overcome that. "The Forum, however, refuses to accede to 64 performances with an actor whom they don't know. They say race has nothing to do with it."

rO 5.6 Tucker, Stephanie. Rev. of *Oleanna*. *David Mamet Review* 1 (1994): 3-4.
Negative review of racial issues raised: "Perceiving themselves as victims of a discriminatory system, had they [Carol and her group] no sympathy for, no understanding of others who suffer from discrimination?" And the final scene took on an uglier resonance: "a black man stood over a white woman who had charged him with rape, a visual reminder of the horror inherent in racial stereotyping. [. . .] Racism, like sexism, remains rampant and cuts both ways— devastating and demeaning perpetrator and victim alike, finally making them indistinguishable and the outcome, for us all, deeply tragic."

Overview of the Scholarship:
A number of critics assume Mamet's misogyny (Bean, Burkman, Garner, and Silverstein). Others seek to understand the play's contribution to current disputes over sexual harassment and political correctness (Piette). A third group looks at abuses of power and/or the nature of language (Bechtel, Elam, Kane), and who has the power to interpret it (Weber). Those who argue the power theme are sensitive to Carol's motivation (Badenhausen, Foster, Goggans, Hardin, Ryan). Those who argue mi- sogyny usually base the argument on the lack of a perceived motive/reason for the change in Carol between Acts One and Two. If there is no motive, then Carol is a "two-dimensional" character and not a serious characterization. There is also concern that Mamet's use of Carol's charge of rape is a trivialization of a serious issue. Those who sympathize with Carol sometimes argue that she has the motivations of a realis- tic character (Goggans) and tend to ascribe her motives to "her group" (Mason); but some see her as other than realistic—postmodern and performative (Elam, MacLeod, Porter, Sauer, Silverthorne, Skloot, and Tomc).

Scholarly Articles:
sO 1 Badenhausen, Richard. "The Modern Academy Raging in the Dark: Misreading Mamet's Political Incorrectness in *Oleanna*." *College Literature* 25.3 (1998): 1-19.
Political correctness and sexual harassment are issues "partially skewed and narrowed by the particular cultural circumstances surrounding the play" (1) and are

dismissed as no longer of importance. What is of importance is the theme of "difficulties of acquiring and controlling language" (2). With this anti-political stance, it is surprising to see citations of Benjamin on Brecht, Eagleton, Fish and Foucault. The argument is that those in power control language, and John is a bad teacher because he does this. He "establishes language as the currency of this environment" (4), "finally sees the class as more teacher-centered than subject-centered" (5), and uses the phone "symbolically controlling the conversation by alternating between live student audience and other unseen voices" (5). Given this negative view of John, one would expect sympathy for Carol, and he has: "Carol is a careful reader who gets better at that vocation as the play progresses" (10). He does not conclude with Carol's better interpretation of language, but with indeterminacy. "Readings of *Oleanna* will resist consensus because the drama investigates how language and gesture signify differently for all involved in the performance. The drama is necessarily provocative because its events take place within a landscape of indeterminacy" (3).

sO 2 Bean, Kellie. "A Few Good Men: Collusion and Violence in *Oleanna.*" *Gender and Genre: Essays on David Mamet.* Eds. Christopher C. Hudgins and Leslie Kane. New York: Palgrave, 2001. 109-25.

A conventional reading of Mamet as misogynist, citing MacLeod and Silverstein: "Disguised as a discourse questioning the power structure of the university, [. . . *Oleanna*] indulges in the mystifying rhetoric of patriarchy that, rather than questioning cultural norms, consolidates power around masculine identity and the ideological center. Even John (or Mamet?) cannot sustain the fiction of equality between himself and his female student for more than a line or two" (120-21).

sO 3 Bechtel, Roger. "P. C. Power Play: Language and Representation in David Mamet's *Oleanna.*" *Theatre Studies* 41 (1996): 29-48.

Bechtel argues that the play is not about sexual harassment because it "does not suggest that John had the slightest of sexual intentions toward Carol"(34). Rather, "It is the issue of power, specifically through and over language, that Mamet is really getting at" (35). This part of the argument depends on an assertion that Mamet is not a realist, and so it is not real characters' actions, but their ideas which are the focus of the play. Later, however, Bechtel essentializes Carol, arguing that she is not just the tool of her Group, because she "does have some feeling of compassion for John" but cannot express it since "The Group has subsumed her identity into its own, and she has become as rigid and unforgiving as it must be" (39). Again, "At the same time, its [language's] confines become inescapable for Carol, who is unable to consider any compromise or compassion despite her natural inclinations" (40). Carol here passes over from character to real person who has "natural inclinations."

sO 4 Burkman, Katherine H. "Misogyny and Misanthropy: Anita Hill and David Mamet." *Delights, Desires, and Dilemmas: Essays on Women and the Media.* Ed. Ann C. Hall. Westport, CN: Praeger, 1998.

"What does finally make this a sexist play, however, is the stereotyping that contributes to a backlash against women, not those who fanatically insist on political correctness, but those who, like Anita Hill, insist on being treated like a person and not like prey in a power game" (112). Her conclusion, however, argues that this view of the play does not work out in the text. "In the melodramatic world of *Oleanna*, in which the evil woman destroys the foolish man, there is finally, in true misanthropic fashion, no debate. The pair are almost equally unattractive, alike, doubles" (117). Though she begins arguing that the play is mere "stereotyping" she concludes that both John and Carol are indicted in this play: "His essentially misogynic agenda is at work as he shows us that Carol may be calculating and destructive but that on some level she is right about John" (116).

sO 5 —. "The Web of Misogyny in Mamet's and Pinter's Betrayal Games." *Staging the Rage: The Web of Misogyny in Modern Drama*. Eds. Katherine H. Burkman and Judith Roof. London: Associated University Presses, 1998. 27-37.

Burkman finds Pinter's direction of *Oleanna* an improvement because he "was seeking to make Mamet's female character a suffering human being who had more than a little justification for her rancor" (28). She quotes Pinter to confirm her view that "What she's doing is a truly revolutionary thing, challenging a value-system that, no matter how liberal, is based on a male system" (28). This is quite different from what Burkman views as Mamet's usual sexist approach in which a female challenges and threatens the machismo world, exposing its misogyny and the attendant misanthropy that is at its core. "Mamet gets caught in his male characters' web of misogyny because he identifies with their hate of women and of themselves, finally sentimentalizing male bonding and celebrating it even while he exposes its basis" (35). For Burkman, Pinter, by contrast, "sympathizes with male and female alike" (35).

sO 6 Burmeister, Beth. "When 'Phaedrus' Meets 'Oleanna': Teaching Composition as Social Justice, or Reconsidering Power (Im)Balances between Students and Teachers." Paper presented at the 48th Annual Meeting of the Conference on College Composition and Communication March 12-15 (Phoenix, AZ, 1997) [ERIC Doc. ED 409565].

Burmeister presents a teaching module: "Reading Plato's dialogue in 'Phaedrus' against David Mamet's 'Oleanna,' and by using it as a site for inquiry [. . .] students are led to question not just the ancient model of education, but all models of education [. . .] as well as models of teacher-student relationships."

sO 7 Elam, Harry J., Jr. "'Only in America': Contemporary American Theater and the Power of Performance." *Voices of Power: Co-Operation and Conflict in English Language and Literatures*. Ed. Marc Maufort. Liege, Belgium: English Dept., U of Liege, 1997. 151-63.

Using Parker and Sedgwick's idea of performativity, Elam examines how in *Angels in America, Oleanna*, and *Fires in the Mirror* "theatrical performance has become an increasingly potent site for the examination and destabilization of the real and for the renegotiation of American identity. By destabilization of the real I mean the ability of the theatre to move beyond the representation of actuality to challenge, critique, and even subvert it" (152). In *Oleanna* Elam uses speech-act theory to examine how "Mamet shows the power of language to confuse as well as connect" (156). Carol "has taken John's words from the first scene out of context and re-ordered them to support her contentions. Her formal accusation, based on John's own language, attests the power of language to affect action" (156). Elam notes that "The word 'rape' [. . .] immediately connotes performative actions. Here Carol proposes that John's words are in fact actions. [. . . Thus] performance of *Oleanna* challenges the meanings of rape as it examines the intersections of speech and action" (157). "Implicit in *Oleanna* is the contention that the context of the times [. . .] not only makes John more susceptible to Carol's accusations, but provides a catalyst for and environment conducive to her raising these false complaints" (158). As a consequence, his judgment of the play is harsh: "Mamet in *Oleanna* overloads the power dynamics, subverts the ideological debate, and creates a situation in which the misogynistic treatment of women can be condoned and even justified in the name of academic freedom and integrity" (161). His conclusion about *Fires*, however, might just as aptly be applied to *Oleanna*. Smith "examines how each's perspective on the truth is shaped by their own belief systems" (159). "Consequently, the performance of *Fires* becomes an arena not only to destabilize the real, but also a site for the examination and critique of one's own perceptions" (160).

sO 8 Foster, Verna. "Sex, Power, and Pedagogy in Mamet's *Oleanna* and Ionesco's *the Lesson*." *American Drama* 5.1 (1995): 36-50.

Foster argues the play "is less an antifeminist statement than it is an indictment of an educational culture in which, in Mamet's view, power-roles and power-games played by both professors and students make teaching destructive and learning impossible" (37). Both John and Carol are seen as playing games, trying to hold onto "expected roles" (42). Concluding that it is unclear "who is the oppressor and who the oppressed" (47), she notes that Mamet denies the audience the comfort of certainty, and "Thus what the audience brings to *Oleanna* becomes more than ordinarily crucial in determining not only how they interpret the drama but also the value they place upon it" (47).

sO 9 Garner, Stanton B. Jr. "Framing the Classroom: Pedagogy, Power, *Oleanna*." *Theatre Topics* 10.1 (2000): 39-59.

Garner feels "that the play was harnessing outrage to a gender politics that it does little to question" (39). In order to remedy this, he taught the play in conjunction with his university's production of the play and discussion—in which he planned to expose to question those assumptions of gender politics he sees as unquestioned. However, the students resisted his efforts; they identified him with John, while he attempted to defend Carol with whom they had no sympathy. "Whatever strategies I might have tried to teach against Mamet's play, I would have had to admit both the limits of classroom framing and the powerful cultural pressures conditioning student response" (49).

sO 10 Goggans, Thomas H. "Laying Blame: Gender and Subtext in David Mamet's
         Oleanna." *Modern Drama* 40.3 (1997): 433-41.
         Goggans argues that Carol is a victim of childhood sexual abuse, and reveals
symptoms of an abused child. She is about to confess this abuse to John at the
end of Act One. When he cuts her off with the phone call, she turns for comfort
to her Group which fortifies her and restores to her power over language.
Freudian slips from *House of Games* are used to support the view of subtext.

sO 11 Green, Geoffrey. "Transference Run Wild: David Mamet's *Oleanna* and the
         Crisis of Human Interaction." *Thirteenth International Conference on Literature
         and Psychoanalysis*. Ed. Frederico Pereira. Lisbon, Portugal: Instituto Superior
         de Psicologia Aplicada, 1997. 43-51.

sO 12 Hardin, Miriam. "Lessons from the Lesson: Four Post-Ionescan Education
         Plays." *CEA Magazine: A Journal of the College English Association, Middle
         Atlantic Group* 12 (1999): 30-46.
         Oleanna has a "more formal resemblance" to Ionesco than the other plays
considered. The article sees the crucial point in whether Carol's accusation of
sexual intent is true or "trumped up." But the analysis bogs down in self-
contradictions: "John, who probably sees himself as a Freirean, (who views
students as empty vessels to be filled) fails to recognize that his control of the
discourse exercises power" (41). John "seems to consider himself an enlightened
post-Freirean educator, willing to look past his expected role to see students as
people [. . .]." (43).

sO 13 Holmberg, Arthur. "Approaches: The Language of Misunderstanding."
         American Theatre 9.6 (1992): 94-95.
         Holmberg recounts the exchange with students at the first performance at
ART and examines Mamet's denial that "political responsibility" is his job. He
amplifies Mamet's answer with quotations from *Writing in Restaurants* on how
the writer's job is not to give answers, but to pose problems of greater complexity
than admit of clear rational solutions. He then addresses Mamet's construction
of the play's language in terms of rhythm in both the writing and the delivery/
direction, and to his philosophy that "the purpose of theatre is to express, not
duplicate" (95). Finally, he examines the issues the play raises as without simple
answers: the value of top notch higher education, the threat of political
correctness, and "the unending struggle for power between male and female"
(95).

sO 14 Kane, Leslie. "The Humanist Fallacy." *Weasels and Wisemen: Ethics and Ethnicity
         in the Work of David Mamet*. New York: St. Martin's Press, 1999. 141-84.
         Kane interprets the play melodramatically, with Carol as villain, and John
as victim. But John is not totally innocent. It is a play of "ethical lapse, ethnic
hatred, and endangered humanity" (183). The "ethnic hatred" refers to John as
"Diaspora Jew" who is disempowered and loses the hope of having a home.
Kane's understanding of the conclusion of the play is unique. "Mamet's

minimalist dialogue opens up a space of awareness that perceptibly widens to accommodate comprehension—however tentative—of the Other. That a moment of significant understanding and agreement is achieved is a direct consequence of the breakdown of humanizing speech" (183). Footnotes for this chapter provide invaluable background on both play and critical responses.

sO 15 Lyons, Donald. "Theater of Academe." *New Criterion* 11.4 (1992): 48-50.

Lyons gets carried away by the sound, and loses the sense of the play. Hence, "*Oleanna* seems written for the sake of its last two scenes of confrontation, and it does have a certain neatness of construction. Those scenes are, of course, totally improbable on the realistic level. Harassees who've filed charges surely don't return for tete-a-tetes with their victimizers. Such a violation of realistic decorum would be unexceptional, of course, if Mamet had a real artistic point to make. But finally it is just an excuse, an occasion for another of his trademark, edgy, ready-to-snap, in-your-face explosive arguments" (49). He notices the parallel with Hellman's *The Children's Hour* as "a melodrama of false accusation" (49).

sO 16 MacLeod, Christine. "The Politics of Gender, Language, and Hierarchy in Mamet's *Oleanna*." *Journal of American Studies* 29.2 (1995): 199-213.

After recapitulating all the arguments for the play as sexist, MacLeod makes the startling assertion that she identifies with John as lecturer, and sees the issues as those of teacher's power, hierarchy, and control of language. She makes a nice parallel with Levene in *Glengarry* who has no control over language until he makes the sale, and then becomes a powerhouse as Carol does. She also parallels Lingk with Carol in the first act, who is wordless and powerless when he comes back to renege on the deal. And Aaronow's innocence which becomes guilt is paralleled with John. Turning from gender neutral arguments, MacLeod attacks the construction of Carol as a tool of her "Group" as an attack on woman as unable to think or act for herself. She parallels the issue to attacks on Anita Hill as a tool of similar "pressure groups" (207).

sO 17 Mason, David V. "The Classical American Tradition: Meta-Tragedy in *Oleanna*." *Journal of American Drama and Theatre* 13.3 (2001): 55-72.

Mason's topic is ambitious: "Insofar as John and Carol represent ideals in which we believe and trust, and which are nevertheless mutually exclusive, Oleanna is a modern tragedy. Given this, *Oleanna* is itself the paradoxical combination of opposites and is a rather unique play for its time. *Oleanna* is both metatheatre and tragedy, the play with no meaning and the play with more meanings than it can bear" (57). Metatheatre, however, is too broadly defined, based on Abel but no current theory—not even a reference to Geis: "If for no other reason than all drama is metatheatrical, *Oleanna* is an example of metatheatre" (64). The main evidence of metatheatre is that the characters are self-conscious: "John and Carol are not only self-conscious, but, on the basis of the confusion their self-consciousness generates, they are prepared to consider whether they themselves are not simply conceptual" (61). In the second half,

Mason argues this play produces two equally committed characters who "act with indomitable commitment to ideals, a commitment so strong that winning and losing—even right and wrong—are irrelevant" (66). This balanced view of the two characters makes his reading unusual—and leads to his conclusion that it is "modern meta-tragedy. In a smashingly grand way, two quintessential American ideals found that there wasn't room enough in this town for the two of them: The Rule of Law and The Will of the People" (71).

sO 18 Nemeth, Lenke. "Miscommunication and Its Implication in David Mamet's Oleana[Sic]." *B.A.S.:British and American Studies/Revista de Studii Britanice se Americane* [Timisoara, Romania] (1997): 167-76.

sO 19 Piette, Alain. "The Devil's Advocate: David Mamet's *Oleanna* and Political Correctness." *Staging Difference: Cultural Pluralism in American Theatre and Drama.* Ed. Marc Maufort. Theatre Arts 25. New York: Peter Lang, 1995. 173-87.

Piette's thesis is based on the view that in Mamet: "language is a form of action and that it often anticipates, if not actually shapes our actions" (175). As a result, "It follows that not only does the characters' lingo echo the predicament of the fractured society they live in, it is at the same time responsible for its downfall, for its empty rhetoric is instrumental in undermining the very structures of that society" (176). However, with the play he has a far less dialectical approach. Instead, political correctness is wrong: "it has resolutely chosen the path of a militant radicalism, so as to become the exact opposite of what it purported to be" (178). John is a perfect innocent, Carol has "systematically twisted the meaning and interpretation of John's words and attitudes" (181). As a result, "So much abuse is piled up by the playwright on the young woman all along the play, that she could not possibly elicit the audience's sympathy" (185).

sO 20 Porter, Thomas E. "Postmodernism and Violence in Mamet's *Oleanna*." *Modern Drama* 43.1 (2000): 13-32.

Porter argues that conventional readings either see the play as antifeminist, or as a power play. But he proposes a third way: "Each of these critiques assumes that the play's action is (or should be) unified around a traditional center: a coherent theme, consistent persona-types, a familiar plot structure" (13). Using Derrida's deconstruction, Porter however argues "this decentering produces an escalating continuum of aggression that culminates in John's physical assault on Carol" (14). But curiously, one of his first moves is to supply a center to John's philosophy of education. He attacks critics who question Carol's transformation between Act 1 and 2 by arguing that the idea of a consistent "'character' and 'identity'" (20) is not longer operable. Rather, backed by her group, "What Carol wants and feels, she avers, is predicated not on an 'I' but on the thoughts and feelings of this collective" (20). But his conclusion rejects postmodernism: "There is not, however, merely a void in the midst of this swirl. Carol's reflective 'that's right' closes the play with a paradox: postmodern difference and its consequent decentering inevitably foster violence at their center" (29). Thus while Porter presents himself as one above the fray of contending parties over this play, he is in fact one with those who sympathize with John, whose liberal "humanism" (23) is much like Porter's own.

sO 21 Ryan, Steven. "*Oleanna*: David Mamet's Power Play." *Modern Drama* 39.3 (1996): 392-403.

Ryan argues that Mamet's dramaturgy is based on a strong "through-line" and he centers its identification around a single theme: "*Oleanna* is developed around one of Mamet's most basic themes: human beings' never-ending battle to dominate one another" (393). He largely takes a sympathetic view of Carol and an unsympathetic view of John. However, he concludes that she too is corrupted: "Unfortunately, Carol's (and her group's) hunger for power is as ravenous and self-serving as John's" (400).

sO 22 Sauer, David Kennedy. "*Oleanna* and *The Children's Hour*: Misreading Sexuality on the Post/Modern Realistic Stage." *Modern Drama* 43.3 (2000): 421-40.

Distinguishing modernist from postmodern realism, the article examines construction of the characters from an actor's viewpoint to distinguish ambiguity from indeterminacy. In *The Children's Hour*, the actor playing Karen must choose between playing her as a (latent) lesbian, or as a heterosexual character confused by the child's accusations. In contrast, the actor playing Carol in *Oleanna* is about to confess at the end of Act One when cut off by John. But what she will confess is never revealed. "To attempt to interpret *Oleanna* by the standards and approaches of modernism can only lead to frustration. Limiting critical choices to the simple either/or of modernist ambiguity results in the critic's having to choose between Carol and John, and to build a case around one choice. But the ambivalence of indeterminacy requires that much greater space be left open in interpreting the postmodern work. Character's motives are not fully knowable, as they are in the revealed-secret form of modernist realism" (434).

sO 23 Silverstein, Marc. "'We're Just Human': *Oleanna* and Cultural Crisis." *South Atlantic Review* 60.2 (1995): 103-20.

The reason for the intense and heated discussion of the play is that "*Oleanna* inscribes a cultural politics of misogyny that lends itself to articulation in terms of neoconservative ideology" (104). Though Silverstein recognizes that earlier Mamet plays were critiques of capitalism, he is still assured that the playwright is at heart a conservative humanist, whose values are displayed by John. "We find here the familiar Mamet theme of the need for a community in which recognition of our commonality becomes the basis for establishing universal values that transcend the limits of strategic, instrumental action" (109).

sO 24 Silverthorne, Jeanne. "PC Playhouse [Exits and Entrances]." *Artforum* 31.7 (1993): 10+.

Mamet still doesn't "get it" (10). "Mamet has invented a woman who seems to 'ask for it' so intensely" (10). But very quickly this melodramatic reading falls apart: "his forte remains ambiguity: it may be hard to sanctify the student in *Oleanna*, but it's impossible to tolerate the teacher" (10). Silverthorne makes a unique point, however, when she argues that "It is the telephone John—his most honest self—who paradoxically produces a corrupt Carol: his bluffing legal threats over real estate teach her to use her accusations as leverage for curriculum change."

sO 25 Skloot, Robert. "*Oleanna*, or, the Play of Pedagogy." *Gender and Genre: Essays on David Mamet*. Eds. Christopher C. Hudgins and Leslie Kane. New York: Palgrave, 2001. 95-109.

Skloot's agenda is unique, to examine "how we can teach and learn better" (104) by exploring "how facts, customs, and feelings are transmitted among inhabitants of the same social and cultural spaces" (96). bell hooks and Friere are used, though apparently without knowing Hardin's article. What makes his study of the play interesting is his balanced recognition that "Carol's pedagogy is as repressive as his [John's] own" (99). Both are seen to conform to Friere's teacher as oppressor. More interesting, because it is so rarely invoked, is Skloot's firm awareness of performance variables—i.e. that "the text seems to indicate a lack of physical desire in John and may also hint at more than a neutral supplicative entreaty from Carol. Here again, a production would have to build these meanings into his intentions" (101).

sO 26 Tomc, Sandra. "David Mamet's *Oleanna* and *the Way of All Flesh*." *Essays in Theatre/Études Théâtrales* [Canada] 15.2 (1997): 163-75.

This is a fascinating but frustrating article. Beginning with an examination of performance theory's approach to the body as a site of "indeterminacy," Tomc contrasts play and subject matter: "Whereas *Oleanna* insists on the possibility of an unproblematic sexual innocence represented by an uncomplicated bodily presence, the discourses of sexual harassment, which are themselves symptomatic of changing perceptions of bodies and social spaces, are preoccupied with that might be called the body's performative possibilities. They emphasize the body's reiterability, its radically unstable erotic significations and indeterminate locations in space and time" (165). This theory is undermined by the assumption that *Oleanna* is one fixed stable entity. [. . .] The play's "thematic of stability is also central to Carol's [character as well as John's] and, indeed, forms the crux of the relationship between them" (165). That Carol insists on fixed meanings is evident, but the case is not so clear with John. Nor is it so clear as Tomc assumes it is with Mamet: "To this end, Mamet in his stage directions carefully delimits the extent and nature of the physical interaction between his two protagonists; and here, too, there is no room for ambiguity. The asexual innocence of John's touch in the first act is carefully anticipated in his escalating concern for Carol" (166). Tomc has an excellent grasp of the indeterminacy of the body in postmodern discourse as it underlies the issue of sexual harassment, but assumes that Mamet and drama are easily fixed in definition.

sO 27 Vargas Llosa, Mario. "Visual Contact." *Making Waves*. Trans. John King. London: Faber and Faber, 1996. 311-14.

Novelist Vargas Llosa sees John "as the victim. "The dialogue in the first act, banal in the extreme, then hangs like a magic object which becomes metamorphosed and unimaginably poisoning in the second and third acts when we discover that, deconstructed and reconstructed by Carol (who is now active in a feminist group), everything that John said—all those that sounded so obvious and insipid—form the basis of an accusation of sexual harassment which will jeopardize the tenure and end up destroying the career of the professor" (312).

sO 28 Walker, Craig Stewart. "Three Tutorial Plays: *The Lesson, The Prince of Naples*, and *Oleanna*." *Modern Drama* 40.1 (1997): 149-62.

Taking John's perspective on the play, the article sees him as wrong in his Foucauldian view of education, leading to Walker's view of the play as a tragedy: "For the degree to which Carol's behaviour is an extension or projection of John's thought becomes evident if we imagine the play to be occurring entirely in John's imagination, like a nightmare. That exercise actually offers a reasonably coherent reading of the play, while imagining the play as taking place in Carol's imagination seems pointless" (159). John's view of education is that "evaluation is '*nonsense*'; he calls tests 'garbage' (23); and suggests that the university constitutes an arbitrary system of control, a cruel trial forced upon students" (159). Carol is confused by his attack on the education she seeks to gain.

sO 29 Weber, Jean Jacques. "Three Models of Power in David Mamet's *Oleanna*." *Exploring the Language of Drama: From Text to Context*. Ed. Jonathan Culpeper et al. New York: Routledge, 1998. 112-27.

This article uses discourse theory to examine a play whose subject, in many ways, is discourse. Weber first distinguishes between the discourse of author/ audience as well as that between Carol and John. Carol and John's discourse depends upon understanding each other in different contexts; so does the audience's: "interpreting involves [. . .] not just understanding the text but also understanding the social context (power relations) and the cognitive context (background schemata), and the extent to which the two are enmeshed. Paradoxically, however, such a (re)construction of the cognitive 'worlds' of the characters, and, by implication, of the author, can only be achieved through the reader's own socio-cultural schemata" (125). In this way, Weber accounts both for the disparities in interpretation between John and Carol, as well as among different readers of the play.

sO 28 Womack, Kenneth. "Performing the Academy: Alterity and David Mamet's *Oleanna*." *Postwar Academic Fiction: Satire, Ethics, Community*. New York: Palgrave, 2002. 98-108.

The chapter is notable for two reasons—it deals mainly with the film rather than the play, but makes no distinction between the two texts. And instead of dealing with power, its focus is on how each character fails at crucial moments to empathize with the other, basing its ethics in Levinas' idea of alterity, recognizing the other as other and "empathizing with [. . .] the subjective experiences of their counterpart" (101). The result is that: "Mamet's pejorative poetics—his satiric interest in revealing the various ways in which his characters ultimately choose the needs of the self over the perhaps more ethical desires of the other—underscores his obvious contention that alterity can hardly sustain itself in an academic world driven by insularity, ideology, and self-interest" (101). The analysis focuses on key moments in which one begins to sympathize with the other, and then John's "rhetorical miscues" (105) or the telephone "short-circuits Carol's capacity for showing compassion" (105). The article takes note of how the "unbelievably spacious office" (103) creates a disjunction between "a seemingly more innocent past and the ethically vacant present" (103). It also notes the bridges between acts that are used in the film. Other than these points, however, it conflates text and film in its analysis.

See also the following scholarly articles covering multiple plays:

sMP2 Andreach, Robert J. "Exemplary Selves in Hell."

sMP 4 Bigsby, C. W. E. "David Mamet: All True Stories."

sC 2 Gidmark, Jill B. "Violent Silences in Three Works of David Mamet."

sC 5 London, Todd. "Mamet vs. Mamet."

sMP 36 McDonough, Carla J. "David Mamet: The Search for Masculine Space."

REUNION, DARK PONY, THE SANCTITY OF MARRIAGE

Scene: Bernie's apartment, Sunday afternoon in early March
Characters: Carol Mindler—24 year old; Bernie Cary—her father in his fifties.
Editions:
> *Reunion; Dark Pony: Two Plays*. New York: Grove Press, 1979.
>
> *Best Short Plays*. Radnor, Pa.: Chilton, 1981.
>
> *Reunion; Dark Pony; The Sanctity of Marriage: Three Plays*. New York: S. French, 1982.
>
> *Reunion* and *Dark Pony*. Lion's Gate Production with ABC Video Enterprises [Videocassette directed by Lamont Johnson, 1982 is in the TOFT Collection.]

Plot Outline:
A reformed alcoholic is visited by his adult daughter for the first time in 20 years. Bernie recounts being a tail gunner, a VA patient, 10 years at the phone company, a furniture mover, having had another wife and another daughter, and his major regret at missing his brother's funeral. Carol relates working in her husband's office and her disappointment in her husband, remembering how she always thought her father was Tonto. Each wants to learn about the other because "the present is important."

Production:
pR/D/S 1 St. Nicholas Theater Company, Chicago January 9, 1976. Midnight showcase performances on Fridays and Saturdays.

Director:	Cecil O'Neal
Set Design:	Carol Doran
Lighting:	Ron Goodman

Cast:
	Bernie:	Don Marston
	Carol:	Linda Kimbrough

Overview:
Reviewers felt the emotion of the piece, and noted that the actors kept it "subdued" (Christiansen) and without "excessive emotion" (Winer), and Syse praised the director for "low-key direction." In each case, the impact of the story is better conveyed because the actors and production worked against it rather than supplementing it.

Reviews:
rR/D/S 1.1 Christiansen, Richard. "*Reunion* Begins Midnight Series." *Chicago Daily News* 12 Jan. 1976.
 Positive review of the director who has: "very sensibly has kept this scene in low gear, emphasizing the emotions by keeping them in check, but with a little too much suppression on Ms. Kimbrough's part." Marston "delivers some deeply realized acting, holding himself under firm control and superbly interpreting a marvelously well-tuned Mametian monolog about a long, drunken holiday in the father's 'happy' past."

rR/D/S 1.2 Syse, Glenna. "A Ray of Light (Comedy) after Some Dark Evenings." *Chicago Sun-Times* 15 Jan. 1976.
 Review of an emotionally touching play: "*Reunion* is a small piece, but a sensitive one, and Cecil O'Neal's low-key direction is perfectly in tune with this story. [. . .] As they make tentative overtures of reconciliation, one can only hope they are able to cushion their regrets about the past and their hesitations about the future. The ending has a touch of bittersweet to it that is nicely done."

rR/D/S 1.3 Winer, Linda. *Chicago Tribune* 15 Jan. 1976.
 Positive review: "Without excessive emotion—indeed Kimbrough could give away a bit more of herself—the two break down twenty years of barriers, going over and over until life truths rub through beneath Mamet's short sentences and patter [. . .] in this short but deft human treatment of a theme heavy with potential for the obvious."

Production:
pR/D/S 2 Double-billed with *Dark Pony*. Yale Repertory production, New Haven, CT, October 14, 1977.
Director:		Walt Jones
Cast:		
	Bernie:	Michael Higgins
	Carol:	Lindsay Crouse

Overview:
The New York critics had glimmers of how this play would work. Cox recognized a strain Mamet would develop years later—"feelings we retain from childhood, about those odd images that haunt us on waking." But such an ephemeral subject was too much for Kerr, who thought "We have not become dramatically involved." Eder, however, saw a resolution— "It is an affirmation that triumphs over incoherence."

Reviews:
rR/D/S 2.1 Eder, Richard. "David Mamet Crafts 'Reunion' with Skill to Stress Tenderness." *New York Times* 22 Oct. 1977: 12.

Positive review: "The play is about their relationship, or, rather, it is about relationship itself. Using his characteristic clipped, oblique, and awkward dialogue—awkward in form only, because its effect is marvelously precise—Mr. Mamet has his characters battle through all the embarrassment and misunderstanding of the reunion, and reach, finally, a kind of heaven. [. . .] It is an affirmation that triumphs over incoherence, and over the failures and evasions of both father and daughter."

rR/D/S 2.2 Fox, Terry C. Rev. of *Dark Pony* and *Reunion*. *Village Voice* 31 Oct. 1977: 83+.

Positive review of Mamet's revision: "The result proves me wrong: 'Reunion' is worth its resurrection. The play still has a glaring fault, but even that is more in focus now. As far as I know this is Mamet's only foray into family—a difficult and painful subject here, since family is defined as a place of broken promises and unfinished homes. [. . .] 'Dark Pony' becomes a piece about what moments and feelings we retain from childhood, about those odd images that haunt us on waking."

rR/D/S 2.3 Fleckenstein, J. "*Dark Pony* and *Reunion*." *Educational Theatre Journal*. Oct. 1978: 417-18.

Positive review of both: "Fragile in its emotional nuances, *Dark Pony* gradually became a reassuring metaphor for life in the modern world. [. . .] Downstage center was the car's bench seat. On either side of the stage were telephone poles, and the periphery of the stage was dark. The Father made the motions of driving. The Daughter sat with a blanket in her lap and a stuffed bunny in her hands. Complementing the simplicity of the staging and the truthful ring of the dialogue was the honesty of the playing of the two actors. [. . .] *Reunion,* although without metaphor, also explores loneliness, in this case arising from attachments broken by divorce."

rR/D/S 2.4 Kerr, Walter. Rev. of *Dark Pony* and *Reunion. New York Times* 30 Oct.
1977: Sec. 2: 5, 21.

Mixed review: "Awkward, tongue tied, hand-conscious, wary, they circle
the table and chairs of a yellowing kitchen without being able to strike an
emotional or even a conversational bargain over tea. [. . .] We have not
become dramatically involved, though. It's as though Mr. Mamet were content to catch nuances of speech—hesitations, confessional impulses—and
let them stand by themselves."

Production:
pR/D/S 3 Triple-billed with *Dark Pony* and *Sanctity of Marriage,* Circle in the
Square, New York, October 18, 1979. The cast was the same as at Yale
above.

Director:	David Mamet
Set:	John Lee Beatty
Lighting:	Dennis Parichy
Costumes:	Clifford Capone

Overview:
Most critics accepted that the audience had to fill in the pauses, to make sense of
the clichéd conversations, and to read what is unsaid from what is said (Jenner,
Oliver, Clurman and Watt). Others (Fox, Novick, Dace) didn't see this and saw
only the alienation and disappointment of the language. Simon, as usual, reduced
it to Mamet as a tape recorder, authentic language without plot. Gussow preferred
the 1977 Yale staging to Mamet's own direction. He also criticized the set and
Mamet's minimalism as: "a bit like a child's coloring book; someone has forgotten to fill in the spaces."

Reviews:
rR/D/S 3.1 Barnes, Clive. "Mamet Falls Short." *New York Post* 19 Oct. 1979:
45+.

Negative review, but not of the acting: "Pinter knows what he is doing,
Mamet seems to be only imitating, and creating, or attempting to create, a
form extraordinarily little substance to it. Lindsay Crouse, particularly in
the last playlet, as the baffled, bewildered daughter was superb. As was
Michael Higgins, an absolute master of evasive honesty and battered
dignity."

rR/D/S 3.2 Clurman, Harold. Rev. of *Reunion, Sanctity of Marriage, Dark Pony.
Nation* 1 Dec. 1979: 571-72.

Positive review: "None have I found more touching" than *Reunion.*
"The daughter has lost her bearings: she is just 'being.' She has come to
find a father, a source or emblem of support in her inner isolation. Both she
and her father are more or less unconsciously yearning to provide some
special service to the other—an affection, a tie, a solace which they timidly
hope will strengthen in time." (572).

rR/D/S 3.3 Dace, Tish. Rev. of *Reunion, Dark Pony, Sanctity of Marriage. Soho Weekly News* 25 Oct. 1979: 51.

Mildly positive review contending *Reunion* consists of "efforts by a voluble, bumbling father and a pleasant but guarded daughter to get to know each other after a lifetime of separation do convey some sort of feeling. As the false intimacy propels the twosome from small talk to acknowledgment of pain, disappointment, and hopes for a real relationship, we may miss the more idiomatic, lyric dialog of better Mamet. But at least we care about these characters."

rR/D/S 3.4 Gussow, Mel. "*Reunion*, 3 Mamet Plays." *New York Times* 19 Oct. 1979: C3.

Positive review [*Dark Pony*] which preferred how: "At Yale, the two actors, sitting in a semblance of a car, magically became their characters—despite the discrepancy of age. With her voice slightly subdued, Miss Crouse seemed like a young child. At the Circle, on an almost bare stage, more brightly lit than necessary, we are much more aware that these are actors—very good actors—pretending, participating in an actor's exercise. We are watching a theatrical performance, and it damages the play's dreamlike, ethereal quality." 'The Sanctity of Marriage' adds nothing to the evening except 10 minutes."

rR/D/S 3.5 Hummler, Richard. Rev. of *Reunion, Dark Pony, Sanctity of Marriage. Variety* 31 Oct. 1979: 102+.

Positive review: "Mamet develops this highly charged situation with admirable delicacy and no false notes. The psychological dynamics of the renewed relationship are utterly convincing, and the playwright's widely praised ear for realistic speech is in top working order."

rR/D/S 3.6 Jenner, C. Lee. Rev. of *Reunion, Dark Pony, Sanctity of Marriage. Other Stages* 1 Nov. 1979: 5.

Positive review: "Mamet seems to be trying to see how much of the usual dramatic paraphernalia he can pare away from his language and still have something recognizable as theater. Plot is gone; the situations are static; character development is sketchy. Even setting has been kept to a minimum. [. . .] All show us isolated people awkwardly trying to make contact. What we see are sketches for a triptych on loneliness."

rR/D/S 3.7 Novick, Julius. Rev. of *Reunion, Dark Pony, Sanctity of Marriage. Village Voice* 29 Oct. 1979: 83-84.

Mixed review: "Many of the best moments in their performances are silent—a reaction, a glance—here as usual a sign of fine realistic acting. The plays themselves, however, are as slight in scope as they are brief in duration. [. . .] Crouse's body tenses subtly all over, when Mr. Higgins moves toward her to give her a present. But the rhythm of the play becomes monotonous: father and daughter gradually achieve a little closeness, then it dissipates in a pause, and they have to start again."

rR/D/S 3.8 Oliver, Edith. "Off Broadway." *New Yorker* 29 Oct. 1979: 81.

Positive review: "Needless to say (for this is Mamet), the humor—and there is plenty of it—is as true as the emotion. By the time the play is over, two lives have been laid bare before us. [. . .] Time after time, the conversation plunges into depths, and time after time the father brings it back to the surface, realizing, after another reminiscent anecdote that comes to nothing, that all they have is the present and that they must go on from there. The ending is moving and right for this most moving play."

rR/D/S 3.9 Simon, John. Rev. of *Reunion, Dark Pony, Sanctity of Marriage. New York* 5 Nov. 1979: 87-89.

Negative review: "They have to give little beyond frequently disconcerting platitudes, but keep staggering toward a relationship. This could be touching—if only Mamet had more insight into heads and hearts instead of merely gluing his ears in arrested development to people's mouths."

rR/D/S 3.10 Watt, Douglas. "Daughter's Search for Answers from Dad." *Daily News* [New York] 19 Oct. 1979, sec. Fri: 5.

Positive review of a play: "surely touching our emotions on an almost bare stage, and then leaving us with an aftertaste of solitude. [. . .] Mamet is careful to make no more of them than that, keeping his dialogue spare and unforced. It may strike some as mannered in its very aloofness, but the style is poetic naturalism, a form the author has often favored."

Performance:
pR/D/S 4 *Reunion* double-billed with *Dark Pony.* King's Head Theatre Club, London, February 23, 1981.

Director:	Stuart Owen
Cast:	
Bernie:	Don Fellows
Carol:	Susannah Fellows

Overview:
Reviewers praised the acting, Grant and Jenkins in particular. Most also understood Mamet's workings; Jenkins and Billington commented on Mamet's use of dialogue to suggest, rather than state, underlying pain. So does Spencer: "Mamet's dialogue charts the tensions, the silences, the intermittent bursts of words which suggest much more than they actually say."

Reviews:

rR/D/S 4.1 Billington, Michael. Rev. of *Reunion and Dark Pony. Guardian* 1981.
Rpt. in *London Theatre Record* 12-25 Feb. 1981: 89.

Positive review: "It would be hard to overpraise the way Mr. Mamet
suggests behind the probing, joshing family chat an extraordinary sense of
pain and loss. [. . . All Mamet needs] is at some point to let his characters
break out of their cocoons and grapple with the rough noisy world beyond."

rR/D/S 4.2 Grant, Steve. Rev. of *Dark Pony and Reunion. Time Out* 1981. Rpt. in
London Theatre Record 12-25 Feb. 1981: 88.

Positive review for "one of the finest performances presently on offer.
[. . .] Fellows, whose portrayal fairly sings with clarity, humour and tightly-
wrapped bitterness, is ably supported by his real life daughter Susannah."

rR/D/S 4.3 Jenkins, Peter. Rev. of *Reunion and Dark Pony. Spectator* 1981. Rpt.
in *London Theatre Record* 12-25 Feb. 1981: 88.

Positive review of "the best play on offer" because "dialogue is masterly.
On the page it looks like prose-poetry but in the theatre it sounds entirely
natural. He knows exactly how to make a character say one thing so as to
mean entirely another. For example, when Carol says of her husband 'you
know he's a hell of a man' we know all at once he isn't." He thought this a
better acted production than Mamet's in New York but preferred *Dark Pony*
as a curtain raiser instead of a trailer.

rR/D/S 4.4 Radin, Victoria. Rev. of *Reunion and Dark Pony. Observer* 1981. Rpt.
in *London Theatre Record* 12-25 Feb. 1981: 89.

Positive review. "The play moves along by tiny scenes—perhaps 15 in
50 minutes—which chart infinitesimal changes of feeling between the pair.
Mamet offers us no theories or conclusions—though a kind of resolution
may be read in 'Dark Pony,' the 10 minute play which follows."

rR/D/S 4.5 Spencer, Charles. *New Standard* 1981. Rpt. in *London Theatre Record*
12-25 Feb. 1981: 89.

Positive review. "Mamet's dialogue charts the tensions, the silences,
the intermittent bursts of words which suggest much more than they actually
say with fine precision and in Bernie he has created a haunting character,
strangely jaunty yet ill at ease, laying bare the whole of his wasted life in
tiny scraps of reminiscence. Yet the play is a bleak one despite its sympathy."

Scholarly:

sR/D/S 1 Carroll. Dennis. "Communion." *David Mamet.* Modern Dramatists
Series. New York: St. Martin's, 1987. 91-117.

Using language as a gauge leads Carroll to place this play in the category
of "Communion" with *Edmond* and *Lone Canoe.* "The dialogue is a
barometer of whether the characters are hiding behind social roles or

lowering them. There are bursts of confident fluency in between stretches of halt in lines in the play and Carol is comparatively silent, her non-verbal responses to Bernie's words, sparsely indicated in the printed text, are crucial" (109).

See also the following scholarly articles covering multiple plays:

sMP 8 Callens, Johan. "David Mamet." *Post-War Literatures in English: A Lexicon of Contemporary Authors* 48 (Sept. 2000): 1-21.

sMP 17 Esche, Edward. "David Mamet." *American Drama.* Ed. Clive Bloom. New York: St. Martin's, 1995. 165-78.

Sexual Perversity in Chicago

Scene: Various spots around the North Side of Chicago, a Big City on a Lake
Time: Approximately nine weeks one summer
Characters: Dan Shapiro, an urban male in his late twenties; Bernard Litko, a friend and associate of Dan's; Deborah Soloman, a woman in her late twenties; Joan Webber, a friend and roommate of Deborah Soloman

Editions:

Sexual Perversity in Chicago, and, the Duck Variations: Two Comedies. New York: S. French, 1977.

American Buffalo; and, Sexual Perversity in Chicago; &, Duck Variations : Three Plays. Methuen's New Theatrescripts; No. 12, London: Eyre Methuen, 1978.

Sexual Perversity in Chicago; and, the Duck Variations: Two Plays. New York: Grove Weidenfeld, 1978.

David Mamet Plays: 1. Methuen World Classics. London: Methuen Drama, 1994.

Awards:

Joseph Jefferson Award for Best New Chicago Play in 1974.

Obie Award for Best Play in 1976.

Plot Outline:

The scenes enacted in two apartments, a library, a bar, a restaurant, a toy department, a gym, an office, a kindergarten class, a porn movie theater, and a beach present the ways the four characters deal with their sexuality. Bernie uses his stories, fantasies and voyeurism to impress and control Dan, his friend. Joan, Deb's roommate, uses cynicism to hide her fear and frustration. Danny and Deb, the innocents, are attracted and attempt a relationship, but ultimately can't commit to its imperfections and return to the protection and world views of their erstwhile friends, Bernie and Joan.

Production:

pSPC 1 Premiere, Leo Lerner Theater, Organic Theatre Company, Chicago. June, 1974.

Director:	Stuart Gordon
Set:	John Paoletti and Mary Griswold
Lighting:	Jeffrey Buschor
Cast:	
Bernard:	Warren Casey
Dan:	Eric Loeb
Deborah:	Carolyn Gordon
Joan:	Roberta Custer

Review:

rSPC 1.1 Winer, Linda. Rev. of *Sexual Perversity in Chicago. Chicago Tribune* 21 June 1974.

Mixed review: "Cliches get courted around as if the words are printed on the singles bar's fake Bauhaus chrome and real sexual perversity lurks in the loneliness behind shallow obsession, the worries about early ejaculations and proper measurements, plus the seemingly inevitable review after each sexual performance. The bed rolls right out from the bar. The play is constructed as a series of blackout skits—sketches, really, that do or do not get colored funny before another one begins."

Production:

pSPC 2 Double-billed with *Duck Variations,* Off-Off Broadway in the Theatre at St. Clement's, New York on September 29, 1975 for 12 performances.

Director:	Albert Takazauckas
Set:	Michael Massee
Lighting:	Gary Porto
Cast:	
Bernard:	Robert Townsend
Dan:	Robert Picardo
Deborah:	Jane Anderson
Joan:	Gina Rogers

Reviews:

rSPC 2.1 Feingold, Michael. "Normal Perversions Come to Second City." *Village Voice* 13 Oct. 1975: 113.

Very positive review: "What's striking is the ease with which [short scenes] can be marshalled into the structure of a play, made to reveal ambiguities and complexities in the characters instead of confirming the obvious. A conventional writer, setting up the same characters for a traditional play, would have noticed that Bernard has latent homosexual tendencies, and duly set up a contrived big scene in which he makes a pass at Danny. We're past that point—the characters may be past it too—so all Mamet needs to show us is Bernard at the beach, ogling chicks in bikinis with his arm around Danny's neck; the sight gag speaks for itself."

rSPC 2.2 Gussow, Mel. "Two Pungent Comedies by New Playwright." *New York Times* 1 Nov. 1975: 15. Rpt. in *Theatre on the Edge.* New York: Applause, 1998. 198-99.

Positive review: "The play is a multipaneled comic strip, with the action merrily hopping from bar to bedroom and finally to the seashore, where the boys are beached in their true avocation: ogling."

rSPC 2.3 Hewes, Henry. Rev. of *Sexual Perversity in Chicago and Duck Variations. Saturday Review* 24 Jan. 1976.

The two plays were not merchandisable for Broadway: "It is an original, funny, and sad theatre piece, but its offhand form, its unfashionably honest use of 'dirty words,' and its one-act play brevity make it an unlikely Broadway bet."

rSPC 2.4 Oliver, Edith. "David Mamet of Illinois." *New Yorker* 10 Nov. 1975: 136.

Very positive review of how "the subtly pointed incidents are so unobtrusively put together that for quite a while the audience is unaware that any story is being told at all—or even, perhaps, that these couples are homosexual. Also, one spends so much time laughing at the funny lines that the underlying sadness of the play comes as an aftertaste. The piece is written with grace and is very well performed."

Production:
pSPC 3 This production moved Off Broadway to the Cherry Lane Theatre, New York City on June 16, 1976 with two cast changes, then closed April 17, 1977 for a total of 8 previews and 273 performances.

Bernard:	F. Murray Abraham
Dan:	Peter Riegert (after Sept., James Sutorius)

Overview:
Some reviewers took the plays as realistic while others sought to delocalize it. This is not just a Chicago problem (Gold), but "could well be set in New York, San Francisco, Los Angeles or Seattle" (Myers). As a result it was mystifying that "no attempt is made to affect realistic locations or timespans, yet one is immediately involved and has no difficulty following the progression of events" (Myers). Others went to the opposite extreme like Simon and alluded to Beckett and Pinter (Kalem) and took the two plays as "absurd" (Oppenheimer). Simon couldn't connect the scenes, and had to keep consulting his program to see if these were the same characters from scene to scene. Still others accepted the blackout and short snippet structure (Watt) and found it both "hilarious" (Watt, Eaker) as well as a way of giving the audience a new way to understand the characters without the usual realistic filling in of the blanks (Watt, Eder). Feingold had the deepest sense that the playwright no longer needed to fill in all the blanks (about homosexuality, Oliver's subtext as well) but could merely hint and let the audience fill in the rest.

Reviews:

rSPC 3.1 Barnes, Clive. "Critic Takes a Bad Seat and Tells All." *New York Times* 30
July 1976: C1.

Pretending to be an out-of-towner: "I certainly had the best time at the
perceptively funny double bill at the Cherry Lane, but that I think did not have
anything to do with where I was sitting [not as reviewer, but mere ticket buyer],
but much more with what I was seeing. "

rSPC 3.2 Da Silva, Beatrice. "Prizewinning Perversity." *Villager* 24 June 1976.

Generally negative review of a play: "with a lack of thematic focus, a more
subtle malady. [. . .] His play is, nonetheless, very entertaining. Scenic locations
change as smoothly as they do on Broadway, aided by Gary Porto's lighting
and a simple, versatile set by Michael Massee. The visuals reinforce the plot's
sick humor."

rSPC 3.3 Eder, Richard. "Mamet's *Perversity* Mosaic on Modern Mores, Moves."
New York Times 17 June 1976: 29.

Positive review of: "a glittering mosaic of tiny, deadly muzzle-flashes from
the war between men and women among the filing cabinets and singles bars."
A "series of blackout skits" is the form, but revealed its own logic: "It is as if
going to bed were the foreplay and conversation the sexual act" as Danny asks
Deb to go to dinner with him after they sleep together. And the other couple's
disconnect is similar. Bernie "with his lean and mustachioed zinginess, his pickup
patter, comes up against her lush mournfulness, her air of a suspicious child. 'I
do not find you sexually attractive,' she declares, finally. 'Is that some kind of
line?' he demands, unbelieving."

rSPC 3.4 Frank, Leah. Rev. of *Sexual Perversity in Chicago* and *Duck Variations*.
WNYC Radio 830, 17 June 1976.

Negative review: "And while some of it is very cute, very funny, and very
much on target, the four characters are brittle, disagreeable people who are so
thoroughly unpleasant that it's difficult to relate to or sympathize with their
problems. The pace of the skits seems uncomfortably slow, and the show itself
is frequently boring."

rSPC 3.5 Fraser, C. Gerald. "Mamet's Plays Shed Masculinity Myth." *New York Times*
5 July 1976: 7.

A promotional piece which quotes Mamet who says: "My sex life was
ruined by the popular media. It took a lot of getting over. There are a lot of
people in my situation. The myths around us, destroying our lives, such a great
capacity to destroy our lives. Voltaire said words were invented to hide feelings.
That's what the play is about, how what we say influences what we think. The
words that the old [character] Bernie Litko says to Danny influences his behavior,
you know, that women are broads, that they're there to exploit."

rSPC 3.6 Gold, Sylviane. "Here's a Romp That Scores." *New York Post* 17 June 1976: 26.

Very positive review of the play: "recalling the comfortably adventurous comedy of Elaine May and Bruce J. Friedman. [. . .] But Mamet knows that sex involves not only the two people who manage to end up in the same bed at the same time, but also, and perhaps more importantly, the people to whom the coupling will be reported, with whom it will be analyzed, for whom it will be embellished, by whom it will be judged."

rSPC 3.7 Hill, Holly. "Play Captures Amoral Desperation of Singles." *Westchester Weekend* 9 July 1976.

Mixed review of the play: "as a picture of debased sexual relationships it is undeniably powerful [. . .] because of the attitude that such language and behavior suggests—the attitude that people are objects without individual dignity and value."

rSPC 3.8 Kalem, T. E. "Pinter Patter." *Time* 12 July 1976: 68.

Positive review: "Mamet, 28, displays the Pinter trait of wearing word masks to shield feelings and of defying communication in the act of communicating. [. . .] This may not sound very funny, but at off-Broadway's Cherry Lane Theater, a most nimble cast unleashes a hailstorm of laughter."

rSPC 3.9 Kerr, Walter. "Easy Does It Playwrighting Comes of Age." *New York Times* 15 Aug. 1976: D5+.

Positive review of Mamet's writing which was not what conventional playwrights would have thought would make a play. *Sexual Perversity:* "makes its shape out of the way words are used, out of an over-arching cadence that replaces the structural authority narrative would once have imposed. Narrative here is elliptical, unimportant, not much more than lightning-flash glimpses into the sexual enthusiasms and hostilities briefly generated by two young men, two young women. But the language in which real and imagined relationships are boasted of, regretted, mocked, makes use of rhythms that are self-stating, then nonstop, finally overriding. You can't fight with an express train."

rSPC 3.10 Myers, Estelle. Rev. of *Sexual Perversity in Chicago and Duck Variations*. *Our Town* 6 Aug. 1976: 12.

Very positive review of the play as realistic in which: "roles of men and women at a sexual or emotional level have become so confused" so the characters are "all too real, and although David's dialogue is very funny, it is, as in real life, very often more than a little sad. [. . .] No attempt is made to affect realistic locations or timespans, yet one is immediately involved and has no difficulty following the progression of events."

rSPC 3.11 Novick, Julius. "The Real Perversity Is Fear." *Village Voice* 16 Aug. 1976: 95.

Very positive review: "The point about Bernie is not, I think, that he is a 'latent homosexual' (whatever that means) but that—like Joan—he is scared, scared, scared. [. . .] Some people have been offended by the misogyny and sexism in *Sexual Perversity*, but it seems to me highly insensitive—or, in another sense, highly oversensitive—to take Bernie's fantastic crudities as the play's statement. On the contrary, this is a compassionate, rueful comedy about how difficult it is, in our fucked-up society, for men to give themselves to women, and for women to give themselves to men."

rSPC 3.12 Oppenheimer, George. Rev. of *Sexual Perversity in Chicago and Duck Variations. Newsday* 19 Sept. 1976.

Rather positive review of Mamet who: "has a decided flair for natural dialogue and humor that borders on the absurd. [. . .] Some of the sketches, for they are more those than a unified play, are highly amusing; other seem pointless. However, the average is high and the playwright shows considerable talent along the highways and low-ways of sexual encounters."

rSPC 3.13 Rich, Alan. Rev. of *Sexual Perversity in Chicago and Duck Variations. New York* 12 July 1976: 64.

Very positive review: "Mamet uses words beautifully, and silences compellingly; his accounting of nine weeks in the lives of two people who come together, and their two friends who sabotage the relationship, is wonderfully told in sharp, jagged blackouts that generate their own cohesive force."

rSPC 3.14 Simon, John. "Our Words as They Speak Us." *New Leader* 16 Aug. 1976: 20-21.

A typically negative extended review: "It is all grotesque and would be preposterous, too, if it weren't, as the saying goes, so true. Early in the play, if you don't consult your program, you may easily assume that these are not the same characters recurring in short scene after scene, but different men and women each time—so widespread are the attitudes, so typical the situations and talk, that you think this is a cross-section of Chicago, indeed the world. And in a sense it is. What, then, is missing? The young playwright cannot be expected to equal Beckett, but he might at least have aimed for a more cosmic despair, a more than sexual laughter." (21)

rSPC 3.15 Stasio, Marilyn. Rev. of *Sexual Perversity in Chicago and Duck Variations. Cue* 4 &11 Sept. 1976: 9.

Rather negative view: "David Mamet has flash. [. . .] As satirical caricatures his quartet of emotional gropers are funny enough, but their lack of depth dooms them as dramatic characters."

rSPC 3.16 Watt, Douglas. "A Serving of Sex and Ducks." *Daily News* [New York] 17 June 1976: 106.

Very positive review which accepts the unusual structure: "Somewhat like the companion piece in structure, 'Sexual Perversity' is all in short takes. The takes are even shorter, though, consisting of perhaps a couple of dozen snippets, blackouts ending with or without laughs. It's hilarious. But somehow, and such is Mamet's artistry, we get to know and like these four very well in this sketchy fashion. We get to know them between the lines, in the pauses and glances and Thurberish distances between male and female. All the while we're laughing."

rSPC 3.17 Wetzsteon, Ross. "The Perversity Is in the Production." *Village Voice* 21 Jun 1976: 118.

    Very positive review of Mamet, but trashing this production which: "with the exception of F. Murray Abraham, is flat, limp, and insecure, while the direction lacks even the most minimal sense of the subtle rhythms in the script. Worst of all, the sets and lighting (crucial in dealing with Mamet's quick jump-cutting) are virtually incompetent, and the silly sound effects should simply be junked."

rSPC 3.18 Wilson, Edwin. "A Broad Sampler from Area Stages." *Wall Street Journal* 20 July 1976.

    Negative review of the structure: "Once again the method is to break things up, this time into a series of vignettes. Some, however, are so short and so pointless that they leave the audience wondering if they have missed something: they haven't."

Production:
pSPC 4 Regent Theatre, London. Opened December 1, 1977 for a six week run.

Director:	Albert Takazauckas
Cast:	
Bernard:	Kenneth Nelson
Dan:	Stephen Hoye
Deborah:	Glory Annen
Joan:	Gina Rogers

Overview:
Critics were divided over the play. Those who liked it saw "sardonic sympathy" (Barber) for the characters, humor (Billington) and "delightful," if minute "observations of behavior" (Young). Chaillet faulted the director for the production; Stothard thought the problem was with Mamet's underwriting the transitions for the character of Dan who was only convincing at the end of the play.

Reviews:
rSPC 4.1 Barber, John. "Mamet Enters with a Talented Eroticism." *Daily Telegraph* 2 Dec. 1977: 15.

    Positive review: "Neither the vulgar poster, nor the catchpenny title, must deter any save the squeamish from seeing 'Sexual Perversity in Chicago' at the Regent, as witty and clever a comedy of intimate relations as I have seen in a long time."

rSPC 4.2 Billington, Michael. Rev. of *Sexual Perversity. Guardian* 2 Dec. 1977: 12.
        Positive review: "Mamet shows that for all the brave bright talk, it is difficult
        to break away from one's sexual past. [. . .] But along the way he provides some
        of the funniest dialogue we have heard come out of America for a while."

rSPC 4.3 Chaillet, Ned. Rev. of *Sexual Perversity in Chicago and Duck Variations.
        Times* [London] 2 Dec. 1977.
        Negative reviews of both plays, Chaillet is offended by the ads and the title
        which: "has been enough to ban its name from some of the national dailies, at
        least as advertising. [. . .] To believe that the woman-baiting the two males
        characters indulge in is no more than it seems may be a slur, but if irony, or the
        more remote possibility that he meant to show how male role-playing separates
        men from women was intended, by the direction by Albert Takazauckas did not
        let it show."

rSPC 4.4 Stothard, Peter. Rev. of *Sexual Perversity and Duck Variations. Plays and
        Players* Feb. 1978: 30-31.
        A somewhat negative review of: "a witty social commentary, brought
        powerfully to life by [Nelson's] brilliant piece of caricature acting." The problem
        is that: "The character of Danny is something of a stumbling block in the
        production and probably in the play itself. He alone has to change over the
        course of the action—from ingenue to cynic, from tender lover to an anti-feminist
        with highly unpleasant thoughts. [. . .] Mamet's skills do not lie in the
        development of character. He makes it a difficult task for Stephen Hoye who is
        totally convincing only in Danny's final conversion to the life of the true Chicago
        male, a tit-and-bum watching trip with Bernie."

rSPC 4.5 Young, B. A. "David Mamet Plays." *Financial Times* 2 Dec. 1977.
        Positive review of *Sexual Perversity* as "the one to go for" because: "The
        skill with which the author has pinned down these little moments in the lives of
        what are by today's standards hommes moyen sensuel is delightful. Sometimes
        we move into fantasy. [. . .] Sometimes we watch perfectly ordinary society or
        sexual encounters cleverly mounted to lead to a point. The observation of
        behaviour, the ear for dialogue, are matchless, the performances exact."

Production:
pSPC 5 Double-billed with *Sermon*, Apollo Theater, Chicago January 16th, 1979.
        Director: Sheldon Patinkin
        Setting: John Paoletti and Mary Griswold
        Cast:
                Bernard: Jim Belushi
                Dan: Scott Jaeck
                Deborah: Bernadette Birkett
                Joan: Kay Kimborough

Reviews:

rSPC 5.1 Christiansen, Richard. "A Powerful Homecoming for 'Perversity.'" *Chicago Tribune* 24 Jan. 1979: sec. 6: 4.

Very positive review: "this piercing tragicomedy on sexual perversity (not perversion) remains a powerful, funny, and tremendously moving work. [. . .] Jim Belushi gives such an intense, full scale, knockout comic performance that he threatens to run away with the show. Scott Jaeck, as Danny, has in his favor a wonderful little kid's face and a real sense of dumb bewilderment and pain in his final loss of innocence. The women, who have weaker parts, do not come off too well here."

rSPC 5.2 Jacobi, Peter. "New Playlet by Mamet." *Christian Science Monitor* 23 Feb. 1979: 19.

Positive review of this production: "Belushi, an actor of tremendous intensity, tends to overshadow the other performers. He is the sort of actor that causes a director to raise the temperature of an entire production. [. . .] He strives for frenzy, for the comic, for the verbal pratfall a bit at the expense of the empty sadness that underlies this Mamet study of the urban singles scene."

Production:

pSPC 6 Double-billed with *Duck Variations* at the Atlantic Theater Company, New York, opened January 12 and closed February 6, 2000.

Director:		Hilary Hinckle
Set:		Alexander Dodge
Costumes:		Rick Gradone
Lighting:		Robert Perry
Cast:		
	Danny	Josh Hamilton
	Bernard:	Clark Gregg
	Deborah:	Kate Blumberg
	Joan:	Kristin Reddick

Overview:

Most of the reviews were negative because the production was excessively realistic, and undercut Mamet's purpose. Feingold blamed the "imitative fallacy;" Hofler and Grode the very realistic set and the direction. Weber, however, liked the "period-perfect" acting and Zinman happily found it "still offensive."

Reviews:

rSPC 6.1 Feingold, Michael. "The History Channelers." *Village Voice* 1 Feb 2000: 65.

Positive review: "Like most things that ought to happen but don't in Mamet plays, this one conveys a flaw in the characters, not in their author. [. . .] Since the characters grate on you, every line offers the performers another chance to slide into imitative fallacy. Josh Hamilton (Danny) and Kate Blumberg

(Deborah) slip now and then, Kristin Reddick (Joan) much more rarely; Clark Gregg, head of the class, avoids all slippage by making Bernie such a chilling creep you have to be fascinated."

rSPC 6.2 Grode, Eric. Rev. of *Sexual Perversity in Chicago and Duck Variations. Back Stage* 21 Jan. 2000: 44.

Negative review: "Momentum is everything with Mamet, and this play is no exception, as the self inflicted obstacles between Danny and Deborah snowball into heartless recriminations at a furious pace. Alexander Dodge's sprawling set, which bounces the foursome around a half-dozen fully realized locations, utterly kills this momentum; some of the scene changes seem to take as long as the preceding scenes. Director Hilary Hinckle exacerbates this problem by directing Gregg and Reddick for laughs that never come; Gregg in particular adds cavernous pauses to Mamet's clipped, terse dialogue."

rSPC 6.3 Hofler, Robert. Rev. of *Sexual Perversity in Chicago/Duck Variations. Variety* 17 Jan. 2000: 140.

Negative review of the women actors, but ultimately at the attempt for realism. Blumberg and Reddick were: "especially diminished by an excessively realistic production, if 'realistic' is quite the right word for Alexander Dodge's set design, which overloads the stage with very used furniture that is supposed to represent a bar, a cocktail lounge, a bedroom, an office, a school room, two living rooms and a few other multi-use playing spaces. On this peculiar playing field, Hinckle's direction ends up giving equal weight to every scene, where, in fact, the actresses might have been better served by a simpler, more stark production that emphasized, rather than tried to negate, their secondary status."

rSPC 6.4 Simon, John. "Two Early Plays Remind Us of a Time When David Mamet Still Mattered." *New York* 24 Jan. 2000: 65+.

A rather positive review: "The men talk about women vauntingly, wantingly, fantasizingly, superiorly, and, above all, grossly. The women talk about men, though less obsessively and crassly. All scenes are essentially self-contained vignettes, sometimes very short, that end on a goofy punch line, an ambiguity, or a non sequitur leaving an aftertaste of puzzlement, a sense of the everyday absurd. And no one learns or changes."

rSPC 6.5 Weber, Bruce. "Mamet? Innocence? Perversity Has Changed." *New York Times* 13 Jan. 2000: E1.

Positive review: "Presented on Alexander Dodge's multitiered set, which manages to contain and economically suggest a half a dozen separate rooms, the play uses brief, jittery scenes separated by blackouts to follow the consummation and subsequent courtship and breakup of Danny and Deborah as witnessed by their best friends. [. . .] In the service of the story, the young actors are reasonably deft with Mr. Mamet's peppery rhythms (and salty language). The women seem period-perfect, managing to capture the 1970s style of feminism, which found all manner of young women trying on newly encouraged postures of self-empowerment."

rSPC 6.6 Zinman, Toby. Rev. of *Sexual Perversity in Chicago and Duck Variations. David Mamet Review* 7 (2000): 3.

Positive review: "I am pleased to report that *Sexual Perversity*, first performed in 1974, is still offensive after all these years. When Bernie Litko (Clark Gregg), the ultra-macho creep, sits on the beach with his less creepy but dorky friend Dan (Josh Hamilton), watching imaginary women walk by, he says 'Hi' to one of them, who ignores him. This provokes the quintessentially Mametian exchange with which the play ends."

Scholarly Overview:
Scholars see the characters as realistic, deformed by the environment evidencing "the pathology of urban life (Begley); "baffled, insecure, essentially solitary" (Bigsby); having too "much freedom to choose in these modern times" (Cardullo); and suffering "the debilitating effects of day-to-day urban routine" (Carroll). Dean, however, notes the "pressures of language exerted by their companions" rather than blaming outside pressures. Instead of taking it realistically, Bruster sees it as a satire; Skeele as "parodic pseudo-religious commentary."

sSPC 1 Begley, Varun. "On Adaptation: David Mamet and Hollywood." *Essays in Theatre/Études Theatrales* 16.2 (1998): 165-76.

This original work examines the movie *About Last Night* with the play and argues that "all art is adaptation" (167). "The film thus begins to flesh out the bare semiotic bones of a play which uses metonymic shorthand—a few barstools, a desk, and a bed—to denote the range of public and private space, so that the stage itself acts as a metaphor for a fragmented, denatured, urban world. Virtually every scene in the film, however, lingers lovingly on the urban landscape— Wrigley Field, the Chicago Art Institute, restaurants, bars, parks, the lakeshore. These images all conspire toward the illusion of filled, integrated, vital space. The play is much more explicitly concerned with the pathology of urban life, the violent pulse of its libidinal energy, the phantasmagoric mythologies of sexual and social identity that structure the experience of its alienated citizens. The film, by contrast, is more quiescent in its representation of the fully reified, monumental environment which, whatever the individual psychological travails of the population, is still fundamentally conceived as a place of benevolent opportunity" (167-68).

sSPC 2 Bigsby, C. W. E. "*Sexual Perversity in Chicago, The Woods." David Mamet.* Contemporary Writers. London: Methuen, 1985. 46-62.

There is no meaning to the lives of these characters: "What they value is style, the hip remark, the quick retort; the fast, almost cinematic intercutting between scenes provides a correlative to this and to the fragmented nature of their lives" (52). Their problem is that: "Sexual anxiety all but incapacitates those who feel impelled to enter into relationships which terrify them; the result is a world in which there is no meeting of minds, and sexual hostility crackles through every scene. This, in part, is generated by a denatured language, by the pragmatics of commerce and the myths of a culture which confuses crude sexuality with intimacy; in part it seems to imply an unbridgeable gap between desire and fulfillment, as the American dream is displaced from an economic into a sexual realm" (51). While Bigsby is also aware "the play is one of Mamet's funniest" he concludes "His characters end the play as they began it—baffled, insecure, essentially solitary" (52).

sSPC 3 Bruster, Douglas. "David Mamet and Ben Jonson: City Comedy Past and Present." *Modern Drama* 33.3 (1990): 333-46.

Bruster sees Mamet as a satirist. The plays, like Jonson's, depict city charlatans and gulls. This is a rather reductive approach, as Geis argues in *Theatric(k)s* (96). In *Sexual Perversity*, Danny is the gull, Bernie the charlatan. But the relationship is more complex. In *Glengarry*, Bruster takes Levene to have been Roma's teacher—but there is little evidence of the play for that. The argument works better for *The Shawl* and *House of Games*.

sSPC 4 Cardullo, Bert. "Comedy and *Sexual Perversity in Chicago*." *Notes on Contemporary Literature* 12.1 (1982): 6.

Cardullo argues that relationships fall apart because couples "have so much freedom to choose in these modern times, they have trouble choosing. So they naturally resort to the security and safeness of friendship with a member of the same sex" (6). The unique point of this article is his reading of the final scene which he says is "widely misunderstood" (6). It is funny not because they "degrade women" but rather "because what we see happening to them is noticeably different from what they think is happening to them [. . .] because we know that finally they have each other. Not in the homosexual sense, as some have suggested, but in the best sense of friendship, of male bonding" (6).

sSPC 5 Carroll. Dennis. "Sex." *David Mamet.* Modern Dramatists Series. New York: St. Martin's, 1987. 51-69.

Very perceptive sense of the play in production, especially the effect of the minimalist set and the direct address to the audience: "Mamet implies that a whole complex of forces—both within Dan and Deb, and without—negates whatever ability they have to open up to each other, even though they desperately want to. The phalanx of inhibiting influences on the lovers is conveyed by the montage pattern of the thirty-four scenes. Their general length and patterning, some with as few as five lines, suggest the debilitating effects of day-to-day urban routine. [. . .] the settings are necessarily spare and minimal—and in Takazaukas' production this very spareness made it possible for one scene to succeed another with the utmost speed. The montage thus underlines the environmental absence of significant, definitional objects to give the characters and audience the reassurance of place" (53-54). Carroll also does nice work breaking out groups of scenes to see how they connect.

sSPC 6 Dean, Anne. "Sexual Perversity in Chicago." *David Mamet: Language as Dramatic Action*. Rutherford, New Jersey: Fairleigh Dickinson UP, 1990. 51-84.

In regard to *Sexual Perversity* Dean is adamant that "the school of opinion which brands him [Mamet] as sexist is completely wrongheaded" (65) because male characters are critiqued as much as the female, and she interviews Colin Stinton and Miranda Richardson to confirm her view. Her view of the play is that the language makes the characters see the opposite sex in a skewed way: "Partly because of the pressures of language exerted by their companions and partly through cultural fiats, any relationship formed between Mamet's male and female characters is doomed to failure. The men are unwilling—or unable—to view women as anything other than sex slaves and receptacles for their pleasure and, not surprisingly, the women regard men as natural enemies and emotional cripples" (54). But curiously she takes a uniquely sympathetic view of Bernie: "What is so tragic about a man like Bernie is that he is, at base, painfully aware of his own inadequacy and fear, and that is why he must behave in the overtly masculine fashion that has become his trademark."

sSPC 7 Skeele, David. "The Devil and David Mamet: *Sexual Perversity in Chicago* as Homiletic Tragedy." *Modern Drama* 36 (1993): 512-18.

Skeele likens *Sexual Perversity in Chicago* to late 16th century Calvinist allegorical sermonizing tragedy, with Danny as the Mankind figure, Bernie as the Vice figure who leads Mankind astray, "delivering a veritable sermon on the necessity of '[giving thanks to a just creator]' every time one is able to 'moisten the old wick' (24). Again, this parodic pseudo-religious commentary is engaging and funny, and through his Vice-like antics Bernie is able to seduce both audience and protagonist, drawing us towards him just as he does Danny" (516). He then universalizes audience response: "Debby [sic] takes on some of the characteristics of virtue," (516) so women are not simply reduced to temptations in this construction.

See also the following scholarly articles covering multiple plays:

sMP 18 Gale, Steven H. "David Mamet: The Plays, 1972-1980."

sMP 20 Geis, Deborah R. "Theatre as *House of Games*: David Mamet's (Con) Artistry and the Monologic Voice."

sMP 21 Herman, William. "Theatrical Diversity from Chicago: David Mamet."

sMP 30 Kim, So-im. "Sexual Myths in David Mamet: *Sexual Perversity in Chicago* and *Edmond*."

sMP 36 McDonough, Carla J. "David Mamet: The Search for Masculine Space."

sMP 41 Quinn, Michael L. "Anti-Theatricality and American Ideology: Mamet's Performative Realism."

sMP 48 Savran, David. "New Realism: Mamet, Mann and Nelson."

sMP 51 Storey, Robert. "The Making of David Mamet."

THE SHAWL AND PRAIRIE DU CHIEN

Editions:

The Shawl and Prairie du Chien: Two Plays. New York: Grove Press, 1985
"Prairie du Chien." *Short Plays and Monologues*. New York: Dramatists Play Service, 1981. 21-38.
The Shawl and Prairie du Chien. London: Methuen Drama, 1989.
David Mamet Plays: 3. London: Methuen Drama, 1996. 67-118.

Characters and Plot Outline for *The Shawl*:

John, a man in his fifties, by observation, conjecture and suggestion, leads a doubtful Miss A, a woman in her late thirties, who has come for guidance about whether or not to contest her mother's will. Charles, John's younger lover, wants to know the tricks of the con, and so encourages John to take her money. During a seance John tells a gory story of the murder of the wife of a Boston merchant, but then says he sees Miss A's mother in a red shawl. Miss A, in the last act, decides to contest the will and believes John has actually seen her dead mother. The play ends with John admitting that he knows something about the shawl that no one else knows, that Miss A burned it in anger five years earlier.

Characters and Plot Outline for *Prairie du Chien*:

On a train traveling from Chicago to Duluth, a storyteller recounts the tale of the murder of a wife and a handyman by a husband who hung himself. The storyteller remembers taking the sheriff with him to prevent tragedy, finding the bodies, and the sheriff moaning to himself and searching the house after seeing a ghost of the murdered wife. As he tells the stories, gin players continue to play until one calls the other a cheater, shoots at him but misses, and the dealer takes his winnings and alights at *Prairie du Chien*. Originally broadcast on NPR's "Earplay" with Charles Durning, Jeff Goldblum, Larry Block, and Bruno Kirby in April, 1979, directed by Daniel Freudenberger.

Production

pS/PdC 1 *The Shawl* and *The Spanish Prisoner* by New Theatre Group at the Briar
    Street Theater, Chicago on April 19, 1985.

Director:	Gregory Mosher
Cast:	
John:	Mike Nussbaum
Miss A:	Lindsay Crouse
Charles:	Gary Cole

Reviews:

rS/PdC 1.1 Rev. of *The Shawl*. *Chicago* June 1985: 24.

"Baffled" review: "Mike Nussbaum is an alleged mystic trying to cheat
Lindsay Crouse, egged on by Gary Cole as his alleged lover but looking more
like his grandson."

rS/PdC 1.2 Abarabanel, Jonathan. "Chicago." *Stages* May/June 1985: 28.

Negative on "Spanish Prisoner" as "a writer's and actor's exercise, not a
play" by the former Literary Manager of the St. Nicholas Theatre. More positive
on "The Shawl" which "is about our need for the mystery of faith and trust to
fill our lives. Also it continues Mamet's fascination with the relationships
between older men and younger men, this time with a homosexual twist. It is a
classic of lean direct story-telling and purity of structure."

rS/PdC 1.3 Morrison, Hobe. "Resident Legit Reviews: 'The Spanish Prisoner'
    and 'The Shawl.'" *Variety* 1 May 1985: 498.

Positive review of a "minor Mamet work, it still has that ability to provoke
and disturb. [. . .] The problem for John and the audience—and here Mamet is
at his two-level best—the more John explains the virtuosity of his guile, the
more he tries to simplify it, so too does he deepen the mystery of what he is and
who he is. The dry after taste of the play is that underneath the layer of John's
deceit is the distinct possibility that he is in touch with something unexplainable,
something given only to a few."

Production:

pS/PdC 2 Double-billed at the Mitzi E. Newhouse Theater at Lincoln Center; previewed
    December 20; opened December 24, 1985 and closed February 2, 1986.

Director:	Gregory Mosher
Sets:	Michael Merritt
Costumes:	Nan Cibula
Lighting:	Kevin Rigdon
Cast:	
Miss A:	Lindsay Crouse
John:	Mike Nussbaum
Charles:	Calvin Levels

Reviews:

rS/PdC 2.1 Barnes, Clive. "Lincoln Center Reopens: 2 by Mamet." *New York Post* 24
    Dec. 1985. Rpt. in *New York Theatre Critics' Reviews* 46.18 (1985): 95-96.

Negative review: "The Mamets were, I think, an unwise choice—the evening is atmospheric and puzzling, but more boring than stimulating. [. . .] When Mr. Mamet is pretentious he can become exceedingly tedious, and as a playwright he seems to lack self-criticism more than self-discipline, for even his apparently empty plays have their vacuums well-crafted, with their vacuity actually given a certain verbal style."

rS/PdC 2.2 Beaufort, John. "Vivian Beaumont Theater Reopens Modestly with Two Mamet Plays." *Christian Science Monitor* 3 Jan. 1986: 19. Rpt in *New York Theatre Critics' Reviews* 46.18 (1985): 97.

Positive review: "In the aftermath of violence, the salesman assumes a new role of quiet authority. Veteran actor Stiller knows how to take command. [. . .] Nussbaum gives a quietly eerie demonstration of how guesswork, inference, and a knowledge of human nature can be used to manipulate a susceptible subject. [Crouse] matches him with her subdued portrait of a Miss A, an intelligent but lonely young woman struggling to decide whether to contest the will from which her late mother has excluded her. John's methods are, however, too soft-sell for his impatient and slightly sinister black accomplice."

rS/PdC 2.3 Brustein, Robert. "The Infidelity Play." *New Republic* 10 Feb. 1986: 25+.

Positive review: "All this is spoken in that terse, elliptical style—replete with interrupted sentences—that is the hallmark of Mamet's writing, but the new element is the suggestion of the supernatural and the mystical, all the more haunting for its quotidian context. Gregory Mosher captures these qualities in a detailed, exacting production, distinguished by Lindsay Crouse, who plays the woman with a tough, repressed scepticism, and Mike Nussbaum as the medium, a forlorn ironist in baggy pants."

rS/PdC 2.4 Freedman, Samuel G. "Theater Returns to Lincoln Center." *New York Times* 21 Dec. 1985: A15.

Interview in which Crouse says: "'he set out to exercise plot-writing as a craft. And I think it came out beautifully. Everybody gets fooled at least once in this play.' For Mr. Nussbaum and Miss Crouse, the Newhouse production provides a chance to return to a play that challenged and, to some degree, defeated them in its Chicago incarnation. Despite the excellent notices *The Shawl* received there, both actors feel their performances were too overt, too arch. 'We didn't realize it at the time,' Mr. Nussbaum said, 'but the thing that became clear in retrospect was that we needed to go for simpler, more direct contact between the actors.'"

rS/PdC 2.5 Hummler, Richard. Rev. of *Prairie du Chien* and *The Shawl*. *Variety* 1 Jan. 1986: 136.

Mildly positive review: "Although the salesman's yarn has a core of mysteriousness involving an apparition, it's intrinsically undramatic (telling rather than showing). [. . .] As a parable of humanity's eternal hunger for faith, 'The Shawl' is a quietly compelling work, written with understated eloquence, especially the role of the dreamy psychic. Nussbaum is touching and absolutely real in the role."

rS/PdC 2.6 Kissel, Howard. "Mamet at the Mitzi." *Women's Wear Daily* (1985). Rpt in *New York Theatre Critics' Reviews* 46.18 (1985): 96.
    Positive review: "The salesman's story and the conversation of the card players has a quality of huskiness that fairly defined masculinity in the heartlands decades ago. The play's dialog is also written in a very self-conscious style, the repetition and interjections creating very deliberate rhythms. [. . .] It is a wonderful piece of 'Then what happened?' storytelling. Two of the actors handle the plot's unexpected turns artfully—Mike Nussbaum has a mesmerizing, liquid voice and a poignant manner as the fortuneteller and Lindsay Crouse has an admirable combination of strength and unexpected vulnerability as his client. The third angle of the triangle, however, is weak. Calvin Levels is quite unconvincing as the medium's test lover."

rS/PdC 2.7 Rich, Frank. "Lincoln Center Presents 2 One-Acts: Spooky Stories." *New York Times* 24 Dec. 1985: C11. Rpt. in New York Theatre Critics" Reviews 46.18 (1985): 94.
    Mildly positive review: "But Mr. Mamet seems to be saying, rather sentimentally, that 'a world without mystery' is a world without romance. The play's narrative twists, more contrived than surprising, leave us with the observation that, in telepathy and love alike, trust and a leap of faith can make one's wishes come magically true. The prime assets of 'The Shawl' are its eerily atmospheric set and lighting (by Michael Merritt and Kevin Rigdon, respectively) and the two lead performances. Mr. Nussbaum, who was the most nebbishy salesman in *Glengarry*, has a touching, frayed sadness about him as the aging homosexual con man. The crisp Miss Crouse brings an aura of mysteriousness to his client. Nonetheless, *The Shawl* seemed underrehearsed at a critics' preview, to the point of exposing the author's own tricks. Mr. Mamet's clipped sentence fragments were often left to dangle separately rather than flow seamlessly together, with the result that one was usually more aware of a playwright's self-conscious stylistic means than the sentiments of his characters."

rS/PdC 2.8 Simon, John. "Girlie Show." *New York* 13 Jan. 1986: 50-51.
    His usual negative review of "two paltry whines by David Mamet—alleged ghost stories that haven't even the ghost of a chance. [. . .] This is playwriting by the numbers, crudely schematic in its pursuit of supposedly depth-giving ambiguity. So it just keeps contradicting itself. [. . .] In the curtain raiser, only Jerry Stiller as the narrator has anything like a part, but he is misdirected into speaking in an affectless monotone that makes things drearier yet."

rS/PdC 2.9 Watt, Douglas. "The Tale of a Traveling Salesman." *Daily News* [New York] 24 Dec. 1985. Rpt. in *New York Theatre Critics' Reviews* 46.18 (1985): 95.
    Mixed review of the play, not of the acting: "either the homosexual relation-ship is extraneous or could have been explored further. Mamet's dialogue is as

crisp and naturalistic as we have come to expect. Yet broken up as it is by breathers and halting deliveries, it begins to assume more of a ritualistic and even unnatural sound than it does when wedded to the stronger material of his more realistic work."

Production:
pS/PdC 3 Royal Court Theatre Upstairs, London. June 9, 1986.

Director:	Max Stafford-Clark
Cast:	
Card dealer:	Michael Feast
Gin Player:	Jerome Flynn
Porter:	Cyril Nri
Storyteller:	Nigel Terry
Listener:	David de Keyser
Listener's son:	Billy Ehninger

Reviews:
rS/PdC 3.1 Coveney, Michael. "David Mamet Double Bill/Theatre Upstairs." *Financial Times* 10 June 1986: 21.

Positive review: "The tension in both plays is admirably maintained. In 'Prairie,' the social circumstances are random, with a pattern imposed by a sudden outburst of violence. In 'The Shawl,' John, the clairvoyant, is poised between deceiving the client and retaining the companionship of Charles (Michael Feast), a neurotic sidekick to whom John explains the tricks of his trade in order to equip him to live in a world without mystery."

Scholarly:
sS/PdC 1 Carroll. Dennis. "Communion." *David Mamet.* Modern Dramatists Series. New York: St. Martin's, 1987. 91-117.

Carroll analyzes the construction of the play: "There are five scenes which contrast the quality of two differing relationships; and the central scene, a séance, is like the apex of a pyramid in which the three characters are onstage together for the only time, and in which the relationships intersect. John is here faced with people antagonistic to one another—rivals for his allegiance" (112).

sS/PdC 2 Kolin, Philip C. "Revealing Illusions in David Mamet's *the Shawl.*" *Notes on Contemporary Literature* 16.2 (1986): 9-10.

Kolin places this play in the context of plays about "corruption in America." He examines the construction of audiences: John as audience of Miss A, Charles, the hidden audience, as well as the play's audience. "The shawl is a rich symbol of the multiple levels of illusions Mamet exposes. On the most literal level, it conjures up memories of a loving mother [. . .]. Farther into the subliminal, the shawl perhaps suggests a mantle suitable for a shaman such as John purports to be. [. . .] Ultimately, though, the shawl is a cover for John's tricks. And, as I have suggested many on stage and in the audience have been wrapped in the illusions of its magic fringe" (10).

See also the following scholarly articles covering multiple plays:

sSTP 3 Brewer, Gay. "The Shawl, Shorts, *Speed-the-Plow.*"

sMP 19 Geis, Deborah R. "David Mamet and the Metadramatic Tradition: Seeing 'the Trick from the Back.'"

Short Plays

Death Defying Acts: "The Interview"

Edition:
"An Interview." *Best American Short Plays 1994-95.* Eds. Howard Stein and Glenn
   Young. New York: Applause, 1995. 55-69.

Production:
pDDA 1 Variety Arts Theatre, New York on March 6, 1995.

Director:	Michael Blakemore
Designer:	Robin Wagner
Cast:	
Attorney:	Paul Guilfoyle
Attendant:	Gerry Becker

Overview:
The play appeared with one-acts by Elaine May and Woody Allen. Most of the reviews were negative, viewing Mamet's play as a one-line joke about lawyers going to
hell. Others, however, saw it as Kafkaesque. Stuart noted that Mamet's dialogue worked
particularly well in this situation, but many others found it "self-parody" (Kissel).
Curiously, none really said anything about the opening of the play, the contest to see
who would speak first—the game of power played with silence rather than speech.

Reviews:
rDDA 1.1 Barnes, Clive. "Death Be Not Proud." *New York Post* 7 Mar. 1995. Rpt. in
   National Theatre Critics' Reviews 56.5 (1995): 126-27.

rDDA 1.2 Blakemore, Michael. "Death Defying Director." *New Yorker* 3 June
   1996: 48+.

rDDA 1.3 Brustein, Robert. Rev. of *Death Defying Acts. New Republic* 24 Apr. 1995: 32+. Rpt. in *Cultural Calisthenics*. Chicago: Ivan R. Dee, 1998. 110-112.

rDDA 1.4 Canby, Vincent. "It's a Jungle out There, a Jungle of Urban Neuroses." *New York Times* 7 Mar. 1995: B1+. Rpt. in *National Theatre Critics' Reviews* 56.5 (1995): 125-26.

rDDA 1.5 Feingold, Michael. Rev. of *Death Defying Acts. Village Voice* 21 Mar. 1995. Rpt. in *National Theatre Critics' Reviews* 56.5 (1995): 123-24.

rDDA 1.6 Franklin, Nancy. Rev. of *Death Defying Acts. New Yorker* 20 Mar. 1995. Rpt. in *National Theatre Critics' Reviews* 56.5 (1995): 124.

rDDA 1.7 Gerard, Jeremy. Rev. of *Death Defying Acts. Variety* 13 Mar. 1995. Rpt. in *National Theatre Critics' Reviews* 56.5 (1995): 121-22.

DDA 1.8 Jefferson, Margo. "Verbal Dexterity May Be the Sum of Three Parts." *New York Times* 19 Mar. 1995, sec. 2: 7.

rDDA 1.9 Kissel, Howard. "*Death-Defying Acts* Rescued by Allen's Hilarious Farce." *New York Daily News* 7 March 1995. Rpt. in *National Theatre Critics' Reviews* 56.5 (1995): 121-22.

rDDA 1.10 Leithauser, Brad. "The Humor of Bile and Bite." Rev. of *Death Defying Acts, The Interview. Time* 20 Mar. 1995: 72. Rpt. in *National Theatre Critics' Reviews* 56.5 (1995): 124-25.

rDDA 1.11 Lyons, Donald. "Staying Alive." *Wall Street Journal* 6 Mar. 1995. Rpt. in *National Theatre Critics' Reviews* 56.5 (1995): 127.

rDDA 1.12 Sauer, David Kennedy. Rev. of *The Interview, Death Defying Acts. David Mamet Review* 2 (1995): 8-9.

rDDA 1.13 Scheck, Frank. "Death Defying Acts Falls Short of Exhilarating." *Christian Science Monitor* 10 Mar. 1995: 12.

rDDA 1.14 Simon, John. "Riches and Rags." *New York* 20 Mar. 1995: 62+. Rpt. in *National Theatre Critics' Reviews* 56.5 (1995): 124-5.

Goldberg Street & Crosspatch
Edition:
Goldberg Street: Short Plays and Monologues. New York: Grove, 1985. 1-19.

Production:
pGS&C 1 WNUR [Northwestern University] Radio, March, 1985.

Review:
rGS&C 1.1 Sachs, Lloyd. "2 Mamet Radio Plays Skillfully Presented [*Cross Patch* and *Goldberg Street*]." *Chicago Sun-Times* 6 Mar. 1985: 49.

Jade Mountain

Edition:
"Jade Mountain." *Best American Short Plays 1998-99*. Eds. Theodore Apstein and Glenn Young. New York: Applause, 2001. 143-154.

Production:
pJM 1 21st annual Ensemble Studio Theater's festival of one-acts, Marathon '98. series C June 1998.

Director:		Curt Dempster
Cast:		
	A:	James Murtaugh
	B:	Chris Ceraso

Reviews:
rJM 1.1 Marks, Peter. "Angst, Guilt, Lust and Loneliness." Rev. of *Jade Mountain. New York Times* 10 June 1998: B5.

rJM 1.2 O'Toole, Fintan. "One-Act Wonders." Rev. of *Jade Mountain. Daily News* [New York] 5 June 1998: 57.

Lone Canoe

Production:
pLC 1 Goodman, Chicago. May 24, 1979 (debuted before the American Theater Critics Association Convention—disastrously according to *File on Mamet*).

Reviews:
rLC 1.1 Ellis, Roger. Rev. of *Lone Canoe. Theatre Journal* 32 (1980): 256-57.

rLC 1.2 Eder, Richard. "'Lone Canoe,' Allegory by David Mamet." *New York Times* 26 May 1979: L6.

rLC 1.3 Winer, Linda. Rev. of *Lone Canoe. Chicago Tribune* 25 May 1979.

No One Will Be Immune

Edition:
No One Will Be Immune. New York: Dramatists Play Service, 1994.

Plot Outline:
Interrogation dialogue between a policeman and a suspect about incidents and actions leading up to his exiting an airplane which later crashes. The suspect's premonition includes strange lights and an alien presence in the countryside. The Interrogator focuses on clarifying the suspect's ambiguous language and feelings.

Production:
pNWBI 1 Marathon '95, Ensemble Studio Theatre, New York, May 3 to June 11,
1995.   Director: Curt Dempster
                        Cast:
                                    A: David Rasche
                                    B: Robert Joy / Paul Fox

Reviews:
rNWBI 1.1 Brantley, Ben. "A Mamet Scorcher in a One-Act Series." *New York Times*
3 June 1995: A13+.

rNWBI 1.2 Sauer, David Kennedy. Rev. of *No One Will Be Immune. David Mamet
Review* 2 (1995): 8-9.

A Sermon

Edition:
Goldberg Street: Short Plays and Monologues. New York: Grove, 1985.

Production:
pS 1 Double-billed with *Sexual Perversity* at the Apollo Theater, Chicago in
February, 1979.   Cast: Cosmo White

Reviews:
rS 1.1 Christiansen, Richard. "A Powerful Homecoming for 'Perversity.'" *Chicago
Tribune* 24 Jan. 1979: sec. 6: 4.

rS 1.2 Jacobi, Peter. "New Playlet by Mamet [*A Sermon & Sexual Perversity*]."
Christian Science Monitor 23 Feb. 1979: 19.

rS 1.3 Simon, John. "Einstein in the Woods [the Sermon]." *New York* 9 Nov. 1981:
70-72.
        Negative review: "But this unmuscular Christianity is not enough."

Uncle Vanya

Editions: Translated and adapted by Mamet
        Uncle Vanya. New York: S. French, 1988.
        Uncle Vanya. New York: Grove, 1989.

Production:
pUV 1 Great Performances WNET/13, 22 Feb. 1991. (136 minute videocassette at
the TOFT collection of the NYPL, Lincoln Center)
                Director: Gregory Mosher

SPEED-THE-PLOW

Dedication: Howard Rosenstone

Scenes: Present time, Los Angeles: Act One, Gould's office in the morning; Act Two, evening at Gould's home; Act Three, next morning, back at Gould's office

Characters: Bobby Gould, a man about forty; Charlie Fox, a man about forty; Karen, a woman in her twenties

Editions:

Speed-the-Plow: A Play. Book Club ed. New York: Grove Press, 1987.
Speed-the-Plow: A Play. New York: Grove Press, 1988.
Speed-the-Plow. A Methuen Modern Play. London: Methuen Drama, 1988.
Speed-the-Plow: A Play. New York: S. French, 1988.
HBJ Anthology of Drama. Fort Worth, TX: Harbrace, 1993. 985-1002.
David Mamet Plays: 3. London: Methuen Drama, 1996. 119-84.

Plot Outline:

Act One. Charlie Fox comes to the office of just-promoted Bobby Gould to report that movie star Doug Brown wants to do a "buddy film" with a studio script Fox had sent him. Fox needs Gould to "greenlight" the script. They are exultant to share producing credit and make a fortune. Gould summons his temporary secretary, Karen, to bring coffee and make lunch reservations. Fox bets Gould he can't bed her. Gould asks her to do his courtesy reading of *Radiation and the Half-Life of Society* by an "Eastern Sissy writer." Then he will choose between it or the sure-hit buddy film.

Act Two. Karen arrives at Gould's house and is full of enthusiasm for the great spiritual allegory about how "all radiation has been sent by God. To change us." Gould explains to her that his job is to produce "good work I hope" but only that which will sell the most tickets. Karen convinces him that instead of being the "whores" he and Fox claim they are, he could reclaim his lost purity by doing something noble and greenlighting the radiation story instead.

Act Three. In Gould's office the next morning, Fox is told the radiation film will be made instead of the buddy film. Fox is outraged and pours invective on Gould because he believes the choice will lead to Gould's being fired. When told to leave, he asks Karen, "If he had said 'No' [to the radiation film] would you have gone to bed with him?" Karen confesses she would not, realizing neither her actions nor his were based solely on purity. Gould responds, "Oh, God, now I'm lost." Karen repeats some passages from the book, but out of context they have no force. She laments "I think I'm being punished for my wickedness." Fox exults, "You ever come on the lot again I'm gonna have you killed." As she leaves, Gould says, "I wanted to do Good . . . But I became foolish." Fox reminds Gould their names will appear as producers and concludes: "How bad can life be?"

Production:
pSTP 1. Broadway production by the Lincoln Center Theater at the Royale Theater, New York. It previewed April 9, for 24 performances and opened May 2, running until Dec. 31, 1988 for 278 more performances. (A four minute excerpt of this performance resides in the TOFT collection NYPL)

Director:	Gregory Mosher
Exec. Producer:	Bernard Gersten
Designer:	Michael Merritt
Costumes:	Nan Cibula
Lighting:	Kevin Rigdon
Cast:	
Bobby Gould:	Joe Mantegna
Charlie Fox:	Ron Silver (Tony for Leading Actor)
Karen:	Madonna

Overview:
Critics were nearly unanimous in their praise of Mosher's direction and for Mantegna and Silver, particularly for their abilities to turn on an emotional dime, as well as for their comic talents in the first half. As for Madonna, there was a marked division of opinion. Henry in *Time* explained how Madonna got the role—Rich was the most outspoken in her defense (see also Oliver and Sauvage); Cunningham lambasted Rich on the air for saying she could act. Kissel's headline was: "No, She Can't Act." A clear majority of the critics, however, seemed to think she was at least adequate in the role; and a number saw the role as "underwritten" (Wilson). Christiansen, the most experienced Mamet watcher, saw her as "a steady performer in the Mamet style, [who] convincingly shows the steely conviction beneath her protestations of being 'only a temporary.'" Most amazing was Hornby's conclusion that Madonna "was not nearly sexy enough for the role." There are two points of confusion here: one group questioned whether she could "really" seduce a producer so easily; another group saw beyond the question of realism to the deeper issue of morality and even "'characters' search for their souls through a cultural labyrinth," (Hill).

The split in opinion had to do with tolerance for ambiguity. Those who took the play as a one note satire found that Madonna did not fit their conception of Karen as con artist and whore. Brustein said "Karen should dominate—the center does not hold." Most offended were Wilson and Beaufort. But those like Rich who saw moral ambiguity accepted Madonna's performance as exactly right. "It is undefinable whether she's another con artist, or a sincere naif." Mosher made the point in Henry's article: "Mamet made the character, rather than a poor soul who is battered to the ground, someone about whom there is an element of doubt." Kroll recognized the duality: "is she more consummate con artist than the two aces themselves?" Two reviewers did note that Michael Merritt's set implied the fluidity of life at the top of a studio—furniture covered in plastic and draped with canvas, repainted perpetually for each new occupant. The set itself sent a signal, as Watt suggested: "the whole epitomizing the transitory nature of these empty lives."

Reviews:

rSTP 1.1 Barnes, Clive. "A Harvest of Riches." *New York Post* 4 May 1988: 29+. Rpt. in *New York Theatre Critics' Review* 48.8 (1988): 274-75.

> Rather positive review: "I have a feeling that, at the rarified level of artistic honesty, his play is not true. It is only words—but what mad, rushing, tumultuous gift for words the man has. He also has a god-given gift for the theater, its dialogs and its methods. He writes lines for actors to play in. [. . .] it is two-thirds perfect and one-third hopeful. Madonna tries hard in a Judy Holliday role, but she sounds more as if she were auditioning than acting."

rSTP 1.2 Beaufort, John. "New Mamet Comedy Dreams up a Trio of Hollywood Opportunists." *Christian Science Monitor* 6 May 1988. Rpt. in *New York Theatre Critics' Review* 48.8 (1988): 276.

> Rather negative review: "Since it lacks heart, there is no need for concern about deeper feelings." Mantegna's "self-important front hides a bundle of insecurities. Mr. Silver's Charlie is the ultimate wheeler-dealer—brash, cajoling, and always outrageous. The glee with which a preview audience greeted his blatant opportunism was almost unsettling. A brunette Madonna completes the human equation. Hers is a quietly modulated Karen, a 1980s climber with a grasp of 'what every woman knows' undreamed by Philip Barry [sic]."

rSTP 1.3 Brustein, Robert. "The Last Refuge of Scoundrels." *New Republic* 6 June 1988: 29+. Rpt. in *Reimagining American Theatre.* New York: Hill and Wang, 1991. 62-65.

> Positive review because: "the play establishes friendship between males and personal loyalty among the corrupted as virtually the last remaining values in an increasingly hypocritical and decaying society. And it insinuates this theme in an insidious, subterranean manner, using the terse, taciturn minimalism for which Mamet has become famous. [. . . Mantegna] brings a dour tenor snap to his deal-making scenes and manages his almost religious conversion with a kind of glazed transcendence." Silver "is a center of primal energy and colloquial fluency, whether rushing across the stage and literally kissing Gould's ass, or blistering him for his treachery with a furious stream of invective ('You squat to pee'). These performances are impeccable, possibly the most powerful acting to be seen on the American stage this year. It is a pity they are compromised by

the female star. Madonna is a charismatic pop singer with an electric performing style and a huge following. She is not a qualified actress."

rSTP 1.4 Christiansen, Richard. "Mamet's Madonna." *Chicago Tribune* 4 May 1988, sec. 2: 3.
Positive review of all three actors: "Mantegna [. . .] is glib and assured at the start, bewildered and deflated at the finish, deftly giving Mamet's raffish dialogue his sly spin. Silver, in a portrayal that grows to awesome proportions, is sensational in his shift from a hesitant and awkward underling to an angry and forceful power of darkness. Madonna, not yet an accomplished actress but a steady performer in the Mamet style, convincingly shows the steely conviction beneath her protestations of being 'only a temporary.'"

rSTP 1.5 Dieckmann, Katherine. "Biting the Hand." *Village Voice* 19 July 1988: 57.
This review paired the play with *The Player*, and was extremely negative about Madonna: "Karen is supposedly fresh, spiritual, uncorrupted, but from Madonna's rigid, monotonous performance of a sketchily written part, it's hard to tell if Karen is naïve or just plain calculating. In fact, Madonna's presence in 'Plow' is an unintentional metaphor for the play as a whole: There is no escape from whoredom, and the possibility of genuineness in the movie industry is reduced to a confidence man's (or woman's) game."

rSTP 1.6 Frank, Glenda. Rev. of *Speed-the-Plow. Chelsea Clinton News* 19 May 1988: 16.
Glowing review: "Mamet touches enough ambiguities and morals to keep scholars in conference papers for a long time. [. . .] Fox, like Macduff, has to hear news over and over before it sinks in—good news and bad. Comedy and something akin to tragedy touch in the rendition, empowering it. [. . . Mantegna and Silver] give performances that are inspired, couldn't be better; and for a stage debut, Madonna walks through her role with a sensitivity and continual insight into the character."

rSTP 1.7 Gussow, Mel. "Mamet's Hollywood Is a School for Scoundrels." *New York Times* 15 May 1988: B5+. Rpt. in *Theatre on the Edge*. New York: Applause, 1998. 208-10.
Positive review: "As the self-impaling lines fly back and forth between the two, the author pinions the characters for their egocentricity and their complete lack of taste. [. . .] Although Madonna is overshadowed by her colleagues, that would seem to be at least partly intentional. She is playing the character as conceived by the author. In the purest sense, she is an ingenue—unknowing in Hollywood—not a crafty Eve Harrington plotting her way to stardom or studio chiefdom. She is sincere, self-effacing and tightly controlled. To further her goals, in this case the filming of the anti-radiation book, she is prepared to be manipulative. As with other Mamet heroines (the few there are) the character has otherworldliness."

rSTP 1.8 Henry III, William A. "Madonna Comes to Broadway." *Time* 16 May 1988: 98+.

Extremely positive review: "right up to the end it is impossible to tell whether the book is brilliance or bilge. If it is the former, then the ending is uncommercially tragic. If the latter, then the ending is a foregone conclusion and, however brief, takes too long in coming. Madonna's awkward, indecisive characterization seems calculated to help paper over those gaps and sustain suspense by keeping the audience from reaching conclusions. Thus the question 'Can she act?' cannot be answered. [. . .] What is troubling in his work is a moral ambiguity that verges on cynicism, coupled with a high-minded tone that verges on sanctimony."

rSTP 1.9 Hill, Holly. "Writer at a Turning Point." *Sunday Times* [London] 8 May 1988: C11.

Very positive review of the play's spiritual dimension: "Yet a state of grace is what Mamet's characters yearn for, and in this play Mamet holds out the possibility of grace. [. . .] Karen, as straight-forwardly and very appealingly played by Madonna, remains an enigmatic character. Joe Mantegna conveys a sense of confident authority as Bobby, and of a possible decency even when frequently calling himself a whore. Ron Silver makes Charlie a wary fox whose surprise attack is ferocious."

rSTP 1.10 Hodgson, Moira. Rev. of *Speed-the-Plow*. *Nation* 18 June 1988: 874+.

Positive review of Mantegna and Silver: "the two main actors' line readings are deft and point up the fact that Mamet is an actor's playwright, creating a language which is less simply overheard and recorded whole-cloth than boiled down, crafted and reassembled to create an intense, hyperrealistic theatrical experience. This, after all, is what art is all about."

rSTP 1.11 Hornby, Richard. Rev. of *Speed-the-Plow*. *Hudson Review* 41.3 (1988): 516-18.

Negative review of Madonna whose: "performance was unexceptional; deprived of an echo chamber, she has little voice, and her features are small and relatively unexpressive, but she is relaxed and sincere on stage, and hence easy to watch. She lacked the driving energy of the men, however, was not nearly sexy enough for the role, and needed more naïve eagerness to convince me that she could have convinced Bobby about the novel."

rSTP 1.12 Hummler, Richard. Rev. of *Speed-The-Plow*. *Variety* 11 May 1988: 135.

Mostly positive review except that: "Madonna gets by as an actress and that's about all. Possessed of a tiny and untrained stage voice and obviously limited acting experience, she does less with her role as an idealistic part-time studio secretary than the part would offer a more capable actress."

rSTP 1.13 Kerr, Walter. "Verbal Witchcraft Produces Magical Responses Out Front." *New York Times* 12 June 1988: B5.

Positive review of the use of language and praise for Madonna who: "is really very good in the part, establishing clearly and sometimes hilariously the points that are most vital to Mamet's tantalizing narrative. [. . .] In a way, the play is about self-consciousness in the presence of language. Madonna, not really all that bright, is in her heart of hearts intensely earnest. [. . .] She is demure; decent; she respects words. Glancing at the prison script, she almost slips a little but she quickly recovers: 'It's the same old—it's despicable.' If a noun or an adverb says something to her, she cherishes it, so much so that she can read aloud [. . .] stressing everywhere the two words 'afraid' and 'love,' only to discover that she is reading from the wrong page."

rSTP 1.14 Kissel, Howard. "No, She Can't Act." *Daily News* [New York] 4 May 1988. Rpt. in *New York Theatre Critics' Review* 48.8 (1988): 277.

Mixed review which loves Mantegna and Silver, but not Madonna: "because they're powerful actors and the piece—a facetious "morality play" about Hollywood—is savagely funny. Then she comes on, and the audience is suddenly quiet. They're not in Mamet's play any more. They're in Madonna's. [. . .] The temp is supposed to be a question mark. The lack of firmness in Madonna's performance adds ambiguity. [. . .] In order to make us believe she has equal power, Madonna has to have equal energy. She doesn't. Being vacant on the stage requires more effort than it does in real life."

rSTP 1.15 Kroll, Jack. "The Terrors of Tinseltown: Mamet's Black Comedy." *Newsweek* 16 May 1988: 82. Rpt. in *New York Theatre Critics' Review* 48.8 (1988): 273-4.

Very positive review: "Mamet's master stroke is to shove these self-justifying, self-loathing clowns smack up against the Big Questions of Our Time. Speed talking. [. . .] Mantegna is very funny and then weirdly touching as he moves from a lordly assumption of power to a state of moral confusion. [. . . Silver] accepts Bobby's bastardry, but when the bastard turns virtuous he explodes into a baroque paroxysm of rage that's both hilarious and terrifying. As for Madonna, she has a lot to learn, but she's a serious actress. [. . .] Or is she more consummate con artist than the two aces themselves? Madonna hits this chord beautifully, turning her confrontation with Bobby into a double seduction that scrambles all the moral angles."

rSTP 1.16 Levett, Karl. Rev. of *Speed-the-Plow*. *Drama*. 169 (1988): 41-42.

Positive review: "The only extravagance is Mamet's language—his arias of commonplace speech, studied with epigrams of the inarticulate. [. . .] And Madonna? Her earnestness and naivety are used to some effect by director Mosher, but where the character is single-minded, the performance is single-toned and one is left wondering what more subtle actresses would find in the part—and what this might do to the moral fable."

rSTP 1.17 Lida, David. Rev. of *Speed-the-Plow*. *Women's Wear Daily* 4 May 1988: 21. Rpt. in *New York Theatre Critics' Review* 48.8 (1988): 281.

Positive review: "Madonna, who is the pivotal figure in the second act, has a charismatic stage presence and is adept at capturing the cadences of Mamet's dialog. She creates an ambiguous character, half idealist and half-loser. This is the play's talkiest act and, unfortunately, Madonna speaks most of her lines in a monotone. The strongest performance is Silver's. When he is called upon to react to a betrayal of an 11-year relationship, he laughs, cries, screams and schemes, and in the process takes control of the stage. His command gives the play a hearty finish."

rSTP 1.18 Lieberson, Jonathan. "The Prophet of Broadway." *New York Review of Books* 21 July 1988: 3+.
    Negative review of the play, and of the production as being too funny: "Mamet's are actors' plays, opportunities for spectacular performances, while not always conveying much of interest in themselves." Lieberson notes that even with a great director and actors, "the play is a disappointment, at moments startling to watch yet morally unchallenging, even insipid. [. . .] One sometimes feels, as here, that the playwright's central concern is the punch line that gets a laugh or a gasp rather than the character or the situation."

rSTP 1.19 "Madonna's Debut." *Women's Wear Daily* 15 Apr. 1988: 20.
    A positive view of Madonna and the play from a preview: "The trio has a remarkable rapport on stage and Madonna's blinding star quality is surpassed only by the impact of the text and Mantegna's and Silver's reading of it. Her presence is a kind of inherent coup de theater [sic]. [. . .] Madonna may be more of a personality than an actress, but in 'Speed-the-Plow' she is captivating. You just want to look at every inch of her—and her co-stars."

rSTP 1.20 Maxwell, Brian. Rev. of *Speed-the-Plow. West Side Spirit* 5 June 1988: 17.
    Negative review of Madonna and the play: Madonna "seems an attempt to raise 'Plow' to a higher plane in which good angel Karen and bad angel Fox battle for Gould's soul. This, however, quickly degenerates into metaphysical mumblings which, with ruminations on art and a debate on morals, soon becomes boring. Madonna brings presence and an apt thin voice, but is undercut by an underwritten role and Mamet's inability to write believable dialog for his female characters the way he does for his male ones."

rSTP 1.21 Oliver, Edith. "Mamet at the Movies." *New Yorker* 16 May 1988: 95.
    Extremely positive review: "The perfectly matched acting of these two men, under Gregory Mosher's direction, is a marvel to behold; not a word or gesture goes to waste. As for Madonna, who, for all her other credits, is just a beginner in the theatre, her performance seemed to me just right. Her temp is the kind of clear-eyed boob who could convince even shrewd Bobby (under the circumstances, of course). [. . .] Her crafty innocence makes a nice contrast to the cynicism and incidental treachery and open greed of the men. The play itself is vintage Mamet, passionate and witty and terribly funny."

rSTP 1.22 Rich, Frank. "Mamet's Dark View of Hollywood as a Heaven for the Virtueless." *New York Times* 4 May 1988: C17. Rpt. in *New York Theatre Critics' Review* 48.8 (1988): 272-3.

Extremely positive review: "The more fun is poked at 'The Bridge' and its lofty warnings about the end of the world, the more it seems that a religious vision of salvation may be presenting itself to one of the hardened moguls, prompting him to change the world and maybe even to make better movies. [. . .] [T]his rock star's performance is [. . .] intelligent, scrupulously disciplined comic acting. [. . .] Mr. Silver's frightening eruptions of snarling anger and crumpled demeanor in the face of defeat make what could be another Beverly Hills caricature into a figure of pathos. [. . .] But when unforeseen circumstances suddenly force this self-assured Machiavelli to declare 'I'm lost,' Mr. Mantegna evinces just the ashen, glassy-eyed pallor needed to convey the vertigo-inducing moral void that Mr. Mamet has opened up before him and the audience."

rSTP 1.23 Rogoff, Gordon. "The Seductions of Cynicism." *Village Voice* 17 May 1988: 105.

Mixed review of play and actors: If Madonna's "unequal, it's partly a response to the wimpy inequality built into the role. Mamet can't let a wise woman into his universe. [. . .] Mamet's not pretending to write characters according to the rules. Forget complexity, roundness, or even 20th century notions of sympathy. Like a latter-day Ben Jonson, he's getting his charge from his own verbal reconstruction of the way masculine evil talks to itself. [. . .] Ron Silver's Charlie, waving his cigar like a rifle, is an astounding talking machine, ingratiating as Jonson's Mosca and Volpone never were; he's thrust, sweat, and parry, a bearded wonder with a mouth like a sewer, so completely in charge of his third-act passion to bring Bobby back from the morality-brink that he begins to transform rottenness into the purest of ideals."

rSTP 1.24 Sauvage, Leo. "Mamet's Unreal Hollywood." *New Leader* 13 June 1988: 20+.

Rather negative review: "Karen does not have a real existence, or a dramatic one for that matter, and it would be idle to invent one for her. Nevertheless, I was moved to play detective and explore the hypothesis that she might be the particularly clever agent of the 'Eastern sissy writer.' [. . .] I cannot appraise her dramatic skills with only the undefined and indefinable role of Karen to go on."

rSTP 1.25 Schiff, Stephen. "Mamet Meets Madonna." *Vanity Fair* Apr. 1988: 32+.

Promotion piece and interview with Mosher: "'But the character does need the strength that it takes to be pure, and Madonna's strength just astonishes you when she walks in the room.' That strength, in fact, may be exactly what the role requires."

rSTP 1.26 Simon, John. "Bringing Up Mother." *New York* 30 May 1988: 88+.

Simon belatedly recognized that Madonna's role itself posed problems of uncertainty: "her character, indeed, by contradictory implications, is both a complete bimbo and a woman of some passionate commitment, honest, and perhaps even taste. A depressing moral and intellectual indeterminacy runs through Mamet's œuvre—enough to leave a much better actress than Madonna stranded."

rSTP 1.27 —. "Word Power." Rev. of *Speed-the-Plow*. *New York* 16 May 1988: 106.
Mildly negative review: "Madonna comes across as vaguely insecure underneath a display of chutzpa and some stylish clothes rather better than temporary help might be expected to wear. In every other way, she is more of a temporary hindrance whenever she is on."

rSTP 1.28 Smith, Liz. "Madonna Plows Right Past Her Critics." *Daily News* [New York] 5 May 1988: 8.
Gossip columnist's view: "I thought she was great. Now I admit about half of those talked to at the opening weren't impressed, but the other half were. The critics shaped up likewise. [. . .] Madonna is a cool, understated antidote to these two onstage Hollywood crazies, these wheeler-dealers who are based loosely on the real-life Ned Tanen and the real-life Art Linson of Paramount."

rSTP 1.29 Stearns, David Patrick. "Madonna Slows Down This *Plow*." *USA Today* 4 May 1988. Rpt. in *New York Theatre Critics' Review* 48.8 (1988): 278.
Rather negative review: "The role would seem to be ideally suited for her alluringly insolent presence. Though she looks terrific, she recites her lines prosaically and without much character. She attempts to stretch a talent she doesn't seem to have developed."

rSTP 1.30 Watt, Douglas. "*Plow* Turns up Dirt on L.A." *Daily News* [New York] 13 May 1988: 53+. Rpt. in *New York Theatre Critics' Review* 48.8 (1988): 277-8.
Rather positive review noted "the year's most apt settings, using a bare stage and draped furniture pieces uncovered as the scene changes, the whole epitomizing the transitory nature of these empty lives. Mantegna and Silver, under Gregory Mosher's split second direction, go about Mamet's deliberately repetitious (Abbot and Costello-like, at times) speech patterns with such skill that you'll be swept away. [. . .] Wouldn't it be funny, though, if in using a rock star Mamet succumbed to the same thinking (name value at the box office) that motivates Gould and Fox?"

rSTP 1.31 Weales, Gerald. "American Theater Watch 1987-88." *Georgia Review*. Fall (1988): 601-02.
Positive review: "The verbal heart of the play is in the wonderful and wonderfully obscene overlap exchanges of the two old friends, for the play is a variation on the typical buddy movie which they plan to make once the intrusive female is pushed aside—as she regularly is in buddy movies."

rSTP 1.32 —. "Rough Diamonds." *Commonweal* 17 June 1988: 371.
Positive review: "Her performance is not as flashily fine as those of Mantegna and Silver, but she does a creditable job with a character who—

unlike Bobby and Charlie—is never clearly defined. [. . .] Bobby and Charlie are a reprehensible pair (each would sacrifice the other for an edge up), but Mantegna and Silver give them so much energy, so much chutzpah, so much tacky charm that we find ourselves rooting for Bobby's return to chicanery. Maybe that is the point. Maybe the target isn't Hollywood, not American business, but the audience itself."

rSTP 1.33 Weiss, Hedy. "'Plow' Slows Actors." *Chicago Sun-Times* 4 May 1988: 39.
        Negative review: "Mamet would have us see her answer as proof that Karen, too, was after something in this buy and sell world—that she was no purer or more idealistic than the men. He never even considers the fact that she may have been attracted to Gould for his willingness to change and to appreciate her point of view. (And you thought Mamet was about to give us a heroine? Not a prayer. Karen ends up looking both more ridiculous and more manipulative than Gould and Fox.)"

rSTP 1.34 Wilson, Edwin. "Mamet's Hollywood." *Wall Street Journal* 6 May 1988: 14. Rpt. in *New York Theatre Critics' Reviews* 48.8 (1988): 275-76.
        Mixed review: "Mantegna and Silver are major-league performers, and though Madonna works hard to hold her own, she cannot be blamed if she appears to be out of her depth. [. . .] As for the secretary, the part is so underwritten it's impossible to know where she is coming from, or even whether or not she is for real. [. . .] And what about Bobby's change of character? Are we supposed to take his overnight conversion seriously? He's been a deal maker, a man with his eye on the main chance, all his life; would he suddenly get religion from a woman he has known one day?"

rSTP 1.35 Winer, Linda. "Mamet's Melodic Voices." *Newsday* 4 May 1988: 9+. Rpt. in *New York Theatre Critics' Review* 48.8 (1988): 278-9.
        Mixed review: "Madonna is OK, sort of, but [this . . .], with the irresistible Joe Mantegna and a riveting breakthrough performance by Ron Silver, is a vicious, scabrous, mean-spirited joy of a play about Hollywood. Based, as Mamet likes to say, 'on an actual idea,' it is a revenge comedy that toys with morality— with the idea that, once in a some secret place, even movie producers may have wanted to do good. In three tightly packed scenes, 'Plow' runs over the perfectibility of mankind with uncompromisingly cynical, dirty-talking, monomaniacal pleasure."

Production:
pSTP 2 This is the same Broadway production at the Royale Theater but with a replacement cast closing December 31, 1988.
        New Cast:

Bobby Gould:	David Rasche
Charlie Fox:	Bob Balaban
Karen:	Felicity Huffman

Overview:
In an interesting experiment, the actors started directly from the script again, but with Mosher still directing—rather than trying to replicate the previous performances. Critics mainly ignored Rasche's performance, most did not like Balaban's, and most liked Huffman. They were far more forgiving than with Madonna as they realized it was the play more than the performance that had frustrated them. Barnes noted that "The style of the playing is far more naturalistic—and as a result, the play [. . .] gathers something in conviction and perhaps even in seriousness." But Rich was more negative about the change to this style, thinking it made the play "diminished in humor and pathos." Critics were puzzled that a better actor as Karen did not improve the play—and Madonna may have had something more than they initially detected working for her. Rich, who had argued all along that Madonna was quite apt, made the point: "Madonna's awkwardness and, yes, star presence, added essential elements of mystery and eroticism to character who doesn't reveal her true, shocking hand."

Reviews:
rSTP 2.1 Barnes, Clive. "New Hands on the 'Plow,' a New Look to the Laughs." *New York Post* 10 Oct. 1988: 26.

Positive review: "Unquestionably Rasche, Balaban, and the deliciously shy and sneaky Miss Huffman show sure hands on the plow, and deliver the laughs on the nose. This remains the funniest hour or so on Broadway. Yes, the men do lack the eclat and aplomb of the originals, and some will miss the tongue-tied and rather endearing amateurishness of Madonna [. . .]."

rSTP 2.2 Hummler, Richard. Rev. of *Speed-The-Plow. Variety* 19 Oct. 1988: 502.

Rather positive review: "Huffman gives the role color and variation, unlike her predecessor. The second scene [. . .] is no longer a stage wait, thanks to Huffman's articulate communication of the character's idealism (tinged with calculation) and to David Rasche's comic susceptibility to her wiles. [. . . Balaban] builds the character nicely to a point where his climactic tirade of enraged disappointment has genuinely ugly bite. The resentment of years of stoogehood comes bursting out as if a boil had been lanced."

rSTP 2.3 Kissel, Howard. "New *Speed* Limits on Broadway." *Daily News* [New York] 29 Sept. 1988: 51.

Rather positive review: "The new cast is mellower, less frenetic." Rasche "has a nice touch of innocence as the young producer. [. . .] It adds wit to Mamet's characterization of this schlockmeister as a kind of modern Everyman." Huffman, he notes, "you know this girl has smarts. With her predecessor, you were never sure. We still don't see her overnight growth from a nervous temp to a power player."

rSTP 2.4 Nelson, Don. "The Second Time Around." *Daily News* [New York] 12 Sept. 1988: 29.

This is a promotional piece about the replacement cast. Huffman says, "Karen is the catalyst. She's the one who defines the choice that Bobby (Rasche) has to make."

rSTP 2.5 Rich, Frank. "'Plow' and 'Butterfly': New Leads, New Light." *New York Times* 23 Sept. 1988: C3.

Not so positive view of the new cast: "The result is a 'Speed-the-Plow' diminished in humor and pathos. Mr. Balaban's Fox is too pathological to permit easy laughter at his vulgarity and conniving in the early scenes. [. . .] But the deep, shudder-inducing chill of the original interpretation is gone. Oddly enough, the altered dynamic between Fox and Gould in 'Speed-the-Plow' has not spilled over to Karen, the temporary secretary who disrupts the men's balance of power. Ms. Huffman's skillful performances in most details similar to Madonna's—in technical expertise, more proficient—and yet less effective. First, that Madonna's awkwardness and, yes, star presence, added essential elements of mystery and eroticism to the character who doesn't reveal her true, shocking hand (and power over powerful men) until late in the play."

rSTP 2.6 Simon, John. "Youth Wants to Know." *New York* 3 Oct. 1988: 78-79.

More positive than his first review. The new cast: "all contribute to humanizing the play, to making the characters people rather than concepts, voicers of feelings (real or false) rather than musical instruments trying to outdo one another by playing louder, faster, slower, softer."

rSTP 2.7 Staples, Brent. "Mamet's House of Word Games." *New York Times* 29 Sept. 1988: B1+.

Analysis of Mamet's work, focused on linguistic minimalism: "To view Mr. Mamet's characters as beneath us is to mistake words for truth and to miss the real truths that underlie the words. If anything, it is we who have not risen to their standard. They resist evasive, obfuscating language to grapple openly with what they want from each other. Honesty is the animus that drives Mr. Mamet's dialogue, even when it is being spoken by cons and thieves. The lies that are told in ordinary conversation are a particular target. His characters don't hide in elaborate webs of words; they slash each other face to face."

rSTP 2.8 Watt, Douglas. "New *Plow* Cast Not up to *Speed*." *Daily News* [New York] 30 Sept. 1988: 47.

Negative review: "Huffman, who has taken over the part of Karen, the designing office temp, is an experienced young actress and quite good in the part except for one thing: while not uncomely, she is almost totally devoid of the sex appeal essential to this character. Worse, the two men—the tall, blond, David Rasche, who looks more like an over-the-wave surfer than the film studio's brash head of production, Bobby Gould. Bob Balaban, a short, bespectacled, wimpish figure turns Bobby's white-hot, money-hungry producer Charlie Fox into a humorless nudnik. The actors, while retaining the rhythms of Mamet's dialogue, drain it of vitality."

rSTP 2.9 Weiner, Bernard. "Whoring in Hollywood." *Tikkun* 4.1 (1989): 77-78.
     Positive review which focused on Mamet's Jewish background: "Because
of Karen, Bobby is forced to confront his moral prostitution in Hollywood. He
opens himself to her love and to the new life of purity and hope that she offers
him. But he sinks back into the pit of greed at the last moment, when his rickety
ego can't handle her confession that she wouldn't have slept with him had he
not been open to changing himself significantly. If Karen is the angelic
personification of Good, Charlie Fox (Ron Silver) is the personification of Evil.
[. . .] Still one aspect of *Speed-the-Plow* continues to confuse and disturb me.
The two Jewish movie producers [. . .] are stereotypically presented as money-
hungry manipulators. Karen, the angel of salvation, is not just offering hope
and change through a nondenominational spiritual force but is definitely a
Christian—apparently born-again. Is the Jewish/Christian dichotomy pure
coincidence?"

rSTP 2.10 Winer, Linda. "Different *Speed* to Mamet's *Plow.*" *Newsday* 22 Sept. 1988.
     Positive view that the new cast "is good news for the play." Huffman "plays
Karen as a clear-eyed, smart woman who is comfortable with the uses of her
sexuality but isn't just a vamp." She has his "most pretentious lines and her
scene with Bobby remains the script's only dead spot. Unlike Madonna, however,
Huffman speaks as if the lines mean something to her. Karen remains a fairly
thankless role, but Huffman relaxes in it and, unlike her colleagues, always
handles the tricky Mamet patter with the grace of an acrobat."

Production:
pSTP 3 Same production as in New York, but now at the National Theatre's Lyttelton
     Theatre in London with a new cast, previewed from January 19 and ran
     from January 25 to August 23, 1989.
          Cast:

Bobby Gould:	Colin Stinton
Charlie Fox:	Alfred Molina
Karen:	Rebecca Pidgeon

Overview:
British reviewers of this National Theatre production mainly faulted Mamet for the
script, rather than Pidgeon for the performance as Karen. Essentially, they expected a
satire on Hollywood in which Bobby and Charlie would be the satiric butts. And
Karen would then supply the counter perspective—Art. But many got frustrated
because the "Art" script sounded hollow, and sympathy began to slide back to making
a profit with the Buddy film—the very script they assumed they were to scorn. That
left critics confused, conflicted, and upset—and so they blamed Mamet. As a result,
they were unanimous in their appreciation of Molina who showed "how making money
together is, for these people, more sexually arousing and emotionally binding than
sex" (Taylor 69). He was also praised for best capturing Mamet's rhythms. Stinton
was also praised, though some had reservations when his characters shifted gears—
soul-searching for a Hollywood magnate broke too many stereotypes and many were

perplexed. Pidgeon was never blamed like Madonna—but she didn't get anyone's full endorsement, either. Several praised her "sincere" delivery of the lines; one praised her enunciation. But they all had trouble, again, when she shifted gears. They felt she hadn't the sexual magnetism to seduce a Hollywood studio head.

Reviews:

rSTP 3.1 Billington, Michael. Rev. of *Speed-the-Plow. Guardian* 26 Jan. 1989. Rpt. in *London Theatre Record* 1-28 Jan. 1989: 73 and as "Hollywood or Bust" *Manchester Guardian Weekly* 13 Feb. 1989: 24.

Positive review as: "much more than an anti-Hollywood satire; it is actually, like all Mamet's plays, about the gap between language and feeling and about the way we use words as a vaporous smokescreen. What makes Mamet fascinating, however, is his sneaking regard for what he satirises. [. . .] and here there is a residual sympathy for these valueless go-getters whose idea of making a movie is to repeat last year's formula."

rSTP 3.2 Coveney, Michael. Rev. of *Speed-the-Plow. Financial Times* 26 Jan. 1989. Rpt. in *London Theatre Record* 1-28 Jan. 1989: 70.

Negative view of the play which liked Molina enormously, but Stinton "disappears when not talking. Blockish and dour, he signals like an automaton and is an implausible oozer of sexual charm, the odour of power. Pidgeon never really lets us know what she thinks, but concentrates on speaking very clearly. Ambiguity over the qualities of the awful radiation novel is permissible. But this girl is a go-getter moving too fast for her own good. She is found out by Charlie, then makes a mistake."

rSTP 3.3 Edwards, Christopher. Rev. of *Speed-the-Plow. What's On* 4 Feb. 1989. Also *Spectator* 4 Feb. 1989: 36. Rpt. in *London Theatre Record* 1-28 Jan. 1989: 72.

Positive review: "But as well as satirising the emptiness of Hollywood, Mamet simultaneously celebrates a sense of compulsive compassion. This is a very American play. [. . .] Gould almost throws his career away on some spurious, pseudo-religious script. The way Karen manages to inveigle him with a mixture of sex and bogus philosophy is terrible funny. But, again, there is pathos beneath the satire. Gould dimly perceives the need for some higher purpose in his life. [. . .] And it is just characteristic of a Hollywood mogul that Gould should fall for something so solemn and bogus."

rSTP 3.4 Gardner, Lyn. Rev. of *Speed the Plow. City Limits* 2 Feb. 1989. Rpt. in *London Theatre Record* 1-28 Jan. 1989: 69.

Positive review: "But despite fine performances (Stinton exuding the stocky sexuality which comes with power; Pidgeon, as neat and unreadable as a closed book until her fatal slip of the tongue; and, best of all, Alfred Molina, murderously insecure beneath his buddy buddy bluster) the characters are mere stooges for Mamet's love affair with the American language: the moral argument sacrificed to virtuoso verbals where the devil gets all the best lines."

rSTP 3.5 Grant, Steve. Rev. of *Speed-the-Plow*. *Time Out* 1 Feb. 1989. Rpt. in *London Theatre Record* 1-28 Jan. 1989: 69.

Positive review: "To make art or to make out, that is the question. And to call the resulting power game a parade of superficiality and cliché is only part of the story." Actors and Mosher conveyed the "constant demands on the audience to weight the worth of what is said and implied."

rSTP 3.6 Hiley, Jim. Rev. of *Speed the Plow*. *Listener* 2 Feb. 1989. Rpt. in *London Theatre Record* 1-28 Jan. 1989: 68.

Negative review that the play rejecting it as satire: "It is nothing of the sort. The play's stance veers between ambiguity and sly celebration."

rSTP 3.7 Hirschhorn, Clive. Rev. of *Speed the Plow*. *Sunday Express* [London] 29 Jan. 1989. Rpt. in *London Theatre Record* 1-28 Jan. 1989: 68.

Positive review: "On Broadway, Madonna played Karen with a vapidity that left a vacuum at the play's core. Ms. Pidgeon is infinitely more convincing and you willingly believe her powers of persuasion."

rSTP 3.8 Hislop, A. "Exposing the Moguls." *Times Literary Supplement* 4479 (1989): 111.

Negative review which oversimplified: "Mamet believes in the artistic purity of a 'true' theatre as opposed to the moral and aesthetic compromises of American film culture. [. . .] Mamet exploits with comic poignancy the tendency in modern Hollywood speech to mouth its own contradictions and deceits so loudly that it does not even pretend to sustain its pretences—there is no need of an ironizing narrator to unmask it."

rSTP 3.9 Hurren, Kenneth. Rev. of *Speed-the-Plow*. *Mail on Sunday* 29 Jan. 1989. Rpt. in *London Theatre Record* 1-28 Jan. 1989: 71.

Negative review: "I expected him [Mamet] to gnaw to the wrist the hand that fed him. Instead he licks its fingers with a phony commerce versus art contest."

rSTP 3.10 James, John. Rev. of *Speed-the-Plow*. *Times Educational Supplement* 3 Feb. 1989: B7.

Saw the play as funny, but without depth: "Mamet's picture of Hollywood is bitingly funny. That the set-up rings hollow hardly matters when brilliant one-liners spark off so much laughter. Chuck [Fox] has the best of them which Alfred Molina deploys with devastatingly comic effect, switching to deadly seriousness with masterful power when threatened. [. . .] Stinton manages Bob's incredible volte-face; Rebecca Pidgeon brings spirit to Karen's almost lifeless part."

rSTP 3.11 Jones, Dan. Rev. of *Speed-the-Plow*. *Sunday Telegraph* 29 Jan. 1989. Rpt. in *London Theatre Record* 1-28 Jan. 1989: 70.

Mixed review: "This is just what the little minx does want [power and money]. She is not naïve at all and she leaves the Head of Production painfully disillusioned. Colin Stinton is quite touching here, but not really repulsive enough for the part."

rSTP 3.12 Marmion, Patrick. Rev. of *Speed-the-Plow*. *What's On* 1 Feb. 1989. Rpt. in *London Theatre Record* 1-28 Jan. 1989: 72.

Positive review: "The play lays bare the bones of institutionalised philistinism practised in Beverly Hills, the land of make believe. [. . .] While the verbal exchanges are slickly directed by Gregory Mosher, making them hugely enjoyable, the story and the flimsy choice presented renders the satire ineffectual. Neurotic as these producers might be, they are also culturally very powerful and no serious questions are directed at that power."

rSTP 3.13 Morley, Sheridan. Rev. of *Speed-the-Plow*. *Herald Tribune* 1 Feb. 1989. Rpt. in *London Theatre Record* 1-28 Jan. 1989: 73.

Positive review: "So much for plot: What Mamet is really writing here is a morality play about power and virginity and sex and the moral epilepsy that more than one critic has always found at the heart of his plays."

rSTP 3.14 Nathan, David. Rev. of *Speed-the-Plow*. *Jewish Chronicle* 3 Feb. 1989. Rpt. in *London Theatre Record* 1-28 Jan. 1989: 72.

Mixed review of the play as "a celebration of the Hollywood hustler, a sly vindication of the values of the tinsel town and its wheeler-dealers, its schemer-dreamers. Whoever said it was a satire on Hollywood needs to have his lampoons examined."

rSTP 3.15 Osborne, Charles. Rev. of *Speed-the-Plow*. *Daily Telegraph* 27 Jan. 1989. Rpt. in *London Theatre Record* 1-28 Jan. 1989: 71.

Positive review: "The confrontation of philistinism and pretentiousness produces some very funny lines. [. . .] Though they are continually assuring one another of their understanding, each of the play's three characters, at one point or another, is forced to admit 'I don't understand.' All of them use language non-intellectually. Emotion has displaced intelligence, and there is nothing to understand."

rSTP 3.16 Paton, Maureen. Rev. of *Speed the Plow*. *Daily Express* [London] 29 Jan. 1989. Rpt. in *London Theatre Record* 1-28 Jan. 1989: 69.

Neutral view: "Two cynical film producers revel in their crassness until Karen the secretary persuades Bobby Gould to give the go-ahead to a movie after a night of sex and soul-searching."

rSTP 3.17 Pit. Rev. of *Speed-The-Plow*. *Variety* 8 Feb. 1989: 161.

Positive review: "A nimble, well-trained cast hits the right serio-satiric chords. [. . .] The versatile Molina is a standout in the flashiest and funniest role, and an obvious candidate for honors anon."

rSTP 3.18 Ratcliffe, Michael. Rev. of *Speed-the-Plow*. *Observer* 29 Jan. 1989. Rpt. in *London Theatre Record* 1-28 Jan. 1989: 70.

Mixed review, but most positive about Pidgeon: "Karen is where 'Speed-the-Plow' begins to go wrong, although Pidgeon's performance is so

mesmerisingly pitched between innocence and knowledge that you can't wait
to hear what she will say next. It is simply not possible to believe that so solemn
a young Head of Production would give in to a Green case so fast."

rSTP 3.19 Shulman, Milton. "And So To Bet . . ." *Evening Standard* 26 Jan. 1989: 34.
Rpt. in *London Theatre Record* 1-28 Jan. 1989: 71.

Mixed review, positive about the performances: "Although Colin Stinton,
as Gould, has the brash bravado of a producer who considers deals are an art
form, his sudden discovery of creative integrity leaves him looking as disoriented
as Al Capone in the Salvation Army. Alfred Molina as Fox, is at least true to his
vulgar self and his panic at the prospect of culture robbing him of a bonanza is
a pleasure to behold. Rebecca Pidgeon, playing the part that put Madonna on the
stage in New York, exuded evangelical passion about the radiation story but she
would have had to possess the sexual power of a Garbo or a Monroe to have tempted
a crass philistine like Gould to incinerate his career on the pyre of high art."

rSTP 3.20 Taylor, Paul. Rev. of *Speed-the-Plow. Independent* 27 Jan. 1989. Rpt. in
London Theatre Record 1-28 Jan. 1989: 68-69.

Positive review: "Art's spokesperson here is not the customary aggrieved
and exploited writer, but a temporary secretary who with a calculated, eye-on-
the-main-chance faux naivete. [. . .] With friends like her, Art needs no enemies.
Apart from being half-baked and virtually unintelligible, her flights of idealistic
enthusiasm are—Rebecca Pidgeon's go-getting Karen alerts you—just a
disguised sales pitch for her own career. [. . .] In the scene where she tries to
persuade Gould of the merits of the radiation book and ends up seducing him,
Mamet's writing, Gregory Mosher's otherwise pointed and lively production
and Colin Stinton's performance all seem to suffer temporary power failure."

rSTP 3.21 Tinker, Jack. "Settling Some Old Scores ... But Without Any Heart." *Daily
Mail* 26 Jan. 1989. Rpt. in *London Theatre Record* 1-28 Jan. 1989: 69.

Rather negative review: "And there was Madonna—symbol of all these
grubby values we are invited to sneer at—giving a performance that would
make an empty space look like talent." But in London production "there is still
a hole where its heart should be. Not even the ringing sincerity of Rebecca
Pidgeon's performance can fill it. [. . .] Suddenly I saw poor, inept Madonna in
quite a new light. Nobody, but nobody, could sell lines like that, even with her
body thrown in as an optional extra."

rSTP 3.22 Wardle, Irving. "Dream Machine." *The Times* [London] 26 Jan. 1989: 18.

Mixed review which liked Molina, but not much more: "Mamet's play
differs from others of this genre in omitting the usual figure of the exploited
writer. It is about the permanent residents of the dream factory; and its
sympathies, if any, lie more with them than with pharasaical visitors. Hollywood,
as Mamet sees it, is just another department of business America. [. . .] Like
Charlie, the girl (Rebecca Pidgeon) begins as an underling and achieves equality

with Bobby through salesmanship; but their encounter is so low on sexual and argumentative energy, that it is only through plot manipulation that he falls under her spell. In this scene, too, the laughs are abruptly cut off."

rSTP 3.23 Wolf, Matt. "From Broadway to London, with Some Surprises." *New York Times* 28 May 1989: B5+.

Positive review: "An early desperation to the men's bravado hints at the rupture to come, and Mr. Stinton's chillingly squat, monochromatic Bobby makes no pretense toward the jocular good ol' guy Joe Mantegna presented in New York. The electrifying Mr. Molina, an actor as rangy as Mr. Stinton is compact, makes Charlie a quickwitted hustler who regards personal loyalty as the last holdout against the Huns. Ms. Pidgeon encounters some of the difficulties faced by Madonna in New York in the play's least rewarding, most difficult part. Sketchily written and ambiguously motivated, Karen benefits from the star presence that Madonna brought to the role and Ms. Pidgeon does not. Still, in a sense, neither actress's deficiencies really matter, since Mr. Mamet is writing about, and on behalf of, his men."

rSTP 3.24 —. "Mamet's Play Greeted Unenthusiastically in Britain." *Chicago Tribune* 2 Feb. 1989, sec. Tempo: 10.

Overview of response of London theatre critics which is surprised that they were mixed because of the usual warm reception Mamet receives in Britain. On Wolf's own "second view, the play's three short acts seem even more brilliantly to constitute a penetrating examination of egos under siege."

Production:

pSTP 4 London production by the Ambassador Theatre Group at the New Ambassadors which previewed March 14, opened March 16 and closed April 22, 2000. (The production was revived with a new cast at the Duke of York's Theatre, June 29 and closing early on August 19, 2000. Director, Rupert Goold, Nathaniel Parker, Bobby, Neil Morrissey, Charlie, and Gina Bellman, Karen.)

Director:	Peter Gill
Designer:	John Gunter
Lighting:	Andy Phillips
Music:	Terry Davies and Paul Higgs
Cast:	

Bobby Gould:	Mark Strong
Charlie Fox:	Patrick Marber
Karen:	Kimberly Williams

Overview:

Most reviewers were positive about this whole production, Woodis noted "it boasts three magnificent performances." Nearly everyone found Williams quite complex and multidimensional in shifting from naïve to manipulative—though several reviewers faulted Mamet for the antifeminist portrait. They all seemed to like Strong's Bobby, but were more divided over Marber. de Jongh echoed the Madonna critiques: "Patrick

Marber is a talented playwright but he should steer clear of the acting area. His performance reeks of physical unease." Brown countered that "he's terrific, beginning rather low-key, quiet and nervy and building steadily to a ferocious climax."

Reviewers became accepting of the many twists and turns of morality and choice here, rather than reducing the play to a "satire of Hollywood" or simple binary of art vs. mammon.

Reviews:

rSTP 4.1 Brown, Georgina. Rev. of *Speed-the-Plow. Mail on Sunday* 19 Mar. 2000. Rpt. in *Theatre Record* 11-24 Mar. 2000: 323.

> Mixed review which is strong for the performances: "Williams brilliantly manages the shifts from girly faux-naivete, through knowing manœuvres to shattered defeat. That's the bit I don't like about this play—the men triumph, the girl gets screwed. There's really no contest."

rSTP 4.2 Butler, Robert. Rev. of *Speed-the-Plow. Independent on Sunday* 19 Mar. 2000. Rpt. in *Theatre Record* 11-24 Mar. 2000: 326.

> Positive review, especially as "Strong's tall, sleek figure lounges back in his office chair, strokes his nose with a long finger and catches every nuance. It's a performance of real quickness and intelligence that is packed with witty detail. He elicits one big laugh with a fleeting furrow of an eyebrow."

rSTP 4.3 Coveney, Michael. Rev. of *Speed-the-Plow. Daily Mail* 17 Mar. 2000. Rpt. in *Theatre Record* 11-24 Mar. 2000: 326.

> Positive review: "On a great, oversized red sofa back at Bobby's place, Karen turns the tables. Bobby's chance of salvation is challenged when Karen says she would not have slept with him if he'd rejected her advocacy of the radiation script. The elegant, brilliantly precise Mark Strong as Bobby mixes a smooth veneer with troubled stirrings in the heart. His own life passes him by. The play is his tragedy."

rSTP 4.4 de Jongh, Nicholas. Rev. of *Speed-the-Plow. Evening Standard* 17 Mar. 2000. Rpt. in *Theatre Record* 11-24 Mar. 2000: 323.

> Mixed review of the performances: "The scene is beautifully played as a power game in which the seductive Kimberly Williams, vehemence in her voice and craziness in her eyes, argues that the films Gould produces should raise the world's morale, not his corporation's bank balance. It's a weakness that Mamet does not allow us to see how Karen, a disturbingly misogynistic creation, works her persuasive magic."

rSTP 4.5 Gardner, Lyn. Rev. of *Speed-the-Plow. Guardian* 17 Mar. 2000. Rpt. in *Theatre Record* 11-24 Mar. 2000: 324.

> Mixed review: "When it comes down to it, Mamet is never on the side of the angels; he's with the cynics. For all their swagger, Bob and Charlie are as much innocents as Karen, and Mamet depicts all three as if they have been gripped by a kind of insanity."

rSTP 4.6 Gross, John. "Mamet Satire Keeps Its Cutting Edge Theatre." *Sunday Telegraph* 19 Mar. 2000: 10. Rpt. in *Theatre Record* 11-24 Mar. 2000: 325.

Positive review: "The play itself starts rather slowly and so does Peter Gill's production at the New Ambassadors. It only really catches fire when Karen turns comically bright-eyed (Kimberly Williams is excellent) and starts rhapsodising about the second script. But after that it never looks back, and the confrontations of the last act, both verbal and physical, are terrific."

rSTP 4.7 Kellaway, Kate. "Cynics of the Best." *Observer* 19 Mar. 2000: 10. Rpt. in *Theatre Record* 11-24 Mar. 2000: 324-25.

Positive review: " The second act, at Gould's house, is fascinating because Mamet never oversimplifies. He gives Karen the right words, set to the wrong music. She argues for quality and passion, but with the help of a lousy book. She is dazzled by it. Williams is superb: her nervous posture has gone. It is as if she had melted between acts; she is translated by her own enthusiasm. Her rapture is described as 'naïve', but there is—even so—a sense that Gould's cynicism might actually be in the balance."

rSTP 4.8 Macaulay, Alastair. Rev. of *Speed-the-Plow. Financial Times* 20 Mar. 2000. Rpt. in *Theatre Record* 11-24 Mar. 2000: 324.

Positive review of performances and the play: "Williams shows that Karen is the most ambiguous —inscrutable—character in the play. How naïve is she and how calculating? How destructive and how liberating? How pretentious and how sincere? The way your reaction to her keeps shifting is the most troubling element in the play, and perhaps the most stimulating."

rSTP 4.9 Morley, Sheridan. "Take Two Buddies." *Spectator* 25 Mar. 2000: 48+. Rpt. in *Theatre Record* 11-24 Mar. 2000: 322.

Positive view of "a morality play about power and sex and moral epilepsy; [. . .] Mamet is savagely energetic in his hatred of a film industry which he clearly sees as one more metaphor, like real estate (in 'Glengarry Glen Ross') or junk shops (in 'American Buffalo') for the moral and spiritual decline of his nation."

rSTP 4.10 Nathan, David. Rev. of *Speed-the-Plow. Jewish Chronicle* 24 Mar. 2000. Rpt. in *Theatre Record* 11-24 Mar. 2000: 323-24.

Positive view: "Not the least of the pleasures of this play is Marber's desperately uneasy search for the right tone that combines big-shot assurance, an old-buddies act and creeping deference to Gould." He observes that when Karen enters, "the men start talking dirty in a display of macho virility."

rSTP 4.11 Nightingale, Benedict. "Grim View of Studio Toil and Trouble." *Times* [London] 18 Mar. 2000. Rpt. in *Theatre Record* 11-24 Mar. 2000: 325.

Mixed view: "Is it plausible that her naive questions—'But is the film good?', 'Do you enjoy your job?'—should so stir the hardened Gould that he thinks of ditching Fox's gilt-edged project for an adaptation of a well-meaning but nutty apocalyptic novel by some 'Eastern sissy'? It seemed so when Madonna brought her charisma to the character on Broadway in 1988. But Kimberly Williams, who plays her here, is too like an artless, eager student of elementary film studies to bring off any such miracle."

rSTP 4.12 Peter, John. "Sour Smell of Success." *Sunday Times* [London] 19 Mar. 2000. Rpt. in *Theatre Record* 11-24 Mar. 2000: 326-27.

Positive review: "Bob and Charlie have now turned her into a commodity, as if she were a script. [. . .] Williams plays her with cool, calm, intelligent detachment: she neither mocks Karen nor portrays her as a pushy little kitten, nor turns her into a victim oozing precious life. The point, hers and Mamet's, is that Karen is simply a wide-eyed gazelle who has blundered into the wrong forest clearing and thinks she is among equals."

RSTP 4.13 Price Steven. Rev. of *Speed the Plow*. *David Mamet Review* 7 (2000): 4.

Mildly negative review: "Karen's is much the most difficult role because it bears the full weight of the play's ambiguity, but here Kimberly Williams and director Peter Gill take the easy option of making her an air-head played for laughs in the first act. If her second-act conversion of Gould becomes incredible as a result, we can always conclude that the play is nothing more or less than a brilliant comic satire on Hollywood. That entails losing faith in the dramatic structure, however [. . .]."

rSTP 4.14 Spencer, Charles. "Spellbinding Tale of Tempting Temp First Night." *Daily Telegraph* 17 Mar. 2000: 13. Rpt. in *Theatre Record* 11-24 Mar. 2000: 325-26.

Positive review: "In the red corner, there's macho Dave, offering a spunky satire of Hollywood values and dog-eat-dog ambition. In the blue corner, there is sensitive David, who clearly has a certain sneaking admiration for a portentously pseudo book that is constantly mocked in the course of the play." Williams as Karen, "just seems like a comic incompetent." But then "she manages to convince him that idealism and art might still be possible in the tarnished world of Tinseltown. It would be unfair to give too much away, but after the slow burn of the first two acts, the play finally explodes into terrific physical and verbal violence."

rSTP 4.15 Stratton, Kate. Rev. of *Speed-the-Plow*. *Time Out* 22 Mar. 2000. Rpt. in *Theatre Record* 11-24 March: 328.

Positive view: "As Bobby, Strong has a marvelous stillness—as if languor and tension had found an equilibrium. Only his trailed-off tones and the shapes his hands sculpt suggest the nervous energy. Kimberly Williams, blank-faced and twitchy, beautifully maintains her character's ambiguity. But it's Patrick Marber's lick-spittle yes man, his body pumping into a graceless sort of war-dance and then subsiding into grovels and genuflections of submission, who holds the stage. When Bobby tells him he's not going to 'greenlight' the buddy movie, his features move from amusement to disbelief to dumbfounded horror in one seamless reaction. 'It's only words,' he says, 'unless they're true.'"

rSTP 4.16 Taylor, Paul. Rev. of *Speed-the-Plow. Independent* 18 Mar. 2000. Rpt. in *Theatre Record* 11-24 Mar. 2000: 322.

Positive view: "Ms. Williams, meanwhile, is wonderfully amusing as she blurs the distinction between cutesy, naïve idealism and on-the-make calculation. Her gasping, choked-with sincerity readings from the appallingly incoherent novel are a riot. The final scene, in which Charlie succeeds in expelling the interloper, is particularly well played. Mark Strong's soulful parade of born-again virtue is hilariously unsure of itself. His eyes keep glazing as he struggles to remember Karen's line on the book so he can piously relay it to Charlie. Groping for a chair in dazed disbelief that something as incongruous as morality has entered the office, Marber eventually lets rip with a brilliant tour de force of baroque scorn."

rSTP 4.17 Woddis, Carole. Rev. of *Speed-the-Plow. Herald* 22 Mar. 2000. Rpt. in *Theatre Record* 11-24 Mar. 2000: 322.

Mixed review: "An acidic, murderously funny dissection of the corrupted Hollywood ethos of money, money, and more money, it works within the framework of a fully fledged morality play—and this is where I part company—setting up his female protagonist, a young secretary tempting in the studio office, as a manipulative Eve. The tussle over a script, between Karen, this bright-eyed researcher after spiritual and ethical meaning, and Patrick Marber's crumpled, cynical Jewish producer, Charlie Fox, is titanic—nothing less than for the soul of Hollywood, embodied in the shape of Mark Strong's Bobby, recently appointed Head of Studio Production."

rSTP 4.18 Wolf, Matt. Rev. of *Speed-the-Plow. Variety* 27 Mar.-2 Apr. 2000: 32.

Very positive view of the production: "This may be the best-balanced of the three productions of the play I've seen. [. . .] Those wanting Fox and Gould played like horses let out of the starting gate may balk at the slow build that Gill deftly insists upon here, a strategy that pays overwhelming dividends in the scabrous third (and final) scene. Under Gill's keen eye, the laughs are there all right, some of them even thunderous. But they can't be separated from the anxiety animating Mamet's study in shifting and traitorous affections."

Scholarly Overview:
More clearly divided than reviewers, scholars largely split 50-50 over the play, mainly on the interpretation of Karen. For some, she is a whore, and Mamet a misogynist for so presenting her. For others, she is an admirable character, an idealist in a world of philistines. Blumberg rebukes Mamet for his "misogynistic, homophobic bent" and for Burkman Karen "is just another kind of whore." Avoiding the sexual grounds for blame, Brewer still finds fault with Karen who is "as guilty as the men." For Kane (1997), Karen's confession "equates all three as whores" but some are "less moral than others;" Stafford faults her for being above work with contempt for "the struggle

of life." For Hall, however through her "the whole power structure is challenged" and Karen is "a feminist disruption." For Nelson the ending of the play evinces "sadism" in "the victimization of the female character" (75) because Karen is pure, "so sure about the incorruptibility of their truth that she wants to share it with the world" (77). For Pearce too Karen is a victim who offers Bobby "the acceptance of the world and the self as they are." Zinman's Karen, however, holds out the possibility of "redemption [by] making an artsy film." The trick here, as Watt indicates, is that the film that Karen supports is for some "artsy" and idealistic—but for others it is abstract, and unfilmable—folly (Kolin). Price deconstructs both sides of the debate by showing how Mamet gives one term dominance, "Hollywood," and then he reverses and "high art" becomes the preferred term, then he discredits that alternative, leaving the audience to sort out the problem. However, most scholars strongly argue for one term's dominance over the other. Reviewers finally saw Karen as an ambivalent character and enjoyed her twists and turns, rather than trying to force her into a single ideological construction. Most scholars have yet to reach this position.

Scholarly Works:

sSTP 1 Blattes, Susan. "The Blurring of Boundaries between Stage and Screen in Plays by Sam Shepard and David Mamet." *Mediatized Drama/Dramatized Media*. Ed. Eckart Voigts-Virchow. Trier, Germany: Wissenschaftlicher, 2000. 189-99.

Blattes covers plays done by Burkman—*True West* and *Speed-the-Plow* as commentaries on Hollywood. She focuses on how both plays display formulaic scripts against seemingly more authentic scripts. But Blattes rightly notes that there is great disagreement over the radiation screenplay in *Speed-the-Plow* and she cites Henry's review which takes Mamet to task for lacking courage to be more clear. In her view, however, this is not a parody, which requires a fixed standard, but a postmodern pastiche, illustrating "the very absence of clearly definable boundaries which characterises contemporary, postindustrial society" (197-98). The same blurred boundaries are found between theatre and film.

sSTP 2 Blumberg, Marcia. "Staging Hollywood, Selling Out." *Hollywood on Stage: Playwrights Evaluate the Culture Industry*. Ed. Kimball King. New York: Garland, 1997. 71-82.

Blumberg dismisses "Mamet [who] perversely celebrates Hollywood's predatory machismo" (72). Fox's "egregious naming of Gould as an 'old woman, experiencing menopause, who squats to pee' denigrates women and equates a feminized man with utter powerlessness, an object of abjection. This misogynistic, homophobic bent has appeared in other Mamet texts and impels me to resist Mametolatory" (72).

sSTP 3 Brewer, Gay. "*The Shawl*, Shorts, *Speed-the-Plow.*" *David Mamet and Film: Illusion and Disillusion in a Wounded Land*. Columbus: Ohio State U, 1992. 29-62.

This is a dark reading of the ending, seeing Karen as a betrayer: "Gould's 'Oh, god, now I'm lost,' in response to Karen's exposed betrayal, is an earnest and primal cry of the forsaken. One can only speculate how quickly and completely he will recover his greedy energy, although with Fox's encouragement may soon return in full. Like other Mamet protagonists, Gould and Fox show courage by their mere dedication to survival; they are fueled by linguistic power and bitterest conceits. In *Speed-the-Plow*, this vision seems at its bleakest." The final line "is an unrivaled celebration of darkness."

sSTP 4 Burkman, Katherine H. "The Myth of Narcissus: Shepard's *True West* and Mamet's *Speed-the-Plow*." *Hollywood on Stage: Playwrights Evaluate the Culture Industry*. Ed. Kimball King. New York: Garland, 1997. 113-23.

Burkman contends that Shepard and Mamet, while seeming to criticize Hollywood in their plays, actually endorse it. To construct this vision, she takes relatively empty signifiers, and makes them univocal. Of *The Bridge* which some critics find compelling, "Mamet never gives any serious credence to the novel as a work of any more substance than the buddy film the male whores agree to make" (117). By reducing what in the text are seemingly opposite works to equivalences, Burkman produces her reading. Though she notes "the ambiguity of Karen as virgin/whore that the director sought" [noted by Ann Hall], Burkman rejects performance: "such ambiguity seems to be sadly missing in the script" (117). All ambiguity is missing in her interpretation. Karen is "just another kind of whore" (117). Thus, Karen is as much a whore as Gould, Gould as much a whore as Fox, and, for creating this, Mamet as much a whore as Shepard.

sSTP 5 Haedicke, Janet V. "Plowing the Buffalo, Fucking the Fruits: (M)Others in *American Buffalo* and *Speed-the-Plow*." *Gender and Genre: Essays on David Mamet*. Eds. Christopher C. Hudgins and Leslie Kane. New York: Palgrave, 2001. 27-41.

In *Speed-the-Plow* "Fox aborts Gould's salvation" and as a result "Once again, Grace is absent from the stage, from the screen, from the world as the illusion of male presence is fostered by female absence. [. . .] Fox sentences his 'buddy' to the 'buddyless,' unredeemed life of the Individual: 'And what if this fucken' grace exists? It's not for you. [. . .] You have a different thing' (81) This 'thing'—the objective linear 'reality'—for the Head of Production is reproducing and producing culture through mythologized image" (36).

sSTP 6 Hall, Ann C. "Playing to Win: Sexual Politics in David Mamet's *House of Games* and *Speed-the-Plow*." *David Mamet: A Casebook*. Ed. Leslie Kane. New York: Garland, 1992. 137-60.

This is a substantial essay using poststructuralist feminism of Lacan and Irigaray. Her thesis is that: "The male characters view women dualistically: they are either Madonnas or whores. The female characters, however, persistently violate such codification" (137). Part of the effect of this is to reveal the lack in the men themselves who, according to Lacan, use women as mirrors in which they find reassurance about their own images. When the women refuse to play that role (particularly Dr. Ford in dress and make-up) then the whole power structure is challenged. Dr. Ford wins out in her world, but Karen does not, "leaving only a trace of that potential [to be 'joyously subversive']" (149). Karen's rejection however, is read as the impossible demand that women be "pure"; "women are not permitted any flaws" (157). When Gould rejects her, "we have seen his insecurity, the lack which he tries to disguise. Even though Fox reestablishes the patriarchal structure in the end, his relationship with Karen has created a place in the text for something more, a feminist disruption" (157).

sSTP 7 Kane, Leslie. "Fuck Money. . . . But Don't Fuck 'People'." *Weasels and Wisemen: Ethics and Ethnicity in the Work of David Mamet*. New York: St. Martin's Press, 1999. 103-39.

    Kane rejects other interpretations of *Speed-the-Plow* which see the play as returning to its starting point. She instead sees religious enlightenment in the ending: "On the contrary, as Fox implies through the technique of indirection, religion—or at least ethnic identity—may provide a source of connectedness, of renewed awareness and redemptive possibility, and ultimately of change" (131). For her, Fox is the center of the play: "we observe him as a friend, one who sharpens Gould's thinking, questions his insights, and helps clarify his dilemma (as the Hebrew word for friend, haver connotes). Even if these actions also serve his own interests, he is empowered to save Gould's professional and spiritual life" (130-31). Karen is reduced to a cipher; her interest in *The Bridge* being simply a device to lead Gould away from his Jewish roots and his true calling.

sSTP 8 —. "Sanctity, Seduction, or Settling Scores against the Swine in *Speed-the-Plow*?" *Hollywood on Stage: Playwrights Evaluate the Culture Industry*. Ed. Kimball King. New York: Garland, 1997. 83-100.

    Kane questions Gay Brewer's view of Bobby Gould as "an inverted Christ figure" since this errs in "missing both the ethnic coding of Mamet's character and the play's intended satirizing of satire" (91). Noting the role of Jews in Hollywood production, Kane sees Mamet's viewpoint as ambivalent. Each character takes a turn as the teacher; first Gould in his new office educates Fox and Karen. In Act Two Kane notes "Her identity and objective cloaked in mystery, at least for the moment, Karen does her best work at night [. . . guiding] Gould into an intercourse characterized by sacred rather than carnal knowledge" (93). In the end, however, it is Fox who educates Gould: "Fox's rhetoric is effective, apparently touching a familiar and familial chord in Gould, whose unity with Fox is communicated linguistically" (96). In the finale, "Karen's confession that she was motivated by ambition and personal gain, critical to the shaping of Mamet's well-made play, equates all three as whores while judging some actions as more or less moral than others" (96).

sSTP 9 Kolin, Philip C. "Performing Scripts in David Mamet's *Speed-the-Plow*." *Notes on Contemporary Literature* 28.5 (1998): 4-6.

    Kolin asserts that "Mamet's perpetual theme is performance; he has a postmodern obsession with how things are played. [. . .] *Speed-the-Plow* is a labyrinth of scripts each wrapped about and through the other. The cumulative effect is that we as audience, too, are unsuspectingly enmeshed in a web of deceptions" (4). In Acts One and Three, the buddy film is played out by Fox and Gould in the office; in Act Two Karen plays out *The Bridge*: "Thus Gould is hoodwinked into thinking that this script is his 'bridge' from sinful commercialism and into glorious redemption" (5).

sSTP 10 Nelson, Jeanne Andrée. "*Speed-the-Plow* or Seed the Plot? Mamet and the Female Reader." *Essays in Theatre/Études Theatrales* [Canada]10.1 (1991): 71-82.

Nelson is the most literal of Mamet interpreters. Ignoring irony or metaphor, she argues that Mamet's male characters are misogynists, and so is he. She quotes his interview with Harriott saying that in the U.S. "we do have a certain amount of misogynistic men. For example, all of them" (72), and uses that to make her case. The play then presents a clear-cut binary between making a bad movie or a good one: "The impact of the prison script was to be measured in dollars. The impact of the novel is emotional, social, and spiritual." (77). This ignores the overblown rhetoric and irony in which the artsy movie is encased: "Karen is so sure about the incorruptibility of their truth that she wants to share it with the world: the novel must see the light of day" (77). Others admit some weakness in her—but not Nelson: "Karen is neither the phallic woman who seeks to undo male authority nor the nurturing angel of salvation who dwells beyond this world. She fits none of these convenient definitions which exist to justify the mutilation and the gagging of women and the construct of male identity and authority." (80).

sSTP 11 Pearce, Howard. "Plato in Hollywood: David Mamet and the Power of Illusions." *Mosaic* 32.2 (1999): 141-56.

Using Godamer and Plato on mimesis, Pearce examines the world of illusions in *House of Games* and *Speed-the-Plow*: "Mamet's habitual playing upon illusions must be recognized as a means of probing the reality of both his characters and their worlds." Karen and Maggie "function as variations on the artist figure in themselves and in terms of their relationship to the audience" (142). In his view, therefore Karen offers Bobby "the acceptance of the world and the self as they are. People in the world are not gods or angels" (151). "Karen, despite succumbing to the machinations of powerful men like Fox in the world of Hollywood, is left no less than Maggie with a privacy, a withdrawal from the audience's desire to know and interpret, and her failed attempt to retrieve the words of the book is an ambiguous performance no less than Maggie's final actions" (154).

sSTP 12 Price, Steven. "Disguise in Love: Gender and Desire in *House of Games* and *Speed-the-Plow*." *Gender and Genre: Essays on David Mamet*. Eds. Christopher C. Hudgins and Leslie Kane. New York: Palgrave, 2001. 41-61.

Price attacks the feminist critics as essentialists, noting that "both Hall and Nelson are led at times into affirming a feminine essence, or at least a knowable subjectivity, the denial of which they elsewhere see as a prerequisite of resistance" (42). In his view Mamet's major works are self-deconstructing: "*Glengarry Glen Ross, Edmond, House of Games, Speed-the-Plow* and *Oleanna* have in common the same dialogic pattern. In all of these works there is a discursive hierarchy, in which an ostensibly privileged ideology (respectively capitalism, free will, psychoanalysis, Hollywood, and academic discourse) is undermined and ironized from within. This newly weakened ideology enters into competition with an alternative: pastoralism, determinism, the confidence game, high art, political correctness. By the end, this alternative has also been discredited. In the resulting aporia the plays seem either to fall between two stools or to occupy both stools simultaneously. On the one hand, the plays offer an Aristotelian resolution. [. . .] On the other hand, the plays present Mamet as confidence trickster, encouraging us to misplace our faith in one of two equally untenable propositions. This constant play of irony accounts for much of the tragicomic vision of his work" (45). Thus Price deconstructs the seeming opposition of terms, first reversing polarities, then discrediting both and leaving the audience to sort out its own position.

sSTP 13 Stafford, Tony J. "*Speed-the-Plow* and *Speed the Plough*: The Work of the Earth." *Modern Drama* 36 (1993): 38-47.

Comparing Mamet's play to a Thomas Morton play of 1800 titled *Speed the Plough* leads to the thematic: "These same motifs—contest, disdain for work, and acceptance of the work of the earth—appear also in Mamet's *Speed-the-Plow*" (41). The whole play is a contest between Karen and Fox—Karen represents contempt for 'the struggle of life' while Fox is a worker who 'takes his part in the contest' (41). Bob Gould is then Everyman "torn by two antithetical forces." Finally, Karen's "action, obviously inconsistent with her appearance of purity, typifies Hollywood values, and it jolts Gould out of his idealism and back to the reality of where it is he works [. . .]" (45).

sSTP 14 Watt, Stephen. "Hollywood on the Contemporary Stage: Image, Phallic 'Players,' and the Culture Industry." *Hollywood on Stage: Playwrights Evaluate the Culture Industry*. Ed. Kimball King. New York: Garland, 1997. 57-71.

Watt approaches *Speed-the-Plow* through an examination of Shepard, Kopit, and films which share a vision of "a postmodern desert aptly theorized by such various commentators as Jean Baudrillard" (52). What results is a view of "The 'un'-postmodern and ultimately retrograde politics of Hollywood [. . .] and the politics of gender reinscription, heterosexuality, and acute misogyny that often results" (55). But in Mamet's play, Watt notes that Fox and Gould are "not nearly so imperious modelers of the consumer's desire as Bigsby implies" (58). He uses the binary of Art equals feminine, Eastern, Sissy writer versus Entertainment equals buddy film, Hollywood, male-male relationship. He argues that the polarity reflects "the recuperation of phallic prerogatives and the creation of images that facilitate this recuperation. This means, inevitably though not always successfully, the attempted vanquishing of the 'feminine challenge' and all that she represents" (55).

sSTP 15 —. "Baudrillard's America (and Ours)." *Postmodern Drama*. Ann Arbor: U of Michigan, 2000. 123-155.

This chapter is similar to the article above. Watt argues that: "The play's narrative demands that Gould negotiate between the Scylla of art—always dangerous when the bottom line is assessed—and the Charybdis of entertainment, the kind Odets's high-minded Castles deplore" (145). In part this defuses the simple binary of art vs. entertainment—Gould is the border between the two.

sSTP 16 Zinman, Toby Silverman. "So Dis Is Hollywood: Mamet in Hell." *In Hollywood on Stage: Playwrights Evaluate the Culture Industry.* Ed. Kimball King. New York: Garland, 1997. 101-12.

Zinman takes *The Cryptogram* as allegorical like Dante of "the death of Innocence" (107). But the great contribution this essay makes is in tracing Bobby Gould through four works, The *Disappearance of the Jews, Bobby Gould in Hell, Speed-the-Plow* and *Homicide.* The Dantean plot begins with the first play, when "Bobby says, 'God damn me.' [. . .] Sure enough, God damns him" (107). In the next, "Bobby Gould visits Hell, comes to understand his wickedness and is, like Dante, sent home, except Bobby Gould is condemned to return to Hollywood" (109). In the third, "Although he flirts with the idea of the redemption of making an 'artsy' film, he comes to his depraved senses. [. . .] His need for spiritual legitimacy [. . .] is overwhelmed by his need for power and money" (109). And in the film, finally, "once again, with still another dramatic chance for rehabilitation, Gould's journey is not salvific" (111). Tracing Bobby through these four incarnations reveals this pattern of chances for reform and salvation which, each time, Bobby foregoes.

See also the following scholarly articles that cover multiple plays:

sMP 2 Andreach, Robert J. "Exemplary Selves in Hell."

sSPC 1 Begley, Varun. "On Adaptation: David Mamet and Hollywood."

sMP 4 Bigsby, C. W. E. "David Mamet: All True Stories."

sMP5 Blansfied, Karen C. "Women on the Verge, Unite."

sO 5 Burkman, Katherine H. "The Web of Misogyny in Mamet's and Pinter's Betrayal Games."

sMP 13 Cohn, Ruby. "Phrasal Energies: Harold Pinter and David Mamet."

sMP 23 Hudgins, Christopher C. "Comedy and Humor in the Plays of David Mamet."

sMP 36 McDonough, Carla J. "David Mamet: The Search for Masculine Space."

sMP 40 Price, Steven. "'Accursed Progenitor': Samuel Beckett, David Mamet, and the Problem of Influence."

SQUIRRELS

Dedication: Linda Kimbrough
Scene: A writer's office
Characters: Arthur, an old writer; Edmond, a young writer; A Cleaning
　　Woman

Plot Outline:

During the four episodes, three interludes and an epilogue, Art, the old writer, and
Ed, the new writer, spend much of the sixty minutes of the play talking about how
to write a scene set in park which includes a man, maybe three men and at least
one squirrel, but maybe a whole squirrel family. The cleaning woman, who is an
ex-writer and Art's ex-lover, continually drops by with her stories and observations on life. Each character contributes monologues on technique, form, meaning, and the nature of writing.

Editions:

Squirrels, a Play. New York: S. French, 1982.
David Mamet Plays: 1. London: Methuen Drama, 1994.

Production:

pS 1 Squirrels opened at the St. Nicholas Theatre Company at the Leo A. Lerner
　　Theatre in Chicago on October 10, 1974.

Director:	David Mamet
Lighting:	Andre Rideau
Set Design:	John Paoletti & Mary Griswold
Costumes:	Cookie Gluck
Music:	Alaric Rokko Jans

Cast:

Arthur:	William H. Macy
Edmond:	Stephen Schachter
Cleaning Woman:	Linda Kimbrough

Overview:

Reviews were mixed. Those who disliked it thought it funny, but rejected it citing the Stanislavsky theory which the program proclaimed the production embraced. Dettmer quoted Mamet's program note: "Using Stanislavsky's definition that 'acting is living truthfully under imaginary circumstances,' we have worked to establish a common vocabulary and a common method which will permit us to bring to the stage [not through our insights but thru our craft] this truth in the form of action." The humor simply did not seem to accord with this, apparently. Ziomek, though negative too, saw a discrepancy and was put off by the wild approval for the crowd: "The play is a tragicomedy—comic in the way the characters present themselves, tragic in what they represent." Even the approving VerMeulen thought the comedy went too far and distracted from the serious dimension. But Christiansen was exultant in the "tremendous zest for language and love of irony." Walker appreciated the language, but found it went on too long. In contrast to much later Mamet minimalism (used as well in the bar-turns-into-the-bed set of the earlier *Sexual Perversity*), Christiansen noted the care which went "down to the smallest prop of its perfectly cluttered set" and others even noted a stuffed squirrel on stage which directly faced the audience.

Reviews:

rS 1.1 Christiansen, Richard. "*Squirrels* Play is Extraordinary." *Chicago Daily News* [about 12] Oct. 1974: 35.

Extremely enthusiastic review of: "a writer with a tremendous zest for language and love of irony. [. . .] Like a poem, the play is packed with metaphor, both verbal and visual; and, almost like magic, it uses some superb piano music (performed offstage by the composer, Alaric Jans) to prepare and punctuate the mood of the action. [. . .] Besides that, Mamet as both playwright and director is sometimes not capable of fully realizing the images of life that he sets out to create; and the three young players [. . .] although clearly tuned in to the play's direction, are not always up to the subtleties this extremely difficult and special work requires. [. . .] Yet this is indeed a striking work of poetic drama, right down to the smallest prop of its perfectly cluttered set."

rS 1.2 Dettmer, Roger. "*Squirrels*: Overrun with Obscurity." *Chicago Tribune* 14 Oct. 1974: sec. 3: 15.

Negative review which mainly deals with the program's assertions about the company's acting system: "The subject is narcissistic, the dramaturgy very talkily turgid. Sartre or Burroughs is more wakening to read than Mamet is to listen to, tho Kimbrough gets off one sly line by virtue of her artistry early on: 'Whether you live in the past or the future, you still gotta pay the rent.' But present time is a vacuum, a problem about which some damn fine plays have been written. For example, 'Butley.' "

rS 1.3 Mamet, David. "Stanislavsky and *Squirrels.*" *Chicago Sun-Times* 6 Oct. 1974: sec. 3.

Promo which notes the acting style: "What that system is depends to a phenomenal degree on who you are talking to. It is a loosely-formed set of techniques, exercises and ideas based on the philosophy that life on the stage is not an imitation of anything, but is real life on the stage. [. . .] It is a fulfilling method, because it relates occurrences in the text and on stage to the artist's own experience, and as the director of 'Squirrels' I have insisted upon using it."

rS 1.4 Rev. of *Squirrels. Theater Northwestern* (University). Oct. 1974.

Very positive review of a play which appeals to the college student facing a blank page. The review notes: "The set is carefully and completely detailed, down to a working candy machine, read [sic] radiator, and the not-so-subtle symbolism of a stuffed squirrel perched on an hourglass. [. . .] William H. Macy, as Arthur, embodies repression in carrying himself tightly while letting his insecurities frame him like the loose hairs of a proper chignon."

rS 1.5 VerMeulen, Michael. *"In Your Town* on WLTD Radio (typescript review) 11 Oct. 1974.

Positive review of "Mamet, that irrepressible cut-up and only playwright to be named by the Reader an official member of the Chicago counter-culture. [. . .] The idea of appealing to the audience's funny bone captivates Mamet and his concentration on humor detracts from the subtle relationship between each of the play's three characters as they feed incestuously off each other's regurgitated ideas. *Squirrels* is a real funny play. It contains the best elements of Marx Brothers' humor with a healthy dose of Eugene Ionesco word games thrown in."

rS 1.6 Walker, Pat. "Theater Coalition Show Great Diversity." Harold Washington Library Archival copy.

Mildly positive review: "*Squirrels* is a treasure for lovers of words and word games, but again, the average or occasional theatergoer will find minimal entertainment here. The play requires concentration and a willingness to tolerate little action; two requirements theatergoers prefer not to meet. *Squirrels* shows us Mamet's beautiful love affair with the English language and his ability to work hard, but about half of the play would have been long enough for me."

rS 1.7 Ziomek, Jon. "*Squirrels* lacks Subtlety." *Sun Times* 10 Oct 1974.

Negative, rather bitter review: "'Squirrels' was rather interesting, yes.

And author-director David Mamet has a good ear for parodying human dialog. But the total package just didn't deserve the wild approval it got from that group of friends in the audience, nor did it seem to fit into what Mamet earlier said he was striving for: a play incorporating the Stanislavsky method—real life on stage. [. . .] The play is a tragicomedy—comic in the way the characters present themselves, tragic in what they represent. All striving for creativity, they wind up stifling it through their meaninglessly structured existence, working on insignificant things."

Production:

pS 2 Revived by St. Nicholas Theatre Company, Chicago for two benefit performances January 7 and 8, 1976 for the theater's building fund, with *Litko* performed by David Stettler, with the same cast.

Reviews:

rS 2.1 Marshall, Steve. "*Squirrels* Revival for Theater Benefit." *Chicago Daily News* 6 Jan. 1976: 22.

Promotional piece which notes that "reviewing the original production, Richard Christiansen, critic-at-large of *The Daily News*, called the drama 'an exuberant and intricate piece of poetry in the theater by a writer with a tremendous zest for language and love of irony.'"

rS 2.2 Syse, Glenna. Rev. of *Squirrels*. *Sun Times* 15 Jan 1976.

Positive review: "Mamet displays a nifty blend of the zany and the shrewd and he has a sly way with a simple sentence. Also, he knows how to pick a cast."

Production:

pS 3 Opened in the Philadelphia Festival Theatre for New Plays at the Harold Prince Theatre of the Annenberg Center on January [26] - February 4, 1990.

Director:	William H. Macy
Set:	James Wolk
Costumes:	Pamela Scofield
Lighting:	Curt Senie
Music:	Alaric Rokko Jans
Cast:	
Arthur:	Roger Serbagi
Edmond:	Todd Weeks
Cleaning Woman:	Natalia Nogulich

Overview:

Negative reviews from most critics for a play which "goes nowhere" (Burbank), "repetitious" (Hari), and "a playful exercise" Weales. Only Collins praised it as not life-like, but "an exaggeration."

Reviews:

rS 3.1 Burbank, Carol. "Oh, Nuts." *City Paper* [Philadelphia] 26 Jan.-2 Feb. 1990.
Negative review: "'Squirrels' goes nowhere, rather bitterly, despite its clever premise that literary clichés piled up on top of each other can poke fun at the funny, dusty nothing that is the usual scene behind a writer's office door. No one seems to have life in this play."

rS 3.2 Collins, William B. "David Mamet's 'Squirrels' Debuts at the Annenberg Center." *Philadelphia Inquirer* 19 Jan. 1990: 15.
Positive review of "a comedy hour" of a play: "It's not life. In life, we are not accompanied by a piano. It's a representation, an exaggeration of how people act when they're really interested in what they're doing. It's a play. A playful play."

rS 3.3 Hari. Rev. of *Squirrels. Variety* 31 Jan. 1990: 88.
Negative review: "Pared to half its repetitious 1-hour length, it could serve as an amusing curtain-raiser for an evening of 1-acters. [. . .] The variations are so numerous—and so shrugworthy—that, on opening night, the junior writer's complaint, 'I'm sick of squirrels,' drew applause."

rS 3.4 —. "Mamet's Tag for His Play on Words." *Philadelphia Inquirer* 29 Jan. 1990, sec. D: 3.
This is a promotional piece: "Mamet's rapid-fire, absurdist approach to the subject pits audiences against themselves. Macy says they've been splitting down the middle, half loving the show, half unsatisfied by the play's free-swinging style. The post-performance discussions have been lively."

rS 3.5 Weales, Gerald. "A Long Way to Broadway: *Traveler & Squirrels.*" *Commonweal* 23 Feb. 1990: 117-18.
Mildly positive review of a lightweight play: "After all, there are more squirrels in this play than the stuffed one [. . .] all three characters squirrel away material pilfered from the minds of the others—or from the wastebasket they share. [. . .] After the production, Macy explained the play as commerce (older writer) vs. imagination (cleaning woman) for the soul of the younger writer." Weales dismisses this as non-Mamet: "*Squirrels* is hardly a statement on art and commerce. It is little more than a playful exercise of a young writer feeling his way through words."

Production:

pS 4 Mandrake Theater Company at the King's Head Theater, Islington, London. Opened March 12, 1993.

Director:	Aaron Mullen
Sets:	Michael Vale

	Costumes:	Tom Pye
	Lighting:	Jonathan Abell
	Cast:	
Arthur:		Edward Petherbridge
Edmond:		Steven O'Shea
Cleaning Woman:		Sara Kestelman

Overview:

More negative than positive reviews of the play. It ranges from "slender" (Armistead), "stalled" (Taylor), "absolutely still" (Wolf). Those who liked it found it "a gloriously superficial play on words" (Rutherford).

Reviews:

pS 4.1 Armistead, Claire. "Dirty Window on the World." *Guardian* 15 Mar. 1993: 8. Rpt. in *Theatre Record* 12-25 Mar. (1993): 285.

Positive review, with some questions about the production: "The trouble with the piece is that, having established that the windows on the world are steamed up, Mamet never bothers to wipe them down. 'Squirrels' remains a slender reflection on the difficulties of writing rather than the problems of seeing and representing. That failing limits the characterization in a way that is beyond the reach of Aaron Mullen's rather drably efficient direction."

pS 4.2 de Jongh, Nicholas. "Cruel and Calculated." Rev. of *Squirrels. Evening Standard* 15 Mar. 1993: 48.

Negative view of "this aggressively boring piece": "The boredom Mamet inflicts is refined, excruciating and extreme. The evening endlessly elaborates upon the original silly conceit. The acting is, however, uniformly fine."

pS 4.3 Hirschhorn, Clive. Rev. of *Squirrels. Theater Week* 19 Apr. 1993: 16.

A neutral review of the play, negative on the production: "Mamet's literary doodling (for that's all it is) has its amusing moments and there are occasional from-the-heart insights into the creative process. But halfway through a paralysis sets in that [. . .] performances are powerless to camouflage."

pS 4.4 Nightingale, Benedict. "Anything but a Blockbuster." *Times* [London]16 Mar. 1993: 39.

Negative review although "Mullen's production perfectly serviceable. The problem is the play. Towards the end, Mamet seems to suggest that writers can learn from their blockages; but it is hard to take him very seriously. How can we do so when before then he has had little that is not facetious to say about either the creative process or the forces stifling it?"

pS 4.5 Rutherford, Malcolm. Rev. of *Squirrels. Financial Times* 15 Mar. 1993: 11. Rpt. in *Theatre Record* 12-25 Mar. (1993): 285.

Positive review: "David Mamet's short comedy at the King's Head in Islington is a gloriously superficial play on words and meanings, here magnificently played by the cast of three. Whether it would stand up to acting and direction any less good must be open to doubt, for I am beginning to think that the best of modern American theatre depends on style and playing rather than writing and substance."

pS 4.6 Showalter, Elaine. Rev. of *Squirrels*. *TLS* 26 Mar. 1993: 18.

A rather negative review: "The Oedipal partnership/competition/romance between an older and a younger man, whether crooks, as in *American Buffalo*, salesmen, as in *Glengarry Glen Ross*, or actors, as in *A Life in the Theatre*, is one of Mamet's favourite subjects. Here, though, it is lightly handled; unlike the plays it is obviously parodying—Albee's *The Zoo Story* and Mamet's own *Duck Variations*—*Squirrels* never transcends the exaggeration and absurdity of its situation."

pS 4.7 Spencer, Charles. "Baffled Agony of a Man Stuck for Words." *Daily Telegraph* 15 Mar. 1993: 17.

Negative review: "[. . .] he is good on the writer's sudden spurts of hope and confidence, and the despair that sets in when what he thought was a bright idea or an elegant sentence turns out to be yet another botched shot. And, as in all Mamet's plays, there are gripping riffs of edgy, sawn-off dialogue, which compellingly chart the shifting balances of power between his characters. But the endless verbal hair-splitting grows tiresome, and the denouement in which the young protégé (suspiciously bright-eyed and bushy-tailed) bites the hands that feed him and assumes dominance over the older man is dismayingly predictable."

pS 4.8 Taylor, Paul. "Completely Nuts." *Independent* 15 Mar. 1993: 14.

A rather positive review: "Anyone who strings words together for a living will wince with recognition, even as he falls about laughing at these desperate, repeatedly stalled efforts to get the show on the road. As one confidently expects, the play traces the transference of power to the younger man. By the end, he has made the revolutionary change of subject matter and replaced squirrels with geese."

pS 4.9 Wolf, Matt. Rev. of *Squirrels*. *Variety* 5 Apr. 1993: 185+.

Negative review: "But while Mamet busily invokes other writers—Ionesco and Joyce among them—the play stands absolutely still, coming to life only in Arthur's sudden outbursts of anger, which seem to belong to another show. Otherwise, 'Squirrels' marks the kind of collegiate come-on best left unproduced, unless you're dying to see a play with the word 'interdigitating' used in it."

See also the following scholarly articles covering multiple plays:

sDV 3 Carroll. Dennis. "Learning."

sMP 54 Zinman, Toby Silverman. "Jewish Aporia: The Rhythm of Talking in Mamet."

The Water Engine: An American Fable

Scene: A radio station in 1934 with or without microphones

Characters: Charles Lang an inventor; Rita, his sister; Morton Gross, patent attorney; Lawrence Oberman, businessman; Mr. Wallace, storekeeper, Bernie, his son; Dave Murray, reporter; Mrs. Varec, neighbor; a barker; Chainletter, a voice-over

Editions:

> *The Water Engine: An American Fable and Mr. Happiness: Two Plays*. New York: Grove Press, 1978.
>
> *The Water Engine: An American Fable and Mr. Happiness: Two Plays*. New York: Samuel French, 1978.
>
> *David Mamet Plays: 1*. London: Methuen, 1996. 259-319.

Plot Outline:

Written for Earplay as radio drama, the play is in two acts. The story is multilayered and multivoiced. With cast members singing, the play opens with an announcer setting the scene: Chicago, The Century of Progress. The main story, a sort of radio drama within a radio drama, concerns Rita Lang and her brother Charles, who has invented an engine that runs on water. Charles goes to patent attorney Morton Gross, who asks him to meet Lawrence Oberman, who wants to buy the invention (presumably to destroy it). Lang refuses, and is threatened since his laboratory is partly equipped by materials from his workplace. The company will sue claiming his work was done on their time, and is theirs. Lang refuses, and is soon confronted by police, from whom he escapes in Mr. Wallace's store, only to discover his sister has been kidnapped because he called a reporter to arrange to tell his story. Lang agrees not to do this, and to meet with Oberman to exchange the plans for his sister. Instead he mails the plans to Wallace's son, Bernie. The announcer reveals that two tortured bodies were found in the lake. Throughout voices are heard, especially a continuing voice of a "Chainletter" which speaks of dire consequences and rewards. The theme is

portentious in the second act: "All civilization stands on trust—All people are connected—No one can call back what one man does." And the voice of the Century of
Progress announces the close of the Hall of "Science, yes, the greatest force for Good
and Evil we possess. The Concrete Poetry of Humankind."

Production:
pWE 1 St. Nicholas Theater Company, Chicago. May 11 through June 19, 1977.

Director:	Steven Schachter
Set:	David Emmons
Costumes:	Jessica Hahn
Lighting:	Kathleen Daly
Original Music:	Alaric Jans
Cast:	
Charles Lang:	William H. Macy
Rita:	Gail Silver
Martin Keegan/Morton Gross:	Michael O'Dwyer
Lawrence Oberman:	Guy Barile
Mrs. Varec:	Belinda Bremner
Mr. Wallace:	Norman Tobin
Bernie:	Joseph Weisberg
Dave Murray:	Dan Conway

Overview:
The unconventional production distanced the reviewers. For VerMuelen, using "the
conventions of traditional radio drama, he burdens 'The Water Engine' with a certain
alienating quality." And for Lowell, "Few of Mamet's characters are given any real
development or depth." However, Christiansen found that in "threading together these
many voices, Mamet has created a rich, varied texture of drama."

Reviews:
rWE 1.1 Christiansen, Richard. "A Dramatic Invention: 'The Water Engine' Bows at
St. Nicholas." *Chicago Daily News* 12 May 1977: 35.
   Positive review: "Coming now, in the midst of our awareness of an energy
crisis, this enduring fable hits a particularly sensitive nerve and receives an
especially keen response. [. . .] To buttress this fable, Mamet has orchestrated a
whole chorus of voices. The myth is mixed with malarkey, gossip, rhetoric,
hack prose, soap box orations, sentimental verse, fact, fiction, corporate
doubletalk and B-movie clichés. By threading together these many voices,
Mamet has created a rich, varied texture of drama, reverberating with powerful
ironies and delicate grace notes."

rWE 1.2 Feingold, Michael. Rev. of *The Water Engine. Village Voice.* 1 Aug. 1977: 63.
   Mildly positive review: "As if conscious of the play's thinness, Mamet
pads it by setting his characters against a hebephrenic backdrop of advertising,
pompous clichés about the fruits of technology, and scabrous, crazy, work-
world gossip and rumors about the Roosevelts, the Lindbergh kidnapping, and

the magical efficacy of chain letters. [. . .] Schachter has visualized it as a radio play, with most of the cast, most of the time, sitting behind a long table whispering into microphones. This device, already well-worn, has little relation to the script, and is not exploited for any of its own imaginative possibilities."

rWE 1.3 Gussow, Mel. Rev. of *The Water Engine. New York Times* 14 May 1977. Rpt. in *Theatre on the Edge.* New York: Applause, 1998. 199-201.

Mildly positive review because it "began its life as a radio play, and the author had not attempted to disguise its origins. He uses radio as a framework for social commentary. [. . .] This is a provocative platform for a play, but 'The Water Engine,' as a theatrical invention, seems to be still in blueprint. It is sketchy and schematic."

rWE 1.4 Kaplan, Sherman. WBBM Radio. no other information. (typescript)

Mildly positive review: "The real drama of *The Water Engine* doesn't begin to flower until the second act of Mamet's tightly compacted play." The audience is key: "Yet in coming to appreciate Lang's technology the audience comes to appreciate at the same time his personal rage and frustration at the power of industry which has robbed his sweetheart of her eyesight and threatens to rob him of his discovery."

rWE 1.5 Jacobi, Peter. "Three Plays in Chicago—A Special Excitement." *Christian Science Monitor* 6 July 1977: 22.

Mixed review of fragmented experience: "Mamet develops his story in too many pieces, short snippets of action held together by a radio-show technique that mimics program style of the 1930s and also permits the author to insert talk of that era's fads and philosophies: chain letters and the utopian nature of science and technology. [. . .] And just as quickly we are asked to deal with issues of science, business, morality, and social consciousness—all through rather stereotyped figures we have seen before. But the Mamet energy is present, too."

rWE 1.6 Loveall, J. M. "'Water Engine' Runs Dry." *Evergreen Gazette* [Chicago] 17 May 1977: 7.

Rather negative review: "Few of Mamet's characters are given any real development or depth. Charles Lang, studiously played by W. H. Macy is case in point. Macy is never given an opportunity to bring depth or development to the role of Lang. It is not that Macy isn't qualified, or doesn't have the ability to do so, since his many fine performances have made him currently one of Chicago's most celebrated actors, and deservedly so. It is simply that the role of Lang has been written sparingly in regard to dialogue. Macy's speeches are short, blunt, and at times, simpish."

rWE 1.7 VerMeulen, Michael. "A Hot Production of Tepid *Water." Reader: Chicago's Free Weekly* 20 May 1977: 27.

Mixed review from one of Mamet's ardent supporters: "in structuring his fable, in playing optimism against pessimism, and in giving his characters enough color to live but not enough to dominate, Mamet has made several significant errors. By keeping his work spare and retaining on stage many of the conventions of traditional radio drama, he burdens 'The Water Engine' with a certain alienating quality. The audience is distanced, presumably so that it can take the play's lessons in on an intellectual level without letting subjective feelings for the characters get in the way. Fine, but Mamet's characters too often seem aborted rather than tantalizingly incomplete. The result is gut confusion."

Production:

pWE 2 Shakespeare Festival Public Theater Cabaret in New York on January 5, 1978. Transferred to Broadway's Plymouth Theatre on March 6, 1978 with *Mr. Happiness* as prologue for 16 performances with the same cast except Rita was performed by Patti LuPone. (A 90 minute video of this production is available at the TOFT collection of the NYPL)

Director:	Steven Schachter
Set:	John Lee Beatty
Costumes:	Laura Crow
Lighting:	Dennis Parichy
Original Music:	Alaric Jans
Cast:	
Charles Lang:	Dwight Schultz
Rita:	Penelope Allen
Martin Keegan/Morton Gross:	David Sabin
Lawrence Oberman:	Bill Moor
Mrs. Varec:	Barbara Tarbuck
Mr. Wallace:	Dominic Chianese
Bernie:	Michael J. Miller
Dave Murray:	Colin Stinton
Lili La Pon:	Patti LaPone

Overview:

Most reviews were positive about play and production. When critical, they took the piece as a failure to be sufficiently realistic. Oliver faulted the play entirely because it was not real radio because "actors pantomime stage business and play to one another; real radio actors play only to the microphone." Barnes, however, raved about "a precise evocation of old-time radio." Most interesting was Clurman, because he grasped the unique features of the play and their satiric purpose—yet he felt too distanced, "desensitized" when what he wanted was to care about the characters. Eder, however, recognized Mamet's purpose was not to make us like the characters, but rather when the actors drop the radio scripts and become the characters, "Reality shimmers back and forth; we are moved, disoriented, and opened up to [. . .] a kind of poetic static, he sets out a vision of American solitariness, innocence, and alienation." Novick also recognized the paradox: "By distancing the story [. . .] Mamet and his director Steven Schachter actually bring it close to us, by disarming our skepticism." Watt, too, recognized the "eerie magic" of the moments when the play stepped away from the microphones and took off on its own—the very devices Oliver found unrealistic—"The total effect is statlingly original, uncanny and chilling."

Reviews:

rWE 2.1 Barnes, Clive. "Mamet's New Play Tops High Water Mark." *New York Post* 6 Jan. 1978: 33.

The play is a precise evocation of old-time radio: "The trick, the involvement, is absolutely remarkable. We are told when and how to applaud, we are told to note when the 'On Air' sign is illuminated, and we are offered a few, desperately convincing messages from someone's sponsor. All at once we are in a time capsule."

rWE 2.2 —. "The *Water Engine* Loses Steam on B'way." *New York Post* 7 Mar. 1978: 21. Rpt. in *New York Theatre Critics' Reviews* 39.6 1978: 333-34.

Saw the move to the Plymouth Theatre as a mistake: "His suggestions reach back into our mythic pasts with a start of guilt and a shiver of remembrance. [. . .] whereas at the Public Theater the audience was established from the beginning as part of the show, as a studio audience, here it was not. This was a grave mistake."

rWE 2.3 Beaufort, John. "Also: A New Mamet Play; Off-Broadway Drama." *Christian Science Monitor* 12 Jan. 1978: 19. Rpt. in *New York Theatre Critics' Reviews* 39.6 1978: 336-37.

Positive review: "Besides its play-within-a-play aspects, 'The Water Engine' touches yet another level with its historical footnotes and ironic undertones. While unfolding the tale of Lang and his invention, Mr. Mamet recalls the confident euphoria of world's fair hoopla as well as such popular aberrations as the chain-letter craze that gulls the superstitious from time to time."

rWE 2.4 Clurman, Harold. Rev. of *Water Engine. Nation* 28 Jan. 1978: 92-93.

A tepid review: "What is ingenious in the handling of this by no means extraordinary material is that all of it becomes grist to the mill of commercial radio. The realities and human tragedy involved in the story are drained of genuine content, their social implication flattened and vulgarized by making nothing more of them than crassly melodramatic entertainment. [. . .] The steely, impersonal efficiency of the procedure becomes, with humorous emphasis, typical of industrial civilization. Thus the sting of the events must fail to produce any cogent public effect. Everything is desensitized, rendered null and void. [. . .] What we may feel at most is a detached and self congratulatory contempt, in almost the same way as the play's radio coverage kills off the implicit drama of its story."

rWE 2.5 Eder, Richard. "Mamet Reinvents Radio." *New York Times* 6 Jan. 1978: C3.

Positive review of an "extraordinary" play: "By the time the play is over, apart from having been delighted, bamboozled and confused, apart from having heard wisps of subversive counternotions underneath each speech and movement, we end up totally seized by Lang. He becomes human innocence and struggle; defeated, but not permanently."

rWE 2.6 —. "'Water Engine' Is Uptown." *New York Times* 7 Mar. 1978: 42. Rpt. in *New York Theatre Critics' Reviews* 39.6 1978: 335.

Eder found it unique: "It is a radio station, all right, but it is also a kind of cockpit receiving peculiar and disquieting signals form the universe. [. . . From] radio actors acting out a radio play, they move into acting out the play itself. Scripts fall away: suddenly Charles Lang, his sister, the sinister lawyers are there at first, and not second hand." These techniques "make us instinctively draw closer to the characters in the radio play."

rWE 2.7 Gottfried, Martin. Rev. of *Water Engine*. *Saturday Review* 4 Mar. 1978: 41.

An extremely positive review which noted Mamet "is an outright original, with a poet's ear for dialogue and a showman's knack for theatricality, and he has the sense of humanity that has been lacking among our playwrights. [. . .] 'All people are connected,' the letter reads. 'No one can call back what one man does.' In this ingenious, satiric way, Mamet indicts the American system."

rWE 2.8 Hughes, Catharine. "Three from the N.Y.S.F." *America* 8 Apr. 1978: 286.

A negative review: "It is a good enough idea, and well enough performed under Steven Schachter's direction. But it is also trying to make substance out of show, comedy out of cliché."

rWE 2.9 Kalem, T. E. "Trickle: *The Water Engine*." *Time* 20 Mar 1978. Rpt. in *New York Theatre Critics' Reviews* 39.6 1978: 335.

A negative review because it was not historical: "No one would dare tell that story with a straight face, so Mamet has told it with a borrowed voice. [. . .] Mamet, 30, who was unborn at the time he writes about, does not realize that resilience, fortitude and fellow feeling were the sustaining forces of the Depression years."

rWE 2.10 Kerr, Walter. Rev. of *Water Engine*. *New York Times* 15 Jan. 1978, sec. B: 3+.

Kerr's first really positive review of a Mamet work: "At the same time that he is involving us, willy-nilly, in the drive of his narrative, he is exposing the narrative for the mere artifice it is. [. . .] 'The Water Engine' isn't simple pastiche, it's not savage parody, God knows it's not gullible melodrama; it comes off as a noncommittal crosshatch of all attitudes done deadpan. [. . .] Mamet wants to get his feet wet in the tricky currents of narrative but is preserving, via the mockery, a lifeline back to shore. I may be wrong, but I did have fun."

rWE 2.11 Kissel, Howard. Rev. of *Water Engine*. *Women's Wear Daily* 6 Jan. 1978. Rpt. in *New York Theatre Critics' Reviews* 39.6 1978: 336.

A rather positive review: "The marvel of 'The Water Engine' is that, though the radio play itself is deliberately artificial, though everything connected with its production, as we plainly see, is equally artificial, it has, nevertheless, an emotional impact, partly because its gloomy theme is perfectly intertwined with its Depression setting, partly because its conceits have a subconscious resonance, despite the artificiality, like certain movie cliches."

rWE 2.12 Kroll, Jack. "Golden Age of Radio." *Newsweek* 16 Jan. 1978: 69. Rpt. in
New York Theatre Critics' Reviews 39.6 1978: 337.
   Positive review of play and a cast which does the "difficult feat of playing
human clichés while evoking the real emotion behind those clichés. They
recapture those baroquely suave radio voices, turning good and evil, idealism
and greed, hope and corruption into smooth arabesques of sound. It is, in fact,
the sound of American innocence that Mamet tunes in through the crackling
static of our sophisticated time."

rWE 2.13 Morrison, Hobe. Rev. of *Water Engine*. *Variety* 8 Mar. 1978: 105.
   A mixed review of "a modestly interesting show but a corny play. […] It's
the stylized narrative form rather than the story itself that is the important thing."

rWE 2.14 Novick, Julius. "The Mamet Show." *Village Voice* 16 Jan. 1978: 89.
   Positive review which recognized the story framed inside radio drama
conventions "would be a heavily tendentious anti-capitalist tract, based not on
fact or serious analysis but simply on paranoid fantasy. But we are not asked to
take it seriously and literally. The wonderful thing about 'The Water Engine' is
that by presenting the invention-fantasy as a radio broadcast, circa 1935, Mr.
Mamet tells us the story without asking us to believe it, except as we believe
any good story while it is being told. By distancing the story—with announcers
and microphones and a highly visible sound effects man and plenty of round,
redolent thirties radio prose—[…] actually bring[s] it close to us, by disarming
our skepticism."

rWE 2.15 Oliver, Edith. "Watered Down." *New Yorker* 19 Jan. 1978: 69-70.
   A negative review because "Mamet's play is a synthetic that doesn't work.
Its ponderous irony (subtitle: 'An American Fable') and its foolishness are poor
substitutes for his usual original humor or his usual subtle tension. Or, indeed
for authenticity. These radio actors pantomime stage business and play to one
another; real radio actors play only to the microphone, and they rarely raise
their eyes from the script or change their expressions (I speak as a veteran of
radio)—it is all done with voices. How much of this is a matter of the writing
and how much a matter of the direction (by Steven Schachter) I cannot tell, but
if one doesn't believe in the radio program, then there is no show."

rWE 2.16 Raidy, William A. "*Water Engine* Gushes Talent." *Star-Ledger* [New Jersey]
9 Jan. 1978.
   Positive review of a surface "parody of the old radio dramas of the 1930s,
corny, melodramatic and filled with the old American dream platitudes of the
honest young man pitted against evil forces. Underneath, it is a powerful
indictment of American hypocrisy of the time, the pipe dream that everyone
(save the 'Bolsheviks') was as good as everyone else, providing you were hard
working, patriotic, and drank your Ovaltine."

rWE 2.17 Richardson, Jack. "*Engine*: A Curious Work." *New York Tribune* 7 Mar. 1978: 24.

A positive review of the play as dark satire: "Truths and happy endings are being cynically manufactured mellow voices send out a soothing message of faith one moment and a commercial harangue the next. [. . .] Mamet can show us clearly the difference between the message and its source. Since it was a medium not meant to be observed, the radio show, when looked at behind the scenes, reveals clearly the tawdry and manipulative manner with which morality and commodities are sold to an audience."

rWE 2.18 Sharp, Christopher. Rev. of *Water Engine*. *Women's Wear Daily* 6 Jan. 1978: 64. Rpt. in *New York Theatre Critics' Reviews* 39.6 1978: 336.

A negative review of the failure of realism: "The play—which is not very strong by itself—is marred by two serious mistakes. [. . .] Beatty centers a live clock over the stage, which is as damaging to any suspension of reality here as a howling baby in the audience would be. The clock makes one hour seem like two. The other mistake is a generally falsetto presentation by the actors—apparently to create a fable-like atmosphere on stage. There is no charm in the approach."

rWE 2.19 Simon, John. "Dirty Pool." *New York* 30 Jan. 1978: 60.

The usual negative review that totally misses the play-within-a-play genre: "I particularly loved those reviews that pondered the ontological or metaphysical reasons for casting *The Water Engine* in the mold of a radio play, when the reason is clearly that it is a radio play, and a rather insignificant one at that."

rWE 2.20 Syna, Sy. Rev. of *Water Engine*. *Wisdom's Child* 17 Jan. 1978.

Positive review: "Nothing in this play is ever said overtly. It is all through nuance, implication, innuendo. Somehow Mamet has fused an anti-capitalist message with Kafka. The tone of the piece is satiric, but so well done and in such well styled language that the characters never become broad caricatures."

rWE 2.21 Wallach, Allan. "An Inventive Spoof of Radio." *Newsday* 6 Jan. 1978: 11A.

Positive review because the play "cleverly manages to be two things simultaneously: A shrill attack on big-business morality and an engaging spoof of early radio. The second aspect not only excuses the melodramatic excesses of the first, it almost makes them necessary. [. . .] The approach works splendidly as a radio-drama parody but inadequately as an attack on business morality."

rWE 2.22 Watt, Douglas. "A Radio Play That Works—on and Off Mike." *Daily News* [New York] 6 Jan. 1978: 5.

Very positive review of play and production: "The evening is unsettling, slightly askew, ever before the play proper, which amounts to an apocalyptic vision—or, at the very least, a frightening view—of a perhaps incurably diseased society, ours. [. . .] We are further surprised to find the actors 'acting'; that is, going through the motions of knocking on invisible doors, opening and shutting them, pouring water, clip-clopping along a sidewalk, and so on, even though a sound effects man with a table full of devices produces the actual sounds. [. . .] But it soon becomes apparent that we are meant to be involved, not only as studio spectators, but as quiescent participants in a corrupt and violent society dominated by big business."

rWE 2.23 —. *"The Engine* Works Uptown." *Daily News* [New York] 7 Mar. 1978. Rpt. in *New York Theatre Critics' Reviews* 39.6 1978: 333.

Positive review of the approach: "the simple and melodramatic little story becomes frighteningly real in its tendency to stray outside the limits of studio practice. [. . .] But the effect of bridging the gap between unreality and reality is accomplished most strikingly by their moving away from the mikes and playing entire short scenes without them."

rWE 2.24 Weales, Gerald. "Stronger Than Water." *Commonweal* 14 Apr. 1978: 244+.

Mixed review focusing on language: "In so far as Mamet is a social playwright—and he certainly sounded like one in the *New York Times* interview on January 15—his concern is with language. His newspaperman, to fill space, dictates a high-sounding paragraph in which the American dream is described in terms of the bargain made and kept. That bargain, on a personal level, delivers Lang to the lawyers and the convivial language of one, the menacing rationality of the other finally destroy him."

rWE 2.25 Wilson, Edwin. "Mamet's 'Engine' Rolls but Where Is It Going?" *Wall Street Journal* 10 Mar. 1978: 21. Rpt. in *New York Theatre Critics' Reviews* 39.6 1978: 334.

A somewhat baffled review that noted four levels, but could not understand why: "The question is, are all the levels of activity in 'The Water Engine' mainly a clever theatrical scheme, or do they give this play a deeper resonance, suggesting meanings not apparent on the surface? There can be no doubt that by cutting away from the main story Mr. Mamet heightens tension and suspense. But what of the play's meaning? Does it have a coherent theme?"

Production:

pWE 3 Goodman Theatre production, Chicago. May 6 through June 2, 1985.

Director:	Steven Schachter
Set:	John Lee Beatty
Costumes:	Jessica Hahn
Lighting:	Dennis Parichy
Original Music:	Alaric Jans
Cast:	
Charles Lang:	William H. Macy
Rita:	Caroline Kava
Morton Gross:	Paul Butler
Lawrence Oberman:	Colin Stinton
Mrs. Varec:	Linda Kimbrough

Mr. Wallace:	Dennis Kennedy
Bernie:	Colin Jensen
Dave Murray:	Bruce Jarchow
Singer:	Annie Hat

Overview:

Extremely positive reviews of this revival which teamed early Mamet stars Macy and Stinton in a version "developed and changed" after the New York production (Syse). Mel Brandon and I saw this production and were impressed with its theatricality.

Reviews:

rWE 3.1 Christiansen, Richard. "'Engine' Runs Well in Revival." *Chicago Tribune* 10 May 1985: sec. 2: 6.

Extremely positive review: "Mamet here is not only a master of language; he's a tremendous storyteller, too. The play's ironic chorus of voices, expressing the sense of fate that hangs over the drama, is woven into a sharp, taut yarn that might have served very well as a thrilling radio drama of the 1930s. Macy, moving from naivete and befudddlement to rage and iron determination, is simply magnificent as the young inventor caught in a web of conspiracy, and he is given wonderful backing by the entire versatile cast."

rWE 3.2 Syse, Glenna. "'Water Engine' Pumped Up." *Chicago Sun-Times* 8 May 1985: 47.

Very positive view of the play's message: "Mamet's philosophy, presented in rather an uncustomary didactic manner, is that all people are connected—if initially for the worst, eventually perhaps for the best. And we're all in this together. [...] Macy is the picture of trust betrayed as the inventor. Colin Stinton doubles with dexterity as announcer and heavy, as does Dennis Kennedy on his soapbox and his grocery store."

Production:

pWE 4 Hampstead Theatre, London, 29 Aug. 1989.

Director:	Robin Lefevre
Décor:	Robin Don
Lighting:	Nick Chelton
Music:	Stephen Boxer
Cast:	
Charles Lang:	Peter Whitman
Rita:	Mary Maddox
Morton Gross:	Peter Jonfield
Lawrence Oberman:	Nick Dunning
Dave Murray:	Stephen Boxer
Bernie:	Aiden Gillen
Mrs. Varec:	Michelle Newell
Mr. Wallace:	Malcolm Terris
Chain Letter:	David Healey

Overview:
Most saw it as a minor play—Spencer arguing that it didn't make the transition from radio to theatre successfully—"Had Mamet not gone on to become one of America's most highly regarded dramatists, it seems unlikely that anyone would have taken the trouble to resurrect this thin little fable." Spencer's critique is acute, in that the production was "never quite sure whether to treat the conspiracy story seriously or to send it up" and as a result the effect of the play not being a contemporary fable, but one historicized by the old medium which, in the USA, had died out in a way it never did in the land of the BBC. Nathan, accordingly, saw "an American fable about the general belief that inventions which threaten existing technology are suppressed." However, the giant radio receiver set made clear that this is a "play within a play."

Reviews:
rWE 4.1 Arro, Isabel. Rev. of *Water Engine. What's On* 6 Sept. 1989. Rpt. in *London Theatre Record.* 27 Aug.- 9 Sept. 1989: 1142.
> A very positive review: " While the plot deals in suppression, the theatre of this piece deals almost obsessively in the dissemination of information, laying hold of every conceivable device with which to effect this."

rWE 4.2 Billington, Michael. Rev. of *Water Engine. Guardian* 31 Aug. 1989. Rpt. in *London Theatre Record.* 27 Aug.- 9 Sept. 1989: 1143.
> Not a positive review: "Radio appeals to the free-wheeling imagination; theatre is inevitably anchored in the concrete and visible. For all its sharp, fast, agile dialogue, *The Water Engine* offers few arresting images. It also buzzes so frantically around Chicago (the Expo, newspaper and legal offices, the violence-haunted streets) that no scene gets a chance to build or character to develop. [. . .] But, because the emphasis is on narrative rather than character, the actors have disappointingly little room for manouevre."

rWE 4.3 —. Rev. of *Water Engine. Herald Tribune* 6 Sep. 1989. Rpt. in *London Theatre Record.* 27 Aug.- 9 Sept. 1989: 1144.
> Mildly negative review because "the fast staccato rhythm means that scenes get no chance to build. Interesting ironies are also placed before us without being developed."

rWE 4.4 Coveney, Michael. Rev. of *Water Engine. Financial Times* 30 Aug. 1989. Rpt. in *London Theatre Record.* 27 Aug.- 9 Sept. 1989: 1143.
> A less than positive review: "By now the play has moved into a contradictory dramatic plane, or maybe Mamet wants to write like Chandler after all. The theatrical impact, however, is confusing and messy, characters hover as aerated speech balloons despite uniformly excellent acting. "

rWE 4.5 Denford, Antonia. Rev. of *Water Engine. City Limits* 7 Sept. 1989. Rpt. in *London Theatre Record.* 27 Aug.- 9 Sept. 1989: 1142.
> This is a positive review: "This funny, nightmarish play [. . .] seems to be a

metaphor for faceless institutional power versus the little person—the helpless listener. Loudspeakers ooze unctuous language over the audience."

rWE 4.6 Edwardes, Jane. Rev. of *Water Engine. Time Out* 6 Sept. 1989. Rpt. in *London Theatre Record.* 27 Aug.- 9 Sept. 1989: 1141.

A tepid review: "This is pretty thin, if enjoyable, stuff probably only for dedicated Mamet groupies, although enhanced by a devastating satire on the infamous chain-letter and a wonderful Bakelite radio set by Robin Don."

rWE 4.7 Edwards, Christopher. Rev. of *Water Engine. Spectator* 9 Sept. 1989. Rpt. in *London Theatre Record.* 27 Aug.- 9 Sept.1989: 1141.

A positive review of play and production which employed "the artful and very entertaining use of a play within a play. As you walk into the theatre you are confronted by the giant front panel of a Thirties radio set, complete with illuminated wavebands. The tuner picks out several stations and then the set slides back to reveal the interior of a Chicago radio station about to go on the air. Some of the dialogue is spoken into huge microphones that descend from the ceiling, while the rest is delivered in highly charged direct exchanges that teeter on the edge of melodrama. [...] Using the form of an earnest radio play from the Depression years, director, cast and designer collaborate brilliantly to project a bewildering world of avarice, deceit, and idealism."

rWE 4.8 Eyres, Harry. "Parable and Pastiche Sustained by Patter." *The Times* [London] 30 Aug. 1989: 19.

Mixed review: "Whether you find it deeply, subtly resonant, or inconsequential, even pretentious, seems almost a matter of taste.[. . .] This distancing effect is beautifully interpreted by Robin Don's set of a stage-wide radio which parts to reveal characters speaking into microphones and reading from scripts. A futher set of sliding doors at the back sometimes opens to reveal the (closed) sliding door of a lift. This gives a claustrophobic sense of mirrors on mirrors or Chinese boxes, but also suggests the Alice-in-Wonderlandish notion that everything is happening not just inside a radio station, but inside a radio."

rWE 4.9 Finch, Tessa. Rev. of *Water Engine. Daily Express* 31 Aug. 1989. Rpt. in *London Theatre Record.* 27 Aug.- 9 Sept. 1989: 1141.

A mixed review which saw the play and performances as "powerful," but finds the plot too much "a world of paranoid distrust. [. . .] The answer too is straightforward. For we see the inventor crushed by the unhealthy interest of the very institution he approaches for help in protecting his discovery."

rWE 4.10 Ford, Mark. "The Process of Distillation." *Times Literary Supplement* 8 Sept. 1989: 975.

Rather negative review: "The main problem is that both production and script try to embody colossal issues about the individual and society through methods that fail to transcend the glib and corny. The play lacks passion and intelligence in about equal measures. Though crisply written and stylishly performed, very little that happens in it carries the conviction necessary to activate the vast themes it is pretending to explore."

WE 4.11 Gross, John. Rev. of *Water Engine. Sunday Telegraph* 3 Sept. 1989. Rpt. in *London Theatre Record*. 27 Aug.- 9 Sept. 1989: 1145.

Gross enjoyed the production, not Mamet: "All very facile, but then Mamet's ideas are the least interesting thing about him. Perhaps he doesn't take them altogether seriously himself. There are times when *The Water Engine* comes close to outright parody—parody with a dash of nostalgia. And at that level it is quite enjoyable."

rWE 4.12 Hirschhorn, Clive. Rev. of *Water Engine. Sunday Express* 3 Sept. 1989. Rpt. in *London Theatre Record*. 27 Aug.- 9 Sept. 1989: 1146.

A negative review which concluded: "By placing the tale against a backdrop of industrial 'progress,' the opposition Lang encounters is meant, of course, to be ironic. Simplistic might be more near the mark."

rWE 4.13 Hurren, Kenneth. Rev. of *Water Engine. Mail on Sunday* 3 Sept. 1989. Rpt. in *London Theatre Record*. 27 Aug.- 9 Sept. 1989: 1142.

A negative review: "Compounding confusion, a thin element of sharp theatricality—in the hounding of a young engineer (Peter Whitman), inventor of an engine powered only by water—is blunted by pretentious inserts to support a wobbly message."

rWE 4.14 Nathan, David. Rev. of *Water Engine. Jewish Chronicle* 1 Sept. 1989. Rpt. in *London Theatre Record*. 27 Aug.- 9 Sept. 1989: 1141.

A positive review which noted the play within a play: "An ordinary thriller writer would have left it at that, but Mamet throws in some heavy complications by having part of the narrative spasmodically played as a 1934 radio play with actors who elsewhere are characters at risk reading scripts into a microphone."

rWE 4.15 Pannifer, Bill. Rev. of *Water Engine. Listener* 7 Sept. 1989. Rpt. in *London Theatre Record*. 27 Aug.- 9 Sept. 1989: 1141.

Positive review of characters who evinced "different kinds of American doubletalk and its embedded hypocrisies, notable the portentously named Oberman (Nick Dunning), a sinister lawyer who asserts that 'if everyone acted in their own self-interest, we would be in paradise.' Meanwhile, the common man is given a non-technological podium at the back of the stage from which to voice his fears of 'America's malevolent destiny as the New World.'"

rWE 4.16 Shulman, Milton. Rev. of *Water Engine. Evening Standard* 30 Aug. 1989. Rpt. in *London Theatre Record*. 27 Aug.- 9 Sept. 1989: 1146.

A rather negative review of the play as "less significant than it looks. Constructed like a dramatic puzzle, it left me wondering whether solving it was worth the trouble. [...] But instead of a simple thriller, Mamet has complicated his film noir story with so many symbols, metaphors and pretentious allusions that one's interest is modified by one's irritation."

rWE 4.17 Spencer, Charles. Rev. of *Water Engine. Daily Telegraph* 31 Aug. 1989.
Rpt. in *London Theatre Record.* 27 Aug.- 9 Sept 1989: 1145.

A mixed review which focused on adaptation: "All this might have worked
rather well on the radio, as a drama that spoofs its own medium. In the theatre,
the idea loses its entire raison d'être and Robin Lefevre's production is hamstrung
as a result. The tone is fatally uncertain, never quite sure whether to treat the
conspiracy story seriously or to send it up, while the show's insistence on its
radio origins becomes a tedious irritant, slowing down and confusing what
might otherwise be an entertaining, if insubstantial, thriller in the film noir
mold."

rWE 4.18 Taylor, Paul. Rev. of *Water Engine. Independent* 1 Sept. 1989. Rpt. in
London Theatre Record. 27 Aug.- 9 Sept. 1989: 1144.

Positive review: "Artfully reversing the normal proportions, Mamet turns
the bulk of *The Water Engine* into an ironically-angled play-within-a-play, a
pastiche of the sort of social protest drama that aimed to give people hope
during the Depression."

Production:
pWE 4 Atlantic Theater Company, New York City, from October 20 to November 21,
1999. Previewed October 18. Double-billed with *Mr. Happiness.*

Director:	Karen Kohlhaas
Set:	Walt Spangler
Costumes:	Rick Gradone
Lights:	Robert Perry
Cast:	
Charles Lang:	Steven Goldstein
Rita:	Mary McCann
Morton Gross:	Peter Jacobson
Lawrence Oberman:	Jordan Lang
Dave Murray:	Josh Stamberg
Mr. Wallace:	Peter Maloney
Bernie:	Carl Matusovich
Chainletter:	Kelly Maurer
Murray's Secretary:	Maggie Kiley
Gross's Secretary & Mrs. Varec:	Maryann Urbano
Ensemble/sound effects:	Jody Lambert

Overview:
This production was not seen to be as good as the original. Feingold faulted it for
missing the "gadgetry" of the original, which covered gaps in the narrative. But the
questions he asked are all not about a radio play, but about realism. Brantley faulted
the director for the production which "is suffused with an air of caution." Only Winer
thought Macy's original version was less effective than Goldstein's.

Reviews:

rWE 5.1 Brantley, Ben. "At the 1934 World's Fair, Speaking the Wrong Language."
New York Times 21 Oct. 1999: B5.

Great appreciation of the play, with some hesitation about this production:
"In most fictive worlds, people who talk like Charles are usually the victims of
lobotomy, brainwashing or hypnosis. In Mr. Mamet's world, they are more
likely to represent an elemental purity, which can translate into either idealism
or brutal primitivism. [...] Language is fate in the dramas of David Mamet, a
key not just to character but to chances of survival, something especially evident
in his short, elliptical morality plays of urban life."

rWE 5.2 Feingold, Michael. "History's Mysteries." *Village Voice* 2 Nov. 1999: 67.

A mixed review of the Atlantic season revival: "David Mamet's 1977 notion
of a 1930s radio thriller is no more than that, a little carpentered thing to divert
you for an hour or so with its suspense—will the genius inventor escape the
baddies who want to steal his engine, or won't he?—while teasing your mind
with hints of the occult, glimmers of Big Brother paranoia, and spoonfuls of
nostalgia for that simpler day when technology meant a better life for everyone.
Mamet's never wasteful: The mind teasing side issues all not only impinge on
the central story but help to build its suspense."

rWE 5.3 Isherwood, Charles. Rev. of *Water Engine and Mr. Happiness. Variety* 1
Nov. 1999: 99.

Positive review of the play, but not so of the production: "Mamet underscores
his story with a variety of evocative touches—a woman promoting the life-
saving powers of a chain letter, the rantings of anarchists in Chicago's Bughouse
Square—to create a kaleidoscopic, surrealistic picture of a particular time and
place. It's an odd play, more style than substance, and thus requiring a perfect
mastery of mood. Unfortunately Kohlhaas and her cast haven't found the right
blend of period authenticity and Mametian mysteriousness to keep it aloft."

rWE 5.4 Simon, John. "Lost in Translation." *New York* 8 Nov. 1999: 67+.

The usual negative review: "*The Water Engine* was designed for radio,
which is to say disembodied voices; in the theater, words must become flesh,
space assume concrete shape. Hence, for example, unindentified characters
spouting chain-letter inanities from limbo do not engage us on the boards as
they would in the air."

rWE 5.5 Winer, Linda. "Moral Naivete/ Mamet's Look Back Boosts Decency and the
Little Guy." *Newsday* 21 Oct. 1999: B3.

Not a very positive review of "a structurally ambitious, unrelentingly earnest
little morality play. [. . .] Director Karen Kohlhaas, a founding member of the
company Mamet and Macy began 15 years ago in Chelsea, squeezes as much
juice as possible out of the alarmingly self-explanatory scripts."

rWE 5.6 Zinman, Toby. Rev. of *The Water Engine* and *Mr. Happiness. David Mamet Review* 7 (2000): 3.

Positive review: "It is worth noting that Mamet's glances are always backwards to the past and that both these implied-radio works are redolent with his signature combination: a yearning of for the old days while ruthlessly unmasking the foolhardiness of that yearning, since the old days were no better than today."

Scholarly Articles:

sWE 1 Bigsby, C. W. E. *"The Water Engine, A Life in the Theatre." David Mamet.* Contemporary Writers. London: Methuen, 1985. 86-93.

Bigsby views the play as an allegory of the artist in translating reality into fiction: "As the barker asks, in such a world, 'Who knows what is true?' His final comment, 'All people are connected' (71), thus becomes an ironic commentary on unlearned lessons rather than the cant of natural unity or the self-justifying mysticism of the chain letter, a desperate article of faith rather than a fact which can be shown to take social form. *The Water Engine* is indeed a fable; but, if its logic is to be accepted, its own coherences must be doubted, as a parable about the decay of form is shaped into an elegant and sophisticated metaphor" (92).

sWE 2 Carroll. Dennis. "The Plays in the Theatre." *David Mamet*. Modern Dramatists Series. New York: St. Martin's, 1987. 131-39.

For Carroll, the work is Mamet's "quintessential play as far as content is concerned. It weaves together 'business,' with its pressure to abrogate trust; the potential for communion in the mentor-protégé relationship; the tensions caused by sexual pressures" (131). "The setting made for a completely fluid presentation of the play's structure, an easy cross-over between the conventions of radio and theatre. Even the chain-letter narrations, which suggest superstition masquerading as just fate, were organically integrated with the play's other formal devices" (135-36).

sWE 3 James, Justin. "Individual Responsibility and the Disintegration of Social Values in David Mamet." *Indian Journal of American Studies* 26.2 (1996): 81-85.

This article presents a simple thesis: "Mamet, through *American Buffalo* and *The Water Engine*, portrays the failure of individuals to redeem society" (81). Individuals fail because "they find pleasure in the existing decay in society." [. . .] The characters presented by Mamet are totally selfish. [. . .] Teach finds it difficult to keep his ideal of friendship. Once he enters into business, he takes advantage of others and denies friendship" (82). Lang's is the reverse: "We find Lang making a genuine attempt to create and maintain a good relationship with his businessmen. [. . .] But the selfish businessmen have no sympathy for Lang" (82).

See also the following scholarly articles covering multiple plays:

sMP 18 Gale, Steven H. "David Mamet: The Plays, 1972-1980."

sMP 19 Geis, Deborah R. "David Mamet and the Metadramatic Tradition: Seeing 'the Trick from the Back."

THE WOODS

Dedication: Gregory Mosher
Scene: Three scenes on the porch of a summer house, early September.
Time: Dusk, Night and Morning
Characters: Ruth and Nick, lovers
Editions:

The Woods: A Play by David Mamet. New York: Grove, 1979.
The Woods; Lakeboat; Edmond: Three Plays. New York: Grove, 1979.
The Woods. New York: S. French, 1982.
David Mamet Plays: 2. London: Methuen, 1996.

Plot Outline:
In Scene 1, Ruth has most of the speeches and they are printed as poetry. She tries to get Nick to talk, and by the end of the act he haltingly tells his father's war story. In Scene 2, she tells stories of her grandmother. She talks to Nick of fantasies, and how "they can be frightening. To do them." As she's about to go for a walk, he tries to make love. She rebukes him for thinking she doesn't want him. She gives him a present, a bracelet that figures in her memory of the grandmother, "Nicholas. I will always love you. Ruth." When he does not respond in kind, and she announces she'll leave in the morning. In scene 3, Ruth wants to go swimming before she leaves. Nick wants her to stay with him—"to fuck her"—she deflects him since he seems not to realize he broke off the relationship. She berates him and finally hits him with an oar—he hits her in the face, and knocks her off the porch. Finally, he reverses and begins to say how he really feels: he's in a hole, alone, and begs her to stay, to hold him. She begins the story about two children in the woods holding each other as *lights fade.*

Performance:
pW 1 Premiered at the St. Nicholas Theater Company, Chicago. Previewed November 11, 12, and 13, opened November 17, ran until December 18, 1977.

Director:		David Mamet
Set:		Michael Merritt
Lighting:		Robert Christen
Cast:		
	Ruth:	Patti LuPone
	Nick:	Peter Weller

Overview:

Reviews liked the actors, and Eder found the play moving. But the others were confused by Mamet's direction. Christiansen said "the production frequently undercuts the text." The text is the mix of "mythic" (poetry?) and "non-poetic" writing. Winer questioned the setting: "Michael Merritt's plain porch isn't pretty—as though Mamet wanted a neutral set in which the characters can see what they want." Goldstein was baffled by the peculiar lighting. After entitling the play's three scenes "Dusk", "Night" and "Morning", "Mamet chose stark, bright front lighting for the entire play." Kaplan questioned his direction of actors "in a style which seems almost stilted. The characters speak at each other rather than to each other."

Reviews:

rW 1.1 Christiansen, Richard. "Mamet New Play in Uneven Debut." *Chicago Daily News* 17 Nov. 1977: 35.

Mixed review of the play, and Mamet's direction: "The play is a beautifully conceived love story, graced with some lovely passages, marred by some mundane moments and directed, by the author, in a most curious fashion that throws its elegant design off balance. [. . .] At its best, this clear, monosyllabic language gives the drama an almost mythical quality, that of a simple story with its roots in the very depths of life. At its worst, alas, the stripped-down dialog ('This is not good, Nick.') approaches the banal and ludicrous range of a soap opera. Much (though not all) of this imbalance might have been solved by a perfect tuning of the production to the script. But, strangely, the production frequently undercuts the text."

rW 1.2 Eder, Richard. "Mamet Expands Range in *Woods*." *New York Times* 30 Nov. 1977: C19.

Extremely positive review: "But 'The Woods' shows real growth, and a decidedly enlarged emotional current between the author and his work. It is less of an artifact and more an act of expression. It has Mr. Mamet's typically restricted cast—in this case a pair of lovers in a cabin in the woods—but a much wider emotional range. Sometimes, it is awkward and slow, and sometimes the deadlocks between the lovers deadlock the play. But it is moving, as well as apt; it intensifies as it proceeds and its end is hair-raising."

rW 1.3 Goldstein, Shelly. Rev. of *The Woods*. *WNUR Radio* [Evanston] 17 Nov. 1977.

Very positive review: "Mamet's *Woods* seem to have their roots firmly planted in soil tended by Freud or Jung. The relationship of Nick and Ruth leave many unanswered questions, but watching LuPone this seems almost unnecessary. LuPone is the sort of actress plays are written for. It is impossible not to be entranced by her deep, rich voice that doesn't waste a consonant. [. . .] This woman possesses magic and it sets the stage on fire."

rW 1.4 Kaplan, Sherman. Rev. of *The Woods*. WBBM Radio. No date available.

Negative review: "The characters speak at each other rather than to each other. They don't use contractions; each word is spoken as if it had been clipped from the printed page and pasted into their working script. [. . . Mamet's] language and style are too self-conscious."

rW 1.5 Leed, Rick. "'The Woods:' Mamet's Poet Drama is an Unqualified Success." *Gay Chicago News* 18 Nov. 1977: 7.

Extremely positive review: "This concern with language is connected to another aspect of Mamet's work—his use of storytelling. People in his plays often tell each other stories rather than directly speak to each to express certain difficult ideas. Somewhere in the language that is crafted into the various stories, there develops a series of eloquent subtexts within the play and within each character's personality."

rW 1.6 Winer, Linda. "Clickety-clack of David Mamet's Typewriter Is Heard Through *Woods*." 17 Nov. 1977: B6.

Mixed review: "One yearns for a reason to care about their trivial traumas, hopes for a suspenseful climax that does not seemed trumped up for the sake of one, and wishes the words self-conscious and affected wouldn't creep even once into the mind. [. . . LuPone's] talent is palpable, if anything, a little too large for the small stage. [. . .] For a while, it seemed that Mamet had written a one-character play for two people."

Performance:
pW 2 New York Shakespeare Festival Public Theater (Newman), New York, April 25 to May 13th, 1979. (The TOFT Collection of the NYPL has a 72 minute videocassette of this production.)

Director:		Ulu Grosbard
Set:		John Lee Beatty
Lighting:		Jennifer Tipton
Cast:		
	Nick:	Chris Sarandon
	Ruth:	Christine Lahti

Overview:
The Woods provoked some surprising discriminations from the critics. Most praised the Chicago production. They were not as positive about Grosbard's New York production with Lahti and Sarandon. Eder, who saw both productions, critiqued Grosbard who "plays for what isn't there, and seems to ignore what is." What is there, according to Eder, are characters "groping for [...] their own feelings." But they use "lame words" to express these which, in the New York production, became "simply lame" talk. Ginsberg found it "overstated" because Grosbard, "has the actors deliver their lines in a modern realistic manner which throws the play off—the poetry sounds

awkward." Oliver simply found the director gave "an extra urgency" as if the play had "some meaning we should be getting and aren't." Those who took the play as mere talk usually praised the director and the performance. The *Village Voice*, however, offered three different views of the play: Feingold, Blumenthal, and Fox all examined it—for the first time trying to create a firestorm of a debate over whether or not Mamet is a misogynist. Like Fox, Gussow found Mamet's Chicago production so tilted toward Ruth that he concluded, "'The Woods' is one-and-a-half character play on the road to becoming another in Mr. Mamet's series of consummate dialogues."

Reviews:

rW 2.1 Barnes, Clive. "'Woods' Lumbers Along." *New York Post* 26 Apr. 1979: 35. Rpt. in *New York Theatre Critics' Reviews* 40.11 (1979): 252.

   Negative review: "Was it worth doing? This Hansel and Gretel couple in from the woods of reality, sharing with us their inarticulate neuroses? No. Mamet's conversation grates on our ears, as futile as sand rubbed on sandpaper. He draws no clear line between fantasy and reality."

rW 2.2 Beaufort, John. Rev. of *The Woods*. *Christian Science Monitor* 9 May 1979: 18. Rpt. in *New York Theatre Critics' Reviews* 40.11 (1979): 251.

   Negative review: "Ruth, the she bore, wants to go for walks in the rain. Nick, the he bore, objects on the defensible grounds that he doesn't wish to get wet. There is more to the dialogue than that, much of it densely symbolic."

rW 2.3 Blumenthal, Eileen. "Mamet a Trois." *Village Voice* 7 May 1979: 103.

   Highly negative review which first raised the charge: "It is deeply infested with misogyny disguised as an enlightened, even feminist, examination of couple interactions. [. . .] It affirms female as victim. But, more disturbing, Mamet ultimately dismisses the woman. 'The Woods' is not really about a couple: It is about a man. It's he who has the grand emotional breakthrough, he who has center-stage finale speech."

rW 2.4 Clurman, Harold. Rev. of *The Woods*. *The Nation* 19 May 1979: 581-2.

   Clurman believed "There is a crucial defect in the text." The fault is that it is too real: "It is all literally 'true to life'[. . .]. The phenomena of nature itself surround and wrap us in an impenetrable dark mystery, unresponsive to reasoned explanation. [. . .] But the realism here dispels the larger dimension sought for. In language and behavior the characters are too concrete and superficially recognizable to take wing."

rW 2.5 Eder, Richard. "Mamet's *the Woods* Redone at Public: Forest's Prime Evil." *New York Times* 26 Apr. 1979: C15. Rpt. in *New York Theatre Critics' Reviews* 40.11 (1979): 250-51.

   Positive review: "What Mr. Mamet has made is not a naturalistic play but a poetic one. The couple's continual talk, with its vaguenesses, its erratic leaping quality, its half-irrelevant sequences, sounds highly realistic; but in fact it is a highly charged super-realism, possessed by the most concentrated kind of emotion. [. . .] Mamet's two characters quarrel, but what they are mainly quarreling with and groping for is their own feelings. They are each numbly, dumbly and very movingly, trying to give voice to themselves and find a mooring in each other."

rW 2.6 Feingold, Michael. "Mamet a Trois." *Village Voice* 7 May 1979: 103.

Positive view of the play, not of the production: "Each has a daydream, and as the play goes from awkward afternoon to sleepless night to irate morning after, each criticizes the other, at first by implication and then aloud, for being real individuals and not daydream-fulfillments. Meantime, woven through their terse and rapidly shifting talk is a picture of how, failing to relate to each other, they fail equally to relate to nature and to their forebears." Grosbard "seems to have been concerned that the parable element would not come clear, and either lets the heightened language pass without comment, or finds unfortunate ways of emphasizing it."

rW 2.7 Fox, Terry C. "Mamet a Trois." *Village Voice* 7 May 1979: 103.

Extremely positive review, countering Blumenthal: "*The Woods* is terrifying, a play which locates sexual tragedy in a pervasive American mythology composed of sentimental ideals, extended war tales, and a belief in a pristine backwoods glory. [. . . Mamet] demonstrates the way in which societal myths shape our most fundamental, personal actions. [. . .] The play is so unstintingly critical of Nick that it is tempting to read 'The Woods' as simply a male-confessional drama of no small power. For while Ruth capitulates to Nick in the end, she has at least found her self-respect.[. . .] For the bitterest notion in *The Woods* is not its understanding of how male fears and ideals destroy men, but how the idea that love saves destroys love."

rW 2.8 Ginsberg, Merle. "Language the Real Star in Mamet's *The Woods*." *Villager* 3 May 1979: 15.

Positive view of the play ("the real star is the language"), not of the production: "Is this the modern sexual dilemma? Women who can speak (perhaps not too much) and men who can only answer with violence? 'The Woods' is a play with much to tell us, but in the present production at the Public Theater it is overstated. Ulu Grosbard, its director, has the actors deliver their lines in a modern realistic manner, which throws the play off—the poetry sounds awkward."

rW 2.9 Gottfried, Martin. Rev. of *The Woods*. *New York* [Cue] 25 May 1979: 14.

Negative view of the play: "Their dialogue, which starts out naturalistically, becomes stylized and absurdist to the point where every other line seems to be either 'yes,' 'no,' or 'I don't know.' Christine Lahti and Chris Sarandon can only be admired for going on stage in such unplayable roles. The estimable director, Ulu Grosbard, did his best."

rW 2.10 Gunner, Marjorie. Rev. of *The Woods*. *Floral Park Bulletin* 10 May 1979: 7.

Backhanded negative review: "It is difficult to conceive of David Mamet's choppily worded two act duo-drama being bettered by another than director

Ulu Grosbard, who emphasizes the stilted dialogue instead of blending it with meaningful action."

rW 2.11 Hummler, Richard. Rev. of *The Woods*. *Variety* 9 May 1979: 554.
Negative review: "Ulu Grosbard's staging magnifies the ostensibly 'poetic' nature of the script and doesn't aid audience involvement. Lahti's performance makes it worthwhile for acting buffs, but Chris Sarandon doesn't overcome the opacity of the male role."

rW 2.12 Jenner, C. Lee. Rev. of *The Woods*. *Other Stages* 3 May 1979.
Negative review: "Musical dialogue swings content by the tail and form overwhelms function. You can't hear the characters for the constant, self-conscious clickety-clack of Mamet's typewriter."

rW 2.13 Kerr, Walter. Rev. of *The Woods*. *New York Times* 13 May 1979: D5.
Negative review: "Rhythms so preoccupy him in 'The Woods' at the Public, that the boy and girl who are spending a weekend in a lakeside summer house tend to alternate long and short lines in precise balance, creating a seesaw effect that is both dizzying and highly uninformative. We can't learn why the two young lovers are so miserable in their isolation if we're going to devote all of our attention to the numbing effect of having syllables counted off."

rW 2.14 Kissel, Howard. Rev. of *The Woods*. *Women's Wear Daily* 26 Apr. 1979: 10. Rpt. in *New York Theatre Critics' Reviews* 40.11 (1979): 251.
Positive view of the playtext; negative view of this production which "seems to have realized very little of the play's potential" because the actors "seem to concentrate most of their efforts on the words, as if this were Noel Coward. We have almost no feeling of intimacy between them, no clear sense of an on-going emotional relationship to which the words act sometimes as an explanation, more often as a counterpoint."

rW 2.15 Oliver, Edith. "Too Many Trees". *New Yorker* 7 May 1979: 130.
Positive review of the play, not of the production: "*The Woods* is a dramatic poem for two voices, incantatory in style, and for other voices, from the past—of his father, of her European grandmother. The dramatic tension between Nick and Ruth, from their loving beginning to panicky loneliness and misery and anger, grows naturally in the play, yet in the performance [. . .] it is given an extra urgency that seems quite unwarranted, as if there were some message, some meaning we should be getting and aren't. If the play were done more modestly [. . .] words would take care of everything and the characters—and incidentally, the shifts of mood and the humor—would become clearer."

rW 2.16 Simon, John. "Permanents and Transients." *New York* 14 May 1979: 75-76.
Negative review: "As usual, Mamet seems to mean his play to be about language—language that under its banalities or eccentricities conceals desperate urgencies. This is the sort of thing that almost every contemporary playwright

has toyed with, and that Mamet often lumberingly toils over. Yet his words stubbornly refuse to reverberate or hint at disturbed depths, whether he flattens them out to echolalia or tries to heighten them into quasi-poetry, or even kicks them sideways into a weirdness that is supposed to tease us with its mystery."

rW 2.17 Watt, Douglas. "They've Lost Their Way in *The Woods.*" *New York Daily News* 26 Apr. 1979: 69. Rpt. in *New York Theatre Critics' Reviews* 40.11 (1979): 250.

Negative review: "In attempting to recreate the cadences of everyday speech, this gifted playwright has achieved a clipped mannered speech pattern peppered with dozens of yesses, noes, goods, and-uhs, whats, whys, ohs, c'meres, you knows and I don't knows. [. . .] Ulu Grosbard's direction unfortunately emphasizes the mannered nature of the script instead of cloaking it. John Lee Beatty's setting is a marvel of economy and suggestion."

rW 2.18 Wilson, Donald. "What Price Passion." Rev. of *The Woods. Soho Weekly News* 3 May 1979: 64.

Negative review: "There is little interesting physical action. Everything is so deadpan and stilted that the play soon becomes unintentionally risible. Mamet never—either in words or action—builds the convincing illusion of an argument for his characters, of hidden irritation and possible violence. Nick and Ruth only posture and say naughty things."

Production:
pW 4 Willful Productions, The Producer's Club, New York City Jan. 1997.

Director:	David Travis
Set Designer:	Devorah Herbert
Lighting:	Dan Scully and Chris Scully
Sound:	Ray Ru
Cast:	
Ruth:	Danielle Kwatinetz
Nick:	Eric Martin Brown

Review:
rW 4.1 Stevenson, Sarah Lansdale. Rev. of *The Woods. David Mamet Review* 4 (1997): 3. [Review from 24 Jan.]

After a twelve year Mamet-imposed hiatus of New York production, permission was finally given for this one. Positive review: "This sudden explosion of explicit language into a play whose language had been quiet, calm, and poetic, was well handled by the actors, for unlike Nick's earlier attack on Ruth, the violence seemed to emerge quite naturally, from a place that had not actually been absent in the previous scenes, but was merely hidden below the surface, awaiting a chance to erupt. When, following this interruption, the language returned to its former controlled state, the undercurrent of left-over tension, though suppressed, was nonetheless palpable."

Scholarly:

sW 1 Bigsby, C. W. E. *"Sexual Perversity in Chicago, The Woods." David Mamet.*
Contemporary Writers. London: Methuen, 1985. 46-62

Though Mamet sees *The Woods* as regenerative, Bigsby sees it "dramatizing
the dislocations in social reality and the apparently unbridgeable gulf between
people than in identifying the means whereby such dislocations might be
transcended. He patently works towards a moment of grace, but this remains
little more than a declaration of faith. In interview he points to restored
relationships as evidence for the possibility of harmony, but, pressed, he admits
that this harmony is more desired than achieved" (58).

sW 2 Brown, John Russell. "The Woods, the West, and Icarus's Mother: Myth in the
Contemporary American Theatre." *Connotations: A Journal for Critical Debate*
[Munster, Germany] 5.2-3 (1995/96): 339-54.

Brown contends that Americans had no Greco-Roman myths to draw upon
as Europeans did, and so had to invent and borrow their own. He uses Mamet's
The Woods, American Buffalo and Shepard's plays. In his view, the buffalo
reference invokes all the myths of the old West. With *The Woods*, however, he notes
how each character invents personal myths, attempts to control what was originally
"an unknowable world of huge trees in woods and forests uncropped by man" (342).
Ruth's depiction of the seagull is done "playfully, and even comically, as Ruth does
her best to fill the sky with heroes" (343). Nick's stories, however, are seen as parallels
to Orestes and Oedipus, "the same stories of inheritance, darkness, dynasties, fire,
and mysteries" (344). McCarthy disputes Brown in sMP 35.

sW 3 Carroll. Dennis. "Sex." *David Mamet.* New York: St. Martin's, 1987. 51-69.

Carroll notes that scholars praise the play, while most critics seeing it in
performance have not (53). He begins with performance, however: "The
summer-home porch set suggests intersection between the spheres of the natural
world and human domesticity; it also suggests openness, vulnerability, lack of
protection" (60). As with *Sexual Perversity*, he sympathizes with the male
character: "It is a last-ditch plea for understanding and sympathy rather than an
authentic commitment or an admission of moral responsibility. It is a plea for
her to enter into his world, to accept him as he is, to accept his inarticulateness
and his insecurities. Her flat 'Thank you' in response surely indicates that she
realises this. She accepts for the time being the role of Earth Mother once again
as she resumes the story of the babes in the woods" (65-66).

sW 4 Hellemans-Van Berlaer, Dina. "Wie Raakte Verdwaald in Het Bos? Over De
Opvoering Van David Mamets the Woods Door Bkt." *Het Teater Zoekt...Zoek
Het Theater. Aspekten Van Het Eignetijds Teater in Vlaanderen.* Ed. Dina van
Berlaer- Hellemans, Marianne Van Kerkhoven and Luk Van den Dries. Vol. 25.
Brussels: Studiereeks van de Vrije Universiteit, 1986. 3-35.

See also the following annotations for the scholarly articles on multiple plays:

sMP 35 McCarthy, Gerry. "New Mythologies: Mamet, Shepard and the American Stage."

Scholarly Criticism of Multiple Plays

sMP 1 Almansi, Guido. "David Mamet, a Virtuoso of Invective." *Critical Angles: European Views of Contemporary American Literature*. Ed. Marc Chenetier. Carbondale: Southern Illinois UP, 1986. 191-207.

Almansi argues "A comic character can never be the writer's mouthpiece. [. . .] A character says 'soft things with a hole in the middle,' but someone somewhere thinks that it is a rather eccentric definition of women. Yet with the most alert modern playwrights, say from Harold Pinter onwards, this voice is kept as muted as possible" (194). His point is that the delight in language itself undercuts taking the lines literally, or as authorial perspectives. "Theatrically, Mamet's plays may not convince everyone, but it would be difficult to deny his prominence as poet of swearwords, artist of invectives, and virtuoso of obscene expressions" (199).

sMP 2 Andreach, Robert J. "Exemplary Selves in Hell." *Creating the Self in Contemporary American Theatre*. Carbondale: Southern Illinois UP, 1998. 89-108.

Without research, this work concentrates on close readings (e.g. "listening" in Act One of *Glengarry*) together with an archetypal/religious approach. He traces images of eating and being eaten in Act One of *Glengarry* where "the act-2 set is a stage image for the hollow self: an image covering nothing. In this hell, predators do to one another what they do to clients in life" (94). *Speed-the-Plow* is seen as a journey into Dante's hell—where Karen is the potential for salvation that Bobby misses. In *Oleanna* the poster outside the Orpheum theatre announced the center, "A Power Play" (98). Andreach's response to Carol is very sympathetic, but both John and Carol are corrupted by power.

sMP 3 Bigsby, C. W. E. *David Mamet.* Contemporary Writers. London: Methuen, 1985.

The first book on Mamet, this work initially places him in the context of American culture of the 1970s and 1980s. It traces his roots in Veblen, in the context of a moralist, "dramatizing the inner life of the individual and the nation" (15). The approach to these early plays presents them as revealing a culture empty of meaning: "alert to the degree to which language deforms experience as experience determines language, [. . .] that leaves the individual severed equally from the past and from the consolation of a shared present" (136).

sMP 4 —. "David Mamet: All True Stories." *Modern American Drama, 1945-2000.* 2nd ed. Cambridge: Cambridge UP, 2000. 199-236.

Bigsby spins out thematic readings with insight but rarely examining the words of the text, though he has much to say about Mamet and language. He begins by defining mythic America in its literature. Telling stories and making myths is the way of filling an empty and meaningless life for the characters. "Yet there is redemption. It lies in the persistence of need, in the survival of the imagination, in the ability to shape experience into performance and in a humour born out of the space between the values of the characters and those of the audience" (205). Bigsby finds "redemption" in this emptiness. "The final irony of David Mamet's plays, however, is that the very faith which makes individuals vulnerable to exploitation and deceit is primary evidence of the survival of a sense of transcendent values for which otherwise he can find no social correlative" (207).

sMP 5 Blansfield, Karen. "Women on the Verge, Unite!" *Gender and Genre: Essays on David Mamet.* Eds. Christopher C. Hudgins and Leslie Kane. New York: Palgrave, 2001. 125-43.

Blansfield notes ambiguity in women's power: "Mamet's women are more potent than initially seems apparent. That power is generated by the man's fear of them, by the male's vulnerability, and by his insecurity. For Mamet's men, rejection by the female is so devastating because of their pathetic dependence on women for their identity. [. . .] Mamet's men have ironically bestowed power upon women by virtue of their own fear—the fear of rejection that will deny their masculinity" (139). Thus "Karen seems to be both manipulative and helpless, worldly yet naïve, an ambiguity that shapes men's reactions to her" (135). Joan's rejection of Bernie, and Teach's anger at Ruthie, both reflect this power of women, and the rage they elicit.

sMP 6 Blattes, Susan. "The Blurring of Boundaries between Stage and Screen in Plays by Sam Shepard and David Mamet." *Mediatized Drama/Dramatized Media.* Ed. Eckart Voigts-Virchow. Trier, Germany: Wissenschaftlicher, 2000. 189-99.

Blattes covers ground previously done by Burkman—*True West* and *Speed-the-Plow* as commentaries on Hollywood. She focuses on how both plays display formulaic scripts juxtaposed against a seemingly more authentic script. But Blattes rightly notes that there is great disagreement over the radiation screenplay in *Speed-the-Plow* and she cites Henry's review because he thought Mamet should be clear about whether it was bogus or authentic. But Blattes argues this is not a parody, which requires a fixed standard, but a postmodern pastiche, illustrating "the very absence of clearly definable boundaries which characterizes contemporary postindustrial society" (197-98). The same blurred boundaries are found between theatre and film.

sMP 7 Blumberg, Marcia. "Eloquent Stammering in the Fog: O'Neill's Heritage in Mamet." *Perspectives on O'Neill: New Essays*. Ed. Shyamal Bagchee. Victoria: U of Victoria, 1988. 97-111.

Using no theory of comparative method, Blumberg lists comparisons and contrasts: "[B]oth portray the failure of the American Dream and the concomitant moral and spiritual bankruptcy of American society at large" (97). The contrasts are almost diametrical opposites, but Blumberg only accounts for this as evidence of a further decline in American society: "instead of stripping the soul naked [as does O'Neill, Mamet's plays] provide explosions of violence, whether verbal, physical, sexual or psychological, when the dam wall of repressions cannot hold back, and cruelty and one-upsmanship dominate. While the subtext cries out for communication, compassion is glaringly absent. Unlike O'Neill's abundant and repetitive dialogue, Mamet's language is stripped down to bare essentials: staccato phrases, monosyllables, simple sentences and invective" (98-99). Given all these opposites, one would expect a better account of the different approaches, but instead what follows is a play by play examination of four plays: *The Iceman Cometh, American Buffalo, Glengarry Glen Ross*, and *Edmond*.

sMP 8 Callens, Johan. "David Mamet." *Post-War Literatures in English: A Lexicon of Contemporary Authors* 48 (Sept. 2000): 1-21.

Callens takes an unusual Jungian approach. "The fable and morality influences in Mamet's plays, partly inspired by Bruno Bettelheim, also help to explain the frequent presence of Joseph Campbell's mythic structure, the protagonist's (1) departure, (2) initiation and testing and (3) return, reintegration or insight. Depending on the critic and the play (e.g. *Edmond, Lone Canoe, Dark Pony, Reunion, We Will Take You There*), the third phase is either ironically subverted or tentatively dramatized" (11).

sMP 9 —. "'You've Gotta Be Where You Are: David Mamet." *Acte(S) de Présence: Teksten over Engelstalig Theater in Vlaanderen En Nederland*. Brussels: VUB Press, 1996. 87-115.

An overview concentrating on Mamet's early plays covering all the themes, but focus is on language, using Wittgenstein's views on the limits of what can be said about the world (93). Interestingly, Callens applies the view to staging, noting that the plays therefore depend on the quality of the actors because of the importance of language (94). Analysis of plays follows, with focus on *Duck Variations* in a 1987 Onfijlbaar Production.

sMP 10 Chakravartee, Moutishi. "Open Theatre and 'Closed Society': Jean Claude Van Itallie and Mamet Reconsidered." *Literary Criterion* 26.3 (1991): 48-52.

This dissertation proposal outlines five chapters. It yokes the most unlikely pairings—one the prime exponent of the "Open Theatre" while he views Mamet as one who "looks at the theatre as a 'closed society'" (49).

sMP 11 Cohn, Ruby. "Eloquent Energies: Mamet, Shepard." *New American Dramatists, 1960-1990*. Second ed. New York: St. Martin's, 1991. 160-84.

Cohn is contradictory, since her point in the 1982 edition is that Mamet is a pure recorder of speech, without ideas, making characters who are not witty in themselves, but causes of wit in Mamet's construction. But in the 1990 edition he has changed and unleashed "eloquent energies." In the earlier edition, Mamet was disparaged quoting Albee on Mamet, now he ranks with Shepard.

sMP 12 —. "How Are Things Made Round." *David Mamet: A Casebook*. Ed. Leslie Kane. New York: Garland, 1992. 109-22.

This is a careful lexicographer's guide to Mamet's use of language to verify the thesis that this is not spoken English, careful transcription, but rather, as with Pinter and Shepard, an invented patois. She is excellent in illustrating all the different uses and shadings of words like "shit" and "fuck." She is also helpful in illustrating passages where words have been omitted. Examples are drawn from the plays she terms "the Business trilogy." Her final example is of all the ways the word "business" itself is used, and she indicates the jargon words in each play.

sMP 13 —. "Phrasal Energies: Harold Pinter and David Mamet." *Anglo-American Interplay in Recent Drama*. Cambridge: Cambridge UP, 1995. 58-93.

Cohn's chapter is an encyclopedic overview of the lexical and definitional variations of Mamet's use of language, mainly in the Business trilogy: *American Buffalo, Glengarry Glen Ross, and Speed-the-Plow*. She traces rhymes, examines expletives, jargon, multiple definitions and puns—every aspect of sound and sense. Both Pinter and Mamet "derive obliquely from Beckett" especially in "the resonance of their dialogue, and their common predilection for repetition" (58). They differ from him in their localized settings: "Although both plays [*Betrayal* and *Speed-the-Plow*] function on realistic sets, the shaped language and its resonance lift them beyond realism into wider significance. Inconspicuously, too, the structure of both plays hits at the residual circularity associated with the theatre of the absurd" (91).

sMP 14 Dean, Anne. *David Mamet: Language as Dramatic Action*. Rutherford, New Jersey: Fairleigh Dickinson UP, 1990.

Each chapter approaches Mamet's characters as tragic victims, rather than dealing with the difficulties their language, their treatment of women and others, might raise. Dean is essential reading to see one dimension—an extremely sympathetic one—to Mamet's plays. It is not the whole picture by any means, but it is a point of view which the critics who take the plays as realistic miss completely. See chapters under individual plays.

sMP 15 Demastes, William W. "David Mamet's Dis-Integrating Drama." *Beyond Naturalism*. Contributions in Drama and Theatre Studies 27. Westport, CT: Greenwood, 1988. 67-94.

Demastes notes that Mamet isn't quite the realist for which he is often taken: "Mamet has found his own unique way of dramatizing that experience, again by beginning with realism to present surfaces and working to illustrate the cracks in those surfaces" (67). One perceptive note of how Mamet does this is the shift from plot to language: "Mamet has granted narrative or plot no more than a secondary role in the great majority of his works, spotlighting dialogue instead, and thereby shifting from a sort of Aristotelian philosophy that argues humans reveal themselves through their actions to one that argues humans reveal themselves through speech" (68). Appropriate to his language notion, Demastes observes of *Glengarry Glen Ross* that Mamet creates a "poetic voice. [. . .] And that fractured, disjointed voice reflects a frustration in all modern conventions and institutions. [Arthur] Miller's rational, generally coherent prose, on the other hand, implies an ultimate faith in current systems, a belief that wounds will eventually heal or be healed. Mamet's plays reveal complex psychological constructs that can't be analyzed through strictly rational, or cause-and-effect means" (92).

sMP 16 Ditsky, John. "'He Lets You See the Thought There': The Theater of David Mamet." *Kansas Quarterly* 12.4 (1980): 25-34.

This introductory survey up to 1978 focuses generally on language: "People really do speak as Mamet's characters do; the sound of his plays has the fascination of an overheard phone conversation" (26). Particular observations are on humor, the parenthesis, and the use of banality to create a blackout line. For example he notes in *Life in the Theatre*: "the curious rituals of power, such as John's using his own saliva to remove a bit of makeup from Robert's face, followed by Robert's making a point of picking up and properly disposing of John's throw away tissue. In these instances, a deliberately bland language is used to mask action of only apparent simplicity" (31).

sMP 17 Esche, Edward. "David Mamet." *American Drama*. Ed. Clive Bloom. New York: St. Martin's, 1995. 165-78.

Esche proposes that Mamet's plays focus on choice—not only for the characters but also for the audience. For example, since Bob is a drug addict, emphasized in the Long Wharf London production in 1984 by continual sniffling, we must side with Donny and Teach. And yet to do so would be wrong, as they discover and as we do. In his reading, Bobby is "immensely sympathetic" (172) and the point is to problematize the audience's own mistaken judgments: "we judge the way we do because we have within us a desire to victimise, a desire to define ourself as not like whatever 'other' we care to identify, and there are few more 'other' than a shifty, scheming, junkie, or so the inner voice might tell us" (173). In *Reunion*, Carol declares that she's "entitled to" a father. "As she stands in front of us claiming her right to have a father, and as we agree with her, we know, by the very depth of our desire, that she is simultaneously demonstrating the impossibility of reclaiming her father in that lost past. The play then presents a dilemma of profound moral dimensions; and our unsureness, the problem of the play, lies in the final irreconcilability of desire with fact" (175).

sMP 18 Gale, Steven H. "David Mamet: The Plays, 1972-1980." *Essays on Contemporary American Drama.* Eds. Hedwig Bock and Albert Wertheim. Munich: Hueber Verlag, 1981. 207-23.

This assessment of Mamet's plays up to *The Woods* (1977) is thematic: "His situations are sometimes realistic and sometimes symbolic, but they all contain a universal kernel around which the action is built and with which the audience identifies" (207). The opening declares, "Mamet's plays are about relationships" (207). *Sexual Perversity* is argued not to be about "the physical act" but rather "the relationship between men and women. [. . .] The relationship between the sexes, Mamet says, is not natural. [. . .] Whatever the reason, male bonding and female bonding have replaced heterosexual relationships and understandings" (210). Yet he views Bernie sympathetically, rather like Dean: "Seen as a reaction to the source of his vulnerability and humiliation and to his powerful fear of rejection, however, these actions are understandable" (211). *American Buffalo* too is about relationships—but Donny's "relationship with Teach has never been verbalized" (212) and "Bob is caught in the middle" (213). *The Woods* ends with a synthesis "with them hanging on, partly in love and partly in a desperate need to be together."

sMP 19 Geis, Deborah R. "David Mamet and the Metadramatic Tradition: Seeing 'the Trick from the Back.'" *David Mamet: A Casebook.* Ed. Leslie Kane. New York: Garland, 1992. 49-68.

Geis has an original approach to dramaturgy, examining the poststructuralist perspective in which all drama is metadramatic. She focuses on the varieties of soliloquy as asides, homiletics, and self-examination with examples from *A Life in the Theatre* (solo to empty theatre, overheard), *The Shawl* (psychic showing "the trick from the back"), and *The Water Engine* (radio as soliloquy). She connects Shakespearean scholarship on soliloquies to *American Buffalo*, takes note of the Greek tradition of chorus in *Duck Variations*, and Roman slave conventions with Roma in *Glengarry Glen Ross* who "does not have to play at being sincere, for he has made his world-weary cynicism into part of his routine—or, more aptly, he is entirely sincere about his utter immersion in deception" (62).

sMP 20 —. "Theatre as 'House of Games': David Mamet's (Con) Artistry and the Monologic Voice." *Postmodern Theatric[k]s: Monologue in Contemporary Drama*. Ann Arbor: U. of Michigan, 1993. 89-115.

Geis notes the Brechtian nature of monologues which break out of the fiction and traces the use of monologues in different ways. In early plays, *Duck Variations, Sexual Perversity*, and *Lakeboat*, "the creation of narrative may be a way of surviving in a world that is depicted as essentially hostile, but its fraudulence and its attractiveness render it troubling and appealing at the same time" (98). The Business plays, are "all preoccupied with the connections between narrative (especially monologic) language and deception" (99).

sMP 21 Herman, William. "Theatrical Diversity from Chicago: David Mamet." *Understanding Contemporary American Drama*. Columbia, SC: U. of South Carolina P., 1987. 125-60.

This is a basic overview, citing Gale, not Bigsby or Carroll. Its tack, however, is unique based mainly on feelings. Of *Sexual Perversity in Chicago*: "There is something chilling about the play, though it is funny and, at times, even moving. Stage images like lonely Bernie, transfixed by the television speaking to him with sex-obsessed, wisecracking voice; the story of King Farouk's lovemaking; and the final images of Bernie and Dan, bitter on the beach—these create an impression that some saving grace has been savagely annihilated" (136). Of *Duck Variations* he insists, contra Bigsby, that "the play insists that there is meaning" and that "the homilies and the allegories are not nearly as interesting as the ultimate connections between Emil and George—nor are they meant to be" (138). Similarly, *American Buffalo* is all about relationships too: "Don would like to define friendship as 'people taking care of each other,' but he cannot. The play won't let him. In the end he is touched by Bob's having bought the nickel for him and hits Teach in a fury at the young man's injury" (144).

sMP 22 Hubert-Leibler, Pascale. "Dominance and Anguish: The Teacher-Student Relationship in the Plays of David Mamet." *Modern Drama* 31.4 (1988): 557-70. Rpt. in *David Mamet: A Casebook*. Ed. Leslie Kane. New York: Garland, 1992. 69-86.

Using Foucault and Barthes, the article depicts powerless characters, aging, who seek to have some power, some control, by playing the role of teacher to someone younger, less experienced: "Whether they be casualties of capitalism—those for whom the American dream never materialized— or outsiders, it is clear that they do not have access to the power conferred either by money, status, or, for that matter, love. Yet their profound need for dominance is very much alive, and because of their disempowerment, can only be expressed through a few particular channels" (74).

sMP 23 Hudgins, Christopher C. "Comedy and Humor in the Plays of David Mamet." *David Mamet: A Casebook*. Ed. Leslie Kane. New York: Garland, 1992. 191-230.

This is a major work of criticism, both because it defines a whole genre of Mamet's work, and because of its towering overview of the issues raised by humor in a satirist who is too often taken to be a realistic writer. Hudgins uses Booth's three kinds of irony, Eric Bentley's concept of humor in drama, as well as Robert Corrigan to create a theory of comic irony and "celebratory humor." This fits Hudgins' response to Mamet's characters: one must be sympathetic to all the characters, though one may laugh at them, one also laughs with them. He uses a wide variety of sources of Mamet quotations to support this view quoted by Schvey: "I always want everyone to be sympathetic to all the characters" (194). Using this approach, Hudgins analyzes *American Buffalo, Glengarry Glen Ross,* and *Speed-the-Plow*. After carefully examining key moments of humor in *American Buffalo*, his reading of the ending deploys more sympathy than is normally seen: "Once the violence is over, a very different tone settles over *American Buffalo's* final moments. Gently humorous and loving would be my description" (210). The paper hat on Teach shifts the tone from the violence the precedes and makes the transition to "the mutual forgiveness and recognition of fault here [between Don and Bobby] is wonderfully gentle" (211).

sMP 24 Hudgins, Christopher C., and Leslie Kane, eds. *Gender & Genre: Essays on David Mamet*. New York: Palgrave, 2001.

The articles in this anthology are cited under the appropriate plays.

sMP 25 Jacobs, Dorothy H. "Working Worlds in David Mamet's Dramas." *Midwestern Miscellany XIV, Being Essays on Chicago Writers* (1986): 47-57.

This is an overview of the plays dealing with workplace. Mamet replaces the usual realistic home setting "with a junkshop, a real estate office, a lakeboat, and a theatre dressing room" (47). The article is descriptive rather than analytic.

sMP 26 Joki, Ilkka. "David Mamet's Drama: The Dialogicality of Grotesque Realism." *Bakhtin: Carnival and Other Subjects*. Ed. David Shepherd. Amsterdam: Rodopi, 1993. 80-98.

Joki applies Bakhtin's theories of language, offering an analysis of the kind of audience needed: "As far as [Mamet's] most characteristic stage plays for adults are concerned, 'it' is a young urban 'person', preferably male, somewhat literary and cultured, but not so cultured that 'he' would find it beneath 'himself' to recognise and appreciate a well-formed utterance in the vernacular. After all, these sociolinguistic realities are exemplary of what

Bakhtin calls 'the eternally living element of unofficial language and unofficial thought.' [. . .] They demonstrate literature in 'a living contact with unfinished, still-evolving contemporary reality.' [. . .]" (84).

sMP 27 Kane, Leslie, ed. *David Mamet: A Casebook*. New York: Garland, 1992. The articles in this anthology are cited under the appropriate plays.

sMP 28 —. "Time Passages." *The Pinter Review: Annual Essays* (1990): 30-49.
Kane has an agglutinating mind which sees multiple connections—here between early (and late) Pinter and early Mamet "in which past events are reported but uncorroborated, past betrayals are paradigmatic, characters are unreliable, chronology is disrupted, narrations are typically erotic and/or fantastic, minutiae are explored in depth" (34). Lists of connections like this abound. She begins by talking about narrative, and the function of story-telling, and this becomes more profound as she links it in "The Disappearance of the Jews" to Jewish tradition: "Joey remembers that biblical narrative is, and was, interpreted 'not by a clear presentation of its theme or meaning, but by the telling of a new tale about an aspect of an old one. This new tale, in turn, discloses by answering one question and conceals by raising new questions" (42).

sMP 29 —. *Weasels and Wisemen: Ethics and Ethnicity in the Work of David Mamet*. New York: St. Martin's, 1999.
Kane's book is invaluable for its footnotes and background material on Mamet. Her readings of the plays, however, are often skewed by her approach through the ethical precepts of Judaism. For example, Karen is faulted in *Speed-the-Plow* because she tries to break up a deal which has the force of a binding contract between Fox and Gould. This is unethical. Despite the sometimes eccentric readings, her interpretations are always challenging and carefully reasoned. Specific chapters are discussed under the appropriate play.

sMP 30 Kim, So-im. "Sexual Myths in David Mamet: *Sexual Perversity in Chicago* and *Edmond*." *Journal of English Language and Literature* [Seoul] 42.4 (1996): 899-922.

sMP 31 Lewis, Patricia and Terry Browne. "David Mamet." *Twentieth-Century American Dramatists*. Ed. John MacNicholas. Vol. 7, Part 2: *Dictionary of Literary Biography*. Detroit: Gale, 1981. 63-70.

sMP 32 Lundin, Edward. "Mamet and Mystery." *Publications of the Mississippi Philological Association* (1988): 106-14.
"What remains at the end of the play is a sense of mystery about people who lack connection with themselves, with each other, and with their environment" (107). Mystery is so broadly defined in this article, that it clearly encompasses everything about *American Buffalo*, as it does the other

two plays: *Glengarry, Glen Ross* [sic] and *Edmond*. No research is included except for the Savran interview. The view of *Edmond* seems homophobic: "Edmond descends from a person who is free, who functions in a marriage relationship with a woman, to being a prisoner in bondage to a homosexual partner" (111).

sMP 33 Malkin, Jeanette R. "Language as a Prison: Verbal Debris and Deprivation." *Verbal Violence in Contemporary Drama*. Cambridge: Cambridge UP, 1992. 145-61.

Malkin analyzes the language games of *Glengarry Glen Ross* and *American Buffalo*: "The act of talking, which already in *American Buffalo* is ambiguously treated by the characters themselves, is here developed into a schizophrenic term: to 'talk' is to act, talk is power, men know how to 'talk'" (156). [. . .] Levene opposes action (i.e. talk which sells) with the other meaning of 'talk' developed in the play: talk as 'the blah blah blah' (p.13), talk divorced from action, talk as theory, as idea" (155-56). "To talk is to become an accomplice; to listen is to be implicated ('Because you listened'). Words can only buy and sell, and they sell trust and friendship just as easily as land" (159). The text is viewed not through performance but as having only one possible interpretation: "they are so thoroughly infected, so basely motivated as to awaken more revulsion than pity. This is especially true of *Glengarry Glen Ross*, in which ethical perversity and verbal restrictedness are totally interwoven and breed a bestiality which, Mamet seems to be saying, endangers an entire society" (161).

sMP 34 Maufort, Marc. "Narrative Patterns in the Plays of David Mamet." *BELL: Belgian Essays on Language and Literature* (1991): 112-19.

"In a number of Mamet's [early] plays, characters often tell stories, either absurd or realistic, which disrupt the flow of dramatic dialogue" (112). Maufort's assertion indicates his structural discovery about Mamet's dramatic construction—one that was taken much further by Deborah Geis in *Postmodern Theatric[k]s*. Maufort classifies these devices as either monologic moments spoken to another person, or those ignoring the other, as if musing or remembering to one's self (a "self-narrated monologue") (116). He does not examine stopped time that Geis does. He concludes, rather, that Mamet's fascination "may well be due not only to his extraordinary themes and characters, but also to his skill at integrating novelistic forms into the framework of the drama" (119).

sMP 35 McCarthy, Gerry. "New Mythologies: Mamet, Shepard and the American Stage." *Connotations: A Journal for Critical Debate* [Munster, Germany] 6.3 (1996/97): 354-68.

McCarthy takes on John Russell Brown's earlier article on myth (sW 2). McCarthy finds in Mamet instead "a nostalgia for myth, in destabilizing the materialist environment" (357). However, "the mythic process is truncated" and so the *American Buffalo*, rich with potential mythic meaning, has very little: "the functionality of myth being exploited in Mamet to degrade the symbol rather than exploit it as a true cultural referent" (358). As a result: "The lesson of *American Buffalo* is that there are images but no narratives. The emblem can denote an aspiration or a nostalgia but it cannot structure the negotiated experience in time" (358). Thus the characters try to use old stories to convey what can't be articulated—and the same difficulty exists for the actor who has to convey having inner thoughts and feelings that can't be expressed. But the stories never work. In *The Woods* he finds that in Ruth's tale of the isolated seagull (7) "the sharing of the image is abortive, lost in incomprehension. The tale itself is without sequence or conclusion. A distant phenomenon is fleetingly viewed, an outcome is suggested but the narrative tails off into an open sky of speculation" (363).

sMP 36 McDonough, Carla J. "David Mamet: The Search for Masculine Space." *Staging Masculinity in Contemporary American Drama*. Jefferson, NC: McFarland, 1997. 71-101.

McDonough sees antifeminism everywhere in Mamet. "His plays are also structured by the search for male identity, for a masculine space, a search that often becomes complicated by competition among men as they seek to establish identities at the expense of other characters. This search for masculine identity is entangled with assumptions concerning women, particularly a fear and hatred of women coupled with an intense physical desire for women or what they can represent to a man. These conflicts are often communicated through obscene, degraded, and inarticulate language that comes to represent characters' insecurities and confusion" (76). This thesis from her book expands sMP 37, and considers *Edmond, Sexual Perversity in Chicago, Lakeboat, Glengarry Glen Ross, American Buffalo, Speed-the-Plow,* and *Oleanna.*

sMP 37 —. "Every Fear Hides a Wish: Unstable Masculinity in Mamet's Drama." *Theatre Journal* 44.2 (1992): 195-205.

Mamet is a misogynist because of his personal sexual insecurities. "Men's confusion and skepticism about women, which often borders on the misogynistic in Mamet's plays, stems from the fear that in losing the definition of women on which patriarchal market society is based, men have lost themselves. Mamet's drama addresses the confusion felt by men such as himself who no longer know where they stand in a patriarchy that is under revision" (196). The men of *Glengarry* and *American Buffalo*, "then, seem to have connections beyond business. They are locked into the competition of their jobs in part because the limited construction of identity they try to enact relies on their work as much as it relies on the positioning of women or, more precisely, of the feminine" (197).

sMP 38 Peereboom, J. J. "Mamet from Afar." *New Essays on American Drama*. Eds. Gilbert Debusscher and Henry I. Schvey. Amsterdam: Rodopi, 1989. 189-99.

Peereboom's brief overview of Mamet's works wobbles a bit as it has no theoretical foundation: "Mamet's characters function most persuasively when their statements are designed to challenge the world and make room for them to act in rather than to represent the complexity of their imaginations" (191); "we are aware of the author, heightening the words they would naturally have said to give resonance to their conflict" [*A Life in the Theatre*] (192). His point is that "Mamet takes the characters' words beyond the point where they could be credible in realistic terms, exaggerates them" (192). "Their irrelevance as material for socio-cultural criticism does not invalidate these statements as signs of life" (193). His conclusion is "thus what one retains from Mamet is not much more his sense of individual moral situations, of people being responsible for themselves, than it is of our culture being responsible for them" (197).

sMP 39 Pinazzi, Annamaria. "David Mamet: Il Teatro Ritrova La Parola." *Ponte* [Florence, Italy] 43.1 (1987): 119-36.

sMP 40 Price, Steven. "'Accursed Progenitor': Samuel Beckett, David Mamet, and the Problem of Influence." *Samuel Beckett Today/ Aujourd'hui: An Annual Bilingual Review* [Amsterdam] 2 (1993): 77-85.

Price delicately sidesteps issues of direct influence using Bakhtin's intertexuality and Wittgenstein's metaphor of family resemblance and thread-spinning. Price notes development in *American Buffalo* toward realistic drama in set and plot—a movement from "episodic to Aristotelian construction, from contraction to expansiveness which represents the precise opposite of Beckett's development." By contrast he notes the parallels: "The figure of salvation who never shows up; the second act which represents both a development and a retraction of the first; the creation of spurious actions and dialogues to cover a very real nakedness" (80). Most important, perhaps, is the "poststructural awareness of the self's subjection to language" (81). While acknowledging the well-made play construction of *Glengarry*, Price tries even more subtle analysis of the "fears which cannot be spoken" in that play as parallel to Beckett. Trickiest of all is the analysis of how "*Speed-the-Plow* gives full articulation on the stage to the sense of inevitable decay and Beckettian denial of free will" (83). The counterweight to this view in the text seems to be the idealistic text of *The Bridge* which Price deconstructs as "incoherent, its apparent pretentiousness confirmed by its fragmentation within the text of the play and by its articulation by Karen [. . .] exposed as incoherent and ineffectual in performance (regardless of its amenability to subsequent scholarly reconstruction, and so it is exorcised." (83).

sMP 41 Quinn, Michael L. "Anti-Theatricality and American Ideology: Mamet's Performative Realism." *Realism and the American Dramatic Tradition*. Ed. W. W. Demastes. Tuscaloosa: U of Alabama P, 1996. 235-54.

This is a complex article using Jakobson, Austin and Searle to create an idea of realism in "genuine performative speech acts" (246). It stretches the definition to cover every play under broad headings: the Business Scam, Hiding Out/Under Cover, Lying About Love in which one's way of speaking equals the performative self, which may or may not be a deception. In the last, for example, "Love, as a kind of contractual performance, is thus potentially transforming, even in a situation in which both fear of commitment and emotional honesty are obviously ideological, that is, 'in Chicago'" (245). The definition of realism is ephemeral: "Yet Mamet's America is rarely dramatized as a place that might actually exist; rather, Mamet's realism is a coming to terms with the difficulty—even the impossibility—of living such ideals" (240).

sMP 42 Radavich, David. "Man among Men: David Mamet's Homosocial Order." *American Drama* 1.1 (1991): 46-60. Rpt. in *Fictions of Masculinity: Crossing Cultures, Crossing Sexualities.* Ed. Peter F. Murphy. New York: New York UP, 1994. 123-36.

Radavich surveys Mamet's plays looking for patterns that conform to Sedgwick's *Between Men.* He lists the homosexual, homophobic, anti-feminist allusions in each play to trace male bonding references. This results in some strange centering: "In yet another all-male play, the cast is now middle-aged, and the focus on male rape ('fucking up the ass') and enslavement (18). And the 'screwing' is not merely verbal" (53). This analysis of *Glengarry* leads to the conclusion: "In the ethos of Mamet's plays, a man symbolically deprived of his penis through personal insecurity or deprecation by other males is, by definition, a faggot or a cunt, debased both sexually and professionally" (54). This leads to a final view of Mamet as "essentially a comic satirist" (58) whose work gives "his dramatic view of a decadent, wounded patriarchy" (59).

sMP 43 Roeder-Zerndt, Martin. *Lesen und Zuschauen: David Mamet und das amerikanische Drama und Theater der 70er Jahre.* Tubingen: Narr., 1994.

sMP 44 —. "Text und Auffuhrung: Rezeptionsasthetische Uberlegungen zum Postmodernen Drama und Theater." *Amerikastudien/American Studies* [Heidelberg] 38.4 (1993): 567-87.

This article examines text versus performance, and the problem of criticism's failure to deal with drama, especially the postmoderns, Mamet and Shepard. "It suggests that the conspicuous absence of poststructuralist theoretical work in the field of drama is due to the fact that theatrical and dramatic texts refuse to be reduced to mere examples of the failure of the text to communicate a specific meaning to the audience or reader" (567).

sMP 45 Roudané, Matthew C. "Mamet's Mimetics." *David Mamet: A Casebook.* Ed. Leslie Kane. New York: Garland, 1992. 3-32.

This essay promises to be "A Postmodern Cultural Poetics" but beneath a little Barthes, mostly that comes back to the thematic approach: "At the center of Mamet's moral vision lies an amoral universe, a postmodernist

American view of Nature spotlighting our organic disconnection from the
historical, cultural, and mythic resonances of the past" (5). Raymond
Williams is not invoked, nor are other cultural critics, while Williams' theme
of Country vs. City is carried out in the essay. There is a long section on
American views of Nature, and the deduction that Mamet's characters have
no relation to nature—though there is some nice work with Barthes' view
of the city as the center of ludic space. But ultimately the point is that
"Teach's self-serving attitude confirms the ontological split between man
and nature" (21). Interestingly, however, he notes that the plays have "traces"
of mythic wholeness.

sMP 46 —. "Theatrician of the Ethical? The Plays of David Mamet." *American
Drama since 1960: A Critical History*. New York: Twayne, 1996. 161-75.
    This is a thematic overview of Mamet's works: "This unity of vision
most often finds its expression in terms of an implicit social critique of a
contingent and decidedly ambiguous universe: a world from which Mamet
eviscerates any moral balance between public virtue and private self-desire.
[. . .] Mamet replicates human commitments and desires in demythicized
forms: commodity fetishism, sexual negotiations and exploitations, aborted
or botched crimes, brutal physical assaults, fraudulent business transactions
enacted by petty thieves masquerading as businessmen, and human
relationships characterized by the presence of physical sex and the absence
of authentic love" (161).

sMP 47 Rouyer, Philippe. "David Mamet: une nouvelle écriture américaine." *Revue
Française D'Études Américaines* 13.32 (1987): 215-26.
    Overview of Mamet's works, focusing on language: "David Mamet s'est
installé dans le texte et l'écriture; la dynamique du langage, l'escrime des
mots, sorte de boxe langagière, la quête du pouvoir par la parole sont les
constantes du théâtre de Mamet" ["David Mamet is incarnated in the text
and the writing; the dynamic of language, the duel of words, like the language
of boxing, are the constants in the quest for power through words in Mamet's
theatre"] (215). Plays examined include *Edmond, Life in the Theater,
Lakeboat, Glengarry Glen Ross, Squirrels, Sexual Perversity in Chicago,
American Buffalo* and *Duck Variations*.

sMP 48 Savran, David. "New Realism: Mamet, Mann and Nelson." *Contemporary
American Theatre*. Ed. Bruce King: St. Martin's P, 1991. 63-79.
    Savran is a gifted cultural critic, who here takes on the philosophical
underpinnings of realism, traces its roots through Ibsen and naturalism using
Raymond Williams, and then argues that the three playwrights "renovated
the very principles that Ibsen used to deconstruct the realism of his day"
(67). Techniques include "populating their plays with figures unable to
express their emotional turmoil or to understand how they are being
manipulated, characters robbed of the ability to speak. [. . .] [T]he subject is
articulated by a discourse over which he or she has little control [. . .] either

stammers out a broken and wounded speech or talks incessantly" (65). He cites the end of *Sexual Perversity*: "Bernie's speech, torn by redundancies, contradictions, ellipses, clichés, false starts and changes in grammatical subject, exposes the basic illegibility of discourse for a character unable to come to grips with his dismemberment" (72).

sMP 49 Schvey, Henry I. "The Plays of David Mamet: Games of Manipulation and Power." *New Theatre Quarterly* 4.13 (1988): 77-89. Rpt. as "Power Plays: David Mamet's Theatre of Manipulation." in *David Mamet: A Casebook.* Ed. Leslie Kane. New York: Garland, 1992. 87-108.

Schvey gives a thematic overview of Mamet's early plays: *Duck Variations* to *Glengarry Glen Ross.* The theme discovered in each is that "Mamet's plays are highly articulate expressions of an attack on the materialistic values of American society. Yet the vision they present is never wholly dark, but it is either illuminated by the pursuit of self-knowledge or by the extraordinary 'wisdom' with which his characters cloak their empty, banal lives" (106).

sMP 50 Smith, Susan Harris. "En-Gendering Violence: Twisting 'Privates' in the Public Eye." *Public Issues, Private Tensions: Contemporary American Drama.* Ed. Matthew C. Roudané. Georgia State Literary Studies 9. New York: AMS Press, 1993. 115-30.

This article brings sociological analysis of the construction of the masculine to the works of Mamet, Rabe, and Shepard. The idea of violence would have worked interestingly with *The Woods* and *Oleanna*—but instead Smith does the famous works: "In Mamet's *Glengarry Glen Ross* 'fuck' appears 142 times and 135 times in *American Buffalo.* The link between violence and threatened manhood, between violence and sexual affirmation of manhood, clearly is made in the repeated 'fuck.' Though most of the verbal abuse in the plays is ostensibly directed at men, the aggressive, assaultive verb is unavoidably associated with violent behavior to women. 'The ultimate proof of manhood,' writes Lucy Komisar, 'is in sexual violence. Even the language of sex is a lexicon that describes the power of men over women'" (118). Since there are no women in the plays she's chosen, and she's ignored the plays that do display violence towards women, the approach is not fully convincing.

sMP 51 Storey, Robert. "The Making of David Mamet." *The Hollins Critic* 16.4 (1979): 1-11.

This early examination of Mamet focuses on language: "The making of Mamet's America is founded upon a verbal busyness, glib, deft, quick; the parenthetical asides that lace his dialogue (destined, undoubtedly, to become as celebrated as Pinter's pauses) suggest minds that abhor verbal vacuums, that operate, at all levels, on the energy of language itself" (2). His characters "behave as their language directs them to behave, with unquestioning faith in its values" (3). In *The Duck Variations* "language does not conceal but rather fabricates emotion" (3). In *Sexual Perversity* he argues that Bernie isn't a conventional "character" if that means a construct of "psychological motives."

sMP 52 Weales, Gerald. "The Mamet Variations." *Decade* Promotional Issue 1.1 (1978): 10-13.

Weales notes that in *The Duck Variations* "the unvoiced bridges" make "logical connections between apparent non sequiturs" (11). He sees *Sexual Perversity* as a step beyond this in its more advanced theory of language which Mamet characterized: "that words create behavior [. . .] our rhythms prescribe our actions" (11). Weales notes in performance "I was particularly taken with the shift at the end, in which a sudden confused look crossed the younger man's face—a suggestion of uncertainty and loss—before he reassumed his role. That moment seemed to me to release the painful implications of the play, to insist that the audience not hide behind its laughter at the behavior of characters who are, after all, 'other' people" (11). In both cases, he argues that Mamet puts the burden on the audience to make the connections. In *American Buffalo* he observes the continual self-contradictions which are placed without comment before the audience, such as Donny's on "business ('common sense, experience, and talent' and 'People taking care of themselves') which come within a few sentences of one another" (13).

sMP 53 Weber, Myles. "David Mamet in Theory and Practice." *New England Review* 21.2 (2000): 136-41.

This article is an overview of Mamet's non-fiction writing, his theories on drama and everything else, bouncing off early interviews as well as the plays to flesh out these writings. Weber considers the general essays, not too reverentially: "If Mamet acquits himself on gender, he has less success with the issues of Judaism and the American Jewish identity, which seem only to make him crabby."

sMP 54 Zinman, Toby Silverman. "Jewish Aporia: The Rhythm of Talking in Mamet." *Theatre Journal* 44 (1992): 207-15.

Zinman analyzes how the words of the characters don't quite name the subject. They use "aporia," the trope of doubt, the real or pretended inability to know what the subject under discussion is. Just about every play has a passage in it that frames the question-filled play with a question; the marriage of form and content aporetically creates a play that seems to withhold from us the very fact/word/truth its characters seem not to know, but which we leave the theatre knowing, and which we—and they—suspect they have known all along" (209). Examples are cited from the ending of *Speed-the-Plow* and a discussion of "nothing" in *American Buffalo*. *Lakeboat, Duck Variations, Goldberg Street,* and *Glengarry Glen Ross* are also cited with a focus on how a Jewish technique of answering a question with a question is used to avoid giving a direct answer.

DISSERTATIONS ON MAMET

D 1 Alvarado, Sonya Yvette. "Dark Visions of America: David Mamet's Adaptation of Novels and Plays for the Screen." Diss. Texas Tech U, 1997.

D 2 Austin, Gayle. "Feminist Theory and Postwar American Drama." Diss. City U of New York, 1988.

D 3 Barton, Bruce William. "'Changing Frames': Medium Matters in Selected Plays and Films of David Mamet." Diss. U of Toronto, 1996.

D 4 Beckwith, Jeanne Joan. "Deviancy and the Stage in the Plays of David Mamet and Peter Barnes." Diss. U. Georgia, 1994.

D 5 Bial, Henry Carl. "Acting Jewish on the American Stage and Screen, 1947-1998 (Woody Allen, Barbra Streisand, David Mamet)." Diss. New York U, 2001.

D 6 Blondell, John Douglas. "Myth and Antimyth in the Work of David Mamet." Diss. U of California, Santa Barbara, 1991.

D 7 Brewer, Gay. "David Mamet and Film: Illusion and Disillusion in a Wounded Land." Diss. Ohio State University, 1992.

D 8 Chi, Wei-jan. "The Role of Language in the Plays of Mamet, Wilson, and Rabe." Diss. U of Iowa, 1991.

D 9 Coperhaver, Bonny Bell. "The Portrayal of Gender and a Description of Gender Roles in Selected American Modern and Postmodern Plays." [Includes *Oleanna*]." Diss. [EdD]. East Tennessee State U, 2002.

D 10 Demastes, William Willis. "American New Realism in the Theatre of the 80s (Fuller, Henley, Norman, Rabe, Mamet, Shepard)." Diss. U of Wisconsin, Madison, 1986.

D 11 Erickson, Steven Craig. "The Drama of Dispossession in Selected Plays of Six Major American Playwrights (O'Neill, Miller, Williams, Albee, Mamet, Shepard)." Diss. U Texas, Dallas, 1991.

D 12 Haedicke, Janet Vanderpool. "'It Is Leviathan': Family, Feminism, and American Drama (Sam Shepard, August Wilson, David Mamet)." Diss. Louisiana State U, 1996.

D 13 Harriot, Esther. "Images of America: Four Contemporary Playwrights (Wilson, Shepard, Mamet, Fuller)." Diss. State U of NY at Buffalo, 1983.

D 14 Haspel, Jane Seay. "Dirty Jokes and Fairy Tales: David Mamet and the Narrative Capability of Film." Diss. U of North Texas, 1997.

D 15 Joki, Ilkka. "Mamet, Bakhtin, and the Dramatic: The Demotic as a Variable of Addressivity." Diss. Abo Akademi [Finland], 1994.

D 16 Kitts, John Stewart. "The Presumption of Gender: Masculinity Construction in the Narratives of David Mamet." Diss. U of Alabama, 1996.

D 17 Klaver, Elizabeth Theresa. "Postmodernism and Metatextual Space in the Plays of Beckett, Ionesco, Albee and Mamet." Diss. U of California, Riverside, 1991.

D 18 Kulmala, Daniel Wayne. "The Absent Other: Absent/Present Characters as Catalysts for Action in Modern Drama (David Mamet, Jason Miller, Edward Albee)." Diss. U of Kansas, 2000.

D 19 Kuo, Chiang-sheng. "The Images of Masculinity in Contemporary American Drama: Albee, Shepard, Mamet and Kushner." Diss. New York U, 1999.

D 20 Lawson, Don S. "The Intertextuality of the Room: A Reading of Selected Plays by Harold Pinter, Joe Orton, and David Mamet." Diss. U of Tennessee, Knoxville, 1989.

D 21 McDonough, Carla Jane. "Staging Masculinity: The Search for Male Identity in Contemporary American Drama (Mamet, Shepard, Rabe, Wilson)." Diss. University of Tennessee, 1992.

D 22 Olszewski, Joseph Francis. "American Theater in the Sixties and Seventies: The Non-Broadway Stage and Its Playwrights." Diss. St. Louis U, 1981.

D 23 Patton, Paul Douglas. "The Prophetic Passion and Imagination of David Mamet." Diss. Regent U, 2002.

D 24 Price, John Alden. "Signs of Shakespeare: Alternative Theory and Postmodern Practice." [Also Pinter, Mamet, Churchill] Diss. U Texas, Dallas, 2001.

D 25 Ryan, Steven Daniel. "David Mamet: Dramatic Craftsman." Diss. Fordham U, 1988.

D 26 Schaeffer, Ira. "Rites of Passage in the Plays of David Mamet." Diss. U of Rhode Island, 1998.

D 27 Stone, Robin Dale. "How Does It Mean? A Discourse Analysis of Four Plays by Harold Pinter, Simon Gray, David Mamet, and Sam Shepard." Diss. U of Missouri, Columbia, 1999.

D 28 Strasburg, Jeffrey Otto. "The Only Way to Teach These People is to Kill Them": Pedagogy as Communicative Action in the Major Plays of David Mamet. Diss. U of Nevada, Las Vegas, 2002.

SELECTED FILM SCHOLARSHIP

F 1 Begley, Varun. "On Adaptation: David Mamet and Hollywood." *Essays in Theatre/ Études Theatrales* 16.2 (1998): 165-76. See sSPC 1

F 2 Berger, Jason and Cornelius B. Pratt. "Class and Power: Exploring with College Students the Ethics and Class Conflict Messages in the Films of David Mamet." *The Image of Class in Literature, Media, and Society. Selected Papers. Conference of the Society for the Interdisciplinary Study of Social Imagery*. Eds. Will Wright and Steven Kaplan. Pueblo: University of Southern Colorado, 1998. 298-304.

F 3 Bilodeau, F. "Film Directors Inspired by Alfred Hitchcock: Gus Van Sant and David Mamet." *Liberté* 41.3 (1999): 105-9.

F 4 Brewer, Gaylord. *David Mamet and Film: Illusion and Disillusion in a Wounded Land*. Columbus: Ohio State U, 1992.

F 5 —. "*Hoffa* and *The Untouchables*: Mamet's Brutal Orders of Authority." *Literature and Film Quarterly* 28.1 (2000): 28-33.

F 6 Carroll, Dennis. "The Recent Mamet Films: 'Business' Versus Communion." *David Mamet: A Casebook*. Ed. Leslie Kane. New York: Garland, 1992. 175-90.

F 7 Deemer, Charles. "Scene & Structure in David Mamet's 'Art Films'." *Creative Screenwriting* 5.3 (1998): 45-47.

F 8 Feaster, Felicia. "*Oleanna*." *Cineaste* 29.3 (1995): 52.

F 9 Gale, Stephen H. "David Mamet's *The Verdict*: The Opening Cons." *David Mamet: A Casebook*. Ed. Leslie Kane. New York: Garland, 1992. 161-74.

F 10 Hudgins, Christopher C. "'Lolita' 1995: The Four Filmscripts." *Literature-Film Quarterly* 25.1 (1997): 23-30.

F 11 —. "'A Small Price to Pay': Superman, Metafamily, and Hero in David Mamet's Oedipal *House of Games*." *Gender and Genre: Essays on David Mamet*. Eds. Christopher C. Hudgins and Leslie Kane. New York: Palgrave, 2001. 209-35.

F 12 James, Nick. "Suspicion." *Sight and Sound* 8.10 (1998): 22-24.

F 13 Johnson, Mary. "*Wag the Dog*: Deconstructing the Dog." *Creative Screenwriting* 5.3 (1998): 20-23.

F 14 La Palma, Marina deBellagenete. "Driving Doctor Ford." *Literature/Film Quarterly* 24.1 (1996): 57-62.

F 15 Louvish, Simon. "Out of the Shadows." *Sight and Sound* 3.6 (1993): 18.

F 16 McKelly, James C. "The Artist as Criminal: *The Zoo Story* and *House of Games*." *Text & Presentation: The Journal of the Comparative Drama Conference* 12 (1992): 65-68.

F 17 Mercurio, James P. "The Edge." *Creative Screenwriting* 5.3 (1998): 12-15.

F 18 Mosher, Gregory. "How to Talk Buffalo." *American Theatre* Sept. 1996: 80.

F 19 Orr, David. "Script Review: *Hannibal*." *Creative Screenwriting* Mar.-Apr. 2001: 31-36.

F 20 Sherman, Ranen Omer. "The Metaphysics of Loss and Jewish Identity in David Mamet's *Homicide*." *Modern Jewish Studies Annual* 11 (1999): 37-50.

F 21 Sherwin, Richard K. "Framed." *Legal Reelism: Movies as Legal Texts*. Ed. John Denvir. Urbana: U of Illinois, 1996. 70-94.

F 22 Van Wert, William F. "Psychoanalysis and Con Games: *House of Games*." *Film Quarterly* 43.4 (1990): 2-10.

F 23 —. "Conspiracy Theory in Mamet's 'Homicide.'" *Western Humanities Review* 49.2 (1995): 133-42.

F 24 Williams, Tony. "Mamet's *Postman*." *Creative Screenwriting* 5.6 (1998): 35-39.

F 25 Yakir, Dan. "The *Postman*'s Words." *Film Comment* Mar.-Apr. 1981: 21-24.

BIBLIOGRAPHIES AND REFERENCE BOOKS

BR 1 Berkowitz, Gerald M. *American Drama of the Twentieth Century*. London: Longman, 1992. 190-94.

BR 2 Callens, Johan. "David Mamet: A Bibliography." *Post-War Literatures in English: A Lexicon of Contemporary Authors* 20 (1993): A 1-21.

BR 3 Carroll, Dennis. *International Directory of Theatre: Playwrights*. Ed. Mark Hawkins-Dady and Helen Ottaway. Vol. 2. Detroit: St. James Press, 1994. 627-30.

BR 4 Charnick, Jason. "David Mamet Info Page." 8 Jan. 2003 <http://www.mindspring.com/~jason-charnick/mamet.html>

BR 5 *Contemporary Authors*. New Revision Series. Vol. 41. Detroit: Gale, 1994.

BR 6 *Contemporary Dramatists*. 5th ed. Chicago: St. James, 1993.

BR 7 *Contemporary Literary Criticism*, Detroit: Gale, Vol. 9, 1978. 360-61; Vol. 15, 1980. 355-58; Vol. 34, 1985. 217-24; Vol. 46, 1988. 245-56; Vol. 91, 1996. 143-55.

BR 8 *Current Biography Yearbook*. 1979. 274-7; 1998. 400-5.

BR 9 *David Mamet Review*. 24 Jan. 2003 <http://mamet.eserver.org>.

BR 10 Davis, J. Madison and John Coleman. "David Mamet: A Classified Bibliography." *Studies in American Drama, 1945-Present* 1 (1986): 83-101.

BR 11 *Drama Criticism*. Vol. 4. Detroit: Gale, 1994. 298+.

BR 12 *Drama for Students*. Vol. 15. Detroit: Gale. Vol 2. 38-53; Vol. 3. 1-21; Vol. 6. 201-15; Vol. 12. 132-159; Vol. 15. 197-214.

BR 13 Jones, Nesta and Steven Dykes. *File on Mamet*. London: Methuen Drama, 1991.

BR 14 King, Kimball. *Ten Modern American Playwrights: An Annotated Bibliography*. New York: Garland, 1982.

BR 15 Kolin, Philip C. "David Mamet's Writing in Restaurants: A Primary and Secondary Bibliography." *Analytical & Enumerative Bibliography* 2.4 (1988): 160-67.

BR 16 —. "David Mamet's Writing in Restaurants: An Index to Names, Key Concepts, and Places." *Researcher: An Interdisciplinary Journal* (Jackson State Univ.) 13.3 (1990): 81-90.

BR 17 Lawley, Paul. "*Glengarry Glen Ross*." *International Directory of Theatre: Plays*. Ed. Mark Hawkins-Dady. Vol. 1. Chicago: St. James Press, 1992. 294-95.

BR 18 Lewis, Patricia and Terry Browne. *Dictionary of Literary Biography*. Vol. 7. pt. 2. Detroit: Gale, 1981. 63-70.

BR 19 *Literature Resource Center*. [database] Gale Group [a k. a. *InfoTrac*].

BR 20 *Major 20th-Century Writers; a Selection of Sketches from Contemporary Authors*. Detroit: Gale, 1991. 1894-97.

BR 21 McNaughton, Howard. *Contemporary Dramatists*. 5th ed. Detroit: St. James Press, 1993. 373-77.

BR 22 *Modern Drama: Scholarship and Criticism 1981-1990: An International Bibliography*. Ed. Charles A. Carpenter. Toronto: U Toronto P. 65-66.

BR 23 Sauer, Janice A. "Bibliography of Glengarry Glen Ross, 1983-1995." *David Mamet's Glengarry Glen Ross: Text and Performance*. Leslie Kane, ed. New York: Garland, 1996. 263-73.

BR 24 Sauer, Janice A. and David K. Sauer. "David Mamet Bibliography." *David Mamet Review* [annually 1994+].

BR 25 Trigg, Joycelyn. *American Playwrights Since 1945: A Guide to Scholarship, Criticism, and Performance*. Ed. Philip C. Kolin Westport, CN: Greenwood, 1989. 259-88.

NAME INDEX

C

Caine, James M. 18
Callens, Johan 63, 122, 123, 139, 142, 262, 49, 367
Caltabiano, Frank P. 187
Canby, Vincent 108, 210, 284
Cantwell, M. 31
Caplan, Betty 236
Capone, Clifford 258
Cardullo, Bert 274
Carroll. Dennis 64, 122, 139, 168, 201, 261, 274, 281, 322, 338, 346, 365, 367
Casey, Warren 264
Cassidy, Claudia 39, 190, 204
Cavendish, Dominic 185
Ceraso, Chris 285
Chaillet, Ned 48, 121, 270
Chakravartee, Moutishi 69, 350
Chancellor, Anna 82
Charnick, Jason 367
Chase, Chris 30
Chekhov, Anton 6, 17, 19
Chelton, Nick 332
Chernomordik, Vlada 17
Cherubin, Jan 30
Chi, Wei-jan 363
Chianese, Dominic 182, 326
Christen, Robert 38, 190, 340
Christiansen, Richard 29, 30, 39, 40, 43, 72, 94, 96, 108, 127, 149, 151, 182, 190, 204, 256, 271, 286, 290, 316, 324, 332, 340
Church, Michael 236
Cibula, Nan 148, 278, 288
Clapp, Susannah 83, 185, 216
Clark, Peter K. 184
Claxton, Richard 100
Clay, Carolyn 79
Clink-Scale, Linda 96
Clites, Robert 182
Cluchey, Rich 126

Clurman, Harold 43, 192, 258, 327, 342
Coe, Richard L. 43
Cohn, Ruby 168, 179, 314, 350
Cole, Gary 278
Coleman, John 367
Collins, Pat 192
Collins, William B. 319
Combs, Robert 140
Connolly, John P. 182
Conway, Dan 324
Cook, James 151
Cook, Ron 161
Cook, William 237
Coperhaver, Bonny Bell 363
Coppola, Sam 165
Core, Susan and George 101
Corliss, Richard 151
Court, Penelope 96
Coveney, Michael 48, 54, 83, 101, 135, 146, 162, 197, 198, 237, 281, 300, 305, 333
Crane, Nancy 75
Cristofer, Michael 19
Cross, Dave 133
Crouse, Lindsay 4, 5, 8, 11, 17, 256, 278
Crow, Laura 326
Crowley, Bob 100
Cullick, Jonathan S. 169
Cummings, Scott T. 206
Cunningham, Dennis 52, 152
Cushman, Robert 146
Custer, Roberta 264

D

Da Silva, Beatrice 118, 266
Dace, Harold 92
Dace, Tish 259
Dahlie, Elizabeth 17
Daly, Kathleen 324

About the Authors

JANICE A. SAUER is a Senior Reference Librarian at the University of South Alabama. Her other writings include the annual bibliography for the *David Mamet Review* and publications on library instruction in journals such as *College Undergraduate Libraries*.

DAVID K. SAUER is a Professor of English and the Altmayer Chair of Literature at Spring Hill College. In addition to assisting in the annual bibliography, he has published articles in journals including *Shakespeare Quarterly, Shakespeare Yearbook, Modern Drama, American Drama,* and *Shaw*.